MAINE AT WAR

Volume I

MAINE AT WAR
Volume I:
Bladensburg to Sharpsburg

By Brian F. Swartz

Copyright © 2011-2019

Portions of the text of this book originally appeared in the Bangor Daily News, in the Bangor Daily News' The Weekly, and on the Bangor Daily News Web site. Any previously published text is copyrighted and solely owned by Brian F. Swartz.

Foreword by Nicholas P. Picerno, copyright © 2018, used with permission.

Publisher's Preface by David M. Fitzpatrick, copyright © 2018, used with permission.

Photos are from a variety of sources, and most are in the public domain. Effort was nevertheless made to credit original photographers throughout.

Edited and designed by David M. Fitzpatrick

Images for the front and back covers were original photos of Civil War reenactors by Brian F. Swartz. They were digitally edited by David M. Fitzpatrick.

ISBN-13: 978-0-9833346-5-1
Published by Maine Origins Publications
an imprint of Epic Saga Publishing
Brewer, Maine, USA
www.MaineOrigins.com
www.EpicSagaPub.com

MAINE AT WAR

Volume I:
Bladensburg to Sharpsburg

by
BRIAN F. SWARTZ

Brewer, Maine

www.MaineOrigins.com

*To my wife Susan
and our son Chris,
who have traipsed
the many battlefields.*

"Out of this suffering
grew a grand resolve
which nothing ever after
caused to waver.

Out of it came a lasting patriotism
and courage that no privation,
no danger could abate.

The few short months developed
a new set of men, and what kind
of men let Fredericksburgh tell.

All that time God was
busy making heroes."

—Major Abner Ralph Small,
*The Sixteenth Maine Regiment in the
War of the Rebellion 1861-1865*

Contents

Foreword by Nicholas P. Picerno i

Publisher's Preface by David M. Fitzpatrick iii

Author's Preface by Brian Swartz v

Acknowledgements vii

Chapter 1: First Blood at Bladensburg 1
Chapter 2: Ill-Prepared to Save the Union 13
Chapter 3: Forming for Battle 19
Chapter 4: This Is Our Colonel 29
Chapter 5: The California Flag 35
Chapter 6: Hot Work at Manassas 43
Chapter 7: Freedom of the Press Takes Flight 51
Chapter 8: Maine Women Mobilize 59
Chapter 9: The 6th Maine Infantry Brawls Apart Portland 67
Chapter 10: Missing the Face of a Pretty Girl 75
Chapter 11: Of Snow and Ice 81
Chapter 12: The Sand and Spiders of Ship Island 95
Chapter 13: Pulaski 101
Chapter 14: Spring Cleaning 115
Chapter 15: Traitor 119
Chapter 16: Old Grizzly Fights 123
Chapter 17: All Ashore Who Are Going Ashore 135
Chapter 18: They Rode to Delay Stonewall Jackson 143
Chapter 19: Slaughter at Middletown 153
Chapter 20: The Inquiry About the Missing 161
Chapter 21: The Ladies of Augusta, the Rains of Seven Pines 167
Chapter 22: The Maine Boys Fired and Fired and Fired... 177
Chapter 23: The Man with the White Handkerchief 193
Chapter 24: Across the Flood 199
Chapter 25: Balloon Handler 207

Continued...

Chapter 26: Morning Carnage at Seven Pines 217
Chapter 27: The Application of Cold Steel 225
Chapter 28: They Sought the Dead Amidst the Disintegrated 231
Chapter 29: A Maine Hero lay Closest to Richmond 237
Chapter 30: Resurrection 241
Chapter 31: Rally Round the Flag, Boys 247
Chapter 32: Angels of the Battlefield 261
Chapter 33: Round Up the Reluctant 273
Chapter 34: Unremitted Fury at Gaines Mill 279
Chapter 35: On the Road Again 295
Chapter 36: The Fighting Retreat 305
Chapter 37: The Battle of Baton Rouge 321
Chapter 38: The Fearful Place Called Harrison's 329
Chapter 39: The Empty Sleeve 339
Chapter 40: The Elephant Approaches 347
Chapter 41: Cedar Mountain Combat 357
Chapter 42: Men Stood Like Statues 365
Chapter 43: Prelude to Slaughter 373
Chapter 44: Encounter in the East Woods 379
Chapter 45: Forward, the 7th Maine 387
Chapter 46: Tramping Tonight on the Field of the Slain 401
Chapter 47: Angels of Mercy 409
Chapter 48: Maine's Most Hated 421
Chapter 49: The Blanket Brigade Presses Onward 427
Chapter 50: They Wanted to Fight 435

Bibliography 439

Military Units Index 445
   Maine Military Units 445
   Other Union Military Units 446
   Confederate Units 448

General Index 449

Foreword

By Nicholas P. Picerno

Many are familiar with the final paragraph of General Joshua L. Chamberlain's address at Gettysburg on October 3, 1889. It begins, "In great deeds something abides." The conclusion to Chamberlain's speech is oft-quoted by Civil War battlefield preservationists as a poignant reminder of why we save battlefields—ground made hallowed by those who sacrificed their lifeblood on it. As useful as Chamberlain's final statement has become, it is the opening portion of that heralded speech that movingly relates Maine's role in the American Civil War.

Chamberlain poignantly stated: "The State of Maine stands here today for the first time in her own name. In other days she was here indeed—here in power—here in majesty—here in glory; but as elsewhere and often in the centuries before, with that humility which is perhaps the necessary law of human exaltation, her worth merged in a name mightier than her own, so here, content to be part of that greater being that she held dearer than self, but which was made more worthy of honor by her belonging to it—the United States of America. For which great end, in every heroic struggle from the beginning of our history until now,—a space of more than two hundred years,—she has given her best of heart and brain and poured out her most precious blood."

In 1860 Maine's population stood at 628,279. Of that number 112,466 Maine men were eligible to participate in the nation's defining struggle. A significant portion of those who could enlist did; 72,945, to be exact. Of that number, 9,398 never returned to their Maine homes. More than 11,000 Mainers who did survive returned home forever scarred by wounds received on the battlefield. Untold numbers returned stricken with psychological trauma inflicted by the ghastly scenes of the battlefield. These statistics offer testament to the valor of Maine's Union veterans and their commitment to the Union's preservation. In the flash of an eye they each risked the wonderment of life, the joy of family, and the fulfillment of old age.

The names of Chamberlain, Berry, Howard, Fessenden, and Beal reside in the pantheon of Maine's history. Yet others whose story has yet to be thoroughly examined are equally as important in telling Maine's Civil War history. Each of them witnessed the horrors of war and if they survived they would never forget the scenes through which they passed. A handful left behind narratives and regimental histories that provided evidence and a unique perspective of unimaginable bravery. These men wrote about their exploits and that of their comrades. Veterans reminisced at regimental reunions and in their local post rooms of the Grand Army of the Republic. Others delivered speeches in which they recounted the glory and deeds they witnessed between 1861 and 1865.

Now Brian Swartz, through diligent and remarkable research, has assembled all of their stories in a three-volume work. Brian conducted his research at archives, libraries, historical societies, and private collections. Known for his ability as a writer, he has demonstrated his other talent as a tireless and dedicated researcher. In addition to those renowned and celebrated luminaries he recounts the stories of lesser-known, but equally determined, Mainers. His passion for Maine's role in the Civil War is evident as he painstakingly uncovers the various participants' accounts. These include John Mead Gould, Abner Small, Thomas W. Hyde, George W. Bicknell, Albert Maxfield, and so many others. Once well-known by their contemporaries, their names have unfortunately faded into history's shadows. Brian has resurrected their contributions and tells their story. He adds them to the historic narrative thereby skillfully weaving a comprehensive history of the many participants from Maine who beheld the five Aprils of the Civil War. Brian's work leaves us, as stated in Chamberlain's last paragraph in his 1888 speech, "to ponder and dream."

Nicholas P. Picerno
Chairman
Shenandoah Valley Battlefields Foundation
New Market, Virginia

Publisher's Preface

By David M. Fitzpatrick

I remember the day that Brian Swartz's Maine at War column first appeared in the Bangor Daily News. It was the beginning of a monthly column intended to run for the duration of the 150th anniversary of the Civil War. Brian and I had worked together for six years, so I was very familiar with his competence as a newspaper writer, but somehow I never saw Maine at War coming.

Perhaps I should have. Brian had always been a dedicated Civil War aficionado, spending his time reading books about the war, traipsing about its hallowed battlefields, and researching. He'd spend endless hours at the Bangor Public Library, the Maine State Archives, historical societies, and anywhere else that might be able to teach him something new—through obscure books, newspaper microfilm, military paperwork, and original letters that Maine soldiers had written to those back home.

I just hadn't suspected how powerfully his twin passions of writing and Civil War history would combine to produce that first column. I read it that morning and met him in our shared office to congratulate him on a job very well done—and to ask him a key question.

"Did you write this on company time?" I asked.

"No," he said.

"Don't," I advised. This was simply a matter of copyright: As employees of the BDN, anything that we wrote on company time belonged to the BDN. Brian spent so much of his personal time researching that it would have been a shame to not own his hard work, born of such passion. More than that, as I suggested, he should save everything that he wrote for that column and, eventually, publish them in a collection.

And, of course, due to the usual space restrictions in print, the lengthy word counts of his initial column drafts typically had to be cut back—sometimes mercilessly—to run in the paper. Much of his research, passion, and flare was lost in the final product. I advised him to keep his original drafts, something that he assured me he was doing.

In 2014, Brian and I both left the newspaper. He'd already amassed a fair number of columns that had run in print, and he continued writing Maine at War as a BDN blog. Brian began asking me about publishing, so I explained the ins and outs of writing nonfiction book proposals, approaching potential agents and publishers, how the world of publishing worked, and so forth.

The challenge would have been finding a major publisher that would let him publish what he really wanted to see in print. I suspect that most publishers would have forced him to tear his work up in order to make it inexpensive to produce and thus sell more copies—do it in one volume, or maybe two with low page counts; cut out this and hack out that; scale back the number of illustrations; reduce it to the bare essentials. In short, he'd probably have to chip away at his passion until it was but a shadow of his vision and dream.

Should Michelangelo have kept hacking away once he'd uncovered David from within the marble? Should da Vinci have removed Mona Lisa's smile? Should Shakespeare have cut his plays in half? No—but that's how commercial publishing usually works.

In 2016, he asked if I would publish it, and I didn't even have to think about it. The chance to support my friend in this marvelous project, and publish something that was truly worthy, was a no-brainer. This was to be no small job. Brian envisioned a three-volume set covering the duration of the Civil War; based on what he had lined up for the first volume, I knew that this would be a big book, and not one with a discount price tag. That never swayed me.

I remember being in seventh grade, some 35 years ago, when the state decreed that students had to get a certain dose of Maine history. I'm not sure where that requirement stands today but, after reading and editing this volume, there's no doubt in my mind that every student in Maine ought to read it. The Civil War is one of the most important times in the history of Maine, not to mention the nation—a time that shaped the future in the many deaths of those who might otherwise have lived, and in the many survivors who would never be the same people they were before the war.

After reading this book at least five times, what I've learned and experienced has been nothing short of stunning. The research that Brian has done, the details that he has reported, the painstaking care that he has taken to accurately quote so many sources, and the countless hours that he has spent putting this together is beyond admirable. More than that, it's engaging. I've leafed through several Civil War books, and to be fair a lot of it reads like typically boring academia.

Not this book. This is a story of courage and valor, allegiance and desperation, satisfaction and frustration, passion and fury. Herein Brian takes you through Maine's vital role in the Civil War, immersing you in the true story of how Mainers answered the call to preserve the Union, and how they lived and died to do so.

May they live on in our hearts and minds thanks to what Brian Swartz has accomplished with this, the first of three volumes of the ultimate authority on Maine Civil War lore. To call this first volume monumental runs the risk of finding myself labeled hyperbolic or sensationalist. I'll take those labels with grace and pride, for "monumental" is perhaps too weak an adjective for what follows.

David M. Fitzpatrick
Editor and Publisher
Brewer, Maine
March 2019

Author's Preface

By Brian F. Swartz

I grew up in Brewer, in central Maine, the place where Joshua Lawrence Chamberlain lived about a century before my grandparents purchased a farm on Chamberlain Street. After Mom built her house on the farm's edge, we had to travel at least a short distance on that street no matter where we were headed.

My elementary education coincided with the Civil War's centennial, highlighted locally by a color cartoon in the Saturday edition of the local *Bangor Daily News*. Based on a particular wartime event coinciding with each publication date, the cartoons let me visualize a Civil War that fascinated me.

Devouring every war-related book that crossed my path, I learned the campaigns, battles, and major players of the Civil War. State law required students to take Maine history in the fifth and eighth grades, so I researched Maine's role in the Civil War while in Mrs. Blethen's eighth-grade history class.

Not much information on that topic was available then and through the decades from the 1970s to 2011—or so I thought. Every mention of Maine's wartime involvement, including the 1993 movie *Gettysburg*, seemed to point toward a certain general, a certain regiment, and a certain Pennsylvania hill. Maine apparently contributed nothing else toward the Union's salvation—and I disparage neither the general nor the regiment.

While working as a *Bangor Daily News* editor in winter 2011, I pitched the top brass on a monthly column titled *Maine at War*, timed to coincide with the Civil War's sesquicentennial. The column would focus on Mainers in the war. Granted permission to publish, I started researching the topic. Surely there was little information to be found—and how quickly the Maine State Archives, the Bangor Public Library, and other sources proved me wrong! Mainers had played intimate wartime roles that, except for a few well-done books published since the war's conclusion, too many history books and courses had overlooked.

Rallying around the flag, men and women from the Pine Tree State went forth to save the United States. Leaving their families and homes in a ruggedly beautiful land from which farmers, fishermen, and loggers still wrestle a hard-won living, more than 70,000 Maine men and boys—so many were so young—joined the Army and the Navy.

At least dozens of Maine women volunteered as nurses, and thousands more women worked in the textile mills or at home to manufacture clothing and equipment for their comrades in arms. Keeping their families and home front together, Maine women—wives, mothers, sisters, and sweethearts—endured loneliness and privation while their men fought far away.

With the initial appearance of *Maine at War* in April 2011, a good friend and colleague, David M. Fitzpatrick, urged me to publish the stories in a book. My column ceased in its print edition with my 2014 retirement, but the online component added in 2012 still publishes weekly.

While select columns and characters evolved into *Maine at War, Volume I: Bladensburg to Sharpsburg*, the book encompasses much more material gleaned from original documents, including period diaries, letters, newspaper accounts, and official reports. Speaking through all this material, specific Mainers share their wartime experiences, which are the essence of *Maine at War, Volume I*.

Come and meet these Mainers, initially strangers when I tramped my first battlefield (Gettysburg) in 1989. Since then, on treks across Maine and as far afield as the Peninsula, South Mountain, Charleston, Fort Pulaski, Chancellorsville and Fredericksburg and The Wilderness, Annapolis, Harpers Ferry, Bentonville, Antietam, Cedar Mountain, Fort Fisher, and Middletown in the Shenandoah, I have crossed paths (sometimes repeatedly) with many *Maine at War* characters.

Among them are Elijah Walker, Sarah Sampson, Oliver Otis Howard, Charles Tilden, Isabella Fogg, John L. Hodsdon, Israel Washburn Jr., John Mead Gould, Jonathan Prince Cilley and the hell-bent-for-leather troopers of the 1st Maine Cavalry Regiment, and the Bradys and the hard-fighting lads of the 11th Maine Infantry Regiment.

Please, let me introduce you to my friends from Maine.

Brian Swartz
Hampden, Maine
April 2018

Acknowledgements

By Brian F. Swartz

The stories woven into *Maine at War, Volume I: Bladensburg to Sharpsburg* could not be told without the support of people interested in Maine history. To everyone who contributed to the book, I express a heart-felt "thank you," and I particularly wish to thank:

Maine State Archivist David Cheever and the dedicated staff at the Maine State Archives;
William Cook and Elizabeth Stevens, the Local History and Special Collections librarians at the Bangor Public Library;
Peter and Cyndi Dalton, whose own books about specific Maine regiments spurred my interest in those units and others;
Nicholas P. Picerno, the leading expert on the 1st-10th-29th Maine infantry regiments;
Megan Pinette, president of the Belfast Historical Society;
The members of Richardson's Civil War Round Table: Glenn Webb, Linda and John Jewell, Jim Roberts Sr., Robert Kuprovich, Duane Wardwell, John Fennell, and the late George Sawyer;
Tom Desjardin, 20th Maine Infantry historian and author;
David M. Fitzpatrick, whose belief in this project kept me inspired when I did not feel like it;
Richard R. Shaw, Bangor historian;
Christopher Swartz, for patiently tramping across the far-flung battlefields with his dad;
Gary Edwards, the Ira Gardner descendant who introduced me to the 14th Maine Infantry;
The Special Collections staff at the Raymond H. Fogler Library, University of Maine;
James Mundy, 2nd and 6th Maine Infantry historian and author;
The Aroostook County Historical and Art Museum;
Eve Anderson and the Thomaston Historical Society;
Dr. William Hopkins;
And most of all, my dear Susan, for her support, patience, and love.

Chapter 1

FIRST BLOOD AT BLADENSBURG

"I know my wound has been a severe one"

Utterly bored by his cushy War Department desk job in Washington, D.C., Maj. Jonathan Prince Cilley of the 1st Maine Cavalry Regiment realized that he wanted to shoot someone, anyone, in late spring 1863, as long as his target wore Confederate gray or butternut.

So to satisfy his blood lust, Cilley fired off a letter to Maine Governor Abner Coburn on Saturday, June 20, 1863.

By his professional acumen and demeanor, Cilley should have been a good bureaucrat after taking his new job the previous winter. Born into a middle-class family in Thomaston, Maine on December 29, 1835, he followed in his father's steps and became a lawyer practicing on the state's Midcoast.[1]

Had Fort Sumter not intervened, Cilley—"Prin" to his siblings—would have married, raised a family, and become a respectable attorney.

And, like his father, Cilley might have pursued politics as a second career.

At 5 feet 6½ inches, Prin Cilley was about average in height for his generation. He had blue eyes and "light" hair and a "light" complexion, physical attributes suggesting English or Nordic ethnicity. He was not a heavy man; inadequate Army rations would have seen to that.[2]

Twenty-five years old on Friday, April 12, 1861, Cilley awoke that morning unaware that Pierre Gustave Toutant Beauregard had ordered the shelling of Fort Sumter at Charleston, South Carolina before dawn. The attack placed Maine at war for the third time in 49 years, including the War of 1812 and the Bloodless Aroostook War.

Desiring to defend his state and country, Cilley joined the 1st Maine Cavalry Regiment within six months. He all but swallowed a Confederate cannonball at Middletown, Virginia on May 24, 1862. Another wounded soldier would have gratefully accepted the medical discharge and hightailed it home. Not Jonathan Prince Cilley: While his mangled right shoulder healed, he petitioned for a war-related job. Figuring that a cavalryman with one usable arm could not ride a horse, an Army bureaucrat decided that Cilley would make a good desk jockey.

And he had better be grateful for the job.

Cilley was not.

Still a 1st Maine Cavalry member in spring 1863, he heard through the regimental grapevine and the Washington press that Col. Calvin Douty had been killed in action at the Battle of Aldie in Virginia on June 17. Hailing from Dover in Maine's Piscataquis County, the 48-year-old Douty had commanded the 1st Maine Cavalry; his death opened opportunities for promotion…

…and Jonathan Cilley wanted back in the saddle.

"In filling this [Douty's] vacancy I earnestly and sincerely, Governor, ask your attention to my claims for promotion," Cilley wrote Coburn from Washington, D.C. on June 20. The governor was only the latest Maine official to hear from Cilley, who had even petitioned Vice President Hannibal Hamlin of Bangor for reinstatement to combat.[3]

He reminded Coburn that, during a previous meeting, Cilley had asked, "If after my return to active service I should act as bravely and efficiently as Lt. Col. [Charles] Smith,[4] so that there should be no preference on that score, and a vacancy should occur in the Colonelcy, whether I should have under the circumstances any claim to promotion?"

Coburn had responded that he could not answer that question until "the actual occurrence" of the 1st Maine's colonel dying, Cilley reminded the governor.

Now Douty had been shot from the saddle in front of a stone wall on the Aldie heights. Cilley told Coburn that while "my return to field service precludes my claiming the position of Colonel … I do think I have a claim to the position of Lieut. Colonel."[5]

Jonathan Cilley (a drawing likely made shortly before his death) **and Deborah Prince Cilley**
Images courtesy of the Thomaston Historical Society

Sergeant Glazier at the Aldie
Col. Calvin Douty of the 1st Maine Cavalry was killed in action at Aldie. This depiction is from Sword and Pen—or, Ventures and Adventures of Willard Glazier in War and Literature *(1890) by John Algernon Owens*

Then Cilley explained why, with Maine at war, he still wanted to fight.

Based on northern New England history, war came naturally to Maine and its residents through the region's first 250 years. Two early 19th-century wars had birthed the state and forged its border with Canada; earlier wars had made the state's existence even possible, and now the Civil War had cast Maine into the national limelight.

Until March 3, 1820, the quintessential "native Mainer"—a self-proclaimed status among (some, fortunately not all) modern Mainers born within the state—did not exist. Massachusetts governed the District of Maine, from which male voters elected representatives to the General Court in Boston and occasionally petitioned that same legislature to establish a new town amidst the far-flung forests north and northeast of the Piscataqua River.

Although colonial settlements dotted its coast in the 1600s, the District of Maine saw its population limited by climate and war. Indians and whites had fought several bloody wars in Maine and elsewhere in New England from the late 1600s to the mid-18th century. Not until after Britain had captured New France during the French and Indian War did white settlers venture east and north beyond Penobscot Bay, a de facto "no-go zone" for the English for almost 150 years.

Devastated by endless war and European disease, the Indian tribes that had limited white settlement to the western shore of Penobscot Bay ended their opposition by the late 1760s. Lured by cheap land—and lots of it—settlers pushed east along the coast and north up the Penobscot River.

Confederate Gen. Pierre Gustave Toutant-Beauregard
Photo by Mathew Brady via National Archives and Records Administration

Maine Gov. Abner Coburn
30th Governor of Maine
Photo via Wikipedia

The Revolutionary War temporarily stopped that expansion. The war impacted Maine; the British blockade hindered coastal commerce, and American and Canadian privateers nipped and bit at each side's merchant ships. On land, serious fighting took place at Machias (an American victory) and at Castine (an American defeat).

There, in July 1779, a land-and-sea expedition financed primarily by Massachusetts attempted to capture a British fort and garrison. American warships cornered a few British warships in Castine harbor, and American soldiers scaled the Dice Head cliffs to chase British soldiers into Fort George. Senior American officers then mismanaged the siege; suddenly appearing in lower Penobscot Bay, a British fleet trapped the American fleet on August 13. Whether captured by the British or scuttled by its crew, every American ship was lost.

The 1779 Penobscot Expedition left Massachusetts broke and unable to defend Maine. Planning to turn the region into a colony named New Ireland, Britain occupied the District of Maine from the Penobscot River east to Passamaquoddy Bay (except for Machias) until the war ended. Britain then returned the region to Massachusetts.[6]

Immediately after the Revolution, Maine owed its population growth (over 57 percent from 1790 to 1800) primarily to in-migration from Massachusetts and other New England states. Unable to pay Continental veterans their promised bonuses, the Massachusetts General Court offered land in the District of Maine as recompense. Many former soldiers and their families moved north into what were literally the wilds of Massachusetts.

The 1810 federal census found 228,705 people living in Maine, primarily along the coast and in the river valleys. Water afforded easier transportation for people and commerce than did the district's inferior roads, and those municipalities where commerce and sea converged did well economically. Portland had grown substantially since Royal Navy Captain Henry Mowat had burned the town (then called Falmouth) in October 1775; at head of tide on the Penobscot River, Bangor would become a major inland port within a generation.[7]

When the War of 1812 erupted, Mainers (like other New Englanders) viewed the conflict as "Mr. Madison's War." President James Madison had sought a fight with Great Britain, and with it Maine lived between a rock (Boston) and a very hard place (British Canada).

The Royal Navy imposed a blockade that devastated Maine's and New England's commerce-based shipping and its affiliated activities, such as shipbuilding. Looking with renewed interest at that New Ireland concept from 35 years earlier, British authorities ordered eastern Maine retaken.

On Monday, July 11, 1814, a British fleet dropped anchor off Eastport on Passamaquoddy Bay. Negotiating at cannon-point, British officers quickly forced the surrender of the small American garrison at Fort Sullivan, overlooking Eastport Harbor.

From there British troops and soldiers skipped westward to briefly occupy Machias and recapture Castine, where the American soldiers garrisoning Fort Madison withdrew on Thursday, September 1. The Union Jack again rose above Fort George.[8]

Meanwhile, American Navy Capt. Charles Morris had moored his frigate, the USS *Adams*, at Hampden about 30 miles up the Penobscot River so that his crew could repair some damage caused by a collision with unyielding Maine granite off Isle au Haut. Hearing about the *Adams*, British authorities went after it.

A British fleet disembarked soldiers at Bald Hill Cove on the Penobscot River in Winterport

Union Lt. Col. Charles Ferguson Smith
Photo by Mathew Brady via National Archives and Records Administration

Kentucky Rep. William Jordan Graves
Illustration by Philip Haas via Library of Congress

on September 2. While warships worked north on the river, the British soldiers marched toward Hampden the next day. There, on the hill occupied then by the original Hampden Academy, they collided with several hundred local militiamen and a few Army regulars.

British troops deployed into line and advanced uphill. In the ensuing action, the militiamen fired a volley and, when the British reciprocated and kept advancing with lowered bayonets, ran away. The British expedition soon captured Bangor, Brewer, Hampden, and Orrington; exacting a high financial price for the militia's chutzpah at defying King George III, British troops returned to Castine.[9]

The Treaty of Ghent officially ended the War of 1812 in mid-February 1815. Not until April 25 did British forces withdraw from Castine. Eastport was later returned (albeit reluctantly) to the United States.

Mainers intent on defending their country duly noted that Massachusetts had done precious little to defend the District of Maine during the war. Anger boiled at this perceived mistreatment; "no event in all the previous history of the union of Massachusetts and Maine so blatantly revealed the extent to which the interests of Maine could be sacrificed to those of Massachusetts proper," author Ronald F. Banks surmised.[10]

With the War of 1812 fresh in their minds and a distrust of Britain in their hearts, Mainers pursued independence from Massachusetts. Boston raised few, if any, objections to getting rid of its northern nuisance, so elected delegates from Maine approved a state constitution at Portland in autumn 1819.

The timing was politically perfect. Missourians also sought statehood, and a Congress seeking to soothe the ruffled feelings between pro-slavery Southerners and anti-slavery Northerners engineered the Missouri Compromise of 1820: Missouri would join the country as a slave state, Maine as a free state. The vote passed Congress that February, and Maine officially became the 23rd state on Friday, March 3.

With the new state came economic opportunity and growth; Maine's population jumped by 100,000 people by 1830. Among the people moving to Maine during that period was Jonathan Cilley, born in Nottingham, New Hampshire on July 2, 1802. He would father the avenging angel, Jonathan Prince Cilley.

While studying law at Bowdoin College in Brunswick, Cilley became friends with classmates and future New England literati Nathaniel Hawthorne and Henry Wadsworth Longfellow and an upper classmate, Franklin Pierce. Graduating from Bowdoin in 1828, Cilley gained admittance to the Maine bar in 1828 and opened a law practice in Thomaston in Lincoln County that same year.

He had a pretty good reason for settling there. Writing to his sister, Elizabeth Ann, on March 15, 1829, Cilley proclaimed that "your brother Jona. is going to take this same dear little Deborah Prince for his wife, a partner for life—the sharer of his joys & sorrows..." Born on July 6, 1808, Deborah was the daughter of Thomaston attorney Hezekiah Prince and his wife, Isabella.[11]

Deborah married Jonathan Cilley in Thomaston on Saturday, April 4, 1829, and bore him five children. Three survived to adulthood: Greenleaf, born in October 1829 and named for his paternal grandfather; Prince, born in 1835; and Julia Draper, born in 1837. A son, Bowdoin Longfellow, died in 1834; his sister, Jane Nealley, died in 1836.

Jonathan Cilley won election to the Maine House of Representatives in 1831 and served admirably until 1836; his party's legislators twice elected him Speaker of the House. Politically a Jacksonian Democrat, Cilley won election to Congress from Maine's Third District and took office in March 1837.

An Andrew Jackson ally, Cilley dealt with state and national issues. The Treaty of Ghent had not solidified Maine's border with Canada, an oversight that grated Maine politicians seeking to expand settlement north in the 1830s. "I made a few remarks in the House a few days ago touching [on] our boundary," Cilley wrote Deborah from Washington, D.C. on January 10, 1838. "They were great, & a sketch of them will be published in a few days."[12]

In a Jan. 16 letter to "My Dearest Deborah," Cilley described a curious House-related incident. Two congressmen, Democrat Samuel Jameson Gholson of Mississippi and Whig Henry Wise of Virginia, "called each other bad names to day in the house of Reps,"

James Watson Webb
Photo from Brady-Handy Collection, Library of Congress

Cilley wrote. "Wise is an impudent & fancy fellow. I do not like him at all. It is thought by some that it will end in a duel. An attempt was made to settle the affair before we adjourned," but to no avail.[13]

Within weeks Cilley would earn Wise's enmity after speaking on the House floor during an investigation of Maine Senator John Ruggles, Cilley's neighbor in Thomaston, a former friend, and now an implacable foe. Ruggles stood accused of corruption by Matthew L. Davis, a correspondent for the New York City-based newspaper *Courier and Enquirer*. The paper was owned by Col. James Watson Webb.

According to Davis, Ruggles had offered to help a New Jersey inventor get a patent for a new style of lock. Ruggles, who allegedly would peddle his political influence for 25 percent of the inventor's earnings, supposedly said, "Merit? Why things do not go here [in Congress] by merit, but by pulling the right strings. Make it my interest and I will pull the strings for you."[14]

During House debate on whether or not to investigate Ruggles (who would be ultimately cleared), Jonathan Cilley stood at his desk on February 12. He asked if Webb, who employed Davis, was the same newspaper owner accused in 1834 of receiving a $52,000 loan from the Second Bank of the United States. The *Courier and Enquirer*, which had opposed renewing the bank's charter, reversed its editorial direction after Webb allegedly received the loan.

Viewing Cilley's question as a personal affront, Webb rushed to Washington and asked a friend, Kentucky Whig Congressman William Jordan Graves, to deliver to Cilley a note requesting an apology.[15] Cilley politely declined to receive the initial note and later a second Webb-written note also carried by Graves, to whom Cilley expressed no "feelings other than those of friendship, and the highest respect for yourself."[16]

Senator Henry Clay, Kentucky's leading politician and a Whig, told Graves that Cilley had insulted him and that a duel was necessary to restore his honor. Henry Wise signed on as Graves's second.

Stating that "New England must not be trampled on," Cilley accepted the challenge to a duel; his second would be Gen. George W. Jones. [17]

In his February letters, Cilley apparently did not mention the impending duel to Deborah. But by Thursday, March 1 she had learned that "you have been challenged by Webber [sic] of New York ... I will never believe you will accept a challenge ... I cannot speak or write about it."[18]

Her letter came too late.

Shortly after 2 p.m. on a cold and sunny Saturday, February 24, the two parties met in Bladensburg, Maryland, just over the District of Columbia line. Eschewing the traditional congressional dueling grounds for a fence-bordered field, Cilley and Graves disembarked from

The United States Capitol, 1831
The Capitol with its original dome, as it looked a few years before Rep. Cilley was killed.
Illustration by John Rubens Smith via Library of Congress

The Bladensburg Dueling Grounds
The date of this photo is unknown, but depicts where Cilley and Graves fought their duel. The two figures in the photo (far left and far right) are standing at the approximate spots that the two men stood for their first shots.
Photo from the Tibbitts family collection, courtesy of the Thomaston Historical Society

their respective vehicles.[19]

Cilley had selected rifles as the weapons du jour. The duelists' seconds, Jones and Wise, paced off 80 yards at a 90-degree angle with the sun.[20] The wind blew at a 45-degree angle toward Cilley. Positioning themselves accordingly, each congressman turned toward his opponent to present a smaller target. Minutes past 3 p.m., the duelists fired at each other and missed.

The duel should have ended there, but during the ensuing discussions, Cilley refused to apologize to Webb, who did not even attend the duel. With a reputation for trying to initiate duels, the blood-thirsty Wise pressured Graves to insist on shooting again; as James Webb's stand-in, Graves claimed that honor had not been satisfied.

The duelists shot and missed.

Jones and Wise spoke with Graves a second time, and Cilley probably realized the duel's intended outcome, especially after Jones reported that, if the third shots missed, Wise proposed "to shorten the distance" between the duelists.[21]

Turning to an accompanying friend, Col. James W. Schaumberg, Cilley said, "I see the disposition of the opposite party and that they thirst for my blood."[22]

Graves insisted on a third shot. Both men fired; Graves's rifle ball struck Cilley in his lower body and apparently severed an artery.[23] "I am shot," Cilley said as he collapsed into Schaumberg's arms.

Jonathan Cilley died within 90 seconds.[24]

Ironically a subsequent Select Committee investigation proved that Cilley had correctly surmised the "thirst for my blood." James W. Webb had rounded up two friends and a few pistols that Saturday before traveling to Cilley's boarding house and then to Bladensburg to force a fight with the Maine congressman. If the three men had stumbled upon the duel, no matter what happened or who tried to intervene, the goal was that "Webb should instantly shoot Mr. Cilley," according to the committee report that described Webb as "an assassin."[25]

On March 2, "the afflicting news of Mr. Cilley's death reached his lovely widow," Sarah Washburn told William Graves in a scathing letter written the same day. "One shriek of horror,

Jonathan Prince Cilley
Photo courtesy of Thomaston Historical Society

burst from her anguished heart, which must bleed, bleed forever…"[26]

The duel shocked the Washington elite and drew outrage in Maine, where the *Lincoln Patriot* headlined "Murder of Mr. Cilley!" The belief became widespread in the state that Graves had murdered Jonathan Cilley, that rather than acknowledge that his honor had been upheld, a Southerner had slain a Maine Yankee.[27]

Jonathan Cilley would be buried in April in Thomaston's Elm Grove Cemetery. Already stricken with tuberculosis, Deborah Cilley would gallantly uphold her husband's name before dying on August 14, 1844 and being buried beside Jonathan.

Deborah bestowed one last honor on her murdered husband. In a September 23, 1838 letter to his sister, Elizabeth Ann Burley, Deborah wrote that "Greenleaf I find clings entirely to me—& I find a solace in his affection & my sweet little Prince (to which I have added the name Jonathan) is affectionate … but my little Julia is my darling."[28]

Raised by their relatives, Greenleaf, Jonathan Prince, and Julia would become well-adjusted adults. They knew that a Southerner, a slavery advocate, had killed their beloved father.

As he wrote Maine Governor Abner Coburn on Saturday, June 20, 1863, Maj. Jonathan Prince Cilley of the 1st Maine Cavalry Regiment explained why he wanted to return to field duty, despite the Confederate cannonball that had mangled his right shoulder 13 months earlier.

"I know my wound has been a severe one, but should that fact be the means of bringing more disgrace upon me, of laying me on the shelf in the springtime of my youth and health, and the very time a man would wish to live that desires to serve his country," Cilley wrote.

"Your father has been killed at the very entrance to public life," he remembered. "Years after, just as you are attaining the full powers of manhood, the same influence that slew your father seeks to destroy the life of your Country.

"You joyfully rush to its aid, glad of the opportunity to avenge the death of your father, and to serve your native land, you are wounded: laid on the shelf; passed by, others passed over you, and your high hopes of usefulness and renown destroyed," Cilley wrote.

"Is such a just reward for those who peril their lives that their country may live?" he asked Coburn. "My character as an Officer and a man, is I think, high and honorable.

"I beg, Governor, a careful and friendly consideration of my claim to the Lieut. Colonelcy of the Regiment," Cilley closed his letter.[29]

Maine was at war; Jonathan Prince Cilley wanted to fight, as did most of the 80,000 other Maine men who answered their nation's call to arms from 1861 to 1865.

But for the Cilley children, the Civil War started at Bladensburg, Maryland on February 24, 1838.

~~~

1. The term "Midcoast" roughly refers to that section of Maine encompassing the shores of Sagadahoc, Lincoln, Knox, and Waldo counties.
2. Jonathan P. Cilley, *Soldiers' File,* Maine State Archives

3. Jonathan P. Cilley, letter to Abner Coburn, June 20, 1863, MSA
4. Charles Smith replaced the slain Douty as colonel of the 1st Maine Cavalry Regiment.
5. Jonathan P. Cilley to Abner Coburn, June 20, 1863, MSA
6. U.S. Census Bureau
7. Ibid.
8. George F.W. Young, *The British Capture & Occupation of Downeast Maine 1814-1815/1818,* Penobscot Bay Press, 2014, pp. 21-22
9. Ibid., pp. 31-41
10. Robert F. Banks, *Maine Becomes a State: the movement to separate Maine from Massachusetts, 1785-1820,* Maine Historical Society, Wesleyan University Press, p. 60
11. Eve Anderson, *A Breach of Privilege: The Cilley Family Letters,* Seven Coin Press, Spruce Head, Maine, 2002, P. 56
12. Ibid., p. 142
13. Ibid., p. 146
14. Ibid., p. 189
15. In an eerie parallel with Cilley, Graves was an attorney who served in the Kentucky House of Representatives.
16. Anderson, *A Breach of Privilege,* p. 190
17. Ibid., p. 192
18. Ibid., p. 155
19. Not until a year after the Cilley-Graves duel would Congress outlaw dueling in the District of Columbia.
20. The final distance apparently was 92 yards, a challenging distance for both duelists. Cilley had hunted with a rifle when younger; having never really handled such a firearm, Graves put in some desperate target practice the morning of the duel.
21. Congressional Globe, House of Representatives, 25th Congress, 2nd Sessions, Library of Congress, pp. 330-331
22. Anderson, *A Breach of Privilege,* p. 179
23. Congressional Globe, p. 331
24. Anderson, *A Breach of Privilege,* pp. 161-162
25. Congressional Globe, p. 331
26. Anderson, *A Breach of Privilege,* pp. 161-162
27. Ibid., p. 181
28. Ibid., p. 214
29. Jonathan P. Cilley to Abner Coburn, June 20, 1863, MSA

Chapter 2

ILL-PREPARED TO SAVE THE UNION

"Our militia system can result in nothing but a miserable failure"

When New Brunswick loggers snatched a Maine land agent and his two companions in the disputed Territory of Aroostook and hustled them over the Canadian border in February 1839, outraged Maine politicians vowed revenge—even if the state must wage war on Great Britain.

In that year of her 19th birthday, Maine prepared militarily and psychologically to beard the mighty British lion.

Yet on Friday, April 12, 1861, "the bombardment of Fort Sumter ... found Maine as little prepared to furnish troops for maintaining the integrity of the Union, as it is possible to conceive," reported an angry and weary Adjutant Gen. John Littlefield Hodsdon.[1]

Within a generation, the state's boiling martial ardor had cooled and coagulated to where of "some sixty thousand men" enrolled as "unarmed militia," perhaps 1,200 men belonging to "merely paper organizations" could "respond to calls for ordinary duty" in Maine, Hodsdon commented. As for duty elsewhere, the men and their equipment were "totally unfitted for service in the field."[2]

Swept into office by the Republican tide that crested in Maine prior to the 1860 general election, Governor Israel Washburn Jr. of Livermore took office in January 1861. The legislature tapped John Hodsdon as the new adjutant general. A Bangor attorney and a militia member in his adult years, he proved a wise choice; Hodsdon had learned the adjutant general's trade a generation earlier during the infamous "Bloodless Aroostook War."

Ratified by the United States Senate in February 1815 to end the War of 1812, the Treaty of Ghent had conveniently overlooked a point critical to Maine: Where was the international border separating Maine and Canada located? Washington really did not care; Augusta (to which the Maine capital was moved from Portland in 1830) and London certainly did.

Hubristic Maine politicians claimed that, according to provisions of the treaty ending the Revolutionary War, the state's northern border reached to within spitting distance of the St. Lawrence River. This boundary would place vast forests of virgin timber and the upper St. John River under American control.

British officials claimed the border lay farther south, along a line that would roughly lop one-third off modern Maine. This border would secure for Britain a land route linking the Maritimes to what was then the Province of Lower Canada, a route that would facilitate troop movements if Britain and the United States decided, in a quaint Maine colloquialism, to "whale away" at each other for the third time.

Ironically, both sides generally agreed that Maine's eastern boundary followed the St. Croix River to its headwaters and then ran due north from there. How far north was open to conjecture, though.

Maine Adjutant General John L. Hodsdon
Photo courtesy of Bangor Public Library

Washington partially solidified the eastern border in 1828 by establishing the Hancock Barracks at Houlton, a settlement on the Meduxnekeag River in the southern Territory of Aroostook. By 1831 the so-called "Military Road" connected Houlton with Mattawamkeag in the Penobscot Valley.

American settlers and loggers pushed north into Aroostook and reached the upper St. John Valley. Conflicts arose with British authorities when some settlers raised American flags and promoted the virtues of Jeffersonian democracy. Finally, in winter 1839, Maine authorities sent a land agent, the Penobscot County sheriff, and an Old Town militia company to clear intruding Canadian loggers from the Aroostook territory. After the legislature appropriated $10,000 to cover expenses, the expedition traveled north in winter snow and cold and camped near what is now Caribou.

On February 12, the Maine land agent and two companions spent the night at a tavern near the New Brunswick border—at least, the invisible line that most local residents assumed was the border. New Brunswick loggers swept into the tavern, grabbed the three Mainers, and presented them to British authorities in Fredericton.

The incident sparked international indignation. Augusta, London, and Washington, D.C. rattled their sabers. Maine called up some 3,300 armed militiamen during the next few years,

Chapter 2: Ill-Prepared to Save the Union

London threatened to send troops to the border, and Congress appropriated $10 million to fund a 50,000-man army to defend American (i.e., Maine) honor and soil against the distrusted John Bull.

In mid-March the Maine Legislature created Aroostook County—and to Adjutant Gen. Isaac Hodsdon assigned responsibility for mobilizing and equipping the militiamen sent north to protect Maine interests. Among his aides was his adopted son, John.

Isaac Hodsdon had married Polly Wentworth in January 1805. They never had biological children; in 1820 the Hodsdons adopted John Littlefield, born in Hallowell, Maine in May 1815 to Jeremiah and Dorothy Littlefield. Jeremiah later died, and Dorothy soon remarried. Isaac Hodsdon adopted Dorothy's son and renamed him John Littlefield Hodsdon.

A Bangor attorney and militiaman in the late 1830s, John learned valuable administrative skills as Maine feinted at war with Britain. While the politicians huffed and puffed, professional soldiers kept close watch on the disputed border, and only one American soldier died—and he from disease. His comrades consigned him to a lonely grave alongside the Military Road in southern Aroostook County.

American and British officials negotiated the Webster-Ashburton Treaty, which when ratified in 1842 established the international border along its modern delineation. The regular troops went to new posts, the Maine militiamen went home...

...and by late 1860, the vaunted militia system so responsive in Maine's 1839 crisis had collapsed. John L. Hodsdon could only shake his head as he reviewed the 1860 report filed by his predecessor, Davis Tillson of Rockland.

Filed with outgoing Governor Lot Morrill, the report indicated that "only thirty six organized militia companies" existed in Maine. Under state law, able-bodied men between 18 and 45 must enroll in local militia companies, far more of which should exist.[3]

Of the 36 companies, "but very few of these ... answer the purposes for which they were designed and chartered," Tillson noted. Most companies had "a fitful and uncertain life, resulting in nothing but vexation and annoyance to their members."[4]

Among the active militia companies was the Castine Light Infantry, based at economically vibrant Castine on Penobscot Bay. Then a busy seaport, Castine had recovered quickly from the 1814-1815 British occupation. Wearing black pants and blue coats adorned with white epaulets, the local militia reported

Davis Tillson
Photo courtesy of Maine State Archives

Maine Gov. Israel Washburn Jr.
Photo by Mathew Brady, Brady-Handy Photograph Collection, Library of Congress

to Captain Seth Devereaux and Lieutenant Charles William Tilden.[5]

By definition a "native Mainer," Tilden was born in Castine to Captain Charles and Mary Tilden in May 1832. The family enjoyed relative affluence; a successful mariner and businessman, Captain Charles sent his namesake son to North Yarmouth Academy in 1849.

Tilden returned home a year later, joined the family businesses, and settled into a comfortable lifestyle. In 1854 he married his first wife, Juliette Osborn of Belfast.

Bangor boasted two militia companies, the Bangor Light Infantry and Grattan Guards. The former, which comprised "a class of men, that would ... be termed the 'top knots' of the town, or 'tony,'" sported uniforms with "red coats and huge bear skin hats." The Grattan Guards encompassed the Bangor-area Irish elite, who wore gray uniforms during their drills.[6]

Then (and now) Maine's largest city, Portland boasted five militia companies: Mechanic Blues, Portland Light Infantry, Portland Light Guard, Portland Rifle Corps, and Portland Rifle Guards. In Androscoggin County, Auburn had an artillery company, and Lewiston—developing into a major textile-manufacturing center—fielded such militia companies as the Lewiston Light Infantry and the Lewiston Zouaves, which was one of only two Zouave companies in Maine.[7]

And Milo, a small town in Piscataquis County, boasted the Milo Artillery, comprised "mostly of farm boys and river drivers."[8]

While these companies remained active in winter 1861, Maine lost other militia companies. On December 27, 1860, the few men still belonging to a light infantry company in Kittery met "at their Armory" and "voted to disband," William L. Tobey wrote Hodsdon from Kittery Point three months later.[9]

As company commander, Tobey dutifully rounded up the militiamen's weapons and equipment; he awaited Hodsdon's instructions as to what to do with everything. "No sudden disaffection or strife in our ranks" had led to the company's disbanding; the state's "gradual disinterestedness and neglect to maintain" the company "with efficiency" had caused the militiamen to abandon their state-mandated duty.

"Unless when organized we can be soldier-like in all that relates to militia[,] we had better not assume the name, under the form of organization," Tobey believed.[10]

Certain militia companies had disappeared years earlier. The annual autumn muster in Eastport of "the citizen soldiery of the Passamaquoddy towns" was "a notable annual event," remembered local historian William Henry Kilby.

But not even the martial excitement generated by the Bloodless Aroostook War adequately fed the militia flames in far-eastern Washington County. Local selectmen balked at paying each militiaman 50 cents per muster day, and "people began to look upon requirements for military service as an unnecessary duty," Kilby recalled decades later.

At the regional muster held at Pembroke in September 1842, only a non-uniformed squad went to represent the Eastport Light Infantry, "and the Lubec Rifles by a single officer," Kilby noted. "That was the end" of the traditional militia system in eastern Washington County, he admitted.[11]

Eighteen years after the poorly attended Pembroke muster, Davis Tillson explained why men deigned to serve in the militia. "I may ... state that the undoubted cause of the lack of vigor and life, the decay and want of interest so apparent in the militia, is solely to be attributed to the fact that no suitable or reasonable compensation is provided for the services requested of our citizen soldiers," Tillson wrote. "This is the real deficiency…"

Unless the legislature acknowledged that militiamen must be paid, "our militia system can result in nothing but a miserable failure," he commented.[12]

John Hodsdon inherited this "miserable failure"—and, on April 12, 1861, a real shooting war. Maine had to respond immediately, because on Monday, April 15, President Abraham Lincoln "called for one regiment of infantry from this State," Hodsdon reminded legislators.[13]

The War Department quickly upped the ante to 10 infantry regiments, so Washburn summoned the legislature into special session on Monday, April 22. Three days later legislators passed a law to raise 10 regiments "to be enlisted for two years unless sooner discharged."[14]

Washburn anticipated the law's passage when he released General Order No. 6 on April 22. The state's militia system was organized into three divisions based on Maine's existing congressional districts. To the major general (a state rank) commanding each division—James H. Butler in the First, William H. Titcomb in the Second, and Wirt Virgin in the Third—he passed word that, as Maine's commander-in-chief, Washburn "orders that TEN THOUSAND VOLUNTEERS, to be organized into Ten Regiments, without regard to present military districts, be immediately enlisted and mustered into the active militia service of the State.

"They are to be armed, equipped and disciplined, and to hold themselves in readiness" to join the "service of the United States when required," Hodsdon indicated. Existing militia companies would be accepted, but current militiamen "who are physically incompetent, or who refuse to take the oath of fidelity [to the United States], must be stricken from the company rolls, and their places filled with new enlistments."[15]

Suddenly John Hodsdon could put to good use the administrative skills learned while working for his father during the Bloodless Aroostook War. Unlike Tillson, who saw the militia system fading away in 1860, Hodsdon encountered in spring 1861 the martial ardor of Mainers intent on saving their country.

And the state's surviving militia companies would lead the way.

~~~

1. *Annual Report of the Adjutant General of the State of Maine, 1861*, p. 5
2. Ibid.
3. Davis Tillson to Lot Morrill, December 19, 1860, Maine State Archives
4. Ibid.
5. James Mundy, *Second To None,* Harp Publications, Scarborough, ME, 1992, p.39
6. R.H. Stanley and George O. Hall, *Eastern Maine and the Rebellion,* Heritage Books, Maryland, 1887, 2008, p. 27
7. *Annual Report of the Adjutant General of the State of Maine, 1861*, MSA, pp. 16-17
8. Mundy, *Second To None,* p. 40
9. William L. Tobey to John Hodsdon, March 20, 1861, MSA
10. Ibid.
11. William Henry Kilby, *Eastport and Passamaquoddy: A Collection of Historical and Biographical Sketches,* 1888, reprinted by Border Historical Society, Eastport, Maine, 2003, pp. 472-473
12. Davis Tillson to Lot Morrill, December 19, 1860, MSA
13. *Annual Report of the Adjutant General of the State of Maine, 1861*, p. 5
14. Ibid., p. 6
15. *Annual Report of the Adjutant General of the State of Maine, 1861*, Appendix A, p. 81

Chapter 3

FORMING FOR BATTLE

"Then with a heavy heart I said good-bye"

Until Confederate gunners opened fire on Fort Sumter in April 1861, Elijah Walker figured that he could skip the potential war promoted by Southern firebrands. He sold coal and lumber in Rockland; while his business partner, Hiram Berry, had decided "that if there was to be a war, he should ... give his services in defence of the Union," Walker "thought I could not do" so.[1]

Already middle-aged by mid-19th-century actuarial tables, the 42-year-old Walker supported a wife (36-year-old Susan) and the seven children (William, Narcissa, Ireson, Winfield, Frank, Annie, and Elenor) enlivening their household. Standing 5 feet 6½ inches, Walker seemed the antithesis of the archetypal Maine farmer or logger, livelihoods that demanded brawn and physical toughness.

But behind his slim build, dark complexion, brown hair, and blue eyes lurked an iron constitution and a sharp mind that benefited Walker immeasurably during the next few years.[2]

And Walker was a natural-born leader of men, although he likely never considered himself as such. Busy with his business and family, he volunteered as foreman of the Rockland-based Dirigo Engine Company, a firefighting outfit. "As the war clouds threatened" while Maj. Robert Anderson and his understrength command hunkered down behind Sumter's brick walls in early 1861, Dirigo Engine's 25 members "urged me, in case troops were called for, to lead them as their captain," Walker noted.

Evidently most of the volunteer firefighters, including Walker, served in the Rockland City Guards, a militia company that Berry had helped establish in 1854.[3]

Some 140 miles to the north in Patten, a Penobscot County town abutting Aroostook County, 18-year-old Ira Bernard Gardner romanticized military life. Local men organized "an Independent Rifle Company" at Patten in the late 1850s; Gardner soon participated in the company's drills, held weekly each summer. He later became the company's orderly sergeant.

"I had studied infantry tactics considerably," Gardner explained his martial fervor. Aware by spring 1861 that "a [national] crisis was approaching," he probably hoped that military service would spirit him far from the house he shared with his parents, John and Mary Gardner, and younger sisters Ida Rosalie, Eva Elberta, and Almy Evelyn.[4]

Sporting brown hair, blue eyes, and a fair complexion, Gardner stood 5 feet 10 inches in his stocking feet. A good education had revealed his administrative skills.[5]

With an active militia company, Patten was a rarity among Maine's smaller towns. With more than 26,000 residents, Portland held title as Maine's largest city—and supported five militia companies.

Twenty-old-year-old John Mead Gould, a Portland native, worked in spring 1861 as a clerk in the Merchants' and Traders' Bank in Portland. Moderate in height at 5-8½, he had brown hair, dark eyes, and a light complexion.[6]

After supper on Sunday, April 14, Gould joined the crowd outside the local telegraph office, where war news dominated the conversations. "I learned that the latest news was that Fort Sumter was fast falling"; later that evening local newspaper reporters informed everyone with earshot of Gould "that Fort Sumter had probably fallen," he told his journal.

Ira B. Gardner
Photo courtesy Maine State Archives

Gould mourned the potential catastrophe that Sumter's surrender entailed. "What an unhappy war. Brother against brother," he commented on April 15. "We could buy their slaves for a mere song compared with the cost of war ... Heaven save us! We can never be a Union after the war!"[7]

The attack on Fort Sumter forced decisions upon Walker, Gardner, and Gould. Walker shed his doubt about military service: "I for the first time, with those brave Dirigo boys, pledged my life and all for the defence of the nation," he announced.[8]

The news was a little slow to arrive in Patten, which "is about one hundred miles from Bangor, and ... at that time it took two days to reach us by letter," Gardner admitted. The time delay proved costly for the adventure-hungry youth; Maine Adjutant Gen. John Hodsdon issued a call for 10,000 men on April 22, and while in business in Bangor about that time, John Gardner chatted with Charles D. Jameson, an Old Town businessman involved in raising the 2nd Maine Infantry Regiment.

Jameson told the elder Gardner that the Patten militiamen "should probably be called upon to go to the front very soon," Ira noted. Then "we found in a few days [later] that the President's call for seventy-five thousand troops had been filled before we could reach the [militia] rendezvous in Bangor."[9]

The Patten militiamen would have to wait their turn.

Men were anxious to enlist. On April 18 Dr. Augustus Choate Hamlin (nephew to Vice President Hannibal Hamlin) informed Hodsdon from Bangor that "the boys are complaining for want of a chance to enlist. Some capital fellows are all ready to enroll themselves as infantry.

"Should you establish a recruiting office here, I would like the appointment of Recruiting Officer and will make use of the Gymnasium [on Columbia Street in Bangor] as [an] office and drill room ... I will guarantee that I will have a company drilling" there "on the night after the arrival of the order," Hamlin told Hodsdon.[10]

Writing Governor Israel Washburn Jr. from Bath a day later, the Reverend John F. Mines lobbied for appointment "as Chaplain to the Maine Reg't of Volunteers." The Bath Grays, a militia company, planned to meet that evening to "probably tender their services to [the state] government, and I am their captain-elect."

Mines admitted to two issues that might inhibit his appointment: "I am a Virginian—but a Union man to the last gasp; a Democrat, but ready to stand by the Government."[11]

A few days later, John Hodsdon learned that H.W. Cunningham of Belfast wanted "to raise two companies of volunteers, men that are hard" and accustomed "to hardship, that will fight on their feet or on their backs." Cunningham sought a major's or captain's commission; successful in raising one company, which later joined the 4th Maine Infantry as Co. A, he settled for a captaincy.[12]

As for Jonathan Prince Cilley, his revenge against the South would involve hurling cannonballs if he had his way. "I have been so full of the Military Spirit for the last week that I have been unable to attend to anything else," he informed his sister, Julia, from Thomaston on April 27.

"I am the recruiting officer for a Company of Flying Artillery from Thomaston & vicinity and been busily engaged the last week raising men," Cilley told her. "If we are successful in obtaining the guns, it will be a splendid Company and composed of picked men as is to be known to future ages as the Knox Flying Artillery."

On May 15 Israel Washburn poured cold bureaucratic water on the hot-blooded Cilley. After going to Boston once and riding "twice to Augusta ... one of the times most of the night" while seeking support and equipment for his proposed battery, Cilley learned from Washburn that "it will cost us [the state] $25,000 to equip" the 100-man unit.

Washburn "does not wish to equip us ... until he has assurance" from the War Department "that the company will be received into

Elijah Walker
Photo courtesy Maine State Archives

the U.S. Service," Cilley wrote Julia.[13]

Many Maine newspapers published detailed accounts of war preparations. "The states are promptly replying to the call of the President with the exception of the border states and men and money are offered in about five times the amount demanded," Gould noticed. His bank "tendered a loan of $250,000 to the state" on April 18, and by now he realized that a war must be fought.

While "I don't have a taste for it [a civil war] at all," Gould realized by the next day that "I am getting my blood up gradually. I felt pitiful and disheartened last week. Next week I shall be ready to go."

A well-educated man who devoured national and state news, Gould likely opted for military service after learning from "the afternoon papers and extras" on Friday, April 19 that a pro-Southern mob had ambushed the 6th Massachusetts Infantry Regiment in Baltimore. "Some 3 or 4 were killed on both sides and many wounded," he noted.

During that chaotic mid-April, the nation's capital lay almost defenseless, with few troops available to deter a Confederate thrust from Virginia or stop the railroad-line sabotage conducted by Southern sympathizers in Maryland. Abraham Lincoln awaited the troops—ironically mobilized militia and not Army regulars—en route to protect Washington.

He looked toward Boston, because "Massachusetts has shown a remarkable degree of activity and patriotism," Gould commented. Born in Windham, Maine in May 1818 (and only weeks older than Elijah Walker), Bay State Governor John Albion Andrew had anticipated Lincoln's call for citizen soldiers; he called up the 6th Massachusetts Infantry, which left Boston on Wednesday, April 17.

The regiment included some Mainers, primarily young men lured south to jobs in Massachusetts's burgeoning textile industry. Born in Norway in Oxford County in March 1828, Corp. Sumner Needham was a lather in Lawrence. Born in October 1839 at Belmont in Waldo County, Pvt. Addison Whitney worked in a Massachusetts textile mill.

Commanded by Col. Edward Jones, the 6th Massachusetts detrained at President Street Station in Baltimore on April 19. The soldiers boarded horse-drawn rail cars for the ten-block trip across the inner city to Camden Station. Jones led six companies on the first trip; by the time the four remaining companies started their journey, a mob estimated at 8,000 people attacked the soldiers.

A running street battle erupted. Rioters

John Mead Gould
Photo courtesy of Nicholas P. Picerno

Chapter 3: Forming for Battle

Massachusetts Militia Passing Through Baltimore (Baltimore Riot of 1861)
Illustration by F.F. Walker, 1861

threw bricks, paving stones, and rocks, and shot pistols and muskets indiscriminately at the Massachusetts boys, who soon returned fire. Whitney and two comrades—Luther Ladd of Lowell and Charles Taylor of Boston—died before the soldiers reached Camden Station; struck on the head by a brick, Needham lingered in a Baltimore hospital until dying on Saturday, April 27.

Twelve rioters also died during the uproar. Bloodied and bruised, the 6th Massachusetts detrained that night in Washington.

Needham and Whitney were the first Maine-born soldiers killed in Civil War combat.

For a few more days John Mead Gould spent his evenings "walking around and thinking of things transpiring." He expressed amazement at Portlanders "flinging out American flags by the wholesale. Horses and even dogs have little flags fastened on their harnesses or collars."

Like other Mainers contemplating military service, Gould realized that "the idea of being shot isn't very pleasant.

"But then it is better for me to die than a married man," he said.[14]

On Thursday, April 25 the Maine Legislature appropriated the funds to clothe and equip the 10,000 volunteers sought by the War Department. By then thousands of men—single or married, young or old—were already flocking to the standards in response to Hodsdon's General Order No. 6, issued three days earlier. The War Department wanted 10 Maine regiments;

Hodsdon would not let a political vote delay the state's recruiting efforts.

After supper on Tuesday, April 23, Elijah Walker and other Rockland residents gathered for a meeting, during which "speeches were made and resolutions were passed, and a twenty-dollar gold coin was tossed on the floor for the first volunteer," Walker said.

Stephen Chapman, a 35-year-old married teacher, bent and picked up the coin. At 6-3, the blue-eyed and dark-haired Chapman towered over most other enlistees and brought to Walker's company a maturity and administrative skills that could benefit his comrades and superiors alike.[15]

Chapman "enlisted in my company and acted as orderly sergeant until appointed by Col. Berry as sergeant-major of the regiment. He was a noble man and a true soldier," Walker praised his first recruit.

Early on Wednesday, militia Maj. Gen. William H. Titcomb came to Rockland from Augusta and handed blank recruiting forms to men anxious to raise infantry companies. "He ... authorized me to enlist a company for ninety days," Walker said.

By 11 a.m. "seventy-three names had been signed to the roll," so Titcomb took it from Walker "and would not allow me to make further enlistments as he wanted others to raise companies." Only three hours later, Walker received from Titcomb a printed order to gather his enlistees in "the [Rockland] Court room" at 5 p.m. "for the purpose of choosing one captain and two lieutenants."

The would-be soldiers dutifully met and elected Walker as their company captain, O.P. Mitchell as first lieutenant, and J.B. Litchfield as second lieutenant.[16]

Aware that "Mother is much opposed to my going to war," Gould had set his affairs in order before walking into the Portland Armory on April 23 to sign "'my death warrant.'" He opted to enlist in the Portland Light Guards, led by Capt. Menzies Raynor Fessenden, a member of a proud abolitionist family.

"To stay at home and only look on seems so cowardly that, big a coward as I am, I can't think of it," Gould justified his decision. "No[,] sir. The United States never was rivalled on this earth and while I live and have power to preserve its greatness I will do it."[17]

Hodsdon needed to send one infantry regiment to Washington immediately, so Maine could not wait until recruiting officers such as Hamlin and Walker filled 100-man companies with volunteers. To be dubbed the 1st Maine Infantry Regiment, this unit would field 779 men rather than the 1,000 men that each succeeding regiment should enroll.

Hodsdon created the 1st Maine Infantry by calling up Portland's five existing militia companies, the Lewiston Light Infantry, the Norway Light Infantry, and the Auburn Artillery. Two other militia companies (the Lewiston Zouaves and a second Portland Rifle Guards company) soon brought the regiment to its ten-company strength.[18]

Gould "was sworn into service this forenoon" on April 24, a day that brought "raw" weather and nighttime rain to southern Maine. He scrambled to complete his preparations; a shoemaker made new boots for Gould, who purchased a 7½-inch "Colt's revolver" and later practiced firing it.

"I couldn't hit [the target] at all," he admitted.

Chapter 3: Forming for Battle

Arranging with bank directors "to hold open" his job, Gould had a tooth filled, bought powder and made bullets for his revolver, made out his will, and drilled daily. The Portland Light Guards would go to war as Co. C, with Fessenden as captain.

Hodsdon's growing but efficient bureaucracy moved fast to equip the 1st Maine Infantry and ship it south. The ten companies "were in quarters and under pay" and sworn into state service at 1 p.m., Saturday, April 27, Gould noted.

Because "the conveniences for sleeping were not sufficient" at the Brown Theatre in Portland, Fessenden dismissed his men that night with the promise that they would "return at 5 A.M." on Sunday.

That afternoon Fessenden marched Gould and his comrades to Portland City Hall to receive "each a pair of shirts, two prs [pairs] drawers, 2 of stockings, and 1 pair shoes with leather strings." Later the company "marched up to the State Arsenal," and each man received a Springfield rifled musket, Model 1858.[19]

But the regiment designated as Maine's first contribution to Washington, D.C. guard duty remained quarantined in Maine due to a measles outbreak. Not until Saturday, June 1 did the fledgling soldiers march through the Portland streets to board a train.

Gould, who had "enlisted because I was unmarried, unloved, and not afraid to die," watched as "wife, sister, mother or lover cried and kissed [their men] despite the orders of the officers.

"At length after much confusion and final kissing[,] the men were got aboard and the cars moved slowly off amid a thunder of hurrahs and the air whited with handkerchiefs," Gould said.[20]

While the 1st Maine formed in Portland, the 2nd Maine coalesced in Bangor and the 4th Maine in Rockland. In Bangor, Augustus Hamlin raised the "Gymnasium Company," which became Co. G of the 2nd Maine; in Rockland, Elijah Walker's 100 men formed Co. B of the 4th Maine.

The militia companies assigned to the 2nd Maine converged on Camp Washburn in Bangor. Seth Devereaux and Charles Tilden brought the Castine Light Infantry from Castine to Bucksport on April 27 to embark on the *Memnon Sanford*, a steamer that "was handsomely decorated with national flags."

Cruising 20 miles up the Penobscot River to Bangor, the steamer "was greeted with cheers from the immense crowds on the wharf." Escorted by the Bangor militia companies and the Bangor Band (the latter of which is still in existence today), the Castine company marched "amid the booming of cannon, the cheering by the excited throng which followed, and the waving of banners" to Camp Washburn, located at the State Arsenal on Essex Street.[21]

The 29-year-old Lt. Tilden was just beginning an adventurous, albeit not unique, military career; his first promotion would occur after Devereaux resigned his commission on May 30. Capt. Tilden would take Co. B into battle that summer.

Wherever their soldiers gathered, Maine politicians scrambled to provide arms, clothing, and food for them. The War Department could scrape up some weapons, but Maine was so desperate for arms that Israel Washburn sent a "special agent," George W. Dyer of Calais, on

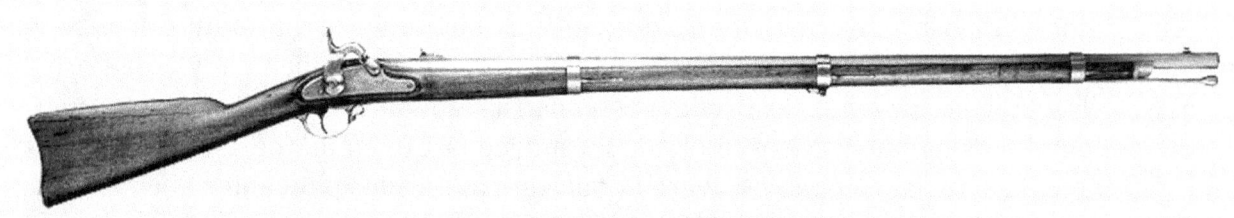

A Springfield 1861 rifled musket, without bayonet.

an international mission to secure functioning rifles.

After making inquiries by telegram, Dyer traveled to Saint John, New Brunswick to meet with the provincial secretary, Samuel Leonard Tilley, on Friday, May 3. They traveled to Fredericton the next day and held a "long, earnest, but unsuccessful" interview with John Manners-Sutton, the lieutenant governor.

Whitehall, the London headquarters for the Royal Army, had recently shipped 3,000 rifles to New Brunswick and a similar number to Nova Scotia to arm each province's militia companies. Per Washburn's instructions, Dyer asked Manners-Sutton if Maine could buy some rifles to equip its regiments.

Stressing that "these arms remain the property of the Queen," Manners-Sutton responded that 2,000 rifles "had been distributed," with the other thousand left in storage until needed. Nova Scotia had handled its rifles in similar fashion.

Manners-Sutton "expressed his warmest sympathy with the Government of the United States, and toward the State of Maine and its Executive," Washburn learned from Dyer, who sensed "that I might have obtained any quantity of muskets, of an inferior rank, from the government, being the property of the Province."[22]

The belief existed in Maine that its soldiers should go heavily armed to war. The Springfield rifled musket came with a 17-inch slotted bayonet, but many officers thought their men should carry small arms, too. After receiving approval to raise a company for the 4th Maine Infantry, H.W. Cunningham contacted Hodsdon on April 22 to ask "if the men I enlist will be furnished with Revolvers & Bowey [sic] Knives at the expense of the State."

The War Department ultimately limited revolvers to officers, sergeants, and cavalrymen; for enlisted men, the bayonet should suffice in lieu of the Bowie knife, ironically a favorite weapon among Confederate troops.[23]

Each militia company sported its own uniform, usually a colorful derivative based on War of 1812 garb worn by fathers or grandfathers. Busy textile manufacturers lacked the time and the pecuniary interest to produce monochromatic uniforms on short notice; to clothe the first five regiments going to war, Hodsdon turned to Mainers who could not legally fight.

Maine women started sewing soon after Fort Sumter fell. In Portland, "the women of the city are fast at work making shirts, scraping lint, and fixing up needles and thread, etc.," Gould noted on April 25. "Women are trumps."[24]

In Bangor, the state awarded a contract to the clothier Wheelwright, Clark & Company to provide uniforms "made of stout cadet grey." The company subcontracted work to all local tailors, "hired all available help, and then gave the balance to the lady volunteers sewing at City Hall."

The contract called for "thirty-two hundred garments ... to be made for our soldiers," according to a local newspaper article. Women working long hours made themselves sick; "many more volunteers will be welcome to work ... on cotton flannel shirts and drawers," the article indicated.[25]

From Wiscasset, Capt. Edwin Smith of the 4th Maine asked Hodsdon if the state could supply some flannel so "the ladies of this town" could sew "underclothing" for the 75 men in his company. He sent the letter along with a member of the local committee charged with ensuring "that the volunteers of this town were provided with the necessary articles of clothing."[26]

While the state purchased much equipment in Boston for the 1st Maine Infantry, the seamstresses working diligently across Maine spelled the difference between sending the first five regiments ill- or well-clad to Washington, D.C. that spring. For many women, wartime sewing represented their first paid employment outside the home; during the next four years, they would continue producing clothing and other items for their men fighting so far away.

State inspectors like Arad Thompson checked human- or machine-sewn clothing; of the contracted "Clothing & Equipment" made for the 2nd Maine, he passed the "Overcoats, Frock Coats, & Wollen [sic] pants" and "the cotton flannel drawers ... (excepting a few Doz. rejected)." Even most socks passed inspection.[27]

Beneath a gray sky that threatened rain, the men of the 2nd Maine Infantry departed Camp Washburn at 8 a.m., Tuesday, May 14. Surrounded by an adoring crowd, the boys—that term would appear so often in future wartime correspondence—marched south along Essex Street and stopped at the First Parish Church on Broadway. There Col. Charles Jameson of Old Town accepted "a handsome American flag" from a local lass, and Hannibal Hamlin delivered an eloquent, albeit long, speech.

Rain fell as the 2nd Maine boys marched to the Bangor train station, where they had 15 minutes to bid farewell to family and friends. Tears flowed freely to mingle with the rain already moistening many faces.

At 10:30 a.m. the soldiers boarded 16 waiting railroad cars that, towed by three locomotives, left the station 15 minutes later "amid the booming of cannon, the shrieking of whistles and the cheers of the multitude."[28]

Charles Tilden and the 2nd Maine Infantry would beat John Gould and the 1st Maine to the war zone. Close behind the 2nd would come Elijah Walker and the 4th Maine, which struck its tents at Camp Knox on the Rockland outskirts after breakfast on Friday, May 17.

Walker "made a hurried farewell on my family of wife and seven children ... then with a heavy heart I said good-bye." William, his oldest son, accompanied the 4th as a servant for Col. Hiram Berry.

At 9 a.m. "we took up our line of march to Atlantic wharf" to board "the steamer Daniel Webster." After walking up the gangway, Walker found a vantage point from which he could watch the ship's departure.

He noticed that as the *Webster* slipped its moorings and started across Rockland Harbor, the city's "streets, windows, [Atlantic] wharf and surrounding wharves were filled with weeping friends and interested spectators."[29]

~~~

1. Elijah Walker, *The Old Soldier: History of the Fourth Maine Infantry,* Tribune, Rockland, Maine, 1895, p. 6
2. Elijah Walker, *Soldiers' File,* Maine State Archives
3. Walker, *The Old Soldier,* p. 6
4. Ira B. Gardner, *Recollections of A Boy Member of Co. I, Fourteenth Maine Volunteers,* Lewiston Journal Company, Lewiston, Maine, 1902, p. 5
5. Ira B. Gardner, *Soldiers' File,* MSA
6. John Mead Gould, *Soldiers' File,* MSA
7. William B. Jordan, *The Civil War Journals of John Mead Gould 1861-1866,* Butternut & Blue, Baltimore, 1997, p. 2
8. Walker, *The Old Soldier,* p. 6
9. Gardner, *Recollections,* p. 6
10. Augustus C. Hamlin to John Hodsdon, April 18, 1861, MSA
11. John F. Mines to Israel Washburn Jr., April 19, 1861, MSA
12. H.W. Cunningham to John Hodsdon, April 21, 1861, MSA
13. Eve Anderson, *A Breach of Privilege: Cilley Family Letters 1820-1867,* Seven Coin Press, Spruce Head, Maine, 2002, pp. 414-415
14. Jordan, *Journals,* p. 3
15. Stephen H. Chapman, *Soldiers' File,* Maine State Archives
16. Walker, *The Old Soldier,* p. 6
17. Jordan, *Journals,* pp. 4-5
18. *Annual Report of the Adjutant General of the State of Maine, 1861,* p. 17
19. Jordan, *Journals,* pp. 4-6
20. Ibid., pp. 16-17
21. R.H. Stanley and George O. Hall, *Eastern Maine and the Rebellion,* Heritage Books, Maryland, reprinted 2008, p. 41
22. George W. Dyer to Israel Washburn, May 6, 1861, MSA
23. H.W. Cunningham to John Hodsdon, April 22, 1861, MSA
24. Jordan, *Journals,* p. 6
25. Stanley and Hall, *Eastern Maine,* pp. 47-48
26. Edwin M. Smith to John Hodsdon, May 11, 1861, MSA
27. A.D. Manson and Arad Thompson letter to John Hodsdon, May 16, 1861, MSA
28. Stanley and Hall, *Eastern Maine,* pp. 51-53
29. Walker, *The Old Soldier,* p. 6

Chapter 4

THIS IS OUR COLONEL?

"The cheers called for were noticeably faint"

Clad in blue wool uniforms, the men belonging to Co. B, 4th Maine Infantry Regiment, sweltered beneath the hot Virginia sun in early afternoon on Sunday, July 21, 1861.

About 1½ miles northeast of the soon-to-be-famous stone bridge spanning Bull Run near Manassas Junction, the Maine soldiers stood "in anxious suspense" as they heard "cannonading a long way to our front," said Capt. Elijah Walker. The distant martial thunder swelled and faded as bitter fighting engulfed Henry House Hill south of Bull Run.[1]

That morning, Union troops had attacked Confederates blocking a Federal advance into northern Virginia. Days earlier, President Abraham Lincoln had sent Brig. Gen. Irvin McDowell and his Army of Northeastern Virginia to provoke a fight with Confederate defenders led by Brig. Gen. Pierre G.T. Beauregard.

Northern politicians wanted the Johnny Rebs "whupped" immediately, despite McDowell's urgent protestations that his green troops were ill-prepared for battle. Now McDowell had his fight, which the 4th Maine boys would apparently sit out.

So would the other three regiments—the 2nd Vermont and the 3rd and 5th Maine—assigned to the 3rd Brigade commanded by Col. Oliver Otis Howard. Only three months earlier, as 1st Lt. Howard, U.S. Army, he had taught mathematics at West Point.

Now Howard led a brigade belonging to the 3rd Division commanded by Col. Samuel Heintzelman.

The division had camped near Centreville late on Saturday, July 20. At 1 a.m. Sunday, Col. Hiram Berry ordered his 4th Maine Infantry boys rousted from their nervous slumber. Soldiers ate breakfast and formed in column, the standard "march" formation.

The hours passed, night faded, and the rising sun promised heat and humidity. Well after dawn, the 3rd Brigade moved out on the Warrenton Turnpike. Howard soon turned his men north on a road that curved northwest and then southwest to Sudley Ford on Bull Run.

The brigade advanced only two miles by 9 a.m. Beside a decrepit blacksmith shop a mile north of Cub Run, McDowell ordered Howard to halt his brigade, now designated as a reserve. Other Union units marched past the waiting troops throughout the morning; Walker soon realized that "all of the army except our brigade had gone forward[,] leaving us in the rear."[2]

Accustomed to cooler, less-humid summer weather, the New Englanders suffered in the Virginia sunlight. Already nervous about fighting in the battle raging to the west, the men sweated profusely.

"I cannot forget how I was affected by the sounds of the musketry and the roar of the cannon as I stood near my horse[,] ready to mount at the first call from McDowell," Howard recalled.[3]

That call arrived at 2 p.m. with Capt. A.W. Whipple, McDowell's chief engineer. Moments after receiving the order to advance, Howard rode past the 4th Maine while shouting, "Forward! Double-quick!"

Since his regiment was the head of the brigade column, "I with Co. B took the advance," Walker said. When Howard ordered him "to deploy a skirmish line 150 yards on both sides of the road," Walker detailed 40 men to take the point. The soldiers "divested themselves of everything except gun and ammunition."

Then for the first time—and definitely not the last—Walker witnessed the suffering inflicted on enlisted men by inexperienced officers. Despite his extensive Army service, Howard overlooked two salient points when he ordered the skirmishers forward.

"The heat was intense," Walker pointed out...

...and led by 1st Lt. O.P. Mitchell, the skirmishers had to run "through brush, bushes[,] and over uneven ground until nearly exhausted," he noticed.

The independent-thinking Walker realized "that the skirmish line was of no benefit." He recalled the exhausted skirmishers to the road, where Mitchell fell prostrate. "I left the oldest man [in Co. B] to care for him and moved on as fast as I could walk."

Howard soon rode up on his horse and again shouted, "Double-quick!"

Walker protested with "qualifying words that could be found in the Bible." Knowing that he had to obey the order, he opted to advance "as fast as was possible and at the same time save the lives of myself and my men."[4]

And Walker probably wondered just who was this "jumped up" colonel foisted onto the Maine and Vermont boys by Maine politicians.

Neither Oliver Otis Howard nor his admirers or detractors would ever define him as a "soldier's soldier," at least physically. Born on a farm in Leeds in northern Androscoggin County in early November 1830, the Howard educated at West Point (Class of '54)

Oliver Otis Howard
Photo by Mathew Brady, Brady-Handy Collection, Library of Congress

was "slender of build," he acknowledged. His voice pitched high, he practiced a devout Christianity scorned by most regular Army officers, and, although stationed in Florida during the latest Seminole war, he had not seen any real combat.[5]

A mathematics instructor at West Point in spring 1861, Howard wrote Maine Governor Israel Washburn Jr. "and offered my services" in a state regiment. Washburn replied that he could not appoint regimental officers; the men must elect their leaders, from second lieutenant to colonel.[6]

Among the regiments coalescing in the Pine Tree State was the 3rd Maine Infantry, comprising a few militia companies and many volunteers drawn from Kennebec Valley municipalities. As with other regiments, the fledgling soldiers elected their noncoms and officers specifically by company and voiced their choices for field staff, including their commanding officer.

James G. Blaine, c. 1860s
Photo from Library of Congress

Gathering at Augusta in late May, the 3rd Maine boys considered Isaac Tucker of Gardiner their top pick for colonel. However, other Maine politicians had heard about Howard's petition; too few Maine soldiers had recent military experience, and Howard did.

In mid-May Howard received an urgent telegram from James G. Blaine, the Republican Speaker of the Maine House. "Will you, if elected, accept the colonelcy of the Kennebec Regiment [the 3rd Maine]?" Blaine asked.

After conferring with his wife, Elizabeth Anne, Howard telegraphed his acceptance to Blaine.[7]

Rather than await the results of the regimental election slated for Wednesday, May 29, Howard set out for Augusta a day earlier. Elizabeth Anne did not know about his trip when, "before entering my front gate" on Tuesday morning, Howard paused and "raised my eyes and saw the picture of my little family framed in by the window.

"Home, family, comfort, beauty, joy, love were crowded into an instant of thought and feeling," he said.

While Howard packed his valise, Elizabeth Anne fixed lunch. They ate together; as Howard said "good-bye" to his family, including the young daughter whom he had recently saved from choking to death on a marble, Elizabeth Anne "said not one adverse word" about his departure.

Crossing the Hudson River on a ferry, Howard caught the 1:30 p.m. train to New York City. There he "went on to Boston by the evening train."

Meanwhile, Blaine and Washburn lobbied the 3rd Maine boys to vote for Howard as their colonel. On Wednesday, another Blaine telegram outbound for West Point caught up with Howard as he rode a Boston & Maine Railroad train from Boston to Augusta.

Dated May 29 (the same day), the message informed "My Dear Howard" that "you were chosen to the command of the Third Regiment yesterday and public opinion is entirely unanimous in favor of having you accept the position ... I understand the Lieutenant Colonel [Tucker] is an admirable military man, one that will be both efficient and agreeable."

Detraining in Augusta at 5 p.m., Howard found rooms in the Augusta House, and "the officers and the friends of the regiment" soon called upon him. On May 30, Blaine introduced him to Washburn "in his office in the State House."

Wrapping both his hands around Howard's extended right hand, Washburn said, "Your regiment is already here—across the way. You must hasten and help us get it into shape."

Maine soldier
His kepi, belt buckle, and bayoneted rifle identify this soldier as belonging to a Maine infantry regiment. A member of Co. H (as indicated by the letter on his kepi), he wears a belt buckle emblazoned "VMM," standing for "Volunteer Maine Militia." Such buckles were issued only to Maine's earliest regiments.
Photo from Library of Congress

Howard was unsure as to how Washburn assessed him during that initial meeting. "At the time pale and thin, I did not seem to those who casually met me to have the necessary toughness" to command rowdy volunteers, "but for reasons of his own, perhaps owing to his nearsightedness, Washburn gave me immediate confidence," Howard said afterwards.

The three men left the State House via "the broad steps to the east, crossed State Street," and took a gravel path across the expansive landscape of Capitol Park, Howard remembered. At the 3rd Maine's camp, he noticed the soldiers had "the choicest of everything," including new gray uniforms, "new guns, new tents, new equipments, and new flags...

"But one glance showed me that the camp itself was in disorder," Howard realized. Many of them relatives, numerous civilians mingled with the soldiers, of whom "some had been drinking and some were swearing."

People soon noticed the short Washburn, who climbed atop an overturned hogshead. "Cheers for our governor!" soldiers shouted, and "a large number responded in strong, manly tones," Howard noticed.

"Thank you, thank you, boys," Washburn responded. "I have brought you here somebody you will like to see. Come up here, Colonel Howard. This is your new colonel."

"All eyes turned steadily toward" Howard as he climbed into position alongside Washburn. Men familiar with Isaac Tucker studied Howard and apparently did not like what they saw.

"The cheers called for were noticeably faint" when compared to Washburn's, Howard admitted. "How young, how slender the new colonel appeared; hardly the man to be placed over strong, hardy fellows whose frames were already well knit and toughed by work."

Howard anticipated such a reaction. The previous evening, several audacious 3rd Maine captains had informed him that "under Tucker, the other candidate for colonel, we could have had a good time," but Howard would "keep us at arm's length."

Now displayed before his new command, Howard gave a short speech that apparently went over well. The cheers were few, but he had not set aside his regular Army commission to win a Kennebec Valley popularity contest; Howard stepped off the ad hoc podium and went to work.

"The proper form and order of an encampment were soon instituted," Howard said. The regiment conducted "some essential drilling ... in a body," and the soldiers learned "to load and fire with some degree of precision."[8]

The 3rd Maine departed Augusta by train on Wednesday, June 5, a day when "the sun shone from a cloudless sky" and "the fruit trees and the luxurious lilacs were in full bloom," Howard remembered long afterwards. Sharing "many last embraces" with the "many sobbing mothers, wives, and dear ones," the soldiers boarded the train cars.

The men peered from windows or sat or stood atop the cars as the train rumbled south toward war.[9]

Howard kept a tight leash on the 3rd Maine through New York City, Philadelphia, and Baltimore. At the regimental camp on Meridian Hill near Washington, D.C., two lieutenants from West Point taught the 3rd Maine boys, officers and enlisted alike, drill and discipline.

As in other regiments, men chafed at military life. At no cost to its participants, Howard quelled a brief, half-hearted mutiny. Men sought leave to see the Washington, D.C. sites, such as the Capitol and White House, but Howard denied their requests.

On July 4 he received a War Department notice: Howard must form and command a new brigade. He tapped the 2nd Vermont and the three Maine regiments.

So this was the "jumped up" colonel who brought his men to Centreville on Saturday, July 20. That evening Howard assembled the four regiments "for the usual parade—then we had them closed in mass and all the men uncovered their heads while the God of battles was entreated for guidance," he recalled.

"Every soldier of my command seemed thoughtful and reverent that night," Howard said.[10]

Never hesitant to point out flaws in senior officers, Elijah Walker remembered that Howard asked his men to prepare for a battle and its potential aftermath. "Before the setting of the sun [on Sunday] some of us will be in eternity," Howard said.

"Many of us thought it poor tactics to instruct us in at the time," Walker commented.[11]

The next day, as the 3rd Brigade soldiers ran toward battle, Walker did not know that McDowell had ordered Howard via A.W. Whipple to "have them [3rd Brigade] move in double time." Rather than the heartless martinet that Walker evidently believed him to be, Howard knew the price his men would pay for obeying the order.

"The heat and fatigue of long waiting had already done its work," he noticed as the brigade raced toward Sudley Ford. To lighten their loads, soldiers shed their blankets, canteens, and haversacks, yet "many fell out of ranks ... overcome by their efforts, more and more [soldiers] left the column and lined the roadside.

"When we crossed the ford, at least one half of my men were absent," Howard reported.[12]

The loss of those men would not affect what happened next to the 3rd Brigade.

~~~

1. Elijah Walker, *The Old Soldier: History of the 4th Maine Infantry*, Tribune, Rockland, 1895, p. 10
2. Ibid., p. 10
3. Oliver Otis Howard, *Autobiography of Oliver Otis Howard, Major General United States Army*, Baker & Taylor Company, New York, 1907, p. 154
4. Walker, *The Old Soldier*, pp. 10-11
5. Howard, *Autobiography*, p. 116
6. Ibid., p. 106
7. Ibid., p. 107
8. Howard, *Autobiography*, pp. 111-118
9. Ibid., pp. 120-121
10. Ibid., p. 152
11. Walker, *The Old Soldier*, p. 10
12. Howard, *Autobiography*, p. 157

Chapter 5

THE CALIFORNIA FLAG

"It was mad, stark, swearing mad"

The 2nd Maine boys detrained in Washington, D.C. on Friday, May 31 and immediately encamped atop Meridian Hill, high terrain surrounding a mansion built on the District's northern edge in 1819 by Navy Commodore David Porter. The camp stood one and a half miles north of Washington and overlooked the swelling Union camps on Arlington Heights in Virginia.

That afternoon Col. Charles Jameson formed the regiment to receive Secretary of State William Seward and his daughter and confidante, 16-year-old Frances "Fanny" Adeline. Then the 2nd Maine camp officially became Camp Seward—and Seward reciprocated the regiment's warm reception by inviting the 2nd Maine officers to a June 6 soiree hosted at his home by Fanny.[1]

Eventually the War Department assigned the 2nd Maine to a brigade (dubbed the 1st) commanded by Col. Erasmus Darwin Keyes.[2] Belonging to the 1st Division commanded by Brig. Gen. Daniel Tyler, the brigade included the 1st, 2nd, and 3rd Connecticut infantry regiments.

On Tuesday, July 16, Irvin McDowell finally advanced his army into northern Virginia. The 2nd Maine left its Falls Church camp at 2 p.m. and reached Vienna six hours later. Wednesday found the regiment deploying with the Connecticut regiments to attack entrenchments defended by about 2,000 Confederate infantrymen. A few Union cannonballs convinced the Confederates to withdraw; "we pursued them all that day, and encamped about half way to Centreville," recalled Sgt. William H.S. Lawrence of Co. H and Bangor.[3]

On Saturday, July 20, the 1st Brigade reached Centreville and camped for the night. Near sunset, Charles Jameson ordered his 2nd Maine drawn into a hollow square; the soldiers formed in lines on three sides and left the fourth side open.

A six-man color guard formed inside the square, into which Jameson rode his horse. Then occurred "a delightful ceremony ... the flavor of which is a fragrance to this day of every surviving member of the battalion," recalled 1st Lt. Horatio Staples of Co. G and Bangor.

During the past few months, wealthy and patriotic Maine women living in San Francisco had spent $1,200 on a spectacular flag to be presented to the first Maine regiment to reach Washington. George Haycock, a civilian, had safeguarded the flag since its arrival at the capital.

Union Col. Charles D. Jameson
Photo courtesy of Maine State Archives

Union Capt. Charles Tilden
Photo courtesy of Maine State Archives

Until measles intervened in Portland, the 1st Maine Infantry should have claimed the flag. Now that privilege fell to the 2nd Maine, which was "the first [regiment] to leave the State" and "the first from Maine to cross the Potomac into Virginia," Staples noted.

Haycock had safely delivered the flag to the regiment. After Jameson finished telling his men about the unexpected honor, an officer called for 36-year-old Color Sgt. William J. Deane of Co. A to step forward and receive the flag.

Employed as a moulder in Bangor, Deane symbolized the archetypical militiamen forming Maine's first six infantry regiments that spring; these regiments drew heavily from the state's best-organized militia companies, many of which enrolled fathers and sons, brothers and cousins, often with many men sharing similar surnames but no blood ties.

Prior to the war, William and his 29-year-old brother James (a house painter) had belonged to the Bangor Light Infantry, mobilized into the 2nd Maine Infantry as Co. A. The company carried on its rolls the Bacons (James and William) from Orono, the 21-year-old Copeland twins (Edward and Edwin) from Dexter, two Bensons (Nathan and Stephen) from Bangor, and James and Joseph Rogers from Orrington.

As Charles Tilden, the recently minted captain of Co. B, watched Deane approach the officer and salute that Saturday evening, the ranks of the former Castine Light Infantry should have included six men named Perkins. However, Tilden had already lost two: Sgt. Elisha of Frankfort and Pvt. John (no relation) of Castine, both discharged for disabilities.

By midnight Sunday, only two Perkinses would answer the Co. B roll call.

Like so many other militiamen, William Deane was married; he lived with his wife and children at 6 State Street Avenue, an obscure address on Bangor's East Side. His family had seen him off at the Bangor train station on May 14, and his wife expected him home soon.

Likely almost all 2nd Maine eyes watched as the officer presented to Deane a new leather harness studded with 13 silver stars symbolizing the 13 original colonies. Deane strapped the harness around his upper body; Jameson then presented the flag to him.

As Staples later attested, the surviving 2nd Maine boys never forgot that "massive India silk" flag. "On a blue field, grouped around an eagle, were thirty-four stars," Staples described the lustrous beauty. "On the reverse were the [coat of] arms of California and Maine on separate shields."

The "California Flag" glimmered in the Virginia sunlight; the Maine ladies of San Francisco had ordered the flag staff adorned with "solid California silver" rings, slides, and sockets; even "the battle-ax" was solid silver, the gaping Staples recalled.

Then, pointing upwards, someone shouted, "Look! Look!"

"All who were present saw hovering over the command a great eagle," the astonished Staples noticed. "Seen through a field-glass it proved to be an American bald-headed eagle of the largest size.

"I know that these stories of eagles that appear in just the nick of time as omens" should "be taken cum grano salis [with a grain of salt]," but "the eagle on this occasion was not an afterthought of a frisky imagination, but a really and truly meat and feather eagle," Staples stated.

The 1st Brigade boys slept fitfully until Tyler ordered his division awakened at 2 a.m., Sunday. The 1st Division crept west through the darkness along the Warrenton Turnpike; sometime after sunrise Keyes pulled his 1st Brigade to the roadside so the division's other brigades could pass.

"While waiting ... for something—we didn't know what," some 2nd Maine boys slipped from the ranks after sunrise and searched a nearby, albeit abandoned, farm for food, Staples said. Discovering "a couple of hives of honey," the foragers shared the honeycombs with their comrades.

Consumed by the hungry soldiers not long after their pre-dawn breakfast of hardtack and salt pork, the honey inflicted "a couple of score of 2d Maine stomach-aches"

Union Gen. William Tecumseh Sherman
*Sherman was a colonel at First Manassas.
Photo courtesy of Maine State Archives*

The "California Flag"
What's left of this flag, financed by Maine women in California, is at the Maine State Museum.
Photos from the Maine State Museum (catalog number 72.36.25)

during the upcoming battle, said Staples. "Moreover, the stickiness of the stuff slobbered our arms and equipments for many a nasty day after."[4]

Into mid-morning the 1st Brigade boys waited a half mile east of the Stone Bridge as the battle raged to the west. At 9:15 a.m., Keyes received orders to leave the turnpike and cross Bull Run at Farm Ford, located some 800 yards upstream from the bridge. Confederate artillery hurled "some twenty-five or thirty rounds of shot and shell" on the 1st and 2nd Connecticut infantry regiments "and wounded several men," Keyes reported his brigade's initial casualties.

Running in the oppressive heat and humidity, the 1st Brigade boys emerged onto high ground north of the Warrenton Turnpike. On the left (east) flank of the 3rd Brigade led by Col. William Tecumseh Sherman, Keyes formed his regiments into two lines facing south: the 3rd Connecticut on the right and the 2nd Maine on the left in front, the 1st Connecticut on the right and the 2nd Connecticut on the left in the rear.

About 2 p.m., Daniel Tyler ordered Keyes "to take a [Confederate] battery on a height

Chapter 5: The California Flag

[Henry House Hill] in front." Commanded by Capt. Henry Grey Latham, the four-gun Lynchburg Artillery "battery was strongly posted, and supported by infantry and riflemen, sheltered by a building, a fence, and a hedge," Keyes realized after scanning the target with his field glasses.[5]

Keyes led his front line downhill and across Young's Branch (a Bull Run tributary). Carrying the heavy California flag, William Deane advanced with Co. C (formerly the Brewer Light Artillery), assigned to protect the color guard of the 2nd Maine Infantry that day.[6]

The front line reached and crossed the turnpike just east (left) of the dirt road rising south from the highway to a frame house owned by James "Gentleman Jim" Robinson, a 62-year-old free black farmer. Flag bearers had already uncased their flags.

When Keyes ordered the 2nd Maine and 3rd Connecticut to advance, "my order to charge was obeyed with the utmost promptness." The two regiments "pressed forward ... up the base of the slope about one hundred yards, when I ordered them to lie down, at a point offering a small protection, and load."[7]

Then the Union soldiers rose to their feet and ascended the northern slope of Henry House Hill. As the 2nd Maine boys reached "the top of the rise, we saw just the other side of a dilapidated Virginia fence, a line or two of rebel infantry, and just back of them—or mingled with them—some field-pieces," Staples noticed.

The two Union regiments had struck in its right flank the Virginia infantry brigade commanded by Col. Thomas J. Jackson, soon to earn the nickname "Stonewall." Beyond the battered fence (many Maine soldiers later noted its existence) Col. Kenton Harper ordered his 5th Virginia Infantry boys to fire "a volley of musketry slap in our faces," Staples said.

Leveling their smoothbores, the 2nd Maine boys fired their first volley in combat. "It was our first gunpowder christening—a species of battle confirmation so to speak," Staples commented.[8] Led by Jameson, who coolly directed his men during the battle, the Maine soldiers advanced some distance beyond the fence and dueled fiercely with the Virginians.

Men went down immediately on both sides. A bullet struck the California Flag's wooden staff and hurled a splinter into the throat of William Deane. He staggered and collapsed, his blood spraying the California Flag as it dropped onto the Virginia grass.

Snatching up the fallen flag, 21-year-old Corp. Americus Moore of Co. K and Old Town yelled at his comrades to advance; he died instantly when a bullet thudded into his head. The California Flag struck the ground again—and lay there as the 2nd Maine boys pulled back and gathered along the fence to shoot at the Virginians.

"There were guns to be fired, and guns to load and fire again; there was a nasty line of grizzly gray scoundrels on the other side of that fence to practice real shooting on," Staples recalled. "It was mad, stark, swearing mad," with the 2nd Maine boys experiencing "a burning desire to get at the gray rats beyond that fence."

Jameson's casualties quickly added up; its bearer killed, another flag went down, as did "twenty, thirty, forty brave fellows," Staples said. He and his comrades "moved slowly forward, loading and firing" as they started to climb over the fence.

Then Keyes ordered the battered 2nd Maine to shift position "to the shelter of some rising ground, a little to the left," according to Staples. The maneuver required the regiment to abandon its wounded and lose its fallen flags.

"Major, the order is to retreat, but I shall not retreat a step while those flags stay!" Corp. Benjamin Smart of Co. H and Portland exclaimed to Maj. George Varney.[9] Smart fought until the flags were retrieved.

Led by Jameson, six soldiers (including Bangor newspaper editor George Brown, Lagrange farmers Leonard Carver and Abiather Knowles, and 19-year-old Henry Wheeler of Bangor) crossed the fence to rescue wounded comrades. Jameson cited the men "for nobly volunteering to accompany me to remove the dead and wounded from the field under a very heavy fire of artillery and musketry."[10]

Confederate bullets punched the air, but Jameson and his men returned unscathed with wounded soldiers Among them was William Deane; during the Union army's subsequent retreat, Lawrence encountered several Co. A soldiers carrying Deane.

"I don't think it possible for him to live," Lawrence said after seeing Deane's horrible wound.[11]

Lawrence was correct. William Deane died sometime during the frantic flight for Centreville

Chapter 5: The California Flag

Robinson House near Bull Run, Manassas, Virginia, c. 1862
The house, on the northern edge of Henry House Hill, was part of Manassas National Battlefield Park, but it is now in ruins, lost to arson in 1993. Only the sill stones remain.
Photo by George N. Barnard, from Library of Congress

and Union-held points beyond. The 2nd Maine Infantry listed 13 men killed, 24 men wounded, and 118 men missing at Manassas; those figures included Pvt. Eben Perkins (killed) and Pvt. John Perkins (captured) of Co. B. The young men hailed from Brooksville; John likely remained behind with Eben as Confederate troops swept north across the Robinson farm.

Charles Tilden lost other men from Co. B that Sunday: Sewall Bowden, a 24-year-old sailor from Castine, was killed, as was John Dealing, a 20-year-old sailor from Bangor. Confederates captured Warren Devereaux of Penobscot, Warren Griffin of Stockton Springs, Jabez King of Orrington, and Charles Morris of Castine; Devereaux contracted typhoid fever and died in captivity.

Other Co. B soldiers were wounded at Bull Run. Tilden never became accustomed to losing men—and he would fight in many battles in the years to come.

As the broken Union army fled toward Washington, D.C. in late afternoon on Sunday, July 21, the 2nd Maine boys brought off their flags, and Jameson expressed to Keyes "my entire satisfaction with the officers and men under my command during the engagement."[12]

The regiment's honor had been upheld.

~~~

1. Charles W. Roberts letter, June 4, 1861, *Eastern Maine and the Rebellion,* R.H. Stanley and George O. Hall, 1887, 2002, Heritage Books, Westminster, MD pp. 58-59

2. Although born in Massachusetts, Keyes grew up in Maine. He was a West Point graduate. Until June 2018, the modern headquarters of the Maine National Guard in Augusta was located at Camp Keyes, named in his honor.
3. William H.S. Lawrence letter, July 23, 1861, *Eastern Maine and the Rebellion,* Stanley and Hall, p. 73
4. Horatio G. Staples, "Reminiscences of Bull Run," Maine M.O.L.L.U.S., War Papers, Vol. III, Portland, 1898
5. Col. Erasmus D. Keyes, *Official Records of the Civil War, Series 1, Vol. 2,* Chapter IX, p. 353
6. Responsibility for protecting the color guard rotated among the companies of an infantry regiment.
7. Keyes, *OR, Series 1, Vol. 2,* Chapter IX, No. 17, p. 353
8. Staples, "Reminiscences of Bull Run"
9. Lawrence letter, July 23, 1861, *Eastern Maine and the Rebellion,* Stanley and Hall, p. 75
10. Col. Charles D. Jameson, *OR, Series 1, Vol. 2,* Chapter IX, No. 18, p. 357. For their heroism. Abiather Knowles and Henry Wheeler received the Congressional Medal of Honor in the 1890s.
11. Lawrence letter, July 23, 1861, *Eastern Maine and the Rebellion,* Stanley and Hall, p. 75
12. Jameson, *OR, Series 1, Vol. 2,* Chapter IX, No. 18, p. 356

Chapter 6

HOT WORK AT MANASSAS

"The enemy is upon us! We shall all be taken!"

Oliver Otis Howard led his thirsty, panting men six miles during their roundabout route to battle at Manassas on Sunday, July 21, 1861. The 3rd Brigade boys ran at the double quick "up hill and down in the swamp, through the bush and brush, through forests, across brooks and little streams," recalled Sgt. William E. Crockett of Co. B, 4th Maine Infantry.[1]

Heat stroke felled men along the way. "It was one of the hottest days of the season, but I stood the march beyond what I had dared to hope," remembered Sgt. Frank L. Lemont of Lewiston and Co. E, 5th Maine Infantry. "While hundreds of stalwart fellows fell out on all sides, I kept on hardly feeling fatigued."[2]

Leading the brigade, the 4th Maine boys splashed across Bull Run at Sudley Ford and passed "the famous brick [Sudley] church, then doing service as a hospital," Crockett commented. "Hundreds of wounded men" lay on the church's "grassy lawn," and "blood [was] here, there, and everywhere, staining the dusty road, soaking the beautiful grass and running in streams from the ambulances."[3]

"Our course was obstructed by the ambulances, filled with the mangled in every shape," Lemont recalled. "We passed along double quick[,] trampling over the wounded, sitting and lying by the way side …"

"I noticed … ambulances in long columns leaving the field with the wounded … men with broken arms; faces with bandages stained with blood; bodies pierced; many were walking or limping to the rear," Col. Oliver Otis Howard described the mobile wounded.

"I was sorry, indeed, that those left of my men had to pass that ordeal," he said.[5]

Survivors recalled the 3rd Brigade receiving Confederate artillery scrutiny some distance south of Sudley Church. When the 4th Maine boys emerged from a tree line somewhere on Matthews Hill, "a cannon shot came whistling through the air, and struck the ground three feet in front of me," said Crockett. "Another passed through the ranks as many feet behind."[6]

The 5th Maine came under a particularly galling fire. Lemont and his comrades ran about a quarter mile "with the six pound shots whizzing just over our heads and falling all around us." Although "the shot and shell were thick," the regiment suffered "but very few casualties"

Union Gen. McDowell's troops meet Confederate Gen. Beauregard's men at Bull Run, July 21, 1861
Chromolithograph by Kurz & Allison from Library of Congress

from the cannonading, said Lemont, a 5-10½ student with gray eyes and light hair.[7]

The fearsome yet ineffectual shelling—whether direct or indirect fire, artillery is the eternal bane of infantrymen—led many 5th Maine soldiers to vanish from the ranks, only to reappear sometime after the battle. Deigning to use the term "cowardice," Lemont decided that "I don't wish to cast any reflections" on comrades who chose self-survival over valor that day.[8]

About 3 p.m., Irvin McDowell sent a staff officer, Capt. J.B. Fry, to direct Howard and his brigade to the Union army's right flank to support an artillery battery. Numbering several hundred men, the four regiments were the last reserves deployed into a battle already lost.

Fry led the 3rd Brigade past the Dogan House and south across Warrenton Turnpike and Young's Branch (a Bull Run tributary). Howard noticed "there was still a fitful rattling of small arms and a continuous roar of heavy guns" to the east along the turnpike "and by the Henry house." He did not know that the final Union assaults on Confederate-held Henry House Hill had failed.

Union troops—"other troops more scattered," Howard commented—retreated north even as the 3rd Brigade deployed into a ravine south of Warrenton Turnpike. There Howard formed two lines: the first with the 4th Maine on the right and the 2nd Vermont on the left;

the second with the 5th Maine on the right and the 3rd Maine on the left.

Mounted on his horse, Howard watched as his men trudged past. "Many were pale and thoughtful," he noticed. "Many looked up into my face and smiled."

Howard ordered the first line to ascend Chinn Ridge to the immediate south "through a sprinkling of trees, out into an open space on high ground." Thickets disrupted the 4th Maine's advance; as they crested the ridge first, the Vermonters encountered "scattered hostile skirmishers" and opened fire.[9]

When the 4th Maine boys emerged on Chinn Ridge, "there was no battery there" to support as Fry had directed, said Crockett; the fought-over battery had long since been destroyed, a fact lost on the Union high command. He estimated that "for twenty minutes we stood ... still, in line" while "receiving a fire from front, and left flank" from unseen Confederate gunners and infantrymen.[10]

Concealed in woods near the Manassas-Sudley Road (modern State Route 234), soldiers from the 2nd and 8th South Carolina infantry regiments and a four-gun artillery battery blazed away at the approaching Union troops.

Elijah Walker noticed that Sgt. Maj. Stephen Chapman, the brave soul whose capture of a tossed $20 gold coin in Rockland on April 23 had identified him as the first man to enlist in the 4th Maine, stood "on the left of the regiment, a few paces in front." Standing "more that six feet high, he was a conspicuous mark for the rebel sharpshooters.

"He was the first to fall and the first to die," according to Walker.[11]

Confederates shot accurately and outranged the 4th Maine soldiers cursed "with poor guns, and worse powder," Crockett snarled. "Powder that was old enough to be your great grandfather's. Powder that would heat our guns so hot we could only hold them by the straps."[12]

The 5th Maine had shed men right and left—and few to enemy fire—before reaching the ravine. After Co. E formed there, Lemont counted ten men: eight enlisted soldiers, himself, and 1st Lt. Aaron Daggett of Greene.

Then "while we stood waiting and taking breath, a shot sped by and struck a fellow in the forehead killing him almost instantly," Lemont witnessed the death of "the first man I saw killed that day.

"He was standing about three feet from me, and I shall never forget the sound the bullet made as it struck him. He fell upon his back, threw up his arms, trembled slightly and was dead," Lemont said.

"You may think that I have grown hard-hearted when I tell you that that sight did not move me, but I assure you it did not unnerve me in the least," he informed his father, "but I did think of his mother, if perchance he had any, as he lay thus uncared for."[13]

On Chinn Ridge, Mainers and Vermonters fell constantly. Crockett saw "one fine young man ... killed, one not withstanding he was a cripple, had come out to do and die for his country." He saw another soldier standing on the left side of Co. B lose his right arm; snatching "a silk necktie" from around the bleeding man's neck, Crockett wrapped the cloth tightly twice around the arm's remnants, shoved a splinter through the silk, took "a few turns" on the splinter, "and the blood stopped!"

Crockett instructed the wounded soldier to "hold on to this [splinter] for your life." Confederates soon captured the man, and a Confederate surgeon tied off the arteries in his bloody stump. The Mainer survived the war.[14]

Seeing his first line rapidly thinning, Howard rode north to bring his second line up in support. He discovered that a straying Confederate cannonball "and a rush of our own retreating cavalrymen" had panicked "a part of the Fifth" Maine; those men fled without firing a shot.

Their remaining comrades and the 3rd Maine advanced uphill, and the 5th Maine boys formed on the 4th Maine's right flank. Howard pulled the 2nd Vermont into reserve.[15]

"I noticed many dead bodies as we passed up through the woods on to the hill," Lemont recalled. He noticed one Union soldier punched through his shoulders by a cannonball; "it was a terrible sight ... I stopped for a moment and thought of his friends at the north, perhaps at the very moment sending up a prayer to God for his safety..."[16]

As the fighting continued, the 4th Maine boys saw another Confederate artillery battery rush into position opposite them. "See! they swing into line to the right, the men jump to their work, home goes the little red bag of powder, down goes the shot to meet it," Crockett watched in fascination.

Ambrose Burnside leads his Union brigade at Bull Run
Image from Harper's Weekly

"A puff of smoke, a whir-r-r in the air, and the ball strikes at my feet," he said.

Crockett ducked, and Adjutant J.B. Greenhalgh shouted, "Don't dodge, Ned!"

Then a cannonball landed behind Greenhalgh, who took a step forward. "The same to yourself!" Crockett shouted.[17]

Time gradually ran out for the 3rd Brigade. Two additional Confederate brigades deployed east to west across Chinn Ridge; partially concealed by trees, the fast-firing Southern riflemen presented few visible targets to Howard's frustrated men.

In the 5th Maine's thinned ranks, "I stood in my place in the company while they discharged 8 or 10 rounds and discharged my pistol once," Lemont said. Figuring "that I might get into a tight place and need the other charges," he stopped firing.[18]

"It was a hot place," said Howard, who rode along his dwindling line. "Every hostile battery shot produced confusion" in the ranks, "and as a rule our enemy could not be seen."

Union Gen. Samuel P. Heintzelman
Photo by Mathew Brady, Brady-Handy Collection, Library of Congress

To the east, shattered Union regiments had abandoned Henry House Hill; Federal soldiers fled in disorder. Although his men had "stood well for a time" under intense enemy fire, Howard realized that his brigade could not hold its position any longer.

Opting for a fighting withdrawal, Howard tried to pull his regiments downhill to regroup in the ravine. The order, delivered to the 4th Maine by an orderly, led to disaster.[19]

When "that order was received, there ended all form of discipline," Crockett realized. "It was a mob from that time to the end. Every man was for himself.

"Back over the hill we went with the rebels in quick pursuit, the shot from their battery, skimming the hill in very unpleasant style," he recalled.[20]

Officers tried to no avail to rally their companies. For a while Capt. William Heath, the 27-year-old Waterville resident who commanded Co. H, 3rd Maine Infantry, "walked … by my horse and shed tears as he talked to me," Howard said.

"My men will not stay together, Colonel, they will not obey me!" Heath cried.

Men ran past regimental surgeons tending to the wounded directly behind the shattered 3rd Brigade line. "For God's sake, stop!" the doctors shouted. "Don't leave us!"

Some men, including at least a few surgeons, voluntarily stayed with the wounded. A cannonball struck Sgt. Alonzo Stinson of Portland and Co. H, 5th Maine Infantry; "his wound was mortal, his arm being broken and his side crushed," Howard recalled.

**Union cavalrymen pause their horses at
Sudley Ford on Bull Run in March 1862**
Image by George N. Barnard from Library of Congress

Stinson died with his brother, Pvt. Harry Stinson, at his side. Advancing Confederates soon swept up Harry, the heroic surgeons, and the wounded; the 3rd Brigade prisoners would suffer a mixed fate, but Harry at least would be released. He would return to war as a commissioned officer on Howard's staff.

"The enemy is upon us! We shall all be taken!" Howard's men shouted as they fled north across Sudley Ford and then east toward the perceived safety of Centreville and the regimental camps. The chagrined Howard tried to rally his men as they approached Sudley Ford.

Near that point, Col. Samuel Heintzelman, "with his wounded arm in a sling, rode up and down and made a last effort to restore order," recalled Howard, who reported to his livid divisional commander.

"He swore at me," Howard succinctly described that embarrassing moment in his life.[21]

Their brigade utterly broken, the Maine and Vermont boys fled into the approaching night. Crockett remembered "a mob of men and horses, fleeing in all directions and a howling enemy in full chase. Out of the woods, and up from the cornfield" the fleeing Federals "came … plenty of them to be seen now as they came running across the valley …"[22]

Except for a few regiments maintaining some order, Federals ran like rabbits from a weary Confederate enemy that failed to capitalize on the battle's disastrous end. Howard and his officers finally rounded up "a good part of my brigade" in Centreville.[23]

But the damage had been done. Initial casualty reports placed the 3rd Brigade's losses at 788 men, an extraordinarily high figure when compared to other Federal brigades. That figure included 50 men killed, 116 men wounded, and 622 men missing; the last number included many men struck down by the heat or fled before the brigade fought on Chinn Ridge.[24]

Between them, Howard's three Maine regiments lost 44 men killed (26 alone in the 4th Maine), 94 men wounded, and 530 men missing, including 335 men from the 5th Maine. The aggregate missing included some men never seen again, as well as a few deserters who never stopped running until they reached their homes in Maine.

Thirteen men of the 2nd Maine Infantry had been killed earlier on July 21; thus Maine had lost 57 men killed at Bull Run. That figure seemed infinitesimal when compared to the 122,238 men of fighting age (from 18 to 45 years) identified in Maine's 1860 census—

—but these 57 men were only the first of 9,398 fatalities to be accrued by Maine during the next four years.

~~~

The reconstructed Henry House
The Maine boys were to the right, perhaps three-quarters of a mile away. The battle of First Manassas flowed around this house on July 21, 1861 and pretty well tore it apart. It was completely rebuilt on the same spot.
Photo by Brian F. Swartz

1. William E. Crockett, *Courier-Gazette,* Rockland, May 26, 1891
2. Frank E. Lemont, letter to his father, *Lewiston Daily Evening Journal,* Lewiston, Aug. 12, 1861
3. Crockett, 1891
4. Lemont, 1861
5. Oliver Otis Howard, *Autobiography of Oliver Otis Howard, Major General United States Army,* Baker & Taylor Company, New York, 1907, p. 158
6. Crockett, 1891
7. Frank L. Lemont, *Soldiers' File,* Maine State Archives
8. Lemont, 1861
9. Howard, Autobiography, pp. 158-159
10. Crockett, 1891
11. Elijah Walker, *The Old Soldier: History of the 4th Maine Infantry,* Tribune, Rockland, 1895, p. 6
12. Crockett, 1891
13. Lemont, 1861
14. Crockett, 1891
15. Howard, *Autobiography,* p. 159
16. Lemont, 1861
17. Crockett, 1891
18. Lemont, 1861
19. Howard, *Autobiography,* pp. 159-160
20. Crockett, 1891
21. Howard, *Autobiography,* pp. 160-161
22. Crockett, 1891
23. Howard, *Autobiography,* p. 162
24. Bradley M. Gottfried, *The Maps of First Bull Run,* Savas Beattie, New York and California, 2009, p. 107

Manassas today
A summer breeze stirs the fields of Manassas.
Photo by Brian F. Swartz

Chapter 7

FREEDOM OF THE PRESS TAKES FLIGHT

"'The Democrat' should not be tolerated at home"

As Manassas devolved into a Union defeat in the Virginia heat, the news initially came on the wind for soldiers like John Mead Gould of the 1st Maine Infantry Regiment. Ensconced on Meridian Hill in Washington, D.C., the 1st Maine boys knew that a battle was being fought that hot Sunday.

As Gould went on guard duty at noon, "I heard a repeated rumbling like thunder" to the west. Other soldiers "seemed to hear the report simultaneously." Their attention riveted on the distant battle, off-duty soldiers shared observations and interviewed incoming camp visitors as "the reports grew louder and kept up a regular and equal rumbling till about 2 [p.m.]," Gould noticed.

Artillery resumed booming at 5:30 p.m.

A civilian, Lewis B. Smith, swung into the 1st Maine camp that afternoon and reported that he had "heard the heavy and brass guns" while some twelve miles from Manassas earlier that day, according to Gould.

Then a courier cantered into the camp about 7:30 p.m. and told Col. Nathaniel James Jackson (a Lewiston mill superintendent just two days shy of his 43rd birthday), "The rebels are surrounded and driven back from Bull Run and can be starved out of their entrenchments."

Later that evening "we commenced receiving reports from town of the battle," noted Gould, who went to sleep that night believing that Gen. Irvin McDowell had soundly beat the Confederate forces at Manassas.

As news about a Virginia battle spread verbally and telegraphically, civilians and soldiers—North and South alike—sought any available information about what was happening a long day's march from Washington, D.C. A wind-driven rain greeted the awakening 1st Maine boys on Monday, July 22, and a comrade returning from the capital "said the people were hurrahing all night at the victory and that we had taken many prisoners," Gould learned.

Union soldiers visit the ruins of Mrs. Judith Henry's house at Manassas after Federal forces reoccupied the area in early 1862.
Photo by George N. Barnard via Library of Congress

"The men acted like maniacs to get the news" because "the morning paper man did not arrive" on time, Gould observed. When the local papers appeared about 7 a.m., the news "turned out much different from what we expected," he realized.

"In fact the victory was not quite so apparent," Gould commented.

After breakfast a passing courier informed Adjutant Elijah Shaw, "We are whipped, whipped badly boys." The upbeat mood evaporated in the 1st Maine camp.

"The men stopped laughing and hurrahing and looked sober," Gould noticed. Scuttlebutt flooded the camp into the afternoon and evening. Unable to sort fiction from fact, Gould "heard that the 2nd Maine had been all shot to pieces by a masked [artillery] battery," an untruth. He called a 5th Maine Infantry survivor "one enormous liar" for claiming that during the battle, "the shots rained down and knocked the men all to pieces," an accurate description of the disastrous minutes the regiment spent on Chinn Ridge.

And Gould dismissed the soldier's claim that "he escaped by running like a stud-horse."[1]

Unlike the newspaper accounts printed on Monday, the 5th Maine soldier accurately described the battle's aftermath. Initially heralding a Union victory based on Irvin McDowell's first jubilant report from Manassas, Northern papers soon shifted their narratives to reflect reality. Those papers often learned the truth from the letters written home by surviving Union soldiers.

Irvin McDowell's "demoralized army" fled in "a disgraceful flight" from victorious Confederates, the pseudonymic "Stephen" admitted to the Bangor-published *Daily Whig & Courier* on July 27 from the 2nd Maine's camp at Arlington Heights, Virginia.[2]

Actually Lt. Col. Charles Roberts of Bangor and the 2nd Maine Infantry, "Stephen" took a pen to paper as news of Manassas shocked Northerners and thrilled Southerners, whose newspapers could not publish sufficient news of the hard-earned Confederate victory. Pro-Confederate accounts would bleed into certain Northern papers, too; the printed aftermath of Manassas would extend through the summer in Maine.

While the 2nd Maine did withdraw relatively intact, some of its men vanished behind enemy lines. Captured that Sunday was Surgeon William H. Allen of Orono; with Confederate troops approaching the regimental hospital set up just off the Warrenton Turnpike, he stayed with his patients rather than flee.[3]

Not so for Assistant Surgeon Augustus Choate Hamlin, the vice-presidential nephew who had helped raise Co. G, the so-called "Gymnasium Company." While caring for wounded men at the 2nd Maine field hospital that Sunday evening, Hamlin earned a figurative white feather from the Bangor press; seizing Col. Charles Jameson's riderless horse from its temporary groom (a young black boy), he fled into the approaching night. Confederates captured Allen, his remaining staff, and their patients; infamy followed Hamlin home.

Bangoreans knew to whom the *Daily Whig & Courier* referred on July 24; "the conduct of Dr. Allen stands out in bright contrast with that of a portion of the surgical forces, who mounted their horses and disgracefully fled," the paper indicated.[4]

As newspapers expounded on the Northern defeat, civilians worried about their relatives or friends in uniform. The War Department would

Union Col. Nathaniel James Jackson,
between 1862-65

telegraph casualty lists later in the war; the casualty-communications system was in its infancy right after Manassas.

Fulfilling a role that would fall to War Department clerks in the future, Bangor resident Llewellyn J. Morse brought home from Washington a detailed 2nd Maine Infantry update. Arriving by train on Friday night, July 26, he shared with *Daily Whig & Courier* Editor William Wheeler "many incidents of interest ... and a list of killed and wounded, so far as they were then known."

The casualties included "Asa Nicholson, Elwin Bradley, T.Y. Burgess, dead."[5] Broken out by company, the long list provided to many Mainers the first information about the fates of their relatives and friends.

Morse's report "that the Second [Maine] fought with unparalleled bravery and gallantry" did little to soften the battle's bloody impact on Bangor, Brewer, Castine, Milo, and elsewhere.

Although 30-year-old Sarah Dustin Deane likely knew the fate of her husband, she learned from the July 27 issue of the *Daily Whig & Courier* that "Mr. Wm. J. Dean [*sic*] of this city, was shot while carrying the new and elegant [California] flag," which "was preserved, stained in the blood of its brave defender."[6]

William J. Deane left behind six children, the youngest a daughter born in 1860.

By July 27, Union soldiers had begun moving past the immediate psychological effects caused by defeat. Roberts accurately assessed that "time alone will heal the present shock" suppressing morale in the loyal states. Anger now simmered in the 2nd Maine camp, he intimated.

"Our boys, owing to fatigue, ragged clothes, no money, &c., are not in the best of humor," and they blamed McDowell for their defeat, according to "Stephen." With "the blessing of God, we soon hope to ... have a Commander-in-Chief in whom we may have implicit confidence," he commented.[7]

Yet while many soldiers sought revenge and civilians mourned their dead or wounded and begged for information about the missing, many Mainers hoped (and prayed) that Manassas would stop the war immediately. While Republicans generally rallied around the American flag, Maine Democrats split into "peace" and "war" factions.[8]

Led by Democratic State Committee Chairman Marcellus Emery, peace Democrats vociferously opposed the war. Emery published two Bangor newspapers: *The Daily Union* and *The Democrat*, a staunchly pro-Southern weekly broadsheet that excoriated the Lincoln Administration and Republicans and published, often verbatim, Confederate press accounts.

Born in Frankfort, Maine in late July 1830, Emery hailed from a politically connected family; his maternal grandfather, Dr. Ephraim Rowe, had helped write the Maine Constitution. Emery went to Maine's better schools: North Yarmouth Academy and Bowdoin College, graduating from the latter in 1849.

Bangor Unionists seethed as Emery ramped up his anti-war diatribes after Manassas. "The loudest advocates of the existing deplorable war, in which the country has been involved, by the Abolition Republican party, are the political demagogues, the partisan priests, and the infamous speculators, who are coining fortunes out of the calamities of their country," he thundered in *The Democrat*.

Chapter 7: Freedom of the Press Takes Flight

The front page of *The Democrat,* Tuesday morning, August 13, 1861
The pro-Southern paper excoriated the Lincoln Administration and Republicans and published, often verbatim, Confederate press accounts. *(Photo by Brian Swartz; archive paper courtesy of the Bangor Public Library)*

55

The demagogues "want offices," the priests advocated freeing enslaved blacks, and the speculators sought wealth, Emery wrote. "The poor unfortunate people—the farmers, mechanics and workingmen—are to be first taxed to death, and then enslaved, as a consequence of all this infamous business."

By that Monday, however, Emery had unknowingly sealed his newspaper's fate (and perhaps his own) by publishing in *The Democrat* on July 30 a post-Manassas report written by Confederate President Jefferson Davis. Local boys were dead, wounded, or missing courtesy of Davis's soldiers, and Emery referred to the conflict in which "the brave soldiers had gone out to peril their lives for their country" as "an 'Unholy War.'"

Bangor Unionists "decided that 'the Democrat' should not be tolerated at home."[9]

Broad Street, Bangor, circa 1880
The Wheelwright & Clark Block, where Marcellus Emery's *The Democrat* had its offices, is at left.
Photo courtesy of Richard R. Shaw

On Saturday, August 10, Unionists packed Norumbega Hall in downtown Bangor and adopted a terse resolution that accused *The Democrat* of "lending ... aid and comfort to the armed enemies of our country" and declared the paper's "editors, publishers and proprietors [to be] guilty of treason."[10]

Emery learned that William McCrillis, a Republican state representative, and Penobscot County district attorney Charles Crosby "made inflammatory speeches and said all in their power to incite a mob." Local attorney Henry E. Prentiss opposed "the efforts then and there being made to create a mob spirit," but "a tempest of hisses" drowned him out.[11]

Emery published *The Democrat* in fourth-floor offices of the Wheelwright & Clark Block, a new brick building adjacent to West Market Square in downtown Bangor.[12] Fearing damage to his property, co-owner J.G. Clark repeatedly begged Emery to relocate his newspaper elsewhere.

Emery would not, even after Bangor mayor Isaiah Stetson declined a request for police protection.

Working to meet their deadlines, Emery and his staff started printing *The Democrat* on Monday morning, August 12. Emery "left ... about 12:25 [p.m.] to go to my dinner, my boarding place being about half a mile distant."[13]

Twenty minutes later, as Emery ate, the bell atop the First Parish Church on Broadway tolled a fire alarm. Other Bangor church bells pealed in unison; "soon the [fire] engines, accompanied by a great crowd," tore "over State Street hill, in the supposed direction of the fire."

The false alarm triggered a well-planned Unionist attack on *The Democrat*.

Pre-positioned when the alarm sounded, a Unionist "crowd" estimated at four to twelve men climbed to the fourth floor of the Wheelwright & Clark Block to sack the newspaper's offices. John Tabor, "a brawny blacksmith," effectively swung a sledge [hammer]; "the large cylinder press was broken into bits" and, along with other equipment, flew out the windows to crash onto West Market Square.

There other Unionists set ablaze a large exterior sign and newspapers tossed from *The Democrat* offices. The "roaring bonfire" and flying debris elicited enthusiastic cheers.[14]

Finishing his dinner, Emery walked toward his office. He met McCrillis at the Broadway-Summer Street intersection; "for the first time since our acquaintance" McCrillis failed to acknowledge Emery.

Then "two gentlemen in a buggy" slowed alongside Emery and revealed that his office "had just been sacked, and all my property thrown into the street." Emery does not indicate if he ran from that point; when he emerged from Central Street, directly across from West Market Square, "I saw the first mob that had ever met my eyes."

He watched Unionists heap "my tables, stands, cases, and other material" onto the bonfire. Forcing his way through a crowd he estimated at "nearly two thousand people," Emery elbowed a passage up the people-packed stairs to his locked office, a sanctuary separate from the destroyed press room.

A Bangor police officer demanded that Emery unlock the office; "unarmed," Emery "told them my object was to secure my account books, notes, bills, and private papers." When he opened the office door, however, rioters surged inside and started throwing everything out the window.

With rioters hot on his heels, Emery abandoned his office. As he emerged onto the sidewalk, other rioters shouted, "Hang him! Tar and feather him! Kill him!"

Emery stepped into the threatening mob, where "friend after friend gathered round me, for my protection." His guards escorted Emery past the mob's fringe, and the gutless Mayor Stetson, "when I was beyond danger ... suddenly conceived an anxiety for my personal safety, and suggested that I had better hurry away," Emery snarled in the immediate post-riot edition of *The Democrat*.[15]

Samuel Smith, a local printer, surreptitiously let Emery use his shop to print a four-page edition of *The Democrat* later that week. In it Emery rebuked the local politicians who failed to protect his property.

"Thus hath the freedom of the Press been stricken down here in Maine ... through the wicked instigation of abolitionist [i.e., Republican] politicians who would willingly subvert all law and all order for the maintenance of a mere party dogma," Emery correctly surmised in that edition.[16]

He quickly folded *The Democrat*, which did not reappear until January 1863.

~~~

1. William B. Jordan, *The Civil War Journals of John Mead Gould 1861-1866*, Butternut & Blue, Baltimore, 1997, pp. 47-48

2. "Stephen" (Charles Roberts) letter, *Daily Whig & Courier,* August 2, 1861
3. Ibid.
4. *Daily Whig & Courier,* July 24, 1861
5. *Daily Whig & Courier,* July 27, 1861
6. Ibid.
7. "Stephen" (Charles Roberts) letter, *Daily Whig & Courier,* August 2, 1861
8. Similar Democratic Party fracturing occurred in the other loyal states early in the war.
9. R.H. Stanley and George O. Hall, *Eastern Maine and the Rebellion,* Heritage Books, Maryland, 1887, 2008, p. 86
10. Ibid, p. 89
11. Ibid, p. 95
12. The Wheelwright & Clark Block still stands at the intersection of Main and Hammond streets in downtown Bangor.
13. Stanley and Hall, *Eastern Maine and the Rebellion,* p. 95
14. Ibid, p. 87
15. Ibid, pp. 95-97
16. John DiMeglio, *Civil War Bangor,* University of Maine graduate thesis, 1967

Chapter 8

MAINE WOMEN MOBILIZE

"Female nurses are much more efficient than men"

A mong Maine women the devil would find few idle hands to work in his shop in midsummer 1861 as women banded together to assist the Maine boys fighting so far away. Patriotic Belfast women established The Ladies' Volunteer Aid Society on Saturday, April 27.

Paying 50 cents apiece to join the LVAS, women sewed blue denim pants, colored handkerchiefs, and other clothing for 4th Maine Infantry soldiers. Working individually at home or collectively in informal groups, the Belfast women supplied much clothing to the local boys before they headed to Washington, D.C.

Similar organizations formed elsewhere in Maine. In Bangor, women related to 2nd Maine Infantry soldiers stitched clothing by hand or sewing machine; ironically, to keep relatively cool while on the campaign trail, New England boys unaccustomed to Virginia's hot and humid weather often tossed away haversacks, bulky blouses, and other clothing lovingly sewn by the ladies at home.

Within days after arriving in Washington, Maine soldiers started complaining about the salty army food. The War Department believed that soldiers had simple dietary requirements: What Uncle Sam provided for food, the soldiers would eat—or go hungry.

Reading the scathing commentary about army fare, many Maine women stuffed food items into the care packages outbound to the various Maine regiments. On Wednesday, August 7, 2nd Maine women staffed the counters at 31 Central Street in Bangor from 9 a.m. to 4 p.m. to receive and sort donated food intended for the city's battle-damaged regiment.

"It is proposed to send cake, cheese, pickles, crackers, lemons, sugar, herring and sardines," noted the *Daily Whig & Courier* in an August 3 announcement. "Such articles only as can be transported in good order will be accepted," with the donated food slated to ship by rail on Thursday, August 8.[1]

Despite the home-front opportunities available for them to assist the war effort, some women knew they should do more. Surprisingly, the Maine Legislature anticipated that desire—which reflected a military necessity—in late April.

On Wednesday, April 24, legislator William McCrillis of Bangor—the same McCrillis who would incite a Queen City riot in mid-August—proposed a bill authorizing women to serve "as nurses for our sick and wounded soldiers mustered into the service of the United States" from Maine.

Nurses would report to the appropriate regimental surgeons. The governor would "make such provision for their [nurses'] comfort and support while so employed, as in his judgment shall be just and expedient," the bill indicated. Already meeting in special session to tackle war-related issues, the legislature overwhelmingly passed Bill 376-174.[2]

Florence Nightingale and other women who served as nurses during the Crimean War set the stage for American women to care for their brethren on the battlefield—or at least close to it. The ink had scarcely dried on Bill 376-174 when one Maine woman decided to sign up as a nurse with the 3rd Maine Infantry Regiment.

In spring 1861, people who knew Sarah J. Sampson could not imagine the life-saving role that she would play during the next four years. Born in 1832, she lived in Ward 5 in Bath, a lower Kennebec River city long affiliated with shipbuilding. Her husband, Charles A.L. Sampson, carved figureheads for sailing ships and served in a local militia company.

Sarah Sampson
Photo courtesy Maine State Archives

Likely taken shortly before the war, a surviving period photograph of Sarah Sampson suggests a petite, smooth-complexioned woman with average features, curly hair, and attention-to-detail eyes; she gazes directly at the camera as if studying its various components. A functional knot tied atop her head indicates long hair; her clothing reveals an eye to period fashion in style and jewelry.

The photograph cannot reveal the inner steel that many people would glimpse by 1865. Sampson remains almost invisible in Civil War lore, although her name was spoken by hundreds, if not thousands, of Maine soldiers during the war—and especially afterwards.

Capt. Charles Sampson, her husband, mustered into Federal service with the 3rd Maine Infantry Regiment at Augusta on June 4. He had brought the largely Bath-area Co. D north on the Kennebec River by steamer in May; a train would take Co. D away to war on June 7.

With Charles Sampson went his bride. Across the North, most officers' wives stayed home, if only because the war was expected to end with one crushing Union victory.

With no young children diverting her attention, Sarah decided to accompany the 3rd Maine as a nurse. She had discussed her impending work with Dr. Alonzo Garcelon, surgeon general of Maine; both knew that with a battle expected in Virginia, Sampson's journey to Washington, D.C. was no tourist excursion.

Unfortunately, Garcelon had not heard from Sampson for "a whole month" when she wrote him from the 3rd Maine camp on Meridian Hill on June 14. "I have been so busy since I came into my present position," she explained her tardiness in contacting Garcelon. Working "with our Surgeon and sick, I have had no opportunity to write to my dear friends at home."

Describing herself as "perfectly well, and never happier in my life than now," Sampson detailed her journey by train in the same passenger car with Col. Oliver Otis Howard and his staff, including his "private secretary" and brother, Charles. The Howards and other officers had "pointed out to me in the most agreeable manner" the passing landmarks, she wrote.[3]

During their swift passage to Washington, the 3rd Maine's staff officers encountered the amiable demeanor that the regiment's enlisted men came to appreciate in Sarah Sampson. She comfortably interacted with "common" Maine soldiers—the farmers, sailors, lumberjacks, mechanics, extra-mouths-to-feed sons, immigrants, and unskilled laborers filling the 3rd Maine's ranks. For Maine boys soon starved for feminine contact, Sarah Sampson came to resemble the mother or older sister left at home. By late June 1862 the 3rd Maine lads would adore her.

The 3rd Maine arrived by train at the Baltimore & Ohio Railroad station in Washington on Friday evening, June 7. Howard and his men spent the night on the "bare floor" in "a vacant building" on Pennsylvania Avenue; Howard's temporary office was "a chairless room without table or lights"; after "the previous hearty, patriotic receptions" the regiment had received en route to the capital, Howard thought his men had received "a depressing welcome to their beloved capital."

The next morning, he marched his men to the four-story Willard Hotel on Pennsylvania Avenue "and arranged to give the entire command a breakfast ... for fifty cents a man" from his own pocket. Howard later sought reimbursement from Maine Adjutant General John L. Hodsdon; "after a spirited correspondence the State finally settled the account," Howard remembered.[4]

Sampson arrived at the Willard at 8 p.m. Friday and, in the relative quiet of her room, she thought about her adventures since leaving Augusta. She realized "that I had entered upon my new life under really favorable auspice."

Dr. Alonzo Garcelon
Photo courtesy Maine State Archives

Garcelon sent with Sampson a letter of introduction to Dorothea Dix, soon to be appointed the first superintendent of women nurses by President Abraham Lincoln. Born in Hampden, Maine on April 4, 1802, Dix had lived her first two years in wretched poverty as her father, itinerant preacher Joseph Dix, wandered from sermon to sermon. Wealthy maternal relations would later welcome Dorothea to Massachusetts and provide her with a well-rounded education; for the rest of her life, she seldom (if ever) mentioned her natal connection to Maine.

American history remembers Dix for her commitment to improving living conditions for mentally ill people and prison inmates. Countless sick or wounded Union soldiers would live—or at least die in dignity between clean sheets—because Dix poured her relentless energy into providing such men with the best nursing care available in North America.

Dix made personal friends and political enemies as she assigned female nurses to Washington-area hospitals. Chauvinistic doctors (especially those commissioned as army officers) disparaged Dix and her nurses; jealous of her official title and ease of access to Lincoln, some physicians expressed their hostility toward Dix throughout the war. Other doctors wholeheartedly supported Dix and her nurses.

With her take-no-prisoners attitude (often construed as arrogance), Dix won no popularity contest with her nurses, either. Many women liked her; others, perceiving her leadership style as autocratic, whispered behind her back.

In the high heat of Saturday, June 8, Sarah Sampson took Garcelon's letter and "made my way to the Capitol" to meet Dix, only to "fortunately (I am confident)" discover that she was away. Sampson encountered instead the fittingly named "Mrs. Healed" (likely "Heald"), an elderly Maine woman who had lived the last eight years in Washington.

Heald taught Sampson "many items, that I trust you will assist me to appropriate to our advantage—state advantage, I mean," she told Garcelon. However, the talkative Heald did Sampson a terrible disservice by painting a darkly biased picture of the absent Dix.

Initially describing Dix as "a good friend, noble, genuine, and patriotic," Heald suddenly revealed a hidden hostility toward her. Dix "had really undertaken more than she was able to get through with," in Heald's estimation.

"In her younger days" Dix "was insane and even now had an insane thirst for Fame," Heald said. Even now, just weeks into the war, sick Federal soldiers "must be under her [Dix's] controll [sic]"—and on this point Heald made a shocking accusation.

Dr. Gideon S. Palmer, the 3rd Maine's senior surgeon, had attempted to admit seven sick

Dorothea Dix in her younger days
Photo from Library of Congress

soldiers to a "General Hospital" on his own cognizance on Friday evening, June 7. Those men were turned away at the door, Sampson informed Garcelon.

"It was through her [Dix] that our sick soldiers ... were not admitted" to the hospital that Friday, Heald told Sampson.

Then "a young German woman who was present" when the incident occurred indicated that she and Heald "could not induce Miss D. to yield to the necessity of the case" and that "it was dangerous" for the nurses to argue any point with Dix, Sampson wrote.

Dix's alleged decision on June 7 stunned Palmer and Sampson, yet they apparently did not speak to Dix about barring the 3rd Maine lads from the hospital—and Sampson possibly did not give Dix an opportunity to defend herself against Heald's slanderous accusations, either.[5]

Sampson quickly put her nursing skills to work. Their bellies full, Howard's men shouldered "their knapsacks, haversacks, and cartridge boxes" and started marching "along Pennsylvania Avenue and Fourteenth Street" toward the 3rd Maine's assigned camp site on Meridian Hill, Howard recalled.

The men labored with the additional weight of "underclothing, books, and keepsakes" donated by "friends at home and along our route" to Washington, he noticed. Overcome by the sweat-inducing heat, men "dropped out of the ranks for water or rest"; then "a sudden storm arose, attended by wind, fierce lightning, and a pouring rain."

Maine boys scattered for shelter. Frantically climbing over a fence, one soldier "pulled his loaded musket after him with the muzzle toward him." When "a rail or stone" struck its hammer, the musket fired, "inflicting ... a desperate, disabling wound" on the young soldier, Howard sadly noted.

Finally arriving on Meridian Hill, the 3rd Maine camped beside the 2nd Maine Infantry Regiment. Its gifted commander, Col. Charles Jameson, arranged for his men to share their "already comfortable tents" with their 3rd Maine comrades, Howard remembered that kindness.

The 3rd Maine boys soon established a proper camp and started learning the art of soldiering. They also discovered that their "radical change of life ... brought illness," Howard realized.[6]

Measles, mumps, dysentery, typhoid fever, and other deadly diseases stalked the Union camps and swept away healthy young men into early graves. Palmer and Sampson believed that sick men should be treated in hospitals to remove the communicable-disease carriers from the regimental camps.

Palmer was finally able to place some patients in the "General Hospital," described by Sampson as "a large & old brick building." Unfortunately, many sick soldiers from the 3rd Maine were dispersed to local homes to be cared for by "strangers," she complained to Garcelon. Only "God knows what" sort of "medical care would be provided."[7]

"Something like cholera" struck down Howard on Saturday, June 29. His illness almost killed him; Howard credited his survival to "my brother's devotion," Palmer's "firmness and skill," the "care given me by" Sarah Sampson," and "the blessing of God."[8]

His reference to Sampson's nursing skills was possibly the first such made by a Maine soldier; it would not be the last.

Regimental surgeons soon discovered that diseases spread as swiftly in the formal hospitals

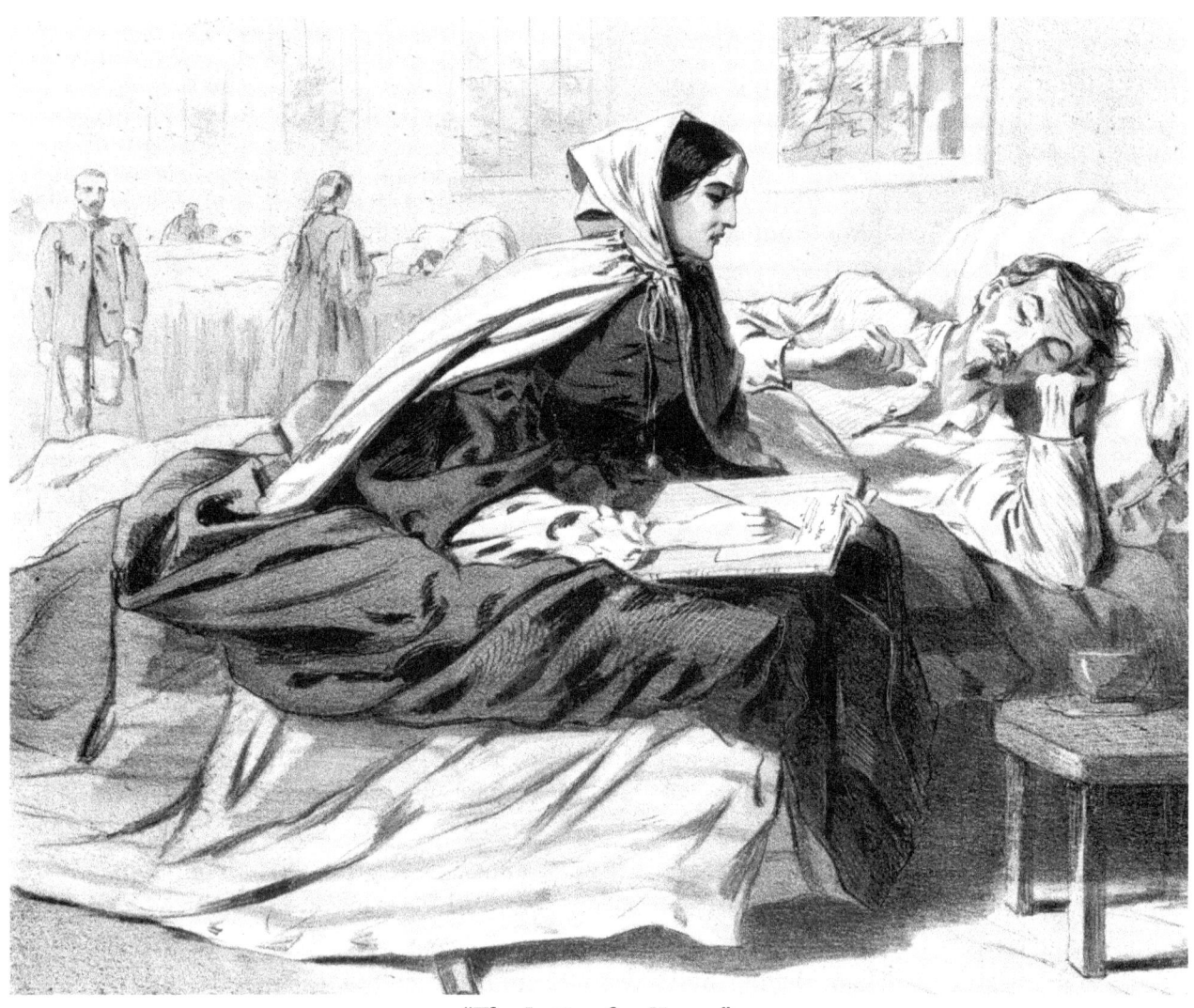

"The Letter for Home"
A nurse writes a letter for a wounded Army of the Potomac soldier confined to a hospital bed.
Illustration by Winslow Homer via Library of Congress

as in the Union camps. Mumps quickly sent one 3rd Maine lad to the "General Hospital," where he "may be exposed" to the smallpox that had appeared in the hospital, Sampson said.

Palmer was so appalled at hospital conditions that while making his rounds on Thursday evening, June 13, he evacuated a sick 3rd Maine soldier "whom he could not in [good] conscience let stay [there any] longer," Sampson said.

In her first week in Washington, she realized that Maine soldiers would encounter "a great deal of sickness from [the] change of climate and diet." Maine boys were complaining about sore throats; Sampson expressed fear that diphtheria and pneumonia, which had "been very prevalent and fatal" in other state regiments, would soon afflict the Maine regiments camped around the capital.

Sampson recommended that the Maine state government establish "a Maine Gen. Hospital" to care exclusively for Maine soldiers. Federal-provided medical care had not impressed the upstart nurse from Bath; the "U.S. government promises so much and [delivers] no more" than promised, she groused to Garcelon.

The prescient Sampson stressed that in caring for seriously ill soldiers, "female nurses are much more efficient than men." Oliver Otis Howard and Gideon Palmer agreed with her, "and our people at home can readily see the advantages," she stated.[9]

In advocating for women nurses, Palmer displayed a foresight rejected by many hidebound officers and physicians. The ghastly hospital-based death rates among Great Britain's wounded and sick soldiers of the Crimean War had declined as Nightingale and other women nurses administered around-the-clock care. In time the skilled care provided by Dix and her nurses would achieve a similar goal in Union hospitals.

Ironically, while initially presented with a negative impression of Dorothea Dix, Sampson shared a similar trait with her; these strong-willed women would focus on patient care and do their respective jobs very well during the next four years.

After posting her letter to Garcelon, Sampson spent the next five weeks assisting Palmer in caring for his patients. The post-Manassas rout scattered the 3rd Maine's casualties hither and yon on July 21, yet just 12 days after the battle, a central Maine newspaper placed Sampson "at the hospital in Alexandria," where she was "unwearied in her attentions to the sick and wounded soldiers."[10]

Sarah Sampson would not labor solo for long. Realizing they were needed more in the field than at home, independent Maine women lobbied Governor Washburn and Hodsdon for placement as nurses with various regiments.

Born in New Brunswick to Scottish immigrant parents in 1823, Isabella Morrison married William Fogg of Calais, Maine when she was 14. Pronounced as "KAL-lus" and not "ka-LAY," the city lay at the head of tide on the St. Croix River separating Maine from the British colony of New Brunswick.

The Foggs had three children before William died. Isabella supported her family by working as a seamstress. As militia companies formed the 6th Maine Infantry Regiment in spring 1861, son Hugh Morrison Fogg (possibly Isabella's only surviving child) went to war with the Calais militia company, designated as Co. D.

Isabella Fogg petitioned Washburn to serve as a nurse with the 6th Maine. He granted her request; in September, Fogg and

Isabella Fogg
Maine State Archives

Ruth Mayhew of Portland arrived in Annapolis, Maryland to work as nurses in an army hospital swept by spotted fever.

A Hancock County native married only a few years to Reverend Andrew Mayhew before his death in Rockland in 1856, Mayhew later moved to Portland to work as a teacher. She, Fogg, and Sampson were among the first Maine women to serve as nurses.

The Maine state government did not equip and staff a hospital to strictly treat Maine soldiers. The cost was a major factor; Maine would likely have fielded the facility's entire expense without Federal compensation.

Precedent was another reason; if Maine established its own hospital, other states would do so, too, and theoretically the battle would come when the regiments from a particular loyal state would suffer disproportionately more casualties than that state's hospital could handle.

Where would the overflow patients go after that state's hospital filled its beds?

The answer, obviously, was to let the War Department provide medical care for all Union soldiers. That choice made sense to Hodsdon, who later explained to state officials, "The admirable provisions made by the United States Government for the relief of sick and wounded soldiers, by establishing general hospitals at Washington and vicinity, rendered unnecessary the establishment of State institutions of a like character at the National Capital."

Instead the state appointed Sarah Sampson and Leonard Watson of Wilton to run the newly established Maine Soldiers' Relief Agency, which set up shop at 273 F Street, Washington, D.C. The purpose of the run-on-a-shoestring-budget agency was to distribute "such donations as it received for the health and comfort of Maine soldiers," Hodsdon noted.[11]

Isabella Fogg later affiliated with the Maine Soldiers' Relief Agency. Other Maine women headed south to serve as nurses; before long, many Maine boys confined to hospitals on the battlefield or in rear areas would hear familiar Maine accents spoken by female voices—and would receive medical care delivered by tender hands.

~~~

1. *Daily Whig & Courier,* Saturday, Aug. 3, 1861
2. *Maine Revised Statutes Annotated*
3. Sarah J. Sampson, letter to Dr. Alonzo Garcelon, June 14, 1861, Maine State Archives
4. Oliver Otis Howard, *Autobiography of Oliver Otis Howard, Major General United States Army,* Baker & Taylor Company, New York, 1907, pp. 131-132
5. Sampson to Garcelon, June 14, 1861, MSA
6. Howard, *Autobiography,* pp. 133-134, 137
7. Sampson to Garcelon, June 14, 1861, MSA
8. Howard, *Autobiography,* p. 137
9. Sampson to Garcelon, June 14, 1861, MSA
10. *Daily Whig & Courier,* August 2, 1861
11. John L. Hodsdon, *Annual Report of the Adjutant General of the State of Maine, 1861,* p. 49

Chapter 9

THE 6TH MAINE INFANTRY BRAWLS APART PORTLAND

"A better representative of Eastern Maine"

Amidst the patriotic fervor sweeping Maine in mid-April 1861, some metropolitan newspapers referred vaguely to an infantry regiment coalescing around companies drawn from the Penobscot River watershed and the Down East coast. Perhaps as colorful a regiment as any mustered in the Pine Tree State, the 6th Maine Infantry would forever reflect the essentially rural character of its soldiers.[1]

After the 2nd Maine Infantry departed Bangor by train on May 14, five unattached companies of soldiers remained at Camp Washburn. A head count taken on Wednesday, May 22 revealed that the companies were "from Ellsworth, Bucksport, Corinth, Old town [sic],[2] and Brownville."[3]

Geographically, Bucksport and Old Town lay on the Penobscot River. Located where the tides surge through the Penobscot Narrows,[4] Bucksport was an actual sea port and mercantile town for western Hancock County. Spreading across most of Marsh Island upriver from Bangor, Old Town was home to various sawmills by 1861.

Brownville, its economy focused primarily on agriculture and logging, straddled the Pleasant River in southeastern Piscataquis County, which borders central and northern Penobscot County. The Pleasant flows into the Piscataquis River downstream at Milo, from which the Piscataquis flows east to reach the Penobscot River at Howland.

A thriving village existed (and still does) in the eastern section of Corinth, a farming town about 20 miles northwest of Bangor. Corinth lay on a stage route between Bangor and Dover, the shire town of Piscataquis County.

The Ellsworth company drilling at Camp Washburn in mid-May 1861 comprised men drawn from central and eastern Hancock County. Although sent to Bangor to await their company's fate, the 100-odd volunteers might have mingled well with five other companies forming in coastal Washington County.

With its thin soil, thick spruce-fir forests, clear and fast-flowing rivers, and island- and peninsula-dotted shore, Down East Maine offered less diverse job prospects than did more prosperous Bangor, Lewiston, Rockland, and Portland. The men living in the towns sprinkled from Bucksport and Deer Isle in the Penobscot River watershed in the west to Eastport and Robbinston on Passamaquoddy Bay in the east pursued physical, hardscrabble employment in fishing, farming, and lumbering or worked at jobs supporting those employment sectors.[5]

Yet from the farms and small towns in Washington County responded sufficient men to form five unattached infantry companies in May 1861. Those companies gathered at Calais on the St. Croix River, tidal Eastport and Pembroke,[6] Machias (the Washington County shire town), and Cherryfield on the Narraguagus River in central coastal Washington County. Volunteers streamed into those municipalities from surrounding towns; on May 6, Theodore Lincoln Jr. took 16 other men by stage coach from Dennysville to nearby Pembroke to join the self-styled Pembroke Rifles.[7]

Then the entire Pembroke contingent converged on Eastport, as did the eclectic and well-officered volunteers from Calais, whose ranks included at least a few British subjects, like 22-year-old laborer Daniel Clark, born on Prince Edward Island; he deserted his company at the first opportunity after leaving Maine. Aaron Hanson, a 20-year-old from New Brunswick, waited more than two years to desert. From Halifax, Nova Scotia came 23-year-old Thomas Macky, who saw the war through to its completion.

Another 19-year-old laborer, Hugh Fogg, hailed from St. Stephen, New Brunswick and Calais. Not the least confused as to where his loyalties lay, he quickly enlisted in the Calais company that was now commanded by Capt. Joel A. Haycock, a surveyor. Haycock's first lieutenant was the 6' 2" Reuel W. Furlong, a schoolmaster who looked at the world through soft gray eyes. The 28-year-old Henry H. Wait went to war as second lieutenant of the Calais company.[8] None of the three officers lived a charmed life; Confederate bullets would find the trio by war's end.

The Calais volunteers boarded the steamer *Queen* and sailed to Eastport, where they disembarked on May 21 and camped at Fort Sullivan overlooking Campobello Island and Deer Island in Canadian waters and Lubec, Maine to the south.[9]

Awaiting the Calais soldiers were the Pembroke Rifles, led by Capt. William Pysell, 1st Lt. John Lincoln, and 2nd Lt. Simon Pottle II. These three men hailed from Pembroke; the highest rank that a Dennysville soldier attained in the early weeks of the company was sergeant, and those three stripes went to Ted Lincoln.

Already present at Fort Sullivan was the Eastport company, led by the 48-year-old Capt. Theodore Carey. Age and inadequate physical conditioning would conspire to sicken him at times; he would later resign his commission, as would 2nd Lt. Charles Day, a 42-year-old sail maker when he joined the company.[10] The company's second-in-command, 26-year-old 1st Lt. Thomas Roche, would not survive the war.

Led by Capt. Benjamin Harris, the Machias Rifles traveled to Eastport with the Cherryfield Light Infantry, led (oddly) by a Rockland carpenter, 37-year-old Ralph Young. His first lieutenant was 20-year-old Frank Peirce of Augusta, his second lieutenant Hiram Sproul of Narraguagus.

Accompanying Peirce's company was an odd man out: a 46-year-old merchant, Washington County commissioner, and natural leader named Hiram Burnham. Technically too old to do much good in the army, he soon showed his mettle in combat.

Born in 1814 in Cherryfield, Burnham hailed from a family of tough Maine Yankees. Grandfather Job Burnham was running the Burnham Tavern in Machias where angry locals gathered in the tap room in June 1775 to debate their response to the threat issued by James Moore, a young midshipman commanding the cutter HMS *Margaretta,* moored nearby in the Machias River.[11]

Job Burnham's brother-in-law, the fiery patriot Jeremiah O'Brien, lobbied his neighbors to capture Moore. The botched kidnapping attempt at a local church on Sunday, June 12 sent Moore fleeing to the HMS *Margaretta* and some 40 Machias-area men boarding two merchant ships and pursuing the British ship the next day. In a close-quarter battle that the U.S. Navy considers the Revolution's

Union Lieutenant Colonel Hiram Burnham
Photo courtesy of Maine State Archives

first sea fight, the patriots boarded and captured HMS *Margaretta* and a Loyalist schooner. Moore was mortally wounded during the fight.

His surname identifying his link with local history, Hiram Burnham grew into midlife as the smart, successful owner of a sawmill. He spent many winters in logging camps well "up" the Narraguagus River; in the close-knit populace of western Washington County, Burnham earned the respect of men who considered themselves the social equals of wealthy neighbors.

Commander of a Narraguagus militia company during the 1839 Aroostook War, Burnham exhibited a striking physical presence throughout his life; "even at fifty he was a stocky and robust figure," wrote late 20th-century author James H. Mundy.[12]

Maine Adjutant Gen. John Hodsdon organized the 10 infantry companies assembled in Bangor and Eastport into the 6th Maine Infantry Regiment. Bangor attorney Abner Knowles, the regiment's first colonel, inherited an essentially blue-collar outfit accustomed to hard physical labor. His men would prove tough in camp and in battle.

"It was a happy combination of the sailor, the lumberman, the student, the farmer, the merchant, and the laborer, with a lucky absence of the politician," said future adjutant Charles Clark, a student from Sangerville who literally "piled up my Greek and Latin books" at Foxcroft Academy on April 24 and enlisted in the Brownville company.

"We were all young," Clark recalled. "The most of us had seen nothing of the world."[13]

Before leaving Bangor and Eastport, the municipality-based companies underwent official re-designation. Commanded by Capt. Albert G. Burton, the Old Town company became Co. I, known as the "Jam Breakers."

"The Oldtown company was composed of big men, they taking uniforms several sizes larger—on the average—than had ever been made, either in Maine or Massachusetts," said a Bangor observer. Sixty-six Co. I recruits "averaged six feet in height and one hundred and sixty-six pounds in weight."

Physical labor had hardened such men. "Many were river drivers[14] and wood choppers … and had reputation for skill and daring in breaking jams of logs when running them on the turbulent waters of the Penobscot and its branches," the observer commented.[15]

The regimental staff included Hiram Burnham, commissioned as lieutenant colonel, and Frank Pierce, a Bucksport man tapped at the 6th Maine's major. All the way down the list to drum major, fife major, and band leader, the men hailed from central and eastern Maine—with one exception.

"The Sixth Maine, which was intended to replace the First [Maine Infantry], was really a better representative of Eastern Maine than the Second," a Bangor businessman said, unfairly disparaging the very Bangor-centric 2nd Maine Infantry.

"With the exception of the Chaplain, every officer resided near the banks of the Penobscot or east of that river," he said.

The "exception" was the Rev. Zenas Thompson, who lived in Portland.[16]

Orders came for the disparate companies to muster into the army. Boarding the steamer *Eastern City*, the 500-odd soldiers camped at Fort Sullivan sailed for Portland in late June. The five Bangor companies boarded a train on Monday, June 24 and chugged south for the Forest City.

For most 6th Maine lads, Portland was the largest city they had ever seen. Housed at Camp Preble in Cape Elizabeth, the fledgling soldiers initially behaved themselves, as had most other Maine soldiers passing through Portland while en route to Virginia and elsewhere. The 6th Maine lads marched in the July 4th parade and drew praise for their military bearing from the *Eastern Argus* editor.

Officially mustered into the Army on Monday, July 15, the 6th Maine soldiers received their first pay the next day before blowing into Portland with money burning holes in their pockets. "Bangor could have warned Portland what to expect of up to nine hundred lumberjacks, laborers, and farm boys suddenly released from the disciplines of camp," Mundy commented 140 years later.[17]

"From appearances, we were led to believe that the 6th was, in point of morality, far ahead of anything which had preceded them," an Eastport newspaper reprinted a Portland paper's shocked report. "But as soon as they were paid off a large number of them became almost unmanageable" in mid-July.[18]

"A little poor rum brought out all the baser passions, and they were gratified to the fullest extent, despite the efforts of the officers," the Portland paper sniffed. Soldiers reeled drunkenly in the city's streets after dark on Tuesday, July 16, "and quarrelling and fighting were the

Chapter 9: The 6th Maine Infantry Brawls Apart Portland

THE STEAMER EASTERN CITY.

The steamer *Eastern City*
The steamer was built in New York City for the Boston to Saint John (New Brunswick) route in 1852. It made stops in Portland and Calais. This engraving is from Gleason's Pictorial Drawing-Room Companion, from March 11, 1854. It transported soldiers of the 6th Maine to Portland.
Photo courtesy of Tides Institute & Museum

order of the night."[19]

The undermanned Portland police battled inebriated soldiers all night and packed them off to Camp Preble to sober up; "we think that about all of them were finally secured, and sent off," a newspaper sighed in relief.

"Physically, the regiment is the finest gone yet from this State ... but a few weeks discipline will bring out their soldierly qualities and make them second to none in the field," the Forest City paper opined.

Fortunately, this particular paper found "a pleasant contrast" to the 6th Maine's carnal occupation of Portland. A reporter discovered sober soldiers packing the Eastern Express Office run by Winslow & Co. Each soldier awaited "his turn to send a package of money to his wife or sisters, or mother or children, which he had left to do battle for his country," the paper reported.

The soldiers "forwarded in this way ... about $1,500," the press claimed.[20]

On Wednesday, July 17, the 6th Maine soldiers—hung over or not—boarded a train comprising "eighteen cars ... drawn by the locomotive *Gov. Goodwin,* which was gaily adorned with flags, and on a shelf in front was placed a beautifully mounted brass cannon, weighing a little over 100 pounds, manufactured by the engineer of the locomotive," reported the *Eastern Argus*. The engineer could fire the cannon "from his platform."[21]

Scheduled to leave Portland early Wednesday morning, the 6th Maine lads encountered "some delay in getting away" from Camp Preble, but as they marched into Portland, "the soldiers made a handsome appearance, fully equal, if not superior, to any Regiment sent from this State," the *Eastern Argus* reporter commented. If any men reeled drunkenly in line, he failed to take note.

Two competing newspapers—the *Argus* and the Portland broadsheet quoted by the *Eastern Sentinel*—disagreed on what happened next at the train station. The *Eastern Sentinel* claimed that the coal-burning *Gov. Goodwin* chugged from the station at 10 a.m.—and not a moment too soon. A large number of people gathered "to see the troops off; but there was little enthusiasm displayed," a Portland reporter read the mood of the crowd.

But "the boys went off in high spirits," he concluded.[22]

Supposedly attending the same event, the *Argus's* reporter claimed that "there was an immense concourse of people present, who greeted the soldiers with hearty cheers and bids of 'God speed.'" He noted the train's departure as "at quarter past 10 o'clock."[23]

Not for the last time would a Maine newspaper publish inaccurate information about the 6th Maine Infantry Regiment.

After Abner Knowles resigned his colonelcy in mid-December 1861, Hiram Burnham took over the regiment. Like his men, he retained a flinty edge that reflected his upbringing in rural Maine.

For the rest of 1861 and much of early 1862, Army officers attempted to knock military sense into the independent-minded 6th Maine soldiers unafraid to question nonsensical orders or defy bullying superiors. In late November 1861, recalled Sgt. Charles A. Clark, the then-acting quartermaster of Co. A, a letter that he delivered to Col. Francis L. Vinton of the 43rd New York Infantry precipitated "an exchange of lively profanity between a colonel and an enlisted man."

Arriving at Vinton's tent, the 20-year-old Clark claimed he "made my best free American military salute." Vinton "yelled at me vociferously to take off my cap," then Clark "stood upon my rights as a free American citizen to wear my cap" when outdoors, and Vinton charged him with "contempt and disrespect" and for refusing to obey the order to doff the cap. The official charge revealed that Clark "did fold my arms in a contumacious manner." That accusation "was probably accurate and correct," he recalled.

Military justice ground Clark through a court martial. On January 19, 1862, "I was found guilty of all charges" and fined $10 a month for two months, he recalled.[24] During a regimental dress parade, "my chevrons were torn off by Doctor Eugene F. Sanger," the 6th Maine's surgeon.[25]

A native of Sangerville in rural Piscataquis County,[26] the talented and conscientious Clark received his second lieutenant's commission about two weeks after being busted to private. Reflecting the obstinate Yankee spirit ingrained in his men, Burnham announced "with vigorous emphasis" that he would not let Vinton "administer discipline in his regiment, or tell his soldiers when to take off their caps," Clark said.

"The episode had rather a happy termination for me after all," he said.[27]

Vinton later gained a brigadier general's stars, suffered a severe wound at First Fredericksburg, and resigned his commission. Clark would not catch his own debilitating bullet until autumn 1864.

~~~

1. The uniquely Maine phrase "Down East" (also spelled "Downeast") refers to the general direction in which ships sailing from East Coast ports steered when approaching the eastern Maine coast. Sea captains described their ships as running with the prevailing northwesterly winds "down" to Maine and "east" from Boston.
2. For consistency, future references to "Oldtown" will use the city's later name, "Old Town."
3. R.H. Stanley and George O. Hall, *Eastern Maine and the Rebellion,* Heritage Books, Maryland, reprinted 2008, p. 63
4. The Penobscot River bends sharply at Bucksport. The main channel flows between Verona Island on the east and the Prospect bluffs on the west; during the Civil War, the incomplete Fort Knox on the Prospect bluffs was occasionally garrisoned to prevent Confederate ships from sailing "up" the Penobscot to attack river ports. The shallower Eastern Channel flows around Verona Island to rejoin the main channel about four miles south.
5. "Down East" now describes the geographical region of Maine stretching from the eastern shore of Penobscot Bay some 100-130 "air miles" east to the delightful Passamaquoddy Bay on the Maine-New Brunswick border. Excluding a few Penobscot River municipalities in adjacent Penobscot County, the term encompasses Hancock and Washington counties.
6. Eastport lies partially on Cobscook Bay, Pembroke wholly on adjacent Pennamaquan Bay.
7. James H. Mundy, *No Rich Men's Sons: The Sixth Maine Volunteer Infantry,* Harp Publications, Cape Elizabeth, 1994, pp. 21-22
8. Ibid., p. 238
9. Garrisoned by an inadequate Army contingent during the War of 1812, Fort Sullivan was surrendered to the British on July 11, 1814 with little fanfare.
10. Buttressed by an Army regulation that infuriated enlisted men, officers could resign their commissions and go home. Enlisted men received no such professional courtesy; they enlisted for the duration, death, or incapacity caused by disease or wounds.
11. Midshipman John Moore had escorted two Loyalist-owned schooners from Boston to Machias to load lumber intended for the construction of British barracks in Boston. When Machias men balked at aiding their perceived British enemies, Moore threatened to open fire on the town.
12. Mundy, *No Rich Men's Sons,* p. 19

13. Charles A. Clark, *Campaigning With the Sixth Maine,* The Kenyon Press, Des Moines, 1897, pp. 3-4
14. Logs harvested on the Penobscot and its tributaries were floated downstream with the springtime snow melt to reach the sawmills and ports on the lower Penobscot River. Loggers known as "river drivers" worked constantly in dangerous conditions to clear log jams and keep the logs moving with the river's current.
15. Stanley and Hall, *Eastern Maine and the Rebellion,* p. 63
16. Stanley and Hall, *Eastern Maine and Rebellion,* p. 68
17. Mundy, *No Rich Men's Sons,* pp. 34-35
18. *Eastport Sentinel,* Wednesday, July 24, 1861
19. Since the 1860s, most historians have assiduously avoided the topic of sex and the Civil War. The Portland press specifically mentioned drunken 6th Maine soldiers; the phrase "baser passions" tiptoed readers past the Forest City brothels, which did a booming trade in 6th Maine Infantry cash after the regiment's July 16 pay out.
20. *Eastern Sentinel,* Wednesday, July 24, 1861
21. *Eastern Argus,* Thursday, July 18, 1861
22. *Eastern Sentinel,* Wednesday, July 24, 1861
23. *Eastern Argus,* Thursday, July 18, 1861
24. Clark was paid a private's $13 per month.
25. Clark, *Campaigning,* pp. 11-12
26. Physically large in square miles, Piscataquis County is the least populated county in Maine.
27. Clark, *Campaigning,* p. 14

Chapter 10

MISSING THE FACE OF A PRETTY GIRL

"The duty I owe my country and Christianity"

Pressured by President Abraham Lincoln to attack the Confederate troops at Manassas, Gen. Irvin McDowell had believed his army ill-trained to wage a proper battle. To add to his anxiety, the 90-day regiments sent by several loyal states to Washington, D.C. in spring 1861 would soon muster out.

McDowell knew that his army would shrink considerably by August 1—and mobilized militiamen like John Mead Gould of the 1st Maine Infantry Regiment knew they would depart military service by late July or early August.

So McDowell marched, fought, and lost, and the loyal states paid the price for political ineptitude and military ill-preparedness. Manassas cost the Union 460 men killed, 1,124 men wounded (many mortally), and 1,312 men listed as captured or missing. The price of defeat hit hard in Maine, then (as now) a state substantial in landscape and inadequate in population.

In Sebec, a small and close-knit town in Maine's immensely rural Piscataquis County, relatives mourned 24-year-old Pvt. Sewall B. Hager. In the northern Waldo County farming town of Monroe, relatives of Ezra Billings learned that the 23-year-old farmer had been mortally wounded and captured.

Hampden residents learned that 19-year-old mariner Martin Jose had died atop Henry House Hill. The body of 18-year-old Stephen Leighton, a Bangor wheelwright, was abandoned on the battlefield. Confederate troops captured 21-year-old James Robinson, a Scot who had enlisted at Bangor; he died of disease in Richmond's soon-to-be infamous Libby Prison.

Wiscasset in Lincoln County lost William Clark, a first lieutenant with Co. G, 4th Maine Infantry. In Belfast, local papers extolled the heroism of Charles Burd, a Co. F, 4th Maine second lieutenant killed on Chinn Ridge.

The 5th Maine Infantry suffered Manassas-related fatalities days before the battle started. As Oliver Otis Howard marched his brigade toward Centreville on July 17, a hungry

Pvt. William McLellan of Casco in Cumberland County left the ranks of Co. K to raid a Virginia apple orchard. He swung the butt of his loaded musket at a juicy apple. A tree limb likely snagged and tripped the musket's trigger; the fired musket ball punched through the body and thigh of McLellan, who died a little while later.

That same Wednesday, another careless 5th Maine soldier accidentally shot and mortally wounded Pvt. Charles Barker of Farmington and Co. E.[1]

The 6th Maine Infantry Regiment arrived in Washington, D.C. on July 19. Four additional regiments were to soon follow, but War Department equivocation had led Governor Israel Washburn Jr. to suspend recruiting efforts.

Manassas ended expectations of a short war. Lincoln called for another 300,000 volunteers, and the War Department needed the four Maine regiments. Recruiting quickly resumed in the state; despite knowing the terrible price paid at Manassas, Maine men enlisted—or re-enlisted.

Union General Irvin McDowell
Photo from the Brady-Handy Collection, Library of Congress

Enjoying the pleasant Washington weather on Saturday, July 27, John Mead Gould dropped by the tent of 1st Maine Infantry adjutant Elijah Shaw. The regiment's 90-day existence would soon end; the men chatted, and when Shaw expressed his belief that "more than half the regiment will come back" to the Army, Gould disagreed. He predicted that perhaps 50 percent of 1st Maine soldiers would return to military service, but to achieve even this re-enlistment rate, the Army "must take the men home" and "let them get sick of loafing."

Envious eyes already eyed the regiment's gear; the 5th Maine's survivors laid claim to "our tents and camp equipage," and early on Tuesday, July 30, the 6th Maine boys arrived to trade "their old flint-lock alterations" for "our rifles," Gould groused. "The meanest weapon on the face of God's earth," the older weapons were useless; "a stick with a bayonet on it would be more effective."

That afternoon, Shaw informed the dyspeptic 1st Maine Infantry lads that they must leave even the old firearms in their camp "and go home bare handed," Gould noted.

On Wednesday, July 31, the 1st Maine left Washington by train for Baltimore. Packed into box and platform cars, Gould and his comrades noticed the passing terrain—and the women.

"The girls grow prettier, less beastly as we advanced north" to Philadelphia and Jersey City, Gould observed. But "the Jersey women are not so plump and pretty as the Penn.

[women]," and he figured that fact was "owing I suppose [to] the Dutch ancestry of the latter."

Two years later, Confederate troops advancing into southern Pennsylvania would comment on how collectively unattractive were the so-called "Dutch girls" watching them march past.

The 1st Maine Infantry hopped the Hudson River by ferry and spent a night in New York City. On Friday, August 2, the steamer *Bay State* carried the Maine boys to Fall River, Massachusetts. From there they traveled 54 miles to Boston and caught a train to Portland. En route, people gathered at whistle-stop stations and rural grade crossings to cheer the passing soldiers.

Gould noticed the summer dresses and slim figures adorning the crowds; "nothing [is] so pleasing as the face of a pretty girl," he commented.

The troop train rolled into Portland "about 2" p.m. on Saturday. Civilians turned out en masse to welcome home their heroes; tossing away their knapsacks as they marched through the city streets, the 1st Maine lads quickly vanished into the humanity.

For Gould, a "fine sail down" Casco Bay marked his return to normality. Then he hustled to where people awaited him.

"Home. Everyone glad to see me. They say I look healthier than ever I think. I have grown tall." His short sentences reflected the chaos surrounding the unwounded warrior now overrun by people who adored him.

Dodging rain drops on Monday, August 5, Capt. Menzies Raynor Fessenden individually discharged the men of Co. C, 1st Maine Infantry Regiment. Each soldier received $23.83 in back pay.[2]

John Mead Gould had arrived home; he did not need to return to war.

Up in Patten in far northern Penobscot County, 18-year-old Ira B. Gardner chafed at his inability to enlist. In July "a large part of our militia company went to the front" as Co. C, 8th Maine Infantry Regiment.

"Being an only son[,] I was not allowed to go with them," he realized.

With "a large share of my comrades at the front," Gardner did what comes naturally to American teen-agers: He whined, wheedled, complained, and moped incessantly until "my presence at home became to my parents so uncomfortable" that they would consent "for me to enlist" just to shut him up.[3]

Amazingly, the patient John and Mary Gardner withstood their son's bellyaching for another five months; keeping their strapping son around through the fall harvest likely played into the delay, too.

A sense of adventure seems the reason why the impetuous Gardner repeatedly begged his parents' permission to enlist. An action-focused youth who seldom recorded his deepest thoughts, Gardner stayed in Patten as wintry conditions gradually descended on northern Maine.

Gould and many other 1st Maine soldiers experienced some difficulty in adjusting to civilian life. He contracted a bad cold after arriving home; on August 13 a northeasterly wind hurled rain across Cumberland County, and Gould, accustomed to the Washington warmth, suffered; "such Siberian weather freezes my very bones," he commented.

He sailed relentlessly around Casco Bay with friends until he "got thoroughly disgusted with salt water." One late August day, Gould was "up at 5 in true soldiers style and went loafing around the silent streets" of Portland.

Some evenings he "walked around town" with 1st Maine comrades. On Saturday, August 17, Gould and a few other ex-1st Maine boys drifted into the Portland Light Guards armory to receive their official federal discharge papers, "as no papers were made out" when the regiment had mustered out 12 days earlier.

Then, upon hearing that the new regiments forming in Maine were needed in Washington, Gould realized "I feel like trying it again myself." He noticed the lamentable response across the North to Lincoln's troop call; "it makes me blue to think of [such] matters," he commented.[4]

Although mustered out of federal service, the 1st Maine Infantry boys remained liable for recall for two years; its members were on "leave of absence without pay or rations," according to Adjutant Gen. John L. Hodsdon. "So far as was practicable," state officials envisioned forming the new 10th Maine Infantry Regiment with "the companies of the First."

On August 28, Hodsdon's office issued General Order No. 50 to disband the 1st Maine and create the 10th Maine Infantry by early autumn. Various 1st Maine companies were dissolved or merged; Hodsdon rounded out the regimental ranks by importing militia companies from Fort Kent and Saco.[5]

Gould considered joining the new regiment, but not before dealing with his internal conflictions. "When I am asked, 'Are you going[,] John[?,]' I have to belie my conscience with the excuse that I have had my turn and [have] a right to stay at home therefore," he told himself.

Yet "I have no right," Gould believed. "I have a mother, father, sisters, brothers, and friends, so have tens of thousands of other soldiers," men "that will be shot. Some one's son or brother or friend must be killed when anyone falls.

"But I have no wife and no little ones[,] and therefore all excuse is gone," Gould said.

From left: **Gould** *(Nicholas P. Picerno)*, **Gardner** *(Maine State Archives)*, and **Hodsdon** *(Bangor Public Library)*

Chapter 10: Missing the Face of a Pretty Girl

The 10th Maine under Col. George L. Beal at Camp Washburn, Patterson Park, Baltimore
Small print noted that this image was "Entered according to Act of Congress in the year 1861 by E. Sachse & Co. in the Clerks Office in the Dist. Court of Md." A handwritten note indicated that the print was received on October 29, 1861, so it was done almost immediately upon the 10th's arrival. In the background are Ft. McHenry (far left, with flag), Long Bridge (middle), and Federal Hill (right). *(Illustration from Library of Congress)*

"The duty I owe my country and Christianity weighs on me," he realized. "I must go or die here of smothered conscience."

Early September saw Gould trying to find a commission in an existing regiment. He occasionally camped and drilled with the remnants of the 1st Maine Infantry. Then, on October 1, John Mead Gould officially became Sgt. Maj. Gould of the 10th Maine Infantry; suddenly immersed in the regimental paperwork, he admitted on Oct. 3 that "the newness of the business makes it hard for me."

At 7 a.m., Sunday, October 6, Gould and other soldiers left camp "in a drenching show of warm rain" and marched to the Portland railroad depot. The train soon left for Boston.[6]

The regiment picked up an additional recruit at Portsmouth, New Hampshire. "There came on board the train … a large, black, Newfoundland, cross-breed dog, weighing considerably upwards" of 100 pounds. Bouncing into the train car assigned to Co. H, the Newfie quickly made himself at home with the men commanded by Capt. Charles S. Emerson.

In time the Co. H boys learned that "Major," as they named the tail-wagging recruit, was a combat veteran, having bounded around the Bull Run battlefield with the 1st New Hampshire Infantry (a 90-day regiment, like the old 1st Maine Infantry). Major had collected "a slight wound" at Bull Run, but chasing bullets seemed like quite good fun for a fur ball who liked having his ears scratched.

By the time the 10th Maine Infantry reached Maryland, Major ensconced himself as a full-fledged member of Co. H and, "never once deigning to recognize a person belonging to any other" company, ate as least as well as his human comrades.[7]

On a cold Wednesday, December 4, Ira Gardner and "about forty others from our section, with our old Captain, James B. Hill, in charge," left rural Patten for the arduous journey to cosmopolitan Bangor and Augusta. Near the State House, the Patten lads joined the 14th Maine Infantry Regiment—and met Col. Franklin S. Nickerson of Searsport. He would soon take the 14th Maine boys places far from the Pine Tree State.

"Our boys with others from Waldo County were designated as Company I," Gardner proudly stated. Hill was tapped as captain, Winslow Roberts as first lieutenant, Charles Smith as second lieutenant, and 18-year-old Ira Gardner as orderly sergeant. Apparently all the free time spent studying "infantry tactics" had paid dividends for the ambitious youngster from Patten.

The 14th Maine spent December and January camped in Capitol Park, the greensward that several other Maine regiments (including the 3rd Maine) had occupied previously. "Quartered in tents," even the soldiers accustomed to bitter northern Maine winters shivered and took ill in the cold; when not drilling or standing guard duty, the soldiers "were obliged to keep a good fire all night to keep warm," Gardner recalled.[8]

The 14th Maine boys would not be the only new recruits to spend that winter in Augusta.

~~~

1. Rev. George W. Bicknell, *History of the Fifth Maine Regiment*, Hall. L. Davis, Portland, 1871, p. 23.
2. William B. Jordan, *The Civil War Journals of John Mead Gould 1861-1866*, Butternut & Blue, Baltimore, 1997, pp. 50-52
3. Ira B. Gardner, *Recollections of A Boy Member of Co. I, Fourteenth Maine Volunteers*, Lewiston Journal Company, Lewiston, Maine, 1902, pp. 5-6
4. Jordan, *Journals*, pp. 54-55
5. *Annual Report of the Adjutant General of the State of Maine, 1861*, pp. 10, 31-32
6. Jordan, *Journals*, pp.65-67
7. William E.S. Whitman and Charles H. True, *Maine in the War for the Union: A History of the Part Borne by Maine Troops in the Suppression of the American Rebellion*, Nelson Dingley Jr. & Co., Lewiston, 1865, pp. 254-256
8. Gardner, *Recollections*, pp. 5-6

Chapter 11

OF SNOW AND ICE

"'Big snow storms' were the rule rather than the exception"

The 6th Maine Infantry Regiment arrived in Washington, D.C. on July 19. Four additional regiments should have followed, but expecting a short war, the War Department had already halted the in-flow of new regiments. Governor Israel Washburn Jr. promptly suspended recruiting efforts in Maine.

By then six infantry regiments had coalesced in Maine; Adjutant Gen. John Hodsdon expected that the four remaining infantry regiments requested by the Lincoln Administration in mid-April could be "sent into the field by the first of July."

However, in "frequent letters and telegrams" sent to Washburn in late May, the War Department "induced" him to send no more regiments. The letters cited the Lincoln Administration's inability to provide "subsistence and quarters, as well as arms" for all the state troops converging on Washington, D.C. as to why Washburn should dispatch only the six existing regiments.

Hodsdon sniffed that federal authorities seemed uncertain as to "the character and amount of force required for the emergency."[1]

Sending home the hundreds of men already listed on the muster rolls, Maine suspended recruiting for regiments 7 through 10—and the first six regiments mustered their full complements.

In Thomaston, Jonathan Prince Cilley believed he had missed the opportunity to avenge his father's murder. "I wish now I had gone with the 4th [Infantry] Regiment and I should had I expected another company might be raised" in Knox County, he admitted to his sister, Julia Draper Cilley, on July 31.

Perhaps Cilley could enlist elsewhere. Julia lived in New Hampshire; did she know if the Granite State might raise a company "in [the] vicinity of Epping or Nottingham? I should be tempted to join them."[2]

Cilley was unlikely aware that Manassas casualties (including deserters) and expiring enlistments for many 90-day state regiments had thinned the Union ranks defending Washington by midsummer. Brig. Gen. Thomas W. Sherman proposed attacking two Confederate forts on North Carolina's Outer Banks in a combined Army-Navy expedition to take place that fall.

Jonathan Prince Cilley
This illustration is later in Cilley's military career; here, he is a general.
Illustration courtesy of the Thomaston Historical Society

Chapter II: Of Snow and Ice

Sherman's expedition would siphon more Union regiments from the manpower pipeline. Secretary of War Simon Cameron suddenly needed more men, and Hodsdon learned in late summer "that additional regiments would be required "from Maine. Recruiting resumed for the four infantry regiments.³

Suddenly Cilley heard rumors about the state forming a cavalry regiment. He "telegraphed to Gov. Washburn for authority to enlist men," and Washburn granted Cilley permission in a Tuesday, September 3 telegram.

Grabbing a muster roll (likely left over from his abortive artillery recruiting efforts), Cilley filled in the regimental details and "signed his name at the head."

Though not yet officially authorized, the 1st Maine Cavalry Regiment had its first recruit. Jonathan Prince Cilley was going to war; the Confederacy would pay dearly for killing his father 23½ years earlier.⁴

Events proved the cavalry-regiment rumor to be true. The War Department informed Hodsdon that Maine could "organize five more regiments of infantry, (with power to increase the number to eight), a regiment of cavalry and six batteries of light artillery."

To this request Cameron quickly added a company of sharpshooters.

On September 11, Hodsdon's office issued General Order No. 46 to recruit sharpshooters and General Order No. 47 to create the 1st Maine Cavalry Regiment. General Orders 48 and 106 followed on September 14 and October 23 to raise five infantry regiments and six artillery batteries, respectively.⁵

Cilley was already recruiting a 100-man company on the Midcoast. He had planned to visit Julia in Epping; now Cilley could not go "as I ... shall be obliged to work hard at it to fill up a Company," he informed his sister on Sunday, September 8.

He admitted that recruiting would be difficult. "Men can not be enlisted as rapidly as they were in May as all the earnest, ardent spirits have already gone to war and fighting is now seen to [be] solid, hard work without the best of accommodations or of food."⁶

Based on their conversations and correspondence with soldiers still in the field or already returned home, civilians had learned "something of what the service really was" and realized that crushing the Southern rebellion would involve "a long and bloody war," Edward Parsons Tobie recalled years later.

A 23-year-old printer living in Lewiston, Tobie joined Co. G as a private in September. His first two years of service with the 1st Maine Cavalry interspersed with bouts of sickness and a brief stint as a Confederate prisoner, Tobie would become the regiment's excellent historian.

Many potential recruits "knew full well that if they enlisted they surrendered their freedom, their personality, in a great measure, their very thoughts and convictions, almost, into other hands, which to many was worse than death itself," he said.⁷

Cilley threw himself with a vengeance into his recruiting efforts—and vengeance could be why "I am forced to spend money freely and work continuously to complete the desired number of men," he told Julia on September 8. Ten days later he could report to her in a three-sentence letter that he had recruited 87 men.⁸

Across Maine, ambitious civilians sought to raise cavalry companies. Recruiting for a three-year mounted regiment often was not difficult; men figured they would rather ride than walk into battle, and "there hung about the cavalry service a dash and an excitement"[9] that lured men raised on the Revolutionary War exploits of Henry "Light Horse Harry" Lee, a dashing Continental cavalry commander who had served under George Washington. Lee was the father of Confederate Gen. Robert E. Lee.[10]

The adjutant general's office stipulated the cavalry recruits must be between 18 and 35 years in age and weigh between 125 and 160 pounds. They had to be physically "sound, able-bodied men ... of correct morals and temperate habits [i.e, not heavy drinkers], active, intelligent, vigorous, and hardy."[11]

In Houlton, located some 200 miles north and east of Thomaston, 23-year-old Black Hawk Putnam decided to take a company of Aroostook County horsemen to war. Named for a Sauk chief who had led several Indian tribes in a brief and tragic war against the United States in spring 1832,[12] Putnam came from solid settler stock.

Black Hawk Putnam
Photo courtesy of the Aroostook County Historical & Art Museum of Houlton

His parents, John and Elizabeth Putnam, hailed from New Salem, Massachusetts, where John was born in 1802 and Elizabeth in 1808. The Putnams were among the first families to settle along the Meduxnekeag River on the southern Aroostook County plateau. That settlement became Houlton and the shiretown for "The County."[13]

John Varnum Putnam set himself up in business and served as the Aroostook County sheriff. He and Elizabeth had four children: Aziel, born in 1835 and dead a year later; Black Hawk, born in 1838; Sarah, born in 1837; and Osceola (named for another well-known Indian chief), born in 1840.

Although the Military Road had connected southern Aroostook County with the Penobscot Valley by 1831, Houlton still remained geographically isolated from the United States. The fastest way to reach New York City or Washington, D.C. involved a short cross-border journey to Woodstock on the St. John River in New Brunswick, then a trip downriver to Saint John on the Bay of Fundy to catch an East Coast-bound ship.

But Houlton residents kept abreast of war news, and Hodsdon's request for cavalrymen electrified Black Hawk Putnam. He lobbied friends and strangers to sign his recruiting papers;

the response was evidently satisfactory.

"It was near night when he came into the [family] store [in mid-October] with his papers & before nine o'clock he had his names of 50 picked young men, the flower of our place," John Varnum Putnam later told a friend.[14]

Recruiters worked diligently that fall to fill the muster rolls for the five infantry regiments, cavalry regiment, and six artillery batteries. "After calmly thinking it over," many new recruits "felt that the country really needed them and they must go, cost what it might ... they were willing, for country's sake, to brave all," recalled Tobie, who would epitomize the men joining the Maine regimental ranks in autumn 1861.[15]

On Wednesday, September 30, Cilley brought 26 men to Augusta; "the first squad that arrived there for the regiment" was "in the immediate charge of Melville B. Cook." After camping that night "on the parade-ground in front of the State House," the squad established a camp on the infield of a nearby race track.

There, under the command of stout Col. John Goddard of Cape Elizabeth, the 1st Maine Cavalry Regiment would spend the winter. Initially named for Goddard, the encampment would become "Camp Penobscot."

Cilley returned to Thomaston to round up the rest of his company. More recruits dribbled into the race-track camp; "a squad of men from Penobscot county arrived" on October 1, to be followed two days later by "a squad from Androscoggin County," Tobie noted.

Each issued "a bed-tick and a towel," recruits "were marched down" to the race track and pointed toward stacked straw bales. Taking the hint, the men stuffed straw into their ticks and, because no tents were yet issued to the regiment, claimed sleeping berths in the available horse barns.

Arriving by train on October 4, one young recruit recalled his first Army-issued supper while writing his father from "in a horse-stall on the Agricultural Fair Grounds, nearly opposite the Capitol." The fledgling soldier "had cold salt beef (good), meat hash (good), hard and soft bread (good), boiled rice (can't say whether or no it was good, never having formed a friendship for the article), and some tip-top coffee, sweetened with molasses, but good."

Listening to one wag ask, "Where is the butter?" the young man noted that "we had a merry time, and ate plenty."[16]

As the acting quartermaster general, Hodsdon started advertising for horses on October 3. Printed in various newspapers across the state, the ads stipulated that horses must stand "from 15 to 16 hands [60 to 64 inches] high" and be "not less than five nor more than nine years old."

Acceptable colors were bay, black, brown, and sorrel, and "a small proportion of grey geldings and dark Mares will be purchased." Horses must be "good square trotters" with a comfortable gait and "be well shod."

The ad listed the first eight locations where "from 20 to 60 HORSES will be purchased [at each site] for our Cavalry Service"; the first round of horse buying began at Brunswick on Monday, October 8.[17]

Jonathan Prince Cilley returned to Augusta by October 9, when he told Julia that "I have just got into my own tent and [am] partly organized." In his newsy letter, he made several prescient points that the approaching winter would brutally reinforce.

"It is very damp and I fear may be uncomfortable for the night," Cilley alluded to the chill that can seep into a person's joints during a Maine fall. He wrote tongue in cheek that he had "the happiness to enjoy Camp Diarrhea to an extent hitherto unknown this season." Many 1st Maine Cavalry "men are suffering from it. Probably owing to a change of diet and strong coffee."

In those sentences, Cilley hinted at the bitter cold and devastating diseases that would strike the military camps in Augusta by January.

Recruiting about 70 men, Black Hawk Putnam brought them south to Camp Penobscot to become Co. E, 1st Maine Cavalry Regiment, on October 19. That same Saturday, Jonathan Prince Cilley and his men mustered into the regiment as Co. B. Cilley's first lieutenant was William Coleman; his second lieutenant was Frank Cutler. The company included "six sergeants, eight corporals, two buglers, two farriers [blacksmiths], one wagoner, one saddler, and seventy-three privates."[18]

As fall shifted to winter, additional units converged on Augusta. O'Neil W. Robinson Jr., a 37-year-old attorney from Bethel in Maine's northwestern mountains, brought the 4th Maine Battery into the capital on Monday, December 16.

U.S. Secretary of War Simon Cameron
This photo is between 1860-65. Cameron was secretary between March 1861 and January 1862.
Photo from Library of Congress

Robinson held the rank of captain, the highest rank available in an artillery battery. He had aimed even higher before the 4th Maine Battery's formation, however; to achieve that goal, Robinson asked his supporters to lobby Israel Washburn en masse.

Benjamin Freeman informed the governor on Monday, Oct. 7 that Robinson, "a lawyer and a gentleman of wealth & mind also a Jamesin [sic] Democrat, is desirous of serving his country on the tented field."

Freeman's point was critical to Robinson's military future. At their August 1861 convention, Maine Democrats had split between peace and war factions. The latter supported the war and took the name of "Jameson Democrats," a reference to Col. Charles Jameson, commander of the 2nd Maine Infantry and the war supporters' 1861 gubernatorial candidate.

The Republican Washburn would understand that Robinson was a Union loyalist despite being a Democrat.

Chapter II: Of Snow and Ice

Robinson asked Freeman "to inquire if the places of [lieutenant colonel] or Major for the eleventh [infantry] regiment was filled." If so, then Robinson would accept a similar rank with "one of the Regts. yet to be formed from this state," Freeman indicated.[19]

Writing with his shaky hand on Tuesday, November 12, R.K. Goodenow of Paris[20] in Oxford County told Washburn that "I have known" Robinson "for ... ten or fifteen years." A Bowdoin College graduate and "a lawyer of good standing in this county," Robinson would be successful "in getting up a company, if the command of one of the batteries ... should be tendered him."[21]

"Having been personally acquainted with Mr. Robinson it gives me great pleasure to say that he possesses all the necessary qualifications for the position he desires & I trust he will receive it," John I. Perry wrote Washburn from Paris on Monday, November 18.[22]

Already swamped with letters recommending many other aspiring officers for commissions in the mobilizing regiments, Washburn got the collective point about Robinson. Perhaps reflecting ongoing suspicions about War Democrats jockeying for staff-officer positions, Washburn made Robinson an artillery captain.

Upon arriving in Augusta, Robinson's men "were assigned to quarters in the tents, which had been erected for four of the Batteries just south of the State House," said Judson Ames, initially a corporal in the 4th Maine Battery's Second Detachment. He hailed from Foxcroft in Piscataquis County.

"Our Battery was camped next to the road (modern State Street)," he noted. Camped nearby were three more artillery batteries (the 3rd, 5th, and 6th); "south of the road toward the [Kennebec] river were located the 14th and 15th [Infantry] Regiments and 1st Cavalry, and across the river at the [Kennebec] Arsenal grounds were located" the 13th Maine Infantry Regiment and the 2nd Maine Battery.[23]

Union Captain O'Neill W. Robinson
Photo courtesy of Maine State Archives

The 4th Maine Battery mustered into federal service on December 21. Winter had arrived by then; it and federal intransigence doomed many Maine boys before they ever fired a shot in defense of the Union.

State authorities had assumed that the War Department would summon the 1st Maine Cavalry (and presumably other fully mobilized units) "to Washington before cold weather set it." Then New York was the destination "for the winter" or perhaps "South Carolina" or "Annapolis, Md." or "Texas," Tobie recalled the scuttlebutt sweeping Camp Penobscot that fall and early winter.[24]

Instead the War Department "held" the Maine regiments and batteries at Augusta for the winter—and a hellish winter it was. Tobie summarized winter 1861-62 as "extremely cold, even for Maine, and 'big snow storms' were the rule rather than the exception."[25]

The miserable weather actually began in mid-autumn, starting with "any quantity of rainy, wet and uncomfortable weather" through October 9 and continuing with "a most violent storm of wind and rain" on November 3, Cilley told Julia.[26]

Not planning on sheltering some 5,000 men in permanent buildings, the budget-constrained state government consigned its enthusiastic volunteers to tents. Inside the 1st Maine Cavalry camp, horses occupied the race-track stables, including some built by soldier carpenters.

The inexperienced cavalrymen moved into tents. So did the other soldiers camped at Augusta. Living in Sibley tents that were "circular and about fifteen feet in diameter," the 4th Maine Battery lads packed 13 men into each tent. Its sole heat source was "a small sheet iron stove in the centre, the stove pipe also answering for a tent pole," Ames recalled. "A board floor was provided upon which we spread our beds at night."

Even for men accustomed to hard winters, that of 1861-62 was particularly brutal. On some nights, "with three feet of snow on the ground and the thermometer ... down to 20 [degrees] below [zero], we found it necessary to lie close together and unfortunate was the man who came next to the door," Ames said.[27]

Soldiers remained ill-clad; expecting to depart for Virginia by late fall, many 1st Maine Cavalry lads had not brought winter clothing with them. The cavalrymen finally started receiving some government clothing in late November and early December.[28] But not until the Maine batteries and regiments mustered into federal service did the War Department start supplying clothing, food, and weapons. Washington's inability to equip its soldiers soon became evident.

"The cold weather is taking my men unprepared—all the clothing [that] government has furnished us has been blankets, shirts, drawers, and stockings—and a few shoes," Jonathan Prince Cilley told Julia on November 3.

"We have had no overcoats, nor anything to protect the men from the rain [while] watering and caring for the horses," he reported. While "200 talmas [oil cloth capes]" had arrived, the troopers could not wear them because government officials had not yet inspected the capes "nor passed [them] through the necessary red tape."

On this stormy Sunday "our men have been forced to go wet and cold in their tents," Cilley wrote.[29]

Food quality suffered, too. Government contractors initially provided the 1st Maine Cavalry with its rations, which "were good enough, and gave general satisfaction to all but chronic growlers," Tobie said.

After the regiment mustered into federal service, the federal government started furnishing the rations. The change in food quality, particularly with bread, was immediately discernible. The first morning that they received government-issued "loaves of soft bread," the troopers discovered its distaste. Claiming the bread "was not good" and refusing to eat the loaves, the men staged a wild food fight by hurling bread loaves throughout the camp; one loaf allegedly struck Goddard.

This impromptu protest by hungry soldiers led to the official decision (Tobie does not say by whom) to suspend the serving of soft bread to the 1st Maine Cavalry for the winter. The troopers "had to do the best they could on hardtack," he commented.

The War Department also "for some reason cut off the supply" of beans, a popular food dish in Maine, Tobie remembered. Trading government-issued rations for beans, entire 1st Maine Cavalry companies improved their menus by cooking bean-hole beans. This process involved digging a hole and building a good fire in it. Soldiers placed a pot filled with beans (usually with molasses and salt pork added) atop the fire and covered the pot with dirt. Left to cook overnight, the pot was uncovered and removed the next day.

The soldiers enjoyed "a good hot dish of baked beans, cooked in the ground, every morning, which, with as good a supper as they could get from what was left in the morning, or from hardtack soaked and fried in pork fat and sugar, lasted until the next morning," Tobie wrote.[30]

Other soldiers shivering in Augusta that winter likely prepared bean hole beans, too. Even such ad hoc nutrition—molasses-sweetened baked beans filled empty stomachs and gave soldiers vitamins and energy that hardtack and salt pork could not—could not postpone the sicknesses that swept the camps.

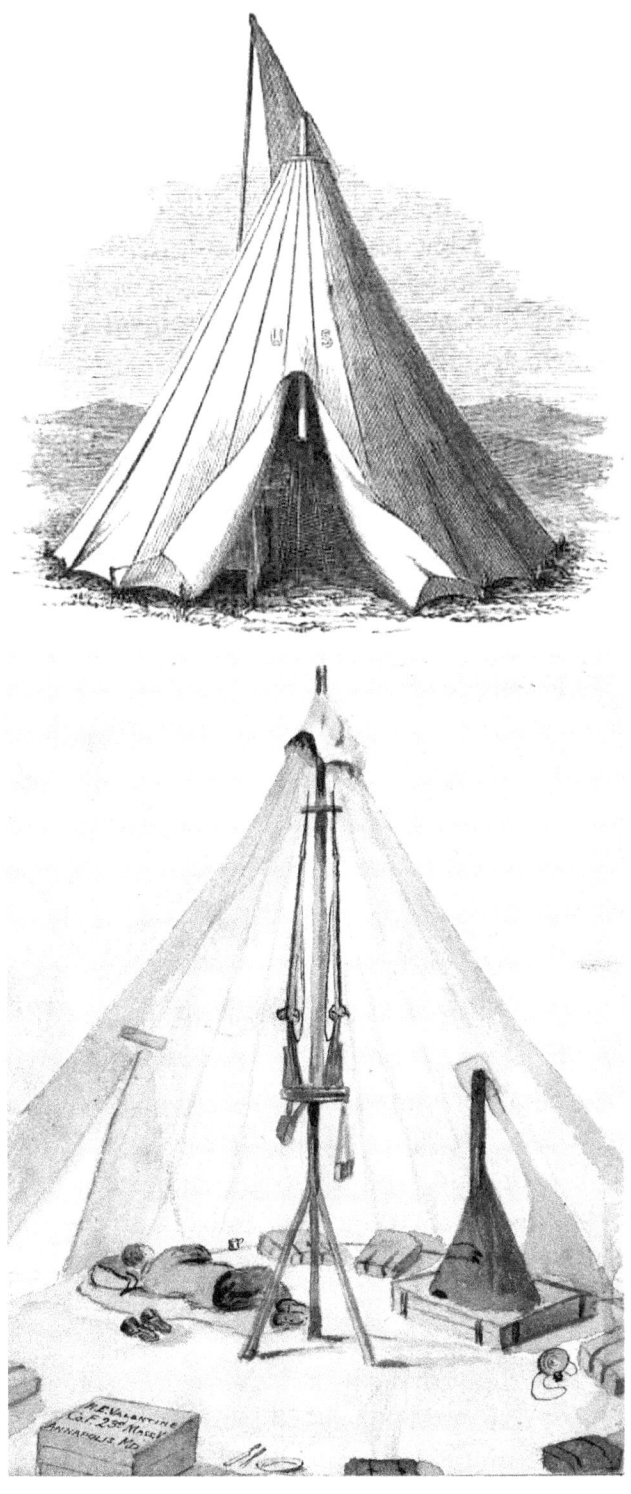

Sibley tent

The Maine boys lived through the terrible Maine winter in these tents. Top: Illustration from *The Prairie Traveler—A handbook for Overland Expeditions* (1859) by Capt. Randolph B. Marcy. Above: A sketch done at Camp John A. Andrew, near Annapolis, Maryland, in December 1861.

Kennebec Arsenal
During the bitter winter of 1861-1862, the soldiers belonging to the 2nd Maine Battery and the 13th Maine Infantry Regiment were billeted at the Kennebec Arsenal in Augusta, Maine, photographed here in 1858.
Photo courtesy of Maine State Archives

Men fell ill. Describing "the heat thus obtained" from the "sheet-iron stoves" as "irregular," Tobie recalled many comrades catching "colds by the sudden changes in the temperature."[31]

Occasionally a 4th Maine Battery soldier would receive a pass to venture into Augusta. If he returned to his assigned tent "after all were asleep" at night, the cold soldier "would build a rousing fire in the little stove," Ames recalled. The surging warmth overheated the sleeping soldiers; then, "as the fire quickly went down an hour later, we would awake shivering with the cold.

"The result was that nearly every man had a cold and cough," he remembered.[32]

Sick men filled the regimental hospitals. Regimental returns for Thursday, January 28, 1862 listed 4,010 men collectively on the rolls for the 1st Maine Cavalry and the 13th, 14th, and 15th Maine infantry regiments. Of that number, the regimental surgeons identified 702 men as being on the sick-lists; 261 patients were from the 1st Maine Cavalry, which had 1,160 men on its rolls that day.

Without firing a shot, the regiment had lost its first man on Friday, January 3 when Thomas Hollis, an 18-year-old from Dead River Plantation in the remote northern region of Somerset County, died from disease. Loading his horse "with his arms and equipments" and leading the animal into the company line with Hollis's boots "reversed in the saddle," his comrades took him out and buried him.[33]

The 1st Maine Cavalry lost other men. In Co. L, 21-year-old Corp. Albert Crocket of Abbot in Piscataquis County died of disease on February 13. Commanded by Capt. Reuben Jennings of Farmington, Co. L was particularly hard hit, and not just with death. A soldier discharged for "disability" (often a euphemism for a debilitating disease or sickness) was as lost to service as if he had been wounded on the battlefield.

Among the Co. L soldiers discharged for disability that winter were Columbus Avery, 18, from Farmington; Almon Haskell, 28, from Industry; Joseph Millett, a 22-year-old farmer from Palmyra; Luther Quint, a 20-year-old farmer from Lexington Township; and Rosalvo York, 26, from Mexico, Maine.

"The first man from my company died this morning[,] John Pillsbury—he had been sick only a week with the lung fever," Cilley informed Julia on February 20, 1862. "To morrow we pay him his last funeral honors, his horse is lead immediately after the band[,] saddled & bridled with boots and spurs attached & followed by the entire Company mounted."[34]

Twenty-three when he enlisted in 1861, Pillsbury came from Belfast.

By late winter "it was estimated by good authority" that the 1st Maine Cavalry lost "more than two hundred men, by death and disability, on account of the cold weather" and the lack of proper clothing and shelter, Tobie remembered.

To ameliorate the situation, Maine legislators adopted in mid-January 1862 "a resolve in favor of distributing blankets to the soldiers now encamped at Augusta." The amended bill authorized Washburn to issue "one blanket to each officer and private" in the nearby camps. The state would fund the blankets "out of any monies not otherwise appropriated."[35]

"This regiment, at least, got no extra blankets" because state officials knew "that every man had a horse blanket, and that many [men] had quilts, comforters, and blankets furnished from home," according to Tobie. The 1st Maine Cavalry troopers were angry about receiving lousy food while camping in cold, poorly heated tents near the State House; Washburn's failure to deliver 1,000-odd blankets only deepened their resentment.

"That the men suffered severely, and needlessly, too, that winter, is simply a matter of fact," Tobie stated.[36]

Fortunately for the Maine soldiers dealing with snow and ice in Augusta, spring comes early in the Deep and Middle South. Campaign planning had taken place far from Maine; the units kept there during the winter started receiving orders to move out.

Mustered into federal service on December 31, 1861, "we remained at Augusta till about February 1st," when the 14th Maine Infantry Regiment received orders to ship to the

Union 2nd Lt. Edward Parsons Tobie Jr.
Photo courtesy of Maine State Archives

LEGISLATIVE RESOLUTION

On January 17, 1862, the Maine Legislature passed a resolve to authorize the purchase of blankets for the soldiers encamped at Augusta. The text of the resolve (top left) and Amendment "A" (bottom left) are as follow (from Maine State Archives):

Resolve

State of Maine
Resolve in favor of distributing blankets to the soldiers now encamped at Augusta.
Resolved, That the governor be, and he hereby is, authorized to procure forthwith for the use of the troops now encamped at Augusta, while they shall remain in said city, such additional number of blankets as their health and comfort may require, and draw his order upon the State Treasurer for the cost of the same, payable out of any monies not otherwise appropriated.
In Ho. Of Reps. Jany 15, 1862. Read twice, rules being suspended, amended as per sheet "A", passed to be engrossed, sufe (?) Chas. A. Miller Clerk
In Senate, January 16, 1862 Non-concurred in amendment of House, and passed Resolve to be engrossed as reported. Sent down for concurrence. James M. Lincoln Secretary

Amendment "A"

Amend by striking out after word "City" the following – "such additional number of blankets as their health and comfort may require" and by inserting - "one blanket to each officer and private"

Deep South, said Ira Gardner. The 14th Maine lads gladly boarded a train four days later for the journey to Boston, where "we were on board the old sailing vessel 'North America.'"

Gardner and his comrades watched other Maine soldiers depart Boston ahead of them. A 22-year-old second lieutenant in the 1st Maine Battery, John Franklin Godfrey of Bangor had boarded "the ship *Idaho*," which was "hauled alongside Commercial wharf."

Once the men and baggage from three artillery batteries and an infantry company were packed on the *Idaho*, "a tug fastening to us like a leech took us amid the cheers of the 14th Me. Regt. who were aboard the North American" to a Boston Harbor anchorage, Godfrey said. The *Idaho* sailed a day or so later.[37] The *North American* followed close behind. Both ships were bound for Ship Island in the Gulf of Mexico. Col. Frank Nickerson and his men were finally outbound for the war zone.[38]

"We were destined to remain at Augusta" until March 14, when the 4th Maine Battery was sent to Portland to stay in "barracks ... located west of the city," Judson Ames recalled. On April 1 the 4th and 5th Maine batteries entrained for Boston and the war.[39]

"We have received orders to leave this uninteresting town of Augusta and join the Army on the Potomac," Cilley informed Julia on Sunday, March 9. "We are leaving in just the right season from this place, as it is beginning to be muddy and nasty here."[40]

Cilley's meteorological observation proved apt; "a heavy snow storm set in,—the heaviest of the season" and postponed the scheduled March 16 departure of companies B, H, I, and M, noted Tobie. As an enlisted man, he likely spent some time shoveling snow around the stables during the storm.[41]

On Thursday, March 20, Cilley and his Co. B troopers arose before reveille, ate breakfast, struck their tents, and started riding to the Augusta train depot around 10 a.m. Eight horses and men went into each boxcar. Placed four abreast at either end, the horses stood tethered with their heads pointed toward the car's center section, where the cavalrymen made themselves comfortable amidst the "two bunches of hay" to be fed the horses during the train ride to Portland and Boston.

"The officers went in a car by themselves," Cilley told Julia.

Loading commenced about 11 a.m.; companies B, H, I, and M departed Augusta a bit after 4 p.m. Until darkness fell, the cavalrymen received all along "the line of the railroad … the glad plaudits of the Crowd and the smiles and salutes of all the fair damsels of Maine," Cilley commented.[42]

The avenging angel was en route to Virginia.

~~~

1. John L. Hodsdon, *Annual Report of the Adjutant General of the State of Maine, 1861*, p. 9
2. Eve Anderson, *A Breach of Privilege: Cilley Family Letters 1820-1867,* Seven Coin Press, Spruce Head, Maine, 2002, p. 416
3. *Annual Report of the Adjutant General of the State of Maine, 1861*, p. 9
4. Edward Parsons Tobie, *History of the First Maine Cavalry, 1861-1865,* Emery & Hughes, Boston, 1887, p. 4
5. John L. Hodsdon, *Annual Report of the Adjutant General of the State of Maine, 1861*, pp. 10-11
6. Anderson, *Privilege,* pp. 418-419
7. Tobie, *History,* p. 2
8. Anderson, *Privilege,* pp. 418-419
9. Tobie, *History,* p. 2
10. Born in Virginia on January 29, 1756, Henry Lee III was a College of New Jersey graduate and an aspiring attorney when the Revolutionary War began. Demonstrating excellent leadership and tactical skills as a cavalry commander, Lee fought primarily—and usually successfully—in the Southern colonies. He had three children with his first wife, Matilda Ludwell Lee (a second cousin) and six children with his second wife, Anne Hill Carter. Robert Edward Lee was their fifth child and fourth son.
11. Tobie, *History,* p. 3
12. Among the Illinois militiamen called up by Gov. John Reynolds to help quash Black Hawk and his warriors was a young attorney named Abraham Lincoln.
13. At 6,672 square miles, Aroostook is the largest county in Maine. Larger in land mass than Connecticut and Rhode Island combined, Aroostook has been called "The Crown of Maine" or, more often, "The County."

14. John Varnum Putnam, letter, Nov. 10, 1861
15. Tobie, p. 2
16. Ibid., p. 5
17. John L. Hodsdon, Warrant 1207, Maine State Archives
18. Anderson, *Privilege*, pp. 419-420
19. Benjamin Freeman, letter to Israel Washburn Jr., Oct. 7, 1861, Maine State Archives
20. Among other Maine municipalities bearing the same names as foreign cities and countries are Athens, Bath, Belgrade, Calais, Cambridge, China, Denmark, Madrid, Mexico, Moscow, Norway, Peru, Poland, Rome, and Sweden. Not all such Maine place names are pronounced the same as their foreign equivalents.
21. R.K. Goodenow, letter to Israel Washburn Jr., Nov. 12, 1861, MSA
22. John I. Perry, letter to Israel Washburn Jr., Nov. 18, 1861, MSA
23. Judson Ames, *History of the Fourth Maine Battery Light Artillery in the Civil War 1861-1865,* Burleigh & Flynt, Augusta, 1905, p. 10
24. Tobie, *History,* pp. 10-11
25. Ibid., p. 13
26. Anderson, *Privilege,* p. 423
27. Ames, *Fourth Maine,* p. 9
28. Tobie, *History,* p. 13
29. Anderson, *Privilege,* p. 423
30. Tobie, *History,* pp. 17-18
31. Ibid., p. 13
32. Ames, *Fourth Maine,* p. 9
33. Tobie, *History,* pp. 12-13
34. Anderson, *Privilege,* p. 428
35. Thomas Hollis Transcript, Jan. 16, 1862, Maine State Archives
36. Tobie, *History,* p. 13
37. Candace Sawyer, *The Civil War Letters of Capt. John Franklin Godfrey,* Candace Sawyer and Laura Orcutt, Portland, ME, 1993, p. 9
38. Ira B. Gardner, *Recollections Of A Boy Member of Co. I, Fourteenth Maine Volunteers, 1861 to 1865,* Lewiston Journal Company, Lewiston, 1902, p. 6
39. Ames, *Fourth Maine,* p 10
40. Anderson, *Privilege,* p. 429
41. Tobie, *History,* p. 26
42. Anderson, *Privilege,* pp. 429-430

Chapter 12

THE SAND AND SPIDERS OF SHIP ISLAND

"The officers of our company paid little attention to our men"

Pvt. Eugene Kincaide Kingman stood at the rail as the steamer *Constitution* approached the western end of Ship Island on Wednesday, February 12, 1862. He and his comrades in Co. H, 12th Maine Infantry had figured prior to leaving Virginia that this Gulf Coast barrier island was their ultimate destination, but as the *Constitution* dropped anchor, the observant Kingman could not yet adequately describe the white-colored shore glimmering in the winter sun.[1]

But another soldier could. "Ship Island is an island of white sand thrown by the winds and waves," said Maj. Gen. Benjamin F. Butler, the man responsible for sending the 12th Maine and its numerical sequels—the 13th, 14th, and 15th Maine infantry regiments—to this dry sand spit.

"It is between five and six miles long and is about ten miles distant from the Mississippi coast," according to Butler. The flat western end "rises only a little above the sea, in places less than two feet," and the eastern end "rises to some considerable height." On the higher terrain grew pine trees that would provide "fuel" and "timber" for the soldiers congregating on Ship Island in winter 1862.[2]

When he joined the 12th Maine on October 12, 1861, the 17-year-old Kingman had imagined he would go to Virginia, where the only serious shooting had occurred so far. Hailing from land-locked Dexter on the border separating Penobscot and Piscataquis counties in central Maine, he had left his parents—Baptist minister Reverend Lebbeus and Ruth Kingman—and a younger brother and four younger sisters to embark on what was to him a grand lark.

To them Kingman would write letters that colorfully detailed adventures, people, and surroundings and often contained rough sketches of various facets of military life.

Commanded by Col. George Foster Shepley, a Portland attorney, the 12th Maine Infantry Regiment coalesced at Camp Chase in Portland and mustered into federal service on November

16. Rather than take his regiment aboard the *Constitution* at Portland as instructed, Shepley had chartered the *Forest City* and set sail for Boston on Sunday, November 24.

Until the *Forest City* slipped its mooring in Portland Harbor, Kingman's only experience with large bodies of water had been Lake Wassookeag in his hometown.³ Now, as the steamer "put out into the ocean" from Casco Bay, "the wind blew like 60," landlubber Kingman noticed.

"It was awful rough and in about ½ hour they were heaving up Jonah all about the deck[,] sea sick enough," he said, admitting that he had hung his head over the rail, too.⁴

Steaming into Boston late on Monday, the *Forest City* disgorged the storm-tossed 12th Maine lads, who caught a Tuesday train to Camp Chase in Lowell. Not until early January 1862 did the 12th Maine lads board the *Constitution* and sail for Virginia. Deposited at Fort Monroe, the men camped near Old Point Comfort and debated if they would stay there or go elsewhere.

Shepley knew, because he owed his commission to Butler, the Massachusetts political general busy assembling an expedition to attack New Orleans.

The odd-duck Democrat in a citizen army run so far by Republican officers, Butler had convinced President Abraham Lincoln and Secretary of War Edwin Stanton to let him "raise, organize, arm, uniform, and equip a volunteer force for the war, in the New England States, not exceeding six (6) regiments." Butler claimed to have shown Lincoln and Stanton the error of their ways in letting the loyal states' governors (predominantly Republicans) appoint mostly Republican officers to the state-raised regiments and artillery batteries.

Because of this, "the Democrats in their localities [including Maine] ... [in] looking substantially upon the war as a Republican war, are taking no part in it," Butler recalled telling Lincoln.

"Your aim should rather be to get every Democrat possible in the war," Butler argued. "Get leading Democrats and they will bring in their rank and file, their clientele, who believe in them and would rally about them."⁵

After visiting the governors of Vermont, Massachusetts, and New Hampshire, Butler "then went to Maine and saw Governor Washburn" and "told him I wanted a regiment and battery." Butler wanted Shepley, "a Democratic leader," to command the infantry regiment.

Union Maj. Gen. Benjamin F. Butler
*Photo from Brady-Handy Collection,
Library of Congress*

"Certainly," replied Washburn. "What a good thing it would be if Shepley would only go."

"I have seen him," Butler said, "and I can assure you that he will."[6]

As to any secrecy about where the 12th Maine would go from Virginia, word about Ship Island had leaked by Monday, February 3, when the regiment left Fort Monroe on the *Constitution*.[7]

Having decided in late 1861 to attack New Orleans, Butler had sought a staging area near the mouth of the Mississippi River. The nearest American-held post was Fort Pickens at the western tip of Santa Rosa Island in Florida, but Pickens was too far from the Mississippi Delta.

But in conjunction with the Navy, ground troops based on Ship Island could approach New Orleans via the Mississippi River or Lake Borgne. Confederate troops had occupied a partially completed fort on the island early in the war, but sailors and Marines had retaken the abandoned fort in September 1861.

After landing on Ship Island on February 12, the 12th Maine soldiers established a camp near the north shore, about a mile east of the island's western end. Damaged by retreating Confederates, the island's round, brick-built lighthouse stood a short distance from the regiment's camp.

Union Col. George Foster Shepley
In this photo, Shepley is a brigadier general. He would earn that commission once he was appointed military governor of the parishes of Louisiana.
Photo from Brady-Handy Collection.
Library of Congress

"Ship Island is sand, sand from one end to the other—fine and white—the kind used to manufacture glass," commented a Midcoast soldier. "Rank grass and rushes, and the cactus here and there in low place are to be found, struggling for existences or drying up in the sun's rays."

The "scrub oak and pitch pine trees" growing on the island's east end fast disappeared after Union troops arrived; "wood is procured at this point for the use of the camp," the Midcoast soldier noted.[8]

Kingman wrote home about the warm weather that caused many Union soldiers to wear straw hats and go barefoot in the sand. The buzzing mosquitoes and flies irritated the men day and night; white spiders crawled up the sides of the canvas tents at night and dropped

Ship Island
The island's fort was renamed Fort Massachusetts in honor of the Union warship that seized the abandoned outpost. Construction on the new fort was halted in 1866.
Illustration from Harper's Weekly, January 4, 1862

suddenly on sleeping soldiers. In one letter, Kingman sketched an alligator that appeared in a fresh-water pool and escaped the best efforts of Union officers to kill it.[9]

Wildlife abounded in the sea and air around Ship Island. "Wild game, such as ducks and plovers are plenty and tame," with "shooting at them being prohibited," a Midcoast soldier wrote home. Hunters' gunfire might ignite a wild Union scramble to repel a perceived Confederate attack.

"Of fish there are many kinds, some very good, and others of the eel species, hideous to behold," he told relatives back home in Maine. "The oyster is found here, and other varieties of shellfish is abundant."[10]

Regiments continued arriving on Ship Island. Sailing from Boston on February 20, the steamer *Mississippi* had on board the 13th Maine Infantry and Benjamin Butler. Surviving a dangerous voyage (as recorded by Butler), the steamer delivered its uniformed cargo to Ship Island on Saturday, March 8.

The *North America* rattled its anchor chain off the island the same day. After boarding that steamer at Boston, Orderly Sgt. Ira B. Gardner of Co. I, 14th Maine Infantry, had inspected

Chapter 12: The Sand and Spiders of Ship Island

the ship's hold in which he would live for several weeks. Pointing out to his friends Charles Blackwell and James Fairfield that "the bunks built around the vessel were not properly secured and liable to break down, I suggested ... that we take the upper berth."

The choice proved prudent; as the *North America* pitched and rolled during "the many nights of rough weather" encountered well into the Gulf of Mexico, the soldier "lying on the outside" of the bunk braced his knees "against the deck overhead to keep the other two from rolling out," Gardner remembered.

Days out from Boston, the 19-year-old Gardner first demonstrated the initiative leadership sorely needed in the "green" 14th Maine. Noticing that "the officers of our company paid little attention to our men," he served the Co. I men "their [daily] rations of salt beef and pork," plus "hard bread." A cooperative quartermaster let Gardner sneak "a dipper of sugar" daily to his men to supplement their bland diet.

As the *North America* steamed south, Gardner attended the funeral for "Charles Reynolds ... the first and only man I saw buried at sea." Weighted down with "a lot of old iron" and sewn into a blanket, the dead Reynolds slid overboard after a brief service. Gardner watched Reynolds "go out of sight beneath the water of the Atlantic Ocean. We all felt that our turn might come next."

A "bad gale" heavily rolled the *North America* in the Gulf of Mexico; the "rough sea" flipped over the ship's coal-fired cook stove. With hot coals "scattering ... over the vessel," the third mate—he "had just escaped from a burning vessel"—emerged on deck and reported to the steamer's captain, "Sir, the ship is on fire."

"Fire!" screamed a nearby 14th Maine soldier. Knocking him through an open hatch, the captain ordered all hatches secured to prevent a thousand frightened soldiers from running amuck on deck. Then crewmen scurried to extinguish the fire.

As the *North America* approached the Gulf Coast, "we saw coming toward us a Rebel gunboat" intent on attacking the steamer, Gardner believed. "Steaming at full speed," the Confederate warship passed the inbound steamer with nary a cannon shot; only then did the 14th Maine boys notice "one of our gunboats" pursuing the enemy ship.

The Maine men cheered lustily "as our gunboat passed with the Stars and Stripes waving over it."

On March 8 the 14th Maine boys disembarked at Ship Island, which Gardner described as "a low, sandy island[,] mostly barren, about twelve miles from the mainland." His regiment camped beside the 13th Maine Infantry at about the island's mid-point; the later arriving 15th Maine Infantry set up camp diagonally south from the 12th Maine's.

The Maine soldiers spent the next few months exploring Ship Island and encountering snakes and wild cattle and hogs. Then 2nd Lt. Charles Smith of Co. I, 14th Maine resigned his commission after "having seen enough of [military] service," according to Gardner, whom Capt. James Hill promptly promoted into the vacancy. The 19-year-old adventurer from Patten was now an officer in the United States Army.

The 12th Maine Infantry departed Ship Island aboard the *Tennessee* on Sunday, May 4 and sailed upriver to New Orleans, which Flag Officer David Farragut and his naval squadron had captured on April 26. The 14th Maine Infantry left Ship Island on May 19.

The steamers transporting several regiments slowly ascended the Mississippi River. At each night's anchorage "the colored people would come out in small boats with milk, fruit and vegetables for sale[,] which were eagerly bought by those having any money," Gardner said. He saw Maine men pay five cents for individual potatoes, which were "eagerly devoured."

Disembarking at New Orleans on Sunday, May 25, the 14th Maine Infantry "formed in column to march through the city" as "the bands commenced to play some popular march," Gardner described the pomp and circumstance.

Assigned by Butler to camp in Lafayette Square, "we were able to secure fresh food, and I have never eaten anything which tasted half as good as that," he remembered. The 14th Maine would not stay long in the Crescent City.[11][12]

~~~

1. The Mississippi legislature ceded the island to federal control in 1858. The Army Corps of Engineers started constructing a fort on Ship Island in June 1859; seized by Confederate troops and named Fort Twiggs in 1861, the partially completed fort returned to Union control after sailors from the USS Massachusetts seized Ship Island that September.
2. Benjamin F. Butler, *Autobiography and Personal Reminiscences of Major-General, Benj. F. Butler,* A.M. Thayer & Co., Boston, 1892, pp. 351-352
3. The 1,152-acre Lake Wassookeag lies entirely within the boundaries of hilly Dexter.
4. *Tramping Out The Vintage, 1861-1864: The Civil War Diaries and Letters of Eugene Kingman,* edited by Helene Phelan, Almond, N.Y., 1983, p. 17
5. Butler, *Autobiography,* pp. 297-299
6. Ibid., p. 305
7. The *Constitution* had previously transported Union troops to Ship Island.
8. "Ship Island," *Belfast Journal* letter, reprinted in *Maine Farmer,* Thursday, May 8, 1862. The writer may have belonged to the 14th Maine Infantry Regiment, which had a strong contingent of Waldo County soldiers.
9. Phelan, *Tramping Out the Vintage,* p. 50
10. "Ship Island," *Belfast Journal,* reprinted in *Maine Farmer,* Thursday, May 8, 1862
11. Ira B. Gardner, *Recollections Of A Boy Member of Co. I, Fourteenth Maine Volunteers, 1861 to 1865,* Lewiston Journal Company, Lewiston, 1902, pp. 6-10
12. Joseph Holt Ingraham, *The South-West by a Yankee,* 1835. Ingraham wrote: "I have termed New-Orleans the crescent city in one of my letters, from its being built around the segment of a circle formed by a graceful curve of the river at this place."

Chapter 13

PULASKI

"The wall of the magazine was badly crushed"

On Sunday, Oct. 6, 1861, Col. Lee Strickland and his 8th Maine lads bumped and thumped into Annapolis on a train sent east from Washington, D.C. via Annapolis Junction. While his men unloaded their baggage, Strickland went to find Brig. Gen. Thomas W. Sherman, who controlled the collective fates of at least a dozen infantry regiments.[1]

With its departure for Washington, D.C., the 6th Maine Infantry was the last regiment raised in the Pine Tree State primarily from militia companies. Adjutant Gen. John L. Hodsdon had all but run out of trained militiamen; beginning with the 7th Maine Infantry in August 1861, regiments comprised "companies ...organized in different parts of the state" with little militia participation.

Hailing from Livermore in the Androscoggin Valley, Strickland had mustered with the 8th Maine at Augusta on September 7; the regiment left the capital by train a few days later.

Southbound from Maine, the 8th Maine had joined the 1st Brigade of Brig. Gen. Egbert Ludovicus Viele at Hempstead on Long Island, then spent three weeks in the District of Columbia defenses. Now the weary Mainers erected a regulation camp at Annapolis.

Not for the first time since joining the Army 29 days earlier did Strickland's men wonder where they were going.

Not until Friday, October 18 did Strickland and his men board the steamer *Ariel* at Annapolis. Men lining the rails watched wide-eyed as the *Ariel* stood down the Severn River and into Chesapeake Bay. A veritable fleet, "one of the grandest sights ever beheld on this continent," surrounded the *Ariel*, which soon took station amidst the ships carrying the rest of Viele's brigade.

With Sherman looking on from his command ship, the *Atlantic*, the transports formed into three brigade-specific columns and sailed south to Hampton Roads.[2]

With the expedition went the 9th Maine Infantry of Col. Rishworth Rich. Carrying thousands of men and hundreds of horses and cattle, the ships soon anchored in Hampton Roads, not far from Fort Monroe and the headquarters of Maj. Gen. John E. Wool, commander of the Department of Virginia.

As far as Wool was concerned, Sherman soon wore out his welcome. Even when lent

"350,000 rounds of ammunition" because "his ammunition was stored at the bottom of his ships," Sherman had not yet left, Wool groused to Secretary War of Simon Cameron on Monday, October 28.³

By now Wool had drawn on his own supplies to give "ten days' rations" to Sherman's soldiers, whose own rations—like their ammunition—were stored deep in the transport ships.

Could Cameron persuade Sherman to sail immediately, if not sooner? What difference would a fast departure make? The Confederates knew what was coming because a young petty officer—"a Mr. Hale, a young officer connected with the Navy"—had stolen a signal book and deserted to enemy lines, Wool groused.

"I will venture to assert that a worse-managed expedition could not be well contrived," he fumed.⁴

He had unfairly maligned Sherman, a hostage to the decisions of the expedition's senior naval officer, Commodore Samuel

Union Brig. Gen. Egbert Ludovicus Viele
Photo by unknown, via Library of Congress

Francis Du Pont. On Sunday, Oct. 27, Sherman rightfully blamed "the unexpected delay of the expedition" on "the stormy and unfavorable state of the weather for our light vessels and tugs."

The expedition's horses "have already been on board some thirteen days and [the] men a week," he told Army Quartermaster Gen. Montgomery C. Meigs. Could the Army "forward immediately to this place 200,000 gallons" of water to replace what had already been consumed aboard ship?⁵

The expedition finally set sail, with the 8th Maine lads aboard the *Vanderbilt* and the 9th Maine aboard the *Coatzacoalcos*. Formed in the three brigade columns behind Du Pont's warships, the transports and support vessels left Hampton Roads on October 29.

Three days later, the fleet steamed into "one of the severest gales which have occurred on this coast for a long time," noted assistant quartermaster Capt. Rufus Saxton. The seas grew so violent that two cattle ships went down (with the crewmen saved), the captain of the *Belvidere* ordered some horses chucked overboard to lighten his load, the steamer *Union* "went ashore on the South Carolina coast," and the *Peerless* went down, albeit "the crew ... was saved."⁶

"Some vessels probably have been lost, but it is believed that the hand of Providence has saved the lives of all," opined Capt. Louis H. Pelouse, Sherman's acting assistant adjutant general.[7]

Arriving off Port Royal, Du Pont's warships promptly bombarded two Confederate forts into submission, and Union troops occupied Hilton Head. The 8th Maine and regiments from four other states garrisoned the island well into the winter.

The 9th Maine and its brigade went to Wassaw Sound, located where the Wilmington River in Georgia flows into the Atlantic Ocean between Little Tybee Island and Wilmington Island to the north and Wassaw Island to the south.[8]

With the occupation of Hilton Head and the February 1862 capture of Roanoke Island in North Carolina by Ambrose Burnside's expedition, Union army and naval forces had started tightening the blockade of Confederate Atlantic ports. Union forces at Wassaw Sound threatened Savannah, guarded by Fort Pulaski on Cockspur Island, an elevated mud flat upriver from Tybee Island.

Located at a latitude of 32 degrees, 2 minutes north and a longitude of 3 degrees, 51 minutes "west from Washington" and named for Revolutionary War hero and American ally Casimir Pulaski, the fort "is a brick work of five sides or faces, including the gorge," reported Army engineer Capt. Quincy A. Gillmore, soon to be brevetted a brigadier general.

Its construction started in 1829 and capably oversaw for a short while by recent West Point graduate Robert E. Lee, Pulaski was "casemated on all sides, walls 7½ feet thick and 25 feet high above high water, mounting one tier of guns in embrasures and one en barbette," according to Gillmore. "An earthen earthwork (demi-lune) of bold relief" covered the gorge, the fort's rear wall.[9]

The "wet ditch" (or moat) was 48 feet wide around the five main walls and 32 feet wide around the demi-lune, Gillmore noted.[10]

Granite, brown sandstone, and perhaps 25 million bricks went into the fort, on which the federal government had spent almost $1 million by late 1860. Unlike granite-blocked Fort Knox in Maine,[11] the construction of Pulaski was essentially completed before the war began, as fewer than 150 Georgia militiamen discovered when they occupied the fort on January 3, 1861.[12]

Now safely in Confederate hands, Pulaski barred upriver passage to Union warships

John Ellis Wool
Photo by Southworth & Hawes, between 1845-61, from Museum of Fine Arts, Boston

and lent protection to blockade runners slipping through the Savannah River channels. With the fort's capture came 20 dismounted cannons and a mud-filled moat; Confederate authorities scrambled to remount the 32-pounder cannons in the casemates and to hire slaves to dig out the moat.[13]

The capture of Hilton Head placed Union soldiers and warships only ten miles from Pulaski—and the War Department ordered the fort captured. The 8th Maine became involved immediately.

The mid-December resignation of the sick Strickland had moved Lt. Col. John Rust of Camden to colonel and Ephraim W. Woodman (the first Co. A captain) to lieutenant colonel. To the latter came an order on Valentine's Day 1862 to report with five 8th Maine companies (A, B, C, G, and K) to Egbert Viele on Daufuskie Island, about 5 miles from Fort Pulaski.[14]

With the 8th Maine boys came detachments from two infantry regiments, the 6th Connecticut and the 48th New York, and the 3rd Rhode Island Artillery, plus some "Volunteer Engineers," noted Viele, charged with building artillery batteries on the Savannah River to cut off Pulaski from Savannah.

Union Col. John Rust
Photo courtesy of Maine State Library

A quick look at a map suggested to Viele no lack of places to site some guns. Flowing toward the sea, the Savannah River split into two channels, north and south, at Elba Island, upriver from Cockspur. Between Elba and Cockspur lay Bird Island and Long Island, plus several small mud flats that essentially passed for islands when exposed at low tide.

Across the North Channel lay Jones Island and Turtle Island, formed by the tidal Mud, Wright, and New rivers; the last meandering waterway separated Daufuskie Island from Turtle Island.

Theoretically an artillery battery set up on any of the larger islands (except Turtle) could sever Pulaski's river-borne supply route. Unfortunately, as Gillmore discovered while searching "for suitable locations for the batteries" and as Viele subsequently noted, "these islands, as well as all others in the river, are merely deposits of soft mud on sand shoals, always covered at high tide and overgrown with rank grasses."

Gillmore's reconnaissance resulted in Union troops finding the telegraphic wires, "both land and submarine," between Fort Pulaski and Savannah and cutting and removing them "for about the distance of 1 mile." Working only at night, Union troops spent three weeks removing a ship sunk to obstruct passage in a side channel; with the hulk and sunken piles yanked aside, shallow-draft Union steamers could enter the Savannah River.

Gillmore determined that Venus Point on Jones Island "and the upper end of Long Island" were "the most feasible locations to be occupied" by artillery batteries.[15]

Working amidst storm-driven rain, wind, and high tides, soldiers dragged "five Parrott guns and an 8 inch siege howitzer" on portable tramways across Jones Island to Venus Point. Constructing a parapet-protected gun platform, the soldiers finished the battery by mid-February.

Three Confederate gunboats dropped downriver on Valentine's Day afternoon and fired on the Venus Point battery from a mile away. The resulting Union barrage, about 30 shells fired all told, struck one gunboat, and all three withdrew upriver.

On Wednesday, February 19, Gillmore ordered "that a battery should be placed on the north end of Bird Island," noted Lt. Patrick H. O'Rorke.[16]

Soldiers from the 8th Maine helped O'Rorke stake out the battery site on February 20.[17] That night, with either sailors or soldiers straining at the oars, rowboats towed flat boats laden with cannons, shells, gunpowder, and buildings materials across the river to Bird Island. Known as Battery Hamilton, the post would mount "one 8-inch siege howitzer, one 30-pounder Parrott, one 20-pounder Parrott, and three 12-pounder James rifles," according to Gillmore.[19]

William McArthur
Photo courtesy of Maine State Library

The next day, 8th Maine lads helped build the gun platforms and mounted the cannons on them. Incoming tides swirled into the battery; sinking into the glutinous mud as they worked, the Maine soldiers erected with the soupy material a levee that defied formation. Finally the levee at least partially blocked the tide water.

Working conditions were horrendous on Bird Island, like Jones Island formed from material "of the most unfavorable description," Viele said. When the firing platforms atop Bird Island started sinking into the mud beneath the cannons' weight, the 8th Maine lads rebuilt them.

Viele praised the "great labor and perseverance of the troops under most trying circumstances, the fatigue parties always standing in water" 24 hours a day.[20]

"Twice each day these islands were covered with water," said an 8th Maine veteran. "Although the men sank deep into mud and water, the work progressed, and was completed.

"But the sufferings of the soldiers ... employed upon the work were almost unendurable," he noted.

This 200-pound Parrott rifle at Fort Gregg, Morris Island, South Carolina, circa 1865, is similar to the smaller Parrott rifles used against Fort Pulaski. (National Archives, War Department photo)

One cold night in late February, Capt. John E. Bryant of Co. C sent three privates—Lindsey O. Goff of Gray, Samuel Holt of Turner, and Maurice Woodbury of Buckfield[21]—to picket an island (likely Bird). The men were "instructed under no circumstances to leave their post."

The incoming tide "came up slowly around them, rising nearly to their breasts" and causing the men to hold their weapons and ammunition pouches above their heads. The tide "as slowly ebbed away; and yet those faithful sentinels obeyed their instructions."

Afterwards the exhausted men struggled to the company's camp and fell sick. "Broken down in health," Goff shipped north to Maine "and soon after died." Holt, too, died "from the effects of the night's exposure." Only Woodbury survived.[22]

The upriver batteries prevented Confederate ships from reaching Fort Pulaski, but the 8th Maine could not shell the fort into submission. To do that, Gillmore needed batteries placed nearer the fort on Tybee Island, already occupied by Union troops.

Working "in the dead of night over a narrow causeway, bordered by swamps on either side," the soldiers hauled with "herculean labor" the 36 pieces of artillery that Gillmore needed for the 11 batteries to be constructed along Tybee's north shore at distances ranging from 1,650 to 3,400 yards from Fort Pulaski. The 13-inch mortars alone weighed "8½ tons … and [the] columbiads but a trifle lighter," Gillmore noted.

"Two hundred and fifty men were barely sufficient to move a single piece on sling carts" after dark, when the soldiers "were not allowed to speak above a whisper," he said.[23]

John Rust had brought his remaining 8th Maine companies—D, E, F, H, and I—from Hilton Head to Tybee Island. Although men from the 7th Connecticut Infantry transported most of the artillery the 2½ miles across the island, soldiers from "the 3d Rhode Island, 46th New York, and 8th Maine Volunteers moved several of the guns under similar circumstances," noted Lt. Horace Porter, the assigned ordnance officer for the Pulaski expedition.[24]

"On arriving here the batteries were incomplete and the whole battalion[25] was put at once at work mounting the monster guns and finishing the embankments," an 8th Maine soldier wrote under the pseudonym "Pulaski" to the Bangor-published *Daily Whig & Courier*.

Digging by day and camouflaging their work each dawn, the tired, mud-splattered Union men gradually created the 11 batteries. Six mounted either 10- or 13-inch mortars, the rest a mixture of rifled cannons. "Much of the work had to be done by night … to conceal what was done from the enemy in the fort," the 8th Maine soldier informed *Daily Whig & Courier* readers.[26]

To the west at Pulaski, Confederate officers scanned Tybee Island with field glasses by day, and scouts slipped out by night to discover what was happening across the South Channel. Built to mount 140 guns, the fort had 48 by late March. Twenty pointed at Tybee Island: five 10-inch columbiads, five 8-inch columbiads, four 32-pounders, one 24-pounder Blakeley rifle, and two 12-inch and three 10-inch seacoast mortars.

With 36 cannons and mortars to man and fewer than 200 Rhode Island artillerymen present to do so, Gillmore ordered infantrymen trained as gunners. To Battery Burnside (a 13-inch mortar) went soldiers from companies E and H, 8th Maine, split into three shifts with each commanded by a U.S. Engineers sergeant. Men from companies D, F, and I reported to Battery Lincoln (three 8-inch columbiads) and Battery Lyon (three 10-inch columbiads); the men at Lincoln shared the post with 3rd Rhode Island gunners.[27]

The unassigned 8th Maine lads were "ordered to the centre reserve, the place that regulation tactics assigned to the best troops," *Whig & Courier* readers learned.

On March 31, the War Department replaced Thomas Sherman with David Hunter, but the move did not affect siege operations against Pulaski. With the bombardment set for Thursday, April 10, John Rust and his ad hoc 8th Maine gunners quietly slipped into their assigned batteries at 1 a.m. that morning. Rust was designated "'Field Officer of the Trenches'" that day.[28]

Thursday's dawn "broke clear and cold," and "a fresh easterly wind whipped the red waters of the Savannah River into whitecaps." Federal gunners had removed the batteries' camouflage, and a sharp-eyed Confederate officer spotted ominous-looking objects jutting above the Tybee shore.

Under a truce flag, a rowboat ferried to Cockspur Island Army engineer Lt. Joseph H. Wilson with a letter requesting that Col. Charles H. Olmstead, the Fort Pulaski commander, surrender his post.

The damage at Fort Pulaski
Left: An interior photo of the breached wall at Fort Pulaski. *(Photo by Timothy O'Sullivan, via Library of Congress)* Above: An exterior shot of Fort Pulaski in April 1862, after it was damaged by Union guns.

He declined the offer.[29]

Union gunners at Battery Halleck opened the bombardment at 8:15 a.m. with a shell from a 13-inch mortar. The other mortar-equipped batteries "opened one after the other," Gillmore noted, and observers watching through field glasses calculated "the approximate ranges [to the fort] by the use of signals."

All 11 batteries were blazing away by 9:30 a.m.

The gunners working the rifled cannons in batteries McClellan, Sigel, and Scott—three of the four batteries nearest Cockspur Island—targeted the corner where Pulaski's south and southeast walls met. Gillmore expected that the rifled guns' high velocity would shatter the exterior brick walls and create a breach. Once the walls collapsed at this point, Union shells could reach the fort's magazine, "located in the angle formed" by the fort's north wall and gorge wall. A shell exploding inside the magazine could detonate everything inside it, including the gunpowder.

As the bombardment began, "unsuitable" pintles dismounted the three 10-inch columbiads in Battery Scott and another at Battery Lyon; what the 8th Maine lads at Lyon thought as the 10-inch gun recoiled off its carriage is not known, but no one was hurt.

All four cannons were soon remounted.[30]

Confederate gunners opened fire, and iron and explosives flew both ways. Pulaski presented a large target for the Federal artillerists, but not so the burrowed-in-the-muck Union batteries to the Confederate cannoneers.

"Owing to the peculiar construction of our batteries," Olmstead's artillerists "could get no shot into them. If he fired at the top of our embankments, his shots flew harmlessly" overhead, and "if he fired lower, the shots fell short or stuck into the embankment, doing no harm," the 8th Maine correspondent noted.

With Rust busy checking the batteries, Capt. William McArthur of Co. I and Limington served as de facto commander of the 8th Maine battalion. Both men were maneuvering across "the open space of about 150 yards between Battery Scott and the protecting bank below" when two enemy shells "passed very near them," the regiment's *Whig & Courier* correspondent noticed.

Rust "took it very coolly and repassed the same spot several times again during the day."[31]

Gillmore and "all experienced officers present" expressed "great surprise and disappointment" at the inaccuracy at the Union's carefully sited 13-inch mortars. Though "the pieces were served with a fair degree of care and skill," fewer than 10 percent of the mortar shells fired at Pulaski actually fell within its walls, Gillmore noted.[32]

Over at Battery Burnside, however, the 8th Maine boys of companies E and H apparently shot with better accuracy. Shells from their 13-inch mortar "knocked over one or two" Confederate guns on the Pulaski barbette, the upper level above the fort's casemates. And a mortar shell from Burnside supposedly "cut down the enemy's flag," too, but Confederate troops quickly raised it again.

Connecticut and Rhode Island gunners in nearby batteries also claimed "the honor" of

The gorge wall of Fort Pulaski today (Photo by Brian F. Swartz)

knocking down the enemy's flag. "Circumstances, however, highly favor the opinion that the Maine boys did it," the 8th Maine correspondent stated.

The bombardment continued unabated until 7 p.m. As daylight faded, Union officers carefully studied Pulaski with their field glasses. Serious damage had been done; "night showed several of the enemy's barbette guns disabled, and deep, ugly looking scars in the wall, and in one spot near the magazine, almost a breech [sic]," *Whig & Courier* readers learned.[33]

Gillmore saw the breach clearly through his field glasses; so did Brig. Gen. Henry W. Benham, commanding the Northern District of the Army's Department of the South. Estimating "that over 3,000 projectiles" were fired at Fort Pulaski during the day, he was pleased with the "successful commencement of the breach."

Sending the exhausted Gillmore to get "the rest which he required," Benham took charge of the land forces "during the first half of the night." He ordered specific Union guns fired at 10- to 15-minute intervals during the night to prevent the Pulaski garrison from sleeping or repairing the fort's damaged walls.

Benham and Gillmore apparently discussed Battery Sigel, located 1,670 yards from Pulaski. On April 10, soldiers from companies H and K, 46th New York Infantry, had worked Sigel's five 30-pounder Parrott rifles and one 48-pounder James rifle.

The guns "appeared not to have been so successfully served during the day," Benham observed. Thursday night he replaced the New Yorkers with "a detachment of 100 seamen from the Navy" and an 8th Maine detachment, commanded by William McArthur.

Commanded by Lt. John Irwin from the frigate USS *Wabash*, the sailors were assigned to the 48-pounder James and three Parrotts; McArthur and his men, who quickly learned the rudiments of gunnery from Army Capt. John Wesley Turner, went to the other two Parrott rifles.

The Union batteries opened fire at 7 a.m., Friday, April 11, and soon "both sides" fired "with great vigor and accuracy," said Benham, who had slept little. The rifled Union cannons pounded at the south-southeast corner of Pulaski; the six rifles at Battery Sigel fired percussion shells that exploded on impact.

Benham, Gillmore, and Rust flitted among the batteries as the morning progressed. Between 10 and 11 a.m., Benham dropped into Battery Sigel and observed the Maine and Navy gunners at work; he found the six rifles "most efficiently served." He "visited all the batteries" and, in late morning, stood and peered at Pulaski through a high-powered telescope.

The high-velocity rifled shells had punched a hole so wide that Benham could see a recess arch inside a casemate. Around 12 noon, "the whole mask and parapet wall" of the damaged casemate "fell into the ditch [moat], raising a ramp quite visible to us," he noticed.[34]

The rifles at Battery Sigel "were worked with fearful accuracy" by the sailors and the 60 men from companies D and I, 8th Maine, noted "Pulaski." Under the targeted and cumulative fire from all the Union rifled cannons, "a breech [sic] was soon made, and then another," the *Whig & Courier* readers learned.[35]

With Gillmore figuring the breach in Pulaski's walls would widen and more debris would fall into the moat, Benham started "arranging for the proper forces, boats, &c." and "scaling-ladders" so Union infantrymen could cross the South Channel, attack Pulaski, and climb the

Dismounted mortar at Fort Pulaski, April 1862
Photo by Timothy O'Sullivan via Library of Congress

debris field to enter the fort.

With Union shells whizzing through the widening breach to pound the magazine walls, Charles Olmstead could guess the outcome. To save his men, he decided to surrender.

"At about 2 p.m., we discovered a white flag thrown up" over Fort Pulaski, Benham reported. "The rebel flag, after filling out to the wind for a few minutes at half-mast, came slowly to the ground." Benham promptly sent Capt. S.B. Ely and Maj. Charles G. Halpine to Fort Pulaski to speak with Olmstead.[36]

But Gillmore boarded a different boat manned by sailors and arrived at the fort prior to Ely and Halpine, who were startled to find Pulaski's main doors closed to them by Gillmore. Seeking glory by sharing the fort's surrender with no one else, Gillmore had ordered the doors shuttered until he and Olmstead came to terms.

Doing so took about an hour in Olmstead's office; afterwards Gillmore vacated Pulaski and left to Ely and Halpine the initial arrangements for rounding up the garrison.

After the white flag had appeared over Fort Pulaski, Union gunners stood in their respective batteries and cheered. The infantrymen particularly realized the bombardment-caused breach meant they would not go into a fort bristling with bayonets and cannons.

"Our shells had penetrated so near the magazine that in two hours more the rebels would have all been blown up together if the firing had continued," wrote "Pulaski" to the *Whig & Courier*.

Benham bestowed an unexpected tribute on the 8th Maine, which "had won that honor by their good behavior, superior discipline and gallantry in the action." The regiment's "flag ... would go up first in the fort," but Col. Edward W. Serrell of the 1st New York Engineers rightfully protested that his men had expended tremendous sweat and toil to site and construct the Tybee Island batteries.

So "Benham decided that the standards [of both regiments] should be lashed together and both raised first on Fort Pulaski," *Whig & Courier* readers learned.

"In consideration of [his] meritorious conduct in the action," Rust was assigned to command the flag-raising detachment. He took with him William McArthur and Sgt. Samuel Gould from Co. D, "and a Captain and Sergeant of the Engineers."[37]

The flags went up over Fort Pulaski, and watching Union soldiers and sailors cheered. A few days later, Rust sent the 8th Maine's flag north to Governor Israel Washburn Jr.[38]

The fort was a mess, "sufficiently ruinous," according to an 8th Maine soldier. "Eleven guns were disabled, the parapet and traverses on all sides shattered, the area torn up by shot and shell, and covered with bricks and fragments."

The soldier noticed that "the wall of the magazine was badly crushed, and the casemates in the rear in ruin. Over [at] the angle where the breach was made, the wreck was nearly complete."[39]

Only the accounting was left after Pulaski fell. During the bombardment, "Rust distinguished himself for bravery and soldier like bearing," and "McArthur evinced much skill in the handling of his guns," according to "Pulaski." He noted that the 8th Maine lads held in reserve "were all very eager to rush into the greatest peril, and all wanted to be at the guns."[40]

One Union soldier, Pvt. Thomas Campbell of Co. H, 3rd Rhode Island Artillery, was killed, and only a few Union soldiers were wounded.

As for the 8th Maine Infantry's other role during the Fort Pulaski campaign, Rust noted that his men had spent far more time digging than actually fighting. Bird, Jones, and Tybee islands had required the frequent application of shovels and pickaxes.

On Tybee Island the 8th Maine had accumulated 3,222 days "employed in building batteries, lugging shot and shell, &c." The days spent "building batteries on Dawfuskie [sic], Bird and Jones' Islands" totaled 1,091days, according to Rust.

His men had run up 100 days "manning batteries, during the bombardment of Fort Pulaski."[41]

Hired to fight Confederates, the 8th Maine lads would see little further combat while assigned to the Department of the South. By mid-April 1862, the action was shifting to Virginia and New Orleans.

~~~

1. Sherman was not closely related to the as yet unknown William Tecumseh Sherman.
2. William E.S. Whitman and Charles H. True, *Maine in the War for the Union: A History of the Part Borne by Maine Troops,* Nelson Dingley & Co., Lewiston, 1865, pp. 192-194
3. A few months later, corruption charges led Cameron to resign and Edwin M. Stanton replacing him as the secretary of war.
4. Maj. Gen. John E. Wool, Oct. 28, 1861 letter to Simon Cameron, *Official Records, Series 1, Vol. 6,* Chapter XV, p. 184
5. Brig. Gen. T.W. Sherman, *OR, Series 1, Vol. 6,* Chapter XV, pp. 183-184
6. Capt. R. Saxton, *OR, Series 1, Vol. 6,* Chapter XV, p. 186
7. Capt. L.H. Pelouse, Nov. 4, 1861, *OR, Series 1, Vol. 6,* Chapter XV, p. 185
8. Correspondence filed in the Official Records officially refers to Wassaw Sound as "Warsaw Sound."
9. Parentheses in the original.
10. Brig. Gen. Quincy A. Gillmore, *OR, Series 1, Vol. 6,* Chapter XV, No. 5, pp. 148-149
11. Built atop the Prospect bluffs at the Narrows on the Penobscot River, Fort Knox was designed to bar enemy warships access to the Penobscot River.
12. Ralston B. Lattimore, *Fort Pulaski National Monument,* U.S. Department of the Interior, Washington, D.C., 1954, reprinted 1961, pp. 7-9 and 13-14
13. The Confederate government routinely hired slaves from their owners to do a lot of the "grunt work." Civilians could hire slaves from slave owners. The slaves were legally viewed as property in the South, and hiring them was seen as no different than hiring horses or mules.
14. Whitman and True, *Maine in the War,* p. 194
15. Brig. Gen. Egbert L. Viele, *OR, Series 1, Vol. 6,* Chapter XV, No. 3, pp. 141-142
16. A native of County Cavan in Ireland and an 1861 West Point graduate, O'Rorke commanded the 140th New York Infantry at Little Round Top at Gettysburg on July 2, 1863. Shot and killed, O'Rorke was honored with a monument mounting a near life-size bronze edifice of his face. Visitors habitually rub the nose for good luck.
17. Lt. Patrick H. O'Rorke, *OR, Series 1, Vol. 6,* Chapter XV, No. 4, p. 143
18. Gillmore, *OR, Series 1, Vol. 6,* Chapter XV, No. 5, p. 153
19. O'Rorke, *OR, Series 1, Vol. 6,* Chapter XV, No. 4, pp. 143-144
20. Viele, *OR, Series 1, Vol. 6,* Chapter XV, No. 3, p. 142
21. Return of Company C, Eighth Regiment Infantry, *Annual Report of the Adjutant General of the State of Maine, 1861,* pp. 379-380
22. Whitman and True, *Maine in the War,* p. 195
23. Gillmore, *OR, Series 1, Vol. 6,* Chapter XV, No. 5, pp. 154-155
24. Lt. Horace Porter, April 12, 1862 report to Brig. Gen. Quincy Gillmore, *Papers on Practical Engineering, No. 8,* Appendix D, D. Van Norstrand, New York, N.Y., 1862, p. 63
25. A battalion nominally comprised five companies, but the numbers could vary depending on the situation.

26. "Pulaski," Letter from the Eighth Maine, April 14, 1862, *Daily Whig & Courier,* Saturday, April 26, 1862
27. In his Special Order No. 32 of April 8, 1862, Gillmore cited only the presence of Co. B, 3rd Rhode Island Artillery, at batteries Lincoln and Lyon. This report was published in *Papers on Practical Engineering, No. 8,* Appendix C, p. 58. The discrepancy between his report and that of the 8th Maine's "Pulaski" cannot be reconciled, but two under-strength Rhode Island companies would have been insufficient to work the six columbiads in the two batteries.
28. *Daily Whig & Courier,* Saturday, April 26, 1862
29. Lattimore, Fort Pulaski National Monument, pp. 31-32
30. Gillmore, *OR, Series 1, Vol. 6,* Chapter XV, No. 5, pp. 157-158
31. *Daily Whig & Courier,* Saturday, April 26, 1862
32. Gillmore, *OR, Series 1, Vol. 6,* Chapter XV, No. 5, pp. 157-158
33. *Daily Whig & Courier,* Saturday, April 26, 1862. The 8th Maine correspondent was incorrect on one point: Pulaski's magazine was located diagonally opposite the targeting point for the Union's rifled guns.
34. Brig. Gen. Henry W. Benham, *OR, Series 1, Vol. 6,* Chapter XV, No. 2, pp. 136-137
35. *Daily Whig & Courier,* Saturday, April 26, 1862
36. Benham, *OR, Series 1, Vol. 6,* Chapter XV, No. 2, p. 137
37. *Daily Whig & Courier,* Saturday, April 26, 1862
38. *Daily Whig & Courier,* Wednesday, April 30, 1862
39. *Daily Whig & Courier,* Thursday, April 24, 1862
40. *Daily Whig & Courier,* Saturday, April 26, 1862
41. "From the 8th Maine," *Maine Farmer,* Thursday, June 26, 1862

Chapter 14

SPRING CLEANING

"Drinking bad whiskey and imposing upon the patriotic credulity of people"

Augusta seemed surreally quiet after wartime exigencies emptied Maine's capital of its uniformed occupiers in late winter and early spring 1862. Though friendly, the boys in blue had taxed Augusta residents to the limit of their collective patience.

Throughout the winter, several regiments had camped in 20-acre Capitol Park, located across State Street from the arched and columned east entrance to the State House. Two parallel rows of planted trees and well-maintained paths lent a cosmopolitan air to the park, which was donated to Maine by Augusta when the state capital relocated there from Portland in 1832.[1]

Numerous Sibley tents peppered Capitol Park's landscaped slopes by late 1861 as several regiments settled into rudimentary camps. Deep snow forced soldiers to march and maneuver in State Street and nearby Capitol Street. Civilians traveling by sleigh or on foot in the preternatural cold of winter 1862 fumed as teeth-chattering soldiers fumbled with their complex drills while blocking the local roads.

Lured to bootleg bars operating behind cloaked doors in ramshackle buildings along Water Street and across the river near the Kennebec Arsenal, drunken soldiers repeatedly challenged both the local watch and the provost guards. Still civilians at heart, most soldiers behaved well, but enough got into trouble that Augusta residents were glad to see them leave, a process that began in February.

Hinting at the gawking they would do upon arriving in Washington, D.C., curious soldiers explored the Charles Bullfinch-designed State House, its cornerstone laid on July 4, 1829. The cupola-capped dome rose above the two-story building, constructed from granite quarried in downriver Hallowell.[2] The Maine Legislature initially met in the State House in January 1832.

With the state government prosecuting a war, uniforms often outnumbered civilian attire inside the State House. Depending on the temperature and weather, soldiers tracked snow, slush, and mud into the building. Their boots and brogans thumping on the interior stairs, commissioned and noncommissioned officers flitted through the offices of Adjutant Gen. John

Maine State Capitol, late 19th century
Photo courtesy of Maine State Archives

L. Hodsdon and his overworked clerks.

His spectacles perched on his nose, diminutive Gov. Israel Washburn Jr. spent his days in meetings with legislators, ambitious civilians lobbying for officers' commissions, contractors, and sometimes ordinary Mainers. Washburn, Hodsdon, and their staffers worked extremely long hours in offices that were poorly lit and poorly heated.

Suddenly, except for those assigned to State House duties, the soldiers vanished from Augusta as Ben Butler summoned four infantry regiments and an artillery battery to the Gulf Coast and the 1st Maine Cavalry went to Virginia. Bugles no longer blatted across Capitol Park, where melting snow revealed the camp-damaged landscape.

Trees budded and flowers blossomed as April transitioned to May. Meeting in the State House on May 2, Washburn and the Executive Council discussed "some matters of importance," including the nomination of a state supreme-court justice. Washburn routinely signed promotion-and-commission forms; the 13th Maine Infantry picked up the Reverend Charles E. Blake of Farmington as its chaplain, and several junior 4th Maine Infantry officers advanced in rank.

Gilman Turner, "the gentlemanly Superintendent" of the State House, carefully checked every nook and cranny inside the well-worn building, from the basement to the cupola. A year at war had left the State House frayed and shabby, needing to be "thoroughly cleaned, painted and carpeted throughout … after its recent occupation by the military."[3]

Turner unleashed his mop-and-bucket brigade.

The bright daylight of June illuminated Augusta, where the war had apparently faded with spring's rising temperatures. Then, by the summer solstice, soldiers suddenly reappeared in the capital—and in Portland, Bangor, Lewiston, Rockland, Houlton, and smaller towns across Maine.

Soldiers "apparently well and able-bodied are lounging about in our cities, drinking bad whiskey and imposing upon the patriotic credulity of people with stories of hardship, exposure and battle," Ezekiel Holmes fumed in his *Maine Farmer* in late June.

Soldiers at a Sibley tent
A group of soldiers from Company G, 71st New York in front of a Sibley tent, 1861. See Chapter 11 for diagrams of a Sibley tent.
Photo courtesy of Library of Congress

Who were these soldiers swapping war stories for cheap booze in Maine bars and saloons? Holmes explained to his readers that "quite a number of soldiers are now absent from their regiments under the plea of sickness, or having furloughs entitling them to visit their families."[4]

Israel Washburn wondered why so many soldiers relaxed at home in Maine rather than face enemy troops in the field. He suspected that the current or allegedly discharged soldiers floating around the Pine Tree State included too many men who had run away rather than fight.

Washburn and Hodsdon considered these men deserters—and, by War Department definition, they were. Maine soldiers had deserted the standards as the first state regiments formed in spring 1861; a trickle that May and June had swelled into a fleet-footed Bull Run skedaddle on July 21.

Casting about for compelling explanations—"excuses" would be the appropriate term—as to why Maine men deserted in 1861, Hodsdon had decided that "by far the most potent cause, and that which occasioned more than half of all the desertions from the Second, Third, Fourth and Fifth Regiments, was the retreat from the disastrous field of Bull Run."

Some Maine-bound soldiers had apparently decided "their organizations had ceased to exist" after the Manassas debacle, Hodsdon told sympathetic legislators. Maine could turn the deserters caught within its borders over "to the authorities of the general government," but he recommended that the state "treat these cases with leniency." Doing so would "be conducive to the best interests of the public services," he explained.[5]

But reality's rising sun gradually dawned on Hodsdon, Washburn, and the other paternalistic state officials initially sympathetic to Maine deserters. Manassas might explain the runner of July '61, but not those of later months.

Dissatisfied with Army life, Pvt. Seth B. Ramsdell of Co. G and Ripley had fled the 2nd Maine on March 10, 1862, not long after being "reduced to [the] ranks" from sergeant "at [his] own request." Canadian-born Pvt. Joseph E. Gagnon had deserted Co. G the previous Oct. 14, less than two weeks after Pvt. Warren W. Bradford of Bangor had deserted the same company while stationed at Fort Corcoran near Washington, D.C.

Two Bangor privates, Elden A. Keene and George W. Pratt, abandoned Co. E, 2nd Maine Infantry on June 6, 1862. Right behind them on June 30 ran Pvt. Russell Poor of Bridgton, a Co. E mutineer transferred earlier to the 2nd New York Infantry. During the bloody July 1 confusion atop Malvern Hill, Pvt. Leander L. Graffam of Bangor and Co. F bolted for parts unknown.[6]

There were many more such runners by late spring 1862, but Hodsdon and Washburn had lost all compassion for skedaddling Mainers, thanks to one particularly vicious deserter.

~~~

1. Capitol Park is part of the Capitol Complex Historic District in Augusta.
2. When the Maine Legislature authorized funding for Maine monuments at Gettysburg in the 1880s, the granite was cut in Hallowell quarries owned by a company whose vice president was Charles Tilden, the enigmatic and heroic colonel of the 16th Maine Infantry.
3. *Daily Whig & Courier,* Saturday, May 3, 1862
4. Ezekiel Holmes, "An Important Order," *Maine Farmer,* Thursday, June 26, 1862
5. Adjutant Gen. John L. Hodsdon, "Deserters," *Annual Report of the Adjutant General of the State of Maine, 1861,* pp.73-74
6. James H. Mundy, *Second to None,* Harp Publications, Scarborough, ME, 1992, pp. 257, 259, 261-262

Chapter 15

TRAITOR

"Even they refused to have his company"

Without informing his commanding officer, Capt. Scollay D. Baker inexplicably sent seven men from Co. I, 9th Maine Infantry Regiment, to guard a Confederate sympathizer's wife in early April 1862. His decision led directly to the deaths of two Maine soldiers, including the man most reviled by his fellow Mainers during the Civil War.

Mustered along with Col. Rishworth Rich into federal service at Augusta on September 22, 1861, the 9th Maine lads participated in the expedition against Port Royal and Hilton Head in South Carolina later that fall. While the 8th Maine Infantry of Col. Lee Strickland worked with picks and shovels to build earthworks outside Port Royal, Rich and the 9th Maine tromped ashore at Fernandina on Amelia Island in northeastern Florida on Saturday, March 5, 1862.

Located on the Amelia River near its confluence with St. Mary's River, Fernandina was the eastern terminus of the Florida Railroad, which crossed the state to Cedar Keys on the Gulf Coast. Florida contributed beef cattle, salt, and other goods to the Southern war effort; while Navy warships blockaded Fernandina, small Confederate coastal schooners could move along the shallower inshore channels and waterways winding around myriad islands and swamps.

Rich[1] scattered his companies around and about Fernandina, a ramshackle port populated by sullen pro-southern whites and frightened ex-slaves who knew their serfdom would resume if Union troops withdrew. Lying on the Amelia's east bank opposite Tiger Island, the town would experience several mysterious fires while occupied by Northern soldiers.

In early April, Rich sent Baker and Co. I to guard the bridge carrying the Florida Railroad over the Amelia River southwest of Fernandina. The 9th Maine's Lt. Col. Horatio Bisbee had arrested a "Mr. Heath" (a Southern sympathizer, the area being loaded with them) and sent his wife to seek safety at "the Judge O'Neal place, which is about two miles and a half from the railroad bridge."[2]

Among the Co. I lads was Pvt. William W. Lunt, who "in personal appearance ... was a remarkable man," noticed *New York Times* special correspondent Henry J. Wisner. "More than six feet in height, and of a proportionately large frame, sinewy and compact, he seemed the very perfection of physical conformation."

Hailing from Hampden, Lunt found life boring in that farming town bordering Bangor on the lower Penobscot River. Born "of respectable parents," he "early betrayed a waywardness which led him into every species of childish vice," Wisner claimed. At 13, Lunt ran away "to fill a menial place in a circus company" that had performed in Hampden, and in time he became a "castanet-player [sic] in a band of Ethiopian Minstrels" traveling with the circus.[3]

After knocking about Maine for several years, Lunt lived in Thomaston a while before joining the 9th Maine as a corporal in Co. I on September 12, 1861. With his enlistment accredited to Orono,[4] he likely kept looking over his shoulder until the regiment cleared the state later that month and breathed a sigh of relief as Maine dropped below the horizon. One can imagine Lunt clasping his hands behind his head, leaning back, and grinning from ear to ear.

Albert W. Lunt, horse thief and convicted felon, had just duped the United States Army into gladly accepting "William W. Lunt" into its ranks. Released from the Maine State Prison in Thomaston "just after the breaking out of the war," Al Lunt had simply changed his first name to escape Maine law.[5]

Finding army life almost as confining as a jail cell, Lunt got into trouble as the 9th Maine worked its way down the Sea Islands. Busted into the ranks with at least three other Co. I corporals before reaching Florida, he marched out with Co. I to guard the Amelia River railroad bridge in April.

On Sunday, April 6, an officer (likely Baker)[6] ostensibly sent Lunt "three miles beyond on our lines … on an improper errand connected with a woman whose existence was made known to them on the previous day while they were scouting." Lunt confronted Mrs. Ellen Manning in her house and "did forcibly take from her" $268[7] "in gold and Confederate currency."[8]

He might have spent the night at Manning's. Later claiming that "he was in danger of being surprised by a party of our own troops, which would have placed him in difficulty," Lunt stated that he "pressed on farther" west of the Amelia River on Monday, April 7.[9]

But the evidence indicates that he had returned to the Co. I camp on Sunday. Lunt apparently listened on Monday as Baker detailed Orderly Sgt. Richard Webster, Corp. James W. Bowman, and privates C. Wesley Adams, Ansel Chase, John E. Kent, Alonzo B. Merrill, and Isaac Whitney of Co. I to guard Mrs. Heath at

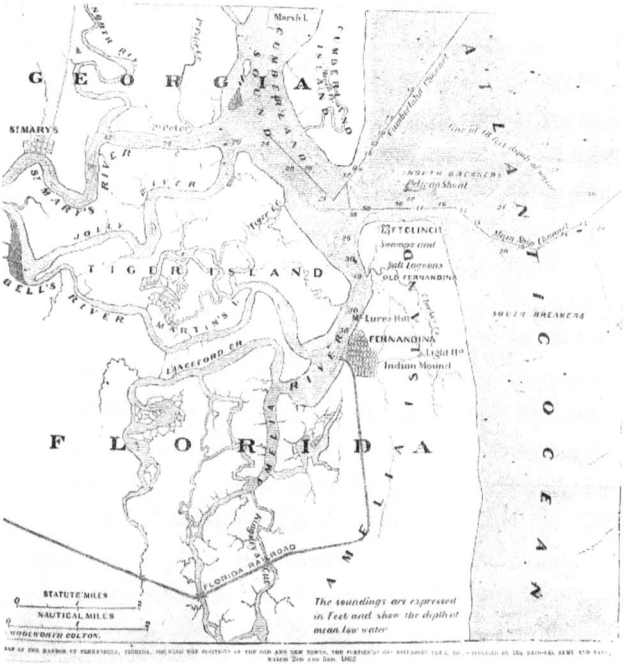

Fernandina, Florida: 9th Maine map
Map from Library of Congress

the O'Neal homestead, located 2½ miles beyond the railroad bridge and Union lines.

"Captain Baker left the party at said place without reporting it to his commanding officer, doing it as an act of kindness and sympathy for Mrs. Heath, and, as his men daily frequented the vicinity with impunity, did not think that he was doing a wrong act or exposing his men," Bisbee noted.[10]

Then the outraged Ellen Manning apparently appeared in the Co. I camp on Monday. No other reason could explain why Albert W. Lunt, a.k.a. William W. Lunt, bolted for the nearby swamps that day.

Meanwhile, Confederate Col. William G.M. Davis, the commander of the 1st Florida Cavalry Regiment, had left 40 Confederate cavalrymen led by Capt. William M. Footman of Co. F "to watch the movements of the enemy near Fernandina and ... repel" any "small parties" of Union soldiers reaching mainland Florida from Amelia Island.

Footman's troopers missed Webster's guard detail, but scooped up two Union soldiers who "landed from a hand car" somewhere along the Florida Railroad west of the river, Davis noted.[11]

Union Lt. Col. Horatio Bisbee Jr.
This photo is sometime between 1877 and 1885. Following the war, Bisbee served in the U.S. House of Representatives from 1877-79 and again from 1882-85.

Were the prisoners Al Lunt and another deserter? Davis did not identify the men; Lunt claimed he left the Manning house with plans "to stop at a house which he had visited before." Perhaps he meant the O'Neal house; no matter his purported destination after robbing Manning, "he came upon a squad of rebel cavalry, and was taken prisoner."

A Confederate officer—Lunt believed him a major, but he possibly was Footman—searched the deserter, who had fled "without arms and accoutrements." As the officer frisked him, Lunt filched his watch.[12]

To prove his deserter status, Lunt told his captors about Webster's detachment. Footman and some cavalrymen approached the O'Neal house on Thursday, April 10. Webster and five other men were inside the house while Pvt. Chase stood watch outdoors.[13]

Spying the oncoming Confederates, Chase offered "resistance" and "was killed, and the rest then made prisoners," noted Footman, who claimed he found "a party of 5 men" at the house. He bundled his six prisoners off to meet Davis at Camp Langford near Jacksonville; Davis shipped them by train to Tallahassee on April 12.[14]

Amidst all the hoopla surrounding Manning's robbery and Lunt's desertion, Baker forgot to recall the Webster detachment until April 10. Two soldiers sent to retrieve the men found "the dead body of 1 man, that from appearances had been shot that day, and the remainder of the party taken prisoners," Bisbee reported. [15]

Despite Lunt's attempt to blend in with his captors, his natural inclinations got the worse of him. His "conduct with the rebels was so bad that even they refused to have his company," and around April 20 Davis "returned him [Lunt] to our lines, with the request" that Confederate deserters "might be treated in a similar manner," Wisner noted.

By now the news was en route to New England that a Maine deserter had betrayed Maine soldiers and cost one man his life and six men their freedom. The state had shipped 15 infantry regiments, a cavalry regiment, and six artillery batteries—all told some 18,000 men, not including Navy recruits—off to war, and Lunt was the first to commit such a heinous act.

Lunt became an anathema in Maine. Serving soldiers and their relatives hated him for allegedly betraying seven Maine soldiers; the slain Chase[16] could be any woman's husband, son, brother, or father, the six captured 9th Maine lads anyone's father, son, brother, husband, or other male relative.[17]

Governor Israel Washburn Jr. and Adjutant Gen. John L. Hodsdon no longer felt merciful toward Maine deserters.

And the Army would exhibit no mercy toward Albert W. Lunt at his autumn court-martial.

~~~

1. Rishworth Rich resigned his command on May 27, 1863.
2. Lt. Col. Horatio Bisbee Jr., *Official Records, Series 1, Vol. 6,* Chapter XV, No. 1, p. 132
3. Henry J. Wisner, "Interesting from Port Royal," *New York Times,* Monday, Dec. 1, 1862
4. *Annual Report of the Adjutant General of the State of Maine, 1861,* pp. 429-430
5. Wisner, *NYT,* Monday, December 1, 1862
6. Scollay Baker seemed to know where he could find lonely, vulnerable white women around Fernandina.
7. Wisner, *NYT,* December 1, 1862
8. "Fate Of A Deserter," *Maine Farrner,* Thursday, Nov. 13, 1862
9. Wisner, *NYT,* December 1, 1862
10. Bisbee, *OR, Series 1, Vol. 6,* Chapter XV, No. 1, p. 132
11. Col. W.G.M. Davis, *OR, Series 1, Vol. 6,* Chapter XV, No. 2, p. 133
12. Wisner, *NYT,* December 1, 1862
13. A picket detail assigned to long-term guard duty would often leave one soldier on guard while his comrades relaxed in a nearby building. When no buildings were available, pickets found whatever shelter they could.
14. Davis, *OR, Series 1, Vol. 6,* Chapter XV, No. 2, p. 133
15. Bisbee, *OR, Series 1, Vol. 6,* Chapter XV, No. 1, p. 132
16. Twenty-three and single when he joined the 9th Maine, Chase had lived in Sebec in Piscataquis County.
17. The six prisoners taken on April 10 impacted families in a small geographical area: Webster, Bowman, Adams, and Whitney were from Bangor, Kent from adjacent Veazie, and Merrill from Holden, two towns over.

Chapter 16

"OLD GRIZZLY" FIGHTS

"The shot and shell were showered around us thickly"

Startled by the letters and newspaper clippings he received by late May 1862, Col. Hiram Burnham sat down in his 6th Maine Infantry Regiment headquarters at "Camp No. 19 in the Field" somewhere on the Virginia Peninsula and penned a report to Maine Governor Israel Washburn Jr. on Saturday, May 24.

"Sir: The people of Maine are much interested in the Battle which was fought at Williamsburg" on May 5, Burnham informed Washburn. "Maine soldiers occupied positions in our line of battle, upon which great results depended, and it is desirable for our citizens to know how they discharged the duties which devolved upon them."

Writing in a flowing cursive, Burnham spent the next 2½ pages detailing the 6th Maine Infantry's role in the Battle of Williamsburg. Ending his report "Very Respectfully," Burnham paused briefly.

Then he vented his spleen in a 1½-page postscript.

"Accounts of the battle contained in letters, purporting to come from Head Qrs [Headquarters] or from members of the seventh Maine Reg.t which have appeared in the Boston Journal, Portland Transcript, Maine Farmer, and perhaps in other papers, contain many mistatements [sic], and are in the main erronious [sic]," Burnham wrote.

"All officers and men under my command behaved in a most gallant meritorious manner," he wrote as an afterthought.[1]

Williamsburg marked the first large-scale Peninsula battle in which some Maine regiments fought. Believing that he could capture Richmond by a flank attack, George McClellan had gradually shifted the Army of the Potomac from northern Virginia to the Peninsula since late winter. Most existing Maine regiments joined the expedition; Burnham brought the 6th Maine ashore at Fort Monroe on Tuesday, March 25.[2]

Whipped into shape by "'Old Grizzly,' as the boys call him," the regiment was ready to fight, a 6th Maine soldier informed a Maine newspaper. Burnham "has brought the Regt. to a high state of discipline and efficiency, and is very popular with us."[3]

Outside Washington, D.C., the 4th Maine Infantry boys struck their tents and broke camp at 10:30 a.m., Monday, March 17, then joined their companion 2nd Brigade regiments—the

Union Maj. Gen. George B. McClellan
Photo by Mathew Brady, 1861

Union Maj. Thomas Hyde
Photo courtesy of Maine State Archives

3rd Maine and the 38th and 40th New Yorks—in marching to Alexandria and boarding transports for the voyage to Fort Monroe.[4]

Disembarking, the 4th Maine lads initially camped near the fort, then shifted with the brigade to a campground near Hampton. Kicked upstairs to wear a brigadier general's stars and to command a III Corps[5] brigade, Col. Hiram Berry took leave of the 4th Maine on Tuesday, March 25.

"The undersigned hereby assumes command of the Fourth Maine Volunteers," Elijah Walker wrote that same day in Regimental Order No. 1.[6] He had survived the regiment's first blood-letting at Manassas, earned promotion to major, helped quell the Co. H mutiny in mid-September 1861, and seen self-styled Professor Thaddeus Sobieski Constantine Lowe and his balloon arrive in early March 1862.[7]

"I suppose it was to see if we could get high enough to view the Confederate army," Walker opined about the balloon. Assigned to assist Lowe during the Peninsula Campaign, Lt. Arthur Libby and 28 enlisted men from the 4th Maine Infantry would participate in the first combat use of "air-craft," as Walker described Lowe's equipment.[8]

The 7th Maine Infantry Regiment "camped some days near Alexandria waiting our time to embark for the Peninsula," recalled Maj. Thomas Hyde of Bath. The soldiers drilled almost relentlessly by day; at night, the young and inexperienced Hyde studied Dennis Hart Mahan's *A Treatise on Field Fortification* by flickering candlelight.

Hyde "almost learned the book by heart, which I found very useful afterward, for there is a right way to dig even a rifle pit."

Chapter 16: "Old Grizzly" Fights

On Sunday, March 23, the 7th Maine Infantry lads boarded "the steamer Long Branch" and sailed for Fort Monroe. Military adventure still excited Hyde; "the next morning we were steaming through the great fleet of transports gathered at Old Point Comfort, gazing with excited interest on the already historic [USS] Monitor," he noted.[9]

The 7th Maine disembarked on Monday and camped with its brigade.[10]

Union soldiers landing at Fort Monroe in late March knew that the USS *Monitor* and CSS *Virginia* had banged, clanged, and dented one another in Hampton Roads a few weeks earlier. Maine lads viewed from a distance the sunken USS *Cumberland* and USS *Congress*, and many commented on the *Monitor*, "the queerest thing in the shape of a steamer I ever saw," said Sgt. William H. West of Machias. "She looks just like a raft only about a foot out of water, when in fighting order, with one of those round cisterns on her."[11]

Assigned to the 1st Brigade (Brig. Gen. Winfield Scott Hancock) of the 2nd Division (Brig. Gen. William F. "Baldy" Smith) of IV Corps (Brig. Gen. Erasmus D. Keyes), Burnham and his men served alongside the 43rd New York Infantry, the 49th Pennsylvania Infantry, and the 5th Wisconsin Infantry. Marching in a pouring rain, the brigade advanced north on Friday, April 4 and approached the Warwick River.[12]

On Saturday, April 5, the 6th Maine lads "engaged in our first skirmish" while probing Confederate positions at Warwick near the James River; a similar reconnaissance conducted the next day with the 5th Wisconsin cost the 6th Maine "our first man, a private in Company

Thaddeus Sobieski Constantine Lowe
*Between 1865-80; Brady-Handy Collection,
Library of Congress*

Union Brig. Gen. Winfield Scott Hancock
*Photo by Campbell Photo Service via
Library of Congress*

Hancock's troops charge at the Battle of Williamsburg
Illustration by Alfred R. Waud, via Library of Congress

E," remembered Charles A. Clark of Co. A.[13]

He likely referred to Pvt. David R. Clark (no relation), who along with Charles Cobb absorbed an exploding Confederate artillery shell around noon that Sunday. These men, the 6th Maine's first two combat-wounded soldiers, survived their injuries, although Clark lost his left arm.[14]

Three days later, during a nasty skirmish along the Warwick River, a Confederate bullet struck Pvt. George Riley of Co. K in the neck. Mortally wounded, Riley died on a sunny Saturday, April 12; he was the first 6th Maine soldier killed in combat.[15]

Deftly handling his numerically inferior troops, the theatrically disposed Confederate Gen. John B. Magruder convinced the nervous McClellan that far more Southern troops defended Yorktown than Magruder actually commanded. "We were in front of the works there just a month," said Charles Clark; not until May 4 did Union troops finally start "on the march to Richmond."[16]

Other Maine soldiers swung north that Sunday. In the 2nd Division's 3rd Brigade marched the 7th Maine Infantry Regiment. "Distant firing was heard at intervals in front from the cavalry and horse artillery," noticed Thomas Hyde.

Meanwhile, believing "the millennium had come," fleeing slaves "pass to our rear," he commented.

That evening, the 7th Maine lads slept "in a potato field, having soft but wet beds between the hills, and as it rained in the night they were softer and wetter by morning," Hyde wrote.[17]

The rain continued into Monday as pursuing Union troops collided with Confederate troops outside Williamsburg. Confederate reinforcements arriving to bolster Magruder's soaked, hungry, and tired soldiers deployed into a series of redoubts southeast of Virginia's second capital and fought most of the day with advancing Union troops.

Burnham recalled that "the battle commenced on our left and centre" at 8 a.m., Monday. Hancock and his reinforced 1st Brigade remained "in reserve perhaps half a mile from where our forces were engaged with the enemy."

The restless Mainers and New Yorkers listened all morning "to the wild uproar of battle," grumbled Burnham. Then Hancock received orders about 11 a.m. "to take the extreme right" on the Union line "and endeavor to turn the enemy's left flank."[18]

Hancock marched about 1½ miles to the northeast with five infantry regiments: his own 6th Maine, the 49th Pennsylvania, and the 5th Wisconsin, plus the 7th Maine and the 33rd New York, borrowed from the 3rd Brigade. Coming along to provide artillery support were 1st Lt. Andrew Cowan and the gunners and six 3-inch ordnance rifles of the 1st New York Battery.

At the first crossroads, Hancock detailed three companies of the 33rd New York as guards while he pushed toward nearby Cub Creek. A staff aide, Lt. George Armstrong Custer of the 5th U.S. Cavalry, accompanied the expedition to show Hancock where his men could cross the creek.[19]

Near the crossroads, "we were in sight of the York River," Hyde said. The soldiers "turned [west] toward the town of Williamsburg" and about 1 p.m. "came to a milldam" spanning Cub Creek, a tributary of Queen's Creek.[20]

Across the mill dam rose a formidable Confederate earthworks. Worried that the position might be occupied, Hancock deployed Cowan's artillery on a hilltop opposite the fort. He then sent Col. Amasa Cobb and his 5th Wisconsin Infantry across the dam (an estimated 75 yards in length) to probe the "very strong earthwork," which "we were surprised to find … entirely deserted," Burnham wrote.

The 6th Maine followed on Cobb's heels. Union soldiers hoisted an American flag above the fort, Hancock left three 33rd New York companies to garrison it, and the brigade "pushed on," Burnham told Washburn. "Passing through a narrow skirt of woods, we came into an open field and discovered a short distance ahead, another rebel earthwork of a formidable nature."

This fort, too, was abandoned.

Hancock estimated that the field extended some 1,200 yards west. Thick woods bordered the field on the north and south; requesting reinforcements to help screen the woods for hidden Confederates, Hancock pushed Cowan's artillery battery "about one hundred rods [1,650 feet]" to the west "and nearly within rifle shot of [two occupied redoubts on] the enemy's left flank," said Burnham.[21]

Moving his 1st New York Battery to a ramshackle farm, Cowan "posted two of my pieces on the right and four on the left of the road, about 350 yards from the fort on our left and 500 [yards] from that on our right, and immediately opened fire on both of these works."

Nervous horses likely snorted and jingled their curb chains as Capt. Charles C. Wheeler brought up the four ordnance rifles of Battery E, 1st New York Light Artillery and "came into battery on my right between the [farm] buildings," Cowan noted.[22] Hancock placed the 5th Wisconsin on Wheeler's right (northern) flank and the 6th Maine on Cowan's left (southern) flank to protect the cannoneers against enemy infantry. The 49th Pennsylvania deployed on the 6th Maine's left flank.

Confederate artillery inside the two redoubts "opened a heavy fire upon us, and our artillery replied with excellent effect," Burnham wrote Washburn. "This artillery duel continued for four hours, with but small loss on our side, though the shot and shell were showered around us thickly.

McClellan arrives at the Battle of Williamsburg
Illustration by Currier & Ives, 1862

"I cannot forbear to remark with what coolness my men withstood this terrible fire," said Burnham. "Less concern could not have been manifested upon dress parade."[23]

Confederate troops hurled more than cannonballs at Hancock's brigade. Charles Clark "felt called upon to show the men [of Co. A] that I was not afraid." Rising "upon my hind legs" from where his men lay on the ground, he was suddenly "struck by a spent bullet from a target rifle, in the immediate vicinity of my watch-pocket, at the waistband of my trousers."

Figuring "that several good-sized grape shot had passed through me," Clark examined his body and found the lead slug, which he "preserved ... as a relic of that day." Bruises discolored the impact point on his body "for several days."[24]

Meanwhile, Hancock protected his flanks by deploying the 7th Maine north of the 5th Wisconsin and the 33rd New York as skirmishers to the south of the 6th Maine. "The 7th was drawn up in line of battle against the woods on the extreme right to guard against an attack by cavalry[,] which was expected from that quarter," wrote a 7th Maine correspondent identified only as "C."[25]

"Companies G and E, were sent to the fartherest [sic] front and right through the woods to watch the enemy in that direction," he recalled.[26]

With the companies went Thomas Hyde, who nervously eyed the surrounding terrain

Chapter 16: "Old Grizzly" Fights

all afternoon.

As the brigade had advanced west with the artillery across the field, "the ground became more open," he said after glancing south along the line of battle. "We could see how few we were," and the men realized that "the danger of being cut off appeared imminent, as the woods on our right were very dense."

Told to scout the woods "with some skirmishers," Hyde looked "from tree to tree to see if a foe lurked behind." Finding the woods devoid of Confederates, he rejoined the 7th Maine soldiers, then "lying down in line in open field" and cussing the muck, the war, the unseen enemy, and everything else that separated the Maine men from their far-away homes.[27]

Later, Hancock would curiously note at 5:10 p.m. how "the clouds had become very heavy over us and the rain was drenching the troops." Seeking reinforcements to help secure a position he thought advantageous to the Federal army, he had traded messages with his higher-ups since midafternoon.

No help came.

Deciding to pull back to the Cub Creek earthworks, Hancock suddenly "observed that the enemy were throwing infantry into the redoubts on my front and that my skirmishers were firing on them.

"I immediately apprehended danger," he commented in classic understatement.[28]

Burnham explained to Washburn what happened next. About 5 p.m., two Confederate generals, Jubal A. Early and Dwight Harvey Hill, made preparations to "drive our Brigade from the field by a desperate charge," wrote Burnham, estimating the oncoming Confederates as "at least six thousand strong."[29]

Hyde figured "some three or four thousand of the enemy" advanced past Fort Magruder—the linch pin of the Confederate defenses at Williamsburg—to attack Hancock's brigade. After successfully repulsing Union attacks elsewhere, the Southerners came to shore up their left flank.[30]

Confederate cavalry emerged from woods near an occupied enemy redoubt. Firing from about 400 yards away, Hancock's skirmishers annoyed the cavalrymen, who apparently intended to charge the Union artillery.

Hancock ordered the guns withdrawn to the Cub Creek earthworks.

Throughout the afternoon the Federal gunners had brilliantly worked their 3-inch rifles. Gradually pounding the opposing artillery to smithereens and scoring some accurate hits inside the occupied redoubts, the weary gunners had dealt with mud and rain.

Each time a heavy ordnance rifle fired, the recoil hurled it backwards to bury its trace and wheels deep in the soupy red Virginia soil. Gunners then shoved their assigned cannon forward to its firing position, reloaded, aimed, and fired again. And back the gun recoiled into the Virginia mud.

The 7th Maine soldiers watched as, after emerging from the woods, Confederate troops "formed rapidly and advanced upon our lines at the double quick, firing as they came," C recalled. "They also advanced through the woods [while] firing upon and receiving the fire of our skirmishers."[31]

Hancock's charge at the Battle of Williamsburg
Illustration by Kurz & Allison, 1893, via Library of Congress

Now Cowan and Wheeler had to pull back as Confederate troops approached. "As my guns were sunk nearly to the hubs[,] it was a work of much difficulty," recalled Cowan, who had already lost one private to a 6-pound Confederate cannonball.

"The ground was so heavy [with mud and pooled water] that it was difficult to draw the pieces," he said. "I succeeded in bringing off all the pieces, and came into battery again" on a rise just west of the Cub Creek earthworks.[32]

Wheeler cut close his battery's withdrawal. Confederate infantrymen already approached as his leftmost ordnance rifle and its gunners limbered up and moved east. At 700 to 800 yards, Wheeler's other gun crews fired case-shot at the enemy troops. At 300 yards his gunners switched to canister. At 100 to 150 yards the remaining ordnance rifles started to limber up.

"Our last piece retired from the [farm] yard as the enemy reached the fence" just to the west, the nonchalant Wheeler reported.[33]

Yelling "Bull Run!" and "Ball's Bluff!"[34] Confederate infantrymen came east across the field. Intent on outflanking Hancock's troops, at least one enemy regiment plunged into the woods to the south, and Hancock saw other Southern troops enter the woods north of the field. Drawn from the 7th Maine and 33rd New York, Federal skirmishers engaged enemy troops in the northern woods. Correctly reading the volley fire and pop-pop-pop of individual rifle shots, Hancock withdrew his infantry.

"As I faced my men about to obey this order, the bullets were already whistling through the air," Burnham recalled. His regiment, the 5th Wisconsin, and the artillery (its progress slowed by muddy soil) "retired [some 500 yards] to the fort in good order," then turned 180 degrees to find the nearest Confederate troops "a few hundred yards" away.[35]

During that withdrawal, Hancock watched from the saddle as Burnham's annoyed skirmishers whirled angrily and fought the pursuing Southern skirmishers "with the greatest pertinacity" and actually stopped the enemy charge in their sector. Burnham halted the 6th Maine, which "faced to the front [west], and waited to collect their skirmishers," Hancock said.[36]

Burnham astutely noticed another potential problem developing on the battlefield as his infuriated skirmishers waged their own private war; doing so "uncovered" the left flank of the 5th Wisconsin and provided an opportunity for charging Confederates to envelop Cobb's unit.

Burnham held his regiment in place, collected his errant skirmishers, and waited until the 5th Wisconsin drew even with the 6th Maine's right flank. Then Burnham pulled back in concert with Cobb, who never forgot Burnham's regiment-saving gesture.

As the artillery and infantry withdrew, "the 7th also faced about" and marched "steadily to the rear" toward the earthworks overlooking Cub Creek, C wrote. Anxious to join the fight, the men growled as they pulled back.[37]

Col. Edwin C. Mason had his men lie down. Hyde surreptitiously watched the Confederates charge: "a fine picture … they made," running "at the double-quick" diagonally across the plowed field toward Hancock's retreating regiments, he remembered.

Enemy troops could not see the 7th Maine boys lying "flat on the ground," said Hyde, stationed on regiment's left flank. Suddenly "I saw General Hancock galloping toward us, bare-headed, alone, a magnificent figure."

"Forward! Charge!" shouted Hancock, seizing the one chance to deflect the Confederate charge. Hyde remembered Hancock uttering profanity: "the air was blue all around him." The 7th Maine lads stood, lowered their bayonets simultaneously, "and with a roar of cheers" charged over the slight crest between them and the nearby Confederates.

Apparently winded by charging across the muddy field, enemy troops "seemed to dissolve all at once into a quivering and disintegrating mass and to scatter in all

Union Col. Edwin Mason
Photo courtesy of Maine State Archives

directions," Hyde realized. "We halted and opened fire."

Through the swirling gun smoke the 7th Maine boys watched enemy soldiers "falling everywhere" or waving "white handkerchiefs ... in token of surrender," Hyde said. His comrades rounded up 300 prisoners before sunset.[38]

And that's how the story would appear in the *Maine Farmer* and other newspapers. The 7th Maine fought gallantly at Williamsburg, news-hungry Mainers would learn in coming days—and of the 6th Maine Infantry, readers would learn little.

But the 7th Maine was not the only Union regiment to charge early that rain-soaked evening. All of the regiments went in with the bayonet, as their commanders indicated in their after-action reports.

Hancock rode to where the 6th Maine lads stood outside the Cub Creek earthworks, just emptied of its 33rd New York garrison.[39] "Colonel Burnham, put five companies of your regiment into this earthwork, and five companies to the left of it, and fight like—! Fight like—!" Charles Clark heard Hancock shout.

Burnham and Hancock later reported that four 6th Maine companies occupied the earthworks.

"In our rear was Queen's Run (Cub Creek), with no avenue of retreat except the narrow causeway across the dam," Clark realized. "If our lines were broken, destruction or capture was the sure fate which awaited us."[40]

Burnham waited. Then "we at once opened fire upon the enemy with such awful execution that it seemed as if every bullet picked its man," he told Washburn.

"With thinned ranks" the Confederates still advanced, then "halted and faltered" about "ten or fifteen rods from us," Burnham recalled. Hancock ordered a charge; "our forces moved steadily forward," Burnham wrote, implicitly including the 6th Maine in that advance.

"Panic stricken and dismayed, the rebels broke and fled as we approached them. A few volleys from our rifles completed the rout, and they cleared the field in wild disorder, leaving it literally black with their dead and wounded."[41]

Hancock reported the 5th North Carolina Infantry as "annihilated," with "nearly all of its superior officers ... left dead or wounded on the field." The 24th Virginia Infantry suffered heavy casualties, too, and "for 600 yards in front of our line the whole field was strewn with the enemy's dead and wounded," he noted.

Hancock reported enemy losses at 120 men killed, 250 men wounded, and 160 men captured. His ad hoc brigade lost 10 men killed, 88 men wounded, and 31 men missing, mostly skirmishers caught in the Confederate charge.

Burnham reported four men wounded, an astonishingly light toll that the 6th Maine would seldom replicate. The fighting over, his men soon "assisted in taking care of their wounded adversaries, until night put an end to their humane effort," Burnham now cast his warriors as angels of mercy.

At least 103 wounded Confederates were carried into the fort and placed on wooden boards to raise them above the earthen floor, described by Burnham as "a perfect bed of mud." Union troops spread their "woolen and rubber blankets" over the wounded enemy

Chapter 16: "Old Grizzly" Fights

troops to protect them from the sheeting rain.

Burnham painted a dark picture for Washburn: The bleeding prisoners emitted "groans and shrieks" that "pierced our ears and attested to the agonies they endured that weary night."[42]

Charles Clark remembered the Battle of Williamsburg as "a fight in a cloud-burst." That night he spread his woolen blanket on two fence rails, pulled a rubber blanket over his weary body, and "slept the sleep of utter fatigue and exhaustion.

"It made no difference that the rain poured in torrents, and the victims of the battlefield lay thickly around us," he admitted.[43]

With his May 24 report, Burnham hoped he had set the record straight with Washburn. "Much has been written by newspaper correspondents concerning this battle which is very wide of the truth," and "facts have been distorted until they are scarcely to be recognized."

As for the 6th Maine lads evidently overlooked by their home-state press, "by your bravery and steady discipline you saved the day," George McClellan told them during a dress parade on Tuesday, May 6. "You have gained honor for the army, for yourselves, and for the state which is proud to own you as her sons."[44]

Passing along McClellan's full comments to Washburn, Burnham implied that no higher praise could the 6th Maine garner than such recognition from "Little Mac."

~~~

1. Col. Hiram Burnham to Gov. Israel Washburn, May 24, 1862, Maine State Archives
2. The 10th Maine Infantry Regiment guarded the vital Baltimore & Ohio Railroad in late winter 1862. The 1st Maine Cavalry Regiment did not deploy to the Peninsula.
3. Letter by "F," July 14, 1862, published in *Daily Whig & Courier,* Thursday, July 24, 1862
4. Commanded by Col. David B. Birney, the 2nd Brigade served in the 3rd Division (Brig. Gen. Philip Kearny) of III Corps (Brig. Gen. Samuel P. Heintzelman).
5. During the Civil War, the Army designated its corps numerically (First, Second, Third, etc.). For brevity and clarity, the author uses the Roman numerals that were instituted for Army corps post-war.
6. Elijah Walker, *The Old Soldier: History of the Fourth Maine Infantry,* Tribune, Rockland, Maine, 1895, p. 22
7. Emulating an August 1861 mutiny by 2nd Maine Infantry soldiers who decided their enlistments had expired, most members of Co. H, 4th Maine Infantry, refused duty on Sept. 21. Claiming that their enlistments, too, had expired, the mutineers planned to return to Maine. Col. Hiram Berry, the regiment's commander, tried, unsuccessfully, to cajole the soldiers to end their revolt. Elijah Walker suggested that Berry turn over the mutineers to Col. John Sedgwick, the brigade commander; Sedgwick promptly swooped into the 4th Maine camp with a provost guard, arrested the mutineers, and assigned them to the 38th New York Infantry. Capt. William Pitcher of Bangor later brought a "new" Co. H to Virginia to join the 4th Maine.
8. Walker, *The Old Soldier*, p. 20
9. Thomas Worcester Hyde, *Following the Greek Cross: Or, Memories of the Sixth Army Corps,* Houghton, Mifflin, United States, 1894, pp. 37-38
10. Commanded by Col. Edwin C. Mason, the 7th Maine Infantry belonged to the 3rd Brigade (Brig. Gen. John

Davidson) of the same 2nd Division to which the 6th Maine was assigned. This divisional association affected both regiments during the Battle of Williamsburg.

11. *Machias Republican,* April 8, 1862
12. Though born in Massachusetts, Ermasus D. Keyes grew up in Maine. He graduated from West Point in 1832. Camp Keyes, the future headquarters of the Maine National Guard, was named for him.
13. Charles A. Clark, *Campaigning With the Sixth Maine,* The Kenyon Press, Des Moines, Iowa, 1897, p.15
14. James H. Mundy, *No Rich Men's Sons: The Sixth Maine Volunteer Infantry,* Harp Publications, Cape Elizabeth, 1994, pp. 58-59
15. Ibid., p. 61
16. Clark, *Campaigning,* pp. 15-16
17. Hyde, *Greek Cross,* p. 49
18. Burnham to Washburn, May 24, 1862, MSA
19. Brig. Gen. Winfield S. Hancock to Brig. Gen. William Smith, May 11, 1862. *Official Records, Series 1, Vol. 11, Part 1,* Chapter XXIII, No. 49, pp. 535-536
20. Some soldiers, including Burnham, identified the stream as Queen's Creek, which flows farther west.
21. Burnham to Washburn, May 24, 1862, MSA
22. 1st Lt. Andrew Cowan, *OR, Series 1, Vol. 11, Part 1,* Chapter XXIII, No. 48, p. 533
23. Burnham to Washburn, May 24, 1862, MSA
24. Clark, *Campaigning,* p. 16
25. A regular contributor to the *Maine Farmer* (a weekly newspaper dedicated to agriculture), "C" may have been Lt. Col. Selden Connor of Fairfield. No matter his identity, "C" enriched his skillfully written letters with vivid details.
26. C, letter of May 14, 1862, published by *Maine Farmer,* June 5, 1862
27. Hyde, *Greek Cross,* pp. 49-50
28. Hancock, *OR, Series 1, Vol. 11, Part 1,* Chapter XXIII, No. 49, p. 538
29. Burnham to Washburn, May 24, 1862, MSA
30. Hyde, *Greek Cross,* p. 50
31. *Maine Farmer,* June 5, 1862
32. Cowan, *OR, Series 1, Vol. 11, Part 1,* Chapter XXIII, No. 48, p. 533
33. Capt. Charles C. Wheeler, *OR, Series 1, Vol. 11, Part 1,* Chapter XXIII, No. 47, p. 531
34. Both battles were significant Union defeats in 1861.
35. Burnham to Washburn, May 24, 1862, MSA
36. Hancock, *OR, Series 1, Vol. 11, Part 1,* Chapter XXIII, No. 49, p. 539
37. *Maine Farmer,* June 5, 1862
38. Hyde, *Greek Cross,* pp.50-51
39. Hancock pulled out the three 33rd New York companies to reinforce the 7th Maine on his right flank.
40. Clark, *Campaigning,* pp. 17-18
41. Burnham to Washburn, May 24, 1862, MSA
42. Ibid.
43. Clark, *Campaigning,* p. 18
44. Burnham to Washburn, May 24, 1862, MSA

Chapter 17

ALL ASHORE WHO ARE GOING ASHORE

"My sick soldiers were scattered everywhere"

As she had so many mornings recently, Sarah Sampson awakened in an empty bed on Wednesday, May 7, 1862. Her husband, Lt. Col. Charles A.L. Sampson of the 3rd Maine Infantry Regiment, had left for the Peninsula weeks earlier as the regiment joined George McClellan's Richmond expedition.

Sarah missed him, missed their private conversations, and missed her "boys," the sick and wounded Maine men whom she had nursed since arriving in Washington the previous June.

Since Charles' departure, Sampson had stayed in Alexandria at the home of Lt. C.B. Ferguson, an Army quartermaster "whose family were friends of ours before we left home." The weeks spent there had refreshed the weary nurse, immersed in a household with "a little boy" on whom she doted.

"We stand him in the window with a little silk flag I have made for him, and when the Soldiers go by, he waves it and hurrahs, and they often bow to him," Sampson told Guy Howard.

Now fully awake in the Ferguson home on this May 7, Sampson arose to begin her morning routine. Momentarily she thought about her desire "to rejoin the regiment, which I hope may be very soon."

This Wednesday would see her desires granted.

During the 3rd Maine's journey to Washington, Sarah had befriended Col. Oliver Otis Howard and his younger brother and aide, Charles. Sarah was not a flirt batting her eyelashes to advance her husband's career; Charles, a ship's figurehead carver from Bath, had risen from captain to lieutenant colonel on his own merits.

The brothers Howard and other 3rd Maine men valued Sarah for her wit, ability, and compassion. A platonic friendship developed between her and Oliver Howard; she soon corresponded with Elizabeth Anne, the beautiful wife with whom Howard would be smitten all his life.

The women probably discovered a common bond; they had married their husbands on Valentine's Day 1855. Trusting her husband, Elizabeth apparently accepted Oliver's friendship with the Maine nurse, who occasionally wrote "my dear little Guy," born 10 months and two days after his parents' wedding. Grace Ellen and James Waite ("Jamie") Howard followed chronologically by late 1860.[1]

Until the 3rd Maine left for the Peninsula, Sarah spent much time daily in the regimental hospital, "moving with it from camp to camp, and whenever serious illness occurred, passed most of my time with the patients."

Her hair often tied in a bun, the demure Sampson nursed many sick soldiers; most recovered, some died. She noted that the first 3rd Maine soldier to die from illness was George I. Blaisdell of Co. I; he succumbed to diphtheria on July 28, 1861.[2]

Union 1st Lt. George W. Bicknell
Photo courtesy of Maine State Archives

The death of John W. Campbell, a 23-year-old private from Livermore in Androscoggin County, had particularly troubled Sampson. Assigned to Co. K, Campbell had contracted typhoid fever in late summer 1861 while the regiment was stationed at Camp Howard in the District of Columbia.

"Delirious all the time," the taciturn Campbell had "bled very profusely at the nose" as nurses cared for him. Soldiers often talked about their families and homes in Maine; Campbell "was very quiet during his sickness," Sampson noticed. He "made no mention of home, friends, living or dying."

John Campbell had died on September 16, 1861. While he lay in state in the 3rd Maine's camp, Oliver Otis Howard and Sampson "took a little walk together" about noon "to the beautiful little Cemetery" located across from the camp of the 23rd Pennsylvania Infantry.

They selected a burial site for the forlorn Campbell. Before his military funeral, Sampson snipped a lock of hair from his head and recovered "some pressed rose-leaves that had lain on his bosom." She "wrote a long letter to his wife (Lucy) ... giving her all the particulars of his sickness" and sealed it, the lock of hair, and the tea leaves inside an addressed envelope.[3]

By the time that Sarah Sampson took her breakfast on May 7, 1st Lt. George W. Bicknell was steering the men of Co. K, 5th Maine Infantry Regiment through "a dense piece of woods" near West Point, a backwater port "at the junction of the York and Pamunkey rivers" in Tidewater Virginia.

Adrenaline stifling his desire to yawn, the tired Bicknell and his men tromped through

Chapter 17: All Ashore Who Are Going Ashore

the "almost impassable" woods for a quarter mile around 8 a.m. He had seldom heard hostile gunfire since Manassas the previous July; now the heavy firing that had erupted minutes earlier grew louder every long stride that the 6-foot, 1¾-inch Bicknell took through the thick undergrowth.

Towering over many comrades, the dark-complexioned Bicknell had worked as a trader in Portland before joining the 5th Maine as a Co. H private in late June 1861. Talented with rifle and pen, he had been promoted to second lieutenant and then to his current rank as military duty and disease weeded out other officers.

Bored with wintertime guard duty near Washington, D.C., Bicknell had welcomed the regiment's transfer to the Peninsula in mid-April. For two weeks the 5th Maine's ship, the lice-infested steamer *John Brooks*, had moored amidst "the large number of transports" collected "at Poquosin flats, near the mouth of the York river" as George McClellan and his staff sorted out which division should go where on the lower Peninsula.

Put ashore on May 3 to reinforce a planned assault on Yorktown, the 5th Maine lads re-embarked two days later and sailed to Yorktown, just abandoned by Confederate soldiers. Venturing ashore in the rain as "severe cannonading" echoed from nearby Williamsburg, Bicknell toured the recently constructed enemy earthworks and "the old works erected by Washington and Cornwallis in ... the Revolution."

Escorted by five gunboats, the Union transports weighed anchor at 9 a.m., May 6 and steamed up the York River. Enjoying the "delightful" day, Bicknell noticed "the farms upon the banks of the river exhibited more ... thrift and prosperity than any we had seen before" in Virginia.

"Really, one felt almost at home as he gazed upon a type of old New England," he commented.

With the Navy gunboats probing for Confederate resistance afloat and ashore, the erstwhile fleet approached West Point, the eastern terminus for the single-track Richmond & York River Railroad. Two rivers—the Pamunkey to the west and the Mattaponi to the east—flowed past West Point to merge as the York River. Just around a hairpin turn in the Pamunkey lay Eltham's Landing, which served the fading Eltham Plantation.

Anchor chains rattled as the transports halted perhaps a half mile off the landing. After "a shell or two from our gunboats" chased away watching Confederate cavalry, Bicknell and the 5th Maine lads clambered overboard

Union Brig. Gen. Henry W. Slocum
Shown here as a Major General
Photo from Brady-Handy Collection, Library of Congress

onto pontoon boats that sailors rowed ashore.

Belonging to the 2nd Brigade (Brig. Gen. Henry W. Slocum) of the 1st Division led by Brig. Gen. William B. Franklin, the 5th Maine's soldiers scrambled ashore at the landing and captured Eltham Plantation, designated by McClellan as his first beachhead beyond Yorktown.

Engineers then assembled pontoon boats and other watercraft in a long line and decked them with lumber to construct a 400-foot floating wharf. Cannons and supplies flowed across it that night.

"Little Mac" intended for Union troops to advance from Eltham northwest along the Pamunkey to capture White House Landing, militarily strategic because the Richmond & York River railroad crossed the river there. The landing served White House, the New Kent County plantation owned in her first marriage by widow Martha Custis, who married George Washington in 1759.

Many Maine soldiers had excitedly studied Mount Vernon while sailing south along the Potomac River; now owned by Robert E. Lee's son, William "Rooney" Lee, "White House" meant nothing to men not yet familiar with the Lee clan.[4]

In planning his march on Richmond, McClellan had determined that White House Landing should serve as a supply base. By occupying West Point, Union troops secured the R&YR railroad, envisioned as an all-weather supply route for the Richmond advance.

The 5th Maine lads camped at Eltham Wednesday. When enemy troops started probing Union lines that night; Slocum turned out his regiments at 4 a.m., Thursday. Spread across "an open field" about "a half mile in diameter," the soldiers stood watch until released for breakfast, Bicknell noted.

Then Confederate Gen. John Bell Hood brought his brigade (comprising the 1st, 4th, and 5th Texas infantry regiments and the 18th Georgia) and Hampton's Legion against the Union pickets. Slocum's 1st Division advanced to meet the threat; a "sharp and severe" fight took place while Bicknell, Co. K, and Co. G under Capt. Alburn P. Harris deployed forward as skirmishers.

Confederate Gen. John Bell Hood
Photo by J.A. Sheldon

Fighting seesawed in the woods, and hard-pressed Federal troops fell back to where the gunboats could provide covering fire. Resulting in 186 Union and 48 Confederate casualties, the battle lasted until an enemy withdrawal around 6 p.m.

"Our loss was small, but our labor was great," Bicknell noted.[5]

Sometime that Wednesday and about 100 miles to the north and west, loud knocking erupted at the Fergusons' front door. The messenger standing there held a telegram addressed to Sarah Sampson.

Calmly unfolding the paper, she read the few words—and exploded into motion.

Charles Sampson had fallen ill "with severe neuralgy" soon after arriving on the Peninsula. Granted permission to report to a hospital at Fort Monroe, he had telegraphed Sarah at Alexandria to join him at the tip of the Peninsula.[6]

She was needed by her husband—and would be needed ultimately by the 3rd Maine lads whom she viewed almost as her adopted children. Sent via an underwater cable strung earlier in the war from Fort Monroe to Cape Charles on the Delmarva Peninsula,[7] Charles's telegram commenced the great adventure that would make Sarah Sampson a legend among hard-bitten Maine warriors.

Maine Sen. Lot M. Morrill
Photo circa 1860-65

While caring for the 3rd Maine soldiers at Camp Howard, she had cultivated influential friends in Washington. After she initiated a chance meeting on July 23, 1861, President Abraham Lincoln had told Sampson, "When you come to Washington, I want you to be sure to come and see me."

She "did go to see him and always found him ready to grant favors, and to help me in every way that he could."[8]

Armed with her husband's telegram, Sampson crossed the Potomac River on May 7 to meet with Maine Senator Lot M. Morrill, the immediate gubernatorial predecessor to Israel Washburn Jr. Morrill, a Democrat whose anti-slavery leanings had led him to join the Republican Party in the mid-1850s, listened to the persuasive Sampson; he "obtained for me a 'pass, and transportation for my supplies to the army for three months,'" she reported.

Sampson hurried back to the Ferguson home to thank her benefactors and to pack.

That evening, a visibly sick Charles Sampson briefly visited with Oliver Otis Howard at his brigade headquarters at Yorktown. "He looks poorly & discouraged," Howard observed.

Sampson shared the news about the telegram sent to Alexandria. "It will do him some good to see his wife," Howard thought.[9]

Early on Thursday, May 8, Sarah Sampson bundled herself and "four large cases of medical

White House Landing, Pamunkey River
Unloading bales of hay for Union Army from barges during the Civil War. The sidewheel steamers Wenoah and New Jersey are in the background.
Photo from Library of Congress

supplies" onto a train for Baltimore, where she boarded a steamer sailing for the Peninsula. Requiring about a day to reach Old Point Comfort, the ship turned into Hampton Roads, where the ghostly masts of the sunken USS *Cumberland* still rose above the sea west of Fort Monroe.

The initial major staging area for Union troops inbound to the Peninsula, the fort now served as a clearinghouse for the outbound Federal sick and wounded. The Army of the Potomac had recently fought a nasty battle at Williamsburg, and as her ship approached Monroe, Sampson noticed "the steamers loaded with the wounded at the wharves" jutting into Hampton Roads.

Immediately going ashore and to work, Sarah discovered that the "Hygeia Hospital was full." Then she "received conveyance to Chesapeake and Hamilton Hospitals, where I found many of our 7th Maine [Infantry] Regiment," wounded at Williamsburg four days earlier.

That night a Fort Monroe ordnance officer and his wife sheltered Sampson in their home; the wife apparently joined her in caring for the Maine soldiers sheltering in the temporary military hospitals. Expressing the goals that carried her throughout the war, Sampson observed, "My sick soldiers were scattered everywhere, and everywhere I would seek for them."

She worked at the Fort Monroe hospitals as McClellan's army pushed toward Richmond. Their days hazily predictable, Sampson and other nurses spent "all our spare time ... with the wounded.

Chapter 17: All Ashore Who Are Going Ashore

"Every moment was precious to somebody" on a hospital cot, she realized, and "those who were the most feeble, or wounded in the face, were our special care." Men with shattered or missing jaws could not eat Army-issued hardtack and salted meat; for these men "we prepared the most delicate food and nourishing drinks," Sampson said.

Finished with routine patient care, nurses "wrote letters for the soldiers" and, as the Virginia sun settled beyond the James River, "did our cooking for the following day," Sampson described their various duties.[10]

The worn-out Charles Sampson recovered at Fort Monroe for a few weeks before rejoining the 3rd Maine, assigned along with the 4th Maine to the 2nd Brigade led by Brig. Gen. David Birney. Part of the III Corps commanded by Brig. Gen. Samuel P. Heintzelman, the brigade camped between Seven Pines and the Chickahominy River in late May.

With the Peninsula's muddy roads hindering wheeled transportation, George McClellan sent troops to seize White House Landing. With the gunboats *Chocura*, *Maratanza*, *Marblehead*, and *Sebago*[11] navigating the curving channel of the Pamunkey River, Union cavalrymen approached White House Landing in the early afternoon on May 11.

Though ambushed, the Federal troopers deployed artillery and chased off the Confederates, who had burned the Richmond & York River Railroad bridge over the Pamunkey. White House Landing, site of the White House Plantation that was then home to Robert E. Lee's ailing wife, Mary, fell to the Union riders on May 12.

"This was the beautiful and romantic spot where [George] Washington wooed, won, and married Mrs. [Martha] Custis," noted Charles A. Clark. He strode into White House Landing

Union soldiers at a Sanitary Commission Tent, White House Landing
Taken during the Civil War; printed between 1880-89.
Photo via Library of Congress

with the 6th Maine Infantry Regiment soon after Confederate troops left.

Hiram Burnham assigned the 5-foot, 7½-inch lieutenant and his company to guard White House on Wednesday, May 14, a week after her husband's telegram propelled Sarah Sampson toward the same destination.

Aware that White House belonged to William "Rooney" Lee, Clark stepped inside the mansion. "In the hall was posted a notice in feminine writing, which besought the Yankee vandals and invaders to respect and hold sacred the spot around which clustered so many memories of Washington," Clark noticed.

"In the dining room was a like notice on the dining table, which contained the information that it was the table from which Washington had eaten his wedding breakfast," he said.

Burnham ordered Clark to bar entry to White House and its ground everyone lacking a pass. Up rode "a distinguished Union general and his staff" lacking "the necessary credentials," Clark said. "I wheeled my guard with fixed bayonets" to stop the glittery cavalcade and send it packing.

Another company relieved Clark's at noon on Thursday, May 15 as Sarah Sampson cared for her patients in the Fort Monroe hospitals. She would step ashore at White House Landing within three weeks.[12]

Bicknell and the 5th Maine and Clark and the 6th Maine had long since marched west toward Richmond.

~~~

1. Sarah Sampson, April 14, 1862 letter to Guy Howard, O.O. Howard Papers, Bowdoin College.
2. "Mrs. Sampson's Report," *Annual Report of the Adjutant General of the State of Maine, 1864-1865,* pp. 108-109
3. Sarah Sampson, October 22, 1861 letter to Oliver Otis Howard, Howard Papers, Bowdoin College.
4. The White House in Washington, D.C., was informally referred to as such before the Civil War, but not officially until 1901. It is unlikely that the soldiers would have known any other meaning for the term.
5. Rev. George W. Bicknell, *History of the Fifth Regiment Maine Volunteers,* Hall L. Davis, Portland, Maine 1871, pp. 84-93
6. Oliver Otis Howard, May 7, 1862 letter to Elizabeth Anne Howard, O.O. Howard Papers, Bowdoin College
7. James Tertius deKay, Monitor, Walker and Company, New York, N.Y., 1997, p. 173
8. "Famous Nurse," *The Bath Independent,* Saturday, Aug. 18, 1906, Bath Historical Society
9. Howard to Elizabeth Anne Howard, May 7, 1862, Bowdoin College
10. "Mrs. Sampson's Report," *Annual Report of the Adjutant General of the State of Maine, 1864-1865*, pp. 109-110
11. The 845-ton sidewheel steamship USS *Sebago* was launched in late November 1861 at the Portsmouth Navy Yard in Kittery. The yard reconditions nuclear submarines today.
12. Col. Charles A. Clark, *Campaigning with the Sixth Maine,* The Kenyon Press, Des Moines, Iowa, 1897, pp. 11-12, pp. 19-20

Chapter 18

THEY RODE TO DELAY "STONEWALL" JACKSON

"Struck by a shell which nearly severed his right arm"

Despite the desire of Jonathan Prince Cilley to get on with the business of whacking Confederates, the Federal government had other plans for the 1st Maine Cavalry Regiment. Rather than keep the unit intact, on Saturday, March 29, the War Department assigned companies A, B, E, H, and M to a "Railroad Brigade" guarding the Baltimore & Ohio Railroad. The regiment's other companies trotted off to a camp in northern Virginia.

Brigade command fell to Col. Dixon S. Miles, a 38-year career Army officer recently recalled from an eight-month leave of absence for supposedly being drunk during the Battle of Bull Run. Based at Harpers Ferry, he assumed responsibility for preventing Confederate troops and guerrillas from "burning bridges" and "tearing up track" along the strategic B&O, recalled Edward Parsons Tobie, then assigned to Co. H, 1st Maine Cavalry.

A 23-year-old Lewiston printer when he mustered with the regiment on Halloween 1861, the blue-eyed, blond-haired Tobie stood an average 5 feet 7 inches, about the right height for a cavalryman. Named for his father and officially a "Junior," the unmarried Tobie would often turn up where the shooting was the heaviest.[1]

The irony of guarding a railroad was certainly not lost on the troopers of companies A and E, who with their horses had left Augusta by train after dark on March 14. Some 12 miles south in Richmond in Sagadahoc County, the last two boxcars containing Co. E troopers and their horses had uncoupled from the train and tipped over.

"Fortunately, no one was hurt," Tobie said. Eight men and horses crammed into the remaining cars for the journey south. The other eight troopers and their bruised horses returned to Augusta to catch a future train.[2]

Reflecting the Army's inept handling of cavalry, Miles scattered the five Maine companies along the B&O line, with Cilley and Co. B stationed at Great Cacapon River.[3] Protecting the railroad "was for the most part arduous and tiresome ... the hardest part of the service, being

Union Col. Dixon S. Miles, c. 1860-62
Photo via Library of Congress

Union Maj. Gen. Nathaniel Banks, c. 1861
Photo via Library of Congress

dull, as well as hard and constant work," Tobie remembered.[4]

Each post along the B&O was held by cavalry and infantry. The latter was assigned "to guard the railroad and bridges by day and night," while the cavalry scouted "the neighborhood and places of rebel resorts," Pvt. Isaac B. Harris of Appleton wrote from "Camp Allen, Great Cacapon, Morgan Co., Va." in mid-April.

The Co. B boys garrisoned Great Cacapon with an infantry company from the 54th Pennsylvania Infantry. Stationed at Harpers Ferry, the Co. M troopers shared guard duty with a company from the 10th Maine Infantry Regiment.[5]

The Maine troopers chased guerrillas, took some prisoners and their horses,[6] and stayed glued to the strategic railroad bridges that, if destroyed, could disrupt train service for days or weeks.

A B&O train carried Cilley and Co. B west to Great Cacapon River from Harpers Ferry.[7] The trip extended into the night; when the train paused briefly at a rural station, Cilley found the conductor talking with the engineer in the engine cab.

Cilley expressed his concern "that it would be difficult and dangerous to unload [the] horses from the cars at night." He hoped the conductor, who was responsible for the train and its passengers, would take the horses' welfare into consideration.

"Sir, the train is under your command," the conductor replied.

Experiencing "the delicious feeling of authority," Cilley responded, "You will go to the nearest turn-out in the vicinity of Great Cacapon, and wait on the turn-out till morning."

The train proceeded to Great Cacapon after sunrise and unloaded the horses and men.[8]

On May 9, the five 1st Maine Cavalry companies received orders from Miles to "March forthwith via Winchester to New Market" and "wait for nobody, but be in haste." Cilley and the other captains must leave "sick men and disabled horses" behind and take "plenty of ammunition."[9]

Just four days earlier, Confederate troops had roughly handled the Army of the Potomac in steady rain during a sharp fight at Williamsburg, Virginia. The Confederates had withdrawn northwest along the Peninsula toward Richmond; the Army of the Potomac, which began its vaunted march into history at Yorktown in April, lumbered after the Southern troops.

Meanwhile, Confederate Gen. Thomas "Stonewall" Jackson and his army lurked in the Shenandoah Valley. Fearful that Jackson's men might erupt from the Valley to swoop upon Washington, President Abraham Lincoln and Secretary of War Edwin Stanton kept thousands of troops near the capital.

The War Department assigned Maj. Gen. Nathaniel Banks and his V Corps to bottle up Jackson in the Valley so they could not reinforce Confederate troops defending Richmond. Banks needed more cavalry, hence the May 9 orders hurrying the 1st Maine to Winchester.

Banks moved his troops "up" the Valley,[10] and his cavalry regiments pulled picket duty and scouted as directed. Michigan and Vermont cavalrymen rode with their Maine counterparts; "we are in the extreme front [of the V Corps], with nothing between us and the enemy but our pickets," George A. Bartlett of Co. M commented.[11]

Recently promoted Lt. Col. Calvin Douty of Dover[12] led companies B, H, and M to Woodstock on Tuesday, May 20 and "had a smart skirmish" with enemy troops there. Jonathan Cilley watched as 2nd Lt. Frank Cutler of Union, Maine, took some Co. B troopers and charged the Confederates, chasing them through Woodstock.[13]

Two days later, troopers from companies H and M skirmished with Confederates near Strasburg. Tobie thought that "these skirmishes, in which the men gave evidence that

Confederate Gen. Thomas "Stonewall" Jackson
Jackson's Chancellorsville Portrait, taken at a Spotsylvania County farm on April 26, 1863, seven days before he was wounded at the Battle of Chancellorsville.
Photo via Library of Congress

Confederate Gen. Richard S. Ewell
Photo via United States National Archives and Records Administration

Union Lt. Col. Calvin Douty
Photo courtesy of Maine State Archives

they had in them such stuff as cavaliers are made of,[14] were good training for what was soon coming."[15]

He was partially correct.

Banks fretted about Jackson, whose army apparently vanished somewhere beyond Strasburg. In a stunning maneuver, Jackson sidestepped the road-bound Union troops and, screened by Massanutten Mountain and the Blue Ridge, slipped his army east through the Luray Valley.[16]

On Friday, May 23, Jackson's troops attacked and all but annihilated an isolated Union garrison at Front Royal. From there Jackson intended to march north and capture Winchester, thus trapping all Union troops remaining in the Valley as far away as Strasburg.

Banks learned about Jackson's Front Royal attack on Friday evening. Knowing that he was heavily outnumbered, he ordered his men to march for Winchester; a long wagon train hauling munitions and sick and wounded soldiers departed Strasburg around 9 a.m., Saturday, May 24. Some infantry went with the slow-moving wagon train.

Banks ordered Brig. Gen. John Porter Hatch and his cavalry to guard the army's rear. In their camp near Tom's Brook, the 1st Maine Cavalry troopers received orders to march at 2 a.m.;[17] saddling up, the men rode north in Saturday's rainy pre-dawn darkness.

Hatch halted his cavalry at Middletown, a somnolent village on the Valley Pike from which "the crop [Chapel] road" ran 7½ miles east "to the Front Royal Pike," Archibald G. Spalding informed Maine Governor Israel Washburn Jr.[18] The crop road intersected the Front Royal Pike at Cedarville; Confederate troops led by Gen. Richard S. Ewell had already passed through that village while en route to Winchester.[19]

Cedarville, Middletown, and Winchester formed a rough right triangle, with the Front Royal Pike from Cedarville to Winchester being the hypotenuse and Middletown being the right angle. Jackson was hurrying his army to Winchester to trap and destroy the retreating Union army.

Banks remained uncertain as to Jackson's location and troop strength. In perhaps the first strategic application of his under-strength cavalry, he told Hatch to find Jackson. Hatch assigned the mission to Douty and "his battalion and two companies of the [1st] Vermont cavalry."[20]

Douty ordered company commanders to send sick soldiers and unhealthy horses on to Winchester. Inspecting his Co. B troopers and their mounts, Cilley saw Pvt. Charles A. McIntyre swaying on his feet beside his horse.

A pale countenance and swollen face indicated that the young cavalryman, "a boy I had enlisted in Warren in front of the schoolhouse where he was a pupil," was obviously sick, Cilley realized.

"What is the matter?" he asked.

"Mumps," McIntyre replied.

Confederate Brig. Gen. Turner Ashby
Image probably drawn from a photo after his death.
Photo via Library of Congress

Union Gen. John Porter Hatch
Photo taken during the war.
Photo via Library of Congress

Cilley ordered him to "fall out" and join the other sick troopers.

"You enlisted me for active cavalry service, and now with the first chance of a fight you order me to the rear," McIntyre responded, refusing his captain's directive. He rode with Cilley toward Front Royal.[21]

Riding through a rain-dampened landscape, Douty led the five 1st Maine Cavalry companies and two 1st Vermont Cavalry companies—A and C, commanded by Maj. William Collins—toward Cedarville. The crop road[22] passed through fields and scattered woods; the Union troopers ran into Confederate soldiers about 1½ miles west of the Front Royal Pike.

An initial exchange of gunfire tumbled the Confederates back for about a mile into "the main body of the army" sent from Cedarville "to strike the [Valley] turnpike near Middletown" and possibly trap Banks and his army, noted "Stonewall" Jackson.[23]

Douty's cavalrymen then encountered "an old woman," possibly a Unionist. She urged Douty to retreat; while Ewell advanced on Winchester, Jackson had marched west on the dirt road to cut off Banks at Middletown.

If Ewell and Jackson sprang their trap, Banks the cat would never get out of the bag; neither would Douty and his 400 men.

Likely thanking the woman for her information, Douty told her not to worry because 40,000 Union soldiers approached from the west. The informer scuttled away; Douty deployed his men "in [a] line of battle in front of a large belt of timber which extended on both sides of the road," Tobie said.

Skirmishers probed east, discovered advancing Confederate cavalry commanded by Turner Ashby, and fired; two Confederates fell. Additional shooting broke out, and Jackson, who was accompanying Ashby and his mixed command of artillery, cavalry, and infantry, realized that he might be facing a Union attack.

Possibly fulfilling a double agent's role, the woman who had recently spoken with Douty now told Jackson about the "forty thousand Yankees" approaching his left flank. While they could see Douty's riders spread along the tree line, Ashby and Jackson could not see what the woods might conceal.[24]

Confederate gunners unlimbered their cannons and fired on the distant Union soldiers and into the trees to flush out hidden troops. Ashby's artillery drew no counter-battery fire, sent no infantrymen scurrying for cover. Only cavalry opposed some of Jackson's best troops, and cavalry could not hold long against artillery and infantry.[25]

But the resolute Douty bought time for the Union troops scurrying north on the Valley Pike behind him. He gradually pulled back his men; for the next four hours, and despite being outnumbered about ten to one, he utilized "every advantageous spot of ground in checking the advance of the entire rebel force on the dirt road to Middletown," Tobie recalled.[26]

Armed only with "pistols and sabres," the Union troopers withdrew through the scattered woods and across adjoining fields, Cilley said. One Maine cavalry captain led his company in a successful charge against Confederate troops; Cilley questioned the charge's necessity, but with no Union men lost, the action was moot.

Douty's appearance upset Confederate plans. "Jackson halted his army on the Front Royal

Chapter 18: They Rode to Delay "Stonewall" Jackson

Molly Camel Run, where Cilley's Yankees ran into the Confederates
Riding east from Middletown in the Shenandoah Valley on May 24, 1862, troopers from the 1st Maine Cavalry Regiment (five companies) and the 1st Vermont Cavalry Regiment (two companies) encountered the advancing Confederate of Turner Ashby at Molly Camel Run about 1½ miles west of Cedarville, just outside Front Royal. The Yankee cavalry approached from the right, Ashby's Confederates from the left.
Photo by Brian F. Swartz

pike, and sent all his cavalry, one battery, and a portion of his infantry (300 Louisianans from "Wheat's Tigers")[27] ... to repel Douty's attack and ascertain his strength," Cilley said. Jackson also ordered Richard Ewell, then not far from Winchester, to halt while the Union threat from Middletown was assessed.

The sun gradually appeared and dried the muddy roads as, a few miles to the west, the cumbersome Union wagon train and its escorting infantry moved "in a straggling manner on the Strasburg pike" toward Winchester, Cilley learned after Douty's battalion trotted into Middletown about 2:30 p.m.[28]

Douty's brilliant delaying tactics had cost the Federal Treasury Department one horse. Multiple communications failures would soon cost the Treasury a great deal more.

Hatch sought to concentrate his cavalry at Middletown, but the Union rearguard (more 1st Vermont companies and the 5th New York Cavalry) had gone missing "up" the Valley Pike.[29] Now Douty and his men trotted into Middletown; ordered to hold the village until

Banks passed through en route to Winchester, Hatch told Douty to form his men in line of battle and fend off the Confederates chasing him.

Banks, however, was already some distance safely beyond the village—and he had not told Hatch. That mistake held the Union cavalry in Middletown too long. Even as Douty deployed his companies into a skirmish line, Turner Ashby abruptly turned the tables.

"Suddenly his [Jackson's] artillery was seen to debouch from the woods in our rear, which fact I instantly communicated to Lieutenant Colonel Douty, who was mounted near me, at the same time handing him my glass," William Collins said.

"The order to mount was quickly given by him, and the rear guard drawn in," he recalled.

Rather than directly attack Middletown, "the enemy, quietly and without being perceived, moved a large force of cavalry, infantry, and artillery to the pike [on rolling high ground north of the village], thus getting ... between him [Hatch] and the main column," Tobie suddenly realized.[30]

"We were drawn up on the turnpike," reported Capt. George M. Brown of Co. M and Bangor. "It was a trying ordeal to see the cannon approaching and taking position within a thousand yards of us, while their infantry had formed behind a stone wall within three hundred yards of us, with another line across the turnpike half a mile in front."

Deploying six cannons, two Confederate artillery batteries—Brown counted only one—fired; a few Union cavalrymen noticed two rifled cannons were "throwing shells." The first salvo struck several Union wagons, plugging the Valley Pike apparently well out of sight of the Union cavalry.

"We were drawn up on the turnpike" as the rifled cannons shelled the horsemen and Confederate infantrymen fired "at [a] safe distance," Brown wrote.

"We were actually a stationary target for them to practice upon," he said. "The courage of our men was tried to the utmost, and not found wanting" as Confederate shells shrieked into Middletown and exploded.

"Not a man left his place," Brown stated.[31]

In the Co. A ranks, Pvt. Clifford N. Mayo of Hampden noticed that initially most Confederate shells "were passing over our heads. But soon they got better range, and then the shells commenced falling amongst us."[32]

Enemy troops blocked potential escape routes to the north and east. Brown noticed "several streets leading to the left [west] by which we might have escaped." The order to retreat did not come as the minutes passed; the cavalrymen and the horses endured the shelling for perhaps a half hour.

Brown "rode up and down the company, talking to and encouraging" his men "to keep their places in the ranks ... I could see in every eye that steady look which convinced me they would follow wherever I led."[33]

Still wearing a cavalry captain's yellow bars, Jonathan Prince Cilley led his company through an orchard.[34] Artillery shells exploded in the trees or plunged through their branches to blow apart in the open; to calm his nervous troopers, Cilley assured them that the noise was much worse "than the actual danger," much like a dog's bark being worse than its bite.

Chapter 18: They Rode to Delay "Stonewall" Jackson

Frank Cutler rode near Cilley as the enemy "shells flew very thick" in the orchard. Suddenly a shell (either a solid cannonball or a shard from an exploding shell) struck Cilley "on the right arm" about three inches below the shoulder, knocked him from his horse, and shattered the bone of his arm" without "severing the main artery," according to Cutler.[35]

"I was in a little orchard looking at them [the enemy], when they threw their first shell," a Maine newspaper subsequently quoted an unidentified Co. B trooper. The shell "came crashing through the trees, knocked me from my horse, burst and mortally wounded Maj. Cilley, who was with me."[36]

"The first man that was hit [by enemy shelling] was Capt. Cilley of Company B," said Pvt. Clifford N. Mayo. "A shell struck him on the shoulder, and took his arm off.

"I was just ahead of him, and saw him fall," Mayo attested. "It is supposed that he was mortally wounded."[37]

Cilley "was struck by a shell which nearly severed his right arm, leaving only a partial connection of skin" and bone, Archibald Spalding informed Israel Washburn.[38]

Tobie watched the explosion hurl Cilley from his horse "in much the deliberate manner in which a squirrel falls to the ground when shot."

Dismounting, Cutler ran to his downed captain "and picked him up" before "cutting of[f] his shirt sleeves to see the wound."[39]

The avenging angel was a goner.

~~~

1. Edward Parsons Tobie, *Soldiers' File*, Maine State Archives
2. Edward Parsons Tobie, *History of the First Maine Cavalry, 1861-165*, First Maine Cavalry Association, Emery & Hughes, Boston, 1887, pp. 26, 28
3. Army brass habitually broke up cavalry regiments and lessened their "hitting power" by scattering companies hither and yon on guard and scouting duty and using individual cavalrymen as headquarters' couriers.
4. Tobie, *History*, p. 28-29
5. *Maine Farmer*, Thursday, May 8, 1862
6. Throughout the Civil War, captured horses invariably vanished into the victor's ranks. A Maine trooper might swap his worn-out nag for a captured thoroughbred. The physical condition of Confederate horses deteriorated so much that by late in the war, a Confederate trooper would be pleased to capture a Union cavalryman and his well-fed horse. The Union soldier walked into captivity; the Confederate rode to battle on a healthy mount.
7. Then located in Virginia, both sites are now in West Virginia.
8. Tobie, *History*, p. 31
9. Eve Anderson, *A Breach of Privilege: Cilley Family Letters 1820-1867*, Seven Coin Press, Spruce Head, Maine, 2002, p. 433
10. General directional movement in the Shenandoah Valley is based on the Shenandoah River, flowing from the southwest (upriver or "up" the Valley) to the northeast (downriver or "down" the Valley) to reach the Potomac River at Harpers Ferry.

11. George A. Bartlett, letter of May 18, 1862; cited in *Daily Whig & Courier,* Thursday, May 29, 1862
12. Older than most 1st Maine troopers, Douty was sheriff of Piscataquis County when he joined the regiment.
13. Tobie, *History,* pp. 31-32
14. Plantation-class officers leading Southern cavalry regiments viewed themselves as cavaliers in the tradition of medieval romances, especially those penned recently by Sir Walter Scott. The most famous Southern "cavalier" was James Ewell Brown "Jeb" Stuart.
15. Tobie, *History,* p. 32
16. While Strasburg marked the western terminus of the Manassas Gap Railroad linking the Valley with northern Virginia, Banks relied on the macadamized Valley Pike for transportation of his army's supplies.
17. Capt. George M. Brown, letter to wife, *Daily Whig & Courier,* Monday, June 2, 1862
18. Washburn sent Spalding and Col. John Goddard separately to investigate the disaster that engulfed the 1st Maine Cavalry at Middletown. Goddard was the regiment's first colonel; he had resigned on March 1, 1862.
19. Archibald G. Spalding, letter to Gov. Israel Washburn Jr., June 4, 1862, Maine State Archives
20. Tobie, *History,* pp. 33-34
21. Brevet Brig. Gen. Jonathan P. Cilley, "The Dawn of the Morning at Appomattox," *Military Order of the Loyal Legion of the United States,* Bowdoin College, 1886
22. Interstate 66 has partially erased this crop road.
23. Maj. Gen. T.J. Jackson, *Official Records, Series I, Vol. 12, Part I,* Chapter XXIV, No. 59, p. 703
24. Tobie, *History,* pp. 38-40
25. Although cavalrymen often fought dismounted during the Civil War, they lacked the "hitting power" afforded by infantrymen armed with longer-range rifled muskets.
26. Tobie, *History,* pp. 38-40
27. The nickname for the 1st Louisiana Special Battalion, organized in 1861 by Maj. Chatham Roberdeau Wheat.
28. Tobie, *History,* p. 40
29. Advancing Confederate troops had cut off these Union cavalrymen at Cedar Creek, necessitating a withdrawal to the west and a cross-country journey to reach Federal lines at Martinsburg, Virginia.
30. Tobie, *History,* p. 35
31. Brown, *Daily Whig & Courier,* Monday, June 2, 1862
32. Clifford N. Mayo, *Daily Whig & Courier,* Thursday, June 5, 1862
33. Brown, *Daily Whig & Courier,* June 2, 1862
34. Jonathan Cilley had recently been promoted to major to replace Douty, but had not received his commission.
35. Anderson, *Privilege,* p. 434
36. *Maine Farmer,* Thursday, June 12, 1862
37. Mayo, *Daily Whig & Courier,* Thursday, June 5, 1862
38. Spalding, letter to Washburn, MSA
39. Anderson, *Privilege,* p. 434

Chapter 19

SLAUGHTER AT MIDDLETOWN

"They shot down our horses that were in front"

As Frank Cutler knelt beside the prostrate Jonathan Cilley, some 1st Maine Cavalry troopers stared aghast. "This was the first shot that had taken effect in the regiment," realized trooper Edward Tobie, "and the first sight of a man wounded and apparently dead, caused some confusion in the ranks."[1]

Briefly leaderless, Cilley's Co. B troopers milled about inside the orchard where their captain lay dying. Confederate artillery fired incessantly as Lt. Col. Calvin Douty hustled to form his four other 1st Maine companies and two 1st Vermont Cavalry companies into column to evacuate Middletown.

Chaos engulfed Co. B; the time to go had come. "Upon arriving" at Middletown "we found the Valley turnpike crowded with the retreating Federal cavalry," noted Confederate Maj. Gen. Thomas J. Jackson.

He did not intend to let the enemy troopers escape.[2]

Douty ordered Maj. William Collins and his Vermonters to form "by fours" on the Valley Pike, just behind Brig. Gen. John Porter Hatch, his bodyguard troopers, and the 1st Maine Cav's Co. H, led by Capt. George J. Summat. A reticent Prussian who had fought Comanches out West with the regular Army,[3] Summat shared little about his life in Europe during his 20 months with the 1st Maine. Considered a good officer, he would gain a warrior's death in less than 13 months.[4]

Douty's Co. E (commanded by Capt. Black Hawk Putnam of Houlton) formed behind the Vermont troopers, and Co. M (Capt. George M. Brown of Bangor) formed behind Putnam's men. Commanded by 1st Lt. Llewellyn G. Estes of Old Town, Co. A formed behind Brown.[5]

Douty would follow after pulling Co. B together.

Cilley's men refused to abandon their captain in the orchard, so Cutler and other troopers carefully carried Cilley to a nearby house owned by John W. Wright, a Middletown businessman.[6] Isaac Harris, the captain's orderly, and Assistant Surgeon George Haley volunteered to care for the dying Cilley.[7]

The other Co. B troopers gradually coalesced behind the cavalry column. "The order was given to advance" by Hatch, who with his bodyguard and staff started north on the Valley Pike.[8]

Appearing earlier that day as the rain-causing cold front slipped east, the sun had quickly dried and hardened the muddy roads. Their horses kicking up dust,[9] Hatch and his caravan trotted north "some distance in advance of ... Douty's battalion," noticed Tobie, riding with Co. H.

Just north of Middletown, troopers suddenly spotted Confederate cannons looming near the Valley Pike, "which at that point was narrow, with a high [stone] wall on each side," Tobie said. Reinforced by Maj. Chatham Roberdeau Wheat's Louisiana infantry, Turner Ashby had plugged the Yankees' escape route by shelling and shattering several Union wagons on the Valley Pike.

Realizing the danger, Hatch and his entourage "turned off on a road leading to the left" and escaped "along a parallel road," said Tobie. Summat and Co. H followed Hatch.

After shoe-marking the Valley mud earlier that day, horse hooves now stirred up "a blinding storm of dust" that prevented Douty from seeing Hatch's sudden direction change and the broken wagons on the pike.

Confederate Maj. Chatham Roberdeau Wheat

Hatch apparently did not send back a staff officer to make sure the remaining Union cavalry took the correct road; this communications failure initiated the "Middletown Disaster."[10]

Lined in column of fours,[11] cavalrymen in the two 1st Vermont Cavalry companies and three 1st Maine Cavalry companies "drew sabers, and put our horses into a gallop," recalled Pvt. Clifford N. Mayo of Co. A. "The horses raised the dust so that we could not see the men ahead of us; of course, we could not see the enemy, but they could see just where we were."[12]

"In the dust and smoke we could not see that the head of our column had turned to the left, and broke for the woods," said Capt. George M. Brown of Co. M. "Companies A, E and M charged straight down the pike under a murderous fire."

Survivors estimated that they had ridden about 100 yards when, firing at extremely close range, enemy cannons eviscerated the cavalrymen. Brown watched horrified as "a section of fours in front of me was destroyed in an instant by a cannon ball" that, sizzling across the Valley Pike from right to left, knocked down all four men and their horses.[13]

As Co. A troopers rode along "the narrow road between two stone walls," Wheat's Tigers stood, slid their rifled muskets across the stone wall, and fired a volley from 20-30 feet away. "They shot down our horses that were in front, and the rest of us ... rushed right upon them,"

Mayo described the developing horror.[14]

That volley "killed and wounded horses and men" and also devastated the Vermont companies and the 1st Maine's Co. E.[15] His horse dying beneath him and "a shell" blowing a hole in the toe of his left boot, Capt. Black Hawk Putnam struggled to his feet; a horse racing along the turnpike knocked him down, the collision dislocating his shoulder.[16]

Troopers at "the head of the column" were "instantly stopped," Tobie said, "and the men next, unable to halt their horses ... and in turn pushed forward by the horses" behind them, "rushed on."[17]

Mayo and his Co. A comrades rode until "our horses lost their foothold, and fell down." He could not avoid the bloody roadblock caused where, "for a number of rods" along the turnpike, "men and horses were piled up two and three tier deep."[18]

Screams of pain and fear rose above the gunfire as "men and animals ... piled up in a mixed mass of humanity, horse-flesh and cavalry arms and equipments, in the utmost confusion," according to Tobie. Rearing horses caught bullets or shell fragments and toppled backwards to trap riders; men "were crushed by the horses and unable to extricate themselves."

The troopers had drawn their sabers prior to departing Middletown. In the wild stone wall-confined melee, men "were wounded by the drawn sabers of their comrades," and men

Marker in Middletown, Virginia today, commemorating battle of May 24, 1862
"Here Stonewall Jackson, on May 24, 1862, attacked Banks retreating
from Strasburg and forced him to divide his army."
Photo by Brian F. Swartz

and horses struggled even as enemy soldiers kept firing.[19]

Cavalrymen and horses piling up behind Mayo forced his horse "on the jam in front, and for about three minutes myself and my horse were wedged in so tight that neither of us could move." His horse, "being a powerful animal, made two or three tremendous springs, and, jumping over the dead horses around him stood across the road in a clear place."

Mayo sat "as well mounted as when I started" riding north from Middletown. He hurriedly looked for an escape route; then "a ball struck my horse, and he fell dead under me."[20]

His horse shot down, too, Brown "was carried into the chaos of struggling and wounded horses." Sliding from the saddle, he "jumped from horse to horse," reached the fence[21] on the western edge of the Valley Pike, and rallied "a few of my men who got out."[22]

Survivors scrambled to escape the carnage. Mayo "picked myself up, and gained the shelter of the [stone] wall" on the west side of the turnpike. Encountering "two or three of our men firing their pistols at some rebel cavalry in the field," he cocked his pistol, then "jumped up and fired over the wall."

Mayo dropped behind the sheltering stones, cocked his pistol again, and "fired two or three [more] times." His comrades emptied their pistols; hesitant to reload in such close proximity to the enemy, the other cavalrymen "left for the woods."

Seeing Confederate troops closing on him, Mayo "thought it about time to leave." He grabbed his saber, vaulted the stone wall, "jumped over the opposite fence [on the far side of the adjoining field], and started for the woods."

Musket "balls were flying around pretty thick" as the cavalrymen raced for the trees; Mayo could only watch helplessly as, just shy of cover, "one man just on the left of me fell."

Mayo saw cavalrymen "flying about in all directions in the woods." He joined eight troopers—including four from Co. A—and headed west beneath "tall oak trees" that provided little cover. Cattle or pigs apparently grazed in the forest, because the Maine cavalrymen saw "no underbrush" in which they could hide as Confederate cavalry chased the escaping troopers and captured some men.[23]

The shooting continued a while longer along the Valley Pike. From his vantage point, "Stonewall" Jackson observed how "in a few moments the turnpike, which had just before teemed with life, presented a most appalling spectacle of carnage and destruction. The road was literally obstructed with the mingled and confused mass of struggling and dying horses and riders.

"Among the surviving cavalry the wildest confusion ensured, and they scattered in disorder in various directions," said Jackson.[24]

Escaping the ambush proved difficult for the survivors. George Brown led his Co. M boys across a field "amid a hail of bullets." Unscathed, the Maine lads reached the woods "and gained cover," then encountered 2nd Lt. Ephraim H. Taylor, a Lisbon soldier who had "rallied the few [Co. M troopers] who were mounted, and retreated with them."

Amidst the sheltering trees, Brown met 1st Lt. John H. Goddard of Co. E and four of his men; the survivors furtively flitted across the Valley, walked 16 miles, and, after placing guards, slept "in the woods near Winchester till daybreak."[25]

The Death of Ashby
Confederate Brig. Gen. Turner Ashby and his cavalry had been a thorn in the sides of Union soldiers, but he ran out of luck on June 6, 1862. This image depicts the 1st Maryland (Confederate) Regiment at Harrisonburg, Virginia. Mounted is Confederate Col. Johnson; in the foreground is the fallen Ashby. His horse shot, Ashby drew his cavalry saber and hollered for his men to charge—and was immediately shot through the heart. There is debate today whether it was intentional, a lucky shot, or friendly fire.
Image from Battles and Leaders of the Civil War (1887)

Clifford Mayo and his comrades played hide-and-seek with pursuing Confederates "until near sunset, when we took a westerly course and struck for a small mountain about five miles distant."

Confederates almost caught the nine Maine cavalrymen as they crossed "a small field" at sunset; bullets whistling around them, the men safely reached nearby woods, and enemy soldiers did not push their pursuit.

The Union lads took stock of their situation. Each man armed with a pistol containing six bullets, the troopers figured they could get off 54 shots before being captured; "we made up our minds that no very small force should take us," Mayo said.

Stumbling into mountainous terrain after dark, the exhausted men slept about an hour without setting a guard. Mayo awoke with a start; rousting his comrades, who had appointed him as their leader, he led them north.

Sometime during the previous few weeks, Mayo "had stretched the map of Virginia" and memorized key points in the Valley until he "understood the lay of the land pretty well." Now, teamed with Pvt. William I. Burrill, a woods-wise youth from Levant, Mayo "kept a pretty straight course" across the mountain and reached lower terrain before dawn on Sunday.

"I took a course about two points east of the north-star and followed it all night," he explained his successful land navigation that ultimately stretched to 18 miles. After sunrise, Mayo figured that Winchester lay somewhere to the east; his party turned in that direction and confirmed the town's proximity while stopping at a house and speaking with its occupants.

Union prisoners in Richmond, Virginia

Union prisoners at Richmond might have ended up at Libby Prison. Brig. Gen. August Willich, captured at the Battle of Stones River, is reading in bed at right. *(Illustration by Act. Maj. Otto Boetticher, via Library of Congress)*

The wood engraving below shows a darker view, but perhaps with a ray of hope. The soldier in the left foreground is writing "United we stand, divided we fall"; in the background, one has written "The union must and shall be preserved." *(Photo from Harper's Weekly, 1862)*

Chapter 19: Slaughter at Middletown

Heavy gunfire from the direction of Winchester convinced Mayo, Burrill, and the others to keep moving north. "The country between the Blue Ridge and Alleghany Mountains is full of small mountains," Mayo said afterwards. "We kept to the sides and to the east of these mountains until we reached the Potomac" and Union lines.[26]

After Black Hawk Putnam vanished in the dust and blood on the Valley Pike, press accounts listed him as "killed."[27] Limping all the way, the tough Houlton soldier joined other uniformed refugees in the woods, quickly worked his way to freedom, and proved the press inaccurate.[28]

"Capt Putnam was among the last to come in," John Goddard assured Israel Washburn.[29]

Occupying the Middletown battlefield, Confederate soldiers rounded up prisoners, shot mortally wounded horses, and stripped saddles and harnesses from the dead mounts. Entering the house of John W. Wright, enemy soldiers captured the dying Capt. Jonathan Prince Cilley and his attendants, Assistant Surgeon Haley and orderly Harris.

When Haley was captured, his "very excellent set of surgical instruments (privately purchased) ... attracted the attention of one of Jackson's surgeons, who ... appropriated them to his own use," according to Tobie. Left with Harris to care for Cilley, Haley was disgusted with the theft.

Sgt. Alanson M. Warren of Co. M, 1st Maine Cavalry, marched into captivity with 41 other Maine troopers. Their route took the prisoners in sunshine and rain up the Valley to Waynesboro and then across the Blue Ridge, where they boarded a train at Charlottesville for transportation to Richmond.[30]

Captured at Middletown, Pvt. Robert Nutter of Co. E escaped at Mount Jackson and captured two Confederate infantrymen before reaching Union lines. He brought his prisoners with him.[31]

Confederate troops also captured 2nd Lt. Joseph C. Hill of Co. A and Kennebunk on May 24. The acting quartermaster of the 1st Maine Cavalry, he watched helplessly as enemy soldiers seized eight wagons under his command.

"He and the seven teamsters and the men that were with them were disarmed and a guard put over them," but their Confederate captors failed to notice a blacksmith hiding in a wagon, Goddard said.

When the opportunity arose, the blacksmith slipped Hill a loaded Colt revolver; suddenly leaping from the wagon, Hill fired and blew a Confederate trooper off his horse. Hill vaulted into the saddle and swiftly recaptured seven wagons and freed the Union prisoners with him.

Hightailing down the Valley, the former prisoners returned the wagons to Union lines.[32]

Not so Jonathan Prince Cilley and his attendants. Confirmed dead within a few days, he was likely confined immediately to a Virginia grave.

~~~

1. Edward Parsons Tobie, *History of the First Maine Cavalry, 1861-1865,* First Maine Cavalry Association, Emery & Hughes, Boston, 1887, p. 36
2. Maj. Gen. T.J. Jackson, *Official Records, Series I, Vol. 12, Part I,* Chapter XXIV, No. 59, p. 703

3. Summat was a first sergeant in Co. K, 5th U.S. Cavalry when he transferred to the 1st Maine Cavalry in fall 1861; doing so earned him a captain's commission.
4. Tobie, *History*, p. 578
5. Capt. Sidney W. Thaxter of Bangor, the commander of Co. A, was away on military business in Baltimore. He forever regretted not being present with his men at Middletown.
6. Private homes, churches, barns, and other buildings often sheltered wounded soldiers after a battle. Jonathan Cilley was the first wounded 1st Maine Cavalry trooper left behind during a retreat; he would not be the last.
7. Many wartime accounts recall the medical personnel who stayed with their patients even as enemy soldiers overran ad hoc field hospitals.
8. Modern Route 11.
9. The Virginia roads were infamous for their dustiness in dry weather and their muddiness in wet weather. Maine soldiers often groused in their diaries and letters about the Old Dominion's thick dust and glutinous mud.
10. Tobie, *History*, p. 36
11. Troopers rode four abreast in this particular formation.
12. Pvt. Clifford N. Mayo, *Daily Whig & Courier,* Thursday, June 5, 1862
13. Capt. George M. Brown, letter to wife dated May 26, 1862; quoted in *Daily Whig & Courier,* Monday, June 2, 1862
14. Mayo, *Daily Whig & Courier,* June 5, 1862
15. Col. John Goddard, letter to Maine Gov. Israel Washburn Jr.., June 5, 1862, Maine State Archives. Goddard, from Cape Elizabeth, served as colonel of the 1st Maine Cavalry Regiment until his March 1862 resignation. He was sent by Washburn to investigate the "Middletown Disaster."
16. *Daily Whig & Courier,* Friday, June 13, 1862
17. Tobie, *History*, p. 36
18. Mayo, *Daily Whig & Courier,* June 5, 1862
19. Tobie, *History*, p. 36-37
20. Mayo, *Daily Whig & Courier,* June 5, 1862
21. Brown specifically used the term "fence," implying that the Valley Pike was not wholly lined with stone walls at the ambush site.
22. Brown, May 26, 1862, quoted in *Daily Whig & Courier,* Monday, June 2, 1862
23. Mayo, *Daily Whig & Courier,* June 5, 1862
24. Jackson, *OR, Series I, Vol. 12, Part I*, Chapter XXIV, No. 59, p. 703
25. Brown, May 26, 1862, quoted in *Daily Whig & Courier,* Monday, June 2, 1862
26. Mayo, *Daily Whig & Courier,* June 5, 1862
27. *Daily Whig & Courier,* Saturday, May 31, 1862
28. Capt. Sidney W. Thaxter, letter to father, May 27, 1862, published in *Daily Whig & Courier,* Monday, June 2, 1862
29. Goddard to Washburn, June 5, 1862, MSA
30. Warren was paroled and released in mid-September 1862.
31. Tobie, *History*, pp. 42-45
32. Goddard to Washburn, June 5, 1862, MSA

Chapter 20

THE INQUIRY ABOUT THE MISSING

"I almost regret that I did not die with the brave fellows"

Reeling from the Middletown ambush, Lt. Col. Calvin Douty ordered his shattered battalion, now "reduced to a mere handful of men," to retreat south along the Valley Pike and take "an intersecting road" away from Middletown. The surviving troopers (including Co. B's, who escaped the ambush altogether) took "a detour to the left [westward]" and "after a hard march, rejoined the main column early the next [Sunday] morning" at Winchester, reported Edward Parsons Tobie.

"After a single hour's rest," the 1st Maine troopers awakened at 5 a.m. to "the rattle of musketry" as Confederate troops attacked Union soldiers at Winchester. Douty and his exhausted men joined the rear guard as Maj. Gen. Nathaniel Banks withdrew his V Corps toward Martinsburg. During an unheralded late-day action at Winchester, companies B and H won "new laurels while covering the retreat of the Tenth Maine Infantry ... by keeping a formidable regiment of cavalry at bay," Tobie recalled.[1]

Capt. George Brown of Co. M and 1st Lt. John H. Goddard of Co. E brought some troopers into Winchester after sunup on Sunday, May 25. Exhausted by their harrowing 16-mile overnight flight through the Shenandoah Valley, the men almost immediately joined the battle against Confederate troops attacking Winchester.

"A few of my men unfit for duty were in Winchester," Brown wrote his wife while referring to the sick men he had shipped north from Middletown 24 hours earlier. He rounded up 25 troopers and 21 horses from Co. M, but when ordered to fight, could only ride out with 2nd Lt. Ephraim Taylor "and fourteen men ... fit for service."

As Union troops retreated from Winchester, Co. M "rode nearly sixty miles" guarding the Federal right flank, Brown estimated. Dodging a company of Confederate cavalry, "my little squad ... finally tricked them and got away safely."

The 1st Maine Cavalry boys had ridden through hell. "I have lived weeks in the last forty-eight hours," wrote Brown, whose pitiful command forded the Potomac River on Monday morning and reported to a Union camp in Williamsport, Md. After eating dinner, he slept three hours, his first lengthy uninterrupted sleep since 2 a.m. Saturday.

"I am unhurt," the weary Brown assured his wife, "but I almost regret that I did not die with the brave fellows who are gone."[2]

Dashing from Baltimore, Capt. Sidney W. Thaxter of Bangor caught up with his shattered Co. A at Winchester on Sunday. He "sent forward with the baggage train the remnant of my company," then stayed with Douty and the two intact 1st Maine Cavalry companies, B and H, as they hovered near the 10th Maine Infantry Regiment "all the way from Winchester to Williamsport."[3]

The footsore men of the 10th appreciated the mounted protection afforded their Maine comrades. The infantrymen had marched fast and long down the Valley; with them, "so crippled from continuous travel that it was with the utmost difficulty he could proceed," came Major, the big Newfoundland cross-breed dog picked up in New Hampshire the previous October.

Union Col. John Goddard
Photo courtesy Maine State Archives

As the 10th Maine boys tramped toward the Potomac River, Confederate troops occasionally came up and harassed the column. At one point, Major "was very nearly taken prisoner by a dastardly attempt on the part of the enemy to 'cut off his rear,'" a human comrade related the dog's tale.

Now caught behind enemy lines, Major traveled two days until he sniffed a familiar odor: a Co. F soldier whom the dog "had never deigned to acknowledge in camp." Now "foot-sore and leg-weary" like any good infantryman, Major followed the Co. F lad back to the 10th Maine's camp, nosed about a bit, and finally raced to where his Co. H friends had set up shop.

"Major was too much of a soldier to tamely submit to such an indignity" as capture, a comrade noted.[4]

Maine cavalrymen trickled into Union lines for at least the next week. Brown mustered Co. M on Tuesday, May 27; he reported 48 men "present aggregate," ten men as "absent, sick, and on detached service," and 32 men as "lost in action and missing." That number included "three sergeants, four corporals and twenty-three privates."

Chapter 20: The Inquiry About the Missing

With only 26 horses, Co. M was essentially dismounted.[5]

The "Middletown Disaster" rocked Maine as the details (accurate and otherwise) filtered into the newspapers. The names of the missing, presumed dead, and wounded appeared in print; not always accurate, the lists provoked consternation and fear in homes across Maine.

From Co. E, "Capt. [Black Hawk] Putnam ... was taken prisoner unhurt," and "Orderly Sergeant [Lorenzo B.] Hill, and Bugler [Evander L.] French are known to be killed.[6] Only nine horses out of the company were saved," the *Maine Farmer* reported in its June 5 issue.[7]

The *Daily Whig & Courier* published running lists of the missing; in a May 27 letter to his father, Thaxter had learned initially that only 18 Co. A troopers had reached Winchester Saturday night. On Tuesday he identified the 39 troopers (including 34 privates) missing from Co. A by name and home town. He was running short of corporals, as four were lost somewhere in the Shenandoah.[8]

Writing from Williamsport on Wednesday, May 28, 1st Lt. Llewellyn G. Estes identified 13 Co. A troopers who "have reported themselves," including Corp. Alonzo Drew of Orono. William H. Luce of Burnham and George F. McDonald of Bangor "have been heard from," Estes reported.[9]

Directly writing Editor William H. Wheeler of the *Whig & Courier* on May 30, Brown identified 23 Co. M troopers still missing six days after the Middletown ambush. "We think it very probable that some may have escaped and got to Harpers Ferry," Brown said.[10]

Late on Friday, May 30, editor Wheeler opened an envelope that had just arrived with the evening mail. Written by Sgt. Julius M. Leuzarder of Lincoln, the letter identified by name and rank the 36 Co. E men who verbally answered roll call at Williamsport on May 26.

Bugler Charles W. Stetson of Mattawamkeag had been wounded, as had Leuzarder, pricked by a saber and struck in the head by "a musket ball." The wounds had not deterred him; "[I] consider myself worth two dead men yet," he bragged to Wheeler.[11]

"A soldier who was taken prisoner and escaped from the rebels at Mount Jackson,[12] reports that there were fifty of the 1st Maine Cavalry prisoners there," Sidney Thaxter wrote on June 7 in a brief summation that identified nine captured enlisted men, including Corp. Milton Chapman of Co. A.

That still left Thaxter with two missing corporals.[13]

News about particular soldiers slowly reached frantic relatives. Houlton's Black Hawk Putnam, "reported a prisoner has been heard from in the mountains, *slightly wounded*,[14] or bruised by horses, it is not known certainly which," the *Maine Farmer* reported on June 12 beneath "Additional From The Maine Cavalry."

A postscript noted, "We have since learned that Capt. Putnam reached here (the 1st Maine camp at Williamsport) on Monday, of the present week."[15]

Arriving simultaneously with the casualty lists from the 2nd Maine Infantry's bloody engagement at Hanover Court House, Virginia,[16] the destruction of three 1st Maine Cavalry companies and the loss of an unknown number of men and horses shocked Governor Israel Washburn Jr. He sent two investigators, Archibald G. Spalding and Col. John Goddard, to find out what had happened at Middletown.

A civilian, Spalding was a competent jack-of-all-trades often involved in projects for Adjutant Gen. John Hodsdon. Commissioned the first colonel of the 1st Maine Cavalry, Goddard had resigned on March 1, 1862; Washburn figured that surviving troopers would trust their former commander and spill the beans about what had occurred at Middletown and afterwards.

In a May 30 telegram to Maine Congressman Samuel Clement Fessenden, Washburn asked that "some one to be sent immediately to look after our wounded in the late disastrous retreat" from the Shenandoah Valley, Spalding wrote Hodsdon from Hagerstown on Monday, June 2. Fessenden had given Spalding Washburn's telegram on Friday and asked "that I would undertake that service."

He would. A Union man to the core, Spalding immediately left Washington. Presenting himself at the Williamsport headquarters of Maj. Gen. Nathaniel Banks on Sunday morning, he located the 1st Maine Cavalry camp and interviewed Douty.

Spalding informed Washburn that "our loss during this two days fight, although severe, is not near as great as, I think, was anticipated." More men had reached the camp; by noon, Sunday, 66 Maine troopers remained missing, including Jonathan Prince Cilley and his attendants.

With so many men missing, "the number of our killed & wounded cannot at present be definitely ascertained," Spalding wrote.

Since the 10th Maine Infantry had transferred to Martinsburg, Virginia, Spalding could not interview Col. George Beal about his regiment's losses.[17] His work done at Hagerstown, Spalding traveled to Frederick by stage on Tuesday and boarded a train for Washington.

Maine Rep. Samuel Clement Fessenden
Illustration by William P. Tomlinson, January 1, 1869

"You may expect to hear from me again," he promised Washburn.[18]

Arriving at Williamsport "after a tedious journey by stage from Frederick" on Wednesday, June 4, Goddard made the 1st Maine Cavalry rounds before turning in for the night. "Happy to say" that he discovered the five companies "in much better spirits and condition than could have been expected considering the fiery ordeal" at Middletown, he wrote Washburn the next day.

Covering eleven pages and written laboriously in cursive, the detailed report dedicated several lengthy paragraphs to the Middletown ambush and expended much ink on the numbers of men and horses lost. Goddard interviewed Brig. Gen. John Porter Hatch and Douty, whose surname both Goddard and Spalding spelled as "Doughty."

As for the 1st Maine's casualties, "I am satisfied that a large number of the missing are prisoners and that the loss of life was primarily among the horses as they [Confederate infantry] fired low" during the Middletown ambush, Goddard stated.

He had some good news for Washburn. "General Hatch, chief of cavalry, tells me that the conduct and coolness of Col Doughty, his officers and men during the entire two days of Banks' retreat and their steadiness under fire were equal to any veterans in the service," Goddard wrote.

"And he [Hatch] said all this and more to them last Tuesday [May 27] when he reviewed them," he told Washburn.

"Col [George] Beal also tells me that Col Doughty covered the retreat of the 10th Me all day on Sunday [May 25] in a most satisfactory maneuver and occupied the position of rear guard all Sunday night, standing by the side of their horses with nothing to eat for either horses or men," Goddard wrote.

After recuperating at Williamsport, Union troops would be "crossing the [Potomac] river today," Goddard wrote. Referring to the 1st Maine Cavalry, he noted that "they are in fine spirits and I hope their companies will be recruited up to their maximum numbers at once."[19]

Reaching Washington, Spalding wrote a well-detailed report to Washburn. Sharing intimate details of Valley geography and Middletown fighting that he had gleaned from 1st Maine Cavalry troopers, Spalding sent with his report (as had Goddard) "a full list of the missing from the Cavalry Battalion.

Union Col. George Lafayette Beal
Photo courtesy of Nicholas P. Picerno

"Some few I think may yet come in[,] but most of them are without doubt prisoners and will[,] I hope[,] be recaptured when we get Jackson and his Myrmidons," he believed.

"Lieut Coln Doughty has, during the trying scenes through which he, and his command were called to pass, evinced qualities, which fully justifies the confidence which has been reposed in him," wrote Spalding.

"The battalion of cavalry under his command are entitled to great credit for their prompt obedience of orders during the [Front Royal] reconnaissance [sic] and their coolness and bravery under fire," he noted.[20]

While Middletown had bloodied the 1st Maine Cavalry, the battle and the regiment's handling of the 10th Maine Infantry's retreat earned Douty and his survivors kudos from other warriors involved in the recent fighting—of that respect, Washburn could be assured.

~~~

1. Edward Parsons Tobie, *History of the First Maine Cavalry, 1861-1865,* First Maine Cavalry Association, Emery & Hughes, Boston, 1887, pp. 37-38
2. Capt. George M. Brown, letter to his wife, May 26, 1862, published in the *Daily Whig & Courier,* Monday, June 2, 1862
3. Capt. Sidney W. Thaxter, letter to his father, May 27, 1862, published in the *Daily Whig & Courier,* Monday, June 2, 1862
4. William E.S. Whitman and Charles H. True, *Maine in the War for the Union: A History of the Part Borne by Maine Troops in the Suppression of the American Rebellion,* Nelson Dingley Jr. & Co., Lewiston, 1865, p. 255
5. Capt. George M. Brown, morning report of May 27, 1862, published in *Daily Whig & Courier,* Monday, June 2, 1862
6. The press accounts often proved inaccurate. Hill was neither killed nor wounded at Middletown, but French was captured there. He was paroled in October.
7. *Maine Farmer,* Thursday, June 5, 1862
8. Thaxter, May 27, 1862, as published in the *Daily Whig & Courier,* Monday, June 2, 1862
9. *Daily Whig & Courier,* Tuesday, June 3, 1862
10. *Daily Whig & Courier,* Thursday, June 5, 1862
11. *Daily Whig & Courier,* Saturday, May 31, 1862. Promoted to first sergeant of Co. E on Sept. 1, 1862, the formidable Leuzarder would be medically discharged in late November.
12. Pvt. Robert Nutter of Co. A
13. *Daily Whig & Courier,* Friday, June 13, 1862
14. Italicized in original account
15. *Maine Farmer,* Thursday, June 12, 1862
16. The Battle of Hanover Court House in Virginia took place on Tuesday, May 27, 1862.
17. George Lafayette Beal commanded the 10th Maine Infantry Regiment in spring 1862.
18. Archibald G. Spalding, letter to Maine Adjutant Gen. Israel Washburn, June 2, 1862, Maine State Archives
19. Col. John Goddard, letter to Maine Gov. Israel Washburn Jr., June 5, 1862, MSA
20. Spalding to Washburn Jr., June 4, 1862, MSA

Chapter 21

THE LADIES OF AUGUSTA, THE RAINS OF SEVEN PINES

"All the signs pointed to an attack on us"

Assigned to picket duty near the Chickahominy River In Virginia early on Saturday, May 31, 1862, Pvt. Robert Brady Jr. would be justified in letting his thoughts drift to the fair women of Augusta—not the last loyal women whom he would meet, but definitely the ladies he remembered the best.

A talented youngster serving with the 11th Maine Infantry Regiment, Brady belonged to Co. D. "Its members were chiefly [drawn] from the towns of the upper Penobscot [River], from Lee, Springfield, Topsfield, Enfield, Prentiss, and contiguous towns," he would recall years later.

"A few [men] from other parts of the State" joined the company in Augusta in mid-autumn 1861, he acknowledged. Physically tough farmers and loggers familiar with the Penobscot River and its adjacent wetlands—marshes, cool and clear lakes and ponds, and fast-flowing streams—comprised the bulk of Co. D.

"Most of them were young men of from eighteen to twenty-four years of age," Brady noticed.[1]

He fit well with his companions. Claiming to be 18, but actually only 16 when he enlisted in the 11th Maine Infantry on November 2, 1861, Brady had received a special dispensation before signing up.

His father, 40-year-old Robert Brady—his surname lacking a "Sr.," but the father of 16-year-old Robert Jr. nonetheless—had agreed to pass off his boy as a full-fledged adult rather than leave him behind in Enfield in the central Penobscot Valley. The decision would benefit the Union for the next 4½ years.

Born in Caran near the Wicklow Mountains in eastern Ireland, the elder Brady may have arrived in North America during the early years of the Great Famine. Born in Houlton circa 1845, the namesake son was working as a farmer when he, his father, and other Penobscot

Carver Barracks
Both were done by the same artist, at different times. The image above is probably 1862. The one on the facing page is 1864 (note the establishment of roads or paths, as well as the addition of a permanent structure).
Lithographs by Charles Magnus, via Library of Congress

Valley lads signed their names (those men who could write) to a muster roll circulated by Leonard S. Harvey.

He may have blinked twice when the Bradys signed the muster roll. Robert Brady stood 5 feet, 8¾ inches, his son 5 feet, 7 inches. Harvey likely realized that Robert Jr., looking suspiciously young, was definitely his father's son; the Bradys shared hazel eyes, the only spots of color in otherwise dark complexions set beneath black hair.[2]

A shoemaker, the elder Brady was a natural leader. When his muster roll evolved into Co. D, 11th Maine Infantry, Capt. Leonard S. Harvey (not to last long in office) named Robert Brady as his first sergeant. John D. Stanwood was the first lieutenant, Gibson S. Budge the second lieutenant, and the younger Brady hefted his rifle and did whatever he was told.[3]

The 11th Maine lads had mustered at Augusta on Tuesday, November 12, 1861. Writing on behalf of Governor Israel Washburn Jr., Maine Adjutant Gen. John L. Hodsdon had just issued "General Order No. 54," summoning the regiment "for immediate service in the field."

In a flowing, informative prose, Hodsdon (a man with an eye to the details) told the 11th Maine's commander, Col. John C. Caldwell, to leave Augusta on Wednesday, November 13. Hours before sunrise, Robert Brady Jr. and his comrades took down their "circular Ellis tents" and tossed the debris that was not portable onto "the camp fires burning with increasing brilliancy."

Into the chaos of a vanishing camp advanced "the throngs of loyal ladies and girls who, in hurried but none the less charming costumes," brought "pails of hot coffee and armloads of sandwiches, cakes, and pies" for the departing soldiers. The awe-struck Brady could barely tear his eyes away from the friendly women long enough to finish packing.

Often accompanied by daughters, granddaughters, and nieces, the women of Augusta "had arisen at an unseemly hour to cheer the hearts of the heroes about to depart for the seat

Chapter 21: The Ladies of Augusta, The Rains of Seven Pines

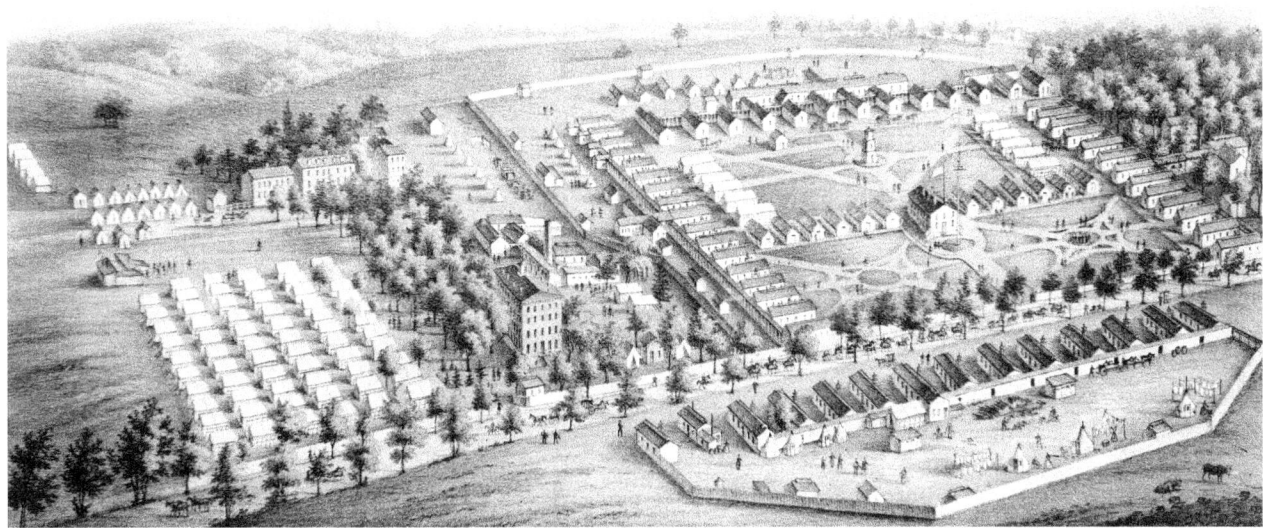

of war," Brady said.

"The ladies of Augusta were always the friends of the Eleventh Maine," he admitted, and the men who outlived the war "have always been respectful admirers of the ladies of Augusta."

The last strain of the 11th Maine's official song, "We'll Hang Jeff Davis From a Sour Apple Tree," had long faded from the regiment's struck camp when Brady and his comrades marched to the train station, boarded their assigned cars, and rumbled off to the cheers of "hurrahing crowds ... at every station."[4]

The 11th Maine lads spent the winter atop Meridian Hill in Washington, D.C., first at Camp Knox and then in hastily built Carver Barracks.[5] The rough-and-tumble regiment fought the wintry Battle of the Sandpits with a neighboring regular Army cavalry regiment before being assigned to the 1st Brigade (Brig. Gen. Henry M. Naglee) of the 3rd Division (Brig. Gen. Silas Casey) of IV Corps (Maj. Gen. Erasmus D. Keyes).[6]

Despite their rather comfortable quarters, his men "suffered severely from sickness," Caldwell told Hodsdon. "No less than four hundred cases of measles" sickened as many soldiers and killed about 30 men, "if I remember rightly," Caldwell figured.[7]

In late March the 11th Maine left Meridian Hill and marched with the division's 14 other regiments to Alexandria. One unidentified Maine soldier recalled "it was a grand sight" as the entire division "marched down Fourteenth Street" in the capital and crossed the Potomac River via the Long Bridge.

Not until Sunday, March 30 did the 1st Brigade boys board the five-deck steamer *Constitution*, owned by the Pacific Mail Steamship Company. "The embarkation was a slow and tedious process, only two men going aboard abreast" at a time, the Maine soldier reported.

Soldiers packed themselves and their gear into "every inch of available space" aboard the steamer. "When all were aboard," the decidedly top-heavy ship was unable "to proceed to sea with safety," the 11th Maine soldier said. The 104th Pennsylvania Infantry Regiment was transferred to another steamer, "the old '*State of Maine*.'"

The *Constitution* "steamed off down the Potomac in fine style" around 8 a.m. on Monday,

169

March 31. About six hours later, the steamer ran aground opposite Aquia Creek, a stream flowing into the Potomac at Brent Point, Virginia.[8]

Three other steamers tugged and prodded the stuck *Constitution* to no avail. The 11th Maine boys finally scrambled over the side to board the steamer *Kent*; then the *Constitution* "was got off the bar" around 7 a.m. on April 1, recalled Robert Brady Jr.[9]

The 11th Maine boys then reboarded the *Constitution*, which "steamed ... merrily onward without mishap" to anchor near Fort Monroe that night. On Wednesday the regiment transferred to the *Hero*, described as a "small tugboat," for the ten-mile sail to Newport News.

The masts and rigging of the USS *Cumberland*, sunk a month earlier by the ironclad CSS *Virginia*, still jutted above Hampton Roads as the *Hero* steamed past. A soldier described

Union Col. John C. Caldwell
Pictured here as a brigadier general.
Photo from Library of Congress

the "masts [as] like arms raised heavenward as if invoking the vengeance of a just God upon the enemies of her country."

Disembarking at Newport News, the 11th Maine lads studied "the outside of the Monitor ... which lay very near us." The Union ironclad "looks as little likely to injure a monster like the Merrimac,[10] as a single log on the Kennebec [River] to carry away the *Free Bridge* at Augusta," one soldier thought.[11]

Amidst the alarums and excursions occurring during the Army of the Potomac's glacial advance up the Peninsula, the 11th Maine lads quickly learned war's reality. Caldwell sent companies A and D "to make a reconnaissance beyond our picket line" on Tuesday, April 29, Brady Jr. recalled.

With Co. A forming a skirmish line, Co. D "moved across a field and through a point of woods" to within sight of a Confederate fort; the other 11th Maine companies followed, he said. Then "a shell came screeching towards us," landed "some twenty feet" away, "burst in a cloud of smoke, and the pieces were flying into the air.

"We heroes waited with open mouths for a half a minute perhaps," he sheepishly admitted, "then at one and the same time we each all ... threw ourselves on the ground and, digging our noses into the dirt, lay there for another full half-minute." Then the men stood "to march on our dignified way."

Heavy shooting erupted along the Co. A skirmish line, and a Confederate bullet killed Pvt. Andrew C. Mace of Farmington. He was the first 11th Maine soldier killed in action.

Chapter 21: The Ladies of Augusta, The Rains of Seven Pines

Brady and his comrades thought they had "seen the elephant"[12] when the artillery shell exploded; as the men returned to camp on that humid day, they viewed the price paid for their combat baptism.

Soldiers carried Mace by stretcher to the camp. Men quietly moved past his body, which "had a fascination for all of us," Brady said. "Few of us but were awe-struck as we looked upon the waxen face now drained of blood, but yesterday blooming with health and spirits."[13]

The Army of the Potomac followed as Confederate Gen. Joseph Johnston withdrew his army to the gates of Richmond. On May 4, Caldwell received a promotion to brigadier general and, with "there being no vacancies in Gen. McClellan's army" for spare one-star generals, departed for Washington, D.C.[14]

A few days later outside Williamsburg, Brady walked across the battlefield where "dead bodies lay where they had fallen." He lost his naiveté that day, especially after stopping at a makeshift hospital where men lay "cut, hacked, shot—dead and dying—a sorry sight there was" to see.

"However hardened we became afterwards, the most indifferent by nature were visibly affected by the grewsome [sic] sights of the bloody field of Williamsburg," Brady admitted.[15]

McClellan's army pushed northwest toward Richmond's eastern approaches. On May 12, the War Department elevated Lt. Col. Harris M. Plaisted to the vacant colonelcy and command of the "green" 11th Maine; seven days later, the 1st Brigade reached the Chickahominy River.

Comprising the 11th Maine, 56th and 100th New York infantries, and 52nd and 104th

Union Gen. Henry Morris Naglee
Photo from Library of Congress

Union Brig. Gen. Silas Casey
Photo from Library of Congress

Union Maj. Gen. Erasmus Keyes
Photo courtesy of Brady-Handy Collection, Library of Congress

Union Col. Harris M. Plaisted
Photo courtesy of Maine State Archives

Pennsylvania infantries, Naglee's 1st Brigade encountered no resistance on the river's east bank. Retreating enemy troops had burned Bottoms Bridge[16] and the nearby Richmond & York River Railroad bridge.

Flowing from northwest to southeast across the relatively flat terrain east of Richmond, the murky and normally slow-flowing Chickahominy River provided the last natural barrier between McClellan and Richmond. Brady estimated that, at the railroad bridge, the Chickahominy was "about forty feet wide, fringed with a dense growth of forest trees, and bordered by low marshy bottom lands" prone to flooding.

After Union pioneers repaired Bottoms Bridge, the 1st Brigade crossed the river on May 20. Then Naglee took some cavalry and two infantry companies, including the 11th Maine's Co. D, and probed south across White Oak Swamp to the James River. The reconnaissance beyond the left flank of the Federal army encountered only Confederate cavalry.

The 1st Brigade advanced west on May 24 to occupy Seven Pines, a town at the intersection of the Williamsburg Stage Road (modern Route 60) and the Nine Mile Road.[17] McClellan sent the entire IV Corps across the river the next day, and Casey moved his division westward to Fair Oaks Station on the Richmond & York River Railroad on May 28.

Erasmus Keyes and Henry Naglee both noticed that the Chickahominy separated IV Corps from the rest of the army. On May 29, Naglee sent "all the pioneers of his brigade" and two companies apiece from the 11th Maine and the 104th Pennsylvania to build a bridge outside the 3rd Division lines at a "place … only fifteen feet wide & three or four feet deep," said 2nd Lt. Harrison Hume, the acting adjutant of the 11th Maine Infantry.

He commanded one Maine company; his friend, 2nd Lt. J. William West of East Machias, the other company. Hume noticed that despite the river's narrow width, "the land is low & after a storm a fellow would have to swim [across the rain-swollen river], most a half mile."

Gen. Caldwell and staff at Fair Oaks, June 1862
Photo by James F. Gibson, via Library of Congress

Wondering about all the noise near their camp, Union soldiers stationed on the left bank of the river "skirmished down to us, thinking we were the enemy," Hume reported. Those men, assigned to a II Corps' division commanded by John Sedgwick, "told us if they wanted any bridges, they could build them, themselves."

Learning that Naglee had ordered a bridge built "some four miles from camp & outside the picket line," Silas Casey ordered the work suspended and the weary soldiers returned to their camps, Hume said.[18]

Meanwhile, soon after his division arrived at Seven Pines, Casey "immediately began a new line of rifle pits and a small redoubt for six field guns to cover our new position," commented Robert Brady Jr. Confederate troops hovered nearby, as the occasional rattle and snap of skirmish-line musketry revealed.[19]

According to Casey, the rifle pits and redoubt were located "about three-quarters of a mile [west]" of Seven Pines, at "the advanced position of the army." His men also built an abatis "about one-third of a mile in front of the [rifle] pits."[20]

By May's final weekend, the work had worn out the 11th Maine boys, now "so reduced by sickness that had our regiment been all together, we could not have showed but 250 muskets," said Harrison Hume. "We had dug trenches, fell[ed] trees & made defensive works," and now "our men are weak from starvation.

"We had not had but four meals of meat for a week [and] not any but hard bread [hard tack] & the whole division was worked to death on picket & other duty," he noted.[21]

By May 28, McClellan had split his army along the Chickahominy. His IV Corps had deployed in and around Seven Pines, and Brig. Gen. Samuel P. Heintzelman had brought his III Corps over to the right bank to take position east of Keyes's divisions. The other three corps remained on the left bank.

Union camps at Fair Oaks
This is a day or two before the battle.
*Illustration by Albert Waud,
Library of Congress*

Aquia Creek, 1863
This swapped hands several times in 1861-62, until the Union established a logistical supply point for the Army of the Potomac.
Photo from Library of Congress

Seizing the opportunity, Joe Johnston decided to attack and destroy the isolated III and IV corps on May 31. His intended two-pronged blow would fall primarily upon Casey's 3rd Division, which with "about 5,000 men" was considered among the numerically weaker divisions in the Army of the Potomac.[22]

Confederate troops probed Casey's "advanced pickets," who successfully fended off "bodies of the enemy" numbering an estimated 300 men on May 29 and 400 men on May 30, Casey reported. The Thursday skirmishes saw the Union pickets suffer four casualties, the Confederates an indeterminate number. Friday's stronger probe cost the Confederates at least six men killed.[23]

Confederate troops were already positioning to attack when "a terrible thunder storm" swept across the Chickahominy watershed on May 30, wrote 1st Lt. Francis W. Sabine of Co. E and Bangor.[24]

"The rain, falling in torrents ... made the roads practically impassable," pulped the Virginia soil into mud, and flooded the lowlands along the Chickahominy, Brady Jr. recalled. Churning debris, the fast-rising river threatened to destroy the bridges; if they went, III and IV Corps would face the Confederate onslaught physically separated from the rest of the army.

The remnants of Co. D "went on picket that [Friday] evening, occupying the extreme right of the line, an entirely unsupported position," Brady said. "The men passed a miserable night, watching in darkness and storm, sheltering themselves as they best could and still remain alert."[25]

Though still inexperienced, the Maine soldiers knew "all the signs pointed to an early attack on us," he said, referring to "the pressure of the enemies [sic] skirmish line, the plain movements of their troops, and the fact that they must either dislodge us or lose Richmond."[26]

Around dawn, Casey learned that the "outer pickets" on his picket line (including Co. D nearest the railroad) "heard [rail] cars running nearly all night on the Richmond end of the railroad," he noted. This report suggested that enemy reinforcements were shuttling by train to a point nearer Seven Pines; Casey decided "to exercise increased vigilance."[27]

Throughout that long night Robert Brady Jr. watched the lightning-rent darkness, shivered in his soaked clothing, and thought about Maine and home. The "loyal ladies and girls" of Augusta must have crossed his mind; he devoted much attention to them years later when writing the regimental memoirs.

The storm blew east early on Saturday, which "broke with the promise of clearness." After sunrise, Brady's father "came out of camp with Private [Jotham S.] Annis," detailed as a cook." Annis carried a kettle full of cold coffee; a fire was kindled, the coffee soon simmered in the kettle, and "the men partook of a rough breakfast," according to Robert Brady Jr.[28]

Suddenly hoof beats sounded in the woods beyond the skirmish line. Maine soldiers seized their weapons.

The Confederates were coming.

~~~

1. Albert Maxfield and Robert Brady Jr., *Company D of the Eleventh Regiment Maine Infantry Volunteers in the War of the Rebellion,* Press of Thos. Humphrey, New York, NY, 1890, p. 3
2. Robert Brady and Robert Brady Jr., Soldiers' Files, Maine State Archives
3. Maxfield and Brady, *Company D,* p. 3
4. Robert Brady Jr. and Albert Maxfield, *The Story of One Regiment: The Eleventh Maine Infantry Volunteers in*

Preparing for the Confederates at Fair Oaks
Left: Union soldiers are watching something in June 1862. Right: Union soldiers with a 32-pounder field howitzer at Seven Pines, Virginia. This photo is also likely before the battle.
Photos from Library of Congress

the War of the Rebellion, J.J. Little & Co., New York, NY, 1896, pp. 7-9

5. Named for Henry Knox, the artillery commander for Gen. George Washington during the Revolution. Knox was an early "land baron" in the District of Maine. Tradesmen from the 11th Maine helped construct Carver Barracks.
6. Although born in Brimfield, Mass., Keyes grew up in Maine. Established during the Civil War, Camp Keyes in Augusta was named for him; the Maine National Guard was headquartered there until June 2018.
7. Brig. Gen. John C. Caldwell, letter to John Hodsdon, *Annual Report of the Adjutant General of the State of Maine, 1862,* p. 128
8. *Maine Farmer,* Thursday, April 24, 1862
9. Brady and Maxfield, *One Regiment,* p. 21
10. Confederate shipwrights built the CSS Virginia atop the hull of the sunken frigate USS Merrimac.
11. *Maine Farmer,* Thursday, April 24, 1862; italics in original document
12. A wartime expression referring to experiencing combat for the first time.
13. Brady and Maxfield, *One Regiment,* pp.24-32
14. Caldwell to Hodsdon, *Annual Report of the Adjutant General of the State of Maine, 1862,* p. 129
15. Brady and Maxfield, *One Regiment,* pp.24-32
16. The modern Bottoms Bridge carries Routes 33/60 over the Chickahominy River east of Seven Pines.
17. Seven Pines was named for the seven pine trees growing near the crossroad.
18. Harrison Hume, letter to "My Dear Father," June 19, 1862, courtesy of Nicholas P. Picerno
19. Maxfield and Brady, *Company D,* pp. 9-10
20. Brig. Gen. Silas Casey, *Official Records, Series I, Vol. XI, Part 1,* Chapter XXIII, No. 92, p. 913
21. Harrison Hume, letter to "Dear Parents," June 2, 1862, courtesy of Nicholas P. Picerno
22. Casey, letter to Brig. Gen. R.B. Marcy, June 5, 1862, *OR, Series I, Vol. XI, Part 1,* Chapter XXIII, p. 752
23. Casey, *OR, Series I, Vol. XI, Part 1,* Chapter XXIII, No. 92, p. 914
24. "Extracts from the private correspondence of an officer of the 11th Maine Regiment," *Daily Whig & Courier,* Friday, June 13, 1862. Although the newspaper did not identify the letter writer, he commanded the skirmishers from Co. E on May 31, as his letter reveals. Plaisted identified the skirmishers' commander as Francis Sabine.
25. By late May, sickness and detached duty had reduced the 11th Maine's ranks substantially.
26. Maxfield and Brady, *Company D,* p. 10
27. Casey, *OR, Series I, Vol. XI, Part 1,* Chapter XXIII, No. 92, p. 914
28. Maxfield and Brady, *Company D,* p. 10

# Chapter 22

THE MAINE BOYS FIRED AND FIRED AND FIRED...

"The exhausted, powder-burned faces to the right and left of you"

Horse hooves sloshed and slopped along a muddy road leading to the Co. D picket line near dawn on Saturday, May 31. Hearing only one horse and not the mud-muted thunder of charging cavalry, 11th Maine Infantry soldiers nervously fingered their rifled muskets.

Deployed about a mile west of the 1st Brigade camps outside Seven Pines, Union pickets "were in sight of the rebel pickets, who were defended by rifle pits and one piece of artillery," a veteran said. The 3rd Division commander, Brig. Gen. Silas Casey, had sensed the increasing enemy pressure on his pickets, who "could not be pushed further without bringing on a general action."[1]

Realizing that a warning about an imminent Confederate attack could not reach him soon enough, Casey had scattered mounted messengers along his picket line. Some Union cavalrymen—certainly not many—prowled around IV Corps in those nervous hours as darkness gave way to dawn; did a lost Union trooper approach Capt. Leonard Harvey and Co. D this morning?

A horse and its rider suddenly emerged from the woods. Maine-accented voices challenged the horseman as infantrymen surrounded him.

Confederate Lt. James Barrall Washington, a staff officer for Gen. Joseph Johnston, had taken a wrong turn in the sodden Chickahominy woods. He had blundered "unexpectedly into the line of D, having mistaken a road in carrying orders to some rebel command," surmised Pvt. Robert Brady Jr. "Quickly halted, he ruefully yielded himself a prisoner."

Perhaps seeking to take credit for the capture, Leonard Harvey marched Washington off to meet Casey. For reasons unclear, Harvey never rejoined Co. D that Saturday; with 1st Lt. John

Captured Confederate Lt. James B. Washington with Union Capt. George A. Custer, May 31, 1862
Washington, a staff officer for Confederate Gen. Joseph Johnston, had taken a wrong turn in the Chickahominy woods and had blundered right into the 11th Maine's Company D; he promptly surrendered.
Photo by James F. Gibson, via Library of Congress

Stanwood being ill, de facto command devolved to 2nd Lt. Francis M. Johnson of Springfield.

"The capture of Lieutenant Washington made the pickets doubly alert," Brady said.[2]

Tension grew along the 1st Brigade's picket line. Rumors flew about Confederates sneaking about the Union lines during Friday night's heavy rain; "prisoners say that a rebel Captain ... came through our lines and explored our position, finding out just how to attack," reported 1st Lt. Francis Sabine of Co. E.[3]

Confederate scouts had indeed explored Casey's extensive, but poorly utilized positions. "For a few days before the battle, we had dug trenches [rifle pits], fell[ed] trees & made defensive works," said 2nd Lt. Harrison Hume, acting adjutant of the 11th Maine.

A 21-year-old student from Robbinston in eastern Washington County, the 5 foot, 9-inch Hume had joined the 11th Maine as its sergeant major in mid-October 1861. Hume had gray eyes and black hair[4] and a low opinion of "that miserable Generalship which has been

Chapter 22: The Maine Boys Fired and Fired and Fired...

displayed throughout all this campaign," he complained on paper to his parents.

He could not understand why "instead of encamping the [3rd] division [of Silas Casey] behind" its defensive positions, "we were placed in front of them."

To Joe Johnston, the haphazard placement of Casey's regiments outside their defensive positions presented a perfect opportunity to smash the 3rd Division in the open. George McClellan concurred, in his fashion, after the battle.

"Fine strategy, splendid Generalship," Hume fumed.[5]

Serving as general officer of the day, Col. Harris Plaisted of the 11th Maine constantly rode among the picket posts after sunrise. Evidence direct and indirect suggested a strengthening enemy presence in the flooded woods beyond the existing picket line, where five 11th Maine companies were already stationed: D on the far right and B, G, H, and K lumped together farther south.

About 7 a.m., Brig. Gen. Henry M. Naglee, commander of the 1st Brigade, ordered his regiments to send additional pickets. With Capt. Francis W. Wiswell and 2nd Lt. Lawson G. Ireland sick,[6] Sabine brought out 27 men, all those available for duty from Co. E, and Capt. Simeon H. Merrill rustled up 22 men from Co. I. Both companies deployed to the northern end of the picket line, not far from Co. D.[7]

Only three companies—A, C, and F—remained in the 11th Maine camp.[8]

The reinforced picket line left Casey with fewer reserves; his division fielded only 4,472 effective fighting men that morning. At their inceptions, each regiment in the 1st Brigade had mustered 1,000 men; in the Chickahominy swamps the five regiments mustered an estimated 1,700 men, an average of 340 men per regiment.[9]

Sometime during the morning, Naglee "himself rode out to their [picket] line to make observations, and warned them [pickets] that they were liable to be attacked at any moment," Brady recalled. The Confederate pickets demonstrated boisterously soon after dawn, and "sharp picket fighting took place during the forenoon," he said.[10]

Barely old enough to shave, he probably looked to his father for guidance as musketry crackled and popped along the Co. D line. At 40, the elder Robert Brady was an old man in this company of young men; within a few hours he would demonstrate the leadership skills that his son would emulate in the years of war to come.

Their attention focused on the west, the 11th Maine lads did not know that God (or nature) had lent the Confederates a crucial advantage. "So rapidly did the Chickahominy ... rise under the influence of the storm" that by Saturday morning, the river "was almost impassable to troops and artillery," the younger Brady explained afterwards.

"Its fords were flooded, and those of its bridges not swept away were submerged," he said.[11]

While benefiting Confederate Gen. Joseph E. Johnston and his advancing troops by trapping the Union III and IV corps against the flooding Chickahominy River, Friday's rain had hindered the Southerners, too. "The operations of the Confederate troops in this battle were very much retarded by the broad ponds of rain-water,—in many places more than knee-deep,—by the deep mud, and by the dense woods and thickets that covered the ground," Johnston acknowledged afterwards.[12]

11th Maine Infantry Regiment flag
The flag is displayed at the Maine State Museum.
Courtesy of the Maine State Museum

Similar conditions plagued the Union soldiers fighting at Seven Pines.

The 3rd Division's picket lines stretched some 3 miles from the Williamsburg Stage Road north across the railroad to the Chickahominy River. Initially responsible for manning the picket line, the 1st Brigade's five regiments "encamped along its length" to fulfill that assignment, Naglee said.

Responsibility for holding the picket line extending from the Stage Road south to White

Oak Swamp fell to the 1st Division commanded by Brig. Gen. Darius N. Couch.[13]

Scheduled to begin about dawn, the Confederate attack finally unfolded "a little after noon," Brady said, when "the roar of the attack on the left [south] was heard."[14]

The Co. D lads were momentarily spared because Joe Johnston had planned for his troops to strike simultaneously east along the Williamsburg Stage Road and southeast along the Nine Mile Road. If conducted as planned, the dual assaults would have outflanked and shattered the 3rd Division.

Instead a serious command error channeled the brigades assigned to both attacks onto the Stage Road. Confederate regiments jammed up for a while as senior officers sorted out the attacking units. Johnston would not be stayed, however.

"Between 11 and 12 o'clock a mounted vidette [picket] was sent in from the advanced pickets to report that a body of the enemy was in sight, advancing on the Richmond [Williamsburg Stage] road," Casey said.

He sent a Pennsylvania infantry regiment to reinforce the picket line, another mounted picket rode back to warn "that the enemy were advancing in force," two Confederate shells "were thrown over my camp," and Casey finally figured out "that a serious attack was contemplated."

He ordered the 3rd Division's camps emptied of every soldier who could carry a rifle.[15]

"The first intuition we had of a battle was some shells thrown in the direction of our camp" 30 minutes before the Union picket line erupted in gun smoke, Hume reported. Similar shelling had occurred in the past, so the 11th Maine boys relaxing in their camp ignored the artillery.

"But in ten minutes after the picket firing commenced, the rebels were right upon us," Hume said.[16]

Led by Gen. Daniel Harvey Hill, the initial Confederate attack swept through the woods either side of the Williamsburg Stage Road. Inside the 11th Maine's camp, Maj. Robert F. Campbell[17] told Hume "to form the regiment," as represented by the only companies (A, C, and F) not already on the picket line.

"There is nothing to form," Hume responded.

"Well, from what there is," round up every available man, Campbell replied.[18]

Hume formed the three companies, and from the regimental hospital staggered the disease-flattened 1st Lt. William H.H. Rice of Co. G and Ellsworth. Urging other sick soldiers to join him, Rice grabbed a rifle and a cartridge box.

At least a few men followed him,[19] and Campbell led out 93 men. Riding in from the picket line, Plaisted met the battalion and led his men to a position north of the Williamsburg Stage Road.

With "the bullets, all the time, falling around us" and striking individual soldiers, the 11th Maine lads pushed their way "through a piece of bushes that had been cut down,"[20] Hume said. Plaisted positioned his truncated battalion between the four cannons and gunners of Battery H, 1st New York Light Artillery to the south and eight companies of the 104th Pennsylvania Infantry to the north. The New York gunners had deployed just north of the Stage Road, on the other side of which spread the 100th New York Infantry, placed there by Casey.[21]

The Confederate onslaught smashed into the pickets astride the Stage Road. As shooting intensified, "the left of the picket line was forced back" and finally broken, Robert Brady Jr. learned later. Men bolted like rabbits or withdrew in relatively good order; no middle ground apparently existed during this retreat as the pickets fell back through the main Union line.

Located north of where Plaisted had deployed his battalion, the four 11th Maine companies (B, G, H, and K) briefly held their positions along the picket line as "the roar of cannon, the shriek of shells, and all the usual din of battle betokened that no mere skirmish was upon us," said a soldier from Co. G and Hancock.[22]

As enemy pressure increased, the four companies retreated some 800 yards before joining the 56th New York Infantry, which Casey had sent days earlier to guard the railroad.[23] Friendly artillery fire "destroyed one poor fellow" from the New York regiment as Union artillery located to the east shot "short of the rebels," the Co. G soldier noticed.

Confederate Gen. Daniel Harvey Hill
Photo via www.generalsandbrevets.com

Then Naglee formed the mixed 11th Maine-56th New York contingent in line some 500 yards from earthworks just lost to the attacking Confederates; swinging around the captured Union cannons, "the enemy turned his whole attention to us, and opened with grape and shells," the Maine soldier said.[24]

Ordered by Naglee to lie down, the Mainers and New Yorkers endured the incessant shelling "for about half an hour," but fortunately the Confederates fired high. "The trees now standing afford unmistakable evidence of the severity of that fire, in being cut or smashed by shells and shot," said another 11th Maine survivor.

He viewed the trees as "standing but silent witnesses" to the mayhem.[25]

"It was uncertain what the pickets should do" on the far right flank, Robert Brady Jr. admitted. Not long after the shooting started, 2nd Lt. Francis Johnson and Corp. Josiah Keene of Waterville disappeared to the north "to learn, if they could, what [Union] force … guarded the [right] flank."

The two men steered through the thick woods and crossed the railroad before encountering Union soldiers hastening to meet Confederate brigades finally making an appearance on the Nine Mile Road northwest of Seven Pines. Those Union reinforcements belonged to Brig. Gen. John Sedgwick's 2nd Division and marked the first reinforcements from II Corps; the infantrymen had tramped across the Chickahominy River on the partially submerged and disintegrating Grapevine Bridge to reach the battlefield.[26]

Heavy fighting engulfed the south end of Casey's line, where Plaisted had "ordered my men to lie down behind a ridge" after maneuvering the 93 men of companies A, C, and F into position "about 30 yards to the right" of Battery H. He told his men to "reserve their fire until the rebels emerged from the woods" to the west.[27]

Confederate troops attacked "in large force on the center and both wings," Casey said. Though the Battery H gunners "kept throwing canister into their [Confederate] ranks with great effect," he soon realized that enemy infantry threatened to turn his division's flanks and capture the artillery's four 3-inch Parrott rifles.

Only the cold steel could save those guns.[28]

Around 1 p.m., "Naglee rode up in front of my line amidst a shower of bullets, and ordered me to charge," Plaisted said. "With the greatest enthusiasm, the order was obeyed."[29]

As Naglee ordered the 11th Maine—"my little Yankee squad," he would affectionately call them—to move, Hume led the 93-odd men in three cheers for their general. Moving simultaneously with the 104th Pennsylvania on its right (north) flank and the 100th New York on the south side of the Stage Road, the 11th Maine boys charged.[30]

Color Sgt. Alexander Katon (a newspaper misspelled his name as "Katen") of Co. B and Pittston "bore our standard bravely in front of the line," Plaisted said.

When he heard, "Forward to the fence!," Katon ran "several yards in advance" of the Pennsylvania line some 200 to 300 yards "across the open space" to the worm fence, Plaisted recalled. Reaching the fence first, Katon "firmly planted our flag" against it.

He held the flag staff "with the greatest steadiness, amidst such a shower of bullets" that no man could possibly survive, Plaisted believed.

Forming along the fence, the Mainers and Pennsylvanians stood about 50 yards from the woods swarming with enemy troops. "We opened fire," said Plaisted, describing the shootout that won the 11th Maine—or at least these three companies—mention in subsequent reports.

The Maine boys fired and fired and

Union Maj. Gen. John Sedgwick
Photo courtesy Maine State Archives

The Battle of Seven Pines, May 31, 1862
Some historians call it the Battle of Fair Oaks. Note Professor Thaddeus
Sobieski Constantine Lowe's observation balloon, *Intrepid,* at top left.
Illustration by Currier & Ives, via Library of Congress.

fired—and caught hell in the Confederate volleys. Assigned to the color guard, Corp. Willis Maddocks of Co. K fell dead beside Katon; 2nd Lt. J. William West of Co. C caught a bullet with his heart "and fell near the fence," Plaisted recalled.[31]

"Men were being shot on all sides of me" as "all around us, the balls were flying like hail," said Hume, who along with his comrades had "lay down" while "the rebels" were "firing it into us in all directions.

"Our men kept firing & we kept telling them to fire low," he encouraged the riflemen in his section of the line.

"Oh, God, for reinforcements," Hume likely thought as he lay "there under that canopy of fire.

"Our Generals have put us in a murderous position & we can't hold it unless those regiments will come up & then we can drive the rebels from the woods," he thought. "A quarter mile" away to the east stood Union regiments positioning to meet the Confederate onslaught gathering additional steam to the south, beyond Battery H.

As lead filled the air around him and the casualties piled up, "all of our little band had no idea of retreating," Hume said.[32]

Fighting like an enlisted man in the 11th Maine ranks, 1st Lt. William H.H. Rice of

Chapter 22: The Maine Boys Fired and Fired and Fired...

Ellsworth got off 17 shots until wounded in the thigh.[33] Evacuated from the field with 1st Sgt. James A. Morris of Cranberry Isles as his attendant, Rice was transported by train to White House Landing, then north by ship to a hospital in Annapolis, Maryland.

Rice died there at 11:30 a.m., July 1; a hospital chaplain had the body embalmed "and sent to his friend" in Ellsworth.[34]

Confederate bullets shattered the flag staff held by Katon. Kneeling on the ground, he leaned over Maddocks' body and held the flag aloft as high as his arms could extend.[35]

Enemy bullets punched 11 holes in the flag, but missed Katon altogether. As 11th Maine casualties accumulated, he emerged unscathed.[36]

Plaisted asked Maj. Robert Campbell to check the men firing along the battalion's left flank. Moving from north to south as bullets filled the air around him, Campbell leaned over and tapped the back of almost every soldier shooting at the nearby Confederates. "Fire lower, boys, fire lower," Campbell told the sweating, gunpowder-stained soldiers. "Aim lower, boys, aim lower."

"His calm, clear commands, as he moved along the line ... can never be forgotten by me," Harris Plaisted said afterwards. "He was unharmed."[37]

After the battle, the Co. G soldier from Hancock heard Plaisted and Campbell described as "no cooler, braver soldiers ... when in the hottest fire" and the men along the firing line as no "braver, calmer men than those who faced a hidden enemy and murderous volleys."[38]

Pvt. Henry G. Prescott of Co. H and Corinth appeared beside Plaisted and raised his blood-covered hand, the middle finger "cut away close to his hand." Blood from the wound had splattered Prescott and his rifle.

Blood and perspiration streaming down his face, Prescott asked, "Colonel, do you think I had better leave?"

"He had kept up his fire until forced, not by pain, but by the inconvenience of the thing, to desist," Plaisted said. "I sent him to the rear."[39]

When a Confederate color bearer emerged from the woods, Pvt. William Parker of Co. C, "a mere boy," cried, "That flag must now come down." Targeting the color bearer, Parker fired and knocked him down.

Plaisted remembered that particular shot "as a specimen of cool and deliberate firing."[40]

Maine boys pitched and fell along the battalion's thinning line. Plaisted lost track of time, but the 11th Maine and 104th Pennsylvania could not have fought for long. With the Pennsylvanians finally falling back and "two-thirds of my commissioned officers and one half of my little battalion ... either killed or wounded," Plaisted "reluctantly ... gave the order, 'Retreat.'"[41]

"Had we stood there twenty minutes longer, we should have all died," Hume admitted. Standing, his comrades retreated east with "the balls falling like hail," the Mainers "being under a cross fire. Many of our men were wounded in retreating," he said.

"Through all the fight, I never lost my sense of danger," Hume commented. As he ran toward the perceived safety of the Federals' main line, bullets whizzed past and overhead; "I expected every moment would be my last but a kind Providence protected me," he said.[42]

Plaisted lost 52 men—six dead, 39 wounded, and seven missing—in that heroic stand at the fence. Now the 11th Maine boys fell back through their camp, where two regimental surgeons, a hospital steward, and an acting quartermaster had evacuated the 56 hospital patients and "all hospital and commissary stores, regimental books and papers," Plaisted said.[43]

The 11th Maine lads then flowed east across the Nine Mile Road and into Seven Pines, where Casey had organized another defense line. There Plaisted learned about the fight that companies B, G, H, and K had made with the 56th New York; the four companies had "behaved nobly and retired from the field in good order" under heavy pressure from advancing Confederates.[44]

That left three 11th Maine companies out on the far right of the picket line. Taking his spy glass, Francis Sabine had climbed an oak tree and then scrambled down to enter a nearby house, where he "had a fine view ... of the rebel pickets."[45]

Union Capt. Francis W. Sabine
Photo courtesy of Maine State Archives

His ears attuned to the violent combat perhaps a mile to the south, 1st Sgt. Robert Brady "realized by the sound of the battle that he was cut off from his camp," his son said later. The elder Brady told his men that if Co. D retreated, they should carefully withdraw "toward the right and rear," where no fighting had yet erupted.

Then around noon, "a rebel line of battle appeared moving towards the line held by D," Brady Jr. noted. His father ordered some men to drop trees across the woods road and block it. The other Co. D lads opened "up a rapid fire on the enemy to give the idea by their boldness that they covered a line of battle," the younger Brady described his father's tactical deception.

Robert Jr. knew that "really between them [Confederates] and Fair Oaks [Station] there was then no force whatever."[46]

Also spotting the advancing Confederates "about noon," Frank Sabine estimated that the battle line comprised "four regiments, with skirmishers deployed in front." The Confederates hesitantly moved, advancing a short distance, then stopping, a process they repeated for a while.

"Finally we saw them sit down," the puzzled Sabine said.[47]

Robert Brady Jr. noticed that "elaborately cautious advance," which resumed sometime in early to midafternoon. The enemy skirmish line "easily flanked our forlorn pickets, and curling them back in spite of their stubborn resistance, finally scattered them through the woods."

Chapter 22: The Maine Boys Fired and Fired and Fired...

Brady became separated from his father as the Co. D boys ran. Many men who heeded 1st Sgt. Brady's instructions reached the hard-pressed Union lines.

Other soldiers (including the elder Brady) vanished.[48]

To the southeast, battered 1st Brigade regiments tumbled into the 3rd Division's main defense line just west of Seven Pines. The strong point on which Casey had based this line was an artillery-filled redoubt not far from the Stage Road; turning the line's left (southern) flank, Confederate troops fired into the redoubt.

Losing one horse to enemy bullets, Naglee "was everywhere, his gray eyes blazing with excitement, his strident voice heard above the roar of battle," 11th Maine survivors told Robert Brady Jr. in the days to come.

Silas Casey "rode up and down his lines that day, bare-headed, his long gray hair floating over his shoulders, encouraging his men by voice and example to a heroic resistance," Brady later wrote.

Their supporting artillery silenced by Confederate rifle fire, Union troops fell back to another line forming along the Nine Mile Road, about 300 yards from the trees lending their name to Seven Pines. The men fought desperately, arriving Union reinforcements received vicious handling from the hard-charging Confederates, and this second line broke.

Its defenders retreated through Seven Pines. "Turning frequently to check the boldest pursuers with withering volleys," the shot-up Federal "regiments arrived at a new line of defense" about a half mile east of the village, said Robert Brady Jr., who evidently reached this last-ditch position after escaping the Co. D trap.

Confederate reenactors fire a 6-pound cannon at Corydon, Indiana
Photo by Brian F. Swartz

House at Fair Oaks used as a field hospital
A soldier's grave is in the foreground. It is unclear when this photo was taken, but it was probably immediately after the end of the battle.
Photo by James F. Gibson, via Library of Congress

"Here were rallied fragments of regiments and of companies, groups and squads of men," he said. Men from various regiments and brigades and divisions mingled together and shot it out with enemy troops as the light faded.

Based on his detailed account, Brady must have fought somewhere in the disorganized Union ranks. "Do you remember that line, the last Union bulwark of that fatal day, the gathering, blessed darkness, the exhausted, powder-burned faces to the right and left of you—faces hard set in firm determination to make one last stand for the bullet-riddled flags flying over

Chapter 22: The Maine Boys Fired and Fired and Fired...

them?" he asked.

Soldiers repeatedly loaded and fired. Their voices hoarse from shouting over the din, the field officers "galloped their foaming horses up and down,[49] while rallying the stragglers" and driving to the firing line "groups and squads of men who had abandoned the day," Brady digested the chaos in which he fought.

"And yonder, what?" he asked, peering west through gun smoke swirling in the day's last light. "Exultant masses of victorious rebels forming to break our last stand?"

"No, as it proved," he concluded. Almost as intermingled as their blue-clad enemies, Confederate troops finally recoiled from "the stubborn resistance" they had encountered since early afternoon.[50]

Darkness ended the day's fighting at Seven Pines, but not before a final 11th Maine drama played out about a mile to the northwest.

Sometime during the afternoon, Francis Sabine had resumed his oak-tree perch as fighting raged to the south before shifting direction to the southeast. Doubtless his men begged him for details, but he could see little with his spy glass.

"We couldn't tell how the battle was going ... only [that] the firing seemed to be in the direction of our camp," he said. The men of companies E and I remained at their posts throughout the afternoon.

Sometime late that Saturday, "we heard a terrible firing" to the east, behind the picket line, Sabine said. Union stragglers fleeing through the 11th Maine posts reported that Confederates were coming west to snatch up the Mainers.

Not quite convinced that enemy troops could have gotten behind him, Sabine took several men and investigated the musketry interspersed with the echoing thumps of well-served artillery. The Mainers "found to our joy" that Sedgwick's men made the noise, Sabine said.[51]

Another Confederate effort unfolding toward sunset sent a "brigade of four or five regiments, with several hundred cavalry" advancing "through a wheat field" west of Seven Pines, Plaisted reported. The maneuver directed the enemy troops toward the woods defended by companies E and I; beyond those woods, the Confederates could turn north by east and strike Sedgwick's division in the rear.

Afterwards, Plaisted speculated that the 60-odd men of the two companies probably "saved Gen. Sedgwick from being surprised by a flank movement of the enemy."[52]

Seeing the Confederates approaching, Merrill and Sabine ordered their men "all on to their posts," a command that "was tough to do, but no one objected," Sabine said. The 11th Maine lads ran into the wheat field, reached a rise, deployed, and immediately fired.

Three Confederate cavalrymen (described by Sabine as "officers") toppled from their horses, and the Confederate advance briefly halted. As "the bullets whistled round us loosely," the Mainers ran for the trees; a messenger took news of the flank attack to Sedgwick, but with darkness descending, the Confederate assault petered out.

Enemy officers "saw us there, and probably supposed we had support" from artillery and infantry, Sabine speculated. "Instead of having support, we knew we were cut off from it."

Rather than sacrifice their men to a possible night attack, Merrill and Sabine pulled back,

Cannons at Fair Oaks
C & G Batteries of the 3rd U.S. Artillery on horses pulling mounted cannons near Fair Oaks, Va. June 1862.
Photo by James F. Gibson via Library of Congress

formed "a new line behind a fence," and waited, Sabine said.

Francis Johnson and a few other Co. D men joined companies E and I sometime after sunset. The 11th Maine lads nabbed many Confederates lost in the dark; sunrise brought great relief to Merrill and Sabine and every Mainer still holding that tenuous picket line.

"It was rainy and dark, and a hard night," Sabine explained.[53]

~~~

1. Observer, "Gen. Casey's Division at the Battle of Fair Oaks," *New York Times,* June 22, 1862
2. Albert Maxfield and Robert Brady Jr., *Company D of the Eleventh Regiment Maine Infantry Volunteers in the War of the Rebellion,* Press of Thos. Humphrey, New York, NY, 1890, pp. 10-11
3. "Extracts from the private correspondence of an officer of the 11th Maine Regiment," *Daily Whig & Courier,* Friday, June 13, 1862. Although the newspaper did not identify the letter writer, he commanded the skirmishers from Co. E on May 31, as his letter reveals. Col. Harris M. Plaisted identified the E skirmishers' com-

Chapter 22: The Maine Boys Fired and Fired and Fired...

mander as Francis Sabine.
4. Harrison Hume, *Soldiers' File,* Maine State Archives
5. Harrison Hume, letter to "Dear Parents," June 2, 1862, courtesy of Nicholas P. Picerno
6. An unusual number of 11th Maine officers reported sick on May 31.
7. *Daily Whig & Courier,* Friday, June 13, 1862
8. "Official Report of Col. Plaisted," *Maine Farmer,* Thursday, June 19, 1862
9. N.H. Davis, Assistant Inspector General, U.S. Army to General Randolph B. Marcy, *Official Records, Series 1, Vol. 11, Part I,* Chapter XXIII, p. 753
10. Maxfield and Brady, *Company D,* p. 11
11. Robert Brady Jr. and Albert Maxfield, The *Story of One Regiment: The Eleventh Maine Infantry Volunteers in the War of the Rebellion,* J.J. Little & Co., New York, NY, 1896, pp. 37-38
12. Gen. Joseph E. Johnston, "Manassas to Seven Pines," *North to Antietam: Battles and Leaders of the Civil War, Vol. II,* p. 215
13. "Brig. Gen. Henry M. Naglee to Lt. B.B. Foster, The Battle of Seven Pines; Report of Brig-Gen. Naglee," *New York Times,* Aug. 11, 1862
14. Maxfield and Brady, *Company D,* p. 11
15. Brig. Gen. Silas Casey, *OR, Series I, Vol. 11, Part I,* Chapter XXIII, No. 92, p. 914
16. Hume, letter to "Dear Parents," June 2, 1862, courtesy of Nicholas P. Picerno
17. Campbell was among the few 11th Maine soldiers who had previously worn a uniform; he was called up with the Cherryfield Light Infantry during the 1837 "Bloodless" Aroostook War. Brady described Campbell as "a brave and intelligent officer."
18. Hume, June 2, 1862, courtesy of Nicholas P. Picerno
19. Brady and Maxfield, *One Regiment,* p. 48
20. Hume, June 2, 1862, courtesy of Nicholas P. Picerno
21. "The Battle of Seven Pines; Report of Brig-Gen. Naglee," *New York Times,* Aug. 11, 1862
22. Hancock borders on the east of Ellsworth, the Hancock County shire town.
23. Brady and Maxfield, *One Regiment,* p. 38
24. "From the 11th Me. Regiment," June 2, 1862, published in the *Ellsworth American,* Friday, June 20 1862. The letter writer was an unidentified soldier from Co. G.
25. "From the 11th Maine Regiment," *Ellsworth American,* Friday, July 4, 1862. The undated latter was signed by "S," who may have been Capt. Winslow Spofford of Co. G.
26. Maxfield and Brady, *Company D,* p. 11
27. "Official Report of Col. Plaisted," *Maine Farmer,* Thursday, June 19, 1862
28. Casey, *OR, Series I, Vol. 11, Part I,* Chapter XXIII, No. 92, pp. 914-915
29. *Maine Farmer,* Thursday, June 19, 1862
30. Hume, letter to "Dear Brother," June 7, 1862, courtesy of Nicholas P. Picerno
31. *Maine Farmer,* Thursday, June 19, 1862
32. Hume, June 2, 1862, courtesy of Nicholas P. Picerno
33. Brady and Maxfield, *One Regiment,* p. 48
34. *Daily Whig & Courier,* Tuesday, July 8, 1862
35. *Annual Report of the Adjutant General of the State of Maine, 1862,* p. 80

36. His heroism earned Alexander T. Katon, 43 years old when he joined the 11th Maine Infantry on Oct. 7, 1861, only this Plaisted-provided footnote in history. Discharged for disability in early July 1862, Katon died aboard a Union transport ship while homeward bound
37. Confederate bullets never did find Robert F. Campbell. He survived the war and lived until May 1891.
38. "From the 11th Me. Regiment," *Ellsworth American,* Friday, June 20 1862
39. Col. Harris Plaisted, letter to Governor Israel Washburn Jr., June 20, 1862, published in *Portland Daily Express,* June 30, 1862. Plaisted identified Prescott as being from Exeter, a town bordering Corinth. Since he was assigned to Co. H, Prescott was evidently serving with the color guard at Seven Pines; he was discharged for his wound in mid-July.
40. *Annual Report of the Adjutant General of the State of Maine, 1862,* p. 80
41. *Maine Farmer,* Thursday, June 19, 1862
42. Hume, June 2, 1862, courtesy of Nicholas P. Picerno
43. Brady and Maxfield, *One Regiment,* p. 48
44. Ibid., p. 46
45. *Daily Whig & Courier,* Friday, June 13, 1862
46. Maxfield and Brady, *Company D,* p. 11
47. *Daily Whig & Courier,* Friday, June 13, 1862
48. Maxfield and Brady, *Company D,* p. 11
49. Of an infantry's combat officers, only the major, lieutenant colonel, and colonel were authorized to ride horses. The captains and lieutenants walked.
50. Brady and Maxfield, *One Regiment,* pp. 39-41
51. *Daily Whig & Courier,* Friday, June 13, 1862
52. *Maine Farmer,* Thursday, June 19, 1862
53. *Daily Whig & Courier,* Friday, June 13, 1862

Chapter 23

THE MAN WITH THE WHITE HANDKERCHIEF

"About midnight I was again ordered forward to my former position"

Inundated by Friday night's hellacious rain, soggy II Corps soldiers remained almost inert in their camps east of the Chickahominy River after sunrise on Saturday, May 31.

Friday's "most terrific storm" had spared neither general nor private, and high winds accompanying the rain had yanked tent pegs from the sodden soil and flattened some tents. Amidst the debris strewn across his 1st Brigade camp, Brig. Gen. Oliver Otis Howard still could not believe how Friday's rain "fell in torrents."

The storm's aftermath particularly impressed him.

Like other Mainers accustomed to "mud season" back home, he thought he knew mud[1]—but as the rain pounded "that peculiarly soft soil" abundant along the Chickahominy watershed, "the mud deepened" until even the soldiers' tents leaned at crazy angles.[2]

Alerted by scouts, pickets, prisoners, and the binoculars of Professor Thaddeus Sobieski Constantine Lowe (chief aeronaut of the Union Army Balloon Corps), Gen. George Brinton McClellan knew that Confederate troops stirred in the woods beyond the IV Corps picket lines west of Seven Pines. With his Army of the Potomac split by the Chickahominy, McClellan hesitated to reinforce the III and IV Corps now isolated beyond bridges disintegrating in the river's freshet.

He ordered II Corps commander Brig. Gen. Edwin V. Sumner to prepare to march at a moment's notice, yet to hold his men in their camps. Sumner relayed this order to his division commanders; 1st Division commander Brig. Gen. Israel B. Richardson warned his brigade commanders, including the 30-year-old Howard.

His brigade comprised four infantry regiments: the 5th New Hampshire, the 61st and 64th New Yorks, and the 81st Pennsylvania, which had mustered in August 1861. The other

Union Brig. Gen. Edwin Vose Sumner
Shown here as a Major General
Photo by Mathew Brady, 1860-63, Library of Congress

Union Gen. Israel Bush Richardson
Photo between 1860-62, Library of Congress

three regiments mustered that fall. Although all four regiments had participated in the Yorktown siege, none had experienced serious combat.

With Saturday's sunrise, Howard's men slogged about their waterlogged camps, stoked smoky fires with wet wood, boiled water for coffee, and ate breakfast.

Noise suddenly stirred the moist air in mid- to late morning. Rising from their breakfast perches on boxes and stumps, the veterans sprinkled through the 1st Brigade's camps cocked their heads.

Edgy new recruits emulated their battle-wise comrades and stood and listened, too. What did the distant thumps and explosions mean?

Artillery, the veterans replied. The steady thumping could mean Union guns shelling an aggressive Confederate probe.

Listen for musketry, patient veterans told the recruits clustering around them. It might sound like a large sheet being torn. If you hear that, someone's got a fight on their hands.

If it gets louder, the fight is coming our way, the veterans cautioned.

At his headquarters tent, Howard "heard the first fitful sound from [Brig. Gen. Silas] Casey's guns" in late morning. Soon came volley-fire musketry, and "before one o'clock we knew that a hard battle was going on," he said.[3]

Chapter 23: The Man with the White Handkerchief

Elijah Walker, colonel of the 4th Maine Infantry Regiment, had already anticipated a battle. Along with Moses Lakeman's 3rd Maine Infantry and the 38th and the 40th New York infantries, the 4th Maine served in the 2nd Brigade commanded by Brig. Gen. David Birney.

The brigade, in turn, belonged to the 3rd Division (Brig. Gen. Phil Kearny) of III Corps (Brig. Gen. Samuel P. Heintzelman), already deployed across the Chickahominy with IV Corps.

With Kearny's division came two Maine brigadier generals who had donned their uniforms only a year earlier. Charles Jameson of Old Town led the 1st Brigade, comprising the 87th New York and 57th, 63rd, and 105th Pennsylvania infantry regiments. The talented colonel of the 2nd Maine Infantry during its bullet-riddled fight at Manassas, Jameson had earned a star despite his political status as a War Democrat.

Hiram Berry of Rockland commanded Kearny's 3rd Brigade, comprising the 37th New York and 2nd, 3rd, and 5th Michigans. The first colonel of the ready-to-rumble or -mutiny 4th Maine Infantry, Berry had led the Limerock Regiment during its fiery combat baptism on Chinn Ridge at Manassas.

He had a reputation of caring for his men; Walker sometimes thought him too lenient with trouble-makers.

Sent across the Chickahominy River days earlier, III Corps had undertaken a "slow and cautious" advance, Walker said. "It was wise on the part of our corps commander to move cautiously" with Confederate troops nearby.

Camping east of Seven Pines, the 3rd Division established an "outpost picket line ... nearly two miles to our front," Walker said. On Friday, May 30, he prowled the picket line "as division officer of the day."

Heavy rain boosted the tension palpable all along the picket lines that day. Walker likely discussed the enemy's proximity with the division's pickets; returning to camp at noon, he rode west again at 2 p.m. and encountered Kearny inspecting his troops with "a few of his staff" in tow.

Kearny, too, expected a fight. "See that the men keep a sharp lookout for the enemy; we shall be attacked soon," he instructed Walker. "I have been to the front and our men are all right. Don't let us be surprised.

"That d----d fool of a Casey is so near his picket line, and his men are lying about so carelessly, he will be surprised," Kearny speculated. "The enemy will be upon him

Union General David Bell Birney
Photo is between 1855-65
Photo by Mathew Brady, via Library of Congress

before he knows it."

The 3rd Division shifted a mile nearer IV Corps on May 30 and another half mile closer about 10 a.m., May 31.[4] As heavy fighting erupted just to the west in early afternoon, Kearny's regiments turned out; the 4th Maine "was first stationed in the woods in front of my encampment," Walker said. The regiment's right flank abutted the Richmond & York River Railroad.

The 4th Maine lads listened a while to the fighting raging to the west before Birney ordered Walker to take his men across a field on the Susan Allen farm. Sloshing over the wet terrain, the Maine boys deployed along "the fence at the edge of the woods," said Walker, his view obscured by trees.

He sent 10 scouts—"one from each company"—to search the woods for Confederates. Reaching a swamp, the scouts shifted south "to find a passage over" the muck; Pvt. Fred H. Rogers of Co. K suddenly encountered a Union cavalryman riding east to find some comrades to help him capture "a squad of rebels near by," Walker reported later.

The enterprising Rogers took on the assignment. He spotted a Confederate infantryman "with a gun in one hand and a white handkerchief on a stick in the other," according to Walker.

Ordering the enemy soldier to drop his gun, Rogers then noticed Col. John Bratton of the 6th South Carolina Infantry Regiment, lying wounded beneath a tree some ten to twelve feet from the first prisoner.[5] Five Maine scouts emerged from the tangled foliage, as did five Confederate infantrymen escorting the twice-captured Capt. John D. McFarland of the 13th Pennsylvania Infantry.[6]

The 4th Maine scouts got the drop on the Confederates and freed McFarland. He "expressed much joy that his captors were now in turn taken by our men," Walker noted.

While the scouts scoured the woods, the 4th Maine "received some shots from the enemy on the left, and one of my officers was slightly wounded in the head," he said. Moses Ford, an acting lieutenant in Co. F, trotted into the lines with a prisoner; before the scouts returned with their happy-to-be-out-of-the-fight Confederates, Birney ordered the regiment to move "to the edge of the next field."

Reaching the vacated fence line, Rogers and his comrades looked around, shrugged their shoulders, and then marched their prisoners to Susan Allen's farm house, now a Union hospital. The wounded Bratton wound up in the care of the 3rd Maine's assistant surgeon, and the intact prisoners and their guards later reported to Kearny's headquarters, where Fred Rogers et al. gave their Confederates to the provost guard.

Unsure as to the 13th Pennsylvania's whereabouts and understandably not desiring to be captured a third time, McFarland stayed with his liberators as they tracked the 4th Maine to its new position. He sheltered with the Maine lads that night.[7]

Around 9 p.m., Walker sent Capt. William Pitcher and companies G, H, I, and K—all deployed on the 4th Maine's left flank—to picket a road that crossed the railroad near Orchard Station. Once in position, Pitcher dispatched scouts "who reconnoitered for a distance of a half mile" beyond his line.

Confused as to where the enemy might be located, Birney shifted his regiments and

Chapter 23: The Man with the White Handkerchief

Lowe sends a dispatch to McClellan
Balloonist Professor Thaddeus Lowe sends word to Gen. George B. McClellan during the Battle of Fair Oaks, also known as the Battle of Seven Pines. In this illustration, the battle is in the distance to the left. Seated is Mr. Painter of the Philadelphia *Inquirer*. Mr. Park Spring is sending the dispatch for Lowe, who is standing.
Illustration by Arthur Lumley via Library of Congress.

ordered Walker to pull back. Similar instructions went to Pitcher, who "drew in my scouts and retired as ordered."

Birney continued confounding his officers; back went Walker and the 4th Maine to their line just vacated, and "about midnight I was again ordered forward to my former position, with instructions to send out pickets a half mile on the railroad," Pitcher said.

With two companies placed in reserve near Orchard Station, he strung his pickets along the railroad and on a line extending south.

Dawn was not long in coming.[8]

~~~

1. "Mud season" marks several weeks in early spring when winter-frozen soil thaws in Maine. Depending on snow melt, the frost depth in the ground, and the air temperature, the start of mud season can vary from year to year. A cold winter can freeze the soil several feet deep.
2. Oliver Otis Howard, *Autobiography of Oliver Otis Howard, Major General, United States Army, Vol. 1,* The

Baker & Taylor Company, New York, 1907, p. 230

3. Ibid., p. 237
4. Elijah Walker, *The Old Soldier: History of the Fourth Maine Infantry*, Tribune, Rockland, Maine, 1895, p. 27. Walker incorrectly listed the date as May 29; his subsequent paragraphs indicate that he actually meant Friday, May 30, 1862.
5. Col. Elijah Walker, *OR, Series 1, Vol. 11, Part 1,* Chapter XXIII, No. 61, pp.859-860
6. Peter P. Dalton, *With Our Faces to the Foes: A History of the 4th Maine Infantry in the War of the Rebellion*, Union Publishing Co., Union, ME 1998, p. 147
7. Walker, *OR, Series I, Vol. 11, Part 1,* Chapter XXIII, No. 61, pp.859-860
8. Capt. William L. Pitcher, *OR, Series 1, Vol. 11, Part I,* Chapter XXIII, No. 62, pp. 861

Chapter 24

ACROSS THE FLOOD

"A few friends were searching for faces they hoped not to find"

If ever Oliver Otis Howard needed bridge builders, midafternoon on Saturday, May 31, 1862 was the time.

As his II Corps arrived near the Chickahominy River in late May, Brig. Gen. Edwin Sumner tapped a few regiments to construct two bridges (designated "upper" and "lower" based on their respective locations) upstream from the Richmond & York River Railroad bridge. The 5th New Hampshire from Howard's 1st Brigade of the 1st Division tackled the "upper" bridge as the river rose close to flood stage.

When Sumner inspired his men to their task by sending them a whiskey barrel, the teetotaling Howard protested. Sumner replied, "Yes, general, you are right, but it is like pitch on fire, which gets speed out of an engine though it burns out the boiler."[1]

Cutting trees along the shore, the New Hampshire lads removed the limbs and used withes and pins to fasten notched logs in place while constructing cribs (also known as "cribwork") to serve as the bridge's abutments and piers. Engineers calculated the desired height for each crib; men added notched logs until each crib was the correct height. Its increasing weight pushed each crib downward until it rested on the Chickahominy's muddy bottom.

To form the deck, the New Hampshire boys laid logs perpendicular to the stringers. To span the swampy approaches, the soldiers constructed "corduroy roads" by placing logs perpendicular to each road's travel direction.[2] Soldiers soon identified this span as the Grapevine Bridge.

Howard had sufficiently examined the Chickahominy to realize that while "it was no more than a creek with low banks," the river and its abutting swamps ranged from 200 to 300 feet in width. That distance perhaps doubled in the rising waters unleashed by the May 30 thunderstorm—and as Confederate troops pounded the outnumbered Union defenders at Seven Pines, reinforcements needed to cross that flood.

About 3 p.m., Saturday, May 31, Sumner sent Brig. Gen. Israel Richardson and his 1st Division to cross the Chickahominy on the "lower" bridge and reinforce the beleaguered IV Corps. To the Grapevine Bridge marched Sumner and Brig. Gen. John Sedgwick and his 2nd Division.

Grapevine Bridge
The bridge was built by the 5th New Hampshire Infantry under Col. Edward E. Cross on May 27 and 28, 1862. The photo's glass was damaged in several locations. *(Photo by D.B. Woodbury via Library of Congress)*

With Brig. Gen. William French and his 3rd Brigade leading, the 1st Division approached the "lower" bridge. Plans called for the division to cross immediately and advance on Seven Pines, but "the crossing of the river was made particularly difficult by the large quantity of rain which had fallen some hours before," Richardson realized.

With "part of the bridge having been swept away," Bill French's "men were obliged to wade ... nearly up to their middles in water, and of course could follow but slowly," Richardson noticed. This bridge might break up at any time, so he let French complete his crossing while detouring "the brigades of Generals Howard and Meagher and all my batteries" to the Grapevine Bridge.[3]

Brig. Gen. Thomas F. Meagher, the 2nd Brigade's commander,[4] had "heard considerable firing in front" at his headquarters "early in the forenoon" on Saturday. The noisy shooting increased "in rapidity and loudness during the day," so around 1 p.m. Meagher ordered his regiments "to place themselves under arms" in anticipation of marching to assist III and IV Corps.

As did the soldiers in Howard's and French's brigades, Meagher's men shed "their overcoats, knapsacks, and blankets" and crammed "two days' cooked rations" into their haversacks. Men stepped off "in the lightest possible marching order," Meagher said.[5]

Northwest slogged Howard's men amidst fast-flowing water that "was now deeper on the flats" and mud that "was well stirred up from the bottom," Howard said.

Ahead lay a nightmare.

The Chickahominy's swift currents tore at the Grapevine Bridge as the 2nd Division got there. Engineers struggled to connect the logs "by ropes and withes," but despite heroic efforts, "great cracks appeared" as Sumner rode up.

The engineers' commander, Lt. Col. Barton Alexander, remonstrated that Sumner and his men "cannot cross this bridge!"

"Can't cross this bridge!" Sumner exploded. "I can, sir. I will, sir!"

"Don't you see the approaches are breaking up and the logs displaced? It is impossible!" said Alexander.

"Impossible! Sir, I tell you I can cross," Sumner replied. "I am ordered."[6]

Alexander expected a disaster as "the solid column of infantry entered upon the bridge," which "swayed to and fro to the angry flood below or the living freight above." The combined weight of the soldiers left the bridge "settling down and grasping the solid stumps by which it was made secure as the line advanced.

"Once filled with men, however, it was safe until the Corps passed," Alexander said. "It then soon became impassable."[7]

Union Gen. Thomas Francis Meagher
Photo from www.generalsandbrevets.com

All the while, soldiers heard the battle raging to the west. Only a few miles away, the 6th Maine boys gathered where they "were stationed on Gaines Hill," not far from the Union Army Balloon Corps camp, remembered one soldier.

"We stood in the ranks and breathlessly listened all one long afternoon ... to the Niagara of Seven Pines," he said. "I say Niagara, for I know no other word so fitting to describe that tremendous roar of artillery."[8]

Just getting to the bridge was difficult. Commanded by 1st Lt. Edmund Kirby, the gunners of Battery I, 1st United States Artillery left some distance between each of the six brass Napoleon 12-pounders they hauled toward Seven Pines. With infantrymen filling the only access road, the gunners took their horse teams onto "the open field contiguous to the Chickahominy swamp," said Col. Charles H. Tompkins, artillery chief for John Sedgwick.

Kirby's men watched their "horses in many instances ... sink to their girths in mud," Tompkins said. With the heavy cannons mired in the water-covered field, the artillerymen unharnessed the horses.

With assistance from men from other 2nd Division batteries, Kirby's men shoved and yanked the stuck cannons across the field. Some gunners hastily assembled a corduroy road so the three remaining batteries could follow Kirby toward Grapevine Bridge.[9]

Sumner's troops crossing the Chickahominy to Fair Oaks
Waud sketched this on May 31, 1862, so this sketch was likely made at the site when the crossing happened. He did this with pencil and zinc oxide (known as "Chinese white") on blue paper; the image has been cleaned up and adjusted for clarity and visibility in grayscale in print.
Illustration by Alfred R. Waud via Library of Congress

There, after struggling along the mucky corduroy road serving as a causeway over the adjacent swamp, men lashed frightened horses dragging the brass cannons across the partially submerged bridge. The water swirled above the cannons' muzzles as the horses snorted in terror and gunners shouted in mingled anger and fear.

Kirby's men reached the opposite bank and "found the road a veritable quagmire," according to Howard. The heavy cannons sank in the gooey mud beneath the flooded bottomland; assisted by infantrymen, the gunners pushed and shoved the stuck cannon wheels and finally dragged three Napoleons and a caisson to higher ground at 4:45 p.m.[10]

Sedgwick's division crossed and advanced southwest toward the railroad line and the station at Fair Oaks. Howard and Meagher and their men followed, with the 1st Brigade starting across the Grapevine Bridge at 3 p.m. Howard and his staff (including his aide and younger brother, 1st Lt. Charles Howard) apparently crossed first; both brigades' muddied infantrymen marched across the gradually disintegrating bridge and left the 1st Division's chief of artillery, Capt. George W. Hazzard, to bring up the rear with his three struggling batteries.

Ordered by Sumner to cross the river at Grapevine Bridge, Hazzard discovered that "the heavy rain ... had rendered the high road [from the "lower" bridge to Grapevine]

Sumner's march to Seven Pines
From Battle-Fields of '61 *(1889) by Willis J. Abbott via ushistoryimages.com*

Union engineers build a corduroy road near Richmond, June 1862
A corduroy road was made by laying logs down. It was rough and dangerous for horses when there were loose logs, but allowed passage over otherwise impassable terrain—such as muddy or swampy areas.
Photo by D.B. Woodbury, via Library of Congress

A close-up side view of a corduroy road's construction
This image was taken sometime during the Civil War, but the location is not recorded.
Photo from Brady-Handy Collection, via Library of Congress

nearly impassable for guns." The gunners traveled through the roadside field "converted into quagmires" by the swirling flood waters, and the cannon wheels "sank at once to the axles.

Hazzard made no mention about finding the corduroy road built by the 2nd Division's gunners. In fact, he believed that "the leading battery [Kirby's] of General Sedgwick's division had cut up every spot by which artillery could move without first" constructing corduroy roads.

So the 1st Division artillerymen, as well as their 2nd Division counterparts left stranded on the east bank while Howard and Meagher led their infantrymen to battle, started cutting trees and building a corduroy road on the approaches to the bridge.[11]

Although "the night proved extremely dark" and the ax-work exceptionally physical in the blackness, the remaining batteries "safely crossed over the river" by 3 a.m., Sunday, June 1, according to Hazzard.

Once on the west bank, he found the terrain "flooded to the width of 200 yards and ... the depth of 18 inches." The corduroy road "was floating on the surface of the water," and two abandoned ambulances teetered on the shifting road.

The gunners started building another corduroy road. Soldiers from the 63rd New York Infantry arrived to guard the mud-covered cannons and caissons, but rather than help the artillerymen construct the corduroy road, the New Yorkers only lent them "some shovels," Hazzard complained.[12]

"The heavy firing" along Sedgwick's divisional line "was over" as Howard and the 1st Brigade "approached the front" late on Saturday. "A thick mist was setting on and a dark, cloudy sky was over our heads, so that it was not easy at 20 yards to distinguish a man from a horse," Howard noticed.

After crossing the Chickahominy River, Howard had sent an aide, 1st Lt. Nelson A. Miles,[14] to monitor the fighting involving Sedgwick's division. As the shooting ended around sunset; Miles rode to find Howard and met him on swampy terrain over which the Confederates had charged and been swept back by the counterchage, Howard recalled.

"General, you had better dismount and lead your horses, for the dead and wounded are here," Miles said.

"A peculiar feeling crept over me as I put feet on the soft ground and followed" Miles, Howard said. Union stretcher-bearers went past; "a few friends were searching for faces they hoped not to find," he realized.

As many soldiers learned for the first time at Seven Pines, a battlefield was a noisy and haunted place at night. The scattered musketry rattling the darkness left nervous soldiers clutching their weapons; horses neighed, "and the shriller prolonged calls of the team mules" echoed across the terrain bordering the Richmond & York River Railroad, Howard noticed.

He listened to the "cries of delirium, calls of the helpless, the silence of the slain, and the hum of distant voices in the advancing brigade." Lantern light briefly illuminated men tossed across the ground like discarded sacks of grain; ghostly shadows flickered amidst the swaying lanterns as "the bearers of the wounded" carried shattered, yet living men "to the surgeons."

The experience stunned Howard. After speaking quietly with a dying Mississippian shivering

Confederates attack Kirby's battery at Fair Oaks
Image from Library of Congress

in the evening damp despite the Union blanket covering him, Howard led his aides "to our allotted lines." He reviewed his written orders, "prepared orders for others," and finally, "with mingled hope and apprehension and conscious trust of God, lay down to dream of home."[15]

He would arrive home much sooner than expected.

~~~

1. Oliver Otis Howard, *Autobiography of Oliver Otis Howard, Major General United States Army,* Baker & Taylor Company, New York, 1907, pp. 228-229
2. In their journals and letters, soldiers from both sides often mentioned building corduroy roads.
3. Brig. Gen. Israel B. Richardson, *Official Records, Series 1, Vol. 11, Part I,* Chapter XXIII, No. 4, p. 764
4. Meagher's three New York regiments (the 63rd, 69th, and 88th) comprised the original Irish Brigade, to which the 28th Massachusetts and 116th Pennsylvania were later added. The regiments recruited primarily among Irish emigrants and their American-born sons.
5. Brig. Gen. Thomas F. Meagher, *OR, Series 1, Vol. 11, Part I,* Chapter XXIII, No. 12, pp. 775-776
6. Howard, *Autobiography,* p. 237
7. Col. Barton Alexander, "The Peninsula Campaign," *Atlantic Monthly,* Vol. 13, No. 77, March 1864
8. Letter by "F.", July 14, 1862, published in the *Daily Whig & Courier,* Thursday, July 24, 1862
9. Col. Charles H. Tompkins, *OR, Series 1, Vol. 11, Part I,* Chapter XXIII, No. 22, p. 794
10. Howard, *Autobiography,* p. 238
11. Hazzard apparently learned from some officers of the three 2nd Division batteries stranded on the river's east bank that Kirby's battery was the first such unit to get stuck in the field bordering the approach road to Grapevine Bridge.
12. Capt. George W. Hazzard, *OR, Series 1, Vol. 11, Part I,* Chapter XXIII, No. 5, pp. 767
13. Howard, *Autobiography,* p. 240
14. After the war, Miles earned a reputation fighting Indians on the frontier.
15. Howard, *Autobiography,* pp. 240-241

Chapter 25

BALLOON HANDLER

"We keep the balloon anchored down with 36 bags of sand"

Fog blanketed the waterlogged terrain along the flooding Chickahominy River as light tinged the dark eastern sky shortly before 4 a.m. on Sunday, June 1, 1862. The poor visibility hampered the ability of 4th Maine Infantry pickets to see what was happening beyond their thin line west of Orchard Station.

North of the river—and about five miles from embattled Seven Pines—movement suddenly disturbed the fog enveloping Powhite, a genteel farm owned by Dr. William Fleming Gaines. Up through the fog rose a balloon, the largest in the Union Army Balloon Corps. Emblazoned on one inflated curve of its 44-foot-diameter gas bag was the capitalized name *Intrepid*; on the opposite curve, a bald eagle clutching an American flag hovered above a painted portrait of George B. McClellan.

In the basket suspended beneath the 72-foot tall gas bag rode Professor Thaddeus Sobieski Constantine Lowe, the United States Army's chief aeronaut, and Park Spring, a Union telegraphist. Below them, Pvt. Joseph B. Wilson and some two dozen soldiers from the 4th Maine Infantry handled the four attached ropes keeping the balloon and its passengers from drifting away.

Working collaboratively, the soldiers gradually played out the ropes from the tubs into which they were coiled after Lowe's final flight Saturday evening. Grouped five or six per tugging tether, men tightly grasped the ropes; Lowe sought no repetition of the aeronautical exploit achieved by Brig. Gen. Fitz John Porter, almost lost to Confederate captivity on April 11 when he climbed into a balloon basket and demanded the handlers ease him skyward with only one rope attached to the inflated gas bag.

That line snapped, and the wind carried Porter over enemy lines before shifting direction and returning him to Union-occupied territory near Yorktown. Later, after the late-August disaster at Second Manassas, some Union troops would wish that the Johnnies had nabbed Porter in April.

Wilson, his comrades, and commanding officer 2nd Lt. Arthur Libby knew each other well, as they all belonged to the 4th Maine. Elijah Walker had bid *adieu* to Libby and 28 enlisted men April 5 when a War Department order had transferred them to Lowe near Yorktown.

Union Brig. Gen. Fitz John Porter, seated, with his staff
The photo is not dated, but the Library Congress indicated that Porter is a major general in this picture. That dates this photo to after July 4, 1862. It appears to be Thaddeus Lowe, the balloonist, reclining on the ground to the left, in civilian garb and with his field glasses. *(Photo from Library of Congress)*

Having seen Lowe and his balloons arrive on the Peninsula in March 1862, Walker did not fully appreciate ballooning, a break-through military technology.

Assigned to assist Lowe during the Peninsula Campaign, Libby and his men participated in the first combat use of "air-craft," as Walker described balloons.[1] And while his colonel evinced little excitement about balloons, Joe Wilson found the temporary duty interesting and challenging.

He had generational roots in Belfast, where his grandfather John Wilson had practiced law, entertained his good friend Daniel Webster, and represented Massachusetts in the 13th and 15th Congresses. John Wilson and his progeny evidently favored the letter "J"; son John married Eliza Townsend, and they had six sons: Jesse, Jones, John, Julius, Justus, and Joseph.

On April 29, 1861, the 5-foot, 10½-inch Joseph B. Wilson joined Co. K, 4th Maine and fell into formation under the watchful eye of Capt. Thomas Marshall. Perhaps reflecting an Anglo-Saxon heritage, Joe Wilson had blue eyes and a light complexion and light hair; he may have been a blond.[2]

Wilson fought at Manassas that July and suffered a serious injury while working with a 4th Maine wood-cutting detail at Lawson Hill near Franconia, Virginia, on December 1, 1861. As Wilson loaded wood into a wagon, he hefted a particular "stick of wood up over the hind wheel" of the wagon, he testified almost 20 years later to Belfast attorney Wayland Knowlton.

"His foot slipped and he sprained himself across the small of his back," Knowlton wrote in Belfast on September 13, 1881. Wilson suffered a painful, almost debilitating injury; after "he received medicine" from a regimental physician, he "remained in his camp" and "was treated by his surgeon all winter for kidney trouble occasioned by the [back] pain," according to Knowlton.[3]

Wilson felt better when the 4th Maine arrived on the Peninsula in late March 1862. How he and Libby and 27 other 4th Maine lads were selected for temporary duty with Thaddeus Lowe remains historically murky, but the transfer occurred quickly on April 5 and saw the Maine boys in action hours later.

Towed to Hampton, Virginia aboard the *George Washington Parke Custis* (a converted coal barge that 20th-century historians would dub America's "first aircraft carrier"), Lowe and his balloons and related gear—particularly his gas generators—went ashore on March 28. Troops from the 13th New York Infantry escorted Lowe, four wagons, and two gas generators to a site near Yorktown.

Libby and his 4th Maine detachment reported to Lowe on Saturday, April 5. Briefly trained as balloon handlers, the Maine boys helped launch a small balloon that afternoon.

Throughout the Peninsula Campaign, the Union balloons and observers provided valuable intelligence about Confederate troop positions and movements. During the month-long McClellan-inflicted delay at Yorktown, Lowe established a second balloon camp at Warwick Court House; assisted by soldiers from Co. A, 85th Pennsylvania Infantry, aeronaut James Allen flew missions there aboard the *Constitution*.

Thaddeus Sobieski Constantine Lowe with his field glasses
Photo from Library of Congress

Maj. Gen. Fitz John Porter, between 1862-70
Photo from Library of Congress

Inflating Lowe's balloon
Above, the 4th Maine inflates Lowe's balloon at Fair Oaks on June 1, 1862.
Photo by Mathew Brady, Library of Congress

Rising above the battlefield
At left, Lowe observes the Battle of Seven Pines from the basket of his balloon *Intrepid* on May 31, 1862.
Photo probably by Mathew Brady, Library of Congress.

Replenishing
On the facing page, Lowe replenishes his balloon *Intrepid* from his balloon *Constitution*.
Photo probably by Mathew Brady, Library of Congress.

Lowe relocated his camps as the Army of the Potomac moved up the Peninsula. The Balloon Corps set up a camp near Powhite Creek east of Dr. Gaines's farm house, and on Thursday, May 22, the 4th Maine soldiers inflated the balloon *Excelsior*, from which Lowe obtained his first view of Richmond.

James Allen flew from a camp set up about five miles west at Mechanicsville. He was assisted by soldiers from the 20th Massachusetts Infantry Regiment.

At Dr. Gaines's farm, "we are camped at the edge of a grove and near by is a deep gulch where we keep the balloon anchored down with 35 bags of sand that weigh 50 to 75 pounds apiece," Joe Wilson noted.[4] The "deep gulch" in which the 4th Maine detachment hid the *Intrepid* from prying Confederate artillery shells was the ravine through which flowed Powhite Creek.[5]

McClellan wanted the balloons flying whenever the weather permitted. As Wilson explained, "When it is calm we take her [*Intrepid*] and carry her up on the hill near by and unhook the [inflated] bags." After attaching "4 ropes, [each] a thousand feet long" to the balloon, the soldiers "slack away" on the ropes, "which are coiled down in tubs" for storage.

Then "up she goes" so Lowe could scout Confederate positions, Wilson said. "Sometimes [the balloon went] higher than others, but never over a thousand feet."[6]

As Confederate troops advanced on Seven Pines in late May, Lowe was up often, peering through his black metal field glasses at Richmond and the roads between there and Seven Pines.[7] He flew the *Constitution* at the Gaines' farm camp, Allen the small *Washington* at Mechanicsville. Having detected Confederate troops concentrating on Seven Pines no later than morning on May 30, Lowe suspended flights as the torrential thunderstorm parked over the Chickahominy River later that day.

Joe Wilson and the 4th Maine detachment remained at Powhite Creek. They saved the *Constitution* and *Intrepid* from destruction during the storm, then started inflating the former while Lowe rode to Allen's camp on May 31.

Climbing into the *Washington,* he ascended "and discovered bodies [units] of the enemy and trains of wagons moving from Richmond toward Fair Oaks" at noon, Lowe later noted. He watched for the next two hours as Confederate troops deployed "in line of battle, and cannonading immediately commenced."

Realizing that "we were facing a great battle," Lowe telegraphed Libby at the Gaines farm to inflate the larger *Intrepid*, which could carry "my telegraphic apparatus and operator." Fighting had commenced at Seven Pines as he rode six miles to find the *Intrepid* only partially inflated.

So Lowe ascended in the *Constitution,* examined the battlefield, and descended to send a message to Union generals that the enemy attack could cause "the destruction of our army."

Wilson and his comrades were still generating hydrogen and filling the *Intrepid's* gas bag. "If only I could get the gas from the 'Constitution' into the 'Intrepid,'" Lowe said. Then he "spied a ten inch camp kettle lying on the ground"; after "one of my mechanics" (likely a 4th Maine artificer) "cut out the bottom," soldiers disconnected the *Intrepid* from the hydrogen-gas generators and connected the balloon to the *Constitution* with the dual-holed kettle.

"In a very short time the gas filled the larger balloon. An hour saved!" Lowe exclaimed.

He and Spring ascended immediately to 1,000 feet and "witnessed the titanic struggle" at Seven Pines. "The whole scene of action was plainly visible[,] and reports of the progress of the battle were constantly sent till darkness fell upon the grand[,] but terrifying spectacle."[8]

Night fell as the 4th Maine lads hauled the *Intrepid* earthward. Men had coiled the ropes into tubs by the time that Lowe and Spring climbed from the balloon's basket.

Keep the *Intrepid* inflated, Lowe instructed Arthur Libby.

Joe Wilson and his comrades did so by using the gas generators devised by Lowe. "We have two tanks which will hold twenty hogsheads [approximately 168½ cubic feet] and they are all on wheels," Wilson explained to his probably disbelieving parents. "We can move them [the tanks] where ever we want to and as we have to use considerable water we set them near some stream [hence the value of Powhite Creek] and move the Balloon within 20 feet of them."

Connecting the tanks with gutta-percha pipe, the soldiers then "put in iron blueings [sic] which they get from the [iron] foundries and then we put in a lot of water and then we put in oil of vitriol which makes the [hydrogen] gas," Wilson noted.

"It generally takes four to six hours to inflate the Balloon," he reported.

The 4th Maine lads also took turns guarding Lowe's tent in one-hour shifts. The professor had attracted considerable enemy attention (including artillery fire and musketry) since his initial April 5 flight. If they could not shoot down Lowe and his balloon, perhaps the Confederates could attack the balloon camp and capture or kill him.

With IV Corps badly mangled and III Corps damaged in Saturday's savagery at Seven Pines, McClellan needed Lowe to identify Confederate troop concentrations and movements. Lowe launched at 4 a.m. Sunday; "owing to fog I was unable to see anything" on the day's initial flight, he noted. The fog left him "unable to see anything until after 6 o'clock."

Chapter 25: Balloon Handler

Union Brig. Gen. Andrew A. Humphreys
In this photo, between 1863-70, he is a major general.
Photo from Brady-Handy Collection, Library of Congress

Union Brig. Gen. Randolph B. Marcy
In this photo, he is a major general.
Photo from Brady-Handy Collection, Library of Congress

Desperate for intelligence, Brig. Gen. Andrew A. Humphreys signaled Lowe at 6:45 a.m., "Have you been able to ascend this morning? Your balloon should be in connection by telegraph, and messages should be sent constantly—at least every fifteen minutes. The balloon must be up all day."

Humphreys, the Army of the Potomac's chief topographical engineer, told Lowe to get "the balloon at Mechanicsville" airborne, too.

But visibility improved considerably by 7 a.m., when Lowe wired Humphreys (their dispatches passed in transit), "I have just obtained a splendid observation from the balloon. I find the enemy in large force on the New Bridge road, about three miles this side of Richmond. In fact, all the roads that are visible are filled with infantry and cavalry moving toward Fair Oaks Station."

He reported that Confederate troops near the Gaines farm remained motionless, a critical observation revealing that Robert E. Lee, who had just assumed command of the Southern troops, was not attacking north of the Chickahominy. Confident that his right flank was secure, McClellan could concentrate on attacking the enemy troops at Seven Pines.[9]

Joe Wilson and his comrades spent the daylight hours Sunday handling the *Intrepid*, which "was up fifteen times," he noted. Skyward, telegraphist Spring busily tapped Morse code as Lowe scanned the Chickahominy River and the Seven Pines battlefield.[10]

"My ascent and observations just completed show the firing of the enemy to be in the same position," Lowe wired Humphreys from "near Doctor Gaines' House" at 11 a.m. His message referred to the battle resumed earlier Sunday by advancing Union troops.

"The road in the rear of the firing is filled with wagons and troops," and "about two miles still farther to the rear of Fair Oaks Station, and on the Williamsburg stage road, Charles City Road, and Central road, are also large bodies of troops," Lowe reported. "In fact, I am astonished at their numbers compared with ours, although they are more concentrated than we are."

Combat raged around and through Seven Pines as Union troops—including Walker and the 4th Maine and the brigades commanded by Hiram Berry, Charles Jameson, and Oliver Howard—clawed their way westward to recapture the IV Corps' abandoned camps. At first the news was good; "the enemy has been repulsed wherever he attacked," Brig. Gen. Randolph B. Marcy signaled Lowe around noon from George McClellan's headquarters.[11]

The world's first aircraft carrier
The Union balloon *Washington* aboard the balloon boat USS *George Washington Parke Custis*, a former coal barge built in the 1850s and purchased by the United States Navy in August 1861. Lowe outfitted it with a gas generator; here it is towed by the tug *Coeur de Leon* as Lowe makes his ascent. Thus did the *GWPC* become the world's first aircraft carrier on November 11, 1861.
Image from the U.S. Navy history Web site

Then the message tone changed. "Can you see General Sumner's corps near the line of railroad about four miles from the Chickahominy?" Marcy suddenly asked. "Was the train of our wagons you saw going toward Richmond or toward James River? Can you see the gun-boats on James River? Which direction does the smoke run?"

Lowe replied that at 11 a.m., he "could see what I understood was General Sumner's corps near the line of [the Richmond & York River] railroad, but not more than two miles from the Chickahominy.

"The [Union] wagons I saw were moving toward James River," he assured Marcy, and "they had not reached the road to Richmond." As for the gunboats, Lowe could not see their hulls, but he saw "heavy smoke arising from the [James River] valley at two points" and could "hear heavy reports from cannon," likely the large-caliber guns carried aboard the Federal warships.

As Sunday wore on, the warm sun heated the Chickahominy woods. The wind picked up, and Allen grounded his balloon at Mechanicsville. Joe Wilson and his comrades struggled to control the breeze-buffeted *Intrepid* and, despite the turbulence, Lowe kept flying.

At 3 p.m. he informed Fitz John Porter (among the various Union commanders bombarding him for information) that "by the appearance of the smoke [seen at Seven Pines] when up I would say that we hold our ground, and more too.

"Chickahominy is fast rising; in front of this point the whole fields resemble a lake," Lowe said, noting the nasty problem that had almost kept Oliver Otis Howard and his brigade from

Thaddeus Sobieski Constantine Lowe's field glasses
These are the field glasses that Lowe used to observe from his balloon. They're currently at the Smithsonian.
Photo courtesy of the Smithsonian National Air and Space Museum

crossing the river the previous afternoon.[12]

Despite the flooding, Howard had already brought his mixed brigade of New Hampshire men, New Yorkers, and Pennsylvanians to the fight earlier on Sunday. That brigade passed in close proximity to the 4th Maine Infantry and Elijah Walker in more ways than one.

~~~

1. Elijah Walker, *The Old Soldier: History of the Fourth Maine Infantry*, Tribune, Rockland, Maine, 1895, p. 20
2. Joseph B. Wilson, *Soldiers' File*, Maine State Archives
3. Joseph B. Wilson, application for Original Invalid Pension, Belfast Historical Society, Belfast, Maine
4. Pvt. Joseph B. Wilson, letter to parents, June 15, 1862, Maine State Archives
5. In mid-June 1862, a Mathew Brady-dispatched photographer visited Lowe's balloon camp on the Gaines farm. Lowe restaged scenes from his Seven Pines' flights with assistance from the 4th Maine soldiers; the photographer captured the images for posterity. In 2011 three Civil War ballooning historians and a Civil War Trust staffer used the photographs and satellite technology to locate the approximate site of the balloon camp at Powhite Creek.
6. Wilson, June 15, 1862, MSA
7. Lowe's field glasses are displayed at the National Air and Space Museum in Washington, D.C. (see the preceding photo)
8. Michael Jaeger, Carol Lauritzen, and T.S.C. Lowe, *Memoirs of Thaddeus S.C. Lowe, Chief of the Aeronautics Corps of the Army of the United States During the Civil War: My Balloons in Peace and War,* Edwin Mellen Press, Lewiston, N.Y., 2004, pages 134-136
9. Professor Thaddeus Lowe, *Official Records, Series 3, Vol. 3*, p. 281
10. Wilson, June 15, 1862, MSA
11. Marcy, who served as chief of staff for George B. McClellan, was also his father-in-law.
12. Lowe, *OR, Series 3, Vol. 3*, pp. 282-283

Chapter 26

MORNING CARNAGE AT SEVEN PINES

"We were startled by a sudden and terrific volley of musketry in front"

"At earliest daybreak" on Sunday, June 1, Capt. William L. Pitcher could sense Confederates lurking near where his command—companies G, H, I, and K of the 4th Maine Infantry—had strung a thin picket line near Orchard Station on the Richmond & York River Railroad.

Aware that heavy firing had echoed to the northwest until sunset on Saturday,[1] Pitcher realized that enemy troops must be nearby. He sent five scouts to find the elusive Confederates concealed by the fog and woods; the scouts spotted, but failed to identify the "men felling trees beyond the houses in front."

Other Pitcher-dispatched scouts got closer and noted the preponderance of butternut and gray uniforms among the ax-men. Seeing an enemy infantry regiment deploying in line beyond the felled trees, the scouts scurried back to Pitcher.

Believing the regiment's presence implied an enemy attack, Pitcher relayed the information to an officer on the staff of Brig. Gen. David Birney, who commanded the brigade to which the 4th Maine was attached.[2]

In the early light, Col. Elijah Walker moved the 4th Maine's six remaining companies (A, B, C, D, E, and F) "on to the railroad" near Pitcher's position. Walker also "sent out scouts" to find the enemy; these men possibly encountered the same regiment spotted earlier by Pitcher's scouts, but by now "the enemy was filing through the woods on the left," Walker realized.

Sending a messenger to warn Pitcher, Walker rode to find Col. John Henry Hobart Ward of the 38th New York.[3] Walker may not have been aware at that moment that Brig. Gen. Phil Kearny, commander of the 3rd Division (of III Corps) to which Birney's brigade was attached, had placed Birney under arrest about dawn and replaced him with Ward.[4]

During the night, Oliver Otis Howard had slept fitfully amidst three of the four regiments of his 1st Brigade. He had last seen Col. Edward E. Cross and the 5th New Hampshire Infantry crossing the Chickahominy River on the "lower" bridge the previous afternoon. Detailed as advance guard for the 3rd Brigade led by Brig. Gen. William H. French, the 5th was Howard's only regiment to bump into Saturday's combat.5

Awakened early Sunday by a messenger, Howard arose. His few aides coalesced around the young general and awaited his orders.

Brig. Gen. Israel B. Richardson had ordered the 1st Division "stood to arms" at 3 a.m., about an hour before there was sufficient light for Thaddeus S.C. Lowe to launch the day's first balloon reconnaissance at Powhite. If the Confederates planned to resume Saturday's battle, dawn on Sunday would be the perfect time.

Union Col. Edward Ephraim Cross
Screen capture from The History Channel's Civil War Combat: America's Bloodiest Battles *(1998)*

The fading darkness gradually revealed the triangular position held by II Corps north of Seven Pines. The triangle's apex rested on Fair Oaks Station (now in Union hands), and one side of the triangle encompassed John Sedgwick and his 2nd Division aligned southwest to northeast along the local road running from the station toward the Chickahominy.

Forming Sedgwick's left flank, Richardson and his 1st Division were the triangle's second side, stretching south-southeast along the Richmond & York River Railroad. Richardson placed French's brigade near Fair Oaks Station and put Howard and his 1st Brigade behind French. Tom Meagher spread his Irish Brigade into a battle line behind Howard's men.

Ordered by II Corps commander Edwin V. Sumner to establish contact with the "pickets of General Birney's brigade on my left" (eastern) flank, the busy Richardson assumed that William French had done so during the night.6

Alert at their posts out on the right flank of Birney's brigade, Elijah Walker and the 4th Maine encountered no friendly troops on their right (western) flank until after daylight on Sunday.

Walker had not reached Ward when "firing commenced on the right" flank, "and I turned and hastened to rejoin my command."7

Tension rippled through the Union lines. Cross and the 5th New Hampshire had "retired before daylight without noise or confusion" from a position facing three Confederate infantry regiments (2nd Mississippi and 2nd and 5th Texas).

Pleased that Cross—whose men nabbed several Confederate prisoners, including a message-bearing orderly grabbed at first light—had evaded contact during his withdrawal to the railroad, Richardson studied the terrain across which Confederate troops would attack... if they did.

Extending some 1,000 yards south from the railroad, "a large open field [lay] opposite my right front," that section of French's brigade nearest Fair Oaks Station, Richardson noticed. The Union skirmishers saw their Confederate counterparts and cavalry emerge from the far tree line not long after Cross had pulled back his regiment.

Union artillery batteries commanded by Capt. George Hazzard and Capt. Rufus D. Pettit[8] fired on the advancing Confederates and scored some hits. The enemy troops "broke and retired into the woods," Richardson said.[9]

Occurring around 5 a.m., "the first noisy collision of this Sunday morning ... became a smart reveille to all," said Howard, by now mounted on a brown horse and moving with his small staff in the early light.

"There was always a strange thrill of interest at such a time," he acknowledged the anxiety felt by most soldiers awaiting their involvement in a developing battle.

Richardson believed the first Confederate probe presaged a major attack on that part of his line; in hindsight, Howard described "the movement" as "only a Confederate reconnaissance."[10]

Suddenly, a mounted messenger pounded through the woods and galloped toward Richardson. The man breathlessly reported the potential disaster on the 1st Division's left flank. A surprised French had discovered a half-mile gap between his easternmost regiment (the 53rd Pennsylvania Infantry, led by Col. John R. Brooke) and Birney's right flank, as represented by the 4th Maine.

Only Brooke's and William Pitcher's pickets lay scattered along the railroad bed. Realizing that enemy troops could pour through this gap, Richardson warned Sumner.[11]

He sent French's brigade across the railroad to spread in line to the left (east), parallel to and about 50 yards south of the steel rails.[12] Richardson pulled the 5th New Hampshire into reserve and ordered Howard to shift the 81st Pennsylvania Infantry (commanded by Col. James Miller) "to prolong the line of General French to the left" along the railroad, Howard noted.

Miller complied and led his men through the thick woods. Connecting with the left flank of the 53rd Pennsylvania Infantry, the 81st Pennsylvania lads extended their battle line farther east with

Union Brig. Gen. William Henry French
Based on his brigadier general's rank here, this photo was taken between September 28, 1861, and November 29, 1862.
Photo from Brady-Handy Collection, Library of Congress

Brig. Gen. French and his staff, September 1863, Culpeper, Virginia
Photo from Library of Congress

the railroad at their backs.

Howard, who would never see Miller again, quickly (and erroneously) learned "that the left of Colonel Miller extended in front and beyond the right of General Birney's brigade."[13] He sent a major to find and warn Birney.

Initially encountering Pitcher, the major told him that the 1st Brigade had deployed "at an acute angle with the railroad" to the west. Howard had anchored his right flank on the railroad "at our farther outposts" and his left flank "near the opening in the vicinity of our reserves," according to Pitcher.

He and his men were no longer needed, the major apparently intimated before riding away.

Pitcher "drew in my pickets" and gathered his four companies into a country lane perhaps 100 to 200 feet south of the railroad and some 800 feet east of where he believed the 1st Brigade to be. He let his men prepare breakfast.[14]

Reinforced by the 81st Pennsylvania, French's brigade faced south toward "a swampy piece of ground, covered with a thick growth of timber," according to Richardson. To the east, "two roads crossed the railroad" nearer Miller's Pennsylvanians.[15]

Pitcher was watching designated soldiers "distributing the morning rations to the men" at 7:30 a.m. when "we were startled by a sudden and terrific volley of musketry in front." Dropping their food and seizing their stacked muskets, the 4th Maine lads waited.[16]

Eyewitness accounts would prove that Pitcher's watch was an hour fast.

Advancing "at a quick walk and owing to prevalence of the woodland," drawing "wonderfully near before they were discovered," Confederate infantry had suddenly struck French's brigade, said Howard.[17]

According to Richardson, "the enemy opened a heavy rolling fire of musketry within 50 yards" of French's line at 6:30 a.m., an hour earlier than Pitcher had figured. At least one enemy column swept up the roads toward the 81st Pennsylvania.[18]

Detecting movement in the thick woods to the south, James Miller spotted soldiers approaching the right flank of the 81st Pennsylvania. "Ready!" he shouted; his men lifted their rifled muskets to their shoulders.

"No, no, colonel, they are our men!" a Pennsylvania officer implored.[19]

Exchanging shouts with cautious Union officers, the approaching Confederates claimed "that they were our friends," said Lt. Col. Charles F. Johnson of the 81st Pennsylvania. After Miller ordered his men to lower their weapons, "in an instant a murderous fire was poured into the regiment at a distance of about 100 feet."[20]

Miller died immediately. Firing fast, the men in the regiment's six right-flank companies pulled back until rallied by Capt. Robert M. Lee Jr. Decoyed by enemy troops led by a soldier carrying a white flag (the deception led some Pennsylvanians to expect a Confederate surrender), the four left-flank companies hesitated to fire.

The Confederates did not; blasted by an accurate volley, the four companies took casualties and broke.

Howard sent Nelson Miles to find them; William Pitcher had already done so.[21]

Elijah Walker had not reached J.H. Hobart Ward when "firing commenced on the right" flank, "and I turned and hastened to rejoin my command." By the time he did, "the enemy had attacked and driven in the ------ Pennsylvania Regiment,[22] of General Howard's brigade, on the right and in front of" Pitcher and his men.[23]

According to Pitcher, "several [81st Pennsylvania] companies on the left of Howard's brigade" retreated "precipitately from the woods, passing by us and down the railroad." Hollering at his own men to form a "line on the railroad," Pitcher cajoled "the retreating companies to make a stand with us."

His "rally round the flag" efforts ultimately unsuccessful, Pitcher advanced his men to "a rail fence a short distance in front and opened fire."[24]

Riding up, Walker saw Howard's Pennsylvanians fleeing "like a flock of sheep with a pack of dogs after them, the enemy following." Confederates "in large numbers came out of the woods within a few rods of us, when a volley from our Austrian rifles put a stop to their further advance," Walker wrote.[25]

Around 7 a.m., Richardson ordered Howard and the 1st Brigade "to fill the interval made worse by the loss of Miller." Howard led forward the 61st New York Infantry (Col. Francis C. Barlow) on the right of his battle line and the 64th New York Infantry (Col. Thomas J. Parker) on the left.

Meanwhile, Nelson Miles found the 81st Pennsylvania's four missing companies "and brought them together at the railroad where was an open space." He "then led them into action," Howard said.[26]

Twin houses at Seven Pines, with 32-pounder Howitzer in the foreground
Union soldiers pose for a photo.
Photo by George N. Barnard, from Library of Congress

He took the New Yorkers through "a woods of tall trees" and "an undergrowth of young oaks" so thick that the soldiers could not "see to any distance before us," Francis Barlow noticed. "The ground in some places was muddy and marshy."[27]

Confederate bullets plucked at oak trunks, limbs, and leaves as the New Yorkers advanced. A bullet punched a hole through the shoulder of his brown horse, so Howard dismounted.

While waiting for an aide to bring up another horse, he turned, gazed across his battle line, and realized that "some [men] had been hit and others were leaving their ranks." Perchance recalling the gradual disintegration of his previous brigade at Manassas, Howard acknowledged that both regiments were encountering "their first experience under fire."

"Lie down!" he shouted. As other officers echoed the command, the New Yorkers went belly to earth behind the railroad embankment about a quarter mile east of Fair Oaks Station.

They could not stay there with French's brigade catching hell just to the southwest.

Up rode aide 1st Lt. Charles Howard leading "my large gray horse," which Oliver Otis Howard promptly mounted. His younger brother rode the general's last spare horse, "a beautiful 'zebra'"; leaning in the saddle, Howard told Charles to place himself in front of the 61st New York.

"In order to encourage the men in a forward movement[,] I placed myself, mounted, in front" of Parker's 64th New York, Howard said afterwards.

He ordered "every field officer ... to repeat each command" before shouting, "Forward!" The order rippled along the line; men rose to their feet behind the embankment.

"March!" Howard shouted, walking his horse southward.

"I could hear the echo of these words and, as I started, the Sixty-fourth followed me with a glad shout up the slope and through the woods," he said. "The Sixty-first followed my brother at the same time.

"We moved forward finely, taking many prisoners as we went and gaining ground," Howard said.

Then "a small Mississippi rifle ball" hit his right forearm. Moments later Charlie Howard "ran to me on foot and said that ... [his] horse was killed. He took a handkerchief, bound up my arm, and then ran back to the Sixty-first."[28]

The 61st New York advanced about 150 yards before drawing even with John Brooke's 53rd Pennsylvania, already "formed in line and briskly engaging the enemy." Barlow asked Brooke to stop shooting "so that we might pass in front and relieve him. This was done."

The advancing regiments pushed the Confederates south and reached the northern edge of the Seven Pines camps abandoned by the 3rd Division of IV Corps on Saturday. In his detailed report, Barlow indicated that Howard's line crested a slight hill about 20 yards north of a road "running parallel to the railroad and directly opposite the camp of [Silas] Casey's division."[29]

Seeing "a stronger force of Confederates, kneeling and firing" from beyond the nearest Union tents, Howard advanced his troops to within 30 to 40 yards, halted the line, and ordered his men to shoot. With the New Yorkers "rapidly firing," Howard rode behind his line.

Suddenly a bullet shattered the left foreleg of the gray horse; struggling to control the injured animal, Howard "was not aware" that "I had been wounded again, my right elbow having been shattered by a rifle shot."

And Charlie Howard had vanished in the melee.[30]

~~~

1. Marching 3 miles from the Grapevine Bridge, Brig. Gen. John Sedgwick had brought his 2nd Division II Corps into action northeast of Fair Oaks Station in late afternoon on May 31, 1862. His arrival anchored the loose right flank of Union troops fighting at Seven Pines.
2. Captain William L. Pitcher, *Official Records, Series 1, Vol. 11, Part I,* Chapter XXIII, No. 62, p. 861
3. Col. Elijah Walker, *OR, Series 1, Vol. 11, Part I,* Chapter XXIII, No. 61, p. 860
4. While filing his official report about Seven Pines, Walker judiciously avoided mentioning the arrest of Birney, whom Walker held in low esteem—and apparently vice versa.
5. Cross was famous for wearing a red bandanna to distinguish himself to his men. On July 2, 1863, he changed

it to black, claiming that he had foreseen his death. He was wounded in battle and died the next day.

6. Brig. Gen. Israel B. Richardson, *OR, Series 1, Vol. 11, Part I,* Chapter XXIII, No. 4, p. 764
7. Walker, *OR, Series 1, Vol. 11, Part I,* Chapter XXIII, No. 61, p. 860
8. Pettit commanded Battery B, 1st New York Light Artillery. He resigned his commission in late May 1863; Pettit's replacement was killed at Gettysburg.
9. Richardson, *OR, Series 1, Vol. 11, Part I,* Chapter XXIII, No. 4, p. 765
10. Oliver Otis Howard, *Autobiography of Oliver Otis Howard, Major General, United States Army, Vol. 1,* The Baker & Taylor Company, New York, 1907, p. 243
11. Richardson, *OR, Series 1, Vol. 11, Part I,* Chapter XXIII, No. 4, p. 765
12. Interstate 64 passes through this area today.
13. Brig. Gen. Oliver Otis Howard, *OR, Series 1, Vol. 11, Part I,* Chapter XXIII, No. 6, p. 769
14. Pitcher, *OR, Series 1, Vol. 11, Part I,* Chapter XXIII, No. 62, p. 861
15. Richardson, *OR, Series 1, Vol. 11, Part I,* Chapter XXIII, No. 4, p. 765
16. Pitcher, *OR, Series 1, Vol. 11, Part I,* Chapter XXIII, No. 62, p. 861
17. Oliver Otis Howard, *Autobiography,* p. 245
18. Richardson, *OR, Series 1, Vol. 11, Part I,* Chapter XXIII, No. 4, p. 765
19. Oliver Otis Howard, *Autobiography,* p. 245
20. Lt. Col. Charles F. Johnson, *OR, Series 1, Vol. 11, Part I,* Chapter XXIII, No. 11, pp. 775
21. Howard, *Autobiography,* p. 245
22. The regiment's number was left out in the original text to avoid embarrassing the outfit.
23. Walker, *OR, Series 1, Vol. 11, Part I,* Chapter XXIII, No. 61, p. 860
24. Pitcher, *OR, Series 1, Vol. 11, Part I,* Chapter XXIII, No. 62, p. 861
25. Elijah Walker, *The Old Soldier: History of the Fourth Maine Infantry,* Tribune, Rockland, Maine, 1895, p. 28.
26. Howard, *Autobiography,* p. 245
27. Col. Francis C. Barlow, *OR, Series 1, Vol. 11, Part I,* Chapter XXIII, No. 9, pp. 772
28. Howard, *Autobiography,* pp. 245-246
29. Barlow, *OR, Series 1, Vol. 11, Part I,* Chapter XXIII, No. 9, pp. 772
30. Howard, *Autobiography,* pp. 246-247

Chapter 27

AN APPLICATION OF COLD STEEL

"Happy to lose only my arm"

Pain emanating from his bullet-shattered right elbow, Brig. Gen. Oliver Otis Howard lingered near his crippled gray horse as the New Yorkers he had led south to the outskirts of Seven Pines fired almost point blank at the tough, unyielding Confederate infantrymen belonging to the 3rd Alabama, 12th Virginia, and 41st Virginia.[1]

Howard had estimated a distance of 30 to 40 yards between the lines when the thunderous volleys erupted; Col. Thomas J. Parker of the 64th New York recalled arriving within "about 50 yards of the enemy's line" when "we opened fire on them."[2]

Francis Barlow, colonel of the 61st New York, watched his men triggering their first volley at "the enemy being plainly in sight by the road-side" and viciously "receiving a very heavy one in return." The musketry "continued for a considerable time, and it was there that our principal loss occurred."[3]

The carnage was terrible. "The bullets whistled in every direction, and the peculiar sound made by their striking a tree or a man was terribly frequent and suggestive," said a Maine soldier. Men in butternut or blue screamed, twirled, pitched, and fell.[4]

Seeing Howard's wounded horse, Lt. William McIntyre dashed from the dissolving line of the 64th New York and, after seizing Howard, pulled the wounded general to "a sheltered place on the ground," Howard remembered.

"General, you shall not be killed," promised McIntyre.

"The bullets were just then raining upon our men," noticed Howard, shock and blood loss now weakening him. At least one bullet struck and killed McIntyre; Howard would never forget the lieutenant for "giving his life for mine."

Gathering his strength, Howard shouted for Barlow, standing not far away amidst the 61st's powder-stained riflemen. "Shall I take command of the whole brigade, sir?" Barlow responded.

"No, only of this portion," Howard told him.

Howard had brought his two regiments south unaware that more Confederate troops hidden by the thickets and scrub oaks had advanced north "beyond my left flank."5 Crossing the railroad, the Confederates came under fire by the separate 81st Pennsylvania contingents led by Nelson Miles and Robert M. Lee Jr.; spotting the men formed on the right flank of J.H. Hobart Ward's 2nd Brigade, the enemy soldiers opened fire.6

Included among these men were the Confederates ambushed by Capt. William L. Pitcher and the rail-fence-hidden lads of companies G, H, I, and K of the 4th Maine Infantry. Enemy troops had "appeared in large force at the edge of the woods" faced by Pitcher's soldiers, irritated that the Confederate attack had interrupted their breakfast.

The Maine boys "repulsed and held in check" the Confederates, said Col. Elijah Walker of the 4th Maine.7

Union Col. Francis Channing Barlow
Here a major general, to which he was promoted after the Battle of Antietam, September 17, 1862.
Photo from Library of Congress

Pitcher's men held the rail fence until the commander of a New York regiment shifting east along the railroad ordered the Mainers to form on his regiment's left flank. Pitcher did so; his men "continued firing with deadly effect."8

Hearing the firing "to my right [flank] and diagonally to my front," Ward "changed front to face the woods from where the [enemy] fire had emanated"; firing fast, Confederate infantry emerged from the woods to threaten Ward's line.

A Trinity College graduate and career soldier wounded during the Mexican-American War, Ward reacted instinctively to the butternut- and gray-clad threat. "I gave the order to fire and immediately thereafter to charge," he succinctly stated.

Delivering an accurate volley, away went the 3rd Maine and 38th and 40th New Yorks to apply the cold steel while Walker, Pitcher, and the 4th Maine anchored Ward's right flank.

"This movement was most brilliantly performed," the admiring Ward applauded.9

"Cheering continually" the 3rd Maine lads "charged over the fence" and "rushed on the enemy with such impetuosity that they broke and fled at the first onset," Col. Henry G. Staples recalled. He and his men—Staples stressed the "we"—chased the retreating Confederates "for a mile through woods and swamps."

Trying to slow the hound-dog Mainers and New Yorkers baying at their heels, enemy troops often turned and fired. Crossing a shallow stream, the 3rd Maine boys suddenly spotted "large numbers" of Confederates "on the top of an eminence"; anticipating the inevitable volley, the fast-thinking Staples told "our brave boys" to throw themselves on the ground about halfway up the hill.

The Confederates, shooting downhill, mostly missed their targets; the 3rd Mainers, targeting infantrymen framed against the skyline, "fired upon them steadily," Staples said. Volley fire spewed lead in both directions, "and most of our casualties took place here," he admitted.[10]

The 3rd Maine boys hoped they swapped casualties at a better than one-for-one ratio as the Confederates retreated from the hill.[11] Ward soon hauled the regiment back into line with his New York regiments and, although reinforcements relieved his brigade, pushed his men west for a while.

Bodies lay strewn along the 3rd Maine's route through the fields and woods. Elijah Walker would report only "2 men killed, 8 wounded, and 1 missing" in the 4th Maine; Henry Staples later received a much higher butcher's bill from the 3rd Maine's surgeon.[12]

With fighting continuing, many wounded Union soldiers—even those shot on May 31—lay where they had fallen. Wounded men who could walk, such as Oliver Otis Howard, staggered toward the rear. Realizing his two New York regiments needed assistance, the bleeding Howard sought John Brooke, asked him to bring up his 53rd Pennsylvania Infantry, then walked to where Dr. Gabriel Grant "was operating under fire beside a large stump."[13]

At his ad hoc facility that gave real meaning to the term "field hospital," Grant bound Howard's right arm. Nearby stood the missing 1st Lt. Charles Howard, the general's younger brother and aide.

"Shot through the thigh," Charlie Howard had tossed aside his sword, then leaned on the empty scabbard while limping to find a doctor. The fox-skin robe once draped across his saddle now lay "thrown across his free arm," Oliver Otis Howard noticed.

"Why weary yourself, Charlie, with that robe?" the general asked.

"To cover me up if I should have to stop," Charlie replied.[14]

Grant dressed Charlie Howard's wound and ordered him into a stretcher. His wound was worse than the young lieutenant had let on; "a Minie ball" punched "through his thigh, boring a hole clear through nearly as large as an inch augur makes, and probably grazing the bone," a friend learned later.[15]

Directed by Grant as to where a more formal hospital might be found, the general

Union Brig. Gen. John Henry Hobart Ward
Photo from Library of Congress

walked north and soon picked up a companion, a soldier "with his fingers broken and bleeding." Their cumulative strengths fading, the men leaned against each other for support.

"We wounded wanderers at last found" the field hospital set up in a private home "a half mile or more north of the Fair Oaks Station" and behind the lines of John Sedgwick's 2nd Division. There, about 11 a.m., "Dr. Hammond, my personal friend, met me near the house, saw the blood, [and] touched my arm," Howard said.

"General, your arm is broken," Hammond stated the obvious after examining the arm and finding the bones at the elbow joint shattered in small pieces. He escorted Howard to a small hut occupied by an elderly black man and woman; they watched as Howard lay down on their bed.

Howard listened as Hammond, a Dr. Palmer, "and several others ... stood by my bedside in consultation. At last Dr. Palmer, with serious face, kindly told me that my arm had better come off," Howard recalled.

"All right, go ahead. Happy to lose only my arm," he responded.

Claiming that "reaction must set in" to the wound, Palmer delayed the surgery for six hours. Not until 5 p.m. did he appear "with four stout soldiers and a significant stretcher." Once his patient was supine on it, Palmer tightened a tourniquet "around the arm close to the shoulder ... above the wound," Howard noticed.

Palmer substantially tightened the tourniquet, and "they then bore me to the amputating room, a place a little grewsome [sic] withal from arms, legs, and hands not yet all carried off,

Fort Richardson and adjacent encampment near Fair Oaks
Photo by George N. Barnard via Library of Congress

Chapter 27: An Application of Cold Steel

Bringing wounded soldiers to the cars after the battle of Seven Pines
Illustration by Arthur Lumley, June 3, 1862

and poor fellows with anxious eyes awaiting their turn," Howard described the hospital's bloody interior.

The hospital orderlies placed Howard "on the long table," Dr. Gabriel Grant loosened the tourniquet, and "a mixture of chloroform and gas was administered and I slept quietly," Howard said. "Dr. Palmer amputated the arm above the elbow.

"When I awoke I was surprised to find the heavy burden was gone," he said, "but was content and thankful."[16]

At Seven Pines, attacking Union troops recaptured the IV Corps' camps and ultimately moved west past the abatis that had not slowed Confederate troops on Saturday. Stretcher bearers found and evacuated wounded soldiers; the extent of the casualties was so great—some 8,400 soldiers wounded, including about 3,600 Yankees—that evacuations would continue by lantern light during the night.

The Howard brothers were fortunate in reaching medical care so fast. Hundreds of wounded soldiers arrived at the hastily created field hospitals, only to encounter the doctor-initiated triage system that sorted men by where bullets or cannon shrapnel had struck their bodies.

A surgeon attending Sgt. B.H. Hall of Co. F, 3rd Maine Infantry described his injury as "wound of abdomen, probably fatal." Pvt. G.H. Gordon of Co. I had seen both legs fractured and an ankle broken; with such "severe" wounds, Gordon "will probably die," an examining surgeon wrote. Gordon did die en route to Fort Monroe at the southern tip of the Peninsula.

The butcher's bill presented to Henry Staples by his regimental surgeon reduced 3rd Maine men to initials, surnames, and status as killed or wounded. The same Co. F in which Gordon and Hall had served numbered four men killed: A.C. Bray, J.H. Gardiner, W.F. Meader, and H.K. Noyes.

While Co. G lost only one man killed (J.E. Cole) and none wounded, no Co. K lads died in battle—but the dying started soon afterwards. The neck wound received by Pvt. D.W. Philbrook was "probably mortal," as was the head wound born by Pvt. D. Freeman. A surgeon wrote that C. Bradbury had been "mortally wounded in the bowels," and "Lieut. Haskell ... will probably die" after his left thigh was fractured.

The 3rd Maine's detailed casualty list and Staples's official June 2 report reached *Maine Farmer* editor Ezekiel Holmes about the same time. When he published them together, the casualty list filled almost one-third of a column.[17]

~~~

1. Col. Francis C. Barlow, *Official Records of the Civil War, Series 1, Vol. 11, Part I,* Chapter XXIII, No. 10, p. 774
2. Col. Thomas J. Parker, *OR, Series 1, Vol. 11,* Part I, Chapter XXIII, No. 10, p. 774
3. Barlow, *OR, Series 1, Vol. 11, Part I,* Chapter XXIII, No. 10, p. 772
4. *Daily Whig & Courier,* Monday, June 9, 1862
5. Oliver Otis Howard, *Autobiography of Oliver Otis Howard, Major General, United States Army, Vol. 1,* The Baker & Taylor Company, New York, 1907, pp. 247-248
6. Brig. Gen. David Birney had commanded the 2nd Brigade, 3rd Division, III Corps. Upon the command of corps commander Brig. Gen. Samuel P. Heintzelman, Birney was arrested after sunrise on June 1. John Henry Hobart Ward, commander of the 38th New York Infantry, replaced Birney as brigade commander. A court-martial later exonerated Birney.
7. Col. Elijah Walker, *OR, Series 1, Vol. 11, Part I,* Chapter XXIII, No. 61, p. 860
8. Capt. William L. Pitcher, *OR, Series 1, Vol. 11, Part I,* Chapter XXIII, No. 62, p. 861
9. Col. John Henry Hobart Ward, *OR, Series 1, Vol. 11, Part I,* Chapter XXIII, No. 59, p. 856
10. Col. Henry G. Staples, *OR, Series 1, Vol. 11, Part I,* Chapter XXIII, No. 60, p. 858
11. By late Sunday morning, Confederate troops were withdrawing from the Union camps and positions captured a day earlier. Union troops swept through the abandoned Seven Pines camps and reached those positions held by the 11th Maine and other IV Corps regiments at dawn on Saturday, May 31.
12. Walker, *OR, Series 1, Vol. 11, Part I,* Chapter XXIII, No. 61, p. 860
13. Dr. Gabriel Grant was the surgeon for the brigade commanded by William H. French. For his heroism under fire at Seven Pines, Grant later received the Medal of Honor.
14. Oliver Otis Howard, *Autobiography,* pp. 247-250
15. *Portland Daily Press,* Saturday, June 28, 1862
16. Oliver Otis Howard, *Autobiography,* pp. 247-250
17. *Maine Farmer,* Thursday, June 19, 1862

Chapter 28

THEY SOUGHT THE DEAD AMIDST THE DISINTEGRATED

"I dread to go upon that battle-field"

As stretcher bearers carried him "to the amputating room" in a field hospital near Fair Oaks Station shortly after 5 p.m., June 1, 1862, Oliver Otis Howard passed a ghastly sight: amputated "arms, legs, and hands not yet all carried off."[1]

Atop those mangled extremities went Howard's right arm, plus many more body parts as wounded soldiers poured into the hospitals, Confederate and Union, where overwhelmed surgeons struggled to save shattered, screaming men. "The wounded!" *New-York Tribune* correspondent Samuel Wilkeson exclaimed upon seeing them "fifty-six hours since they received their injuries."[2]

Not trusted by some Union generals, yet embraced by other generals seeking public acclaim,[3] news correspondents hung around Army camps and headquarters while begging generals and other officers for noteworthy military information, rumors, and scandals. "Recognized by General [Samuel P.] Heintzelman as a volunteer aide-de-camp," Wilkeson had almost unfettered access to the III Corps commander and was present during the Battle of Seven Pines.[4]

For the past two days he had "worked, and slept, and ate, and served among a thousand wounded soldiers," and by Monday evening, June 2, Wilkeson could not contain the horror.

The abattoirs passing for field hospitals were sufficient to almost sicken him; "the wretchedness of the unfortunates who are brought in [to the hospitals] in an uninterrupted stream of tardy discovery, and lie under foot everywhere, waiting surgical help," wrote a stunned Wilkeson.

"I dread to go upon that battle-field," he said.[5]

The carnage was indescribable. Lead and iron had torn men apart at Seven Pines. The day after the battle, Col. Armor A. McKnight of the 105th Pennsylvania mentioned how, during the battle, he had watched as the head of a young lieutenant from Co. D was "blown off by

Union Brig. Gen. Philip Kearny Jr.

Samuel Wilkeson
Correspondent for the New-York Tribune, operating with the Army of the Potomac. This was well over a century before we would hear the term "embedded" to describe a journalist traveling with a military outfit.
Photo courtesy of Dickinson College

a cannon ball" as the officer led "his men forward to repulse a charge of the enemy."[6]

Observing the almost hand-to-hand fighting at Seven Pines on May 31, Maj. Robert M. West of the 1st Pennsylvania Light Artillery saw a Confederate case-shot knock down "a majority of the detachment which was trying" to haul a disabled Union cannon to safety. The Pennsylvania battery of Capt. Theodore Miller fired "a discharge of canister from a section of his guns" and "mowed down ... whole rows of the enemy," West said.[7]

Flitting amidst disintegrated and intact bodies, Union soldiers searched the battlefield for dead and injured comrades, the latter "wounded in every possible form, and with possible degree of severity," said Wilkeson. Bringing the casualties to the field hospitals, stretcher bearers deposited wounded men wherever space permitted.

At one such hospital, Wilkeson saw "groaning" men spread "everywhere over three acres of lawn." He listened to "the piteous cries for help, for drink, for shade—the delirium of the dying—the blood and discoloration, and disfigurement, and dirt."

Wounded men unable to move and not yet helped by the exhausted hospital stewards and surgeons suffered where they lay. Men "away from water" begged for water; left outdoors

Chapter 28: They Sought the Dead Amidst the Disintegrated

A battlefield ambulance at some point during the Civil War
A Zouave ambulance crew demonstrates removing soldiers from a battlefield.
Photo from Library of Congress

across Saturday and Sunday nights, men "undergo wintry torments from the night cold!" Wilkeson exclaimed.[8]

The patched-up Howards, who had fortunately received relatively prompt medical attention, left the field hospital in an ambulance on Monday morning. Oliver climbed up next to the driver while the other patients (including Charlie) lay in back.

The ambulance soon arrived at nearby Fair Oaks Station on the Richmond & York River Railroad. Trains carried wounded soldiers from there to White House Landing, the temporary Federal port on the Pamunkey River. Carried aboard transport ships staffed by doctors and nurses, the wounded men received medical care as the ships sailed to Annapolis and other designated ports.[9]

At Fair Oaks Station occurred an incident later immortalized in Civil War lore. As Howard eased himself from the ambulance, up clattered Brig. Gen. Philip Kearny and his staff. Kearny led the 3rd Division of III Corps at Seven Pines; his brigade commanders included Hiram Berry and Charles Jameson from Maine, and his regiments included the 3rd and 4th Maine infantries.

"General, I am sorry for you," quietly said Kearny, who had lost his left arm while fighting in the Mexican War. "But you must not mind it; the ladies will not think the less of you!"

Howard "glanced at our two hands of the same size" and laughed. "There is one thing we can do, general. We can buy our gloves together!" he said.

"Sure enough!" Kearny replied "with a smile."

Then he rode away, and "I never met him again," said Howard.[10]

As would so many other men wounded at Seven Pines (and later during the Seven Days

Battles), the Howards and other patients caught a train east to White House Landing. The only intact soldier aboard the freight car carrying the Howards was Capt. F. D. Sewall, the general's aide.

Some wounded men stood while leaning against the car's sides. Others sat, but "the majority were lying or reclining upon straw which covered the floor of the car," Howard noticed. The car jerked as the engine started eastward; to keep his "peculiarly, sensitive" human cargo from suffering more than necessary, the conductor told the engineer to run "at a snail's pace," Howard said.

The steamer *Nelly Baker*

Traveling on a fought-over roadbed that "was in rough condition," the freight cars tilted, swayed, and shuddered every time their wheels ran over rough seams between the rails. Some wounds broke open as men bumped into one another or a freight car's steel and wood sides; when the train pulled into White House Landing three hours later, waiting soldiers swiftly unloaded the patients and took them aboard several transport ships.[11]

The Howards and Sewall boarded the steamer *Nelly Baker*, aboard which Oliver Otis would write his official Seven Pines report on Tuesday, June 3.

With their Monday evacuation, the Howards escaped from hell, the hospitals where Sam Wilkeson listened to "the screaming of stout men under the surgeons' knives." He witnessed "the ceaseless labors on the operating table in the great hospital tent" and "the use of knife and probe by lantern-light all around this country seat, and the dressing of ghastly wounds all night and all day, and all day and all night.

"'Tis a memory that shall make the Seven Pines painful until I die," Wilkeson admitted.[12]

~~~

1. Oliver Otis Howard, *Autobiography of Oliver Otis Howard, Major General, United States Army, Vol. 1*, The Baker & Taylor Company, New York, 1907, p. 250
2. Maine Farmer, Thursday, June 26, 1862. Wilkeson was not identified by Maine Farmer editor Ezekiel Holmes.
3. William Tecumseh Sherman vehemently detested journalists throughout the war.
4. Brig. Gen. David B. Birney, *Official Records, Series 1, Vol. 11, Part I,* Chapter XXIII, No. 58, p. 854
5. Maine Farmer, Thursday, June 26, 1862
6. Col. Armor A. McKnight, *OR, Series 1, Vol. 11, Part I,* Chapter XXIII, No. 57, p. 851
7. Maj. Robert M. West, *OR, Series 1, Vol. 11, Part I,* Chapter XXIII, No. 72, p. 883
8. *Maine Farmer,* Thursday, June 26, 1862
9. The War Department established receiving hospitals at Annapolis, Md., from which men and supplies could be transported by railroad.

Chapter 28: They Sought the Dead Amidst the Disintegrated

Houses converted into Union field hospitals
Both of these were used by Brig. Gen. Joseph Hooker's division in June 1862.
Photos by James F. Gibson via Library of Congress

Burying the dead and burning the horses after the battle—June 3, 1862
Illustration by Alfred R. Waud via Library of Congress

10. Philip Kearny was killed during the September 1, 1862 Battle of Chantilly, Virginia
11. Howard, *Autobiography,* pp. 251-252
12. *Maine Farmer,* Thursday, June 26, 1862

Chapter 29

A MAINE HERO LAY CLOSEST TO RICHMOND

"We did not know that our missing ... might be killed or wounded"

Somewhere amidst the human debris strewn across the Seven Pines battlefield lay 1st Sgt. Robert Brady, his teen-aged son believed while commiserating with his Co. D, 11th Maine Infantry comrades on Sunday morning, June 1, 1862.

One infinitesimal Union entity among the regiments, brigades, and divisions chewed up during the two-day battle known as Seven Pines or Fair Oaks,[1] "Co. D was somewhat scattered," Pvt. Robert Brady Jr. admitted. Many lost comrades had wandered the Union lines throughout Saturday night's rainy darkness; not until late Sunday morning did the dispersed Co. D coalesce under 1st Lt. Francis Johnson.

The company's official commander, Capt. Leonard Harvey, had exited Seven Pines stage right with a Confederate prisoner early on Saturday. Convinced that he was needed at home in Weston,[2] Harvey submitted his resignation and transferred Co. D to Francis Johnson within the next 24 hours.

The survivors off-handedly dismissed the departing Harvey, who would merit only two lines under "Personal Sketches" in a subsequent history of Co. D.[3]

Serious fighting took place about a mile away as Johnson counted his men on Sunday morning. The unabated carnage piled more bodies atop the battle's casualty scales, but the fight was over for Co. D and the shot-to-pieces 11th Maine.

Lt. Col. Harris Plaisted, who had precious few men left, was amazed there were any survivors at all. "My little battallion [sic] stood the fire of the enemy for hours, until more than half their number had fallen, and would have stood longer had I said so," he said, describing the behavior of the companies (A, C, and F) directly under his command on May 31.[4]

Plaisted had gathered his eviscerated regiment as dusk fell on Saturday. The survivors "saluted with cheers" the "regimental colors," then "for our Colonel three [cheers] were given and received by him" with great emotion. Trooping into nearby woods, the men "built fires and laid for a short night's rest."

And out of the dark came Maj. Robert Campbell, "seeming almost as one from the dead, as we had been told he was killed," said a Co. G soldier.[5]

Plaisted demanded casualty lists on Sunday. Francis Johnson counted eight D men missing: 1st Sgt. Robert Brady, Sgt. Abner F. Bassett, Corp. Freeman R. Dakin, musician Robert Strickland, and privates Daniel Gray, Mathew P. House, Moses E. Sherman, and William Sherman.

"We did not know that our missing ... might be killed or wounded," said Robert Brady Jr., worried about his father. After Union reinforcements shoved Confederate troops out of Seven Pines on June 1, the 11th Maine lads searched for their friends.

The regiment's "hastily abandoned camp had been rummaged by the Confederates," but no Co. D men lay there, according to the younger Brady.[6]

Only later did Brady learn that, while retreating on May 31, his father had captured two Confederate soldiers. He got them as far as the Richmond & York River Railroad track before enemy infantrymen suddenly emerged from the sodden thickets and captured him.[7]

The 11th Maine's survivors retrieved some wounded comrades. Badly wounded on May 31, Pvt. John Whitcomb Jr. of Co. K and Newburg[8] "lay on the ground two days and nights before he was discovered and cared for." Whitcomb's bullet-busted leg was amputated near the hip; evacuated to a hospital ship at White House Landing, Whitcomb underwent a second amputation on June 15.[9]

Discharged at Philadelphia, Whitcomb came home and "sufficiently recovered to get about on crutches," a newspaper reported. He became "one of the many dismembered but heroic memorials of the war for the salvation of the Union."[10]

Plaisted   **Casey**   **Naglee**

Soon to be singled out by Gen. George Brinton McClellan as the primary cause for the pummeling received by Union troops on May 31, Brig. Gen. Silas Casey compiled casualty lists for his 3rd Division of IV Corps.[11]

Calculating that the divisional firing line numbered 4,380 men, Casey initially reported 1,425 men killed, wounded, or missing; that figure rose by eight men in mid-June. The 1st Brigade led by Brig. Gen. Henry M. Naglee had suffered 637 casualties, 44 percent of the divisional total.[12]

On June 2, Plaisted reported 79 casualties, including 12 men killed, 50 wounded, and 17 captured.[13] Although first reported as missing, Daniel Gray was found dead on the battlefield; Co. D.'s missing men represented 41 percent of the regiment's captured soldiers.

Sometime after the battle, Plaisted and some 11th Maine soldiers searched the worm fence where companies A, C, and F had fought. Digging with whatever makeshift tools they could find, the men buried their slain comrades.

Union Maj. Gen. George B. McClellan
Photo by Mathew Brady via Wikipedia

They did a lot of digging. Into their graves went Privates Thomas Deray and George W. Warren of Co. A, Jerry McCarty and John F. Moore of Co. C, and George Farrow, John Flagg, and James Lang of Co. F. Also buried near the fence were 2nd Lt. J. William West of Co. C, Corp. James A. Scoullar of Co. F, and Corp. Willis Maddocks of Co. K, detailed on May 31 to serve with the color guard.

The survivors mourned their slain friends. "Poor West, we all feel bad about him for he was much respected by all," acting Adjutant Harrison Hume said. "I miss … West very much but I can't realize that he is gone, poor fellow.

"We found his body after the battle & buried it in a soldiers [sic] grave[,] which is not a desirable one for it is always slight, & the dead are poorly buried," Hume noted.

He wrote West's wife to let her know how her heroic husband had died. Hume felt as if he almost knew the widow; one day in late May, West had showed a photograph of his wife to Hume. "She is not pretty, but she is smart," West had said, anxious to return home to his family.

"He thought a great deal of his children," Hume had long since learned.[14]

Plaisted gazed across the earthen mounds before returning to the regimental camp. "The 11th boys are buried nearer Richmond than any soldiers of the Union army," he proudly noted. "That is true of Lieu [William] West's grave, and he fell several rods in rear of some others fell.

"Willis Maddocks ... fell at the very front, and his grave marks the extreme point where the Union men fought," Plaisted said.

"If I had a thousand men—*Maine men*—such men as I now have, God helping us, we would make a name for our good old State," said Plaisted, not realizing that his men had already done so.[15]

~~~

1. Seven Pines referred to the crossroads village where Brig. Gen. Silas Casey had established the main defense line of his 3rd Division; Fair Oaks was a nearby station on the Richmond & York River Railroad. Union officers often interchanged the names when describing the battle in their after-action reports.
2. Weston is a small town in the southeast corner of Aroostook County.
3. Albert Maxfield and Robert Brady Jr., *Company D of the Eleventh Regiment Maine Infantry Volunteers in the War of the Rebellion,* Press of Thos. Humphrey, New York, NY, 1890, pp. 11, 73
4. Col. Harris Plaisted, letter to Gov. Israel Washburn Jr., June 20, 1862, published in *Portland Daily Express,* June 30, 1862
5. "From the 11th Me. Regiment," June 2, 1862, published in the *Ellsworth American,* Friday, June 20 1862. The letter writer was an unidentified soldier from Co. G.
6. Maxfield and Brady, *Company D*, p. 12
7. The five months that Robert Brady spent in captivity damaged his health. Later promoted to second lieutenant of Co. B, 11th Maine Infantry, he resigned his commission on March 14, 1863 and went home to Enfield and his wife, Cordelia, and their young children. Robert Brady Jr. served capably through the remainder of the war.
8. Today spelled "Newburgh"
9. There is no indication of what else was amputated.
10. *Maine Farmer,* Thursday, January 15, 1863
11. McClellan exposed his Army of the Potomac to potential attack when he left his five corps separated by the Chickahominy River in late May. Failing to properly oversee the deployment of III and IV Corps south of the river, McClellan sought a scapegoat to explain the disaster of Seven Pines; the hapless and low-ranking Silas Casey made a perfect patsy.
12. Brig. Gen. Silas Casey, *Official Records, Series I, Vol. 11, Part I,* Chapter XXIII, No. 92, pp. 916-917
13. Robert Brady Jr. and Albert Maxfield, *The Story of One Regiment: The Eleventh Maine Infantry Volunteers in the War of the Rebellion,* J.J. Little & Co., New York, NY, 1896, p. 49
14. Harrison Hume, letter to "Dear Parents," June 2, 1862 and letter to "Dear Brother," June 7, 1862, courtesy of Nicholas P. Picerno
15. Plaisted, letter to Washburn, June 20, 1862, published by *Portland Daily Express,* June 30, 1862. Italics in the original.

Chapter 30

RESURRECTION

"He was inclined to damn the men of that state"

As Capt. Jonathan Prince Cilley lay dying in Middletown, Virginia, his sister Julia Draper Cilley and other fearful relatives and friends heard terrifying reports about Confederate troops massacring their prisoners.

Initial reports had already listed Captain Cilley as dead. The war news telegraphed from New York on May 28 indicated that Confederate troops had "deliberately attacked our sick train,[1] firing into the ambulances, and upon fainting men by the wayside; killing in cold blood all incapable of making resistance."[2]

After destroying the Maine and Vermont cavalry companies at Middletown, "the rebels kept up a yell and killed many with their sabres and bayonets who lay wounded on the ground," another press account noted.[3]

Published in various newspapers, a letter confirmed that several Union soldiers who had "engaged in that fearful massacre" in the Shenandoah Valley had witnessed "the inhuman ferocity" of Confederate soldiers. They had bayoneted wounded men and "mutilated and desecrated" dead Yankees.[4]

At her home in Epping, New Hampshire, Julia Draper Cilley received conflicting information about her next-to-the-oldest brother. His hands barely wiped clean of Jonathan Prince Cilley's blood, 2nd Lt. Frank Cutler wrote "Miss Cilley" on May 28 that Jonathan "was slightly wounded and taken prisoner" at Middletown.

In examining Cilley's shattered shoulder, Cutler had discovered "the bleeding was *very*[5] little as it was more bruised than cut." Though admittedly "bad is the tidings I have communicated," Cutler felt "it is much better told in a direct & certain form by letter" than "by the uncertain reports" appearing in Maine newspapers, he explained to Julia.

Referring to "our worthy Captain," Cutler assured Julia that "all respected him & deeply regret" his capture. Company B troopers promised "many threats of vengeance" upon the Confederacy "at the first chance."[6]

But the press reports referring specifically to Jonathan Prince Cilley and generally to Confederate massacres indicated a different fate for the captain. On Thursday, June 12, *Maine Farmer* editor Ezekiel Holmes reported that "this gallant young officer [Cilley] of the Maine

Jonathan Prince Cilley and his sister, Julia Draper Cilley
Photos courtesy of the Thomaston Historical Society

Cavalry was mortally wounded, and probably died soon after he was struck. Later reports confirm the statement."

Holmes reminded his readers that Rep. "Graves of Kentucky" had killed Cilley's father "in a duel ... nearly twenty-three years ago." The recently killed son "is said to have possessed all the noble and chivalric characteristics of his father ..."[7]

Sent by Maine Governor Israel Washburn Jr. to investigate the "Middletown Disaster" (which received remarkably little attention from Army authorities),[8] Archibald G. Spalding interviewed surviving 1st Maine troopers. His detailed report noted, among other things, that Jonathan Prince Cilley had "died immediately after being taken prisoner."[9]

Then news filtered into Union papers that early accounts of perfidious behavior by bloodthirsty Confederates might be untrue. While visiting the 1st Maine Cavalry camp "near Williamsport," Maryland on June 4-5, Col. John Goddard learned the troopers had heard rumors about Southern atrocities.

Apparently based on the testimony of escaped Union prisoners, as well as news carried between the lines by civilians, Union officers confirmed "the hospitals were not burned by the rebels," Goddard told Washburn, "and our sick are usually kindly treated by them, but there have been instances of shocking barbarity," especially the sight of "the women at Winchester" firing "on our retreating troops."[10]

Julia Draper Cilley could rest easy that vengeful Confederates had not slaughtered her brother and his comrades. That Jonathan Prince was dead, the press was sure; no soldier could survive having his arm blown apart.

Julia received other letters from friends and relatives seeking to console her upon Jonathan's death. "I know of your present great affliction ... that your beloved brother was wounded mortally at Front Royal," Elizabeth T. Grimes wrote Julia on June 6.

Grimes dealt at length with her last memory of Jonathan, incurred when she had met him in Washington in late March. "He was looking better than I had ever seen him before, bronzed, by exposure, & more muscular from active exercise," Grimes recalled.

As was occurring in other towns where slain 1st Maine Cavalry troopers had lived, "many friends bear you in their hearts in this sad hour[,] longing to make your burden of anxiety light," Grimes told Julia.[11]

But—and with Thomaston's avenging angel there was always a "but"—"we still have some hope that his injury is not fatal—it is possible," Grimes wrote, expressing a hope similar to Julia's.

Like a sputtering candle, hope repeatedly dimmed and flickered in Middletown throughout May 25 and May 26. Confederate authorities cared less about a cannonball-struck Yankee officer; officially Southern prisoners, Assistant Surgeon George Haley and Pvt. Isaac Harris (described by Frank Cutler as Cilley's "waiter) cared for the dying Jonathan Prince Cilley in the house of John W. Wright.

Despite her "guest" being a hated Yankee, Wright's wife, Anna,[12] assisted with Cilley's care. Frank Cutler and other Co. B troopers had laid their broken captain on a lounge in the Wright home; sometime on Monday or Tuesday, the dying Cilley awakened to hear "the steps of a woman crossing the room."

Cilley gradually examined himself and his surroundings. His shattered right "arm felt as though it looked green, and something seemed foreign to him."

Having often examined Cilley's ghastly wound, Haley believed that the captain would die from it. Alerted that Cilley was awake and making noise, Haley asked Mrs. Wright to deliver the bad news. She demurred, so Isaac Harris told Cilley, "Captain, do you know that you are mortally wounded and cannot recover?"

"Thunder!" Cilley exploded. "I am not going to die. What do you mean?"

"The—the doctor—told me so," stammered Harris, surprised by Cilley's outburst.

"Well, the doctor doesn't know as much about it as I do. I intend to see the war finished," growled Cilley.

The avenging angel wanted to accomplish his one goal in life.

Equipped with "a common handsaw and a butcher knife," a captured 1st Vermont Cavalry assistant surgeon soon darkened the Wrights' door "and insisted that the [Cilley's] arm should be amputated."

Cilley begged to differ, and when the sawbones revealed that in his six months of military service, he "had not seen a single amputation performed," someone apparently threw the Vermonter out of the house.[13]

A few weeks later, Julia Draper Cilley opened a letter delivered to her Epping home. She

Union cavalry escort
This illustration is representative of the 1st Maine Cavalry
Illustration by Edwin Forbes, 19 September 1863, via Library of Congress

read, in an unfamiliar handwriting, "Dear Sister ... You have probably heard before now that I was wounded and taken prisoner," Jonathan Prince Cilley had dictated via Isaac Harris on Wednesday, June 4. Detailing the May 24 battle involving his regiment, Cilley accurately told Julia that "a small piece [of shell] injured my arm so much so that I have been unable to care for myself."

But he was receiving "the best of care" and "every comfort that I can ask for" in the Wright home. "Mrs. Wright is never tired of doing and seems to study for my care!"

The letter revealed a Cilley who was startlingly upbeat despite his wound. Confederate officers had paroled him, Haley, and Harris on June 1, "and in a few days [we] shall all be ready for home," he informed Julia. Union troops had pushed Thomas J. "Stonewall" Jackson and his army "up" the Shenandoah Valley to Strasburg, "and we hear that Gen [James] Shields and other staff officers are in hot pursuit [of Jackson] and giving him what he deserves."[14]

Three days after Harris jotted down Cilley's thoughts for Julia, Frank Cutler wrote another letter to "Miss Cilley" from Williamsport. After escaping his Confederate captors at Mount Jackson, Pvt. Robert Nutter of Co. E had apparently traveled through Middletown while en route to Union lines.

Nutter spoke with Surgeon Haley, who reported that Cilley "is doing well," Cutler assured Julia Cilley.

And "P.S. Our forces occupy" Middletown, "so your brother is in the hands of the Union forces," Cutler concluded his good news. Julia learned from subsequent letters that Haley had removed some bone fragments from Jonathan's right arm.

Cilley did not leave Middletown as soon as he desired. His wound healing slowly, he tried writing with his left hand. "Can you read it?" he asked, referring to his penciled June 23 letter to Julia. On July 3, he reported to her that "my arm continues to improve & my strength to gain."

Not until August 9 could Cilley finally tell Julia, "Out of secess[15] I am once more and on my way home."[16]

Jonathan Prince Cilley returned to Thomaston that autumn and later underwent additional surgeries in Washington, D.C. to remove some 40 fragments (bone and possibly metal) from his right arm and shoulder.[17] Though he still lusted for vengeance, Cilley had changed... had admittedly softened a bit.

Cilley, "who had the unusual experience of reading his own obituary," would forever believe "that he owed his recovery to be carried immediately" to John Wright's home "and receiving there the motherly care and nursing of his wife, Mrs. Wright," Edward Parsons Tobie wrote long afterwards.

"Indeed, his comrades attributed his chivalrous esteem of the women of Virginia to Mrs. Wright's kindness, as he was inclined to damn the men of that state," Tobie said.[18]

~~~

1. Ambulances and wagons carrying sick and wounded Union soldiers during the retreat "down" the Shenandoah Valley. Direction in the Valley is based on the flow of the two branches (North and South) of the Shenandoah

River: "down" (northeast) toward the Potomac River or "up" (southwest) toward the Shenandoah's headwaters.
2. *Daily Whig & Courier,* Thursday, May 29, 1862
3. *Daily Whig & Courier,* Friday, May 30, 1862
4. *Daily Whig & Courier,* Saturday, May 31, 1862
5. Italics in the original.
6. Eve Anderson, *A Breach of Privilege: Cilley Family Letters 1820-1867,* Seven Coin Press, Spruce Head, Maine, 2002, pp. 434-435 (italicized in original account)
7. *Maine Farmer,* Thursday, June 12, 1862
8. After Confederate soldiers drove Maj. Gen. Nathaniel Banks and his V Corps from the Shenandoah Valley, the War Department had greater disasters to explain than what had occurred at Middletown.
9. Archibald G. Spalding, letter to Governor Israel Washburn Jr., June 4, 1862, Maine State Archives
10. Goddard, letter to Governor Israel Washburn Jr., June 5, 1862, MSA. Some Union soldiers noted Winchester women shooting at fleeing Federal troops; at least one Union soldier was shot down by a distaff sniper.
11. Anderson, *Privilege,* pp. 438-440
12. 1870 U.S. Census, Frederick County, Opequon Township, p. 81. The Wrights, whose sons would have been approximately 7 and 5 in 1862, apparently moved to Middletown after the war began. The family was not listed in the 1860 census for Opequon Township.
13. Edward Parsons Tobie, *History of the First Maine Cavalry, 1861-1865,* First Maine Cavalry Association, Emery & Hughes, Boston, 1887, p. 41. This footnote applies to the dialogue reported in this entire scene.
14. Anderson, *Privilege,* pp. 437-428
15. "Secess" or "secesh" was a derogatory term referring to Southern sympathizers and Confederate troops alike.
16. Ibid., pp. 441-444 (italicized in the original account)
17. Although his wound did not fully heal until September 1863, Cilley developed his own form of occupational therapy; he regained the use of his right arm.
18. Tobie, *History,* p. 41

Chapter 31

RALLY 'ROUND THE FLAG, BOYS

"We shall not all return"

By early spring 1862, Union armies stood poised to crush Confederate forces in Virginia. Planning to capture Richmond from the southeast, George McClellan started shipping men and material to Fort Monroe at the tip of the peninsula formed by the James and York rivers. There he would concentrate the 121,500-man Army of the Potomac before advancing northwest to attack Richmond's defenses.

In the Shenandoah Valley, Maj. Gen. Nathaniel Banks commanded Federal divisions charged with pinning Confederate Lt. Gen. Thomas "Stonewall" Jackson and his troops (perhaps 5,000 men in late winter) between the Appalachian and Blue Ridge mountains.

Farther west in the Appalachians, Maj. Gen. John Fremont commanded Union troops guarding key cities and transportation centers. In northern Virginia, Maj. Gen. Irvin McDowell and his I Corps—which would ultimately swell to 40,000 men—defended Washington, D.C. and its approaches from possible Confederate attacks.

With so many soldiers available to destroy Virginia's vastly outnumbered Confederate defenders, the Lincoln Administration (via Adjutant General Lorenzo Thomas) ordered that recruiting cease in the loyal states. On Thursday, April 3, Maine Adjutant Gen, John Hodsdon issued General Order No. 11, directing that "all officers and others engaged" in "Volunteer recruiting service in this state" should "close their several offices and [points of] rendezvous."[1]

Then Jackson waged his brilliant Valley Campaign that bruised and battered three Federal armies. Afraid the elusive Jackson might attack the capital, President Abraham Lincoln prevented McDowell and I Corps from reinforcing McClellan in the Chickahominy River swamps just east of Richmond.

Suddenly the War Department reopened the recruiting spigot.

On Thursday, May 22, Hodsdon's office issued General Order No. 12 to create "one Regiment of Infantry, the Sixteenth of Maine Volunteers ... to serve for three years or during the war, if sooner ended." The new regiment would field "not less than" 866 men and "nor more than 1,046 men, in the aggregate."

Recruiters must accept only "able-bodied men" from age 18 to "under the age of forty-five years." Youngsters under age 18 could enlist with "the written consent of their parents or guardians."2

A few mornings later Sgt. Maj. Abner R. Small of Waterville "was laying out the work on my desk" inside the State House recruiting office. A year earlier he had enlisted in Co. G, 3rd Maine Infantry, and had fought at Manassas. Utterly bored with camp life by early winter, he had requested a transfer to a recruiting job in Maine.

Small now worked for Maj. John Gardiner, a former regular Army dragoon and the current Federal superintendent of recruiting services in Maine. Since April 3, work had slowed in Gardiner's office; suddenly the major told Small, "Sergeant-Major, the governor wishes to see you at once ... I've recommended you for a commission."

Taking "the stairs three at a leap," Small reported to Governor Israel Washburn Jr. He

U.S. Adjutant General Lorenzo Thomas
Photo from Library of Congress

Union Sgt. Maj. Abner R. Small
Photo courtesy of Maine State Archives

"swung round in his chair" and informed Small that "we're to raise a new regiment." If Small could raise Co. B, 16th Maine Infantry, then "I'll commission you captain. When can you go?"

"This afternoon, sir," Small replied.

Moments later he blew into the recruiting office and thanked Gardiner for his recommendation. "Make good my promises to the governor," Gardiner replied.

Other ambitious young men also fanned out across Maine in late May to recruit companies for the 16th Maine.

Small enthusiastically preached about the joys of soldiering to anyone who would listen; his first afternoon on the hunt, he secured his first recruit in Vienna. After signing up a second recruit in Mt. Vernon, Small suddenly struck out.

In Readfield he "painted the town red with patriotic posters ornamented with pictures of proper soldiery" and enrolled a youngster under age 18. Arriving promptly on the scene, the boy's father "threatened to make a dead hero of me if he should find me in town by Saturday night," recalled Small, facing a danger as real as a discharging Confederate cannon.

The irate father "led him [his son] home by the ear," and Small decamped for safer environs.

He soon realized that "recruiting was a discouraging business. I called up all the eloquence of my ancestors, if they had any; I pleaded, cried, swore, and prayed, yet only two

Secretary of War Edwin McMasters Stanton
Photo taken between 1855-65
Photo from Library of Congress

Union Col. Adelbert Ames
In this photo, taken by 1865, he's a major general.
Photo from Library of Congress

patriots were enrolled to my credit."

Out-hustling and out-recruiting Small, Charles Hutchins of Augusta enlisted enough men that he dared lobby Washburn for the Co. B captaincy. A deal was a deal; because Small admitted, "I was failing to raise" Co. B, Hutchins received the promised commission instead.

But his fortunes improved when he opened a letter on Friday, June 6. Washburn had appointed Asa Wildes of Skowhegan as colonel of the 16th Maine; writing Small from Augusta on June 5, Wildes reported that "I have appointed you Adjutant of the 16th Regiment. Please report here at once."

The position gained Small a lieutenant's commission and a heavy workload; "in Room No. 9, off the rotunda of the State House, I began in earnest my work" to organize the 16th Maine, "and ... I had my hands full," Small admitted.[3]

Competition immediately developed for potential 16th Maine recruits. Now under the management of the jumpy Secretary of War Edwin M. Stanton—who, like the equally gullible McClellan, saw a Confederate lurking behind every Virginia tree that spring—the War Department asked for more "troops from this State ... at the earliest moment possible," Hodsdon announced in General Order No. 13, written on May 26.

"The Commander-in-Chief [Washburn] ... directs that three regiments of infantry" be created "for three months service" with the Army, Hodsdon wrote.

Within 24 hours, Lorenzo Thomas telegraphed Washburn that Stanton had withdrawn his request for the short-term regiments. On May 27, Hodsdon instructed recruiters to "cease enlisting from this date" and discharge all 90-day recruits.[4]

Such Washington-based equivocation distracted the collective loyal states' adjutant generals from serious duties that May.

Ironically, after tallying the recruits who had rushed to join the three-month regiments, Hodsdon and his staff believed that "the action of our citizens in volunteering, in all parts of the State, was so prompt" that the regiments would have reached their quotas "in three or four days at the most."[5]

Recruits dribbled into the 16th Maine camp at Augusta as May faded from the calendar. "From every part of the state, recruits came forward slowly in June," Small said.[6] Of the recruits reporting for duty, failed medical examinations sent some patriotic men home on the next available stage or train.

Under General Order No. 12, each 16th Maine recruiter had to find "some reputable physician to examine candidates for enlistment." Paid 25 cents per recruit "finally accepted by the United States mustering officer," a doctor had a pecuniary interest in passing every physically flawed specimen of Maine manhood who darkened his examining room's doorway.

The wonder is that the freelancing physicians, who received no compensation for rejecting ill or elderly men, failed as many recruits as they did.[7]

Then on Saturday, July 5, Hodsdon's office issued General Order No. 16 to create two full-term infantry regiments. The 17th Maine would form at Portland, the 18th Maine at Bangor—and this time President Lincoln, not Secretary Stanton, had requested the reinforcements.

Three days later Lincoln telegraphed Washburn to create a third infantry regiment; consecutively numbered the 19th Maine, this regiment would "rendezvous at Bath," Hodsdon wrote.[8]

Officers and recruits gradually populated the 16th Maine's camp. "One day, as I was busy ... at guard mounting," Small saw "a handsome young man" watching the hubbub inside the camp. "He sported a white beaver hat ... and carried himself with the dignity of a senator."

The civilian kept watching as Small went about his duties; soon "a feeling came over me that he was my military superior," Small thought.

Chapter 31: Rally 'Round the Flag, Boys

The man finally approached Small and quietly said, "Farnham, late of the 2nd Maine."

Newly appointed as major of the 16th Maine Infantry, Augustus Bowman Farnham "requested me to show him through the camp," Small recalled.

Born in Bangor on March 10, 1839, Farnham was only 22 when commissioned as a first lieutenant in Co. G, 2nd Maine Infantry Regiment, in late May 1861. A Manassas veteran, Farnham had left the 2nd Maine on Jan. 2, 1862. An up and coming merchant in Bangor, he had found civilian life not to his liking; with Washburn seeking experienced officers to lead the 16th Maine, Farnham applied for a staff slot.

On "another day," a uniformed captain "came briskly into No. 9 [office inside the State House] and informed me that his name was Tilden, that he was the new regiment's lieutenant-colonel, and that I was to take my orders from him," Small remembered his succinct introduction to Charles Tilden of Castine.[9]

After shaking a few hands at the State House, Tilden explored the 16th Maine's camp. As did other Maine officers that spring and summer, he climbed the career ladder by seeking higher rank in a new (or at least a different existing) regiment. Leaving the 2nd Maine Infantry as a combat-tested captain, he brought valuable leadership experience to the 16th Maine.

At least its bumbling and stumbling recruits behaved well. A few regiments assembling at Augusta during the past year had trashed the capital, but not the men and boys of the 16th Maine; they "are ... remarkable for their orderly and civil conduct," a correspondent commented in the *Portland Daily Press.*

Asa Wildes brooked no foolishness; if the recruits thought they could pull the wool over the eyes of their new lieutenant colonel, Tilden's steely gaze—honed in combat at Bull Run, Hanover Court House, and Gaines Mill—convinced them otherwise.

And Tilden subtly reminded the fledgling soldiers about the cavernous gap between a veteran and a recruit. He brought "a secesh [secession] flag, taken by the 2d Maine from the 5th Alabama regiment" at Gaines Mill, the correspondent said. "The flag is of silk, about four feet wide and seven feet long, and bears the stars and bars of the rebel confederacy ... It is stained with blood."

The 16th Maine recruits could figure how blood had splattered that flag.[10]

Civilians also eyed commissions in the new regiments. Sitting at a desk in Brunswick on Monday, July 14, the 33-year-old professor of modern languages at Bowdoin College

Maine Attorney General Josiah Hayden Drummond
Photo via Wikipedia

wrote "His Excellency Governor Washburn" to ask if he "desires and will accept my service.

"Perhaps it is not quite necessary to inform your Excellency who I am," the erudite academician wrote, identifying his father and describing a seven-year career at Bowdoin, then (and still) a top private college in Maine.

"I have always been interested in Military matters, and what I do not know in that line, I know how to learn," claimed the husband of Frances Caroline Adams and father of Grace and Harold. He told Washburn that Bowdoin administrators had granted him "leave ... to spend a year or more in Europe, in the service of the College."

The aspiring warrior stated that "this war must be ended, with a swift and strong hand; and every man ought to come forward and asked to be placed at his proper post." Almost 100 of his former students "are now officers in our army," he claimed.

Asking Washburn to decide "whether I can best serve you here [at Bowdoin] or in the field," the Brewer-born Joshua Lawrence Chamberlain concluded his letter, then posted it to Augusta.[11]

Washburn received many similar letters in midsummer. Some came from ambitious officers, others from educated men like Chamberlain, unknown to the politically astute governor. He quietly inquired about Chamberlain; writing Washburn from Portland on July 21, Maine Attorney General Josiah H. Drummond excoriated Chamberlain.

"His old classmates etc. here say you have been deceived: that C.[hamberlain] is nothing at all: that is the universal expression of those who knew him," Drummond wrote.[12]

Evidently hearing other more positive reports about Chamberlain, Washburn sought an officer's slot for him. Spurred by "liberal bounties"—the governor raised to $45 the bounty for men joining the new regiments and to $55 the bounty for "recruits for old regiments," with the money "to be paid" before the recruits left Maine—recruiting went well in July.

In fact, based on recruiters' reports, the four regiments were attracting more men than authorized. When Stanton asked Washburn for yet a fifth infantry regiment in early August, Hodsdon responded that "all companies already enlisted for new regiments," yet "not necessarily" needed in the four now forming, should report to Island Park in Cape Elizabeth by August 12.

There these companies would form "the Twentieth of Maine Volunteers."[13] To lead this regiment, Washburn tapped Adelbert Ames, an 1861 West Point graduate from Rockland. Severely wounded while serving with the 5th U.S. Artillery at Manassas, Ames had seen additional combat during the Peninsula Campaign. Although brevetted an Army lieutenant colonel on July 1, 1862, he lobbied Washburn for a command position with a state regiment.

Washburn made Ames colonel of the 20th Maine Infantry, Joshua Chamberlain its lieutenant colonel, and Charles Gilmore of Bangor its major.[14]

Some hometown supporters viewed Chamberlain's rank as a demotion, because Joshua Chamberlain, "the son of Colonel Joshua Chamberlain of Brewer" had already "accepted the Colonelcy of the Maine 20th Regiment," William Wheeler bragged in the *Daily Whig & Courier* on July 22, a day after Attorney General Drummond had trashed Chamberlain.

Now Drummond's "nothing at all" was apparently commanding the 20th Maine. "This is a

Chapter 31: Rally 'Round the Flag, Boys

Gen. Joshua Lawrence Chamberlain
Photo by Mathew Brady, Brady-Handy Collection, Library of Congress

significant and gratifying index to the State of public feeling in the present crisis," Wheeler believed.[15]

He was, of course, incorrect.

Stanton clamored for the new regiments as July transitioned to August. Beginning with Southern successes in the Shenandoah Valley (where Jackson's only loss had come at Kernstown on March 22), Union fortunes had ebbed since spring. Outside the gates of Richmond, a new Confederate field commander—Robert E. Lee—had outfoxed and outfought McClellan in late June and had chased his numerically superior army to Harrison's Landing on the James River.

In early to mid-July, John Hunt Morgan and his hard-riding Confederate cavalry had run amuck in Union-held central Kentucky. By mid-August a larger Confederate army under Maj. Gen. Edmund Kirby Smith would invade Kentucky and, on August 29-30, would thrash a Union army at Richmond. This battle occurred simultaneously with the Union debacle at Second Manassas.

Everywhere that Lincoln and Stanton looked that summer, the Confederacy was on the ascendancy. The Union needed more men now, not later, Stanton informed the loyal governors.

In Maine, Governor Washburn "orders and directs, that all enlisted men ... shall report to the general rendezvous ... without delay" and "must come in at the latest, before Saturday," August 9, Hodsdon stressed on July 31.

The 16th Maine boys were ordered to report to Augusta by Tuesday, August 5.[16] They came from cities, towns, and unorganized plantations and townships.[17] Often British- or Indian-centric, Maine place names developed almost haphazardly until the region's 1820 separation from Massachusetts. As settlement pushed northward (especially after the 1842 Webster-Ashburton Treaty settled the border with Canada), state officials delineated additional internal political boundaries by sending surveyors into the regions beyond the cities and towns.

Starting at the New Brunswick border and working their way west until stopped by a political or natural boundary, surveyors laid out lines ostensibly six miles apart from south to north. Called a "range," a surveyed section was divided into 36-square-mile political entities called "townships," each measuring six miles on a side (more or less).

The state identified each township by its township number and range number. This methodology led to Maine's numerical place-naming system, where Township 1, Range 1 (also T1R1) abutted the St. Croix River in eastern Washington County and Township 20, Range 11 (also T20R11) bordered the St. Francis River in northernmost Maine.

In Co. A, Capt. Charles Williams led men from Anson, Augusta, Benton, Fairfield, Madison, and Waterville on the Kennebec River and Detroit and Newport on the Sebasticook River; those municipalities spread across Kennebec, Penobscot, and Somerset counties.

Hailing from Skowhegan, Williams had five men—Corp. Winslow Morrill, Owen Cunningham, Alden Hackett, John McKeen, and Alonzo Tripp—from Township 4, Range 5; 23-year-old James Witham came from Township 3, Range 3.

John Kealiher hailed from Moose River Plantation, 18-year-old Josiah Nutting from

Canaan, and 40-year-old Cyrus Hall from Concord Township. James Leavitt was the only recruit from Lincoln, 22-year-old Austin Poor the only one from Patten. How 26-year-old William Nelson wandered into Co. A from New York City, the muster rolls did not explain.[18]

Prospective recruits faced one gauntlet not run by the volunteers of '61: tougher medical exams. Fourteen months earlier, doctors had approved recruits because they had sufficient fingers and toes and a palpable pulse. Stunned by the multitudinous soldiers shed from the ranks because of disease and physical infirmities, the War Department had tightened the medical criteria.

The contrast was conspicuous, particularly to the combat veterans like Ames and Tilden sent to whip the new regiments into shape, literally and figuratively. "The *physique* ... of this regiment will be admirable, [with] most scrupulous care being taken by the examining surgeon, Dr. Briggs of this city, not to admit any men into its ranks who are not thoroughly able-bodied," a correspondent said in Augusta. "The critical examination of Dr. Briggs has excluded many a man who has therefore been compelled, much against his desires, to go home."[19]

Daniel Chaplin
Photo courtesy of Bangor Public Library

Unqualified recruits still slipped past the medical screening. Seeking to accompany "her lover, who had enlisted" in the 16th Maine, an Androscoggin County woman "passed the Surgeon's examination as to health" and traveled to Augusta "with the recruits from Lewiston," Ezekiel Holmes appended a juicy *Kennebec Journal* tidbit in his *Maine Farmer*.

The woman was "of masculine frame, is sun burnt, and to all general appearances would pass as a hardy man," said a KJ reporter who apparently met the distaff recruit.[20] "She is patriotic, is willing to expose herself to hard marches and hard fighting for her country," the reporter ironically listed the reasons given for letting women serve in the American combat arms 140 years later.

Detected and "rejected from the service" on Thursday, June 26, the woman "was furnished with the means of reaching her home, for which she departed in her male attire, which really looked adapted to her make and manners.

"She would probably be as efficient a soldier as most men who in engage in battle," the reporter commented.[21]

At Saco in York County, 22-year-old John West Haley wondered if he should enlist at that time. "In 1861 I concluded I had a duty to perform[,] but hesitated about embarking on this troubled sea," said Haley, recently a Saco Water Power Shop employee.

"I feared I lacked those qualities which soldiers so much need," so he had avoided enlisting a year earlier, he said.

After Hodsdon announced the formation of the 17th and 18th Maine infantries, "a very intimate friend became fired up" about joining; along with "some other friends, five of us in the same class in Sunday School ... were getting hot under the collar," Haley recalled.[22]

One friend enlisted on August 5, and "the rest thoughtlessly followed, like sheep over a fence," said Haley, realizing he had agreed to enlist "in a momentary spasm of enthusiasm."

Describing himself as "naturally timid and shrinking," he wondered why "I had, even for a moment, thought seriously of going into the service." Rather than reveal "a white liver [cowardice] by backing out," Haley signed his enlistment papers on Wednesday, August 6.

Passing a medical examination the next day, Haley officially joined Co. I, 17th Maine Infantry. The company was "composed almost entirely of men from York and Cumberland counties" in southern Maine, "with a few 'Oxford [County] bears' sandwiched in," he said.

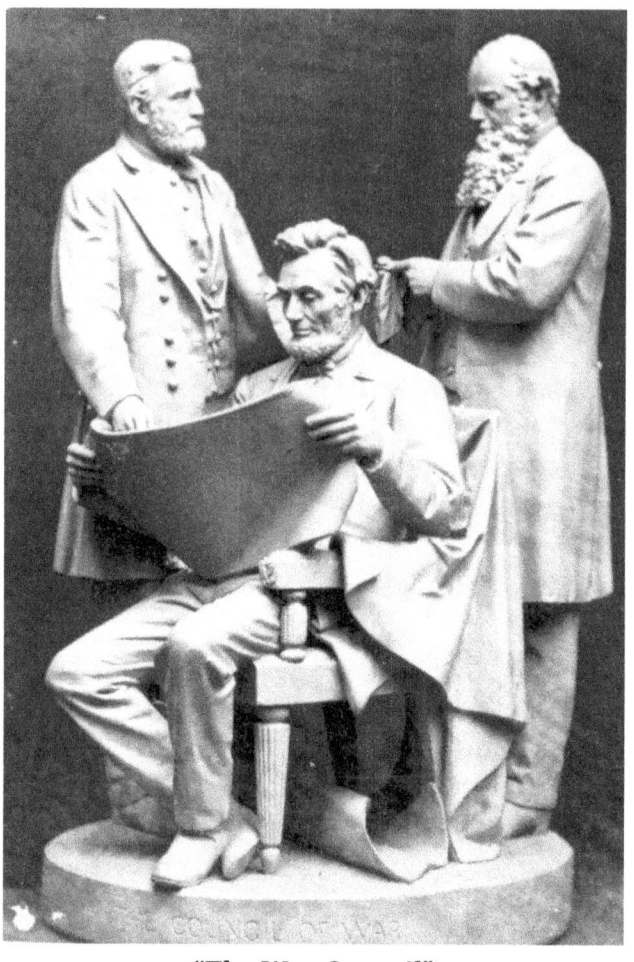

"The War Council"
This c. 1870 statuette depicts President Abraham Lincoln (sitting), Gen. Ulysses S. Grant (left), and Secretary of War Edwin McMasters Stanton.
Sculpted by John Rogers; image published by George Stacy, via Library of Congress

Shipped to Portland on Thursday, August 7, the new recruits were "mustered into the state service by Captain Joe Perry," Haley recalled. The fledgling soldiers then crossed the Fore River and reported to their first official post, Camp King in Cape Elizabeth.

Taking stock of his Co. I comrades, Haley counted 16 high-school graduates, "nine collegians, two clergymen, and one lawyer." He figured "patriotism prompted most of these" to join the 17th Maine; "as far as my own case is concerned, I lay claim to but very little of what goes by that name.

"Love of a change, an overwhelming desire to see the country ... furnished the key to my conduct," Haley commented.

That night the Co. I boys ate "salt horse" and drank "copious draughts of some kind of tea which tasted strongly of turkey stuffing," he noticed. The recruits slept two men per shared blanket inside a Sibley tent; only "a few wisps of hay" formed the tent's floor, and the recruits evidently chatted for a while. Not until "the 'wee small hours'" did Haley and his tent mates fall asleep.

"The next morning dawned on a tired and disgusted set of mortals," he remembered.[23]

Unlike the 20th Maine Infantry's ten companies, each drawn from specific counties, the 18th Maine Infantry forming at Bangor strongly represented central and eastern Maine. Bangor (known as the Queen City of Maine) provided Col. Daniel Chaplin, Adjutant Russell B. Shepherd, Quartermaster Horatio Pitcher, and two of the ten infantry captains. Maj. Charles Hamlin came from Orland; Surgeon R.E. Paine and another captain hailed from Hampden. The seven other company captains came from Bucksport, Columbia, Eastport, Ellsworth, Lincoln, Orono, and Sangerville.

Because he listed Portland as his place of residence, only Lt. Col. Thomas Hammond Talbot could be considered "from away." Although technically a New Brunswick-born British subject, the 42-year-old Chaplin had lived in Maine since age three. A skilled horseman and a veteran of First Manassas and the Peninsula Campaign, he had resigned as major of the 2nd Maine Infantry in mid-July to take command of the 18th Maine. Its ultimate fate would intertwine with Chaplin's.

In mid-August 1862, however, the regiment was "now fully organized, armed and equipped, and are fast learning the routine of the duty." Battalion drill commenced on August 12, and Chaplin's men were "ready now and willing to receive the bounty and pay."[24]

On Sunday, August 16, Capt. Christopher V. Crossman marched his Co. D to the State Street home of William P. Wingate, customs collector for the Port of Bangor. Under the adoring collective gazes of "the ladies of Ward Seven," Crossman and his soldiers stopped in the street, spun as one toward the house, and snapped to attention.

Wingate's vivacious daughter, Ada, stepped toward Crossman, "presented an elegant flag" for the 18th Maine, and delivered a short patriotic speech in which she asked the Co. D lads to "accept this flag and its accompaniments with our best wishes for your welfare."

When Ada Wingate finished speaking, her male admirers doffed their caps and "gave three rousing cheers for the flag, and three more for the ladies who presented it."

Aware "that there are men in these ranks near and dear to many of you," Crossman looked at the flag and thanked the women for "this emblem of liberty," which "shall be our talisman for good." A few appropriate sentences later, he fell silent; the Ward 7 ladies served their soldiers refreshments and gave each man "a needle case containing many useful articles, which had been prepared" by the women.

Crossman received a new revolver from a local businessman, and the Co. D lads marched back to Camp Roberts. Many of them would never return to Ward 7.[25]

As the five regiments rapidly formed in August, Hodsdon (as acting quartermaster general) and his staff scrambled to fully equip the 5,000 men. Among other items, the state issued to the 16th Maine "1000 Enfield Rifle Muskets, Bayonets and Appendages, calibre 58."

The regiment also received "1270 Drawers, pairs of"; "1009 Hats, trimmed, infantry"; "1010 Great Coats"; "1010 Trowsers [sic]"; "1000 Blankets"; "50 Sibley Tents" and "50 Tent

Poles"; "28 Wall Tents" and "28 Wall Tent Flies"; and "1010 Knapsacks, complete."

The other four regiments headed to war were similarly equipped.[26]

On Thursday, August 14, Small watched in satisfaction as the 16th Maine "was formed in line and formally mustered" into federal service by his former boss, John Gardiner.

"One moment we were free men to go and come as we pleased, and the next saw us amenable to all the arbitrary and despotic rules of the war department," Small realized. "In fact we were machines to be perfected and used as men like ourselves, holding commissions of authority, saw fit for the good of the service."[27]

John Gardiner traveled to Cape Elizabeth to muster the 17th Maine Infantry into federal service on Monday, August 18. Haley remembered him as "a full-blooded West Pointer who has a crushing hatred for all volunteer troops," a viewpoint with which Small would have vigorously disagreed.

Formed in "the ranks of dress parade," the 17th Maine boys stood at attention "for hours while one company at a time was inspected," Haley said. "Several men fainted and fell" as Gardiner continued with his inspection; "by the time the first three companies were inspected," all the enlisted men but one lay "flat on the ground."

For whatever reason, that single soldier, Jim Jose, "stood as a monument of endurance and folly" as the ceremony dragged on, Haley said.

Gardiner finished mustering the 17th Maine boys, who also received "our guns." According to Haley, Gardiner discovered one recruit who "was given permission to retire from service"; citing a "desire to escape domestic tyranny," the soldier declined.[28]

Unlike many Maine other regiments, the 16th Maine never called a specific municipality "home." The 5th Maine Infantry would always be associated with Portland[29] and the fledgling 18th Maine Infantry with Bangor.[30]

Not even Augusta sufficed for the 16th Maine. Local residents had watched many regiments occupy their city during the previous 15 months; the 16th Maine was just one more polyglot collection of amateur soldiers headed out to play at war. Neither the capital city nor the new regiment shared a special bond.

So when the 16th Maine "left Augusta quietly, without ostentation or parade" on Tuesday, August 19, "we neither expected or received any marked expressions of profound gratitude or boundless enthusiasm to cheer us on our way to the seat of war," Small said.

He thought about the future as the regiment's train rattled south toward the New Hampshire border. "We shall not all return," Small realized. "Many lives will have gone out, and with them the light of many homes and the hope of many hearts, ere the war closes.

"But there comes home to us the thought that these will have not died in vain," he prophesized.[31]

Other regiments swiftly followed the 16th Maine. Marching across Tukey's Bridge into Portland about 6 a.m. on Thursday, August 21, the 17th Maine boys discovered that they were horribly out of shape. On that warm morning "the sweat ran down our faces," Haley recalled, and the "dust filled our eyes and ears and throats."

Boarding their train, the new soldiers rolled south "amid a great hurrahing at a speed of not less than a mile a minute," he believed. The train "flew through Saco so fast" that the soldiers could not "recognize friends ... assembled at the depot to see us off.

"But it was best to go in this way; it prevented many trying scenes," Haley admitted.[32]

The 18th Maine Infantry also mustered on August 21, then left Maine three days later. Under Col. Frederick Sewall, the 19th Maine Infantry mustered on August 25 and entrained for Virginia on August 27.

As the last regiment to form that month, the 20th Maine mustered into federal service on August 29 and left the state on Tuesday, September 2.

All five regiments would indeed encounter glory and horror on Southern battlefields.

~~~

1. John L. Hodsdon, *Annual Report of the Adjutant General of the State of Maine, 1862,* Appendix A, p. 3
2. Ibid., Appendix A, pp. 2-3
3. Henry Adams Small, *The Road to Richmond: The Civil War Letters of Major Abner R. Small of the 16th Maine Volunteers,* Fordham University Press, New York, 2000, pp.33-36
4. Hodsdon, *Annual Report of the Adjutant General of the State of Maine, 1862,* Appendix A, pp. 3-4
5. Ibid., Appendix A, p. 6
6. Small, *Road to Richmond,* p. 37
7. *Maine State Adjutant General's Report 1862,* Appendix A, p. 3
8. Ibid., Appendix A, pp. 5, 7
9. Small, *Road to Richmond,* pp. 39-40
10. Letter by "Skirmisher," July 11, 1862, published in *Portland Daily Press,* Saturday, July 12, 1862
11. Joshua L. Chamberlain, letter to Governor Israel Washburn Jr., July 14, 1862, Maine State Archives
12. Josiah H. Drummond, letter to Governor Israel Washburn, July 21, 1862, MSA
13. Hodsdon, *Annual Report of the Adjutant General of the State of Maine, 1862,* Appendix A, pp. 8-9
14. Ibid., Appendix A, p. 9
15. *Daily Whig & Courier,* Tuesday, July 22, 1962
16. Hodsdon, General Order No. 24, *Annual Report of the Adjutant General of the State of Maine, 1862,* Appendix A, pp. 8-9
17. Under Maine law, incorporated cities and towns are self-governing. Unorganized plantations and townships are governed by the state.
18. *Annual Report of the Adjutant General of the State of Maine, 1862,* Appendix D, pp. 542-543
19. Letter by "Skirmisher," July 11, 1862, published in *Portland Daily Press,* Saturday, July 12, 1862. Italicized in the original.
20. Still published in Augusta, the venerable *Kennebec Journal* is habitually called the KJ.
21. *Maine Farmer,* Thursday, July 3, 1862
22. John Haley, *The Rebel Yell & the Yankee Hurrah,* edited by Ruth L. Silliker, Down East Books, Camden, Maine, 1985, pp. 12-13
23. Ibid., pp. 23-24
24. "The Eighteenth," *Daily Whig & Courier,* Tuesday, Aug. 12, 1862

25. "Presentation," *Daily Whig & Courier,* Monday, Aug. 18, 1862
26. *Annual Report of the Adjutant General of the State of Maine, 1862,* Appendix G, pp. 19-21
27. A.R. Small, *Sixteenth Maine Regiment in the War of the Rebellion 1861-1865, Volume I,* edited by Peter and Cyndi Dalton, B. Thurston & Company, Portland, 1886, reprinted by Union Publishing Co., p. 19
28. Haley, *Rebel Yell,* p. 27
29. After the war, survivors of the 5th Maine Infantry Regiment constructed a memorial hall on Peaks Island in Casco Bay. Operated by the Fifth Maine Infantry Community Association, the hall now houses an excellent Civil War museum and hosts many private and public events.
30. The 18th Maine Infantry would be designated the 1st Maine Heavy Artillery Regiment in January 1863.
31. Small, *Sixteenth Maine,* pp. 22-23
32. Haley, *Rebel Yell,* p. 21

Chapter 32

ANGELS OF THE BATTLEFIELD

"The number of sick here is large, alarmingly so"

White House Landing hummed with activity as nurse Sarah Sampson first gazed upon the Federal supply base from the deck of a hospital transport on Monday, June 2, 1862.

As the ship had steamed northwest along the York River, Sampson had studied the Tidewater shore so exotic to a Maine woman accustomed to the granite-clad ledges against which cold Gulf of Maine waves pounded.

Even after sailing from Baltimore to Fort Monroe, Sampson found her war-bound journey exciting. She noticed the York's rain-swollen, muddy waters spilling back from the steamer's bow; even from her perch on the ship's rail, Sampson sensed the water's warmth, so unlike the Kennebec River that varied in temperature with the summer tide's directional flow at Bath.

As the steamer stood off Ferry Point northeast of Williamsburg, many seabirds rarely seen in Maine wheeled and called overhead. Flanked by creek inlets, salt-water marshes, and forests that grew trees unlikely to survive Maine's cold winters, the York raced onward to the Chesapeake.

After passing marshy Terrapin Point to port, the steamer approached the York's headwaters at West Point. Viewed on a map, the non-descript headland and its abutting land mass resembled a fisted left hand with its thumb extended. The smaller Mattaponi[1] and Pamunkey rivers merged at West Point to form the wider York River, introduced into American lore during the 1781 siege of Yorktown.

Until the last few weeks, West Point had served as the eastern terminus of the Richmond & York River Railroad, tying the eastern Tidewater to the Confederate capital. Union troops had captured the headland, sailed around the Pamunkey's first clothespin turn to seize Eltham's Landing, then marched overland to seize White House Landing.

Slowing inside the narrower Pamunkey, the steamer swished past Eltham, rounded the Mississippi-like horseshoe bend upriver, and followed the winding river past Cumberland Landing. Navigating the marked channel past the island called "Indian Town,"[2] the steamer approached the haphazard port operations at White House Landing, where engineers and laborers scrambled to complete massive wharves.

Across the landing's temporary docks moved supplies vital to the Army of the Potomac, bloodied these past two days at Seven Pines to the west. In the opposite direction came "the wounded ... in large numbers, in the [railroad] cars, to be placed on Hospital transports," Sarah Sampson observed upon arriving at the landing.

Bearing their broken, living freight, trains rumbled constantly into White House Landing. Crossing the planks laid from the shore to ships' decks, stretcher bearers carried the casualties directly to hospital steamers moored parallel to the river bank.

Soon after reaching the landing, Sampson encountered the wounded Howard brothers (Oliver Otis and Charles), carried aboard the steamer *Nelly Baker*. Pleased to see a friendly and familiar face, the Howards asked Sampson to accompany them to Fort Monroe; late that Monday she asked an army surgeon to dress the brothers' wounds before the *Baker* sailed to Baltimore.

Returning to White House Landing on Tuesday, June 3, Sampson "made myself generally useful among the wounded men on shore and on transports." Until now she had cared for soldiers in Army hospitals, but at White House Landing, the incoming wounded lay outdoors beneath shade trees or in the broiling late spring sun.

"Such suffering and confusion I never before witnessed," admitted Sampson, surprised at the poor supervision and care extended the arriving casualties. "Many serious wounds had not been dressed for several days."

Flies laid eggs in suppurating flesh; larvae hatched into wriggling maggots chewing on rotting flesh. Sampson understood the medical implication; "indeed, the loss of many limbs was the consequence of inattention to lighter wounds," she said, careful to add that "this was not the fault of surgeons, but from circumstances beyond their control"—specifically the overwhelming number of wounded.

Sampson cared for many 3rd Maine soldiers, at least a few of whom died from infections caused by neglected dressings. Aboard the steamer *Elm City* she nursed Brig. Gen. Charles Jameson, the initial commander of the 2nd Maine Infantry. "Ill with the fever that terminated his life," Jameson "was my patient for several days," Sampson noted some time later.[3]

Among the nurses with whom she associated at White House Landing was Ellen Orbison Harris, wife of a prominent Philadelphia physician and the secretary of the influential Ladies' Aid Society of Philadelphia. Both women worked aboard the hospital transport *Louisiana*, where amputated limbs piled up on deck and blood splattered the nurses' aprons.

Like the slight Sampson, Harris exemplified polite society's vision of the proper middle-class wife—and her friends believed her physically incapable of the grand adventure she had undertaken. She "was one of those delicate, fragile, and feeble-looking ladies ... apparently condemned to lives of patient suffering and inactivity by constitutional defect of physical vigor.

"Yet she it was, this pallid and low-voiced lady, who" when the war broke out "glided from her sick chamber" to pursue "a self-imposed and self-directed career of Christian and sanitary labors" greater than similar efforts past in past wars, a biographer described Harris.

Chapter 32: Angels of the Battlefield

Steamers at White House Landing during the war
Photo from Library of Congress

His words could apply to Sampson, Isabella Fogg, and other women eschewing their comfortable homes for duty in military hospitals in spring and summer 1862.[4]

As Union troops moved west toward Richmond in mid- to late May, Army engineers repaired the Richmond & York River Railroad bridges burned by retreating Confederates. Ships brought to White House Landing six locomotives and 80 railroad cars purchased in the North and loaded at Baltimore;[5] once the railroad was reopened, trains "loaded with supplies were constantly running to the front ... from 15 to 20 miles in advance," noted Brig. Gen. Stewart Van Vliet, chief quartermaster for the Army of the Potomac.

"All of" the army's "immense supplies were thrown forward by the railroad and the large supply trains of the army," said Van Vliet, figuring that McClellan's army needed six hundred tons of supplies of all sorts daily. That total included "3 pounds of provisions per day" for each soldier and "26 pounds of forage" for each horse.[6]

By May 27 the massive hospital at White House Landing encompassed "105 hospital tents," all those that could be obtained, according to Dr. Charles S. Tripler, Army of the Potomac medical director.[7] Frederick Law Olmstead of the United States Sanitary Commission managed the non-military medical personnel (including the nurses) working at the landing.

With even the railroad line plagued by the rains sweeping across the Peninsula in early June, supply became critical as the Army of the Potomac nudged nearer Richmond. Logistics were challenging as the supplies for particular army corps went to specific stations. Savage Station was the whistle stop for the III Corps of Brig. Gen. Samuel P. Heintzelman and the II Corps of Brig. Gen. Erasmus Keyes, a Maine native.

Medical personnel also created a major field hospital at Savage Station. That hospital remained in operation as II and III Corps shifted their supply points west to Orchard Station,

White House Landing with supply ships
This view downriver is between May and late June 1862.
Photo from Library of Congress

located seven miles from Richmond.

Representing the United States Sanitary Commission, Isabella Fogg of Calais had reached White House Landing not long after its capture. During the previous winter she and Rockland nurse Ruth Mayhew had cared for spotted-fever patients at an Army hospital in Annapolis.[8]

"Indifferent to the danger of infection," the two Maine nurses "were on duty in the fever ward," working "all day, and often a considerable part of the night" as winter transitioned to spring. Fogg and Mayhew avoided catching spotted fever and helped many of their patients recover.

When the 6th Maine Infantry shipped to the Peninsula, Fogg sought a way to follow her beloved son, Hugh, and his comrades to Virginia. Before the spotted-fever outbreak, she had cared for sick 6th Maine lads at Annapolis; when the hospital transport *Elm City* arrived at Annapolis in early May with "the mutilated heroes of Williamsburg" aboard, Fogg lobbied the USCC to let her care for the sick and wounded soldiers closer to the front.

Fogg and other nurses shipped south on the *Elm City*; she was at White House Landing on May 31 when Federal trains started transporting from Fair Oaks Station an "unbroken stream of the wounded and the sick." Overwhelmed by the influx of casualties, the medical personnel worked around the clock to get men aboard the hospital ships and shipped north to Annapolis, Baltimore, and other ports.

Dr. John Swinburne, a New York physician, noticed "the skill and activity of Mrs. Fogg" in caring for the incoming wounded. Aware that wounded men were receiving insufficient medical care at the front, Swinburne relayed to Fogg via Frederick Knapp of the USCC a request for her to work at the forward Federal hospitals.

"Mr. Knapp, that is just where I would like to go," replied Fogg, anxious to be nearer her son and the 6th Maine. She caught a train to Savage Station, the collection point for all the Union casualties piling up due to sickness and war. Fogg arrived there about two weeks ahead of Sarah Sampson.[9]

Riding in "an open freight-car loaded with barrels of beef, upon which we sat," Sampson and other nurses took the Richmond & York River Railroad to Savage Station on Friday, June 13, not an inauspicious date for the nurses. Unloading their trunks, they visited the III Corps' headquarters near Savage Station.[10]

Meanwhile, Confederate Gen. James Ewell Brown Stuart met with his senior cavalry officers at Old Church in Hanover County, northeast of Savage Station. The previous day, Stuart had led some 1,200 troopers "and a section of the Stuart Horse Artillery" north and east from

Boxcars and wagons at McClellan's headquarters at Savage Station
Sometimes called Savage's Station, this was a key outpost for the Army of the Potomac on the Richmond & York River Railroad. This photo was taken shortly before the Battle of Savage Station.
Photo by James F. Gibson via Library of Congress

Richmond to find the right flank of the Army of the Potomac; the Confederates skirmished with Union forces on Thursday before resting briefly that night "near South Anna Bridge ... 22 miles from Richmond."

The Southern cavalrymen pushed eastward on Friday to confirm that the Union right flank was "up in the air," according to period parlance. Essentially completing his reconnaissance mission when he clattered up to Old Church somewhere around the time that Sampson's train rattled and swayed into Savage Station, Stuart debated with his officers their return route to Richmond.

"Here was the turning point of the expedition," Stuart realized. "Two routes were before me. – the one to return by Hanover Court-House, the other to pass around [Union lines] through New Kent ... and make a bold effort to cut the enemy's lines of communication."

Figuring that senior Union officers "would naturally expect me to take that [Hanover Court-House] route," Stuart decided to ride around McClellan's army by proceeding nine miles southeast to Tunstall's Station on the Richmond & York River Railroad.

Union Brig. Gen. Stewart Leonard Van Vliet
Photo taken between 1865-70
Photo from Brady-Handy Collection, Library of Congress

As Sarah Sampson toured the Union field hospital at Savage Station, Stuart approached Tunstall's Station well to the east. Sending two cavalry squadrons to attack the Union supply post at Garlick's Landing on the Pamunkey River, he "pushed [scouts] forward rapidly to Tunstall's to cut the wires and secure the depot."

At Garlick's Landing, Confederate troops burned "a large number of wagons" and "two transports loaded with stores," Stuart learned. At Tunstall's, the Confederate riders captured "15 or 20 infantry" pickets "and set about obstructing the railroad."

Lacking tools to tear up the track, Confederates piled material on it instead. As his vanguard approached Tunstall's, "a train of cars came thundering down from the Grand Army," Stuart said.[11]

Probably not until the next day did Sampson learn about her potentially close call. The train crew that had brought her to Savage Station unloaded freight and passengers there, then picked up some outbound passengers, including six 11th Maine Infantry Regiment officers sent home on a recruiting expedition.[12]

The train soon departed for White House Landing. "On its return" there, the flat car on which she had ridden earlier that day "was fired into by the rebels, and the bridge at

Tunstall's station, over which we had crossed, burned," Sampson learned.[13]

The Union train approaching Tunstall's Station "had troops on board and we prepared to attack it," Stuart reported. Slamming aside the Confederate obstructions "without being thrown from the track" and taking heavy fire from enemy cavalrymen, the train rolled toward White House Landing.

Then "the railroad bridge over Black Creek was fired," Stuart noted.[14]

Since early June, the battle-mauled 11th Maine had recuperated in a camp east of Seven Pines. The regiment still belonged to the 1st Brigade of Brig. Gen. Henry M. Naglee, but after the near Union defeat at Seven Pines, the vengeful McClellan had replaced 3rd Division commander Brig. Gen. Silas Casey with John J. Peck.

Through most of June "our position did not seem to be one of much importance," commented Maj. Robert F. Campbell, the unflappable warrior from Cherryfield. Stuart's raid changed all that.[15]

As Stuart rode around the Union army, Naglee hustled his brigade to guard the Chickahominy River bridges. The 11th Maine lads occupied Bottoms Bridge[16] en masse early on June 14 and guarded the vital span until relieved on June 17, long after Stuart had returned to Richmond.

Then the Maine boys relocated their camp "to a high bluff by the railroad and about one mile from the railroad bridge," upon which Campbell and his men kept close watch.[17]

Unperturbed at being cut off temporarily from White House Landing, Sampson and the

Confederate Gen. J.E.B. Stuart
From National Archives and Records Administration

Frederick Law Olmstead, Sanitary Commission
From The World's Work *via Wikipedia and archive.org*

other nurses slept that night (June 13) in Heintzelman's telegraph office. The next morning, they dined on Army rations "and found a home with a family [the Dudleys] formerly from Massachusetts," Sampson expressed her pleasure with her new quarters.

Then the nurses met with Sam Heintzelman and his one-armed 3rd Division commander, Brig. Gen. Phil Kearny. Both men "were exceedingly kind to us" and sent "their private carriages to convey us and our supplies to the various hospitals," Sampson said.

Stewart Van Vliet also met with the nurses at Savage Station. Advising the women to base their operations at the station, he "also offered us transportation to any point," Sampson observed.

The warm and colorful Virginia spring passed into early summer as the nurses spread good cheer, food, and comfort through the original field hospital. Others had popped up around Savage Station; "we were constantly being sent to come to this hospital or that," Sampson said.

"Every day was full of interest," she said. While traveling in the vicinity of Savage Station, the nurses poked their noses and piercing eyes into every nook and cranny and often "came across some sick [men], who by accident, were not in regularly organized hospitals."

Sick, shot-up, and abandoned soldiers sometimes crawled into the nearest available refuge; others wound up shoved into attics heated into the low triple digits by the Virginia sun. No matter where the neglected men sheltered, they could not escape their determined rescuers. Alerted by a sentinel one day, Sampson and Harris entered "an old building without windows or doors" and discovered a 3rd Maine Infantry captain, George W. Harvey, "very ill and delirious with fever." He had "only a canteen from which to take his drink."[18]

Harvey lay on a stretcher as the Death Angel flitted about him. Harris remembered him as "an elegant-looking youth."

Seeing the nurses approach, the hallucinating Harvey blurted, "Is it not cruel to keep me here, when my mother and sister, whom I have not seen a year, are in the next room! They might let me go in?"

Sampson and Harris knelt beside Harvey and ministered to him. His mind alternating between the battlefield and home, "he drew two rings from his finger, placed there by a loving mother and sister," and gave them "to an attendant" (probably Sampson), Harris said.

"Carry them home," Harvey begged.

Taken to a Union hospital, he died the next day.[19]

Patients and nurses alike suffered at Savage Station "during the long, hot days of June." Physically tough, Isabella Fogg placed "a wet towel" on her head each day before tugging on a hat; periodically moistening the towel in any available water container, she avoided the sunstroke that was felling even healthy men.[20]

Casualties continued arriving at Savage Station, often faster than the trains could transport patients to White House Landing. "The number of sick here is large, alarmingly so," Sarah Sampson realized. "We found between three and four hundred sick" in Kearny's 3rd Division, to which the 3rd and 4th Maine infantry regiments were assigned.

"They nearly all needed a change of clothing, which we could not obtain," Sampson told a friend in Maine. Despite the fields and pastures scattered around Savage Station, sick soldiers "had nothing under them but their blankets, not a spire of straw, and nothing to rest their poor fevered heads upon, but their leather knapsacks."

Malnutrition stalked the sick and wounded soldiers sheltering in Sibley tents and beneath every bit of available canvas. The nurses delivered to their patients "the first corn starch and farina which they had," as Sampson described the diet she introduced to those men under her care.

"Think of typhoid fever patients having nothing to eat but hard bread [hardtack]. There is fault somewhere," Sampson excoriated the unidentified senior Army commanders responsible for the patients' care at Savage Station.

"In this hospital are the sick of the 3rd and 4th Maine," she reported. "The patients were all glad to see us" that "they feel gratitude for any expression of kindness."

As the nurses worked, delirious patients "often ... happily think their mother or sister has come at last and 'thank God,'" Sampson noticed. Nurses cooled sweat-beaded foreheads with cloths soaked in spring water, held hands with the dying, and by candlelight penned letters dictated by amputees.

"I can give you no idea of an every day experience" at Savage Station, Sampson wearily wrote her friend. "Yet we do so little of what should be done."

On June 25, Union troops launched their last attack toward Richmond. Fighting determined enemy defenders during the Battle of Oak Grove, Federal regiments racked up casualties and accomplished precious little in the swamps west and southwest of Seven Pines.

Union Brig. Gen. Joseph Hooker
Photo from Library of Congress

"We had heard firing all the morning and knew what must follow," said Sampson, associating such martial noise with broken and bleeding men. "We finished our rounds in double quick time, and went ourselves."

A "four mule wagon" laden with supplies hauled Sampson and Harris and their supplies to "within a mile of the scene of action, and were fully appreciated I assure you," Sampson said.[21]

Earlier that morning, Brig. Gen. Joseph Hooker had pushed his 2nd Division of Heintzelman's III Corps west from Seven Pines to capture the forest dominated by Oak Grove, appropriately named for the oaks growing there. George McClellan wanted Confederate troops ejected from the forest before sending other Union forces northwest on Nine Mile Road to capture Old Tavern.

With the high elevations of Old Tavern in Union hands, McClellan could place siege guns there to bombard the Confederate defenses between his army and Richmond.

As his brigades encountered stiffening enemy resistance, Hooker requested that Heintzelman send in Kearny's division, then held in reserve. David Birney had already "marched my [2nd] brigade .... to the line of fortifications in front of the [3rd] division."

The 3rd Maine Infantry held a picket line as the 2nd Brigade moved to the front. Still weakened by his neuralgia, Lt. Col. Charles Sampson rode among his men as he listened to the same shooting his wife could hear at Savage Station.

Hooker's men shed blood for every yard gained that morning. In early afternoon, Kearny ordered Birney to relieve the Hooker brigade commanded by Brig. Gen. Cuvier Grover; taking with him the 4th Maine, 40th New York, and seven companies from the 101st New York, Birney sent a staff officer to bring up the 3rd Maine.

Making only minimal contact with enemy troops, the 2nd Brigade occupied woods near Grover's positions and stayed there until dusk. Charles Sampson kept close watch on his 3rd Maine lads in the field that Kearny had ordered them to defend.

The sun set before Grover received orders to withdraw his damaged brigade. Miffed after Kearny "took command of the troops" in the afternoon, the prickly Birney ordered the 4th Maine and the 101st New York's "to move out of the woods by the [Williamsburg] road and report to me at the 'lookout tree,' where General Grover was stationed."

Leaving an aide to guide those two regiments, Birney rode to the 3rd Maine. His conversation with Sampson went unrecorded. Sampson ordered his men to follow Birney; despite "the night being very dark and foggy," Birney and Sampson found Grover's staff officer assigned to take the 3rd Maine to its assigned position.[22]

As the 3rd Maine lads followed the 101st New York's seven companies through the woods around 10 p.m., a Confederate volley suddenly shattered the darkness and men's nerves. The frightened New Yorkers bolted, but officers swore and swatted backsides with sword flats until the men reformed and marched to their proper posts.

The volley also rattled the 3rd Maine. Not a fan of Maine soldiers,[23] the disgusted Birney claimed that while "most of this hitherto reliable regiment remained at post ... some retired to camp some mile in [the] rear" as the Confederate volleys died away.

"The commanding officer," Charles Sampson, "left his command and post and was next morning in camp," according to Birney. "I could not find him during the night. He left without my permission or knowledge."

Birney placed Sampson under arrest on Thursday, June 26. Regimental command devolved to Maj. Edwin Burt.[24]

Unaware that her husband commanded his regiment only a few miles away, Sarah Sampson nursed wounded soldiers on the battlefield's edge until Wednesday's darkness made such work impossible. Returning to the Dudley house that night, she "found notes from several surgeons, begging for stores." Blankets and clothing ran short in the Federal hospitals; with Union gunners and infantrymen burning through their ammunition farther afield,

Chapter 32: Angels of the Battlefield

The Battle of Savage Station
This image was published in 1887, based off a sketch made at the time.
Illustration from Library of Congress

munitions received preferential loading on the trains at White House Landing.

Sarah Sampson awoke on Thursday to find that more shattered bodies had arrived at Savage Station. She hoped to work among the 3rd and 4th Maine lads at the 3rd Division hospital, "but after I once got to work" nearer the station, "I could not leave.

"We began where the groans of the wounded and dying soldiers met our ears," she said.

On June 26, Gen. Robert E. Lee hurled his Army of Northern Virginia against Federal troops north of the Chickahominy River. As fighting raged at Beaver Dam Station (also called Mechanicsville) on that Thursday, surgeons, orderlies, and nurses treated the wounded men flooding into Savage Station.

"Our supplies being somewhat reduced, and learning that others had reached White House Landing for us," Sampson and Harris caught a train to the landing in late afternoon Thursday and stayed the night; they planned on returning to Savage Station with the supplies early on Friday, June 27.

But Robert E. Lee had intervened. Although his attack at Beaver Dam Station on Thursday resulted in heavy losses and a de facto Union victory, Lee had thoroughly rattled George McClellan. Deciding to shift his supply base from White House Landing to Harrison's Landing on the James River, "Little Mac" decided to abandon White House.

"Orders had been already given for the evacuation of White House, and ... the wounded were being rapidly moved from that point," Sampson discovered Thursday night.[25]

She and Harris would not return to Savage Station.

~~~

1. Also spelled "Mattapony," this river resulted from the upstream merger of four lesser rivers: the Ma, Ta, Po, and Ni (or "Ny").
2. Named for the Pamunkey Indian Tribe, which has a nearby reservation.
3. "Mrs. Sampson's Report," *Annual Report of the Adjutant General of the State of Maine, 1864-1865,* pp. 110-111
4. Frank Moore, *Women of the War: Their Heroism and Self-Sacrifice,* S.S. Scranton & Co., Hartford, Conn., 1866, pp. 176-177
5. "Report of Col. D.C. McCallum, General Manager of the U.S. Military Railroads, 1866," Edwin P. Alexander, *Civil War Railroads & Models,* Clarkson N. Potter Inc./Publishers, New York, 1977
6. Brig. Gen. Stewart Van Vliet, *Official Records, Series I, Vol. 11, Part I,* Chapter XXIII, No. 7, p. 159
7. Dr. Charles S. Tripler, *OR, Series I, Vol. II, Part I,* Appendix S, p. 205
8. Lynda L. Sudlow, *A Vast Army of Women: Maine's Uncounted Forces in the Civil War,* Thomas Publications, Gettysburg, Penn., 2000, pp. 92-93
9. Moore, *Women of the War,* pp. 114-116
10. "Mrs. Sampson's Report," *Annual Report of the Adjutant General of the State of Maine, 1864-1865,* p. 112
11. Brig. Gen. J.E.B. Stuart, *OR, Series I, Vol. XI,* Chapter XXIII, No. 21, pp. 1036-1039
12. William E.S. Whitman and Charles H. True, *Maine in the War for the Union,* Nelson Dingley Jr. & Co., Lewiston, Maine, 1865, p. 269
13. "Mrs. Sampson's Report," *Annual Report of the Adjutant General of the State of Maine, 1864-1865,* p. 112
14. Stuart, *OR, Series I, Vol. XI,* Chapter XXIII, No. 21, p. 1039
15. Maj. Robert F. Campbell, July 18, 1862 letter to Gov. Israel Washburn Jr., Maine State Archives
16. Bottoms Bridge carried the Williamsburg Road over the Chickahominy River.
17. Whitman and True, *Maine in the War,* p. 269
18. "Mrs. Sampson's Report," *Annual Report of the Adjutant General of the State of Maine, 1864-1865,* p. 112
19. Dr. L.P. Brockett and Mary C. Vaughan, *Women's Work in the Civil War: A Record of Heroism, Patriotism and Patience,* Ziegler, McCurdy & Co., Philadelphia, and R.H. Curran, Boston, 1867, pp. 154-155
20. Moore, *Women of the War,* p. 116
21. "Aid For Maine Soldiers," *Maine Farmer,* Thursday, July 10, 1862
22. Brig Gen. David B. Birney, *OR, Series 1, Vol. 11, Part II,* Chapter XXIII, No. 70, pp. 179-181
23. The attitude was reciprocal. Elijah Walker, colonel of the 4th Maine Infantry, held Birney in low esteem.
24. Birney, *OR, Series I, Vol. XI, Part II,* No. 70, p. 181
25. "Mrs. Sampson's Report," *Annual Report of the Adjutant General of the State of Maine, 1864-1865,* p. 111

Chapter 33

ROUND UP THE RELUCTANT

"The secesh is at home in a nest of secessionists"

As he edited the popular *Maine Farmer* in early summer 1862, Ezekiel Holmes noticed the Union soldiers suddenly appearing on the Augusta streets. Some belonged to the 16th Maine Infantry then converging on the capital, but many men behaved like veterans.

Why were they home in Maine and not with their regiments in the field? Holmes investigated a bit before telling his readers, "There is reason to believe that a large number of soldiers are now absent from their regiments, on the pretense of sickness, and drawing their monthly pay and rations, who are in good health and perfectly well fitted for duty."[1]

Instructed by Governor Israel Washburn Jr. to determine the status of the returned soldiers, Adjutant General John L. Hodsdon released General Order No. 15 on June 20. He directed "that all soldiers belonging to Maine, at home on furlough or otherwise, not having been discharged from service, will report themselves in person or by letter to the Adjutant General at Augusta forthwith.

"All such persons, except those whose furloughs have not expired, who fail to report themselves immediately, will be liable to be treated as deserters," indicated No. 15, which covered officers and enlisted men alike.

"All invalid and wounded officers of Maine who are able to travel" had to "report in person to the General commanding the camp of Instruction at Annapolis,"[2] Hodsdon stressed. After arriving there, the officers could rejoin their regiments or appear before "an examining board" that would determine "their ability to return to duty."[3]

Soldiers reporting in person or by letter to Hodsdon's State House offices must deal with Maj. John William Tudor Gardiner,[4] "the United States' Military Commander" in Augusta, Holmes informed his *Maine Farmer* readers. A letter sent in lieu of a personal appearance must "give full particulars" of a soldier's situation, including his "regiment, company, residence and Post Office address."[5]

The issue of missing soldiers was not unique to Maine. The War Department soon issued General Order No. 61 requiring all sick and wounded (and not medically discharged) soldiers who could travel to report to Annapolis. Unfortunately for Washburn, Hodsdon, and the colonels commanding undermanned regiments in the field, General Order No. 15 convinced too few recalcitrant Maine soldiers to return to their units.

Washburn tried again with an executive order released on July 7. "It is known that large numbers of soldiers are absent from their regiments, some on furlough and some on sick leave, who are now able to return to the regiments where they are needed for the service of their country," he wrote.

Washburn also cited the "invalid or wounded soldiers who are able to travel" and who had not been medically discharged. The Union needed all these men, including the healthy soldiers showing up in most cities and towns, and by God if they failed to report to Annapolis or Augusta, they would "be reported as deserters and liable to be treated as such."

And Washburn asked "all officers of the militia, all magistrates and all good people of the State" to alert Hodsdon "of the presence of such soldiers in their vicinity, giving their names, the company and regiment to which they belong when known, with the places they are now." His request marked the first time that a Maine governor had asked Mainers to spy on their neighbors statewide.

Ezekiel Holmes
Publisher of *Maine Farmer* and the
"father of Maine agriculture"
Illustration courtesy of University of Maine archives

Washburn's executive order identified six serving officers, scattered from Eastport to Norway, who could issue free travel passes for soldiers traveling to Augusta. A letter could suffice, but many men intended to appear in person at the adjutant general's office.[6]

Some soldiers apparently did not get the message—or chose to ignore it. The implicit threat of a deserter's punishment—docked pay, public humiliation, incarceration, even execution—failed to spur as massive an influx of soldiers to the front-line regiments, nor soldiers or letters to Augusta, as Washburn had desired.

In July, he started appointing at least one reliable Unionist man in each county as an agent "for looking up deserters and absentees from their regiments." Most agents came from small towns, as did many of the missing soldiers whom they sought.[7]

The state paid each of its 19 agents $2.50 per day, plus $5 per apprehended deserter. While scouring Kennebec County for potential deserters in August, Gilman J. Page boosted his earnings by charging $7.50 per day" for three days for "subsistence of myself and horse." The extra $22.50 boosted Page's August invoice to $66.75.[8] Meanwhile, a Maine private earned $13 a month (or 43 cents a day) for defending the country.

Hodsdon's agents pursued soldiers across the state. In Piscataquis County, Sebec farmer

Maine Farmer, May 28, 1863
Image courtesy of Fogler Library, University of Maine

John H. Gilman received from Hodsdon's office a list of men home on some sort of authorized leave from the military. Traveling along the county's wretched roads, Gilman tried to find each man and confirm the paperwork indicating his relationship to the army.

In Milo (home to many men of Co. D, 2nd Maine Infantry), Gilman tried to meet with 15 veterans. Most had their discharge papers, issued primarily for medical reasons.

Hearing about Gilman's mission, Eliazer Tolman had gone immediately "to Augusta to report in <u>person</u>," Gilman noted. Captured at First Manassas, R.A. Monroe was "home on a <u>parole</u>." He had just traveled to Augusta to see an army surgeon and obtain a medical discharge.

But Edward Ricker had "<u>No Papers</u>," and Gilman "could not see him." Perhaps giving Ricker the benefit of the doubt, Gilman nosed around about his physical condition. "I am satisfied from reliable information that he is used up for life," Gilman informed Hodsdon.

"All Milo folks say he never will be good for <u>anything</u>," Gilman noted.

Elsewhere in Piscataquis County, Gilman called upon Aaron Wilson of Co. E, 14th Maine Infantry. Wilson was seriously ill; Gilman "did not call for [his] papers as his maker will discharge him from all trouble in this world in a <u>few hours</u>."[9]

Agent Augustus Stevens of Blue Hill pounced on John J. Carter, medically discharged from Co. A, 14th Maine Infantry Regiment in Louisiana. Stevens surmised "Carter is apparently well and able to work," despite his discharge certificate.

Signed on June 30 by Col. Frank Nickerson of the 14th Maine and approved on July 5 by Capt. R.P. Davis, an aide to Maj. Gen. Benjamin Butler, the "Surgeons Certificate of Disability" was legitimate. However, someone had erased the penciled sentence, "no objection to his [Carter's] being reenlisted is known to exist."

Was Carter actually healthy enough to rejoin the army? The discharge certificate kept Stevens from nabbing him as a deserter, but a bona fide deserter sheltered "on Long Island in Blue Hill bay"—or so Stevens believed.

"William G. Pirs. [Pert]" of Co. B, 2nd Maine Infantry, had "from what I can learn deserted at the Battle of Bull Run" in July 1861, Stevens noted. "Absent without discharge or furlough," Pert was asked to appear before state officials in Augusta.[10]

As summer passed, the Maine regiments in Virginia continued bleeding men, a few to desertion and many more to medical incompetence and chicanery. Still camped at Harrison's Landing on the James River weeks after the Peninsula Campaign's seven-day finale, the 11th Maine Infantry hemorrhaged men.

Disease did not claim them all.

"I have processed the discharge of 12 men ... who were never fit for the service in consequence of physical disability of long standing," Dr. Nathan F. Blunt, the 11th Maine's surgeon, informed Maine Surgeon General Alonzo Garcelon on August 8.

"It is to be hoped that in future none but sound men will be sworn in to service," Blunt hinted at the inept Maine doctors approving physically unqualified men for Army duty.[11]

Maine Surgeon General Alonzo Garcelon

Corrupt physicians were also thinning the ranks, claimed Lt. Col. William H. Shaw, the temporary 11th Maine commander in the absence of Col. Harris Plaisted. Shaw had just reviewed "a long list of ... soldiers that have been discharged," he informed Adjutant General John L. Hodsdon on August 16.

Many soldiers on the list "are known to be as strong rugged men as we have in the Service," Shaw rumbled in the August heat and humidity at Harrison's Landing. How had such healthy soldiers been medically discharged?

Venality, Shaw thundered. Rumors circulated in the 11th Maine and other state regiments that some surgeons in Maine were "being hired to give Certificates of Disability for as small a sum as $5.00," he scratched his charge across a foolscap page.

"I hope it is not so with the [examining] surgeons at Augusta," Shaw said, his ardor momentarily cooled.

"But it is well known that men have been discharged there and at other places who have deceived the Surgeon," Shaw growled. "The moment they were free," such soldiers "would kick up their heels and tell how neat[ly] they" had escaped the army.

"It has a bad effect upon them in the field," Shaw informed Hodsdon.[12]

And at home in Maine, a medically discharged soldier's blatant defiance infuriated Jeremiah Bartlett, living in Lockes Mills village in rural Greenwood in Oxford County. Dennis W. Cole, a 24-year-old married farmer from Greenwood, had mustered into Co. F, 17th Maine Infantry Regiment on August 18; by Saturday, September 20, Cole was "at home[,] riding

Union attitudes towards secessionists were often quite strong
Illustration by Thomas Butler Gunn, December 7, 1861, via Library of Congress

around as large as life," bragging about the bounty money he had earned, Bartlett wrote Hodsdon.

Greenwood had paid Cole $60 to enlist, and he also received $80 in state and federal bounties. "He went on from Portland with the Reg't as far as New Jersey and by some maneuver got back here, as <u>he says</u> with his discharge," Bartlett complained. "He takes good care not to show it.

"The secesh is at home in a nest of secessionists that should be broken up," Bartlett opined.

Cole should have been arrested, apparently because Bartlett considered him a deserter. He had asked two policemen and a justice of the peace to do something about the "full blood secesh" who was faking his medical condition, in Bartlett's opinion.

"This playing sick by such men should be punished—he is a well man," Bartlett stated. "He only enlisted to cheat the bounty out of the Government."

Identifying himself to Hodsdon as "your old friend," Bartlett believed that "such cusses" as Cole "ought to be hung …"[13]

Despite Bartlett's doubts, Cole had been discharged for disability at Philadelphia on September 6. His Army service had lasted all of 19 days.

He kept that part of his bounty that he had received.

~~~

1. Ezekiel Holmes, "An Important Order," *Maine Farmer,* Thursday, June 26, 1862
2. The War Department had established medical facilities at Annapolis to treat returning wounded soldiers and freed prisoners of war. Hospital ships often transported soldiers wounded during the Peninsula Campaign to Annapolis.
3. Adjutant General John L. Hodsdon, General Order No. 15, June 20, 1862, Maine State Archives
4. Born in Gardiner in June 1817, Gardiner graduated from West Point in 1840. A veteran of the Mexican War and Army assignments in the Upper Midwest, he was shipwrecked while en route to an Army post in California in December 1853. Medically discharged on Nov. 14, 1861, Gardiner capably served at the state level. He was a no-nonsense individual.
5. Ezekiel Holmes, "To Returned Maine Soldiers," *Maine Farmer,* Thursday, June 26, 1862
6. Governor Israel Washburn Jr., July 7, 1862 executive order, MSA
7. *Daily Whig & Courier,* Tuesday, Aug. 12, 1862
8. Gilman J. Page, invoice to Adjutant Gen. John L. Hodsdon, Aug. 22, 1862, MSA
9. John Gilman, August 7, 1862 report to John L. Hodsdon, MSA; all notes in this chapter that are underlined were underlined in Gilman's original
10. Augustus Stevens, August 1, 1862 letter to Hodsdon, MSA
11. Dr. Nathan F. Blunt, August 8 1862 to "Dr. A Garselin (Garcelon), MSA
12. Lt. Col. William H. Shaw, August 16, 1862 letter to John L. Hodson, MSA
13. Jeremiah Bartlett, September 20 1862 letter to John L. Hodsdon, MSA

Chapter 34

UNREMITTED FURY AT GAINES MILL

"It was like a phantom battle as it appeared to us"

Busy with his administrative duties, Maj. Thomas Hyde cocked an ear as distant thunder echoed across the Chickahominy River soon after lunch on Thursday, June 26. Artillery: Someone was taking a pounding "in the direction of our right and front," he figured.[1]

Over that way, beyond the north or "left" bank of the Chickahominy, General Robert E. Lee had just launched his audacious attempt to destroy the Army of the Potomac piecemeal. Late June found the army dangerously divided by the winding Chickahominy; *à la* the days leading to Seven Pines in late May, George McClellan had split his army, this time by placing four of his five corps south of the river.

Only V Corps, led by Brig. Gen. Fitz John Porter, was stationed above the Chickahominy. Forming an under-strength Union right flank, Porter's three divisions held positions close to Richmond.

South of the river, so did the III Corps commanded by Brig. Gen. Philip Kearny. "At the point we occupied, we could see the spires of the churches of Richmond, and hear much that was transpiring in the enemy's camp near us," said Brig. Gen. Hiram Berry of Rockland; he commanded Kearny's mixed Michigan-New York 3rd Brigade.[3]

Opposite the Union troops south of the Chickahominy were some 25,000 Confederates commanded by Maj. Gen. John B. Magruder. McClellan had planned on June 25 to hold the Confederate troops in place north of the river with V Corps and punch through McGruder to Oak Grove, high terrain from which Union siege guns could shell Richmond.

Lee intended the June 25 attack to be Little Mac's last.

Confederate scouts and patrols probed Porter's lines across Beaver Dam Creek (a Chickahominy tributary) and farther to the east prior to Lee revealing his single-minded determination to demolish McClellan's army. In mid-June, gray-clad cavalry led by J.E.B. Stuart had ridden a literal ring around McClellan by dashing past Porter's under-defended rear areas and

Confederate Gen. Robert E. Lee
Although a general, Lee wore the three stars of Confederate colonel, equal to his last rank in the U.S. Army. This photo was taken in March 1864.
Photo by Julian Vannerson via Library of Congress

Union Brig. Gen. Hiram George Berry
This photo was taken between March 1862 (when he was promoted to brigadier general) and November 29, 1862 (when he was promoted to major general)
Photo from National Archives and Records Admin.

turning south near the Pamunkey River.

Damaging the Richmond & York River Railroad at Tunstall's Station, Stuart's troopers had crossed the Chickahominy on a hastily assembled bridge, then dashed on to Richmond.

Now aware that Porter was vulnerable, Lee ordered an attack on the Beaver Dam Creek positions on June 26. Entrenched along the creek's east bank and aided by well-handled artillery, Union troops inflicted heavy losses on the enemy infantry.

"All the afternoon we heard heavy cannonading," noticed Hyde, nominally third-in-command of the 7th Maine Infantry Regiment. The previous weeks he had served on the 2nd Division staff of Brig. Gen. William F. "Baldy" Smith. Part of the VI Corps of Brig. Gen. William B. Franklin, Smith's division included the 7th Maine and the press-competitive 6th Maine, as well as the five-regiment "Vermont Brigade."

The division occupied the fields and woods directly across the Chickahominy from V Corps. Hyde sensed the growing nervousness around divisional headquarters; that shooting across the river could come Smith's way.

By sunset Hyde and his companions "could see the quick flashes of the guns, and later" as artillery fire lessened, could hear "the low surging sound of distant musketry." Darkness ended the battle, the second of a sequential seven, and Porter's men still held their lines.[4]

Rumors spread about a Union victory. "Bands played, joy seemed to almost illuminate the night," said 1st Lt. George Bicknell of the 5th Maine Infantry, commanded by Col. Nathaniel J. Jackson and located south of the Chickahominy with VI Corps.

Officers told their men to stuff "two days' cooked rations" into their haversacks and get ready to march. "Richmond was to be ours," Bicknell repeated the principal rumor circulating through the camps. "No one doubted it. Our triumph was soon to be heralded in every part of the world."[5]

He had spoken too soon.

Until 9 p.m. on June 26, the 11th Maine Infantry soldiers heard the cannonading from their camp near the Richmond & York River Railroad bridge over the Chickahominy River. Shortly before midnight, the regiment turned out en masse to guard the span. Taking along some 100 men, Capt. Jonathan Hill plunked the bulk on the bridge's western end and deployed pickets a quarter mile beyond its eastern end.

All other 11th Maine lads "stood by their arms as a reserve, twelve hundred yards from the bridge," a comrade remembered.[6]

Union Brig. Gen. William Farrar "Baldy" Smith
Photo via Library of Congress

Union Col. Charles Roberts
Photo courtesy of Maine State Archives

Union Col. Nathaniel James Jackson
Jackson was promoted to brigadier general on September 24, 1862, his rank in this photo.
Photo courtesy of Maine State Archives

Union Brig. Gen. Daniel Adams Butterfield
Photo courtesy of United States Army

Nurse Isabella Fogg had spent Thursday with her favorite warriors, the soldiers of the 6th Maine Infantry Regiment, assigned to the 1st Brigade of Brig. Gen. Winfield Scott Hancock.

Learning that his mother was working at Savage Station, Hugh Fogg had obtained permission from Col. Hiram Burnham to travel there. He shared with Isabella "a moving account of the sufferings of his comrades at the extreme front," where bug- and water-borne diseases felled more men than did Confederate bullets. The enervated Isabella packed an ambulance with medical supplies, rounded up a teamster, and ventured west on June 26.

She found 60 to 70 sick men in the 6th Maine's camp, located just behind the fairly static front lines. Suffering "with typhoid fever and chronic diarrhea," the sturdy Maine soldiers refused evacuation to even the 1st Brigade's hospital; distrustful of doctors and hospitals, the men could see the Richmond church spires in the distance.

Isabella Fogg discovered that the sick men "hoped to be well enough to march through the streets of Richmond," a victory the soldiers expected would occur "in a few days."

With a Confederate artillery round occasionally "screaming over the lines," Fogg cooked food for men subsisting on hard tack and rancid salt pork, distributed the medical supplies she had brought, and held canteens and cups so feverish men could drink water.

As the sun dropped toward Thursday's horizon, Isabella climbed into the ambulance, bid farewell to Hugh, and endured the bouncing and jouncing until she reached Savage Station.

Chapter 34: Unremitted Fury at Gaines Mill

She spoke that night with her civilian superiors about "the possibility of bringing constant relief" to sick men refusing to leave their positions at the front.[7]

Robert E. Lee lost some 1,500 men and technically the Beaver Dam Creek battle (also known as Mechanicsville for the nearby hamlet), but the fight alerted McClellan to the danger facing Porter. Ordered to pull back toward the Chickahominy, Porter left a relatively strong skirmish line to watch the Confederates brigades opposite the Beaver Dam Creek defenses.

Porter redistributed his divisions early on Friday, June 27 to new lines along Boatswain's Creek, a Chickahominy tributary flowing through a ravine east of a local landmark called Gaines' Mill. The 1st Division commander, Brig. Gen. George W. Morrell, deployed his three brigades along the high east bank of the creek.

Nearby stood a house owned by 77-year-old widow Sarah Watt.

Brig. Gen. Dan Butterfield—soon to be of "Taps" fame—and his 3rd Brigade held Morrell's left flank. Anchored against Butterfield's right flank (northeast along the creek) were Brig. Gen. John H. Martindale and his 1st Brigade.

As the sun rose, Martindale conferred with his regimental commanders, including Col. Charles W. Roberts of the 2nd Maine Infantry, shot up at Hanover Court House exactly a month earlier. We have to hold this line, no matter what, Martindale indicated.

Exchanging banter and salutes as he rode through the 4th Maine Infantry's camp south of

Union Brig. Gen. Joseph Jackson Bartlett
Photo from Brady-Handy Collection,
Library of Congress

Union Brig. Gen. Henry Warner Slocum
Shown here as a major general.
Photo by Mathew Brady via Library of Congress

the Chickahominy around 8:30 a.m. on Friday, Brig. Gen. Hiram Berry found Col. Elijah Walker and let him in on the secret not shared with most Union soldiers, including Fitz John Porter's men, soon to be fighting for their lives across the river.

"A retreat had been ordered," the surprised Walker learned.

Actually on a bit of a secret mission, Berry asked Walker to ride with him to the headquarters tent of Brig. Gen. Phil Kearny, the one-armed 3rd Division commander. The 3rd Maine and 4th Maine still belonged to the 2nd Brigade commanded by David Birney, who in turn reported to Kearny. As much respected by his men as Birney was deprecated by Walker, Charles Sampson, and other Maine soldiers, Kearny chatted quietly with Sam Heintzelman while Berry and Walker rode up, dismounted, and saluted.

Walker raised an eyebrow as Heintzelman, the III Corps commander, confirmed the order to retreat. McClellan had conferred with his corps commanders Thursday night; rather than fall back along the Richmond & York

Union Brig. Gen. William Buel Franklin
Pictured here as a major general
Photo from the Library of Congress

River Railroad to White House Landing and the Pamunkey River, the army would withdraw south to the James River, where Navy gunboats could literally protect McClellan.

Snake-infested White Oak Swamp obstructed the army's southward passage. The swampy terrain restricted the Union infantry, artillery, and massive supply trains to only the few bridges over White Oak Creek, which flowed generally west to east while en route to the Chickahominy.

Several fords allegedly existed, however, and the army needed experienced ax men to cut trees for bridges and corduroy roads. Hiram Berry had immediately suggested the 4th Maine lads, known for their ability to flatten a forest.

Perhaps knowing about the testy relationship between Birney and Walker, Kearny asked Berry to bring Walker directly to the headquarters tent.

Could Walker and the 4th Maine "find Jordan's Ford and make it passable for troops as soon as possible?" Heintzelman inquired.

Certainly, Walker responded.

Rousting out his men in mid-morning, he marched them southward, each soldier hauling "all his clothing, a shelter tent [half], one hundred rounds of ammunition," plus his rifle, gear, and three days' rations. Walker also issued "axes, shovels and picks" to about half of his men.

After tramping for two miles toward the ford's perceived location, Walker realized his error. Nabbing "a citizen" and ordering him "at the peril of his life" to guide the Maine men to Jordan's Ford "by the shortest and best road," Walker was pleased when the crossing came into view another four miles later.

As his men started cutting trees to corduroy a road to White Oak Creek, Walker dispatched a rider to Kearny. The man returned at 3 p.m. with orders "to suspend work," Walker grunted.

Does the army want this place ready or not? he thought.

The inherently impatient Walker rode to the 3rd Division camp, found Kearny at 5 p.m., and asked him to check Jordan's Ford. Kearny quickly inspected it before returning to his headquarters for the night.

Wondering what was going on, Walker could only scratch his head at the confusion.[8]

North of the Chickahominy, the 2nd Maine Infantry held a position along the high east bank of Boatswain's Creek approximately due north of the Watt House, which still stands. As his men stacked tree limbs and fence rails to form rough breastworks, Charles Roberts spoke with his line officers and waited.

Union Brig. Gen. George Sykes
Pictured here as a major general
Photo from Brady National Photographic Art Gallery, via Library of Congress

Poor communications, difficult terrain, and other factors delayed the disparate Confederate attacks. Heavy skirmishing "opened fiercely" at sunrise, "but more to our right" (east) than where Thursday's fight had occurred, Hyde noticed across the river.

As Friday wore on, "we saw fires and heard heavy explosions in the direction of Porter's camps," said Hyde, unaware of McClellan's plan to withdraw. Vast troop columns "appeared on the flats across the Chickahominy above us"; raising his field glasses, he studied the distant infantry.

"Dirty gray uniforms," Hyde realized.[9]

Confederate troops directly attacked the strong Union positions along Boatswain's Creek. Against the 2nd Maine and Martindale's 1st Brigade rushed Alabamians, Mississippians, North Carolinians, Texans, and Virginians, many screaming the feared "Rebel yell." Federal cannonballs, Minie rounds, and shells eviscerated the oncoming Confederates, who

Union Gen. Martindale with staff near Richmond
Martindale is in the center. The photo was taken July 1, 1862.
Photo from the Library of Congress

plunged down the ravine's brushy bank and splattered across the narrow stream.

The fighting reached the rear areas, including the 1st Brigade hospital where 2nd Maine assistant surgeon Dr. Alden D. Palmer helped care for the wounded soldiers pouring eastward from the battle. The 1st Brigade's chief surgeon, Dr. William H. White, remembered that as "the battle raged fiercely… our hospital was struck frequently by [incoming Confederate] cannon balls and shells."[10]

As the afternoon wore on toward early evening, Union soldiers—including the 2nd Maine boys—gradually ran low on ammunition and warm bodies, the latter problem created as the casualties piled up. The wounded filtered rearward to the brigade hospital.

Yet not every Union soldier leaving the lines along Boatswain's Creek was wounded. Skulkers[11] used any excuse to leave from the regimental line and seek shelter. As the Union fortunes waned on June 27, such men appeared at the 1st Brigade hospital and spread tales of impending disaster.[12]

The surgeons discussed quietly what they should do if Confederates overran the hospital. Palmer "spoke out bravely and said he would never desert the wounded soldier, but would remain with me to the last, and perform his duty cheerfully," White recalled.

By now, Palmer had "performed many capital operations in a surgical manner, and become very expert and skillful in the use of the knife," White noted.[13]

Besides the 2nd Maine, Martindale's brigade included two Massachusetts and two New York regiments. The 13th New York "and the fire-proof and scarred veterans of the 2nd Maine" held the left of Martindale's brigade, according to a *New York World* reporter.

Employing Napoleonic tactics, Confederates from the 5th Alabama Infantry "moved up over the crest of a hill opposite, in splendid style, even, steady and resolute, with arms at right shoulder shift, ready for a charge," the reporter noted.

The Mainers and New Yorkers lay "concealed in the low growth of timber in the valley." As the Alabamians appeared atop the hill, Union officers yelled, "Up and at them!" The Maine and New York boys "sprang to their feet" and unleashed "one piercing, terrible volley ... into the ranks of the confident enemy," the reporter wrote. "The hill was cleared as though swept by a hurricane."

Union troops scurried to retrieve the fallen regimental and battle flags of the 5th Alabama. Into the ranks of the 2nd Maine a soldier carried the 5th's red-silk regimental flag, a trophy that must not be lost. Even as enemy troops finally broke the Boatswain's Creek line and the 1st Brigade withdrew into the night, the 2nd Maine boys brought all their flags off the field.[14]

Perhaps thousands of Union bystanders watched the battle without participating. "We witnessed this bloody contest across the valley of the river, but the atmospheric condition was such that no sound of artillery or musketry reached our ears," said Charles Clark of the 6th Maine.

"It was like a phantom battle as it appeared to us," he said.[15]

"We could hear the ... unintermitted fury on our right," said Hyde after hugging the ground himself to avoid incoming Confederate cannonballs.

"Still the heavy gray columns were pouring in upon Porter," he realized. "We all felt that we ought to attack to make a diversion."[16]

Nathaniel Jackson had started the 5th Maine toward the fighting at 5:30 a.m. with the 2nd Brigade led by Col. Joseph J. Bartlett. Fleshed out with the 16th and 27th New Yorks and the 96th Pennsylvania, the brigade belonged to the 1st Division commanded by Brig. Gen. Henry W. Slocum.[17]

Sent initially to guard Duane's Bridge (the Union-held river crossing nearest Confederate lines), the 5th Maine soldiers went belly to earth as enemy artillery "opened a severe fire of shot and shell upon us," Bicknell said. Around 11 a.m. (Bartlett recalled the time as 10 a.m.), Slocum recalled the 2nd Brigade, and "we had proceeded but a short distance before the enemy sent shell after shell whizzing upon us," Bicknell noted.[18]

Slocum sent the brigade back to the bridge, which Bartlett's men sufficiently

Union Gen. Daniel Butterfield on horseback
From The Photographic History of The Civil War in Ten Volumes: Volume Four, The Cavalry *(1911).*

ripped apart to stop Confederate troops from using it. The shooting intensified across the Chickahominy; about 2 p.m., Bartlett received orders from Slocum "to cross Woodbury's Bridge and hasten" to reinforce Porter's hard-fighting infantry.[19]

Bartlett responded immediately; thumping across Woodbury's Bridge (about 500 yards downriver from Duane's Bridge) with the 16th New York Infantry in the van, Bartlett's men marched "up the hill on which the battle was then raging" along Porter's left flank at Boatswain's Creek, recalled Lt. Col. Jacob G. Frick of the 96th Pennsylvania Infantry.[20]

Busy just then with his regiment, Frick would soon join the 5th Maine, now approaching "where death's winged messengers flew fast and thick," Bicknell noticed.[21]

With Confederate reinforcements commanded by Thomas "Stonewall" Jackson now pressuring his right flank, Porter was in serious trouble. As yet unaware of that threat, Slocum sent Bartlett and the 2nd Brigade first to reinforce Porter's left flank, then "to the extreme right of the field" (and Porter's battle line) to assist a division of Army regulars commanded by Brig. Gen. George Sykes.

Tired by their forced march in the hot, still air, Bicknell and his comrades lay down when Nathaniel Jackson halted the 5th Maine in a ravine behind Sykes' brigades. Bartlett, who had ridden to this point, let his men "rest, of which they were greatly in need."

Stonewall Jackson's Confederate divisions continually hammered the Union right flank. His men "unable longer to withstand the fierce attacks and withering fire of the enemy," Sykes told Bartlett to bring his brigade up to the battle line at 5 p.m.

The 16th New York advanced first "under the most terrific fire of musketry" and two enemy artillery batteries, Bartlett described the lead rain driving horizontally across the battlefield. "Giving three cheers long and loud," the New Yorkers rushed forward with Bartlett and their colonel leading them.

Anchoring the regiment, Bartlett summoned the 96th Pennsylvania to take position on the left of the 16th. "The murderous fire across the plain" enervated the Pennsylvanians, particularly "some of the line officers," the disgusted Bartlett complained, so he rode through the hellacious fire "to lead forward the third regiment in line," the 5th Maine.[22]

Nathaniel Jackson ordered his men to stand, and moving "with an unbroken, unfaltering front" in two lines, the 5th Maine lads "passed over the brow of the hill" and appeared in view of Confederate troops. Bullets zipping past his ears, the sweating Bicknell counted off "some fifteen rods" (about 250 feet) before Jackson told his men to "'lie down.'"

"In a moment every man was on his face," perhaps a moment before an enemy brigade "unleashed "a full volley ... without the slightest effect," Bicknell said.

Bartlett needed the 5th Maine lads farther to the front. "On," Jackson ordered.

"Up rose every man," said Bicknell, standing as "the air was full of bullets.

"No eye turned backward" in search of safety, he noticed. "Intense eagerness pervaded every file" as "home, comfort, life, death" were "all forgotten. Victory was alone thought of, alone desired."

As "the whistling bullets chimed music to the soldier's ear," the 5th Maine lads stepped off with Jackson and his second-in-command, Lt. Col. William S. Heath of Waterville, presenting

Boatswain's Creek, which flows through the Gaines Mill battlefield
Photo by Brian F. Swartz

large targets atop their horses. Bicknell and his men advanced firmly with "no short, timid step."[23]

From the saddle, Bartlett watched while the "regiment ... changed its front in the most soldierly manner, and under the sweeping storm of iron and leaden hail sent up their battle-shout and rushed upon the enemy." He rode alongside the advancing 5th Maine.[24]

Nathaniel Jackson waved forward his two lines. His men "advanced with a shout" and "involuntarily bent forward their heads" as they marched through "a perfect storm of bullets, shot and shell, which whizzed through the air as thick as hailstones in a storm."[25]

In the brief silences between enemy volleys, Bicknell could hear the swish, swish, swish as Maine men marched through tall grass. Bullets thudded into a Maine lad here and there, but the lines kept "on—now quicker—quicker still," Bicknell said, keeping pace with his company.

"No one seemed to breathe," then the regiment charged, and "the brow of the hills was ours," he exulted.[26]

The slope behind Bicknell was strewn with 5th Maine bodies. "The wonder is not that they lost so many, but that any escaped," Jackson said afterwards.

His command had captured the hilltop and the farm and outbuildings that stood upon it. Still in the saddle, Jackson "raised his sword over his head to cheer on his men." Suddenly "a piece of a shell" ripped past him "so closely" that it sliced the sword strap and struck "the fleshy part" of Jackson's arm "just above the elbow."

Battle of Friday on the Chickahominy
"Porter, McCall, Slocum, Sykes, and Sumner attacked by a superior force of the rebels under Jackson and Lee," the artist wrote across the top of the image. Pencil and zinc oxide on tan paper.
Image by Alfred R. Waud, June 27, 1862; published in Harper's Weekly, July 26, 1862.

The concussion blew Jackson "from his horse into the grass" and left him senseless "for more than an hour."[27]

The blond-haired and blue-eyed Heath took charge as the 5th Maine boys opened fire on Confederate troops regrouping in the distance. Bartlett summoned the 27th New York to form alongside the 5th Maine, and the Pennsylvanians finally came up.

Reinforced enemy brigades advanced toward the 2nd Brigade; amidst heavy firing, Heath noticed that the farm house and outbuildings (likely those comprising the McGehee Farm) had separated four 5th Maine companies—I, G, C, and H—from the regiment's other six companies.

Riding up to the four companies, Heath ordered them to "move ... to the left and perfect the line." Suddenly "shot directly through the brain," Heath fell from his horse "without uttering a groan," Bicknell said.[28]

Comrades bore away the dead Heath and left him beneath a tree "in woods near the Chickahominy ... with the intention of securing" the body "after dark" for burial. Adjutant

George W. Graffam of Portland did retrieve Heath's "sword and belt, cap, diary, and the valuables in his pocket."[29]

With the 5th Maine's third field officer, Maj. Edward S. Scamman of Portland, sick in an army hospital, "here we were in a terrific fight, without a field-officer in command," Bicknell realized. Surviving line officers rallied their companies and continued the battle; regimental command fell to Clark S. Edwards, the senior captain.

Each soldier fought "on his own responsibility," according to Bicknell. "Comrade after comrade fell upon either side, yet there was no faltering." Two Maine companies charged with bayonets to chase away Confederates gathering on the regiment's left flank, and "still the battle raged, and still we held our position," Bicknell said.[30]

Fighting raged all along Porter's lines, almost two and a half miles in length. Slocum's three brigades were helping hold—just barely—the Union right flank as disaster struck on the hotly defended left.

The day's last Confederate assault across Boatswain's Creek began after 7 p.m. With Union lead shredding their ranks, Southern infantrymen plunged into the ravine, splashed through the creek, and climbed its east bank.

History still disputes where Confederate troops initially scythed into the Union lines; struck hard, Charles Griffin's 2nd Brigade fell back, exposing the 2nd Maine's right flank. Other Confederates pried apart the seam between Martindale's and Butterfield's brigades over on the left; with enemy troops already passing his flanks, Roberts pulled his boys back under heavy fire.

Gaines Mill cost the 2nd Maine more than 90 casualties, including many men captured. The ill Lt. Col. George Varney of Bangor vanished during the retreat; "although not wounded" during the fight, Varney "was not entirely recovered from his late illness" when he and Adjutant Lewis P. Mudgett of Stockton Springs went missing.[31]

Bartlett's 2nd Brigade was still on the firing line as the distant Union left flank crumbled. Throwing "fresh troops in double numbers against my line," Stonewall Jackson pounded the brigade, according to Bartlett. On his left flank, the 27th New York and 5th Maine "staggered back under the fearful fire," and Bartlett scurried over to harangue his men.

Stabilizing their lines, they "nobly maintained the fight, without giving an inch of ground ... until long after darkness showed the flash of every musket," he said.[32]

The 2nd Maine lads were retreating toward Alexander's Bridge on the Chickahominy as the 5th Maine boys fought near the McGehee Farm. More Confederate brigades deployed into line; "about sunset the fire came too hot," admitted Bicknell, surprised that he remained intact.

"It was more than flesh and blood could resist, and backward the men began to fall," he noticed.

Around 8:30 p.m., as his men pulled back with their ammunition almost expended, Bartlett noticed a regiment's flag left behind by bullet-tossed color bearers. "Brave as a lion," Bartlett "came dashing up amid a perfect shower of bullets," Bicknell said.

"Boys, don't leave your colors," yelled Bartlett, believing the flag was the 5th Maine's. "About face!"

"Back the boys charged with a perfect yell, gained the colors, and held ... the position" until told to pull back, Bicknell said.[33]

Like a corpse suddenly resurrected from the dead, Nathaniel Jackson stirred where he lay in the two-foot grass (probably wheat). Hearing his name called repetitively, he regained consciousness, blinked, and listened. Unaware that Bartlett had pulled his 2nd Brigade downhill, Jackson did not know that the McGehee Farm now stood "between the fire of the two armies." Infantry volleys and artillery fire thundering in his ears, Jackson could scarcely hear his rescuer belly-crawling through the grass as "bullets whizzed overhead, so close as to even cut off the tops of the grass."

"I'm here," Jackson must have grunted. His name lost to history, the 5th Maine volunteer squirmed toward his wounded colonel.

"Lie close to the ground," the man warned.

No one could stand and live in that "awfully grand" scene stretching from the farm downhill to the 5th Maine's attenuated line. "It was near night-fall, and the thick smoke which hung over the field shut out from view the opposing armies, their positions being disclosed only by the sheets of flame which burst forth almost continuously from either line of battle," a Maine veteran recalled.

"The course of the shells could be distinctly seen overhead, and the whizzing of passing bullets and shot was anything but pleasant," he remembered.

The rescuer reached and quietly checked the wounded Jackson. "Follow me," the soldier must have said before crawling south on his hands and knees.

His wound leaving blood on the grass stalks, Jackson worked his "way slowly along in a prostrate position." The two soldiers soon felt the ground flatten beneath them; touching Jackson, the rescuer would have told him to "get up and run when I do."

Volleys ripped along the lines, then stopped. The men "arose and ran within our lines," a surprised 5th Maine survivor watched the two wraiths sweeping past him.

They soon met "an empty stretcher" and its bearers; they placed the bleeding Jackson on it and headed him toward the 5th Maine's camp. Dr. George E. Brickett tended the colonel's wounded arm.

The 2nd Brigade withdrew quickly across the Chickahominy River at Alexander's Bridge; Bicknell figured he reached the right bank about 9 p.m. Hours later his men fell asleep at the campground they had left early Thursday morning.

Learning that William Heath had been shot and killed, Nathaniel Jackson ordered Brickett to take "a detachment of men" and search for the corpse.

Finding Confederate troops swarming through the woods north of the Chickahominy, Brickett and his men abandoned their mission. A talented attorney by profession, William S. Heath went into an unmarked grave, if buried at all. He left behind a young wife and two young children.[34]

The Confederate victory at Gaines Mill had shoved V Corps south, thus reuniting the Army of the Potomac even as McClellan passed orders to retreat to the James River.

"The loss in the whole army was terrible," Bicknell said. The 5th Maine had lost 10 men killed and 69 men wounded, he noted. Another 16 men were missing.[35]

Temporarily transferred to command the 5th Maine Infantry due to its lack of staff officers, Jacob Frick reported a final total of seven officers and 59 "enlisted men" killed or wounded. Although the regiment had "received a very galling fire from a greatly superior force," the "officers and men behaved nobly," he reported.[36]

Bartlett reported "the loss of 500 officers and men" in his brigade; the 16th New York reported 201 casualties, the 27th New York lost 151 men, and the 96th Pennsylvania 87 men dead, wounded, or missing. Adding the 66 men lost in the 5th Maine, and Bartlett's initial estimate of losses was very close; the 2nd Brigade officially reported 505 casualties.

Bartlett described all his warriors as "brave, energetic, and efficient."[37]

~~~

1. Thomas Worcester Hyde, *Following the Greek Cross; Or, Memories of the Sixth Army Corps,* Houghton, Mifflin, United States, 1894, p. 67
2. The terms "right bank" and "left bank" refer to a waterway's banks looking downstream. Technically the "left bank" of the Chickahominy was north of the river, its "right bank" to the south. However, some reports written during the Peninsula Campaign mistakenly flipped the banks of the Chickahominy to "right" (north) or "left" (south), based on looking upriver. These references are erroneous.
3. Hiram G. Berry, January 8, 1863 report to John L. Hodsdon, *Annual Report of the Adjutant General of the State of Maine, 1862,* p. 121
4. Hyde, Greek Cross, pp. 66-67
5. Rev. George W. Bicknell, *History of the Fifth Regiment Maine Volunteers,* Hall L. Davis, Portland, Maine 1871, p. 99
6. William E.S. Whitman and Charles H. True, *Maine in the War for the Union,* Nelson Dingley Jr. & Co., Lewiston, Maine, 1865, p. 269
7. Frank Moore, *Women of the War: Their Heroism and Self-Sacrifice,* S.S. Scranton & Co., Hartford, Conn., 1866, pp. 116-117
8. Elijah Walker, *The Old Soldier: History of the Fourth Maine Infantry,* Tribune, Rockland, Maine, 1895, pp. 29-30
9. Hyde, Greek Cross, p. 67
10. Dr. William H. White, July 30, 1862 letter to Maine Gov. Israel Washburn Jr., Daily Whig & Courier, Thursday, August 7, 1862.
11. The term "skulkers" referred to soldiers who often vanished from the battle line with the first shot and did not reappear until the fighting ended. Recognizing the difference between a brave comrade who suddenly panicked under fire and a skulker seldom found on the firing line, Maine soldiers held the latter individual in low esteem.
12. During battle, a skulker often excused himself to help a wounded comrade reach a field hospital. A surgeon might draft a skulker as a hospital steward, but many skulkers kept walking until safely off the battlefield.
13. Dr. William H. White letter, *Daily Whig & Courier,* Thursday, August 7, 1862. White reported that Dr. Palmer and Hospital Steward Daniel E. Edgerly "were taken prisoners at the battle on the 27th of June." Palmer, from Orono, was named surgeon of the 9th Maine Infantry in 1863.

14. *Daily Whig & Courier,* Tuesday, July 8, 1862
15. Col. Charles A. Clark, *Campaigning with the Sixth Maine,* The Kenyon Press, Des Moines, Iowa, 1897, pp. 11-12, 21-22
16. Hyde, *Greek Cross,* p. 67
17. Displaying no imagination, War Department officials consecutively numbered the divisions in each corps and the brigades in each division. During the Peninsula Campaign, four of McClellan's five Army corps fielded a 1st Division; all five fielded a 2nd Division.
18. Bicknell, *History,* pp. 99-100
19. Col. Joseph J. Bartlett, *Official Records, Series I, Vol. 11, Part I,* Chapter XXIII, No. 176, p. 447
20. Lt. Col. Jacob G. Frick, *OR, Series I, Vol. 11, Part I,* Chapter XXIII, No. 177, p. 450
21. Bicknell, *History,* p. 100
22. Bartlett, *OR, Series I, Vol. 11, Part I,* Chapter XXIII, No. 176, pp. 447-448
23. Bicknell, *History,* pp. 101-102
24. Bartlett, *OR, Series I, Vol. 11, Part I,* Chapter XXIII, No. 176, p. 448
25. "The Fifth Maine in Battle," *Maine Farmer,* Thursday, July 17, 1862, reprinted from Lewiston Journal
26. Bicknell, *History,* p. 102
27. "The Fifth Maine in Battle," *Maine Farmer,* Thursday, July 17, 1862
28. Bicknell, *History,* p. 102
29. "The Fifth Maine in Battle," *Maine Farmer,* Thursday, July 17, 1862. William Heath's clothing and valuables were given to his brother, Capt. Francis Edward Heath of the 3rd Maine Infantry Regiment. After William Heath pitched from his saddle, his horse bolted and ran south across the Chickahominy River to the 5th Maine's camp. Francis Heath also received the horse.
30. Bicknell, *History,* pp. 102-103
31. Col. Charles W. Roberts, July 4, 1862 letter to father Amos M. Roberts, *Daily Whig & Courier,* Friday, July 11, 1862. Varney and Mudgett were captured and later paroled.
32. Bartlett, *OR, Series I, Vol. 11, Part I,* Chapter XXIII, No. 176, p. 448
33. Bicknell, *History,* p. 103
34. "The Fifth Maine in Battle," *Maine Farmer,* Thursday, July 17, 1862. On Tuesday, August 25, members of the Kennebec County Bar presented to the Maine Supreme Judicial Court in Augusta resolutions praising William S. Heath and four other deceased attorneys.
35. Bicknell, *History,* p. 104
36. Frick, *OR, Series I, Vol. 11, Part I,* Chapter XXIII, No. 177, pp. 450-451
37. Bartlett, *OR, Series I, Vol. 11, Part I,* Chapter XXIII, No. 176, p. 449

Chapter 35

ON THE ROAD AGAIN

"The Eleventh went down into the swamps of the Chickahominy"

Run.

That's all that George Brinton McClellan could tell his troops, who despite the 6,837 comrades lost at Gaines Mill believed they needed only one solid punch to capture Richmond as the sky brightened on Saturday, June 28.

Even excluding the mauled V Corps debouching onto the Chickahominy River's right (south) bank via the bridges Alexander and Woodbury, the reunited Army of the Potomac numbered sufficient rifles and artillery tubes to thrust westward through John Magruder's 25,000 Confederates and take Richmond.

The bulk of Robert E. Lee's army lay north of the river. Lee knew that Union troops would destroy the bridges to stall Confederate pursuit. To secure a crossing and attack the Yankees would take time, perhaps too long to stop McClellan's divisions from entering the Confederate capital.

The Billy Yanks in the ranks instinctively knew they could still win.

Their commander did not.

Run, run for the James River, McClellan had told his generals at night on Thursday, June 26.

Run—and do not stop moving.

Without being officially told, the 11th Maine lads guarding the Richmond & York River Railroad bridge east of Seven Pines knew that something awful had happened north of the river on Friday. As the afternoon wore, V Corps stragglers—likely skulkers deliberately straying from the battlefield—started appearing at Jonathan Hill's outposts across the bridge.

The stragglers voiced loud opinions about the fate of V Corps. Pointed west toward Seven Pines, the fleet-footed stragglers crossed the railroad bridge even as 11th Maine soldiers commanded by Sgt. Benjamin F. Dunbar of Belfast pried up 200 feet of deck boards. Momentarily left in place, the planks could be tossed into the Chickahominy to deny the bridge's use to Confederate troops.

Men also prepared torches for burning the bridge. No Chickahominy span could be left intact.[1]

Born in Deer Isle and living in Belfast when he enlisted in the 11th Maine in mid-October 1861, the 5-foot, 11-inch Ben Dunbar had worked as a sailor prior being made a sergeant in Co. F. His height gave him a bit of a commanding presence; when the brown-haired and gray-eyed Dunbar told his men to move, they moved fast.[2]

Capt. James Brady[3] deployed three cannons from Battery H, 1st Pennsylvania Light Artillery, to a hilltop position overlooking the railroad bridge. Soldiers constructed earthworks to shelter the guns and screened them with small, cut trees. Six additional 11th Maine companies joined Hill's at the west end of the bridge.[4]

With the cannons "placed on the hill behind us, the Eleventh went down into the swamps of the Chickahominy" and "formed a long skirmish line," said Robert Brady Jr.[5] Concealing themselves amidst the thick leafy growth along the river's muddy shore, the skirmishers nervously watched the left bank and the murky water flowing past.

During the day, troops posted south of the Chickahominy and opposite the Gaines Mill battle had nervously eyed each other's lines. Maj. Gen. David R. Jones commanded the Confederate division facing the 2nd Division of Brig. Gen. William F. "Baldy" Smith; his 1st Brigade, which included Col. Hiram Burnham and the 6th Maine Infantry Regiment, had "occupied Golding's Farm, which joins the [Chickahominy] River," since early June, recalled a 6th Maine veteran.

Friday morning had found the regiment on picket duty. Sent to probe the Union lines at Golding's, Confederate Brig. Gen. Robert Toombs attacked instead. His artillery "vigorously shelled us until 6 P.M.," when enemy troops "suddenly rushed on us, out of a piece of woods opposite our position, in great force," the 6th Maine soldier recalled the Battle of Golding's Farm.

"The old 6th stood up like a solid wall, and for an hour poured an incessant sheet of fire into them," he said. Now short 271 men, Toombs withdraw his battered regiments.

The 6th Maine lost no more than 25 men. Pvt. Silas Page, a teen-age farmer from Bucksport, was "torn to pieces" by a Toombs-inspired cannonball. Another shell tore a leg off Pvt. Charles Mitchell of Hudson, a small town in Maine's Penobscot Valley; evacuated to Savage Station, Mitchell died the next day. A Confederate soldier got close enough to punch a bullet into Sgt. Elias Ketch, a laborer

Confederate Brig. Gen. Robert Augustus Toombs
Between 1870-80
Photo from Brady-Handy Collection, Library of Congress

The first cabinet of the Confederate States of America
Unlike the late-in-life photo on the facing page, at the time he joined the Confederate Army, Toombs looked more like he did here. This wood engraving was made using photographs. From left to right: Judah P. Benjamin, Stephen Mallory, Christopher Memminger, Alexander Stephens, LeRoy Pope Walker, Jefferson Davis, John H. Reagan, and Robert Toombs. Toombs wanted the Confederate presidency; he settled for Secretary of State, but quickly resigned to join the army.
Illustration from Library of Congress

from Lincoln. He, too, died at Savage Station on Saturday.[6]

Throughout the night, Yankee survivors of Gaines Mill struggled to reach Union lines. Comrades carried wounded men. Foot- or leg-wounded, other soldiers staggered along on makeshift crutches crafted from rifles or tree limbs. Most survivors crossed at upriver bridges, but some "three thousand officers and men, mostly Pennsylvania reserves" of George McCall's division "were passed over the [railroad] bridge to the right bank" and sent west along the tracks to Savage Station, an 11th Maine soldier remembered.[7]

Gloom stalked the camp of the 5th Maine Infantry Regiment as 1st Lt. George Bicknell and the Co. K survivors awoke early on Saturday. Exhausted, powder-stained men instinctively sought familiar faces now forever lost.

Ordered "to be ready for immediate movement," most soldiers wrote letters home "to assure those far away, who may be thinking of us, of safety up to the moment of writing," Bicknell said.

"The mail-bag left the camp ... heavier than usual," he noticed.[8]

Men wounded at Oak Grove, Beaver Dam Creek, and Gaines Mill poured into the field hospitals at Savage Station. Isabella Fogg and other nurses ministered to the casualties, loaded into boxcars and shipped east to White House Landing as soon as possible. Friday saw 600 to 700 casualties arriving at Savage Station, where rumors circulated about the army's fate.

No matter how fast the nurses worked, more wounded men arrived as the sun set. Fogg could not sleep that night; mules braying and dry axles screeching, ambulances rumbled into Savage Station, and soldiers bore their wounded comrades directly from the battlefield on their shoulders or on stretchers.

Saturday's dawn unveiled the human detritus accumulated during the night. Fogg worked amidst the horror recalled by a Pennsylvania chaplain, Reverend James Junius Marks.

"All the open grounds around the house of Mr. Savage, all the floors of the barns and stables and outhouses were covered with a ghastly multitude, bleeding, groaning, and dying," he said.[9]

Doctors, nurses, and hospital attendants flitted constantly among the men laid beneath every tree. Photographer James F. Gibson, a Scot who with his wife Elizabeth had immigrated to Washington, D.C. by 1860, had accompanied Union troops on the Peninsula for his employer, Mathew Brady.

On a Saturday not yet disrupted by distant gunfire, Gibson set up his cumbersome camera near the Savage farmhouse and focused on the wounded men and their attendants filling the yard. Restricted by the technology of this time to a slow shutter speed, Gibson caught on glass plate the "ghastly multitude" described by Marks.

The photograph would become among the more famous created during the war.[10]

Union wounded on train flatcars at Savage Station
This grainy photo shows at least 40 visible heads, and probably that many more not visible.
Photo from Brady's National Photographic Portrait Galleries, via Library of Congress

Chapter 35: On the Road Again

Union field hospital at Savage Station after the June 27, 1862 Battle of Gaines Mill
Photo by James F. Gibson via Library of Congress

In such scenes did Isabella Fogg and other nurses work Saturday. A trainload of wounded soldiers left for White House Landing around breakfast, and the hospital attendants gradually loaded another train with 500 casualties.

The 11th Maine soldiers guarding the railroad bridge over the Chickahominy noted that "a long train of cars filled with sick and wounded, passed early in the morning" for White House Landing, a Maine soldier said. Around 9:30 a.m., the same train "returned loaded with forage.

"This was the last train that passed the bridge to the Army of the Potomac," he later recorded.[11]

Around 3,000 sick and wounded men were still at Savage Station as James Marks stepped into the telegraphic office near the railroad tracks around 10 a.m.

The wire connection with White House Landing "suddenly ceased working," Marks said, perhaps shuddering at the implication. The telegraph operator told his audience that the wires were down.

"Our worst fears were now realized," Marks admitted. "It was certain the enemy was in our rear."[12]

After the Union V Corps withdrew south of the river on Friday night, Lee had wondered where McClellan would move next. Stuart's cavalry troopers and infantrymen commanded by Richard Ewell probed east along the river Saturday to determine if McClellan was falling back on White House Landing.

He was not.

By mid-morning, Jeb Stuart's Confederate cavalry had ridden up to Dispatch Station on the left bank of the Chickahominy River, just a short distance from the 11th Maine's easternmost outposts. About 9:30 a.m., Maine scouts spotted "a brigade of rebel troops with artillery and cavalry" only a mile off, a soldier recalled.

Col. Harris Plaisted recalled his far-flung pickets; men rushing across the bridge at 10 a.m. claimed the Southerners were a half mile away. Thirty minutes later, the Federal cavalrymen fleeing Stuart's riders at Dispatch Station raced across the railroad tracks within a hundred yards of the railroad bridge and vanished downriver toward Bottoms Bridge.

Surprised Maine soldiers watched as Confederate cavalry rode after the retreating Yankees. Then Southern infantrymen appeared not far up the tracks.

Burn the bridge, Plaisted snarled.

Blue-clad Maine vandals tossed the bridge's planks over the side, and "the torch was applied to the prepared combustibles" by the arsonist du jour, Ben Dunbar himself.

The railroad bridge went up in flames; located two miles downriver, Bottoms Bridge burned after the Union cavalrymen crossed it.[13]

Federal troops destroyed all the Chickahominy bridges that they guarded. Elements of McClellan's army already crept south on the dry, dusty roads; to screen the withdrawal, some units nearest enemy lines south of the river demonstrated against Confederate positions.

Joe Bartlett advanced his mangled 2nd Brigade toward the Confederate lines around 8 a.m. His men had pitched their tents to simulate a permanent camp, but struck those same tents about two hours later and marched off "leaving our knapsacks and other equipage" where the tents had been located, according to Bicknell.[14]

If intended to confuse enemy troops as to McClellan's intentions, the ruse did not work. After the 5th Maine lads stacked their arms, Jacob Frick sent one company at a time to retrieve its knapsacks. Curious Confederates watched for a while, then started shelling the fourth or fifth company to reach the temporary camp site.

Later that day, Henry W. Slocum advanced his 1st Division (including Bartlett's brigade) to screen "our retreating army" and "to check any advancing movement which the enemy might see fit to make," said Bicknell.

Bartlett's four under-strength regiments engaged in minor fighting that faded with sunset.[15]

Not far from Slocum's division, Confederate troops sensing movement in the Union camps again probed the lines held by Baldy Smith's 2nd Division. The divisional wagon train had already started south when Smith sent the ax-wielding 7th Maine Infantry soldiers of his 3rd Brigade into the woods alongside the roads along which enemy infantry could advance.

Chapter 35: On the Road Again

George Alfred Townsend, war correspondent
Townsend kept good company. He is pictured here (at left) in 1871 with Mark Twain (center) and David Gray, editor of the *Buffalo Courier*. He was likely with the New York Herald during the war, until 1865.
Photo from Brady-Handy Collection, Library of Congress

Swinging away, the Maine men felled trees across the roads "to delay pursuit," said Maj. Thomas W. Hyde.

The 3rd Brigade had missed Friday's fight at Golding's Farm; now, on Saturday morning, curious Confederates listened to the axes thumping into tree trunks opposite the Southern lines.

Wanting to know what the Yankees were doing, Gen. Jones again sent Robert Toombs and his Georgia brigade to find out.

The Confederacy's first secretary of state, Toombs habitually expressed opinions at odds with his superiors. Ordered to discover the reasons for the Yankee activity and not to pick a fight, Toombs promptly disobeyed the second command to accomplish the first.

After Confederate artillery shelled the 3rd Brigade's empty camps, gray- and butternut-clad infantry emerged from the woods and precipitated the Battle of Garnett's Hill. Engaging their enemies "in an hour's fight," the 7th Maine and the 3rd Brigade inflicted "severe losses" on the Georgians and drove them off, Hyde said.[16]

To reach the James River, George McClellan and his army had to cross White Oak Swamp, a snake-infested, thickly wooded, and partially impenetrable wetland created by White Oak Creek, flowing east to the Chickahominy. A few roads crossed the swamp; infantrymen could use the nearby fords, but wheeled vehicles could not.

Elijah Walker and the 4th Maine had spent Friday night swatting mosquitoes at Jordan's Ford, the nearest to the III Corps camps. Walker's division commander, Phil Kearny, finally appeared early on Saturday; he and Walker crossed White Oak Creek at Jordan's Ford and examined the terrain.

Resume work, said Kearny, who had suspended the regiment's corduroy-road construction about 16 hours earlier. Swinging their axes with a vengeance, the 4th Maine lads "built about 250 feet of corduroy bridge" over the creek and wielded "picks and shovels" to construct approaches on both banks, Walker said.

His men worked continuously as the Saturday sun swung to the west. If Union troops must retreat across the creek at Jordan's Ford, the 4th Maine would have a bridge ready.[17]

Orders had gone by Thursday to Brig. Gen. Stewart Van Vliet (the army's chief quartermaster) at White House Landing to remove all personnel and as many supplies as possible by ship, then torch the remaining stores.

Stuck at the landing since Friday, nurses Sarah Sampson and Ellen Harris helped load the sick and wounded soldiers onto available transports. Doing so might have saved the lives of many Union men by removing them from the miasmatic environs in which senior Army officers had placed them.

Visiting White House Landing in early June, Reverend James Marks had noticed "a city of hospital tents" pitched "in one of the great fields.

"The ground was swampy," and June's rains often pooled runoff on the surface, often beneath the tents lacking wood-plank floors, Marks noticed. "The men suffered from much dampness."[18]

The hospital complex at White House Landing had not impressed war correspondent George Alfred Townsend during a late June visit. "There was quite a town of sick men" who sometimes lay 20 men packed into a single wall-tent, he noted.

The hospital tents "were pitched in a damp cornfield," where "the sun shone like a furnace upon the tents, and the rains drowned out the inmates," Townsend said.

Apparently the Union commanders "so reverenced their national shrines" that neither White House nor its lawn were "used for hospital purposes," Townsend said.[19]

Marks had also picked up on that point. The grounds around White House "were high, well drained, and covered with grass, and the whole surface protected by shade-trees," he noted. "No more genial and delightful spot could be selected" for the hospital complex, "but for some unexplained reason a boggy field was chosen."[20]

Amidst such damp contamination flitted the tired, sweaty nurses who cared for the suffering patients. Amidst the evacuation, not until the last possible minute did Sampson finally board a steamer that soon stood down the Pamunkey River and entered the York.

Isabella Fogg remained at Savage Station on Saturday. Medical personnel desperately cared for the sick and wounded, but many men went neglected without blankets, food, and medicine. As Reverend Marks walked about the hospital complex, men begged him for help.

More wounded soldiers arrived during the day, and every building and tent—at least 300 of those—brimmed with casualties. Marks estimated that 15 to 20 men occupied each tent; with each nurse responsible for three tents, Fogg would have cared for 45 to 60 men until she was ordered to leave.[21]

When she had time, Fogg watched the dust clouds kicked up by Union troops marching past Savage Station while en route for the James River. The tramping continued into the night. Fogg could tell that the columns were moving east, away from the enemy; how long before there would be no Union troops between Savage Station and Lee's advancing Confederates?

And what would happen to the casualties piling up in the hospital complex?

Aware by now that their army was retreating, those Union troops still holding the line glanced over their shoulders as darkness fell on Saturday. Not until 2 a.m., Sunday, June 29 did the 1st Division of Henry Slocum receive orders to withdraw. Reflected by the faces of tired men and the metallic components of rifles, uniforms, and gear, flames danced merrily in the Chickahominy dark as "everything which we could not carry was burnt," George Bicknell said.

Smart soldiers stuffed their haversacks with abandoned food. "Forward, march!" officers called, "and with light step [we] moved out upon the road," Bicknell said.[22]

~~~

1. William E.S. Whitman and Charles H. True, *Maine in the War for the Union,* Nelson Dingley Jr. & Co., Lewiston, Maine, 1865, pp. 269-270
2. Benjamin F. Dunbar, *Soldiers' File,* Maine State Archives. Later promoted to second lieutenant and then first lieutenant, Dunbar mustered out in mid-November 1864.
3. James Brady was no relation to the Robert Bradys, senior and junior, of the 11th Maine Infantry.
4. Whitman and True, *Maine in the War,* p. 270
5. Albert Maxfield and Robert Brady Jr., *Company D of the Eleventh Regiment Maine Infantry Volunteers in the War of the Rebellion,* Press of Thos. Humphrey, New York, NY, 1890, p. 57
6. "Letter from the Sixth Maine Regiment," July 14, 1862, *Daily Whig & Courier,* Thursday, July 24, 1862
7. Whitman and True, *Maine in the War,* p. 270
8. Rev. George W. Bicknell, *History of the Fifth Regiment Maine Volunteers,* Hall L. Davis, Portland, Maine 1871,

p. 105
9. Rev. James Junius Marks, D.D., *The Peninsula Campaign in Virginia*, J.B. Lippincott & Co., Philadelphia, 1864, pp. 226-227
10. Gibson would work with fellow Scot Alexander Gardner at the Antietam and Gettysburg battlefields, but he remains best known for his Peninsula Campaign photography
11. Whitman and True, *Maine in the War*, p. 270
12. Marks, *The Peninsula Campaign in Virginia*, p. 228
13. Whitman and True, *Maine in the War*, p. 270
14. History does not record why the knapsacks were left but the tents were taken.
15. Bicknell, *History*, pp. 106-108
16. Thomas W. Hyde, *Following the Greek Cross*, University of South Carolina Press, Columbia, S.C., 2005, p. 66
17. Elijah Walker, *The Old Soldier: History of the Fourth Maine Infantry*, Tribune, Rockland, Maine, 1895, p. 30
18. Marks, *The Peninsula Campaign*, pp. 184-185
19. George Alfred Townsend, *Campaigns of a Non-Combatant and His Romaunt Abroad During the War*, Blelock & Company, New York, NY, 1866, pp. 149-150
20. Marks, *The Peninsula Campaign*, pp. 184-185
21. Marks, *The Peninsula Campaign*, pp. 228-231
22. Bicknell, *History*, pp. 105-109

Chapter 36

THE FIGHTING RETREAT

*"Maine may consider herself honored
in the bravery of her sons"*

After spending Saturday, June 28 constructing a corduroy bridge over White Oak Creek at Jordan's Ford, the sweat-soaked men of the 4th Maine Infantry Regiment did not rest on their ax handles on Sunday.

Throughout the day, retreating Union soldiers tramped south through the heat and humidity as other comrades held their positions near the destroyed Chickahominy River bridges or in the swamps and woods west of Seven Pines. The front-line Union regiments maintained a semblance of normality in the Federal camps as the battered V Corps and the cattle herd and wagons trains of the Army of the Potomac struggled to cross White Oak Swamp.

Until Friday, June 27, George McClellan had treated the swamp as an impenetrable left flank. Now his army needed additional crossings of White Oak Creek.

Pleased with the rude span and its corduroyed approaches that his 4th Maine lads had engineered at Jordan's Ford, Col. Elijah Walker told Brig. Gen. Phil Kearny at noon on June 29 that the bridge was ready.

Focused on extracting his 3rd Division from its positions near Seven Pines, Kearny acknowledged Walker's news. At 1 p.m., he ordered Walker to explore the downstream Fisher's Ford and determine "how soon I could have it in readiness for the passage of troops."

Selecting an aide or two, Walker rode to Fisher's Ford, "personally made the examination," and reported to Kearny that the 4th Maine lads could whip up a bridge and corduroyed approaches that infantry could use "with three hours from [the regiment] receiving an order so to do."

A courier rode up with Kearny's response at 3 p.m.: Get busy.

Walker promptly marched a third of his regiment to Fisher's Ford and left his men at work under the watchful eye of Lt. Col. Edwin Carver.[1]

The 3rd Maine Infantry boys had departed their camp at 5 a.m. Sunday as Kearny contracted his divisional lines. In the American military's best "hurry up and wait" tradition, the Maine soldiers finally crossed White Oak Swamp on the Jordan's Ford bridge "late in the afternoon" before

Union Col. Edwin Burt
Photo from Library of Congress

Confederate Gen. Benjamin Huger
Photo from Library of Congress

probing carefully toward the Charles City Road, said Maj. Edwin Burt, the acting colonel since the June 26 sacking of Lt. Col. Charles Sampson.[2]

As Union troops retreated almost due south toward the James River, Robert E. Lee maneuvered his divisions to catch and shatter the Army of the Potomac. Three roads—Charles City, Darbytown, and River, in order from north to south—ran southeast from Richmond to intersect the route selected by George McClellan.

The Charles City and Darbytown roads were especially vital to McClellan and Lee. Union divisions and wagon trains retreating along the Williamsburg Stage Road either east from Savage Station or west from Bottoms Bridge funneled onto two roads that angled south to merge above White Oak Swamp. From this intersection a single road crossed White Oak Creek to meet the Long Bridge Road, which ran from the Chickahominy River some nine miles southwest to New Market on the River Road, near the James River.[3]

Upon crossing White Oak Creek and reaching Long Bridge Road, Union troops turned west and marched approximately two miles to Glendale, a crossroads formed by Long Bridge Road, Charles City Road, and Willis Church Road. Charles City Road angled toward this crossroads from the northwest; from Glendale, the Willis Church Road (also called the Quaker Road) pointed south toward Malvern Hill and the River Road—and safety.

Although a recently discovered woods road was soon siphoning off some wagon trains,

Chapter 36: The Fighting Retreat

most Union formations turned south on the Willis Church Road.

Extending southeast from the Richmond defenses, the Darbytown Road intersected the Long Bridge Road about a mile west of Glendale. Lee envisioned his troops attacking along the Charles City and Darbytown roads to capture the crossroads, which McClellan must defend until his army passed by.[4]

Lee also planned to attack along the River Road to strike the Union troops retreating over Malvern Hill. Meanwhile, "Stonewall" Jackson would push his divisions south across the Chickahominy River and strike the rear of McClellan's army.

Somewhere, surely, the Confederate divisions would pry apart the Union lines and roll up a Federal corps or two. Lee could attack anywhere from White Oak Swamp to Malvern Hill; McClellan had to defend everywhere, but the Glendale intersection must be held—to the last man, if necessary.

Unsure as to where to find Confederate troops on Sunday afternoon, David Birney ordered Burt "to proceed cautiously toward Charles City road." Deploying Co. B as skirmishers, Burt probed south for a mile, then ran into "a superior force of the enemy posted in the woods, with field artillery."[5]

The Co. B lads had encountered skirmishers from the Confederate division of Maj. Gen. Benjamin Huger. Expected by Lee to play a central role in trapping the retreating Union army, Huger advanced cautiously on June 30 before bivouacking his mixed Alabama-Georgia-Louisiana-Virginia division on the Charles City Road, about three miles from Glendale.

Burt's men drove the Confederate skirmishers into their lines; "our flankers on the left were fired on by the enemy," Huger described the noisy buzzing along his flank. He "pushed light troops into the woods" to find out how many Yankees threatened his division.[6]

"We were finally obliged to yield the ground to superior forces," Burt admitted. As Co. B fell back on the 3rd Maine's line of battle, he noticed two men absent: Corp. William McDavitt Jr. was "either killed or wounded and taken prisoner," and someone reported that Pvt. Harrison Hobbs was dead.[7]

Burt reported the enemy roadblock to Birney, who passed the news to Kearny. Riding to Jordan's Ford, Kearny suddenly appeared beside Elijah Walker. "Some misunderstanding arose" between the two men, Walker remembered, and Kearny promptly arrested Walker.

But the startled Walker would not vanish like the Birney-arrested Charles Sampson had after Oak Grove. To his credit, Kearny "then rode to the front, saw the condition of affairs, returned, came up to me," and offered his right hand—his only hand—to shake Walker's.

Kearny acknowledged his error "and asked me to again take command of my regiment," Walker said.[8]

Although Benjamin Huger believed "I was leaving Kearny's division behind me,"[9] he need not have worried about Kearny attacking across White Oak Creek; because enemy troops held the Charles City Road in considerable numbers, Kearny ordered Birney and Brig. Gen. John C. Robinson[10] to pull their brigades back across White Oak Creek; he then rode downstream to find another crossing.

After the 1st and 2nd brigades recrossed the Jordan's Ford bridge to the left bank of

White Oak Creek, 4th Maine vandals attacked the span with their axes, "displacing nearly all the corduroy," Walker noted. Meanwhile, acting on Walker's recommendation, Hiram Berry had marched his 3rd Brigade east to cross White Oak Creek at Fisher's Ford.

Amidst all the comings and goings late that Sunday, Walker had grabbed a passing ammunition wagon and ordered his men to toss out the ammunition boxes and place "six sick men and some hospital stores" inside the wagon bed.

The wagon rolled away as 4th Maine Infantry property. Walker was no McClellan, who had abandoned his wounded so that he could flee faster.[11]

David Birney and his four regiments tramped six miles east through dense, snake-infested thickets before crossing White Oak Creek and reaching higher ground to the south. The 2nd Brigade reached the Charles City Road not far from Glendale at 10 p.m. Exhausted after marching and skirmishing in Sunday's high heat and humidity, the 3rd Maine boys "bivouacked for the night," Edwin Burt said.[12]

Union Gen. John Cleveland Robinson
Photo by Mathew Brady, via Library of Congress

Walker did not catch up with the 3rd Division until Monday morning.

Dawn on Sunday found the 11th Maine pickets still "lying concealed behind breastworks and trees" along the Chickahominy and sniping at Confederate troops appearing on the left bank, according to a veteran. The Yankees were glad to see the sunrise; though the regiment-set fire had burned away the deck of the Richmond & York River Railroad bridge the previous day, the "green and water-soaked" heavy timbers of its substructure still stood, the Maine lads had noticed during the night.

A courier riding from George McClellan's headquarters had found Col. Harris Plaisted at midnight Saturday. "Destroy the foundation of the bridge, utterly," McClellan ordered because he did not want the deck "repaired for the passage of artillery."

With flames still flickering on the bridge deck, Sgt. Benjamin Dunbar again turned out his pioneers "and a body of picked men" from the 11th Maine and went to the bridge. Guarded by tired, but grim-faced comrades standing watch on the right bank, ax-wielding soldiers ran onto the shattered deck of the bridge and waded into the river to attack the substructure.

Axes thudded into the beams as Dunbar's experienced pioneers chopped down "all the posts and uprights" supporting the 80-foot section of bridge between two piers, a veteran

Chapter 36: The Fighting Retreat

reported. Confederate troops on the opposite shore vanished during the early morning destruction; not until after Sunday's dawn did enemy infantry start probing the 11th Maine's defenses again.[13]

As the Union lines contracted that torrid Sunday, many wounded men at Savage Station speculated as to when they would be evacuated. A confusing late-day battle near the extensive hospital complex diverted Baldy Smith and his division—including the 6th and 7th Maine infantry regiments—to support the II Corps of Brig. Gen. Edwin Sumner; the shooting ended around 9 p.m. with another 919 men added to the Federal casualty rolls.

By then the 2,500-plus sick and wounded hospitalized at Savage Station realized that they would be abandoned. White House Landing had fallen to Confederate cavalry, and McClellan lacked sufficient wagons to carry off both his casualties and supplies.

With too much of either to evacuate, he abandoned both at Savage Station.

Reverend James Junius Marks spent Sunday morning checking on patients and managing the nurses assigned to his particular area of responsibility, a small hospital encompassing only 150 "sick men, some of them in a dying condition."

Afraid that advancing Confederate troops—Marks heard them "cutting a road and constructing a bridge" somewhere to the north, toward the Chickahominy—would soon reach Savage Station, Col. John Burke of the 63rd New York arrived at "the gate of the hospital" and urged Marks to evacuate his patients. McClellan had ordered all ambulances sent south empty in expectation of picking up casualties incurred during the retreat; Marks lacked wagons and figured he "had not more than six men well enough to help the others away."[14]

Similar conditions existed across Savage Station. Cannon fire grew louder as Confederate troops of John B. Magruder pushed east; stragglers (including officers) passing through the hospitals spread frightening rumors, and hurting soldiers cried in apprehension.

"Through all these fearful scenes and agonizing fears" about the hospital's abandonment, Isabella Fogg "continued her labor for the sick till the last moment." Ordered to leave, she loaded "sanitary supplies" into an ambulance, apparently among the last at Savage Station, and joined the southward-shuffling columns.

Her thoughts about abandoning wounded men from the 6th Maine Infantry went unspoken.[15]

Reverend Marks learned from Sam Heintzelman that McClellan decided to abandon the Federal casualties because their presence could make the army's "escape ... impossible."

Returning to his hospital section, Marks gathered the medical personnel and as many patients as possible around a mulberry tree. He implored those still mobile to leave with the retreating army; "I entreated the stronger to help the weaker," he recalled.[16]

As Sunday wore on, apocalyptic scenes unfolded around that length of the Richmond & York River Railroad still in Union hands. The abundant supplies stacked alongside the tracks must be destroyed; riding along with Baldy Smith's 2nd Division, Maj. Thomas Hyde of the 7th Maine slowly looked around as he approached Savage Station, where "fires and explosions were the order of the day.

"Here an immense pile of hard bread in boxes ... was blazing; there a long line of whiskey

Malvern Hill house, before being destroyed by fire

This 17th-century house survived the Revolutionary War (Lafayette camped there twice in 1781) and later the Battle of Malvern Hill, but was destroyed by fire in 1905. All that remains today are the end gables and a fireplace, but it is architecturally significant as one of the few cruciform-design houses in Virginia (i.e., from above, the floor plan forms a cross). The Virginia Landmarks Commission says that "The one surviving chimney is perhaps the finest example of seventeenth century diaper brickwork in the state."

Photo from Library of Congress

barrels was being destroyed; farther on was a huge holocaust of hospital stores, and new clothing was at the will of every chance comer," Hyde described the widespread devastation.[17]

By late afternoon Marks "could see, mounting above the trees, the flames from the vast commissary stores at Fair Oaks Station" to the west. He discovered that Union soldiers were loading a "long train of cars, forty or fifty in number ... with shells, kegs of powder, and cartridges" at Savage Station.

Plans called for setting the munitions-packed train afire and rolling it east toward the Chickahominy bridge destroyed earlier by the 11th Maine.[18]

Bandaged, bleeding, and feverish refugees fled the Confederates approaching Savage Station, even as Union troops battled them. As the sun set, "the fight of Savage Station was made, and it was short, sharp, and decisive," Hyde noted.

"The enemy were quickly rolled back into the woods from whence they came," he said.

Baldy Smith kept his division on the field well into the night. Hyde watched as "the lights of those helping the wounded mingled with the fireflies' glimmer in the fields" where

Chapter 36: The Fighting Retreat

the battle had occurred. To the south, bonfires lit the road along which the 7th Maine would soon retreat.[19]

Riding from Savage Station in early evening, Marks "beheld a long, scattered line of the patients staggering away, some carrying their guns, and supporting a companion on an arm, —others tottering feebly over a staff which they appeared to have scarcely strength to lift up."

Sick men toppled onto the road, then crawled to their hands and knees, "and stimulated by the fear of the enemy," teetered away toward the James River, he said.

"Never had I beheld a spectacle more touching or more sad," Marks realized.[20]

As "Stonewall" Jackson's veterans crowded the left bank of the Chickahominy River, Union soldiers still guarding the destroyed bridges received orders to fall back. About 4 p.m., Col. Harris Plaisted recalled the 11th Maine men watching the broken R&YR railroad bridge.

Emerging from the woods bordering the railroad tracks on the opposite bank, a Confederate soldier suddenly ventured onto the shattered bridge. Multiple Maine rifles cracked; witnesses described the Southerner—perhaps more than one—as dead.

Enemy artillery started shelling nearby Bottoms Bridge around 5 p.m. Union artillery replied, and the cannonballs flew noisily. As the remaining 11th Maine pickets (those hidden downstream from the railroad bridge) withdrew, everyone within a mile or two of the railroad bridge suddenly heard a train coming from Savage Station.

What happened next lasted a lifetime in Mainers' memories.[21]

Returning to Savage Station sometime in the afternoon, Reverend Marks watched as "hundreds of barrels of flour and rice, sugar and molasses, salt, and coffee, were consigned to the flames."

Yankee soldiers merrily tossed boxes onto burning piles. "The scene was altogether unearthly and demoniac," Marks shook his hand. Soldiers "blackened with smoke and cinders" threw "into the fire boxes of goods, tents, fragments of broken [railroad] cars, and barrels of whiskey and turpentine."

Explosions thundered across Savage Station as burning ammunition detonated.

Incredulous at all the destruction, Marks noticed the munitions-laden train, now poised "to spring on the track." Darting alongside the track, torch-wielding soldiers fired the box cars' wooden sides. With flames curling around the box cars, an engineer released the brake in the lead locomotive; its throttle already tied open, the engine accelerated immediately.

Marks had ridden to a slight rise beyond the train, now moving on "a descending grade." Flames streamed behind the locomotives;[22] resembling "one long chain of fire," the train "plunged past me like some vast monster from a sea of fire," the Pennsylvanian said.[23]

The train hurtled east two and a half miles (Marks' estimation) before reaching the 11th Maine-busted bridge. Sent earlier to retrieve the regiment's pickets along the Chickahominy, Sgt. Lemuel E. Newcomb and the right-flank pickets were about 250 feet from the bridge "when the train came rushing on."

The Mainers "were in anxious suspense" as the train rushed "nearer to the chasm. We first heard a crash, and then there was a terrible explosion," Newcomb recalled.

He and his men hit the dirt. Iron flew everywhere; "the tops of the trees were shivered by

The train goes over the bridge destroyed by the 11th Maine
Pencil, zinc oxide, and black ink wash on brown paper.
Illustration by Alfred R. Waud via Library of Congress

the flying fragments, and a large ball buried itself in the mud about ten feet from me," Newcomb said.

The Union retreat continued through Sunday night. Located on the far left flank of McClellan's army (now moving south), the 11th Maine and its brigade crossed White Oak Bridge. Harris Plaisted formed his men in line of battle facing north, deployed guards, and let his exhausted soldiers sleep on their arms.[24]

Withdrawing from Savage Station, the 3rd Brigade of Baldy Smith's 2nd Division crept southward through the darkness. After Thomas Hyde fell asleep in the saddle, his horse wandered into the ranks of another brigade; loose horses or mules racing along the road frightened "thousands of Yankees" into believing they were under attack by Confederate cavalry.[25]

Hyde jerked awake; "as far as I could see, the road was ... vacant." Chagrined Union soldiers soon emerged from the woods, reformed their regiments, and resumed shuffling toward the James.

Smith got his 2nd Division across White Oak Swamp at White Oak Bridge as Monday, June 30 dawned clear, absolutely cloud free, and hot. Dog-tired soldiers dropped in their tracks when the regiments bivouacked; Hyde took 200 men to picket the division's right flank.[26]

Federal skirmishers north of White Oak Creek traded shots with approaching Confederates. South of the creek, drowsy Union soldiers listened to the pop-pop-pop musketry as regiments, brigades, and divisions shuffled away toward the James River.

Suddenly, as officers' pocket watches ticked toward noon, massed Confederate artillery concealed across the creek opened fire on the Union bivouacs. "Shrieking shells" exploded "in puffs of white smoke," and "broken iron" struck men, horses, and the ground, an 11th Maine veteran said. Soldiers assigned to a pontoon train "drawn up by the roadside" slashed the harnesses on the draft horses and rode away.

Sheltered along a tree line, the Maine soldiers watched as chaos erupted "on the great cleared field in which the troops and [wagon] trains were massed," the veteran said. The 11th Maine boys formed "behind the rails of a torn-down fence" and watched the artillery duel, of which the Confederate guns got the upper hand.[27]

With White Oak Bridge destroyed, Jackson could not push his artillery over White Oak Creek, but Confederate officers found nearby fords suitable for infantry. Advised of these discoveries, the ailing Jackson failed to shove his foot sloggers over the narrow creek and onto McClellan's rear guard.[28]

Lee's northernmost opportunity to snag McClellan's army never really got started.

As the afternoon wore on, Benjamin Huger cautiously probed toward Glendale along the Charles City Road. After marching their divisions southeast along the Darbytown Road, Confederate generals Ambrose Powell Hill Jr. and James Longstreet reached Long Bridge Road and turned east. Encountering Union pickets about a mile from Glendale, the advance Confederate regiments halted.

Fighting had broken out to the south along the River Road, where an effective bombardment from Navy gunboats deterred the rather sluggish efforts by Confederate Maj. Gen. Theophilus Holmes to strike the Federal columns retreating over Malvern Hill.

Holmes settled for sending six three-inch ordnance rifles to shell the Union columns from "some 800 yards" away. Later sending his 6,000 infantrymen to join the artillery, Holmes rode east and found Robert E. Lee, "just returning from an observation of the enemy's position." Lee okayed Holmes's maneuvering before riding away.

Union observers had spotted the six Confederate guns; gunboats started hurling big shells at the hapless Southern artillery, and 25 to 30 Federal guns placed atop Malvern Hill opened fire, too. The one-sided duel damaged Confederate gun crews and stopped Lee's southernmost attack on Sunday.[29]

The last chance to break apart McClellan's army would have to come at Glendale. Lee ordered Longstreet and Hill to attack around 5 p.m. Confederate brigades advanced eastward to strike the Union line extending from above the Charles City Road south a few miles to a point near the Willis Church Road. Bloody fighting erupted as the sun slowly dropped in the western sky.

Phil Kearny's 3rd Division held terrain between the Charles City and Long Bridge roads. Birney and his 2nd Brigade defended Kearny's right flank, Robinson and his 1st Brigade the

Confederate Gen. Ambrose Powell Hill Jr.
*Photo from National Archives
and Records Administration*

Confederate Gen. James Longstreet
Pictured here as a lieutenant general.
Photo via Wikipedia

division's left flank. Hiram Berry and his 3rd Brigade stood in reserve.

Three Confederate brigades soon struck Kearny's line. Fighting was especially brutal where Capt. James Thompson and the six cannons and crews of Battery G, 2nd U.S. Artillery repeatedly shredded charging Southern infantry, initially with case-shot and then, as the enemy troops closed to within 150 yards, with double canister.

"Of all the fighting I ever witnessed this was about the most desperate," said Elijah Walker, his 4th Maine not directly involved in the combat and he an eyewitness from a safe distance. "The enemy hurled their legions upon that small brigade [Robinson's] and Thompson's battery, taking two of the latter's guns."

The 63rd Pennsylvania Infantry charged, engaged Confederate infantry hand to hand, and regained the cannons. Fighting seesawed around Thompson's battery, but arriving Union reinforcements helped drive off the valiant Southerners. Afterwards, "dead and dying Confederates lay in piles within a few feet of Thompson's brass Napoleon guns," Walker said.[30]

Glendale represented Robert E. Lee's last opportunity to destroy a portion of McClellan's army. In horrific fighting along the Long Bridge Road, Confederate troops cracked open the lines held by the 3rd Division (Pennsylvania Reserves) of Brig. Gen. George A. McCall. When a brigade commander named George G. Meade went down with multiple wounds, for a few minutes McClellan's army was only a strong Confederate thrust from being pried apart. Federal reinforcements hustled forward to close the breach.

The battle petered off with sunset; scattered skirmishing continued in the thickets and woods for some time. The failure of Holmes, Huger, and Jackson to aggressively attack the retreating Federal army had left Lee with nothing to show for his 3,673 casualties.

Noticeably absent from the battlefield, McClellan had sacrificed 3,797 men to save his army. While his warriors fought and died at Glendale, he had boarded the USS *Galena* at Haxall's Landing on the James River before cruising upriver to where the gunboat helped shell Theophilus Holmes's heroes.

Then McClellan dined with Navy Commander John Rodgers. Sometime during that meal—or perhaps shortly afterward—George McCall and his aides accidentally bumped into Confederate infantry in the Glendale darkness. While McClellan drank the best wine that a Navy steward could serve, McCall started walking west to a prison camp in Richmond.

During the night, Union survivors on the front lines collected as many wounded comrades as they could find. Federal lines continued retracting as regiments tramped south on

Confederate Maj. Gen. Theophilus Hunter Holmes
Photo courtesy of www.generalsandbrevets.com

Union Gen. George Archibald McCall
Photo is circa 1862.
Photo courtesy of www.generalsandbrevets.com

"The Gunboat Candidate"

Two poor decisions by Gen. McClellan returned to haunt him in 1864 when he vied for the Democratic presidential nomination, both involving the ironclad USS *Galena.* In May 1862, while the *Galena* led a flotilla of Union gunboats in an attempt to capture the Confederate capital of Richmond, an onslaught from Confederate batteries drove them back; McClellan refused to send ground troops to the Navy's aid. And when McClellan's Peninsula Campaign ended disastrously at Malvern Hill, McClellan's troops retreated to the protection of the naval guns, which ended any chance of taking Richmond. McClellan was aboard the Galena, safe and secure, while his troops fought and died on land. This 1864 political cartoon features McClellan watching the land battle through a telescope from the safety of the *Galena.* The word balloon reads, "Fight on my brave Soldiers and push the enemy to the wall, from this spanker boom your beloved General looks down upon you."
Illustration probably by Louis Maurer for Currier & Ives, via Library of Congress

Willis Church Road.

Recalled from the picket line before sunrise on Tuesday, July 1, Edwin Burt and the 3rd Maine lads arrived on Malvern Hill around 5 a.m., took a short breather, and "moved to the front, and formed in line of battle" to support Capt. George E. Randolph and Battery E, 1st Rhode Island Light Artillery.

As Burt expected, Confederate gunners paid attention when Randolph fired a few ranging shots in their direction. Enemy artillery promptly replied, and the 3rd Maine men endured "a severe fire" for "some six or eight hours," Burt noted.

Around them raged the Battle of Malvern Hill. Lee hurled his infantry against the Union artillery parked almost hub to hub across Malvern's southernmost fields. Open terrain rose slightly toward the distant treeline about a mile north; as Confederate artillery and infantry emerged from the woods, the Federal gunners tore apart the Southern batteries and blasted the charging infantry.

Onward came Confederates determined to breach the Union lines. Opposing infantry made contact in places, but the Southerners never really had a chance. Darkness ended the fighting that cost the Union 3,007 men and the Confederacy 5,650 casualties.

To occupy their minds and protect their bodies, the industrious 3rd Mainers first tossed up a fence-rail barricade, then dug the earth with whatever equipment was at hand to convert the barricade "into a formidable rifle pit or breastwork," Burt said. His men lay behind their fortifications until 2 a.m. Wednesday, then quietly withdrew in the pouring rain to the James River.[31]

Elijah Walker remembered that appalling "march of seven or eight miles through a drenching rain." His 4th Maine lads had not eaten for at least 24 hours. Coming "upon some wagons loaded with pork and hard tack," Walker spurred his horse to where he could find an ax, then rode back and hacked the barrel hoops and chopped open the hardtack boxes.

"The men marched by, helping themselves" to "this hard and homely but welcome fare," he said.

Their stomachs partially filled, the 4th Maine soldiers marched into the Union lines at Harrison's Landing around 2 p.m. July 2, assembled in the wheat field assigned as their bivouac area, and "sank to the ground and slept," their equally weary colonel reported.[32]

Briefly shelled by pursuing Confederates on Thursday, July 3, the men of the 3rd Maine Infantry traipsed another three miles before finding their designated bivouac site. Edwin Burt found a camp stool and a makeshift table at which he could sit while composing an after-action report for David Birney.

Faces and names ran through Burt's mind as the report coalesced on foolscap. Combat and disease had shrunk the regiment significantly since its arrival on the Peninsula; Burt knew every man and his habits, and he probably paused and thought a while after writing particular names.

Burt identified at least 20 men as "missing, supposed to be a prisoner." Ben Huger's "light troops" had evidently swept up William McDevitt of Co. B on June 29, but Burt could no longer remember exactly where other men had vanished. Hiram Coburn and John Dennis of Co. C, Sgt. Charles Lowe and five Co. G privates, and Luke Shattuck and Perley Smith of Co. F: the list ran on for a ways.

Reviewing the names, Burt noticed—and perhaps with pleasure—how few specific casualties he had identified as killed. Only Pvt. Harrison D. Hobbs was confirmed dead, and some of the missing might have been dead, of course. Sgt. Charles H. Sampson had lost his "right leg shot off above the ankle," and Corp. Hiram A. Turner had been "wounded in left hand and leg."

As the 3rd Maine's survivors rested at Harrison's Landing, a familiar figure moved through their truncated camp. The regimental chaplain, Reverend Henry C. Leonard, "was ever present with us" while sharing "our hardships and dangers," Burt noted.[33]

Union troops at a reenactment of the Battle of Perryville, Kentucky
Smoke obscures regimental colors on the Union firing line.
Photo by Brian F. Swartz

During the weeks since the Battle of Seven Pines, Leonard had spent considerable time at the 2nd Brigade hospital at Savage Station. He had "worked with the Brigade Surgeon and our own excellent and faithful Surgeon," Dr. Thaddeus Hildreth of Gardiner.

They had done "the best that could be done for our own and other soldiers coming in from the battle ground with broken limbs and bleeding faces," said Leonard, a Universalist minister. "Not a man of our wounded came to us with a faltering spirit or complaining tongue."

From Seven Pines to Harrison's Landing, Leonard had accompanied the 3rd Maine lads on their marches and, whenever possible, onto the battlefield. An eyewitness, he noted how "the dead were buried on the field of battle carefully and tenderly by their own comrades."

Leonard watched as tears streamed down the dusty cheeks of survivors now leaning on dinged shovels, if the men had access to such precious tools. Heads bent as Leonard—a soldier's chaplain—spoke appropriate words over the deceased.

Then comrades wielded bayonets or knives to inscribe on "neat head boards" (often ripped from hardtack boxes) "fitting inscriptions" indicating the names of the dead and their companies and regiments.

"Maine may consider herself honored in the bravery of her sons," Leonard realized.[34]

~~~

1. Elijah Walker, *The Old Soldier: History of the Fourth Maine Infantry,* Tribune, Rockland, Maine, 1895, p. 30
2. Maj. Edwin Burt, July 5, 1862 report to Gen. D.B. Birney, *Maine Farmer,* Thursday, July 31, 1862
3. Elko Road (Route 156) follows the main road taken by Union troops retreating from the Williamsburg Stage Road to White Oak Swamp.
4. Modern renaming has altered place names at the crossroads. That section of Long Bridge Road extending from the intersection to the Chickahominy River is now Charles City Road; the section of Long Bridge Road running southwest from the crossroads is now Darbytown Road as far as the intersection where that road turns northwest toward Richmond. River Road is now New Market Road, connected to Darbytown Road by Long Bridge Road.

Union Napoleon cannon at Malvern Hill
Placed near the southern end of Malvern Hill, this bronze 12-pounder Napoleon and other nearby cannons mark where Union artillery deployed on July 1, 1862 as the Army of the Potomac retreated south across the hill toward the James River. The woods to the left soon flow onto Malvern's steep western slope; the cannon points north toward the distant treeline—about a mile away—from which Confederate artillery and infantry emerged to attack the Union forces. Among the Maine units that fought at Malvern Hill was the 3rd Maine Infantry Regiment.
Photo by Brian F. Swartz

5. Burt, *Maine Farmer,* Thursday, July 31, 1862
6. Maj. Gen. Benjamin Huger, *Official Records, Series 1, Vol. 11, Part II,* Chapter XXIII, No. 307, p. 789
7. Burt, *Maine Farmer,* Thursday, July 31, 1862
8. Walker, *The Old Soldier,* p. 30
9. Huger, *OR, Series 1, Vol. 11, Part II,* Chapter XXIII, No. 307, p. 789
10. Promoted to brigadier general since Seven Pines, Birney commanded Kearny's 2nd Brigade. Robinson had replaced the injured Brig. Gen. Charles Jameson of Old Town as commander of the 1st Brigade.
11. Walker, *The Old Soldier,* p. 30
12. Burt, *Maine Farmer,* Thursday, July 31, 1862
13. William E.S. Whitman and Charles H. True, *Maine in the War for the Union,* Nelson Dingley Jr. & Co., Lewiston, Maine, 1865, pp. 270-271
14. Reverend James Junius Marks, D.D., *The Peninsula Campaign in Virginia,* J.B. Lippincott & Co., Philadelphia, 1864, pp. 236-237
15. Frank Moore, *Women of the War: Their Heroism and Self-Sacrifice,* S.S. Scranton & Co., Hartford, Conn., 1866, pp. 116-117
16. Marks, *The Peninsula Campaign,* pp. 238-240
17. Thomas W. Hyde, *Following the Greek Cross,* University of South Carolina Press, Columbia, S.C., 2005, p. 71
18. Marks, *The Peninsula Campaign,* pp. 243
19. Hyde, *Following the Greek Cross,* p. 72
20. Marks, *The Peninsula Campaign,* pp. 243-244
21. Albert Maxfield and Robert Brady Jr., *The Story of One Regiment: The Eleventh Maine Infantry Volunteers in the War of the Rebellion,* J.J. Little & Co., New York, NY, 1896, pp. 58-59
22. James Marks referred to "engine" in the singular; other Union eyewitnesses claimed seeing two locomotives hauling the train.
23. Marks, *The Peninsula Campaign,* pp. 245-246
24. Maxfield and Brady, *The Story of One Regiment,* p. 59
25. Many other soldiers stampeded by the frightened animals remembered this incident, too. It was indicative of the general panic experienced during the retreat.
26. Hyde, *Following the Greek Cross,* pp. 72-73
27. Maxfield and Brady, *The Story of One Regiment,* pp. 60-61
28. Although the debate continues to this day, many historians believe that Jackson, utterly exhausted by lack of sleep and nutrition during the days his troops spent marching from the Shenandoah Valley and fighting outside Richmond, had reached the end of his physical endurance. The tactically brilliant mind evident during the earlier Valley Campaign could not process critical information on June 30.
29. Maj. Gen. Theophilus Holmes, *OR, Series I, Vol. 11, Part II,* Chapter XXIII, No. 352, p. 907
30. Walker, *The Old Soldier,* p. 31
31. Burt, *Maine Farmer,* Thursday, July 31, 1862
32. Walker, *The Old Soldier,* p. 31
33. Burt, *Maine Farmer,* Thursday, July 31, 1862
34. Rev. Henry C. Leonard, "Third Maine," *Maine Farmer,* Thursday, July 31, 1862

Chapter 37

THE BATTLE OF BATON ROUGE

"They are right on us"

Along with most members of the 14th Maine Infantry Regiment, 1st Lt. Ira Gardner had not yet "seen the elephant" when he and Co. I stepped ashore at Baton Rouge, Louisiana on Monday, July 7, 1862.

Since arriving in New Orleans on May 25, the regiment had performed little more than guard duty in a city still reeling from its Union occupation. Commanded by Col. Frank Nickerson of Searsport, the 14th Maine boys had initially camped in Lafayette Square.

The largest city in the Confederacy, New Orleans was now run by Maj. Gen. Benjamin F. Butler, a Massachusetts Democrat among the first "political" generals appointed by Abraham Lincoln. Earning the sobriquet "Beast" from white, pro-Confederacy New Orleanians enraged at his perceived high-handedness as the city's military governor, Butler had less interaction with the civilian populace than did his soldiers.

They caught particularly virulent attention from—"had some curious experiences ... with," Gardner politely observed—Confederate women.

Gardner noticed that such women "think it proper to show their contempt" for Union soldiers "by turning their backs to us, and in some cases spitting on us." He evidently was not targeted by local women leaning from upper-floor windows to hurl chamber-pot contents onto passing Union soldiers.

Butler "put a stop to their insults" by promising to treat any woman caught insulting Federal troops as if she was "'a woman of the town'" (or prostitute), said Gardner.[1]

In early July Butler ordered the 14th Maine and several other regiments and artillery batteries to occupy Baton Rouge, the Louisiana state capital. By now the first lieutenant of Co. I, Gardner had already participated in one brief expedition into the Louisiana bayous.

Taking the 14th Maine Infantry ashore at Baton Rouge on July 7, Frank Nickerson reported to Brig. Gen. Thomas Williams, the Union garrison commander. Union regiments defended a line "extending from the [Mississippi] river above the city to the river below" Baton Rouge, Gardner noticed.

Williams told Nickerson to camp where the Bayou Sara and Greenwell Spring roads intersected on the Union left flank. The 21st Connecticut Infantry deployed to the 14th Maine's immediate left; to the right were the 6th Massachusetts (Carruth's) Light Artillery and the 21st Indiana Infantry. Other units held the Union line south to the Mississippi River.[2]

The Maine boys settled into the ennui of garrison life. Smothered and sickened by the summer heat, humidity, and malarial mosquitoes, Gardner and his comrades constantly drilled when not manning the picket posts.

Discussing the 14th Maine and Baton Rouge in an August 16 letter to Maine Governor Israel Washburn, chaplain George Washington Bartlett commented that "one who has not experienced it can hardly conceive of the tedium and weariness of being with an army [in camp] and nothing to do, -- [of] the difficulty of keeping up the spirits and discipline of the men."

Born in Litchfield, Maine in 1827, the adventurous Bartlett had traveled around Cape Horn to prospect for California gold, returned to New England to graduate from Bowdoin College ('54) and Harvard College Divinity School, and, as a Unitarian minister, pastored at Christ Church in Augusta in the years prior to the Civil War.

In December 1861 Bartlett had joined the 14th Maine Infantry as its chaplain, and Nickerson later promoted Bartlett to a captaincy, albeit with no leadership responsibilities.[3]

Sensing an opportunity to capture the isolated Baton Rouge garrison, Confederate Maj. Gen. John C. Breckinridge collected troops at Camp Moore near Kentwood, Louisiana. Like their Yankee enemies, the Confederate soldiers lost men weeks before the fighting started.

Stricken with dysentery and malaria, many of Breckenridge's men filled the Camp Moore hospitals. Despite his lengthy sick

Union Capt. Ira Gardner
Photo courtesy of Maine State Archives

Union Col. Frank Nickerson
Photo courtesy of Maine State Archives

Chapter 37: The Battle of Baton Rouge

Union Chaplain George W. Bartlett
Photo courtesy of Maine State Archives

Confederate Gen. John Cabell Breckinridge
Photo from Library of Congress

rolls, Breckenridge set his army in motion toward Baton Rouge on Monday, August 4.

By late afternoon Union scouts had spotted the Confederate advance guard negotiating the Comite River some ten miles to the east of Federal-held Baton Rouge. The Southern troops approached the town along the Greenwell Spring Road during the night.

About 4 a.m. on Tuesday, August 5, Southern irregulars collided with 21st Indiana pickets outside the Union lines.[4] Routed by Hoosier gunshots, the partisans slammed rearward into the advancing Confederates regulars. In the ensuing friendly fire, the horse ridden by Brig. Gen. Hardin Helm fell and pinned him. A Confederate bullet also killed Lt. Alexander H. Todd.

The gray-upon-gray bloodshed echoed as far as the White House. Helm was married to Alexander Todd's sister, Emilie; the Todds were half-siblings of Mary Todd Lincoln.

Breckenridge had coordinated his ground attack with a naval assault by the CSS *Arkansas*, a 165-foot ironclad that had shot its way through a U.S. Navy squadron blockading Vicksburg in mid-July. Confederate strategy called for the *Arkansas* to attack the small Union naval squadron moored off Baton Rouge as Breckenridge's men assaulted the land defenses.

Broken-down engines cast the ironclad ashore about ten miles north of Baton Rouge on August 4; setting fire to their warship, crew members fled the *Arkansas*, which soon blew up.

As a thick fog descended on Baton Rouge during the night, Gardner "did not go to bed but lay down with my equipments [uniform and gear] on." The "long roll"[5] sounded as dawn brightened the sight-limiting fog. Claiming that he was sick, Capt. James B. Hill told Gardner, "Ira, you will have to take the company out."⁶

The 14th Maine boys moved quickly into line. "Our boys went in with their old blue trousers on," said the excitable Bartlett as he watched the ten companies form with Co. I on the regiment's far right flank.⁷

Then "the long roll was changed to the reveille," so Gardner assumed a false alarm had turned out the 14th Maine. Stacking their arms, his men started preparing their breakfasts.

Suddenly "I heard the clatter of an approaching horse," Gardner realized. He watched as "an officer on a foam-covered animal" emerged from the fog and rode past.⁸

"Lieutenant, turn your men out! They are right on us!" the officer shouted.

Yelling at the Co. I boys to fall in, Gardner ran through the camp while "calling for the regiment to form." He entered Nickerson's tent to tell the sick colonel that the camp was under attack.⁹

Union Brig. Gen. Thomas R. Williams
Photo courtesy of www.generalsandbrevets.com

Hurling some 6,000 men at Baton Rouge, Breckenridge dispatched Maj. Gen. Charles Clark and his division to deal with the 14th Maine and the 21st Indiana. Preliminary gunplay had led the Hoosiers' commander, Lt. Col. John Keith, to march his men 600 yards east from their original position. Capt. William Carruth deployed the four 12-pounder cannons and gunners of the 6th Massachusetts Light Artillery near the 21st Indiana.

The fog obfuscated Nickerson as he walked along his regimental line. To the east, Carruth's guns and Keith's infantry banged away in the murk. Where were the Johnnies?

Gunfire suddenly erupted nearer the assembled 14th Maine. Dim figures appeared in the fog and shouted the countersign. Unsure whether the shooting presaged a full-scale attack or a minor probe, Nickerson learned from his retreating pickets that Confederate troops approached from the east.¹⁰

Skirmishers out front, Clark's Confederates carefully sought the Yankees waiting somewhere in the fog. Seeing movement "only a short distance away" from the 14th Maine's camp, Gardner yelled at his men to fire at "a brigade of rebel troops."

The Co. I volley tripped additional shooting along the regimental line.

The vaguely seen Confederates apparently drifted away from the unexpected resistance. Nickerson then maneuvered the 14th Maine in a left wheel through the regiment's camp; his new line spread "at right angles" to "the rebel brigade" deflected by the 14th's initial volley, Gardner noticed.

"Next came an order to [move] forward, which we did, marching through the tents," he said.¹¹

Still in line, the 14th Maine boys marched quietly through nearby woods until brought up short by a rail fence. Unable to see even 25 yards in front of him, Nickerson ordered his men to remain silent as Confederate artillery shelled the regiment's abandoned camp.

The Maine soldiers heard Confederates probing noisily across the fog-shrouded terrain. Suddenly Confederate infantrymen coalesced in the fog about 100 yards away; Nickerson yelled for volley fire. The 14th Maine delivered five volleys and shattered the enemy attack.[12]

Gardner remembered those volleys, which "proved to be a check to a brigade of infantry advancing on our [left] flank, as the dead in our front were numerous the following morning."[13]

The gunfire animated Bartlett, who hung close to Nickerson throughout the battle. "We had a nice fight—and splendidly did the boys conduct themselves," Bartlett told Washburn afterwards. "Most of them had never heard such [combat] music before, and maybe didn't understand its nature, at any rate, they paid no attention but moved about with as much precision as tho' they were on a common battalion drill."

Nickerson discovered that the Confederate brigade repelled by the 14th Maine's initial volley now approached from the east, "right thro' our camp," Bartlett realized. Belonging to Clark's division, the Confederates captured every bit of regimental baggage.[14]

Nickerson quickly wheeled the 14th Maine Infantry by the right and faced his men east. Spotting the maneuver through the thinning fog, Confederate gunners opened fire with their cannons and tore holes in the 14th Maine's relatively straight lines.[15]

"Our organization was completely broken up and had lost very heavily in men," recalled Gardner, who rallied some 200 soldiers and "crossed the road" to where William Carruth and his men worked their bronze Napoleons. Gardner remembered that the battery "had lost their horses and [we] helped them retake their guns."

Forming his little band on the 21st Indiana's left flank, Gardner joined the Hoosiers and Bay Staters in shooting at Clark's Confederates. Nickerson rounded up the diminished 14th Maine, including the men whom Gardner led.

"Lieutenant Gardner, you have behaved nobly to-day," he told the surprised Gardner.[16]

With Bartlett—surprisingly no shrinking violet in terms of avoiding combat—shadowing him, Nickerson was everywhere that bloody morning. "Oh, it was beautiful to see the Col. manage that reg't in action," Bartlett told Washburn.

His sickness (possibly dysentery or malaria)

Confederate Maj. Gen. Charles Clark
Photo courtesy of www.civilwararchive.com

The Battle of Baton Rouge, Louisiana, August 4, 1862
Illustration from Currier & Ives, believed done in 1862

momentarily forgotten, Nickerson walked back and forth among his men; "wherever the fire was hottest[,] there he was[,] cheering and holding his men steady," Bartlett said. The exhausted colonel finally "borrowed a horse and mounted," and with an aide helping him stay steady in the saddle, "continued to ride up and down the line[,] giving orders."

Then "a friendly bullet killed the horse" and dismounted Nickerson. He rested briefly before going "on foot again," Bartlett said.[17]

Three Confederate infantry regiments—the 4th Kentucky, the 31st Alabama, and the 31st Mississippi—finally shoved aside the 14th Maine boys. After tearing down a fence blocking their way, the Mainers retreated through the abandoned camp of the 7th Vermont Infantry and rallied in a ravine just south of the Louisiana state prison.[18]

Facing strengthening Union resistance and naval gunfire (including shelling from the Maine-built gunboats USS *Katahdin* and USS *Kineo*), Breckenridge initiated a withdrawal about 10 a.m. Before pulling back, Confederate survivors looted the captured Union camps, then burned them.

"On occupying the old camp ground the next day[, we discovered that] everything of any value was gone," Gardner said. The 14th Maine boys had lost their tents, belongings, and all clothing except for the tattered uniforms worn into combat.

The thefts and vandalism were thorough. "In passing along through the [14th Maine] camp" on August 6, Lt. Col. Thomas Clark of the 6th Michigan Infantry "saw something in the dirt" and picked it up, Gardner said. The debris was "my commission as a lieutenant, which the rebels had torn in two."[19]

Telling Washburn that "there never have been many neater little battles than that of the 14th, [at] Baton Rouge," Bartlett indicated that in the confusion and terror of their first battle, his comrades had "no idea at the time that it was anything at all!"

In fact, the 14th Maine boys "were never more surprised than when we learned that they [enemy troops] were running away, leaving their dead on the ground."

Eleven days after the battle, "you c'd scarcely [sic] guess how the spirits of the men were improved by" the fight, Bartlett believed. "They are in the best mood and condition except that they have no white gloves now[,] and their clothes are not quite so clean[,] but since they behaved so well 'tisn't so much matter about the clothes."[20]

Bartlett's assessment echoed Nickerson's comments to Washburn on Saturday, August 9. Nickerson reported "the Rgt. was never in better condition—the boys are jolly—get into a fight among themselves once in a while[,] while disputing who was 'ahead in the fight.' Then someone laughs at them and then they sit down and smoke and talk about the next fight."

The Destruction of the Rebel Ram 'Arkansas'
The United States gunboat *Essex* destroys the Confederate ram *Arkansas* on the Mississippi River near Baton Rouge on August 4, 1862.
Illustration from Currier & Ives via Library of Congress

He reported the regiment's losses as 36 men killed, 71 wounded, and 12 missing, for a total of 119 casualties. Of the wounded, "eight have since suffered amputations of a leg," Nickerson wrote.[21]

Ira Gardner and his comrades had finally seen the elephant on a Deep South battlefield.

~~~

1. Ira B. Gardner, *Recollections Of A Boy Member of Co. I, Fourteenth Maine Volunteers, 1861 to 1865,* Lewiston Journal Company, Lewiston, 1902, pp. 10-11
2. Ibid, pp.13-14
3. George Washington Bartlett, letter to Governor Israel Washburn Jr., August 16, 1862, Maine State Archives
4. Edwin C. Bearss, "The Battle of Baton Rouge," *The Journal of the Louisiana Historical Association,* Vol. 3, No. 2, Spring 1962
5. The "long roll" was a steady, rattling drum beat sounded to call a regiment into line. Senior officers often had the long roll sounded to assemble regiments before dawn, always a favorite time for sudden assaults as had occurred at Shiloh on April 6, 1862.
6. Gardner, *Recollections,* p. 15
7. Bartlett to Washburn, August 16, 1862, Maine State Archives
8. Referring to a sweat-soaked horse.
9. Gardner, *Recollections,* p. 15
10. Bearss, " Baton Rouge"
11. Gardner, *Recollections,* p. 15
12. Bearss, "Baton Rouge"
13. Gardner, *Recollections,* p. 16
14. Bartlett to Washburn, August 16, 1862, MSA
15. Bearss, "Baton Rouge"
16. Gardner, *Recollections,* p. 16
17. Bartlett to Washburn, August 16, 1862, MSA
18. Bearss, " Baton Rouge"
19. Gardner, *Recollections,* p. 16
20. Bartlett to Washburn, August 16, 1862, MSA
21. Col. Frank Nickerson, letter to Governor Israel Washburn Jr., August 9, 1862, MSA

Chapter 38

THE FEARFUL PLACE CALLED HARRISON'S

"The flies are so thick that the boys shoot them with cartridges"

Torrential rain soaked all the Union troops approaching Harrison's Landing from Malvern Hill on Wednesday, July 2. The 5th Maine Infantry lads "awoke to ... a severe rain-storm," commented 1st Lt. George W. Bicknell. Tramping "some five or six miles" through the poorly drained fields and woods bordering the River Road—horse-drawn vehicles had priority there—Bicknell and Co. K reached Harrison's Landing and "finally pitched our tents in the mud."[1]

"Fighting by day and retreating by night," the "completely exhausted" survivors of the 6th Maine Infantry Regiment marched into Harrison's Landing "in excellent spirits" on Thursday, July 3, one veteran proudly wrote.

"The line officers behaved well throughout the retreat, in which their labor was very arduous," he noted. The middle-aged Col. Hiram Burnham "was everywhere found, encouraging the men by his voice."[2]

Burnham's men could not yet appreciate the 15 square miles of Tidewater real estate into which Gen. George McClellan would cram his army, which "occupied a space of 5 miles on the James River by 3 miles broad," noted Robert Knox Sneden, the topographical engineer for III Corps and Sam Heintzelman.[3]

The overall region known as Harrison's Landing was bordered by Kimmage's Creek on the west and Rawlins Mill Pond on the north. Draining the pond and flowing southeast to the river, Herring Creek and its pestilential swamps formed a secure and essentially impenetrable eastern flank for the badly damaged Federal army. High ground known as Evelynton Heights ("Evelinton Hills," wrote Sneden) rose beyond Herring Creek.[4]

Swamps also adjoined Kimmage's Creek and the mill pond. Feeling secure behind these

Harrison's Landing
Illustration from Harper's Weekly

natural defenses, men dug in. "We are well protected by artillery and heavy siege guns, and shall soon have extensive earthworks thrown up, beside rifle pits in proportion ... our defences will be ample enough and strong enough to defy any force that the enemy can bring against us," noted a 7th Maine Infantry veteran.[5]

After the slow-moving cold front slid to the east by Thursday morning, the 6th Maine's dog-tired veterans—the older men sporting stubbly beards, the youngsters fine facial hair—tromped across a Kimmage's Creek bridge and reached relative safety for the first time since June 26.

Behind them—behind everybody—came the 2nd Division of John Peck and the thinning ranks of the 11th Maine Infantry Regiment. The incredible din of Malvern Hill had scarcely disturbed Robert Brady Jr. of Co. D on July 1; "I must confess that I slept ... the sleep of the thoroughly tired out" as cannons roared on the plateau, he admitted.

Shuffling into line after Wednesday's sunrise, the 11th Maine lads "marched hither and thither" as rain pummeled them, Brady commented. "The heavens opened and torrents of rain descended" as the 2nd Division took "a covering position" to protect the retreating Union troops against a Confederate attack.

That same rain delayed enemy pursuit; water dripping from their battered visors, the 2nd Division warriors peered into the murk all day and through Wednesday night.

Few Confederates appeared.

The Union columns "floundered through mud into Harrison's Landing," Brady said. The rain had eased considerably by early Thursday; Peck and his division guarded the retreat, "and not till all were past us, the last wagon and the last straggling man, did we of the rear guard move into that haven of rest and safety."[6]

Thinking they had left behind "Chickahominy fever" during their retreat, surviving Union soldiers would quickly discover that malaria had followed them to the James River—and the jaundiced Col. Elijah Walker soon grasped the trap into which George McClellan had led his army. The same streams and swamps keeping the Confederates out also hemmed in the Union soldiers, initially forced to drink "water ... obtained from bogs," Walker wrote.

Chapter 38: The Fearful Place Called Harrison's

That water "was the poorest kind of bog water imaginable," he realized. "Its debilitating effects, in conjunction with those of malaria" gave Walker "serious fears of losing all my men by sickness.

"Harrison's Landing was a fearful place," he concluded.[7]

The actual Harrison's Landing had served Berkeley Plantation, long past its economic prime and historical significance. Two miles to the east lay Westover Landing and its eponymous plantation.

Anchor chains for the hospital transport *State of Maine* rattled into the river off Harrison's Landing after dark on Tuesday, July 1. Aboard ship, an anxious Sarah Sampson stood near the rail and peered at the darkened shore.

So near and yet so far from her beloved 3rd Maine boys and all other Maine soldiers needing her help, she awaited the dawn.

Sampson and Ellen Harris, her companion in J.E.B. Stuart-enforced exile from Savage Station, had eventually departed White House Landing aboard the *Louisiana*. Convincing the steamer's captain to deposit them at Yorktown, the nurses had tended Army patients there for a day before catching "the mail steamer for Fortress Monroe.

"Here we passed a few days usefully" tending the sick and wounded, including Maine men "whom we had cared for at the front," Sampson commented. Another woman "kindly loaned ... clothing" to Sampson, left sartorially destitute since Confederate troops had captured her trunk and wardrobe at Savage Station.

The eastern horizon gradually brightened on Wednesday, July 2. As the Tidewater shore emerged from the darkness, Sampson heard oars splashing, and watercraft soon bobbed alongside the *State of Maine*.

"The wounded were brought out to us in small boats" because no wharves extended into the James, noted Sampson, thrust suddenly onto the front lines. "The groaning of the poor fellows, as they were lifted from one boat to another, was heart-rending."[8]

Over the next several days, Army engineers supervised construction of new wharves. Freed slaves became stevedores, unloading incoming supplies and hauling out to the wharves whatever McClellan wanted removed.

The soldiers gathered in their shrunken regiments needed clothing, food, shelter, and even cooking utensils. Elijah Walker had inventoried

Union Brig. Gen. John James Peck
Pictured here as a major general, sometime after his promotion on July 25, 1862.
Photo from Library of Congress

Berkeley Plantation today
Photo by Brian F. Swartz

"15 tin dippers, 12 shelter tents, and 4 rubber blankets" after his 4th Maine camped within the Union lines.

"These were all we had for the accommodations of the entire command," he sighed.[9]

Initially many Union soldiers went hungry, unless they had adapted well to "the outrageous food ... provided for the men," groused Lt. George Bicknell of the 5th Maine Infantry.

Issued as "*sides of hogs*," rancid pork was "frequently covered with blisters," the iron-stomached Bicknell complained. Senior army officials considered "bacon ... of the meanest description" and "wormy hard bread" sufficient fare for the frontline soldiers; a civilian at heart, Bicknell believed that "at home it would make a decent man sick to look at" such food.[10]

Fortunately the food situation soon improved. Rather than join a state regiment, Adelbert Knight of Lincolnville had enlisted in the regular Army. Now a private in Co. F, 11th U.S. Infantry Regiment, he described the food served at Harrison's Landing as "first rate grub," with the fare including "bacon side, apples[,] onions[,] cabbage[,] and new potatoes twice a week and soft bread every 4 days."[11]

As soldiers settled into some semblance of ordinary life in early July, Sarah Sampson spent every waking moment caring for the sick and wounded. "I went several times on the transports" to Fort Monroe "and occupied my time on the return passage in writing letters for the [sick or wounded] soldiers" who had provided her with friends' names and addresses, she said.

When able at Harrison's Landing, Sampson went ashore and visited the hospitals, where "I found many Maine soldiers." She "was able to relieve much suffering" by distributing clothing "sent me by our friends at home.

"I always had a good supply" of clothing at Fort Monroe, and sympathetic "quartermasters and surgeons in charge of [the] transports" forwarded whatever she needed, Sampson noted.[12]

During the retreat to Harrison's Landing, Isabella Fogg had constantly dispensed medical supplies from the ambulance entrusted in her care. The teamster handling the team delivered Fogg safely to the new Union camps; already aware of her skills, Army surgeon Dr. Jonathan K. Letterman placed Fogg in "special care of the diet of the amputation cases."

As amputees were evacuated to Fort Monroe and then to Northern hospitals, Fogg "subsequently distributed the much needed supplies furnished by the Sanitary Commission to the soldiers in their lines."[13]

Having yanked his army from its positions five miles shy of Richmond to a pestilential hole 20 miles away, George McClellan still envisioned attacking the Confederate capital. As supplies poured into Harrison's Landing and sick men floated out, McClellan hatched a few schemes that ultimately went nowhere. He briefly advanced Joseph Hooker and his division toward Malvern Hill late on August 2, but Hooker could only report that due "to the incompetency of guides furnished me ... I have deemed it expedient to return to camp" the next day.[14]

Meanwhile, brigade and division commanders shifted men to meet perceived staffing needs. Now back with the 11th Maine Infantry since recovering from a bug- or water-caused illness, Maj. Robert F. Campbell vented his frustration in a mid-July letter to Governor Israel Washburn Jr.

"Sir, a few days since we were ordered by our division commander [Brig. Gen. John J. Peck] to make a detail of 5 men to fill up a New York Battery. We accordingly made the detail," the 6-foot, 45-year-old Campbell wrote.

"But [we] protested that they had no right to put a man that is enlisted as an <u>infantry man</u> into the artillery service," the Cherryfield lumberman growled with quill pen and ink.[15]

The Peninsula Campaign had shriveled the 11th Maine to the equivalent of a few under-strength companies; many other Union regiments had suffered similarly. The 11th Maine had fought gallantly at Seven Pines with the 3rd Division of Brig. Gen. Silas Casey, blamed by McClellan for the near Union defeat.

McClellan had then replaced Casey with Peck, a New Yorker, and Bob Campbell suspected a bit of favoritism in his raiding Maine men for an Empire State artillery battery.

Campbell was having nothing of it. "If the service demands that the New York Batteries be filled up[,] there are plenty of New York regiments that are small and without officers and could be well used for that purpose," he told Washburn.[16]

So passed the weeks at Harrison's Landing. Sent to the front one day in late July, the 4th Maine lads discovered and "impetuously attacked" on "much higher and firmer ground ... a large field of blackberries," noticed the feverish Elijah Walker, who checked himself off "the sick list" so he could command the movement "to the front, as a support to the picket line."

Declining to divulge the location of the blackberry patch, Walker's men raided it daily. Dining on the fresh berries "and some fine ripe tomatoes ... so revived me that I had no [future] occasion to be reported on the sick list," Walker said.[17]

Plagued by flies, snakes, and other Virginia critters that bit or stung, soldiers waited for McClellan to do something—*anything.* Meanwhile, the War Department had created a new army in northern Virginia. President Abraham Lincoln had tired of McClellan's empty promises and unremitting demands for more men. The Army of the Potomac served no military purpose fading away in the Tidewater summer, so Army Chief of Staff Henry W. Halleck ordered McClellan to abandon Harrison's Landing and send his men where they could do some good.

The evacuation of Harrison's Landing began quietly on Monday, August 10, "when General McCall's division[18] received orders to strike tents, provide six days rations and be ready to move at a moment's notice," noted a *New-York Tribune* reporter.

McCall's men tramped to the wharf at 9 p.m. "and embarked quietly on steamers," he observed. "They left the Landing some time during the night for Aquia Creek" on the Potomac River.[19]

Union Maj. Gen. Henry Halleck, c. 1865
Photo by John A. Scholten via Library of Congress

McClellan spared his remaining soldiers—at least those fit to walk—such transportational ease; most soldiers would march overland to Yorktown and other designated Peninsula destinations. Even with approximately 500 ambulances and wagons lost during the retreat to Harrison's Landing, some 3,000 wheeled vehicles were still available to haul baggage during the upcoming retreat.[20]

"They have sent all the men away from here that were not able to march and by that I think there is agoing [*sic*] to be some grait [*sic*] move within a few days," figured Adelbert Knight.[21]

Orders came down for soldiers to send their knapsacks to the wharves. The exhausted 11th Maine survivors piled them into wagons Monday night; the knapsacks went into a canal boat on Tuesday, August 11.

Harris Plaisted's men were happy to be leaving the pestilential Harrison's Landing, where one veteran said that "the flies are so thick that the boys shoot them with cartridges."[22]

Wednesday brought a flurry of excitement as Navy gunboats saturated the James River's wooded right bank with artillery shells after a Confederate cavalry patrol suddenly appeared near the shore. The 11th Maine soldiers learned to their disgust that their precious knapsacks had gurgled into the river when the seams opened on the overloaded canal boat; "the knapsacks are now on a schooner in a rather wet condition," complained Co. D chronicler Albert Maxfield.[23]

Chapter 38: The Fearful Place Called Harrison's

"We have been under marching orders the last week for where I do not know," Adelbert Knight wrote August 12. The Army regulars had seen their knapsacks "put aboard of vessels to carry down the river," Knight commented, and "we have to keep three days grub on hand so as to be ready to march at a minute's notice."

"Ordered to move to light marching order" at 2 p.m., Monday, August 11, the 4th Maine lads finally stepped off on August 16 for Yorktown; so did the 11th Maine Infantry.[24] "The sick were sent away in transports," Elijah Walker noted, and on Friday, August 15, his men lit bonfires onto which they hurled "every combustible thing which they did not wish to take."

"Joy shone on all faces and all hearts were lighter," Walker said.[25]

Thumping over the Chickahominy River on a 2,000-foot pontoon bridge, the 11th Maine Infantry boys marched stolidly along dusty roads to Yorktown. The pace was relentless; "the Colonel told us when we started not to fall out until dead," one veteran recalled. Hungry soldiers raided Confederate orchards, corn fields, and pig sties; a few resourceful Mainers stole one farmer's "corned beef, and chickens, and set his cider mill to making cider of his apples."[26]

Arriving at the coast, most Army of the Potomac regiments boarded ships for transportation north to Washington. A battle had just taken place at Cedar Mountain in central Virginia, and some units leaving the Peninsula would fight at Bull Run in late August.

Isabella Fogg remained at Harrison's Landing almost to the end. Among the last nurses to evacuate the landing, Fogg sailed on the *S.R. Spaulding* "with a ship load of the wounded" to Philadelphia; she "saw them safely removed to the general hospital, and then returned to Maine."[27]

Sarah Sampson had reluctantly left Harrison's Landing weeks before her boys. After resigning his 3rd Maine commission, Charles A. L. Sampson had spent "a few weeks of quiet and

Union commanders at Harrison's Landing, August 1862
From left: Col. Albert V. Colburn, Col. Delos B. Sacket, and Gen. John Sedgwick
Photo by David B. Woodbury via Library of Congress

Soldiers at Harrison's Landing, probably July 1862
Above: Soldiers cooking. Facing page: Soldiers repairing a cannon.
Illustrations by Alfred R. Waud via Library of Congress

rest" at a Fort Monroe hospital, his wife told Maine Adj. Gen. John L. Hodsdon on Wednesday morning, July 10.

While Sarah wanted to continue caring for her boys, Charles had no logical reason to remain on the Peninsula. He expected his wife to accompany him home to Bath, so she packed up her supplies and sailed from Harrison's Landing aboard the hospital transport *Nelly Baker* that Wednesday.

"It is with great reluctance that I leave at a time when my services are so much, ever so much needed, and when my opportunities and facilities for affording relief to the suffering are daily extending," Sarah admitted to Hodsdon.

Friends had exerted "earnest persuasions and importunities ... that I should remain from a sense of duty," she noted, "but I feel my first duty is to my husband, who would not on my account permit me to remain even were I disposed to."[28]

The *Nelly Baker* churned toward Fort Monroe with the battered ironclad gunboat USS *Galena* as escort on July 10.[29] Sampson apprehended the danger; sudden and accurate fire from a concealed Confederate artillery battery had hit the steamer *Daniel Webster* six times during its upriver passage earlier that Wednesday. One cannonball had pounded through one side of the pilot house and out the other while spewing wood splinters that wounded the steamer's pilot.[30]

Consequently "there is considerable excitement on board" the *Nelly Baker*, Sampson admitted. She soon went below decks to care for patients. Later she learned that "quite a number of [enemy] guns" had fired at the *Nelly Baker*, "but as yet none has hit us."

Sarah Sampson hoped her husband, having "lost none of his patriotism … may again be able to offer his services to his Country.

"And I will return with him," she assured Hodsdon.[31]

~~~

1. Rev. George W. Bicknell, *History of the Fifth Regiment Maine Volunteers,* Hall L. Davis, Portland, Maine 1871, pp. 116-117
2. "Letter from the Sixth Maine Regiment," July 14, 1862, *Daily Whig & Courier,* Thursday, July 24, 1862
3. Robert Knox Sneden, "Map of Harrison's Landing," Library of Congress
4. Confederate cavalry commanded by J.E.B. Stuart arrived on Evelynton Heights on Thursday morning. Instead of waiting until Confederate infantry could arrive and fortify this high ground overlooking the Union campsites, Stuart let his artillery commander, Capt. John Pelham, open fire with one 6-pounder howitzer. Boiling from their camps, Union troops quickly moved onto the heights and drove off Stuart's troopers. In his July 5 report to Brig. Gen. David Birney, Maj. Edwin Burt of the 3rd Maine Infantry noted how "the rebels shelled our camp … with great vigor" on July 3.
5. "Letter from the Maine 7th," *Portland Daily Press,* Wednesday, July 16, 1862

6. Albert Maxfield and Robert Brady Jr., *Company D of the Eleventh Regiment Maine Infantry Volunteers in the War of the Rebellion,* Press of Thos. Humphrey, New York, NY, 1890, pp. 65-66
7. Elijah Walker, *The Old Soldier: History of the Fourth Maine Infantry,* Tribune, Rockland, Maine, 1895, p. 33
8. "Mrs. Sampson's Report," *Annual Report of the Adjutant General of the State of Maine, 1864-1865,* pp. 111-112
9. Walker, *The Old Soldier,* p. 31
10. Rev. George W. Bicknell, *History of the Fifth Regiment Maine Volunteers,* Hall L. Davis, Portland, Maine 1871, pp. 118-119. Italics in original.
11. Pvt. Adelbert Knight, letter to his mother Julia Ann Fletcher Knight, Aug. 12, 1862, copies in possession by Brian Swartz, courtesy of Larry Knight.
12. "Mrs. Sampson's Report," *Annual Report of the Adjutant General of the State of Maine, 1864-1865,* p. 113
13. L.P. Brockett. M.D. and Mrs. Mary C. Vaughan, *Women's Work in the Civil War: A Record of Heroism, Patriotism and Patience,* Ziegler, McCurdy & Co., Philadelphia and R.H. Curran, Boston, 1867, p. 507
14. Brig. Gen. Joseph Hooker, *Official Records, Series I, Vol. 11, Part II,* Chapter XXIII, No. 2, p. 951
15. Underline in the original.
16. Maj. Robert F. Campbell, July 18, 1862 to Maine Governor Israel Washburn Jr., Maine State Archives
17. Walker, *The Old Soldier,* p. 33
18. George A. McCall commanded the 3rd Division (Pennsylvania Reserves) of Fitz John Porter's V Corps.
19. "The Evacuation of Harrison's Landing by McClellan's Army," *Maine Farmer,* Thursday, August 28, 1862
20. Stephen W. Sears, *To the Gates of Richmond: The Peninsula Campaign,* Ticknor & Fields, New York, N.Y., 1992, pp. 338-339
21. Pvt. Adelbert Knight, Aug. 12, 1862 letter to Julia Ann Fletcher Knight.
22. Robert Brady Jr. and Albert Maxfield, The *Story of One Regiment: The Eleventh Maine Infantry Volunteers in the War of the Rebellion,* J.J. Little & Co., New York, NY, 1896, p. 76
23. Brady and Maxfield, *The Story of One Regiment,* p. 76
24. William E.S. Whitman and Charles H. True, *Maine in the War for the Union,* Nelson Dingley Jr. & Co., Lewiston, 1865, pp. 95, 276
25. Walker, *The Old Soldier,* p. 34
26. Maxfield and Brady, *Company D of the Eleventh Regiment Maine Infantry Volunteers,* p. 77
27. Brockett and Vaughan, *Women's Work in the Civil War,* p. 507
28. Sarah Sampson, July 10, 1862 letter to Maine Adj. Gen. John L. Hodsdon, MSA. Sampson underlined specific words in her letter.
29. Commissioned in April 1862, the USS *Galena* had participated (along with the USS *Monitor*) in the abortive naval bombardment of Confederate defenses at Drewry's Bluff on May 15. Confederate gunners got the better of the *Galena,* badly damaging the ship and killing 12 crewmen.
30. *Daily Whig & Courier,* Saturday, July 19, 1862
31. Sarah Sampson, July 10, 1862 letter to Maine Adj. Gen. John L. Hodsdon, MSA.

Chapter 39

THE EMPTY SLEEVE

"Waldoboro is to be redeemed"

Elizabeth Anne Howard soon learned that her husband had taken two bullets for the Union on June 1. She did not know that she would soon hug her soldier tightly.

According to a press account reprinted from the *Lewiston Journal*, Brig. Gen. Israel Richardson had sent "a private dispatch" from his 1st Division headquarters upon learning that Oliver Otis Howard had been shot. The message "states that Brigadier General Howard was wounded in the arm in the battle of Saturday,[1] and that the limb would probably have to be amputated. Gen. Howard's brother, C.H. Howard … was also wounded in the leg."[2]

As wartime press reports went, this one was fairly accurate (O.O. Howard had been wounded on Sunday, of course). Before boarding the train at Fair Oaks Station with the wounded Howards on June 2, Capt. Frederick D. Sewall stopped by Richardson's 1st Division headquarters and left a message for "Mrs O O Howard" in Lewiston.

Dated June 2, the telegram informed a startled Elizabeth, "The General is wounded. Fear he will lose his arm[;] he will come home as soon as possible. Do not come unless you hear again. Charles slightly wounded in the leg." Sent from "Richardsons … via Ft Monroe," the message soon reached Elizabeth Anne Howard.[3]

When her husband took command of the 3rd Maine Infantry in spring 1861, Elizabeth—"Lizzie" as the general so affectionately called her—brought the couple's three children (5-year-old Guy, 4-year-old Grace, and baby James) home to Maine. She anxiously awaited word from her "Otis," now under the attentive care of nurse Sarah Sampson aboard the hospital transport *Nelly Baker*.

Although in pain from his wound, Howard took ink and pen near dawn on June 3 and "made my first effort at writing with my left hand." Addressing the letter to his fearful family, he wrote with a "backward slant."[4]

The salutation "Dearest" opened the letter, written in a forced penmanship that left Elizabeth trying to translate specific words and phrases. Explaining that he wrote "with only my left arm," Howard indicated that he and Charlie "shall go to Fort Monroe today and probably to Baltimore tonight."

Some words almost fell apart as Howard struggled to write cursive with his left hand.

Union Brig. Gen. Oliver Otis Howard
Pictured here as a major general, sans right arm.
Photo from Brady's National Photographic Portrait Galleries, Library of Congress

Elizabeth Anne Howard
O.O. Howard's wife.
From The Autobiography of Oliver Otis Howard, Major General, United States Army *(1907)*

"Charlie is very comfortable & so am I," he assured Elizabeth. "We miss you & the children. Shall see you soon."

Charlie Howard informed his "Dear Sister" in a postscript written at 6:30 a.m. Tuesday that he had received "only a flesh wound in the thigh. You will see us at Auburn soon," he promised his sister-in-law.[5]

As the *Nelly Baker* steamed south on the York River on Tuesday, June 3, Howard either wrote or more likely dictated his official "report of command as engaged at Fair Oaks Station on the 1st instant." Addressed to Capt. J.M. Norvell, the 1st Division's assistant adjutant general, the report detailed the performance of the 1st Brigade until immediately after Howard's wounding.

Ever the professional soldier, Howard did not let a missing arm stop him from fulfilling his duties. Compiling a list of regimental officers killed or wounded, he profusely praised his staff officers by name. As for the 1st Brigade's enlisted soldiers, "all the men behaved most gallantly," Howard told Richardson. "I cannot speak too highly in praise of such troops."[6]

Disembarking at Baltimore, the Howards entrained for New York City and crossed the Hudson River on Wednesday, June 4. After resting for about 24 hours, they left for Lewiston, traveling by ship and train.

"Gen. O.O. Howard, who was wounded in the late battle near Richmond, was enthusiastically received by our citizens upon his arrival here this afternoon," indicated a Friday, June 6 telegram wired to Maine newspapers from Lewiston.[7]

"The whole population appeared to have turned out to greet us" at the Lewiston train station, a surprised Howard said. Politicians welcomed home the brothers-in-birth-and-arms and Sewall, the general's only permanent aide not shot at Seven Pines. Expressing their "patriotic love," civilians cheered robustly as "words of welcome and appreciation had been spoken and acknowledged."

Finally the Howards and Sewall "hastened to the hotel in Auburn where my wife and children were," Oliver Otis said.[8]

Arriving at the Maine Hotel,[9] he enveloped Elizabeth Anne with his left arm and mingled with his children; "sweet, indeed, was the rest of a few subsequent days when we enjoyed the nursing and comforts of home," Howard remembered.[10]

He could have spent the summer recuperating under the tender loving care of Elizabeth Anne. Closely following the war news and casualty lists already appearing in Maine newspapers,

Union officers in front of the incomplete new Capitol dome
Judging from Oliver Otis Howard's missing arm at far left and the incomplete dome, this illustration was probably done between 1862 and 1863, assuming that the artist would have drawn a finished dome if it had been done later. The artist presumably worked from existing portraits; the group did not take a break from the war to get together and pose. From left: Howard, Philip Kearny, George H. Thomas, Ambrose Everett Burnside, Winfield Scott Hancock, Winfield Scott, Goerge B. McClellan, W.S. Rosecrans, Joseph Hooker, Lew Wallace, Benjamin Franklin Butler, George Armstrong Custer, and John A. Logan.
Illustration by Augustus Tholey via Library of Congress

he refused to shed his uniform while the stump of his right arm healed.

Howard decided that if he could not fight, he could still help the war effort. Governor Israel Washburn Jr. contacted Howard, who "volunteered his services ... to address the people in various parts of" Maine "for the purpose of encouraging enlistments in the army," editor Ezekiel Holmes told *Maine Farmer* readers.[11]

Elizabeth Anne (and perhaps the children)[12] accompanied Howard as he traveled by buggy, train, and wagon to mingle with civilians anxious to meet a war hero. In mid-June he "visited Portland and participated in [a] State religious convention, where I gave two public addresses" that "were the beginning of a canvas of Maine for filling the State quota of volunteers."

Norumbega Hall, Bangor, Maine, c. 1870
Photo courtesy of Richard R. Shaw

Independence Day found Howard speaking in Livermore in Androscoggin County. Descending "a flight of steps[,] I slipped and fell"; he reflexively reached for the stair rail "with the hand which did not exist" and plummeted down the stairs.

The fall "thrust the stump of my amputated arm into the ground, making the hurt from the fall very severe," Howard said afterward. "It would have been worse, except for a sole-leather protection," the stump cap fastened over the arm stub at the Fair Oaks hospital.[13]

Howard crisscrossed the state in mid-July. Arriving in Augusta on Friday, July 11, he attended an evening worship service at the First Baptist Church and enjoyed the musical escort provided him by the Citizens Band to the home of J.S. Turner, where Howard spent the night.

The next day he mingled with the local folks before catching a train to Portland.[14] That night Howard was the keynote speaker at a Grand Patriotic Rally held in Portland City Hall. Its music featuring "soul-stirring strains," the band from the 17th U.S. Infantry Regiment[15] entertained the guests, "the door-ways and passages leading to the Hall were densely packed, and hundreds [were] turned away disappointed," a newspaper reporter observed.

Waiting until the requisite civilian illuminati had almost lulled the audience to sleep, Howard went to the lectern and exhorted Mainers to support the war effort. "I will not say now this country is in danger of being broken, but is it threatened," he said.

His speech touching upon the Peninsula Campaign, the army, and McClellan—many Mainers now doubted the man's ability to win a fight—Howard asked Mainers to "lay aside all partizan [sic] spirit, for the good and welfare of our country," and enlist. "My friends, let every man think for himself. Let him be thoughtful, and let him come up to his duty like a man,"

Howard concluded.

He stepped back "amid a perfect storm of applause and cheers, ladies waving their handkerchiefs, and gentlemen swinging their hats, all perfectly frantic with enthusiasm," the reporter scribbled on his note pad.[16]

Howard then traipsed through Oxford County on Monday, Tuesday, and Wednesday, July 14-16.[17]

Reverend Rowland Howard, the general's brother, wrote Elizabeth from Farmington on July 16 that "I hope you can go to Bangor. Otis ought to have somebody with him & no one so good as a wife."[18]

The Maine Central Railroad transported Howard to Bangor on Thursday, July 17, where he spoke at a War Meeting held in Norumbega Hall on Central Street. Bands escorted the "large number of people ... arriving from the neighboring towns," and militia companies brought Howard from the train station to the hall, where carpenters had built a platform outside the main entrance.

Perhaps the grace of God spared Howard that Thursday night like He had at Seven Pines, as the general believed. Crowds so packed the streets around Norumbega Hall that Howard could not reach it; rally organizers opted to shift the event outdoors, then inexplicably threw open the building's front doors.

The crowds outside thinned as men and women elbowed their ways indoors. Then "the procession marched in to the inspiring strains of the Band," and the rally opened with a ministerial prayer.

Now jammed with onlookers who could not squeeze into Norumbega Hall, the platform outside the front doors partially collapsed, dropping "men, women and children ... some ten or fifteen feet" to a level with the Norumbega Hall foundation.

Swirling protectively around Howard, supporters hustled him out the rear doors as gas pipes broken by the collapsed platform spewed coal gas outside the hall's main entrance.[19] Howard went to the Bangor House, where he and other dignitaries soon stood on the balcony overlooking the intersection of Main and Union streets.

U.S. Vice President Hannibal Hamlin
Hamlin, from Maine, was the 15th vice president, serving under Abraham Lincoln from March 4, 1861–March 4, 1865.
Photo by Mathew Brady or Levin Corbin Handy, via Library of Congress

Howard delivered a heart-felt, rousing speech repeatedly interrupted by applause and cheers. Vice President Hannibal Hamlin spoke next, and rally organizers called it quits after businessman Lewis Barker finished a steam-winding speech at 11:45 p.m. People straggled home; Howard crawled into bed before returning to the Maine Central station the next morning.[20]

Hamlin's presence that night was not unexpected. A native of Paris in Oxford County, Hamlin had practiced law in Hampden and politics in Augusta and Washington, D.C. prior to the war. He lived in Washington when the Senate was in session; President Abraham Lincoln essentially ignored his vice president, little more than the warm body designated by the Constitution to replace the president upon his death or incapacity.

At this point, Hamlin lived in Bangor with his second wife and his younger children from both marriages. His first wife, Sarah Jane Emery, had died of tuberculosis in 1855; after a year's mourning, Hamlin married her much younger half-sister, Ellen Vesta Emery. He also served as a private in Co. A, Maine Coast Guards.

Friday found a crowd cheering for Howard at Skowhegan in Somerset County, and Saturday he appeared before an enthusiastic crowd in Bath, which had sent two militia companies to war a year earlier under Howard's command.[21]

Wherever he spoke, Howard wore his general's uniform with the right sleeve of the jacket pinned shut. *Cartes de visite* taken of the uniformed Howard early in the war and again post-Seven Pines powerfully contrast the price paid by this Christian warrior; the people listening to Howard saw the empty sleeve and understood its meaning.

"Honorably and gallantly has Gen. Howard discharged his duty," Ezekiel Holmes wrote. "Maine is proud to own such men, and to honor such deeds of courage."[22]

Howard's demonstrable patriotism electrified loyal Mainers. After listening to the general deliver "his effective speech at the War Meeting" held in Bangor, poet David Barker of Exeter felt inspired to pen a four-stanza poem titled "The Empty Sleeve," dedicated to Howard:

> *"By the moon's pale light to a gazing throng,*
> *Let me tell one tale, let me sing one song;*
> *'Tis a simple song of a one arm man.*
> *Till this very hour I could ne'er believe*
> *What a tell-tale thing is an empty sleeve—*
> *What a weird, queer thing is an empty sleeve."*

According to Barker, the empty sleeve "tells ... of a county's need and a country's call, of a kiss for a child and wife, and a hurried march for a nation's life," as well as "of a battle-field of gore—of the whizzing grape—of the fiery shell—of a scene which mimics the scenes of hell.

"To the top of the skies let us all then heave one proud huzza for the empty sleeve—for the one arm man with the empty sleeve," Barker wrote.[23]

Whether or not Barker's poem motivated men to enlist is not known, but Howard's mere presence certainly did. After authorizing Governor Washburn in late May to raise one infantry regiment (designated the 16th Maine), the vacillating War Department requested two more

David Barker/"The Empty Sleeve"
The poem as it appeared in the *Bangor Daily Whig & Courier,* August 15, 1862, page 2.
Poem image courtesy of the Bangor Public Library; Barker image from his book Poems by David Barker

THE EMPTY SLEEVE. The following beautiful poem is from the pen of our friend David Barker, Esq., of Exeter, whose productions entitle him to rank among the first New England poets. Mr. Barker was in the city when Gen. Howard made his effective speech at the War Meeting, and the "silent eloquence of that empty sleeve" made such an impression upon him, that he felt an inspiration to write. Unlike many poets, Mr. Barker cannot write at all times and upon all subjects, but only when impelled by some unseen power, which we think will be frequently the case.

[For the Whig and Courier.
The Empty Sleeve.

[Inscribed to Gen. Howard, of Maine, who recently lost his right arm in defence of his Country.]

BY DAVID BARKER.

By the moon's pale light to a gazing throng,
Let me tell one tale, let me sing one song;
'Tis a tale devoid of an aim or plan,
'Tis a simple song of a one arm man.
Till this very hour I could ne'er believe
What a tell-tale thing is an empty sleeve—
What a weird, queer thing is an empty sleeve.

It tells in a silent tone to all,
Of a country's need and a country's call,
Of a kiss and a tear for a child and wife,
And a hurried march for a nation's life;
Till this very hour who could e'er believe
What a tell-tale thing is an empty sleeve—
What a weird, queer thing is an empty sleeve.

It tells of a battle-field of gore—
Of the sabre's clash—of the cannon's roar—
Of the deadly charge—of the bugle's note—
Of a gurgling sound in a foeman's throat—
Of the whizzing grape—of the fiery shell—
Of a scene which mimics the scenes of hell—
Till this very hour would you e'er believe
What a tell-tale thing is an empty sleeve—
What a weird, queer thing is an empty sleeve.

Though it points to a myriad wounds and scars,
Yet it tells that a flag with the stripes and stars,
In God's own chosen time will take
Each place of the rag with the rattle-snake,
And it points to a time when that flag shall wave
O'er a land where there breathes no cowering slave.
To the top of the skies let us all then heave
One proud hussa for the empty sleeve—
For the one arm man with the empty sleeve.

such regiments in early July. President Abraham Lincoln then telegraphed Washburn a few days later to request yet a fourth infantry regiment, to be designated the 19th Maine.[24]

Enlistments lagged. When Waldoboro-area men expressed little interest in military service, Howard swept into town with Reverend T.J. Brown, the 15th Maine Infantry chaplain. The general "addressed a vast crowd in his usual forcible and impressive style," and Brown "also talked to the people."

Afterwards, "Waldoboro is to be redeemed," a newspaper correspondent claimed. "The loyal Union men of that town are aroused" and promised "to smoke out every rebel sympathizer" living in the Midcoast seaport. After meeting with Washburn in Augusta, several "loyal citizens" promised "to raise a full company" of infantrymen and, together with Waldoboro voters, pledged money to pay a $125 bounty to each local recruit.[25]

"I went over the State ... visited the principal cities and villages, and often made two addresses a day, urging my countrymen to fill up the ranks," Howard later said.

He could not be credited exclusively for rousing sufficient patriotic fervor to fill the five infantry regiments (not the War Department-mandated four) that Maine raised in summer 1862. However, "the quota of Maine was filled," Howard realized, and in late August "I returned to the field."[26]

~~~

1. Howard was wounded on Sunday, June 1.
2. *Daily Whig & Courier,* Thursday, June 5, 1862
3. Oliver Otis Howard Papers, George J. Mitchell Department of Special Collections & Archives, Bowdoin College Library, Brunswick, Maine
4. Oliver Otis Howard, *Autobiography of Oliver Otis Howard, Major General United States Army,* Baker & Taylor Company, New York, 1907, p. 252
5. Oliver Otis Howard Papers, Bowdoin College Library, Brunswick, Maine
6. Brig. Gen. Oliver Otis Howard, *The War of the Rebellion: Original Records of the Civil War, Serial 12, The Peninsula Campaign, Va., No. 5,* Chapter XXIII, pp. 768-770
7. *Daily Whig & Courier,* Saturday, June 7, 1862
8. Howard, *Autobiography,* pp. 253-254
9. *Portland Daily Press,* Saturday, June 28, 1862
10. Howard, *Autobiography,* pp. 253-254
11. *Maine Farmer,* Thursday, July 17, 1862
12. The Howards later had four more children: Chancey, born May 3, 1863 during the Battle of Chancellorsville; John; Harry Stinson; and Elizabeth.
13. Howard, *Autobiography,* pp. 254-255
14. *Maine Farmer,* Thursday, July 17, 1862
15. A regular Army regiment, the 17th garrisoned the Casco Bay forts protecting Portland.
16. *Portland Daily Press,* Monday, July 14, 1862
17. *Maine Farmer,* Thursday, July 17, 1862
18. Oliver Otis Howard Papers, Bowdoin College Library, Brunswick, Maine
19. The gas was manufactured from coal.
20. *Daily Whig & Courier,* Friday, July 18, 1862
21. *Maine Farmer,* Thursday, July 17, 1862
22. *Maine Farmer,* Thursday, June 12, 1862
23. *Daily Whig & Courier,* Friday, August 15, 1862
24. John L. Hodsdon, *Annual Report of the Adjutant General of the State of Maine, 1862,* Appendix A, pp. 5, 7
25. *Daily Whig & Currier,* Thursday, August 7, 1862
26. Howard, *Autobiography,* p. 255

Chapter 40

THE ELEPHANT APPROACHES

"The dust was so thick and suffocating"

As his 4th Maine Battery crossed hot and dusty Virginia in July 1862, Capt. O'Neil W. Robinson Jr. and just about all his men had yet to see a serious "elephant." They had not fired a cannonball at Confederate soldiers—and neither had Confederates fired at them.

The 10th Maine Infantry Regiment and 2nd Lt. John Mead Gould traveled directionally with the 4th Maine Battery. Baptized by hostile fire during their May retreat from Winchester, the soldiers of Col. George Lafayette Beal had met the elephant, albeit a small critter.

Now trekking toward Culpeper in central Virginia, both units headed for a collision with a real big elephant.

Robinson, the Bethel attorney whose Democratic Party leanings had concerned Maine's Republican Governor Israel Washburn Jr. the previous autumn, had detrained with his battery in Washington, D.C. on Thursday, April 3, 1862. After freezing all winter in their Augusta camp, the gunners had camped briefly in Portland in mid-March before boarding a southbound train with the 3rd and 5th Maine Batteries.

Robinson brought with him four officers and approximately 100 enlisted men. His battery fielded six 3-inch wrought-iron ordnance rifles, each weighing 820 pounds and capable of firing a 9½-pound projectile at least 1,850 yards. In Army fashion, the gun crews and their guns were numbered one through six and were paired in two-gun sections. Each gun crew consisted of "a Sergeant, two Corporals and thirteen men," noted Corp. Judson Ames of Foxcroft, assigned to the Second Detachment (No. 2 gun) commanded by Sgt. Algernon S. Bangs of Augusta.[1]

"The extra men of the Battery are divided among the detachments," noted Ames, a 5-foot, 10-inch machinist.

Accompanied by the 6th Maine Battery of Capt. Freeman McGilvery (a Searsport ship's captain), Robinson and his men initially trained at Fort Ramsey in Alexandria; the 6th Maine went to nearby Fort Buffalo. To pay for tobacco, some thrifty Yankees from Robinson's battery earned money by gathering and selling "old bullets" as "old lead." Scrounging "an old shell" on Saturday, May 10, privates Lewis Davis and Charles Robie "attempted to extract the fuse plug," Ames said.

Union Capt. O'Neill W. Robinson Jr.
Photo courtesy Maine State Archives

George L. Beal
Photo courtesy of Nicholas P. Picerno

The exploding shell mortally wounded both men. Robie died that day; Davis lingered until May 29.

Receiving their horses on May 25 and their six cannons on May 26, Robinson's men entrained for the Shenandoah Valley on June 13; McGilvery and the 6th Maine Battery boarded the same train. On the hilly journey from Harpers Ferry to Charles Town, the 4th Maine gunners helped push their train up a steep incline; the underpowered engine chugged so slowly in places that the Maine men, still fresh from their farms, got out and picked blackberries alongside the tracks.

Catching up with the train took only a short run afterwards.

The blue-clad tourists visited the John Brown-related Charles Town jail and gallows, "still standing in a field near by," Ames noted. "Here we first met the genuine Secesh[2] and about the only good looking girls that we saw in Virginia.

"They did not smile very sweetly on us," he admitted.[3]

Like the five other artillery batteries that Maine had sent to war by mid-spring 1862, the 4th Maine Battery (often called "Robinson's Battery" in deference to its commander) received far less attention in the hometown newspapers than did the larger infantry regiments and the 1st Maine Cavalry, often cited in the press after being shot to pieces at Middletown. The 1st Maine Battery of Capt. Alden W. Bradbury had gone to Louisiana in mid-winter, the next five batteries to Virginia.

The Maine press had published accounts of the 3rd Maine Battery not even receiving its

Chapter 40: The Elephant Approaches

Union Brig. Gen. Christopher C. Augur (above) and Union Brig. Gen. Alpheus Starkey Williams
Both pictured here as major generals.
Augur photo from Brady-Handy Collection, Williams from Brady National Photographic Art Galleries; both via Library of Congress

cannons. Instead, the battery "was transferred into the Infantry service, and stationed on the Rappahannock [River] to protect a company of Pontoniers,"[4] noted Capt. James G. Swett. "We were furnished with infantry arms for our own protection in case of need."

Swett was proud of what his gunners-turned-infantry had accomplished "opposite Fredericksburg" by mid-May. After erecting the pontoon bridge across the Rappahannock, his men noticed that heavy use left the span "wearing ... out too fast."

Shouldering their axes, the 3rd Maine gunners went "into the woods to cut timber," took up the pontoon bridge, and "put a tressle [sic] bridge across," Swett bragged.[5]

The War Department attached the 4th Maine Battery to the 2nd Brigade (Brig. Gen. Henry Prince) of the 2nd Division (Brig. Gen. Christopher C. Augur) of II Corps, commanded by the Stonewall Jackson-manhandled Maj. Gen. Nathaniel P. Banks.[6] As part of the Army of Virginia commanded by Maj. Gen. John Pope, Augur started his division east from the lower Shenandoah Valley on July 5; breaking camp that afternoon, the 4th Maine Battery crossed the Blue Ridge Mountains at Manassas Gap and rolled toward Warrenton.

Accidents and smallpox cost Robinson men as his battery reached the Piedmont. Blacksmith Albert V. Thompson and brother privates Asa and Charles Coombs obtained permission to leave the battery's camp near Warrenton to pick the "very abundant" blackberries—and promptly deserted. Ames figured the trio "got on the wrong road and did not discover their mistake until they arrived in Canada."⁷

Other men fell sick during the battery's early summer stay in Little Washington. A few died; two "were buried under a large locust tree in a field near our camp" before Augur started his 2nd Division on the road to Culpeper, Ames noted.⁸

Nathaniel Banks brought both his divisions, the 2nd of Augur and the 1st of Brig. Gen. Alpheus S. Williams, east to central Virginia. Early July saw the 10th Maine Infantry on the march through the "very hilly" lower Shenandoah Valley, "covered with a thick growth of wood," said Pvt. Harrison A. Tripp of Co. F and Sedgwick.

Commanded by the tough, no-nonsense Beal, the 10th Maine belonged to the 1st Brigade (Brig. Gen. Samuel W. Crawford) of Williams' division. The other regiments tromping east with Crawford were the 5th Connecticut of Col. George D. Chapman, the 28th New York of Dudley Donnelly, and the 46th Pennsylvania of Col. Joseph Knipe.

Union Maj. Gen. John Pope
Pictured here as a brigadier general
Photo from Library of Congress

On Sunday, July 6, the artillery- and cavalry-accompanied 1st Brigade "started on a scouting expedition ... through as pretty a country as you ever laid eyes on," Tripp said. The 10th Maine broke camp about noon on Monday and climbed "a steep hill."

As the vistas widened around him, Tripp gazed as "encircled with towering mountains, the lovely valley of Luray, with its green fields, its pretty streams and its golden grain bowing its yellow head to the reaper's sickle, burst upon our sight, as it lay spread out before us like a map."

He had no time to gawk. The 1st Brigade approached Luray, "said to be occupied by the enemy," and the Union cavalry soon "made a dash into town." A brief skirmish saw two Confederates killed and four captured.⁹

The expedition steered the 1st Brigade southeast toward Warrenton in Fauquier County. Crossing the Blue Ridge at Chester Gap as "the sun grew hot and the boys began to straggle," the 10th Maine boys marched only 8 miles before camping Sunday night, said Adjutant John Mead Gould, also a second lieutenant in Co. E.

On a "terribly hot" Monday, the regiment marched at 4 a.m. Men strayed from the column to glean and gobble blackberries and cherries; the abundance of the latter "is surprising," noticed Gould as he rode a worn-out horse.

In a company in the regiment marching ahead of the 10th Maine, each soldier "carried a huge limb full of cherries," he commented. "The appearance was of a moving forest."

That night the 10th Maine camped near a 100-acre field filled with ripening low-bush blackberries, which Maine soldiers harvested until darkness approached. The hot weather continued as the Maine boys finally reached Warrenton on July 11.[10]

Camping on a hill some three miles from Warrenton, the Union soldiers ate well by raiding "lamb, mutton, beef, poultry, honey, milk, butter," and other supplies from surrounding farms, Tripp noted.[11]

The practice gained official sanction. On July 18, Pope issued General Order No. 5 to his Army of Virginia. "As far as practicable, the troops of this command will subsist upon the country in which their operations are carried on," he instructed his men.

Officers commanding the foraging parties would issue vouchers to Virginian farmers whose food stocks and farm animals had been purloined. The vouchers would "be payable at the conclusion of the war" if the recipients could prove they were "loyal citizens of the United States."[12]

Not until July 24 did the 10th Maine reach Culpeper Court House and camp "on a hill east of the village," Gould noted. The Maine lads passed the next two weeks in typical mid-Virginia summer weather: "pleasant" on most days, "hot" and "very hot" on others, according to Gould.

On Wednesday, July 30, the quartermaster traded the regiment's well-worn Sibley tents for "the famous shelter-tent or dog tent as they should be called," Gould groused. Each soldier received a "piece of cloth about a yard square with buttons and button holes around three sides."

By fastening two pieces together, soldiers could create a suitable tent—or so the theory went.

"Rain and even dew will penetrate the thin cloth and I fail to see the actual benefit myself," Gould complained.

More troops suddenly appeared around Culpeper Court House, described by Gould as "much neater than Front Royal." Along the town's streets stood "quite a number of pretty good brick houses and stores" not yet ravaged by war, a fact that surprised him.

Gould particularly noticed the gardens and trees surrounding many houses; "it looks more like a forest, in fact quite Portlandish," he commented.

Suddenly the 10th Maine soldiers sensed

Union Brig. Gen. Samuel Wylie Crawford
Photo by Mathew Brady via Library of Congress

a change in the air. The 1st Maine Cavalry rode past the camp on August 6, to be followed later by elements of the III Corps of Maj. Gen. Irvin McDowell, "not a very fat man [,] but is bloated with liquor and turkey-diet as much as any man I ever saw," Gould said after encountering McDowell and his entourage at the 1st Maine Cavalry's camp on Thursday, August 7.[13]

About noon on Friday, August 8, Samuel Crawford received orders to march southwest from Culpeper Court House to support the cavalry brigade commanded by Brig. Gen. George D. Bayard. Pressured by Confederate troops advancing across the Rapidan River, the cavalrymen skirmished as they withdrew northeast past an 814-foot monadnock rising from the countryside some seven miles southwest of Culpeper.[14]

Known alternately as Cedar or Slaughter (for the farm of Reverend Philip Slaughter), the mountain dominated the countryside to-

Union Capt. Freeman McGilvery
Image courtesy Maine State Archives

ward Culpeper. Cedar Mountain would give its name to the upcoming battle.[15]

The 10th Maine had just received new clothing; men particularly scrambled to acquire "shoes and rubber blankets," Gould noticed the hubbub within the camp. The soldiers of Co. H tucked in their new blue blouses and tied their rubber blankets around their bodies "with the white cloth side out to prevent them from slipping."

He thought the H boys resembled "a company wearing regalia."[16]

Tripp recalled that the regiment stepped off "about noon ... to march towards Gordonsville" (well behind enemy lines). Marching "about 5 miles from camp," Beal's soldiers bivouacked near Knap's Pennsylvania Independent Battery E, which was deployed on a hill south of the Culpeper Road.[17]

Although accustomed to campaigning, Crawford's men suffered along the "extremely hot, dry, and dusty" road toward the Rapidan, according to Gould. Despite their "soldierly appearance and ... fine marching," men "fainted from the excessive heat" before the regiment had "marched a mile.

"One by one they blanched and reeled over," and though the 1st Brigade occasionally halted in the shade,[18] more men fell out along the march, Gould noticed. A few men suffered sun stroke, "three old English soldiers of Co. D" who had previously deserted a British regiment in New Brunswick to join a Maine regiment "took this occasion to desert us forever," and most 10th Maine stragglers "came up in the cool of the evening."[19]

Crawford learned that his lead regiment had encountered the Union cavalrymen by 4 p.m. "between Colvin's Tavern and ... Cedar Run." Riding ahead with his staff, the general saw Confederate pickets and cavalry and deployed his four regiments and their supporting artillery "on the low ground of the [North Branch of Cedar] run, completely concealed from the enemy."[20]

Beal and his 10th Maine remained in position past sunset. Guarded by pickets, the Maine boys slept under arms Friday night and awakened early on Saturday.

Christopher Augur's 2nd Division had reached Culpeper late on Friday. Trailing along with the 2nd Brigade's hard-marching infantrymen (plus a cavalry company), O'Neil Robinson and the 4th Maine Battery went into camp a mile north of Culpeper about midnight. Robinson's boys knew that a battle lurked somewhere in the warm Virginia darkness; couriers galloped to and fro in the Union camps in the wee hours of Saturday, horse hooves thudded continuously through the darkness, and the Maine men slept little.

By 6 a.m. on Saturday, August 9, Col. Samuel H. Allen had deployed his 1st Maine Cavalry Regiment one to one and a half miles from the center of the Confederate lines spreading northwest from the base of Cedar Mountain. The bulk of Jackson's troops still marched toward Culpeper, and Alpheus Williams and his division represented the bulk of Union troops present on the battlefield.

Union Maj. Gen. Irvin McDowell
Photo from Brady National Photographic Art Galleries via Library of Congress

Union Brig. Gen. George Dashiell Bayard
Photo courtesy of www.generalsandbrevets.com

With little shooting taking place, Allen shifted his cavalry troopers "some 300 yards to the extreme left" of the 1st Division around 11 a.m. and posted "a strong force as pickets still a mile farther to the left [southeast] ... extending quite to the foot of the mountain."[21]

Curiosity drew some 10th Maine men to ascend the hill occupied by Joseph Knap's Pennsylvania Independent Battery E. Gould and his comrades watched "a few mounted men riding back and forth on a ridge, at the base of Cedar Mountain," he said. The clustered infantrymen gave Confederate gunners a target; Knap chased away the Mainers, but some returned to see Union cavalry come under enemy fire.

Knap "would not have us there," admitted sightseer Gould. Shooed downhill, the curiosity-seekers "flanked the battery" and the guards assigned to keep them away from Knap, "lay down out of sight, and watched" the distant Confederates until George Beal rode over and "ordered us to remain behind the [hay] stacks."[22]

Union Brig. Gen. John W. Geary
Photo from Brady-Handy Collection, Library of Congress

At their camp outside Culpeper, the 4th Maine gunners had hitched up their horses around 7:30-8 a.m. As the rising sun beat down on the suffering animals, Robinson sent a lieutenant to ask brigade commander Henry Prince for orders.

"When I have orders for Captain Robinson, I will send them," Prince snarled in response.

Stunned by the brusque response, Robinson ordered his "horses ... unharnessed and taken by the drivers to a field some distance away to graze" around 9 a.m., Ames said. Quietly spreading his one-star general peacock's fan, Prince suddenly sent a courier to Robinson with orders to limber up.[23]

The 4th Maine's drivers hustled the hungry horses back to camp and re-harnessed them.

"We marched from Culpeper Court-House before noon," noted Prince. His 2nd Brigade followed the brigade of Brig. Gen. John Geary; "the booming of artillery in front indicated that the march ... was not a long one," good news for infantrymen marching on "the warmest day of the season."[24]

O'Neil Robinson took the 4th Maine Battery "through Culpeper ... at a trot," according to Ames. With artillery fire thudding in the distance, the gunners maneuvered their caissons, cannons, limbers, and wagons along the Culpeper Road,[25] "crowded with troops of all kinds with their ammunition and baggage wagons hurrying to the front."

"The day was intensely hot," Ames realized. "The dust was so thick and suffocating that at

Chapter 40: The Elephant Approaches

times it was difficult to get our breath." The gunners (many of whom walked) passed many Union soldiers "lying by the road completely prostrated and others suffering from sun stroke."

The 4th Maine Battery "halted in a piece of woods nearly a mile in the rear of our line," already skirmishing with Confederates near Cedar Mountain, Ames noticed the slightly cooler air beneath the trees. Other Union soldiers at Cedar Mountain commented on the difference in temperature, if only a few degrees, between being in the direct sunlight or being in shade. The weather was terribly hot.

Prince remembered that his brigade "rested and obtained water" in "a strip of woodland" spreading across the Culpeper Road from north to south, "six miles from Culpeper." Relaxing in the shade, his men filled their canteens in the North Branch of Cedar Run.

Then Henry Prince "placed Captain Robinson under arrest for some reason, the exact nature of which was never clearly understood," the stunned Ames learned.

Except for shooting at Confederates at Winchester, Virginia on May 25, the 10th Maine Infantry had not really "seen the elephant" since arriving in the Old Dominion State. Likewise, the 4th Maine Battery had not experienced serious combat these past four months.[26]

But now the elephant approached from the Rapidan River, and the 4th Maine boys had just lost their captain.

~~~

1. Foxcroft lay on the north bank of the Piscataquis River in southern Piscataquis County, opposite Dover on the south bank. Both towns merged as Dover-Foxcroft on March 11, 1922.
2. "Secesh" was a derogatory term applied liberally to all white Southerners, of whom perhaps one-third actually remained loyal to the United States. Many pro-Unionists would pay dearly for doing so.
3. Judson Ames, *History of the Fourth Maine Battery Light Artillery in the Civil War 1861-1865,* Burleigh & Flynt, Augusta, 1905, pp. 8-14

Cedar Mountain battlefield, August 1862
Panoramic view from the center of the battlefield of Cedar Mountain. Union tents abound.
Photo by Timothy O'Sullivan via Library of Congress

4. The term "pontoniers" referred to pontoon-bridge builders.
5. Capt. James G. Swett, May 19, 1862 letter to Editor William H. Wheeler, *Daily Whig & Courier*, Friday, May 30, 1862
6. Jackson had driven Banks from the Shenandoah Valley in late May 1862 during a whirlwind campaign that had included the May 24 ambush of the 1st Maine Cavalry at Middletown, Virginia.
7. Thompson was never seen again. Originally identified as deserters, the Coombs brothers rejoined the 4th Maine Battery on May 18, 1865.
8. Ames, *Fourth Maine*, pp. 15-16
9. "Harrison" letter to his parents, "From the 10th Maine Regiment," *Ellsworth American*, Friday, August 22, 1862. The only 10th Maine Infantry soldier from Hancock County with a first name or surname of Harrison was Pvt. Harrison A. Tripp of Sedgwick.
10. William B. Jordan, *The Civil War Journals of John Mead Gould 1861-1866*, Butternut & Blue, Baltimore, 1997, pp. 152-155
11. Tripp, *Ellsworth American*, August 22, 1862
12. *Ellsworth American*, Friday, August 1, 1862
13. Jordan, *Journals*, pp. 163-168
14. Brig. Gen. Samuel W. Crawford, *Official Records, Series I, Vol. 12*, Chapter XXIV, No. 8, p. 149
15. Cedar Mountain is approximately half the height of a similar monadnock, Mars Hill, that dominates the skyline in east central Aroostook County in Maine.
16. Maj. John M. Gould, *History of the First-Tenth-Twenty-Ninth Maine Regiment*, Stephen Berry, Portland, ME 1871, p. 165
17. Tripp, "From the 10th Maine Regiment," *Ellsworth American*, Friday, August 29, 1862. Often identified as "Knapp's," Pennsylvania Independent Battery E was commanded by 1st Lt. Joseph Knap.
18. Because neither army had yet established long-term camps in the Culpeper area, the region was still wooded in places.
19. Gould, *History*, pp. 166-167. The Co. D rolls published on pp. 320-321 identify nine men as having served in the "English Army." According to the Nov. 1, 1862 Co. D returns as published on pp. 273-274 of the *Annual Report of the Adjutant General of the State of Maine, 1862*, only two Co. D soldiers deserted on August 8 near Culpeper; both Gould and the 1862 MAGR list Fort Kent as the hometown of deserter William D. McDonald. According to the 1862 AGR, Fort Kent was also the hometown of deserter Hugh Murphy, who is not listed in Gould's "History."
20. Crawford, *OR, Series I, Vol. 12*, Chapter XXIV, No. 8, p. 149
21. Col. Samuel H. Allen, *OR, Series 1, Vol. 12*, Chapter XXIV, No. 3, p. 140
22. Gould, *History*, p. 170
23. Ames, *Fourth Maine*, pp. 17-18
24. Brig. Gen. Henry Prince, *OR, Series 1, Vol. 12*, Chapter XXIV, No. 19, p. 167
25. Some soldiers, including Gould, knew the Culpeper Road as the "Orange road." For consistency, the author refers to the Culpeper Road.
26. Ames, *Fourth Maine*, pp. 17-18

Chapter 41

CEDAR MOUNTAIN COMBAT

"Give them three Down East cheers!"

Surprised by the sudden arrest of their captain, O'Neil Robinson Jr., the 4th Maine Battery gunners stayed near their ordnance rifles as the broiling Virginia sun hung motionless above Cedar Mountain in midafternoon on Saturday, August 9, 1862.

Artillery thudded intermittently in the distance. Their heads drooping in the heat, Robinson's horses flicked their tails at gyrating flies. Mopping sweaty brows and swigging at canteens containing warm water, Maine soldiers quietly speculated as to why Brig. Gen. Henry Prince had arrested Robinson.

Hostile thunder echoed off Cedar Mountain as the petulant Prince pondered Robinson's fate. Then, 30 minutes after arresting Robinson, Prince inexplicably released him.

The 2nd Division's commander, Brig. Gen. Christopher Augur, sent orders for Prince to shift south of the Culpeper Road "for the purpose of meeting the enemy." The 4th Maine rumbled along as four infantry regiments—the 3rd Maryland, 102nd New York, and 109th and 111th Pennsylvanias—and two Army battalions filed "to the left" and navigated a Cedar Run tributary for three-quarters of a mile.

Crossing the flowage, the 2nd Brigade soldiers "halted in its hollow to wait for orders" that were not long in coming, according to Prince.

With Gen. Thomas "Stonewall" Jackson feeding Confederate brigades onto the battlefield, artillery fire "became continuous, and both sides were placing more batteries," Prince said. Up rode a courier on a sweating, wild-eyed horse; he handed a folded paper to Prince, then saluted and rode away.

Prince read the orders that effectively trisected his brigade. Augur wanted the two Army battalions marched to his headquarters, Prince's four regiments formed on the left (southern) flank of a brigade deploying south of the Culpeper Road, and the 4th Maine Battery sent "to relieve … the battery on the hill nearby."[1]

Robinson steered his battery "across an open field about a half mile" to pull up "behind some hay stacks at the [Robert] Hudson House on the north side of the Mitchell Station road," said Corp. Judson Ames, assigned to No. 2 gun. From its intersection with the Culpeper Road, the Mitchell Station Road ran southeast past Cedar Mountain.[2]

Knap's Pennsylvania Independent Battery E takes on Confederates at Cedar Mountain
Illustration by Edwin Forbes, from the Morgan Collection of Civil War Drawings, Library of Congress

Near the two-story, wood-framed Hudson House rose a slight hill occupied by Union artillery. Throughout the morning the gunners of Pennsylvania Independent Battery E of 1st Lt. Joseph Knap had dueled with Confederate gunners hidden in trees on the northern slope of Cedar Mountain, about a mile due south.

The 10th Maine Infantry had supported Knap's battery since Friday evening. Now, as Chris Augur's infantry deployed in line south of the Culpeper Road, Col. George Beal received orders to move the 10th Maine north of the Culpeper Road to rejoin the 1st Brigade of Brig. Gen. Samuel Crawford.[3]

He had summoned the 10th Maine while reassembling his brigade to meet Confederate infantry appearing in strength to the west. Crawford's brigade extended from the Culpeper Road north; Brig. Gen. George H. Gordon deployed his 3rd Brigade of the 1st Division on Crawford's right (northern) flank, and action seemed imminent as the commander of the Union II Corps, Maj. Gen. Nathaniel Banks, appeared with his staff on the battlefield.

Bringing his men across the road, Beal maneuvered "pretty near a piece of woods in front of the battery," said Pvt. Harrison Tripp, referring to Battery F, 4th U.S. Artillery, commanded by 1st Lt. Edward D. Muhlenberg.

The movement brought the regiment under Confederate artillery fire; "the shot and shell was flying about quite lively" for "about two hours," Tripp noticed.[4]

A 21-year-old shoemaker living in Sedgwick when the war began, the dark-haired and gray-eyed Tripp had enlisted in the 10th Maine on September 5, 1861. Unmarried, he wrote home frequently; his letters provided richly detailed glimpses of 10th Maine and military life that relatives forwarded to William P. Burr and N.K. Sawyer, who published the *Ellsworth American* in Ellsworth.[5]

About the time that the 10th Maine shifted north of the Culpeper Road, horse teams pulled the 4th Maine Battery's guns across the field toward the Hudson House. "We first heard the music of shells ... tearing through the air over our heads," Judson Ames recalled of the moment he saw the elephant.

The shells "passed high enough over us to be harmless," and Maine men laughed as an exploding shell sent feeding calves stampeding in a nearby field around 3 p.m.

Reality sank in 15 minutes later when Robinson received orders to deploy his battery to the north side of the Hudson House, on the left (southern) flank of the Union batteries already in action. Capt. Freeman McGilvery then moved his 6th Maine Battery to a position on the south side of the house.

As the gunners assigned to Robinson's No. 2 gun ascended the hill, Ames watched stretcher bearers carry away "some severely wounded men" from a shell-damaged battery, perhaps Battery K, 1st New York Artillery, commanded by Capt. Lorenzo Crounse. Ames also saw several harnessed horses, just struck and gutted by enemy shells.[6]

Robinson had deployed his ordnance rifles in three two-gun sections. That of Junior 1st Lt. Hamlin F. Eaton "occupied lower ground" on the battery's left flank, where the terrain partially sheltered the men from incoming fire, according to Ames. Positioning himself near Eaton's section, Robinson watched the effect that his battery's outgoing shells had on the opposing artillery.

Suddenly the elephant walked across Ames and his comrades. Firing from their higher

Cedar Mountain today, seen from the northeast
Photo by Brian F. Swartz

Hudson House at Cedar Mountain, site of Gen. Pope's headquarters
Photo by Andrew J. Russell via Library of Congress

perch on Cedar Mountain, Confederate gunners swung their tubes to target the unlimbering 4th Maine Battery.

An incoming shell fragment struck Pvt. Abel Davis of No. 6 gun in the leg. Pvt. Charles H. Sally stepped into Davis's position—and another shell fragment laced a "severe scalp wound" across Sally's skull.

Bleeding profusely, the private "did not have to be carried off the field, because none of the boys could catch him," said Ames, too busy to pursue the fleeing Sally.[7]

Senior 1st Lt. Lucius M.S. Haynes[8] commanded the right-flank section, comprising the No. 1 gun of Sgt. Jere Owen and the No. 2 gun of Sgt. Algernon Bangs. Ames furiously worked with Bangs' gunners as both ordnance rifles fired some 50 rounds. Suddenly "a shell struck the wheel of Sergeant Bang's piece," ricocheted, and "struck Byron Phillips, tearing away part of his chin and shoulder."[9]

Confederate gunners utilized every weapon in their arsenals to silence the Union artillery. Striking and breaking the axle of No. 1 gun, a shell[10] hurled wood splinters that wounded some gunners.

The concussion of the shell's explosion permanently deafened Ambrose Vittum in one ear.

A case shot hurled a round steel ball into a boot worn by Hannibal Powers of No. 1 gun. Feeling the ball lodged in his sock, Powers assumed he was wounded; he had started for the rear when someone suggested that he remove the damaged boot "and see how bad the wound was," Ames noted.

"When the boot was pulled off the bullet rolled out and Powers resumed his duties," he said.

Robinson lost other men as the dueling continued. From their elevated perches on Cedar Mountain, "the enemy's batteries ... were nearly concealed [and] they had much the advantage of us," realized Ames. With No. 1 gun out of the fight and No. 2 short on men, Robinson transferred Haynes and his section to the left of Eaton's section around 5 p.m. Haynes joined the No. 2 gun crew as they shelled Confederate artillery hidden by foliage and smoke.[11]

About 5 p.m., Alpheus Williams ordered Samuel Crawford to advance his 1st Brigade west through "a thick belt of woods [that] skirted an open wheat stubble field on three sides; a road [the Culpeper Road] running across formed the fourth." Deploying five companies of the 3rd Wisconsin Infantry as skirmishers. Crawford formed a line of battle with the 46th Pennsylvania on the right, the 28th New York in the center, and the 5th Connecticut on the left, nearest the Culpeper Road.

Reining in among the trees on the eastern edge of the field, Crawford surveyed the terrain on which his regiments would fight. "In front of the line the field sloped downward toward the woods directly opposite, the point of which terminated at the road," he noticed.[12]

Confederate artillery focused on Muhlenberg's four twelve-pounder Napoleons[13] as Union batteries—including three from Maine—fired steadily from "the knoll where we had been all morning," said 2nd Lt. John Mead Gould. Infantrymen battled nearby; the incessant shooting "was so terrible that we did not notice the cannonading much."

With the time approaching 6 p.m.—Gould remembered "the sun ... nearing the tree tops"—the advancing 1st Brigade collided with three Confederate brigades, and amidst "the report of the most tremendous volleys we had ever heard" resounded "the hurrah of the boys of our brigade," he said.[14]

Crawford estimated that his three regiments and the 3rd Wisconsin must cross "a space of nearly 300 yards ... to reach the opposite woods" now invested by Confederate infantrymen supported by an artillery battery near the Culpeper Road. Crawford asked Alpheus Williams to send two Battery F cannons to support the 1st Brigade's attack; the messenger passed a staff officer sent by Williams to order Crawford to charge the Confederates immediately.

His men went forward with bayonets fixed and glimmering in the sunlight. Clambering over or through a fence bordering the trees, the approximately 1,600 Union soldiers gave "one loud cheer" (the hurrah heard by Gould) and "charged across the open space in the face of a fatal and murderous fire" from enemy "concealed in the bushes and woods on our front and flank," Crawford recalled.

Running between hay shocks scattered across the wheat field, the 5th Connecticut, 28th New York, and 46th Pennsylvania plowed into the Confederate-held woods "and engaged in a hand-to-hand fight with vastly superior numbers of the enemy," according to Crawford. More Confederates came up as Jackson fed in late-arriving brigades; "my gallant men, broken, decimated by that fearful fire," came back across the wheat field, now strewn with Union bodies.

"The slaughter was fearful," especially among the field officers, he admitted.[15]

Reenactors of Battery F, 1st Pennsylvania Artillery prepare to fire a cannon at Gettysburg
Photo by Brian F. Swartz

"While all this wonderful fighting was going on[,] we were lying idle on the northern edge[16] of the woods" while supporting Edward Muhlenberg's battery, Gould noted.

Beal sent him to scout the situation out in front. Reaching the eastern edge of the wheat field, Gould spotted the Ohioans of Brig. Gen. John Geary's brigade of Augur's 2nd Division moving west along the Culpeper Road, south of Crawford's regiments.[17]

Running back through the woods, Gould ran into the approaching 10th Maine. Beal had spread his approximately 450 men into line of battle, beginning on the left flank (nearest the Culpeper Road) with Co. F and proceeding to the right (north) with A, E, D, C, I, G. K, and B. The line ended on the right flank with Co. H, its men identifiable by the white cloth of their slung blankets.[18]

As the 10th Maine lads emerged into the wheat field, "we could see and hear a large force" across the way, Harrison Tripp observed. Astride his horse, Beal led his regiment past the wheat shocks as "the [rifle] balls were flying in all directions," Tripp noticed.[19]

Gould recalled that the regiment "passed down the hill, then up and then down again, for the wheat field has a ridge in it running at right angles to the road." Rushing from the enemy-held tree line, 1st Brigade survivors slipped to the north to escape around the right flank of the advancing 10th Maine boys, who quickly figured out "that we were the only [Union] regiment left in the vicinity," Gould said.

Rising in his stirrups, Beal waved his doffed hat and shouted, "Give them three Down East cheers!"

The tree lines echoed the resulting hurrahs, but effusive shouts could not carry the day. Beal saw Confederates—hundreds, maybe thousands—milling in the woods that drew closer with every step his 10th Maine lads took. Halting the line of battle, he turned his companies around and started them toward the tree line along the field's eastern edge.

Up rode Maj. Louis H. Pelouse with orders from Nathaniel Banks for Beal to stop the retrograde movement. Beal refused, then engaged the "furious" Pelouse in such a verbal and hand-animated quarrel that the officers "appeared to be having a fist-fight," Gould watched the altercation.

Pelouse-cum-Banks ordered Beal to halt the 10th Maine in full view of Confederate artillery and infantry. Stopped "on the northern slope of the ridge," the Maine boys turned around; "the officers dressed their companies so as to gain the slight protection" the ridge provided, Gould noticed.[20]

Many 10th Maine lads probably prayed "for which we are about to receive" as they gazed across the wheat field.

Some of them would only take a few more breaths.

~~~

1. Brig. Gen. Henry Prince, *Official Records, Series I, Vol. XVI,* Chapter XXIV, No. 19, p. 167
2. Judson Ames, *History of the Fourth Maine Battery Light Artillery in the Civil War 1861-1865,* Burleigh & Flynt, Augusta, 1905, p. 18
3. Some soldiers, including John Mead Gould of the 10th Maine, knew the Culpeper Road as the "Orange road." For consistency, the author refers to the Culpeper Road. Modern Route 15 bypasses that section of the

1st Pennsylvania Artillery reenactors fire a 10-inch Parrott rifle at Gettysburg
Photo by Brian F. Swartz

Culpeper Road lying south of where the 10th Maine fought at Cedar Mountain. The Civil War Trust has erected a period fence along a portion of the 1862 road.
4. Harrison Tripp, "From the 10th Maine Regiment," *Ellsworth American,* Friday, August 29, 1862
5. Harrison A. Tripp, *Soldiers' File,* Maine State Archives
6. Although habitually moved as far away from deployed cannons as possible, harnessed horses provided a large and valuable target for enemy gunners.
7. Soon hospitalized in Washington, D.C., Sally completed his three-year enlistment with the Invalid Corps.
8. Haynes was a minister from Augusta. He and Robinson's three other lieutenants—Matthew Coffin and Charles White of Skowhegan and Hamlin Eaton of Readfiel—received their commissions after helping Robinson recruit men for the 4th Maine Battery.
9. Comrades carried the mortally wounded Phillips to the rear, "where he died about two hours later and was buried" in the Hudson family's garden, Ames observed.
10. Ames' testimony indicates this was a shell, not a solid shot.
11. Ames, *Fourth Maine,* pp. 18-19
12. Brig. Gen. Samuel W. Crawford, *Official Records, No. 8, Series I, Vol. XVI,* Chapter XXIV, pp. 150-151
13. At one point Gould identified Battery F as "Best's battery," but Capt. Clermont L. Best commended the II Corps artillery at Cedar Mountain.
14. Maj. John M. Gould, *History of the First-Tenth-Twenty-Ninth Maine Regiment,* Stephen Berry, Portland, ME 1871, pp. 171-172
15. Crawford, *OR, No. 8, Series I, Vol. XVI,* Chapter XXIV, p. 151
16. Gould's directional compass was slightly off; the 10th Maine was actually on the eastern edge of the woods.
17. Consisting of four Ohio infantry regiments, Geary's brigade formed the right flank of Augur's division. Its other brigades advanced west through a corn field stretching between the Culpeper Road to the north and the Mitchell Station Road to the east.
18. Gould, *History,* pp. 172-173, 180
19. Tripp, *Ellsworth American,* Friday, August 29, 1862
20. Gould, *History,* pp. 173-174

Chapter 42

MEN STOOD LIKE STATUES

"I raise my piece, take hurried aim, and fire"

John Mead Gould remembered forever those last relatively quiet seconds before the 10th Maine Infantry Regiment unleashed a leaden hell.

The Maine boys had "waited a moment more" as their retreating 1st Brigade comrades withdrew across the wheat field, now filling with Confederate infantrymen along its western verge, Gould said. The setting sun hovered just above the distant trees, "and the smoke had settled like a thin mist over the ... field."[1]

Sharpshooters pushing east into the wheat-shocked field targeted the officers and non-coms leading the opposing Union regiments. Soldiers had practiced similar tactics in North American wars since the mid-18th century; by picking off the opposing officers and sergeants, soldiers left enemy infantry leaderless and less effective on the battlefield.

Capt. Andrew Cloudman of Co. E and Portland sported a Hardee hat, "a splendid hat" decked out "with bugle, eagle and cord and ostrich feathers," noticed Gould, himself preferring a less ornate chapeau. The hat made Cloudman "a perfect target"; he caught a Confederate bullet above one ear and fell dead amidst his astonished men.

Wearing "a splendid hat" led to 1st Lt. Herbert Sargent of Co. E being "wounded in the face," and 2nd Lt. Abel Rankin of Co. F "wore a hat and was wounded," Gould said.[2]

On the left flank, Sgt. Charles Marston of Co. F and Lewiston "was among the first" to fall, said Gould, remembering the foreign-born Marston as a former "English marine and a model of all that was correct in soldierly deportment."

To the northwest, a Confederate emerging from "those dark and smoky woods" across the field waved a flag, whether a regimental or national banner Gould could not confirm as he squinted into "the bright sunset dazzling our eyes." He saw flames spouting from enemy muskets firing along the deeply shadowed tree line.

Individual Mainers started shooting. Still in the saddle, Col. George Beal checked his ten companies for proper alignment.

"Fire!" he shouted.

"We who were in the line can never forget the tremendous crash and echo it made," Gould said. "This first volley had a marked effect on the enemy."[3]

Their ranks thinning, Confederates from the 42nd and 48th Virginia infantry regiments pushed forward into the wheat field. Other enemy troops appeared to the northwest, amidst scrub brush covering the field's upper section. Their position let them fire into the 10th Maine's right flank.

Made conspicuous by the white of their out-turned blankets, the men of Capt. Charles Emerson's Co. H attracted nasty attention. Emerson emerged unscathed; bullets killed 1st Lt. James C. Folsom and mortally wounded 2nd Lt. Albert W. Freeman. Emerson lost four privates killed and another mortally wounded. Nineteen other Co. H enlisted men were wounded.

The bullets whizzing from right to left through the ranks left men realizing "we are flanked," said Pvt. Harrison A. Tripp of Co. F, commanded by Capt. William Knowlton of Lewiston. Tripp knelt in the company's front line; behind him stood Sgt. Reuben Pratt of Mercer, a man "as dark as an Indian, with his black hair sticking through a dozen holes in his hat."[4]

Union "Hardee hat"
This Hardee hat at the Gettysburg National Military Park museum, is pinned up on the right, inconsistent with regulations.
Photo by Hal Jesperson via Wikipedia

Enemy bullets buzzed fast and effectively. "Our line began to wilt in a way none of us ever knew before or since," Gould recalled years afterwards.

Maine soldiers adopted individualized shooting stances; "the sight was ludicrous in the extreme," Gould noticed. Many soldiers instinctively made themselves smaller targets by kneeling or lying on the ground; other men stood and fired.[5]

"The bravery of the men is astonishing, perfectly astonishing," Gould watched the 10th Maine boys fight. Men stood "like so many statues," while others lay prone. Most men knelt, and a few stood and went "through the movements of load and fire almost as regular as on drill."[6]

Maine soldiers burned through their ammunition. By his count, Tripp fired 23 times. His baptism to combat did not frighten him; he "felt no more concern after I had fired twice, than if I had only been out snow-balling," Tripp informed his parents. "If I did not put some of the foes to our dear old flag out of the line of fighting, for a couple of months at least, then it is because I can't shoot straight."[7]

Walking past the color guard, Gould "noticed nearly all the corporals were gone." Lying down by a stump, he tucked his head against it as "the bullets flew more thickly than at any other time."

Gould watched incoming bullets "hitting the ground and throwing up dust in every direction. They passed by almost in sheets, just as rain comes down in the heaviest part of a thunderstorm." A bullet "passed directly under my neck and spattered the bosom of my blouse full of dust."

The startled Gould rose; a hard object slapped his left temple. "I could see nothing but stars" as he lay "half senseless some five minutes," he remembered. Examining his body with both hands, "I could not find any hole and no blood and concluded that I wasn't dead yet."[8]

Soldiers chided and cursed their enemies as bullets struck home all along the regimental line. "The enemy were armed with almost every kind of rifle or musket," and because the lines of the opposing Confederate brigades "exceeded ours three times" in length, "we were under a cross fire almost from the first," Gould said.

With "huge gaps" appearing in the 10th Maine Infantry's double lines, "every man, with hardly an exception, was either killed, wounded, hit in his clothes, hit by spent bullets and stones,[9] or jostled by his wounded comrades," he realized.

Bullet-struck soldiers "threw up their arms and fell over backward," and "some reeled around and around," Gould described the bodies being tossed aside by the bloody elephant tromping through the regiment's ranks. A few soldiers fell face forward, "and a very few fell dead."

Other soldiers assisted wounded comrades to the rear, "and a few managed to skulk off," Gould said, referring to men who disappeared when the shooting started.[10]

More Confederate regiments shoved eastward across the wheat field. Union reinforcements came up, the 2nd Massachusetts Infantry assuming a position "a little to our rear and perhaps 300 yards to our right" flank and elements of the 3rd Wisconsin Infantry fighting beyond the Bay Staters, "out of view of our right," Gould said.[11]

Tripp fought untouched on the firing line. Men fell around him; "poor John Gordon, on my right [in the front line], is shot through the face from the right flank and falls by my knee," he said.[12]

Reuben Pratt was there, but "at last I do not see him," Tripp realized. "I look to the right; there is no company, no regiment. I turn my head to the right rear, and nearly in the edge of the woods I see the regiment, with the colors, in retreat!"

Pvt. Harrison Tripp, Co. F, 10th Maine
Photo courtesy of Nicholas P. Picerno

Confederate pressure had driven back the Union regiments north of the 10th Maine's position. A 46th Pennsylvania Infantry survivor fighting on the regiment's right flank brought a warning to Beal, "The rebels are on your right, sir."

Confirming the sergeant's message, Beal yelled, "Retreat!" Tripp did not hear him.[13]

Clustering around the shrunken color guard, the 10th Maine lads pulled back disjointedly as the national and regimental flags were carried rearward into the woods. Some men lingered behind to rescue wounded comrades.

Watching the 10th Maine seemingly melt away—"there was no skedaddle," Gould stressed—triumphant Confederates charged across the field.[14]

Realizing he was almost alone on the abandoned firing line, Tripp turned "my head to the front" to "find that the rebels have climbed the fence [along the field's western edge] and are advancing into the field, singly and in groups, but I see no colors."

Just 25 yards away approached "a tall, lank, red-whiskered man, with his gun at a trail," Tripp saw the closest threat. "I raise my piece, take hurried aim, and fire, and he falls headlong, and I *run*!"

Making "a bee-line for the woods in my rear," Tripp passed a few Maine soldiers hiding behind wheat shocks. He entered the woods, got "behind the first tree I come to," and looked

The Battle of Cedar Mountain. August 9, 1862
Crawford's Charge is on the right.
Illustration by Currier & Ives via Library of Congress

Chapter 42: Men Stood Like Statues

The Battle of Cedar Mountain. August 9, 1862
Illustration by Currier & Ives via Library of Congress

around. Reloading his rifled musket, Tripp looked across the field, covered with approaching enemy troops. He looked south to the Culpeper Road, where 1st Lt. Joseph Knap still commanded the men and ten-pound Parrott rifles of Pennsylvania Independent Battery E.

On the southern horizon rose Cedar Mountain, its lower wooded slopes covered by gun smoke from enemy artillery. Between the mountain and the Culpeper Road stretched the corn field through which Confederate and Union infantrymen had battled the past few hours; enemy infantry was driving back those Federal regiments, and Knap's guns faced capture.

Union cavalry suddenly charged to cover Knap's withdrawal. Confederate infantrymen hesitated in the wheat field; some 10th Maine lads escaped during the delay.

"Look at that small band of heroes as they form for the charge," said Tripp, witnessing a deliberate sacrifice of four companies and 164 men of the 1st Pennsylvania Cavalry, led on this suicidal assault by Maj. Richard J. Falls. Told to attack without infantry support, Falls ordered "the fence in the edge of the woods [on the eastern side of the wheat field] … thrown down," according to Tripp.

Drawing their sabers, the Pennsylvanians walked their horses into the wheat field. Now regrouped, Confederate infantry advanced again toward the watching Tripp. He saw (or perhaps heard) Falls give the order to attack; his men kicking their horses directly into the charge, "with a rush like the swoop of the eagle they dash for the enemy."

Confederate cohesion briefly broke as, yelling at the top of their lungs and cutting, slashing, and thrusting with their sabers, Falls and his men rode through three lines of Confederate infantrymen. As the Pennsylvanians approached the fence on the wheat field's boundary, heavy gunfire tore apart the tree line. Horses and riders went down, Pennsylvanians reeled in the saddle, and survivors raced for shelter in the woods from which they had emerged short minutes earlier.

Tripp then decided to find the 10th Maine, vanished somewhere to the east.[15]

Passing through the woods, the sweat-soaked and filthy Gould crossed a large field. At Cedar Run "I took off my blouse and trappings, pulled [my] shirt off over my head and such a refreshing bath I never had in my life."

Gould finally caught up with his regiment, but 10th Maine flotsam and jetsam still floated about the battlefield. Men rejoined their companies, and Beal asked for a head count. "We went into action with 461 men, lost 170 killed, wounded and missing," all lost in the half hour or so the regiment had fought, Gould figured.[16]

Harrison Tripp believed the 10th Maine Infantry had taken 483 men into battle; on Saturday night, "all that we can find now is about 180," and of the 43 Co. F lads who marched into the wheat field, only 19 men came off it.[17]

Where his 4th Maine Battery gunners worked their ordnance rifles alongside the Hudson House, Capt. O'Neil Robinson learned toward dusk—shortly after the 10th Maine started fighting in the wheat field to the northwest—that Confederate infantry had ejected Union infantry from the corn field faced by his guns.

"A volley from the corn field, not many yards in front of us, passed just over our heads," said the lanky, blue-eyed Corp. Judson Ames. Orders came to withdraw; gunners brought up an intact horse to replace a wounded animal in its harness, and the horse team pulled away its caisson.

Confederate infantrymen suddenly erupted from the corn field and charged the Union artillery. Just beyond the Hudson House, Capt. Freeman McGilvery and his 6th Maine Battery "stoutly resisted the charge made on them" and "held their ground until all others had time to get by," Ames said.

Swept into the mad race for survival, Robinson and his gunners escaped capture. Thumping across Cedar Run and through woods, the Mainers encountered lead elements of the reinforcing III Corps of Maj. Gen. Irvin McDowell, moving up to stop the Confederate advance.

"As we passed through their line a sense of security at once prevailed and the mad rush ceased," Ames breathed.[18]

Remaining on the battlefield until well after sunset, Brig. Gen. Samuel Crawford collected his 1st Brigade near Colvin's Tavern, a landmark noted by men marching to battle the previous

Chapter 42: Men Stood Like Statues

Union reenactors demonstrate the two-line firing line at Perryville, Kentucky
This is the firing line that infantry regiments typically adopted on the battlefield.
Photo by Brian F. Swartz

day. Weary 10th Maine soldiers thumped like laden grain sacks onto the ground and fell asleep.

In their first battle, George Beal and the men of the 10th Maine Infantry had "engaged the enemy with great vigor," noted Brig. Gen. Alpheus Williams, commanding the 1st Division to which the regiment and Crawford's 1st Brigade were attached.

"Though suffering less in loss of officers than regiments farther to the right, its list of killed and wounded abundantly testifies to the persistent gallantry with which it fought," Williams wrote.[19]

The 4th Maine Battery suffered eight casualties: one man killed, six wounded, and one missing. Positioned south of the Hudson House, the 6th Maine Battery of Freeman McGilvery had lost 18 men: four dead, nine wounded, and five missing.

After arresting and releasing O'Neil Robinson prior to the battle, Brig. Gen. Henry Prince vented his irritation with his 6-foot artillery captain in print. Not writing his official report until Nov. 10, Prince acknowledged that the 4th Maine Battery "was in action four hours and a quarter, gallantly and efficiently served."

He mentioned Robinson only once by name—and lavished much more praise on his three aides-de-camp.[20]

~~~

1. Maj. John M. Gould, *History of the First-Tenth-Twenty-Ninth Maine Regiment,* Stephen Berry, Portland, ME 1871, p. 174
2. William B. Jordan, *The Civil War Journals of John Mead Gould 1861-1866,* Butternut & Blue, Baltimore, 1997, p. 168
3. Gould, *History,* pp. 174-175
4. H.A. Tripp, "Cedar Mountain," *National Tribune,* Thursday, May 6, 1886, p. 1
5. Gould, *History,* p. 175
6. Jordan, *Journals,* p. 170
7. Harrison Tripp, "From the 10th Maine Regiment," *Ellsworth American,* Friday, August 9, 1862
8. Jordan, *Journals,* pp. 172-173
9. This term may have referred to buckshot.
10. "Skulkers" existed in many regiments. Sometimes a skulker fled danger by helping remove a wounded soldier from the battlefield.
11. Gould, *History,* pp. 175-177
12. From Mt. Vernon in Kennebec County, Gordon survived the battle. So did Reuben Pratt.
13. Tripp, *National Tribune,* May 6, 1886, p. 1
14. Gould, *History,* p. 178
15. Tripp, *National Tribune,* May 6, 1886, p. 1. Italics in earlier passage in the original.
16. Jordan, *Journals,* p. 173
17. Tripp, *Ellsworth American,* Friday, August 29, 1862
18. Judson Ames, *History of the Fourth Maine Battery Light Artillery in the Civil War 1861-1865,* Burleigh & Flynt, Augusta, 1905, pp. 20-21
19. Brig. Gen. Alpheus S. Williams, *Official Records, Series I, Vol. XVI,* Chapter XXIV, No. 9, p. 147
20. Brig. Gen. Henry Prince, *OR, Series I, Vol. XVI,* Chapter XXIV, No. 19, pp. 169-170

Chapter 43

PRELUDE TO SLAUGHTER

"We had a boogerish time"

Sometime during the morning of Saturday, September 13, an awe-struck 1st Lt. John Mead Gould stood examining the western horizon after he emerged from woods south of Frederick in central Maryland.

He saw a future battlefield.

For the past two days the 10th Maine Infantry Regiment had marched northwest from Rockville as George B. McClellan and his Army of the Potomac pursued Robert E. Lee and the Army of Northern Virginia. At Manassas in late August, Lee and his lean warriors had shellacked Maj. Gen. John Pope and his (Union) Army of Virginia.

Despite heavy Confederate losses, Lee swung his army to the northwest to invade Maryland. He hoped to capture Harrisburg in Pennsylvania and perhaps attack Baltimore or Philadelphia. After crossing the Potomac upriver from Leesburg, Virginia in early September, his men occupied Frederick on September 10.

The invasion stunned Northern leaders. Quickly sacking Pope, President Abraham Lincoln named McClellan commander of all Union troops in Maryland and Virginia. Ever a slow mover, McClellan gradually disentangled his Army corps from their camps around Washington, D.C. and sent his men marching by various Maryland roads to find the will-o'-the-wisp Confederates.

Leaving their camp near Fort Ward in Alexandria, Virginia on Thursday, September 4, the 10th Maine boys crossed the Potomac River and spent that night north of Tennallytown (modern Tenleytown). The stark contrast between secessionist Virginia and loyal Maryland astounded Gould and his comrades.

"We made a few halts" while marching through Tennallytown, Gould said. "The women and young ladies opened their doors and windows to give" the soldiers "bread and butter, meat, apples, peaches, and preserves.

"I tell you it was cheering to see their [Maryland women's] pleasant faces after having been so long in the Virginia wilderness where women have spoiled their faces by looking sour," said Gould, a fan of the fair sex.

Maryland's "green fields, painted fences and luxuriant crops" surprised Maine soldiers accustomed to Virginia, a "vast fenceless wilderness which grows little but weeds," Gould commented on September 4. As the 10th Maine boys marched through farm fields to reach the Rockville Turnpike on Friday, he relished the verdant prosperity; "the character of the country is so different that it is very pleasant to ride along even at the slow rate we go," he said.[1]

Assigned to II Corps, Army of Virginia, the 10th Maine spent four days at Rockville before moving gradually toward Urbana.

Reflecting McClellan's glacial mentality, the Army of the Potomac's divisions averaged six miles a day while probing toward Frederick.[2] McClellan moved faster administratively by melding the Army of Virginia into the Army of the Potomac, which already had a II Corps.

He redesignated the 10th Maine's parent command as the XII Corps on Friday, September 12. Within that corps's organization, the 10th Maine belonged to the 1st Brigade (Brig. Gen. Samuel Crawford) of the 1st Division (Brig. Gen. Alpheus Williams).

After a vicious little fight with rear-guard Confederates, Federal troops liberated Frederick on September 12.[3] Lee's army had already vanished beyond Catoctin Mountain, the north-to-south ridge separating Frederick from Middletown to the west.

A bugler sounded reveille in the 10th Maine camp at 3:30 a.m. on Saturday. Marching at 7 a.m., the Maine boys soon passed the Baltimore & Ohio Railroad station at Ijamsville and headed west.[4]

Meanwhile, McClellan encountered a rapturous reception from Union sympathizers as he rode into Frederick about 9 a.m. Civilians swarmed their perceived savior;[5] Union troops pushed west along the National Pike (modern Alternate Route 40) and crested Catoctin Mountain.

Below the soldiers spread Middletown Valley, named for its largest town. Some ten to twelve miles west rose high and rugged South Mountain, running from the Potomac River north to Pennsylvania as the Maryland extension of the Virginia Blue Ridge. South Mountain naturally obstructed Union soldiers headed for Confederate-held Hagerstown and Union-held Harpers Ferry, then under siege.

Later that morning Gould reached open ground downriver from Frederick. Trees no longer blocked the horizon; as he enjoyed "a splendid view" of "the long chain of mountains forming the right bank of the Monocacy" River near Frederick, he suddenly heard the sounds of war.[6]

Confederate troops—artillery, cavalry, and infantry—had deployed along the undulating spine of South Mountain to block the National Road at Turner's Gap to the north, the Old Sharpsburg Road a mile south at Fox's Gap, and a country road at southerly Crampton's Gap near Burkittsville.[7]

Federal troops had already encountered the enemy when Gould caught up with the action. "In two of the gaps [Fox's and Turner's] cannonading was going on, not very sharp but evidentially a hard place to dislodge artillery," he said.

"The rebels are understood to be in retreat and this is to delay our advance on them," he explained the distant slam-banging.[8]

Chapter 43: Prelude to Slaughter

On Sunday, September 14, thousands of Union soldiers attacked the Confederates defending the South Mountain passes. The 1st Brigade and 10th Maine Infantry marched through Frederick, where "the morning bells of the churches rang out clearly, reminding us of home, peace, and Christianity," said Gould.

Throughout Frederick "the American flag swung from the roofs and windows, and every one, from the old women down to the babies, joined in giving us a welcome," he said. "The ladies gave us water in glasses, and that was delicious."[9]

The 10th Maine boys "took a very crooked course to get out of town" as fighting raged along the slopes leading to Turner's and Fox's gaps, Gould said. "Firing was heard all day," and as the 10th Maine lads crested Catoctin Mountain, "the discharges of artillery [on South Mountain] could be easily seen."

Union Maj. Gen. Jesse Lee Reno
Photo from the Civil War Photograph Collection, Library of Congress

The regiment dropped into Middletown Valley and, for the rest of Sunday, marched "first up and then down and round and round and back again," Gould said.[10]

The fighting at Turner's and Fox's gaps continued through the afternoon and into the evening. The 10th Maine "were two or three miles away" when Union soldiers from IX Corps (commanded by Maj. Gen. Jesse Reno) made their "final charge" against Southern defenders at Fox's Gap, according to Gould.

"We saw the smoke and heard the sound of the muskets; we could also hear the shells burst; but besides marching, swearing and halting often in sight of the battle, we took no part," he admitted.

Near dusk a 35th Massachusetts Infantry lad mistook Reno and his staff for Confederate cavalry and fired a bullet that toppled Reno from his saddle. Mortally wounded, he died as stretcher bearers carried him down South Mountain; riding white horses—the monotone color remained embedded in Gould's memory—some troopers from Co. G, 1st Maine Cavalry escorted the sad procession past the watching soldiers of the 10th Maine Infantry.[11]

"Who is that wounded?" Gould asked.

"It is General Reno. He is dead," replied a soldier, possibly a Maine cavalryman.

"My heart went down like a piece of lead," Gould recalled later. During "the last week" the 10th Maine boys had repeatedly heard the names of Ambrose Burnside and Jesse Reno, "two stars just rising into glory," Gould explained.

The 10th Maine kept moving. That night "we had a boogerish time poking through

The Battle of South Mountain, Maryland, September 14, 1862
Illustration via Library of Congress

cornfields and ploughed lots" until the Maine boys discovered a road, Gould said.

Union troops captured the three passes on September 14 at a total cost of 4,500 Union and Confederate casulaties. The 10th Maine camped near the National Pike; awakening Monday, Gould and his comrades "had a long talk" with some 50 captured Confederates under guard nearby.

With his regiment not marching until noon, Gould ventured into Fox's Gap. Passing ambulances and stretcher bearers "bringing off the dead and wounded," he noticed the wounded men filling the roadside houses and "adjoining yards," in which many men sheltered beneath the shade trees.

Along the Old Sharpsburg Road, Gould saw details from the 45th Pennsylvania Infantry burying dead Union soldiers. Wrapped in blankets, the fully clothed corpses attested to the Federal victory; had the Confederates won the battle, they would likely have stripped the dead Yankees of clothing and shoes.[12]

"Each corpse had a grave to itself, and a head board made of a cracker box," Gould noted.[13]

But "still further up was the principal battle ground[,] and from my birth I never saw such a sight," the appalled Gould admitted. Confederate troops had fought behind the cover afforded by several stone walls and rail fences; "I must have seen more than a hundred" unburied dead Confederates, said Gould, not realizing that the horror he encountered this Monday was a prelude to the slaughter he would witness outside Sharpsburg on Wednesday.

"They were lying there, a mass of grey flesh, loose dust, blood, blankets, grey cloth rags, guns and equipment," Gould described the carnage. Only recently promoted to first lieutenant, he noticed a similarly ranked Confederate officer, "a fellow of splendid build and good uniform," who lay with "his face ... in the dirt, his clothes almost hid by clots of blood and dirt."

Gould saw "old men and boys," including a particular "little fellow scarcely 14 years old. His face showed him to be one of those sprightly little rogues which are into every scrape that is up ... but for the blood you would have thought him in sound and peaceful sleep."

Gould discovered one head-shot Confederate left "nearly in a standing position" by the thick brush that caught him as a bullet hurled him backwards. "There he was, with his hands thrown to the front, apparently shrinking from something he feared, and with his staring eyes and bloody face, made the most horrible and frightful sight I ever witnessed."[14]

Walking amidst the carnage at Fox's Gap, Gould noticed that "all the dead [Confederate soldiers] had been robbed of their valuables, their pockets were turned, and the accoutrements were thrown about and haversacks emptied."

He had heard the ghoulish tales about dead Union soldiers being stripped naked by Confederates. While the enemy dead were left clothed at Fox's Gap, Gould expressed his disgust that blue-clad vultures had searched their slain enemies for money, watches, and other valuables.

"Don't let us accuse rebels alone of robbing the dead," he said.[15]

In death, the Confederates attested to the hunger they had experienced while invading Maryland. The slain Confederate soldiers "are mere skeletons and have an ashy hue against

Union Maj. Gen. Joseph King Fenno Mansfield
Photo by Mathew Brady via Wikipedia

which the dust that here is ash colored hardly shows," Gould noticed.

The accumulated gore revolted him; finally "I had seen enough ... and came off as quick as my legs could carry me," he admitted.

Though a Union officer, Gould could not rejoice at the deaths of so many enemies. "The waste of life, [of] human beings was so new, so awful, so revolting that I lost all heart for rejoicing and all hate for my foes," he said.

On that warm Monday, Brig. Gen. Joseph K.F. Mansfield took command of XII Corps. Gould and the 10th Maine marched west along the National Pike in early afternoon, crossed Turner's Gap, and descended its western slope to enter Boonsboro, "quite a thriving village and not small."

There "we took a road to the left" and marched a short distance toward Sharpsburg, he recalled.

While camping that "warm night," Gould "had a glorious rest ... in our tent with warm atmosphere, plenty of clothes and protection from the dew."[16]

He would not sleep well for some nights to come.

~~~

1. William B. Jordan, *The Civil War Journals of John Mead Gould 1861-1866*, Butternut & Blue, Baltimore, 1997, pp. 186-187
2. Ronald H. Bailey and the editors of Time-Life Books, *The Civil War: The Bloodiest Day: The Battle of Antietam*, from the series *The Civil War* by Time-Life Books, Alexandria, Va. 1984, p. 23
3. Bailey, *The Bloodiest Day*, pp. 26-27
4. Jordan, *Journals*, p. 190
5. Bailey, *The Bloodiest Day*, pp. 27-29
6. Jordan, *Journals*, p. 190
7. Bailey, *The Bloodiest Day*, p. 44
8. Jordan, *Journals*, p. 190
9. Maj. John M. Gould, *History of the First-Tenth-Twenty-Ninth Maine Regiment*, Stephen Berry, Portland, Maine 1871, p, 225
10. Jordan, *Journals*, p. 191
11. Gould, *History*, p. 226
12. Jordan, *Journals*, pp. 191-192
13. Gould, *History*, p. 227
14. Jordan, *Journals*, pp. 191-192
15. Gould, *History*, p. 227
16. Jordan, *Journals*, pp. 190-193

Chapter 44

ENCOUNTER IN THE EAST WOODS

"Almost as good a target as a barn"

As drummers beat the long roll in the 10th Maine camp about 8 a.m. on Tuesday, September 16, John Mead Gould and his tent mates collapsed, folded, and packed their mobile home on the designated regimental wagon.

Maj. Gen. Joseph King Fenno Mansfield, the new commander of XII Corps, wanted his men to march, so march they did on this "hottest day for a month"—and for all of a mile on the road from Boonsboro to Sharpsburg in central Maryland, Gould acerbically commented.

Then the 10th Maine boys halted "in a valley beyond which a very sharp cannonading was going on," he recalled. An intervening hill caught most incoming Confederate shells; "three or four solid shot came whistling over" to explode beyond the relaxing Mainers, Gould noticed.

Throughout that hot Tuesday, Union troops converged on Sharpsburg, a small town nestled among the hills between meandering Antietam Creek and the Potomac River. South of the creek, Robert E. Lee had drawn up his Army of Northern Virginia to fight the Union boys trying to evict him from Maryland.

Against Lee came George B. McClellan and the Army of the Potomac. Commanded by Col. George L. Beal of Norway, the 10th Maine had crossed Turner's Gap on South Mountain on Monday (hours after Mansfield took command of XII Corps) and camped south of Boonsboro that night.

Like moths drawn to a late-summer flame, Confederate and Union forces converged on Sharpsburg on Tuesday. His Northern invasion blocked by McClellan's September 14 victory at South Mountain, Lee should have withdrawn his smaller army across the Potomac at the Sharpsburg fords.

Instead he decided to fight. Under pressure from President Abraham Lincoln to damage or destroy Lee's army, McClellan devised a multi-corps assault scheduled to start about dawn on Wednesday, September 17.

After resting for an hour or so on Tuesday, September 16, the 10th Maine lads "advanced a few yards" and "remained here all day" while listening to cannoneers and pickets exchange fire into the evening. "Then we pitched our tents" and settled in for a night's sleep, Gould said.

Shortly after 10:30 p.m. he awakened to discover XII Corps assembling for war. In McClellanite genius, the Union's I Corps under Maj. Gen. Joseph Hooker would strike Lee's left flank north of Sharpsburg early on Wednesday. Twelfth Corps would support Hooker's attack; to do so, Mansfield would have to march his 7,200 men through the darkness to form up near I Corps.

Tramping along the Sharpsburg road (modern Route 34), the 10th Maine went through Keedysville, turned west, "and marched in all about 4 miles, but where we went from and where we went to[,] I haven't the least idea and can not find out," Gould admitted.

John Mead Gould
Photo courtesy of Nicholas P. Picerno

"That we went round Robin Hood's barn I can swear to," he groused.[1]

Twelfth Corps "took up position about 1½ miles in rear of General Hooker's corps" about 2 a.m. on Wednesday, recalled Brig. Gen. Alpheus Williams, the 1st Division commander. Reporting to him were the 1st Brigade (to which the 10th Maine was attached) under Brig. Gen. Samuel Crawford and the 3rd Brigade, commanded by Brig. Gen. George H. Gordon. Mansfield's XII Corps also included the three-brigade 2nd Division of Brig. Gen. George S. Greene.

A 40-year Army veteran, the aging and white-haired Mansfield had lobbied for a combat command for months. He now commanded men—about half were raw recruits in new state regiments—from Connecticut, Indiana, Maine, Maryland, Massachusetts, New Jersey, New York, Ohio, Pennsylvania, and Wisconsin.

"The First District of Columbia Volunteers, nominally attached to this [3rd] brigade [2nd Division] has wholly disappeared from this command by desertion and sickness," commented Williams.[2]

About 2 a.m., Wednesday, the 10th Maine bivouacked on the farm of George Line, located a short distance east of the Smoketown Road. Mansfield slept on the west side of a farm fence, the Maine boys on the east side; late in the night, "some of our boys who indulged in loud talk were ordered by the General to lower their tones to a whisper," Gould recalled.[3]

Hooker and his I Corps rolled toward Confederate lines at 5:30 a.m. "In a few minutes the ball [was] opened by cannonading and musketry," Gould awoke to the not-so-distant din.

Mansfield ordered the 10th Maine boys to tear down the farm fence; then, "in advance of all the Corps,"[4] the 1st Brigade marched west across the Smoketown Road and almost reached the John Poffenberger farm. Turning left (south), the brigade crossed other farm fields and paused about 6:20 a.m. between the Joseph Poffenberger farm to the west and the nearer Samuel Poffenberger wood lot to the east.

Mansfield rode ahead to watch the furious fighting raging across David Miller's 30-acre cornfield and the East Woods abutting it.[5] Inconceivable slaughter was taking place across this terrain, which would change hands several times during the morning.

Meanwhile, the 1st Brigade's regiments went belly to earth. Lying down "under a small hill," the 10th Maine boys listened to the Confederate artillery shells passing overhead. Enemy gunners "fired few fuse shells, no cap shells, but quantities of bass [notes], probably railroad iron, which makes a very singular fluttering," Gould commented.

"There was a projectile which came along making a perfect whistle and without the least whir or harsh sound," he noted.[6]

The Maine boys watched "the flight of one great solid shot, that went jumping along 50 yards or more at a bound" and "plowing up cart loads of dirt" before "landing at last" in a cornfield behind the 1st Brigade, Gould said.[7]

At 7:20 a.m. (according to his watch, "which may have been five to ten minutes fast," Gould suspected), Mansfield started the 10th Maine south by east to cross the Smoketown Road. Tearing down its adjoining fences, the Maine boys marched onto a large field owned by Sam Poffenberger; the East Woods bordered the field to the south and west.

Suddenly Joseph Hooker rode from the woods and, upon learning that Col. George Beal commanded the 10th Maine, told him, "The enemy are breaking through my lines; you must hold these woods."[8]

To this point the 1st Brigade's regiments had advanced "closed in mass, that is ten ranks deep (of fifteen ranks counting the file closers)," Gould noted. From west to east (right to left), companies I and G formed the first two lines; behind in two-line increments came companies E and B, K and D, A and C, and H and F.

Gould "followed the regiment generally

Union Brig. Gen. George Henry Gordon
Photo courtesy of Nicholas P. Picerno

381

behind Company E."

Believing "that the men could be handled better in mass," Mansfield maneuvered all his regiments in similar large rectangular formations and "forbade our being deployed into one line," Gould said.

His men already under fire by Confederates crouching behind a fence bordering the East Woods, Beal turned his regiment to the right and started marching toward the trees, as directed by Hooker. The 10th Maine boys marched tightly grouped, and Gould felt the Confederates could hardly miss.

"We were almost as good a target as a barn," he wryly commented.

Some 50 to 100 Confederates crouched behind the East Woods fence and aimed while resting their rifles on the fence rails. Bullets whizzed past the marching Mainers; swallowing hard, Gould thought that "it is terrible to march slowly into danger, and see and feel that each second your chance for death is surer than it was the second before.

"The desire to break loose, to run, to fire, to do something, no matter what, rather than to walk, is almost irresistible," Gould voiced the fear probably gripping almost every Maine lad marching southwest at perhaps 7:45 a.m. that bloody Wednesday.

The closer the 10th Maine approached the fence, the more accurate the Confederates fired. "One man after another fell," Gould saw from his vantage point.[9]

Up front, Beal heard and saw his men grunt, scream, tumble, and spin. Minutes earlier Mansfield had denied Beal's request to deploy the 10th Maine into line to place more rifled muskets on the firing line and shrink the target offered the Confederate skirmishers.

Waiting until Mansfield rode away, Beal deployed his men into line at the double quick. Hustling through whizzing enemy bullets, the Maine boys responded as smoothly as if deploying on a parade ground. Gould admired how specific companies ran great distances to reach their assigned sections of the line; from west to east (right to left) it comprised companies H, A, K, E, I, G, B, D, C, and F.[10]

With Co. H nearest the Smoketown Road, the 10th Maine boys reached the East Woods fence and fired on Confederates hiding inside the woods. Beal apparently turned his horse at the fence; a bullet aimed at him struck the already wounded horse in the head instead.

In agony the horse reeled and tried to buck; Beal hurriedly dismounted—and went down himself, a bullet "passing through one [leg] and entering the other slightly." Beal was out of action.[11]

Nearby, Lt. Col. James S. Fillebrown of Lewiston dismounted from his horse. Blood flowing down its neck, Beal's mortally wounded horse ran up to Fillebrown, "turned about[,] and planted his hind legs [hooves] in Fillebrown's chest and stomach," Gould said.[12]

Fillebrown remembered that the 10th Maine boys had gone "into the woods some few rods" to duel with men from the 20th Georgia Infantry. He reported that Beal's "mortally wounded" horse collided with his mount, and "I was knocked from my horse.

"Returning," the wounded horse "gave me a severe kick in the stomach, entirely disabling me for three days," Fillebrown noted.[13]

The wounded Beal crawled a short distance to shelter beneath a large oak alongside the

Smoketown Road.[14] Regimental command devolved to Maj. Charles Walker of Portland. Sick for the past month, he had doggedly kept pace with the 10th Maine during its advance across Maryland.

By now many 10th Maine boys had climbed the fence or gone into the East Woods to shoot at the retreating Confederates. "We saw the men we were firing into, dodging from tree to tree, aiming at us, yelling, shaking their fists sometimes, and saucy generally," Gould said.[15]

He recalled that "the woods were like Deering's Oaks [sic] [in Portland], large trees, no underbrush." Despite the gun smoke swirling amidst the East Woods, the Maine boys had good sight distance; Gould "could see a rebel regiment marching by the flank toward our right" flank, where "a brave color sergeant" from the shattered 105th New York Infantry stood waving "his flag, a signal for his company to rally around him."

Union Lt. Col. James Sullivan Fillebrown
Photo courtesy of Nicholas P. Picerno

At least 30 comrades already clustered around the brave New Yorker, "and more were running out to him," Gould remembered that incredible sight.[16]

Dueling with Confederates hiding behind "numerous ledges, logs, trees, and piles of cord wood," the 10th Maine boys fought like frontiersmen, picking individual targets and working deeper into the East Woods as resistance slackened. "We had a bloody time of it," Gould admitted.

He saw other XII Corps regiments deploying through the woods on the 10th Maine's right flank. Mansfield, Crawford, "and other mounted officers" sat their horses "over on the Croasdale Knoll," a slight rise to the west, Gould noted.

Suddenly Mansfield raced his horse down the knoll and through the woods. "Cease firing! You are firing into our men!" he shouted while riding past the 10th Maine.

Riding "very rapidly and fearlessly," Mansfield reached a point where the regimental line bordered the fence, Gould recalled. Confused by Mansfield's command, which some 10th Maine officers had enforced, Union troops stopped firing.

Their enemies did not. On the 10th Maine's left flank, Capt. William P. Jordan and Sgt. Henry A. Burnham—both from Portland—stood at the fence (Jordan actually climbed atop a boulder to get Mansfield's attention) and "pointed out particular men of the enemy, who were not 50 yards away, that were then aiming their rifles at us."

"Look and see!" Jordan implored Mansfield.

"Yes, you are right," Mansfield replied. Leaving Jordan, he rode along the fence and attempted to pass through a section that was down. When the horse balked, Mansfield dismounted and led it into the Samuel Poffenberger field.

Confused while watching Mansfield gesticulate during his brief conversation with Burnham and Jordan, Gould hurried along the fence to learn what Mansfield wanted. "I met him at the gap in the fence," Gould said. "As he dismounted his coat blew open, and I saw that blood was streaming down the right side of his vest."

His horse safely across the fence, Mansfield attempted to remount; he could not. Gould found three 10th Maine boys—1st Sgt. Joseph Merrill of Readfield and Co. F, Pvt. Storer S. Knight of Portland and Co. B, and Pvt. James Sheridan of Portland and Co. C—to help him and a black civilian cook carry Mansfield in a blanket "to find a Surgeon."

The ad hoc stretcher bearers found an ambulance at the southern edge of Samuel Poffenberger's woods. Transferring the dying Mansfield to the "younger doctor" found with the ambulance, Gould hurried south to rejoin his regiment.[17]

By then reinforced by another Union regiment, the 10th Maine had all but driven the Confederates from the East Woods. Learning that the Maine lads were running low on ammunition, George Greene (now commanding XII Corps) relieved the regiment; when Gould "hastened back to the battlefield," he "found the place cleaned out of everything but killed and wounded."

With the East Woods "very vigorously shelled" by enemy artillery, Gould headed north to find his men. He assisted two Union soldiers trying to evacuate a wounded "107th N.Y. boy" who, "as is usual with the wounded ... was in good humor and very thankful to us." Confederate artillery shells repeatedly exploded nearby as Gould helped carry the wounded soldier about three-quarters of a mile to the rear.

The battle was over for the 10th Maine, which Gould found "scattered over the whole country."[18]

The regiment had been shot to pieces in less than an hour's work in the Poffenberger field and the East Woods, where the opposition had included Alabamians, Georgians, and Texans. According to Gould, "the 10th Maine went into battle with 21 officers, and 276 men with muskets."

Thirty-one men (three officers and 28 enlisted men) were killed or mortally wounded; five officers and 35 enlisted men were wounded. The 10th Maine counted no men missing.[19]

Fillebrown later claimed that "the lifeless remains of 43 rebels, among them Lieutenants, Captains, and one Colonel, [discovered] as we advanced [through East Woods], proved the unerring aim of our men's rifles.

"It was a squirrel hunt on a large scale, as you could see our men creep along from tree to tree," he said.[20]

Gould numerated the dead. Company F had lost Pvt. James E. Covell of Durham; he "was for some time my clerk and orderly" and "a fine fellow, intelligent, sprightly, and honest," and the "son of a minister from Pownal," Gould eulogized the young man.

Chapter 44: Encounter in the East Woods

Gunsmoke obscures the firing line of Union reenactors at Perryville, Kentucky
Photo by Brian F. Swartz

Company I had lost Capt. Nehemiah Thompson Furbish of Portland and 2nd Lt. William Wade of Westbrook. The latter "was so honest, rough and fearless," Gould said.[21]

Actually an acting second lieutenant, Wade had "carelessly" sat atop the East Woods fence with "sword in hand, waiting to jump at the first man of [Co.] I who should offer to run," Gould learned. "A bullet struck him—the thud of it was heard away up in Co. H—and he dropped over backward, lifeless."[22]

That night the surviving 10th Maine lads camped near the George Line farm. Ninety-two enlisted men stacked their rifled muskets, and officers met with the ill Maj. Walker. "The boys feel happy at their general success but the constant loss of men by one cause or another has made it now anything but the jolly crowd of a year ago," Gould realized.

"More than half of our men are recruits," he said. "'The best men are always killed' seems to be proved true. Hard life and sickness reduces the weak and sickly. Battle takes the life blood from our army and although more fall by sickness than by battle[,] I question whether the country loses more in that way."[23]

~~~

1. William B. Jordan, *The Civil War Journals of John Mead Gould 1861-1866,* Butternut & Blue, Baltimore, 1997, p. 193
2. Brig. Gen. Alpheus S. Williams, *Official Records: Series 1, Vol. 19, Part 1,* Chapter XXXI, No. 164, p. 475
3. John Mead Gould, *Gen. Mansfield at Antietam,* S. Berry, Portland, Maine, 1895, pp. 8-9
4. Jordan, *Journals,* pp. 193-194
5. Gould, Gen. *Mansfield at Antietam,* p. 9
6. Jordan, *Journals,* pp.193-194
7. Maj. John M. Gould, *History of the First-Tenth-Twenty-ninth Maine Regiment,* Stephen Berry, Portland, Maine, 1871, p. 234
8. Gould, Gen. *Mansfield at Antietam,* p. 9
9. Gould, *History,* pp. 236-237
10. Gould, Gen. *Mansfield at Antietam,* pp. 11-12
11. Lt. Col. James S. Fillebrown, *Official Records, Series I, Vol. 19, Part 1,* Chapter XXXI, No. 169, p. 489
12. Gould, *History,* p. 240
13. Fillebrown, *OR, Series I, Vol. 19, Part 1,* Chapter XXXI, No. 169, p. 489
14. Gould, Gen. *Mansfield at Antietam,* p. 7
15. Gould, *History,* pp. 237-240
16. Jordan, *Journals,* p. 194
17. Gould, Gen. *Mansfield at Antietam,* pp. 14-17, p. 20
18. Jordan, *Journals,* p. 195
19. Gould, Gen. *Mansfield at Antietam,* p. 12
20. Lt. Col. James S. Fillebrown to Anna Fillebrown, September 19, 1862, *Lewistown Falls Journal*
21. Jordan, *Journals,* p. 195
22. Gould, *History,* p. 242
23. Jordan, *Journals,* p. 197

Chapter 45

FORWARD, THE 7TH MAINE

"The 7th Maine were to find their Balaklava"

After waiting patiently for the 7th Maine Infantry to arrive at Antietam, the Angel of Death reaped a terrible harvest from the regiment late on Wednesday, September 17. Drawn primarily from central and southern Maine (with companies A and I recruited in Aroostook County), the 7th Maine mustered into federal service at Augusta on Wednesday, August 21, 1861. His prior military experience involving only a short stint with a Chicago infantry regiment, 20-year-old Capt. Thomas Worcester Hyde of Bath brought Co. D to the regimental camp near the State House.

Col. Edwin C. Mason of Portland assumed command of the 7th Maine Infantry, and Selden Connor of Fairfield became its lieutenant colonel. Casting their votes for major, the captains and lieutenants—one and two per company, respectively—selected Hyde as the third staff officer (a major) authorized for the 7th Maine.

A dyed-in-the-wool Yankee, Hyde hailed from solid New England stock. His father, the quaintly named Zina Hyde Jr., was born in Connecticut in mid-October 1787. Moving to Bath on the lower Kennebec River in 1802, Zina apprenticed in "a store for retail trade" that was owned by his half-brother, Jonathan Hyde.

Zina learned the retail trade while gaining social prominence with his peers; he served as major of a coastal militia brigade kept busy by British seaborne raids during the War of 1812. By now a well-established merchant, he married Harriet Buck of Bucksport in 1816; she died less than seven months later.

In mid-April 1840 Zina married Eleanor Maria Little, a 36-year-old widow originally from Jamaica Plains in Boston. Sailing for Europe with her husband, she gave birth to son Thomas Worcester in Florence, Italy in January 1841. A daughter, Mary Eleanor Hyde, followed in November 1842.

Zina Hyde died in 1856. His son graduated from Bowdoin College and Chicago University ('61), served briefly with a Chicago-raised regiment that never left Illinois, and returned to Maine later that summer. Thomas Hyde raised a 100-man company for the fledgling 7th Maine Infantry that August.[1]

Now, less than 13 months later, Maj. Hyde commanded the 7th Maine and led his men

The 7th Maine at Antietam
Sent to attack the Piper Farm in the distance, 7th Maine soldiers cross the Bloody Lane
packed with Confederate dead and wounded.
Illustration by Capt. James Hope, courtesy of National Park Service

through the drifting road dust toward the slaughter at Sharpsburg, Maryland. Based on the distant cannon thumps and the less distinct rattle and rip of musketry, Hyde knew that "the angel of death was already hovering" over the unseen, but noisy battlefield.[2]

The 7th Maine Infantry and four New York infantry regiments (20th, 33rd, 49th, and 77th) formed the 3rd Brigade (Col. William H. Irwin) assigned to the 2nd Division (Maj. Gen. William F. Smith) of the Army of the Potomac's VI Corps, commanded by Maj. Gen. William B. Franklin. An official order had thus far spared Franklin and his corps from the carnage outside Sharpsburg.

On Sunday, September 14, Gen. George McClellan had dispatched Franklin and VI Corps to clear Confederates from Crampton's Gap on South Mountain in Maryland and then relieve the besieged Federal garrison at Harpers Ferry, Virginia. To reach the gap, Franklin marched his three divisions and 12,000 men southwest across Middletown Valley to Burkittsville, a crossroads town tucked against South Mountain.

In late afternoon, Brig. Gen. Henry W. Slocum deployed the three brigades of his 1st Division in the fields abutting the mountain's lower eastern slope. Trailing behind Slocum on the Middletown Road (modern Route 17), the 2nd Division under Smith "drew near the South Mountain range" after conducting "several slow and deliberate marches," said Hyde.

As the 7th Maine boys tramped into Burkittsville, "the smoke of a [Confederate] battery on the far mountain side was soon followed by round shot shrieking overhead," Hyde noticed. Ordered to move at the double quick, his men ran through Burkittsville "while cannon balls crashed among the houses and the women young and old with great coolness waved their handkerchiefs and flags at us."

Charging across Burkitt's Run and up South Mountain, "Slocum's people went right up the pass[,] driving all before them[,] and we after," Hyde said.³

Slocum's men captured Crampton's Pass around sunset. Provided with faulty estimates of enemy strength, the cautious Franklin dithered that night rather than push south several miles in the darkness to take the rugged Maryland Heights opposite Harpers Ferry.⁴

The 7th Maine and the 2nd Division debouched into Pleasant Valley on the west side of South Mountain on Monday. Hyde could see "a rebel line stretching across the valley a mile or so in advance" even as "the faint boom of cannon from distant Harpers Ferry could be heard.

"We expected a fight of our own," he said.⁵ Franklin deigned to move, though VI Corps heavily outnumbered the Confederates defending the approaches to Maryland Heights. A hard "shove" by Franklin likely would have placed his artillery on the heights and his infantry on the Potomac River shore opposite Harpers Ferry.

The Union troops encircled there surrendered that day.⁶

Sixth Corps rested in Pleasant Valley until Wednesday morning. Awakening from "a refreshing" night's sleep "in a half filled hay cart," Hyde mounted his horse and led a "high spirited and happy regiment toward we knew not what."

The 2nd Division moved out around 5:30 a.m.

By 9 a.m. "the firing ahead of us became louder" as the 3rd Brigade approached Sharpsburg, Hyde said. "We were soon meeting hundreds of wounded [Union soldiers] coming to the rear."

The 7th Maine followed the 77th New York Infantry, which kicked up road dust that drifted amidst Hyde's men. He brought to Sharpsburg only 15 officers and 166 enlisted men, more than 80 percent fewer than the 1,000-odd men who had mustered with the regiment in mid-August 1861.

With the dust blocking his views beyond the 77th New York and his veteran's ears detecting how "the artillery and the rattle of small arms grew louder," Hyde turned in the saddle. He looked "back ... at the firm set of faces behind me[,] every one of them known to me personally and never known to lack nerve in danger."

Hyde noticed that "the regiment looked so small." He ordered "our eight or ten drummers and fifers to arm themselves with guns picked up by the roadside [after abandonment by wounded soldiers] and join their companies." Only one 7th Maine lad—"and he was sick"—fell out of the column and "went to the rear," Hyde said.

Union Capt. Thomas Worcester Hyde
Photo courtesy of Maine State Archives

Irwin pushed the 3rd Brigade across Antietam Creek at Pry's Ford. Suddenly the 77th New York lads sped into the "double quick as we came to some woods," so the 7th Maine boys started running, too, Hyde said.

The 3rd Brigade soon reached the Smoketown Road. Hyde suddenly realized his men were passing the 10th Maine, now disengaged from its early morning shootout in the East Woods.

Shocked "that [the] splendid regiment [was] reduced to a small squad," he ventured among the 10th Maine survivors and "asked for [George] Beal and [James] Fillebrown[,] and [I] was told they were down."[7]

"About 11 o'clock a.m." the 20th New York "formed in line of battle in the woods on this [south] side" of the creek, recalled the 20th's Col. Ernst von Vegesack, a Swedish nobleman who had offered his services to the Union in 1861. The 20th New York Infantry was comprised primarily of German immigrants.[8]

Union Col. Ernst Mathias Peter von Vegesack
Photo taken on June 1, 1863
Photo from Library of Congress

"I could see the long line of Germans moving obliquely to the left" as the 77th New York lads went "straight on," Hyde said. An Irwin aide ordered him to maneuver the 7th Maine onto the left flank of the 20th New York; Hyde deployed his companies into line and conducted a left half wheel.

Then his men emerged from "the woods and the whole magnificent [battlefield] panorama ... was in full view," he described the vista from his saddle.

With the 33rd and 77th New York regiments forming its right flank, the 3rd Brigade charged south toward the Dunker Church. Hyde saw that Vegesack's "Germans, some eight hundred strong, were moving in fine line and looked so well that the whole fire of the enemy was being concentrated upon them."

Enemy artillery fire tore up the right-flank regiments as well.

Confederate marksmen loitering "about some barns on our left flank" forced Hyde to divert the 7th Maine to the outbuildings on the William Roulette farm. Hyde lost "a dozen men" while clearing out the buildings; then the 7th Maine lads "dashed back again at the run" to go to ground "on the left of the Germans, who had lost heavily."

The Maine boys passed through "a Confederate regiment of perhaps four hundred men" who put up no resistance, Hyde recalled. The enemy, enlisted men and officers alike, lay "as they fell" in aligned ranks; "so few had been the survivors it seemed to me the whole regiment

Chapter 45: Forward, the 7th Maine

was lying there in death," he believed.

"Their clothing was of gray or butternut color[,] and my impression was that they all had red or very light hair," Hyde said.

As the 7th Maine boys approached the 20th New York's left flank, a bullet struck Lt. Augustus F. Emery of Co. E and Fairfield squarely in his waist. Hyde watched him "jump in the air and fall[,] rolling over several times apparently in great agony." Other soldiers heard Emery screaming from some distance away.

By 1 p.m. the 7th Maine lads "hugged the ground" amidst "a lot of boulders in front [that] protected us fairly well," Hyde noted. Several Union batteries deployed behind the 3rd Brigade dueled with the Confederate artillery spread near the Dunker Church.

Shot and shell whistled and zipped overhead as Hyde watched the Irish Brigade (identifiable by its magnificent green flags adorned with Irish harps) charge "up[hill] to the line over to the left" beyond the Roulette farm. Out of sight of Hyde, the Irish Brigade attacked Confederates defending a sunken farm lane.

Enemy artillery targeted the 3rd Brigade all afternoon, but the 7th Maine lads lay fairly sheltered by the boulders. Hyde watched as "the Vermonters [2nd Brigade, 2nd Division] came up deliberately to our left and rear." Late in the afternoon "we could see … in the far distance the long delayed efforts" of Maj. Gen. Ambrose Burnside and his IX Corps to dislodge "the sturdy lines of the Confederates opposing him" south of Sharpsburg.

Augustus Emery suddenly rejoined Co. E, where some men likely blanched at the perceived ghost. They had last heard him screaming in pain and seen him writhing in the Maryland grass. He lived, however, because the "bullet had struck his belt plate" and not penetrated his body, Hyde learned.[9]

Sometime between 4 p.m. and 5 p.m. (Hyde was unsure as to the exact time), Capt. John Wolcott deployed his Battery A, 1st Maryland Light Artillery near where the 7th Maine boys sheltered in the boulders. Wolcott's battery was assigned to Henry Slocum's 1st Division, which had attacked and carried Crampton's Gap on September 14.

Slocum's artillery commander, Capt. Emory Upton, accompanied Wolcott's men as they placed their six three-inch rifled cannons on slightly higher ground. The Maryland gunners opened fire on the central section of the Confederate lines; the opening salvo attracted

Union Maj. Gen. Ambrose Everett Burnside
Photo by Mathew Brady, restored by Michel Vuijlsteke, via Library of Congress

attention from angry gray-clad infantrymen sheltering amidst the haystacks on the Henry Piper Farm, located almost due south and less than a mile downslope from Battery A.

The farm lay deep inside Confederate lines.

Gun smoke puffed near the Piper buildings, and Maryland gunners dropped. Irwin had scurried to join Upton; dodging Confederate bullets, Wolcott "complained bitterly" to William Irwin "that sharpshooters were picking off his men" and pointed out the sharpshooters' positions on the Piper farm, Hyde said.

Soldiers' watches ticked toward 5 p.m. Except for the enemy bullets scouring Battery A, shooting had slackened along the 3rd Brigade's front. Hyde figured his regiment and brigade had done enough for the day; "we were expecting soon to be relieved[,] little knowing that in a few minutes more the 7th Maine were to find their Balaklava," he said.[10]

Turning his horse, Irwin rode from Battery A to find Hyde. Not bothering to dismount, Irwin told the startled Hyde "to send a company to dislodge" the Confederate sharpshooters at the Piper farm, Hyde later told Maj. Charles Mundee, the assistant adjutant general of the 2nd Division.

Hyde ordered a depleted company to engage the enemy troops; doing so meant crossing almost a mile of open terrain. After assessing the situation, Irwin quickly rode back to Hyde and said, "That is not enough, sir. Take your regiment and drive them from those trees and buildings."[11]

Hyde saluted Irwin, then said, "Colonel, I have seen a large force of rebels go in there, I should think two brigades. What I had seen must have been reinforcements going to repulse Burnside."

"Are you afraid to go, sir?" Irwin snarled before repeating the order.

"Give the order so the regiment can hear it, and we are ready, sir," Hyde replied.[12]

Pointing again at the Piper farm, Irwin repeated his order, swore, and then spat, "Those are your orders, sir."[13]

Calling his men to attention, Hyde sent Johnny Begg and George Williams, the "two young boys carrying the marking guidons," to the rear so they could not participate in the attack. Waiting until their major's attention was elsewhere, the boys slipped into the regimental line.

"Left face!" Hyde shouted. The 7th Maine lads snapped 90 degrees to the left.

"Forward!" Hyde ordered. His men marched past the five Vermont regiments of the 2nd Brigade (the so-called "Vermont Brigade") and formed behind a fence. Hyde's original second lieutenant in Co. D, Joseph G. Butler of Presque Isle, deployed 15 skirmishers in front of the 7th Maine, which Hyde now turned to the right to face south toward the Piper farm.

The Maine lads marched south and "crossed the sunken road, which was so filled with the dead and wounded of the enemy that my horse had to step on them to get over," Hyde said. "We stopped in the trampled corn on the other side to straighten our line."

Atop his Virginia thoroughbred, Hyde took position to the right side of that line. Riding "a big white horse" borrowed from a colonel, Adjutant William L. Haskell of Portland took position on the left flank.

Steering the 7th Maine toward "a point on the right of Piper's barns," Hyde paused, then shouted, "Charge!" The Maine lads rushed "at the double quick down into a cup-shared valley" that gradually rose onto higher ground near a barn on the Piper farm.[14]

"With fixed bayonets the men dashed forward in line with a cheer, advancing nearly a quarter of a mile at the double-quick," he said. Awaiting the Maine lads with loaded weapons were the 1st Texas Infantry, the 2nd Mississippi Battalion, the 7th Georgia Infantry, and what Hyde later described as "a fragment of a Louisiana regiment."[15]

Watching Confederates may not have believed the suicidal audacity they witnessed during the next few minutes. Charging unsupported, the 7th Maine presented a target that no Confederate could miss. Many Yankees watched, too; along the Vermont Brigade's lines, regimental commanders "begged to follow our charge," Hyde learned later.

Lacking orders from William Smith to support the 7th Maine, Vermont Brigade commander Brig. Gen. William T.H. Brooks responded, "You will never see that regiment again."[16]

Union Brig. Gen. Thomas Harbraugh Brooks
Photo courtesy of www.generalsandbrevets.com

"Finding the regiment so severely engaged, I was very anxious to support them, but my orders were positive not to advance my line," William Irwin explained why he failed to send his men to support the 7th Maine.

Instead he "rode rapidly forward" past the boulders that had sheltered the 7th Maine, located "the officer commanding the right [flank Vermont] regiment of the Second Brigade," and asked the man "to support Major Hyde."

The officer properly "declined to do so without orders from General Brooks"; Irwin shifted blame to the Vermont regiment.[17]

Comprising fewer than 175 men, the 7th Maine's line covered a considerable distance and moved perpendicular to the stone wall-lined Hagerstown Pike, slightly more than 100 yards away from the regiment's right flank. "My feeling was first of great exhilaration, which was quickly dashed by that wretched Maryland battery," Hyde growled. Trying to fire beyond the charging 7th Maine, a Battery A crew "took out four men of my right company at their first shot."

Confederates defending the Piper farm fired fast and furiously. Haskell went down on the left flank when Confederate bullets felled him and his mount (called "old Whitey"), so Hyde steered his horse "in front of the regiment" so his men could see him.[18]

By now enemy troops in the Piper orchard had fled, and "those directly in front, behind haystacks and outbuildings, also broke, and their colors having fallen, we dashed on up the hill to secure them."

Confederate infantrymen concealed by the Hagerstown Pike stone wall "rose suddenly ... poured in a volley" at the 7th Maine lads, then turned to their left and started "double-quicking ... to cut off our retreat," Hyde said.[19]

Because the Maine boys "were going so fast," the Confederate volley did little damage. Assessing the terrain, Hyde ordered a "left oblique" to place "a rise of ground" between his men and the pike.

The hill on which retreating Confederates had abandoned their flags lay "just to the right of and beyond Piper's barns," Hyde noticed from where he rode about 20 feet ahead of his men. Just as "we breasted this hill ... I saw over its top" that "there were several times our number [of Confederates] waiting for us."

To avoid his men being silhouetted and shot against the Maryland sky, Hyde ordered, "Left flank!" The 7th Maine lads angled to the east, ran past the Piper barns, tore apart a fence delineating a "cow yard," and "went up a rise of ground into the [Piper] orchard," he recalled.

Color Sgt. Harry Campbell of Co. D carried the regimental flag during the attack. Somewhere near the Piper barns a bullet struck Campbell "in the arm," Hyde said. "He held it up to

The reconstructed Dunker Church today.
Photo by Brian F. Swartz

Chapter 45: Forward, the 7th Maine

Union reenactors prepare to fire a 3-inch ordnance rifle at Sharpsburg, Maryland
Photo by Brian F. Swartz

me, all bloody, waving the flag.

"Take [the flag in] the other hand, Harry," Hyde told Campbell.

Spotting the Maine soldiers, the Confederate troops concealed behind the first hill "fired several volleys and then charged after us," Hyde watched the developing encirclement of his regiment.[20]

"Here we received a severe fire from three directions, and the enemy advanced in force," he said. Confederate artillery opened fire with grapeshot, and although "shielded some" by the orchard's trees, "we met a heavy loss," he admitted.[21]

Struck in its hip and mouth by bullets, Hyde's horse reared and plunged. Hyde "slipped off over" the horse's tail and landed on the ground; he noticed that overhead "the twigs and branches of the apple trees were being cut off by musket balls, and were dropping in a shower."

Although its blood had splattered Hyde, the thoroughbred "only lost his back teeth" and had "a charge of buck and ball" lodged "in his hip." Remounting, Hyde found his men formed into line in the orchard; delivering "a terrible fire" on the Confederates pouring into the cow yard, the Maine boys left a "pile of dead ... there."

Hyde had earlier counted four enemy regimental flags, including one emblazoned "Manassas." Badly outnumbered and running low on ammunition, the 7th Maine boys were slowly withdrawing "through the tall picket fence" along the northern edge of the orchard.

As Hyde rode toward his men, he heard Harry Campbell "call out as in pain behind me." Turning his thoroughbred, Hyde "went back to save the colors if possible." The apple trees apparently (and only briefly) concealed Hyde from Confederates pursuing the 7th Maine;

"Battle of Antietam—Army of the Potomac: Gen. Geo. B. McClellan"
September 17, 1862.
Painting by Kurz & Allison, via Library of Congress

enemy troops swept past and cut him off.

Turning his horse again, Hyde rode into a fence corner, where perhaps a dozen Confederate soldiers surrounded him.

"Rally, boys, to save the major!" a Maine sergeant bellowed. Rushing to the picket fence trapping Hyde and his horse, 7th Maine lads pushed "the muzzles of their Windsors ... between the pickets" and fired a volley that "few of my would be captors" escaped, Hyde vividly recalled that moment for the rest his life.

"Sgt. [Henry F.] Hill [of Co. I] with his sabre bayonet cut through the rails[,] and I was soon extricated," Hyde said.

As the 7th Maine boys poured from the orchard, Union artillery fired grapeshot into it. While the friendly fire support blocked Confederate pursuit beyond the orchard, Hyde acknowledged that "we were more afraid of the [Union] grape than the enemy."

The Maine boys delivered a final volley. Hyde "then formed the regiment on the colors, sixty five men and three officers, and slowly we marched back toward our place in line."

Confederate artillery deployed east of the Dunker Church fired a few rounds at the diminutive line, then fell silent. All along the Federal lines, and particularly "when we came in front of our dear comrades, the Vermonters," men "rose up and waved their hats" and cheered raucously, according to Hyde.[22]

As the bloodied 7th Maine lads marched toward their initial position on the 3rd Brigade's left flank, Corp. Warren Ring of Co. A—the sole survivor of the color guard—"brought off our flag riddled with bullets," Hyde proudly stated. Harry Campbell lay somewhere in the Piper orchard, and all but one member of the color guard had been wounded.[23]

Irwin "had the extreme pleasure of seeing the shattered[,] but brave remnant of the Seventh Maine in good order return to my lines.

"No words of mine can do justice to the firmness, intelligence, and heroic courage with which this regiment performed its dangerous task," he commended in his after-action report. "Their killed and wounded and their colors riddled by [musket] balls are the proud, yet melancholy witnesses of their valor."

Irwin's praise came five days too late.[24]

Estimating that the charge and its repulse "lasted perhaps thirty minutes," Hyde reported twelve enlisted men, Sgt. Maj. John B. Parsons, and two lieutenants (Harlan Brown of Co. I and Charles Goodwin of Co. D) as killed in action. Sixty enlisted men and three officers had been wounded and rescued, and 16 enlisted men were missing.

So were Adjutant Haskell and captains Granville Cochrane of Monmouth, John Cook of Lewiston, and James Parnell Jones of China.[25] Haskell would later die of his wounds. Cochrane was shot in an ankle, Cook suffered a bad leg wound, and Jones was slightly wounded.

As for the boys who carried the marking guidons, George Williams was killed and "buried on the field," Hyde sadly noted. John Begg lost the arm shattered by a Confederate bullet.[26]

Other men had survived close calls. Capt. John Channing of Co. E and Fairfield and 1st Lt. Eli Webber of Co. B and China discovered three bullet holes apiece in their clothing after the fight. The only officer who "escaped untouched in clothes or person" was 1st Lt. Albert Nickerson of Co. Co. E and Fairfield.[27]

Hyde suffered a minor hand wound, which he hardly noticed as the shrunken 7th Maine resumed its position on the left flank of the 20th New York. "We did not take a large space on the line as we lay down in the falling darkness," Hyde noticed.

That night he shared a single blanket with Channing, Nickerson, and Webber. Talking late into the night about "our dead and crippled comrades," the four men cried their hearts out, Hyde admitted.

No one knew why Irwin had ordered the 7th Maine Infantry to charge unsupported into the enemy lines. Hyde evidently shared his concerns with 3rd Brigade officers—and from them he learned why the Angel of Death had swept so many Maine boys into eternity.

By Thursday morning "we knew our efforts were resultant from no plan or design at headquarters," Hyde said.

In his after-action report filed with VI Corps, 2nd Division commander William Smith detailed the September 17 accomplishments and bravery of his 3rd Brigade, which had "charged upon the enemy, and drove them gallantly until abreast the little [Dunker] church at the point

Burnside's bridge
The photo above is the bridge as it looks today.
Photo by Brian F. Swartz

The bridge after the battle
The photo at left was taken after the Battle of Antietam. Confederate guns on the hill pounded Union troops below.
Photo from The Photographic History of The Civil War in Ten Volumes: Volume Two, Two Years of Grim War.

of [the West] woods."

Citing "the report of Major Hyde, Seventh Maine Volunteers, with reference to the gallant conduct of that regiment, acting under the orders of Colonel Irwin," Smith stated that "these orders were not made known to me till after the regiment had moved" against the Piper farm.[28]

Smith and VI Corps commander William Franklin evidently confirmed on September 18 that Irwin had ordered the suicidal attack "from an inspiration of John Barleycorn," said Hyde, politely declining to describe his brigade commander as "drunk" when he sent the 7th Maine to meet its Balaklava.[29]

Franklin and Smith sacked Irwin as the 3rd Brigade commander on September 18.

In their post-Antietam reports, many commanding officers mentioned specific soldiers for bravery or outstanding conduct. In his September 22 report, which included one paragraph lifted partially verbatim from Hyde's report of three days earlier, Irwin cited "the distinguished gallantry of my aide, Captain E. Martindale, and my assistant adjutant-general, Lieutenant William H. Long."

Likely aware that his drunkenness had killed or wounded more than 75 Maine boys, Irwin wrote, "I cannot forebear calling the attention" of William Smith "to the gallant soldier and gentleman, Major Thomas W. Hyde" of the 7th Maine.

"He led his regiment into action with spirit and courage, handled it under severe fire with judgment, and retired in compact order and with a steady front," according to Irwin. "Conduct like this requires soldierly qualities of the highest order."[30]

As for Hyde, "I cannot make exception for [any 7th Maine lads] for special mention," he succinctly stressed in his September 19 report. "Where all behaved so nobly, and obeyed orders so readily, distinction would be invidious."[31]

On Thursday morning, Franklin assigned the shattered 7th Maine Infantry to guard duty at VI Corps' headquarters. Later in the day George B. McClellan "came to see our colors, which … were riddled with balls," Hyde learned afterwards.

"I was told he had said many kind things, but at the time I had gone out to the [Piper] orchard to see if I could find any wounded" 7th Maine lads, he explained his absence from corps headquarters.

Dodging enemy bullets—Robert E. Lee did not evacuate his broken army until Thursday night—Hyde located eight wounded comrades who were too crippled to move on their own but who were only too happy to see him. He reached the apple orchard and discovered the lonely fate of one Maine soldier.

"I found Harry Campbell hardly cold, propped up against a tree with his pipe beside him," Hyde described that moment years later. He had last heard Campbell cry out when a Confederate bullet caught him inside the orchard.

The mortally wounded Campbell had pulled himself to an apple tree (or perhaps a kind Confederate soldier had helped him) and, after propping himself against its trunk, enjoyed a last smoke of his pipe as he bled to death. Given his body's partial warmth, he may have survived until early Thursday.[32]

From the orchard, Thomas Worcester Hyde could see the human cost of Irwin's command. The 7th Maine lads had inflicted great damage on their opponents; "their [Confederate] loss I find, on visiting the field, to be much heavier than ours," he noted.[33]

The Angel of Death had reaped a terrible harvest because of a command issued by a drunk colonel. Reflecting on those moments when he protested Irwin's instructions, Hyde admitted, "I wished I had been old enough or distinguished enough to have dared to disobey orders."[34]

~~~

1. Parker McCobb Reed, *History of Bath and environs,* Sagadahoc County, Maine, 1607-1894, Lakeside Press, Portland, Maine 1894, pp. 322-325
2. Thomas Worcester Hyde, *Following the Greek Cross; Or, Memories of the Sixth Army Corps,* Houghton, Mifflin,

United States, 1894, p. 94
3. Hyde, *Greek Cross*, pp. 92-93
4. Ronald H. Bailey and the editors of Time-Life Books, *The Bloodiest Day: The Battle of Antietam*, from the series *The Civil War* by Time-Life Books, Alexandria, Va. 1984, p. 55
5. Hyde, *Greek Cross*, p. 94
6. Bailey, *The Bloodiest Day*, p. 59
7. Hyde, *Greek Cross*, pp. 94-95
8. Col. Ernst von Vegesack, *Official Report, Official Records: Series I, Vol. 19, Part 1,* Chapter XXXI, No. 133, pp. 413-414
9. Hyde, pp. 95-98
10. Hyde, pp. 98-99. Fought on Oct. 25, 1854 in the Russian Crimea, the Battle of Balaklava involved the mistaken charge and resulting destruction of a British cavalry brigade, a military disaster commemorated by Alfred, Lord Tennyson in his epic poem, "The Charge of the Light Brigade."
11. Maj. Thomas W. Hyde, *OR, Series I, Vol. 19, Part 1*, Chapter XXXI, No. 132, pp. 412-413
12. Hyde, *Greek Cross*, p. 100
13. Hyde, *OR, Series I, Vol. 19, Part 1*, Chapter XXXI, No. 132, p. 412-413
14. Hyde, *Greek Cross*, pp. 100-101
15. Hyde, *OR, Series I, Vol. 19, Part 1*, Chapter XXXI, No. 132, p. 412-413
16. Hyde, *Greek Cross*, p. 104
17. Col. William H. Irwin, *OR, Series I, Vol. 19, Part 1*, Chapter XXXI, No. 131, pp. 409-412
18. Hyde, *Greek Cross*, p. 101
19. Hyde, *OR, Series I, Vol. 19, Part 1*, Chapter XXXI, No. 132, p. 412-413
20. Hyde, *Greek Cross*, pp. 101-103
21. Hyde, *OR, Series I, Vol. 19, Part 1*, Chapter XXXI, No. 132, p. 412-413
22. Hyde, *Greek Cross*, pp. 102-104
23. Hyde, *OR, Series I, Vol. 19, Part 1*, Chapter XXXI, No. 132, p. 412-413
24. Irwin, *OR, Series I, Vol. 19, Part 1*, Chapter XXXI, No. 131, pp. 409-412
25. Hyde, *OR, Series I, Vol. 19, Part 1*, Chapter XXXI, No. 132, p. 412-413
26. Hyde, *Greek Cross*, p. 100
27. Hyde, *OR, Series I, Vol. 19, Part 1*, Chapter XXXI, No. 132, p. 412-413
28. Maj. Gen. Franklin F. Smith, *OR, Series I, Vol. 19, Part 1.* Chapter XXXI, No. 125, pp. 401-403
29. Hyde, *Greek Cross*, pp. 104-105
30. Irwin, *OR, Series I, Vol. 19, Part 1*, Chapter XXXI, No. 131, pp. 409-412
31. Hyde, *OR, Series I, Vol. 19, Part 1*, Chapter XXXI, No. 132, p. 412-413
32. Hyde, *Greek Cross*, p. 107
33. Hyde, *OR, Series I, Vol. 19, Part 1*, Chapter XXXI, No. 132, p. 412-413
34. Hyde, *Greek Cross*, pp. 104-105

Chapter 46

TRAMPING TONIGHT ON THE FIELD OF THE SLAIN

"With the swinging gait peculiar to Maine"

Maine men kept dying weeks after the sun set across Sharpsburg on Wednesday, September 17, 1862.

Rousted from their restless night's sleep around dawn on an overcast Thursday, 1st Lt. John Mead Gould and the 10th Maine Infantry survivors—those men with four intact limbs apiece—left their camp "and marched out past the ground" across which the regiment had fought a day earlier.

After the enlisted men stacked their rifled muskets, Gould explored the battlefield as far as Union pickets let him walk. Anticipating the battle's resumption, both armies warily watched the opposing troops. Gould heard "a continual crack of [picket line] musketry" in the morning; that shooting soon lessened as an informal truce let Confederates and Yankees rescue their respective wounded.

But the dead remained. Antietam had killed 2,108 Union soldiers and 1,546 Confederates. By the time Gould arrived at a cornfield where dead Southerners "lay in scores," he noticed that "nearly all of our dead had been removed to heaps near the fences and all that remained were the rebel dead."

Near the corn field spread a pasture; "behind many projecting rocks they [dead Confederates] lay as thick as grasshoppers," and "the fences were piled with dead," Gould noticed as he spent "about two hours among the corpses."

Clad in "everlasting grey and dirty homespun" and splattered with "blood and dirt on every face," the dead Confederates shared "the same vacant and unmeaning expression," he said. "You look at them as so much trophy, so much evidence of the days [sic] work, and of the uselessness of secession.

"It seemed as if human life was worth nothing and a man's soul a myth," Gould thought.[1]

After spending some hours on Thursday trying to find men missing from the 7th Maine

Union Lt. Col Selden Connor in 1893
Photo via Wikipedia

Union Brig. Gen. George Lucas Hartsuff
Photo via Wikipedia

Infantry's suicidal charge, a weary Maj. Thomas E. Hyde rejoined his shattered regiment. With the survivors bedded down for the night, Hyde "saw two officers under a blanket, and turned in close beside them to be safe in one direction from being run over in the night.

Dawn found his blanket mates still sleeping. "They were so quiet I looked to see who they were," Hyde said.

His silent companions were dead.[2]

By late Friday, September 19, Confederate troops had withdrawn across the Potomac River. Believing he lacked sufficient men and equipment to pursue the battered enemy, Gen. George McClellan dithered and dallied. National honor called for the restoration of occupied Harpers Ferry. That Friday, the 10th Maine and 1st Brigade were sent "crawling along [the Hagerstown Pike] toward Sharpsburg," Gould recalled.

The brigade's ultimate destination was Harpers Ferry; in McClellanite fashion, Union troops would take their sweet time arriving there.

Halting by the bullet-pocked Dunker Church late on Friday morning, the 10th Maine lads "all took a peep at the wreck on the knoll in front of the church. Here a rebel caisson had exploded," according to Gould, "and the piling up of its fragments with the dead bodies of horse and man, was one of the most hideous sights our regiment ever beheld."[3]

Confederate artillery had defended the knoll[4] on September 17. No sooner than Friday, likely after the 10th Maine marched past the Dunker Church, civilian photographer Alexander Gardner set up his camera on the knoll and focused on a battered caisson, beyond which stood the Dunker Church and the rail fence bordering the Hagerstown Pike.

Gardner's haunting daguerreotype reveals at least six dead Confederate soldiers and a dead horse near the caisson. The dead men were laid out for burial.

Passing through Sharpsburg and crossing Antietam Creek "upon the bridge which Burnside [had] carried," the 10th Maine lads ascended South Mountain, thrashed around in the dark early Saturday, and went down and up and down the mountain later that day. Sunday finally found Gould and the regiment camped on Maryland Heights opposite Harpers Ferry.[5]

The decimated 7th Maine remained near Sharpsburg, where Lt. Col. Selden Connor (recently ill with chronic catarrh) rejoined his men. "We were very glad to see him again, as well as some chickens he brought with him," Hyde said.

In "his first official act" after returning to the 7th Maine "a few days" later, Col. Edwin Mason arrested Hyde, "nominally for not having kept him informed of the doings of the regiment, but I didn't know where he was and 'had other fish to fry,'" Hyde fumed.

Mason was angry because Hyde "had recommended" to Maine Governor Israel Washburn Jr. "a lot of sergeants for promotion," with each man selected "'for especial gallantry at Antietam.'" Hyde preferred "to make bravery the only test for promotion," while Mason "preferred to advance men of cleanliness and faultless equipment."

Bad blood already existed between Hyde and Mason, who would certainly have learned of Hyde's bravery at Piper Farm. "He soon repented and released me," Hyde said.

Still lingering north of the Potomac, McClellan declared the 7th Maine Infantry unfit for further duty. Obtaining War Department permission, he informed Washburn via Special

Confederate dead gathered for burial after the Battle of Antietam
Photo by Alexander Gardner via Library of Congress

"A Lonely Grave"
The title was given to this image by its photographer. Union soldiers stand guard at a comrade's grave at the foot of the tree after the Battle of Antietam in September 1862.
Photo by Alexander Gardner via Library of Congress

Order No. 271 and an October 4 letter that he was "returning this gallant remnant of a noble body of men ... to the State whose pride it is to have sent them forth."

The 7th Maine lads were promptly shipped to Maine to "be recruited and reorganized under your personal supervision," McClellan told Washburn.[6]

Meanwhile, a "new" Maine regiment tramped into Sharpsburg on September 19.

Led by Col. Asa W. Wildes, the 16th Maine Infantry Regiment had arrived in Washington, D.C. in late August. Forming inside Fort Tillinghast in Arlington at 4 a.m., Sunday, September 7, the 16th Maine boys departed "with the swinging gait peculiar to Maine" soldiers, crossed the Aqueduct Bridge over the Potomac River at sunrise, and marched through Georgetown, according to Adjutant Abner R. Small.[7]

The Maine boys were laden "with two days' rations and forty rounds of ammunition," and orders had forced the enlisted men to leave "our tents, knapsacks, and overcoats behind," he noticed.[8]

"There was some grumbling at this, but in our greenness we expected that they would follow us in a few days ... or that we should soon return to them," Small commented.[9]

The men marched with essentially the clothes on their backs, enough ammunition to shoot off in a noisy skirmish, and food that probably disappeared by the regiment's first evening

Chapter 46: Tramping Tonight on the Field of the Slain

meal. At Leesboro in Maryland on September 9, the 16th Maine gypsies joined the 3rd Brigade commanded by Brig. Gen. George Lucas Hartsuff. The brigade included four infantry regiments: the 12th and 13th Massachusetts, the 9th New Hampshire, and the 11th Pennsylvania.

On Thursday, September 11, the 16th Maine camped at Ridgeville. The officers sheltered in their tents, which had "followed the regiment," Small said. Enlisted men built crude shelters with cornstalks and fence rails foraged from local farms.

Afraid his ill-trained men might be sent into action soon and "bring disaster ... and disgrace to the regiment," Wildes protested vigorously and futilely as far as the I Corps commander, Maj. Gen. Joseph Hooker. An angry Wildes resigned on Saturday, September 13, leaving the combat-experienced Lt. Col. Charles Tilden in temporary command of the 16th Maine.

Four days later Hooker summoned the regiment to Sharpsburg; marching 18 miles on September 18 and ten miles on September 19, the 16th Maine's weary soldiers camped near the Antietam battlefield that Friday.

With Small in tow, Charles Tilden reported that evening to Brig. Gen. Alpheus S. Williams, the temporary commander of the battle-damaged XII Corps. Astounded at the sudden appearance of the 16th Maine, Williams informed its officers (and Wildes, who had not wandered far) that the regiment should not have left the Washington forts. A "mistake or ill judgment" had sent the regiment marching into the late Maryland summer.

Likely relieved that his former command had missed the Antietam slaughter—a putrid pall clung to the battlefield for days afterwards—Wildes sought reinstatement as colonel. McClellan granted his wish in Special Order No. 262, issued on September 25.[10]

Riding onto the battlefield on Sept. 19, Small realized what could have happened to the 16th Maine at Antietam. "Many of our officers and men were disappointed that we had not been in the fight; they feared that the reputation of the regiment must suffer," he commented.

"I felt no deep regret when I went over the field," Small stated. "The dead were still there. They lay in windrows, in some places almost entire companies together.

"The sunken road southeast of the Dunker Church was heaped with grey corpses ... the

The dead at Antietam
Left: An unburied Rebel lies next to a buried Yankee at Antietam (photo by Alexander Gardner). Right: At Dunker Church on September 17, 1862, after the battle of Antietam, Confederate soldiers lie dead together on the field.
Photos by Alexander Gardener, via Library of Congress

cornfield north of the church was strewn with blue," Small discovered. The church, "a small, plain building, was battered terribly; solid shot had gone through it, and thousands of bullets had pitted its brick walls."[11]

By later that weekend, the 16th Maine had "camped near the Potomac River, three miles west of Sharpsburgh," Small said. Worn out by their relentless marching on bad roads, men sought shelter wherever they could. With their baggage and tents still ensconced in a D.C. warehouse (Small figured the location was somewhere in Arlington, based on the assigned duty station for Quartermaster Isaac Tucker of Gardiner), the 16th Maine boys suffered.[12]

So did thousands of other men.

The dying had not stopped with the shooting, which had wounded 9,716 Union soldiers and 8,600-8,700 Confederates. Many wounded Confederates had been recovered during the September 18 truce, but hundreds of seriously wounded men were abandoned in Sharpsburg.

Most buildings became ad hoc hospitals. The horrific casualties overwhelmed the ability of the War Department to care for the combat-injured; disease and exposure hurled more men into understaffed hospitals.

Early autumn 1862 brought daytime heat and sunshine, cool nighttime temperatures, heavy dews, morning fogs, and occasional rain to central Maryland. "The exposure to cold night, after being heated by long and rapid marching, frequently through drenching rains, sowed seeds of disease in the system of many noble fellows, and sent to the hospital, and to death, scores of our best men," Small recalled.

Men in the other 3rd Brigade regiments were "well clothed in flannel and overcoats, and supplied with rubber blankets" and shelter tents, which shed precipitation on "dark and stormy nights," Small said.

The 16th Maine boys constructed shelters from cornstalks and tree boughs; huddling inside such inadequate cover, men shivered, coughed, and wheezed as rain dripped on them "long after the storm was over," he remembered.

Wind blowing through the shelters chilled the soldiers clad in wet shirts, often the only outerwear the men possessed. Dampness seeped into joints and lungs; while rheumatism often afflicted soldiers later in life, respiratory diseases killed other men sooner.

Each morning, allegedly sick men reported for examination to the 16th Maine's surgeon, Dr. Charles Alexander of Farmington, and assistant surgeons, Drs. Joseph Baxter of Gorham and William Eaton of Brunswick. Since the Revolutionary War, American soldiers had matched wits with medical personnel while attempting to gain medical

Lincoln meets with McClellan at Antietam
Lincoln meets with McClellan in the general's tent at Antietam on October 3, 1862
*Photo by Alexander Gardner
via Library of Congress*

President Lincoln with Gen. McClellan and officers, October 3, 1862
Photo by Alexander Gardner via Library of Congress

release from duty, if for even a day; in the 16th Maine camp, the doctors soon learned to identify habitual malingerers and send them packing.

But by early October the slackers numbered only a few, the sick too many. "Alexander and his assistants were untiring in their attempts to succor the [regiment's] sick," Small said. Finding dry shelter for the ill required innovation because the regiment's baggage and tents had not yet arrived at Sharpsburg.

Trying to help, Wildes, Tilden, and other officers distributed their tent flies as shelter for the sick men.

Sickness finally overwhelmed Alexander's limited resources. On Wednesday, October 15, the official morning report listed 698 men as "present" in the 16th Maine camp. The medical staff identified 256 men as sick; of that number, 68 men were confined to the regiment's hospital.

During those weeks when Maine boys and their clothing literally dissolved before his eyes, Small watched as "the worst cases were sent" to "a division hospital" set up in Smoketown, a village north of Sharpsburg. That hospital's medical staff struggled to shelter and treat their patients.

Small saw the result; "in a little field beside the [Smoketown] road rests a majority" of the sick 16th Maine lads sent to the division hospital, he noted. These men were "victims to inefficiency, neglect, and red tape."[13]

Prodded by President Abraham Lincoln, McClellan finally pushed his Army of the Potomac across its namesake river and into Virginia in late October. The army took most medical personnel, supplies, and transportation with it.

By Halloween the patients left at Smoketown and elsewhere seemed to be forgotten.

Some civilians from Maine came looking for them.

~~~

Confederate dead in the "Bloody Lane"
In the Sunken Road used as a rifle pit, many Confederate soldiers died.
Photo by Alexander Gardner via Library of Congress

1. William B. Jordan, *The Civil War Journals of John Mead Gould 1861-1866*, Butternut & Blue, Baltimore, 1997, pp. 197-198
2. Thomas Worcester Hyde, *Following the Greek Cross: Or, Memories of the Sixth Army Corps,* Houghton, Mifflin, United States, 1894, p. 107
3. Maj. John M. Gould, *History of the First-Tenth-Twenty-ninth Maine Regiment,* Stephen Berry, Portland, Maine, 1871, p. 262
4. The knoll lies between the reconstructed Dunker Church and the Antietam National Battlefield Visitors Center.
5. Gould, *History*, pp. 263-264
6. Hyde, *Greek Cross,* pp. 108-110
7. No explanation is given to describe the gait that was "peculiar" to Maine soldiers.
8. Major A.R. Small, *The Sixteenth Maine Regiment in the War of the Rebellion 1861-1865,* editors Peter and Cyndi Dalton, B. Thurston & Company, Portland, Maine 1886, pp. 32-33
9. Major Abner R. Small, *The Road to Richmond, editor Harold Adams Small,* reprinted by Fordham University Press, New York, 2000, p. 44
10. Small, *Sixteenth Maine Regiment,* pp. 33-36
11. Small, *Road to Richmond,* p. 47
12. Small, *Sixteenth Maine Regiment,* p. 36
13. Small, *Sixteenth Maine,* pp. 36-37

Chapter 47

ANGELS OF MERCY

"The misery and suffering beggars all description"

Sheltering in a cold, unheated Maryland school house, an ill 57-year-old Maine soldier watched disbelievingly as two angels suddenly appeared beside him in early November 1862.

Pain from his injured spine radiating through his body, the old warrior listened as the angels, who resembled middle-aged white women, spoke soothingly to him. Did he hear correctly? Did not one angel speak in the Down East accent peculiar to coastal eastern Maine?

That angel was Isabella Fogg, late of Calais and the 6th Maine Infantry. Talking in cultured Bay State tones to the startled veteran was Harriet Eaton; she and Fogg were there to help, Eaton told the incredulous soldier.

No greater polar opposites could assist this particular soldier on this cold November day. Although five years older than Fogg, Harriet Eaton lacked Isabella's martial experience. Assigned in June 1862 to the burgeoning Union field hospital at Savage Station on the Richmond & York River Railroad in Virginia, Fogg had cared for many wounded men during the Seven Days Battles and afterwards.

The physically tough Fogg worked in a Harrison's Landing hospital in Virginia until August, then returned to Maine. Filing detailed reports about the primitive medical care that Maine soldiers were receiving,[1] Fogg shared her experiences with government officials, churches, and women's organizations.

She evidently met Harriet Eaton while speaking in Portland. Born into relative economic comfort in Massachusetts in August 1818, Harriet Agnes Hope Bacon married Jeremiah Sewall Eaton, pastor of the First Baptist Church in Hartford, Connecticut, in 1840.

The Eatons had a son, Franklin (or "Frank" to his mother) in 1842. Two years later, the members of Free Street Baptist Church in Portland hired Jeremiah Eaton as their pastor; he brought his family to Portland, where daughters Agnes and Harriet were born during the next 11 years.

Jeremiah's death in 1856 (likely from tuberculosis) should have left his family destitute, but Harriet displayed a gumption that, along with assistance from church members, ensured the family's survival.

Ironically, Eaton and Fogg shared one wartime bond: sons serving in the Army. Fogg's 18-year-old son, Hugh, had gone to war in spring 1861 with the Calais militia company forming the backbone of Co. D, 6th Maine Infantry Regiment. Isabella had worked with the Co. D boys outside Richmond in late spring 1862.

When the 25th Maine Infantry Regiment mustered at Portland on September 29, 1862, Franklin "Frank" Henry Eaton had joined Co. A as a private.[2] Formed as a nine-month regiment, the 25th Maine would not leave Portland until mid-October.[3]

Its disbandment postponed by the Gettysburg campaign, the regiment would spend the next nine months garrisoning various Washington, D.C. forts.

Fogg's reports, letters penned by Maine soldiers, and lobbying by their friends and relatives led the Maine Legislature to estab-

Isabella Fogg

lish the Maine Soldiers' Relief Agency and appoint Col. John W. Hathaway as its commander and Charles C. Hayes as his assistant. Hathaway quickly opened an office at 273 F St. in Washington, D.C.; the agency soon had offices in New York City and Philadelphia, major transit points for Maine troops traveling to and from the war.

Representing the Ladies Committee of the Free Street Baptist Church, Eaton and Fogg left Portland by train on Monday, October 6. With the women went the medical supplies and other items acquired and packed by committee members; Eaton and Fogg would distribute the supplies to Maine soldiers after arriving in Washington.[4]

Enduring "almost suffocating" dust along the railroad "between Baltimore and Washington," the women arrived at the latter city about 7 p.m., Tuesday. The next morning, with the "heat intense," they searched for Maine soldiers at Armory Square Hospital and Douglas Hospital.

Eaton described Armory Square Hospital as "perhaps the best in the city, every thing in fine order," and she and Fogg "talked with many Maine soldiers" and "found the nurses warm hearted and kind.

"In this Hospital each ward has a separate building, and each bed a mosquito netting over it, everything sweet and clean," Eaton said of a hospital that probably seemed like paradise on Earth to soldiers convalescing at a nightmarish facility across the Potomac River in Arlington.

Speaking to Maine soldiers at Douglas Hospital, Eaton learned that "they seem to feel great horror of entering Convalescent Hospital."[5]

Chapter 47: Angels of Mercy

On Sunday, October 12, John Hathaway crossed the Potomac River to visit the Maine soldiers confined at this hospital, actually a complex of "convalescent camps in Alexandria," Hathaway told Governor Israel Washburn Jr. in a letter written on October 15.

"The soldiers have very appropriately" dubbed the facility "Camp Misery"—and justifiably so, he informed Washburn. "It is a beastly place," and "I ... found things in a wretched state—most of the men were without blankets lying on the bare ground—four or five in a little shed tent—and the entire camp as filthy as possible—and that was the place to which convalescents were sent to fully recover.

"Of course many [recovering soldiers] have become sick and the others do not gain," Hathaway wrote.[6]

He discovered that "Camp Misery" sheltered 10,985 convalescing soldiers; an adjoining facility could shelter 38,000 paroled Union prisoners.[7]

"The existence of the camp in its present condition is a disgrace to the Government," Hathaway stated. "The Medical Inspector General informs me that he has reported its condition to the proper authorities—but it does no good."

Hathaway already knew that Eaton and Fogg needed a horse-drawn conveyance—an ambulance would suffice—with which to deliver the supplies so carefully packed in Maine.

Hathaway could really use a horse—and an office staff.

Vice President Hannibal Hamlin strolled into 273 F St. on Tuesday, October 14 and, after listening to Hathaway, "obtained for me an audience" with Secretary of War Edwin M. Stanton. "I broached the subject of transportation," which involved use of a government horse, but Stanton "immediately said that he could not grant it," Hathaway told Washburn.

Stanton "assumed all State associations would pay their transportation." He promised to "dismiss ... from the service" any officer "granting use of Government horses to any State Association or to the [civilian-run United States] Sanitary Commission," Hathaway indicated.

He detailed the reasons why "I must have someone (a male clerk) to remain in the [agency] office" when he was away "visiting hospitals—I have more demands on me now for that purpose than I can supply."[8]

In mid-October Eaton and Fogg traveled by train to Frederick and Harpers Ferry and visited a few hospitals. The women returned to Washington on October 21.

Charles C. Hayes
Photo courtesy of Maine State Archives

By then Hathaway was fielding unremitting reports that Maine soldiers either wounded at Antietam or taken ill afterwards were suffering terribly from inadequate medical care at hospitals upriver from the capital. He had not yet obtained official permission for Eaton and Fogg to travel alone to disperse their supplies.

That situation changed dramatically at 7 p.m., Friday, October 24, when the women arrived invited at the private room that Hathaway rented. After the obligatory social niceties, he informed Eaton and Fogg that Leonard Watson, an MSRA representative, would leave for Frederick on Saturday.

"Are these ladies to go with me?" Watson asked, entering the room on cue.

"Well, they will go with you as far as Frederick and <u>then take their own course poking around the [Maine] Regiments</u>," Hathaway responded.[9]

Arriving in Frederick by train on October 25, Eaton and Fogg met Capt. Edward A. Snow of Rockland. Commander of Co. I, 19th Maine Infantry, he was sick with an "ulcerated throat and fever" when the women had stopped in Frederick in mid-October; by then on the mend, Snow "very politely took a carriage and carried us to our lodgings," Eaton said.

On October 28, Eaton and Fogg met sick 1st Maine Cavalry lads in a Frederick hospital. "These poor men ... have to dress their own wounds, wash themselves if they are washed at all," she said.

Walking back to their quarters, the women passed a soldier—his right arm missing—jumping up and down beneath an apple tree and swatting at a dangling apple with his left hand. Fogg "sprained her foot badly" while getting the apple for the man.

"I am afraid she will have a sorry time of it," Eaton commented.

Charles Hayes and Leonard Watson joined the women on Halloween. On Saturday, November 1, Hayes accompanied the two women as "we took our departure" with a driver and ambulance borrowed from the 1st Maine Cavalry. Eaton described the "day [as] summer like, scenery beautiful indeed, autumn tinted foliage covered the mountain tops while villages nestled in the valleys."[10]

The intrepid civilians visited Maine soldiers at a Middletown hospital. "We ... found them very comfortable, [the] men happy, and the [local] ladies were kind" while working as volunteer nurses, Fogg wrote Hathaway.

Crossing South Mountain at Crampton's Gap, the investigators discovered at Keedysville "a painful contrast" with the military hospitals east of the mountain. "There we found several Maine men, in a church and three other buildings ... laying on the bare floor with their coats for pillows. Their [food] stores consisted of hard bread, beef and coffee," Fogg noted.

"As we had no supplies with us ... we could not relieve" the men's hunger, so the soldiers said they would apply to the U.S. Sanitary Commission for food the next day, she said.[11]

Briefly losing the road to Smoketown and its military hospital, the party "arrived just at dark," said Eaton. The women lodged in a private home for the night. Forced to sleep on the sitting-room floor without a sheet to cover her, Eaton huffed about "a wounded southwestern Virginia rebel" who had a private room.[12]

The women arose early on Sunday, November 2 to visit Smoketown Hospital, where

> # MAINE SOLDIERS' RELIEF ASSOCIATION,
> ### AND
> ## MAINE STATE AGENCY.
>
> Office and Store-rooms No. 273 F St., near Corner 13th St.,
>
> TWO SQUARES EAST OF PAYMASTER GENERAL'S OFFICE,
>
> WASHINGTON, D. C.
>
> ### LEONARD WATSON, AGENT.
>
> Officers and Soldiers in hospitals, wishing assistance, advice, or information, will receive attention. SOLDIERS are CAUTIONED not to pay money to Claim Agents or Clerks, as all needed information is given FREE, on application to the Agent or Visitors, concerning Back Pay, Furloughs, Transportation at "Government Rates," SETTLEMENTS OF DISCHARGED SOLDIERS—their Pension and Bounty. Information given concerning Soldiers on application by their friends.

Maine State Soldiers' Relief Association card
The MSRA handed out these small cards to apprise soldiers of the services offered by the MSRA and the Maine State Agency Sanitary Commission in Washington, D.C. These agencies assisted soldiers with getting leaves and furloughs, getting paid, receiving mail and packages, and more.
Image courtesy of Maine Historical Society/Maine Memory Network

they found about 30 Maine soldiers among the 700-odd patients. One reality immediately assaulted the women's senses.

"This place is in a most miserable condition ... the effluvia arising from the condition of these grounds is intolerable, quite enough to make a man in perfect health sick, and how men can recover in such a place is a mystery to me," Fogg vented her anger.[13]

Eaton "was quite disgusted with the place. Stench and filth dreadful." The stink was so bad in one ward that she suffered a "bad head ache" and "could not enter" the ward.

"Dirty rags and filth meet you at every turn," she noticed. Patients lacked "enough to eat," and the "men well enough to be up [are] laying in bed for want of clothes."[14]

In typical soldierly fashion, the sick Maine men "complain very much" despite "a great quantity of supplies" and the medical care provided by Pennsylvania nurses, Fogg indicated.[15]

The livid Eaton expressed a different opinion about those same nurses. "Here ... were five ladies with hospital tents, abundance of stores, cook stoves, and with all other appurtenances," she spat in a November 5 letter to Irene Francis Bosworth in Portland. "To their shame, I say, because they had not taken measures to see that the filth was removed that was producing malarious diseases to add to their other sufferings.

Confederate dead along a fence on the Hagerstown road after Antietam
Photo by Alexander Gardner via Library of Congress

"Sick men were lying here who begged, as we were passing, for clothing to put on that they might rise from their beds and walk about a little," Eaton told Bosworth. "They had not even drawers."[16]

That patients remained at Smoketown Hospital more than six weeks since Antietam demonstrated the army's inability to provide adequate medical care. The failure was widespread as the Army of the Potomac finally lurched into Virginia in late October and scattered sick and wounded men across the landscape.

Later that Sunday at Bakersville, Maryland, Fogg and her companions found 25 patients from the 5th Maine Infantry Regiment "left in a schoolhouse in care of the [hospital] steward without supplies." The steward, William Noyes of Saco, made "every effort to keep them [his patients] comfortable."

The investigators asked Noyes why he did not seek assistance from the U.S. Sanitary Commission, which had facilities nearby. Noyes replied that after encountering "so many difficulties in obtaining" supplies "from this source[,] hr preferred purchasing [supplies] himself," Fogg observed.

Sharing with Noyes a box of canned jellies obtained from Hathaway, the investigators then went to the USSC facility and submitted a list of needed supplies. Then Fogg and her companions traveled to Sharpsburg; "the Maine troops had crossed the river" there, and "only five Maine men" and a captain from the 20th Maine Infantry "were left here," Fogg told Hathaway.[17]

Approaching Sharpsburg from the north, the ambulance crossed Antietam battlefield. Fogg, while not actually fired upon during her Peninsula Campaign service, had witnessed the immediate horror of battle.

Eaton now "was deeply affected" to see a battle's aftermath. She saw "the graves" and "the famous cornfield where the battle was so fierce, the orchard where our Maine 10th tried to fight under cover of the trees," and the dead, rotting horses scattered over the battlefield.

Eaton tried to imagine "the scene of that awful day."[18]

Fogg and her companions "then proceeded to Harpers Ferry," where on November 3 they discovered "the sick are in a fearful condition, [sheltering] in every old house and church and hundreds on the ground." The assistant surgeon of the 19th Maine Infantry, Dr. John Q.A. Hawes, cared for "upwards of 50" men from that regiment; while visiting these sick men, Fogg learned that Hawes "does all in his power for their comfort."

Maj. Gen. Henry Slocum, the official XII Corps commander since October 20, asked the Maine civilians to travel to the Loudon Valley in Virginia "to learn the condition of several hundreds, who had been sent [there] the previous day" without proper medical care being arranged for them, Fogg reported.[19]

Crossing the Shenandoah River on a pontoon bridge, Eaton, Fogg, and Hayes "took ... a large load of Hos.[pital] stores" to "a new convalescent camp" in the nearby Loudon Valley, Eaton said.

Bearing no resemblance to Portland's cobble-stoned streets, the road to the valley wound "under rocky crags, over precipices, still onward."[20]

The sick soldiers suffered in the November cold in the Loudon Valley. "We found them lying on the ground,[spread] in all directions, many convalescent, but a great many very low," Fogg wrote, her words suggesting that such men lay near death. Clad in their filthy clothing, ill fed, and weakened by respiratory diseases, hundreds of Union boys endured this medical hell.

The federal government had literally abandoned these suffering heroes to their collective fates. "At this time no surgeons, nurses or cooks were on the ground and hard bread [was] their only food," Fogg fumed.

Only Sanitary Commission representatives ministered to the poor men. That morning Fogg and her companions had, "after much pleading," procured "a few supplies from the Commission" members, who acted "as if they were contributing out of their own pocket."

Watson had evidently left the investigative team by now to deliver a report to Hathaway. With the purchased supplies "we went to work to administer to the wants of the sick," Fogg wrote, Harriet Eaton "to wash and clean them, which they stood greatly in need of, while I prepared food for them."

Charles Hayes searched for "Maine men, but found none," Fogg noted. Soldiers were famished; the Mainers fed "every one who could not help themselves."[21]

Eaton, Fogg, and Hayes retraced their steps to Harpers Ferry, then crossed the Potomac River on a pontoon bridge and traveled by ambulance to Berlin, Maryland (now called Brunswick, not to be confused with a different Berlin, Maryland in Worcester County). After spending a comfortable night in a private home, the civilians awoke on Wednesday, November 5, and sought sick Maine soldiers.[22]

Despite all the malaise they had encountered, the Mainers were not prepared for the

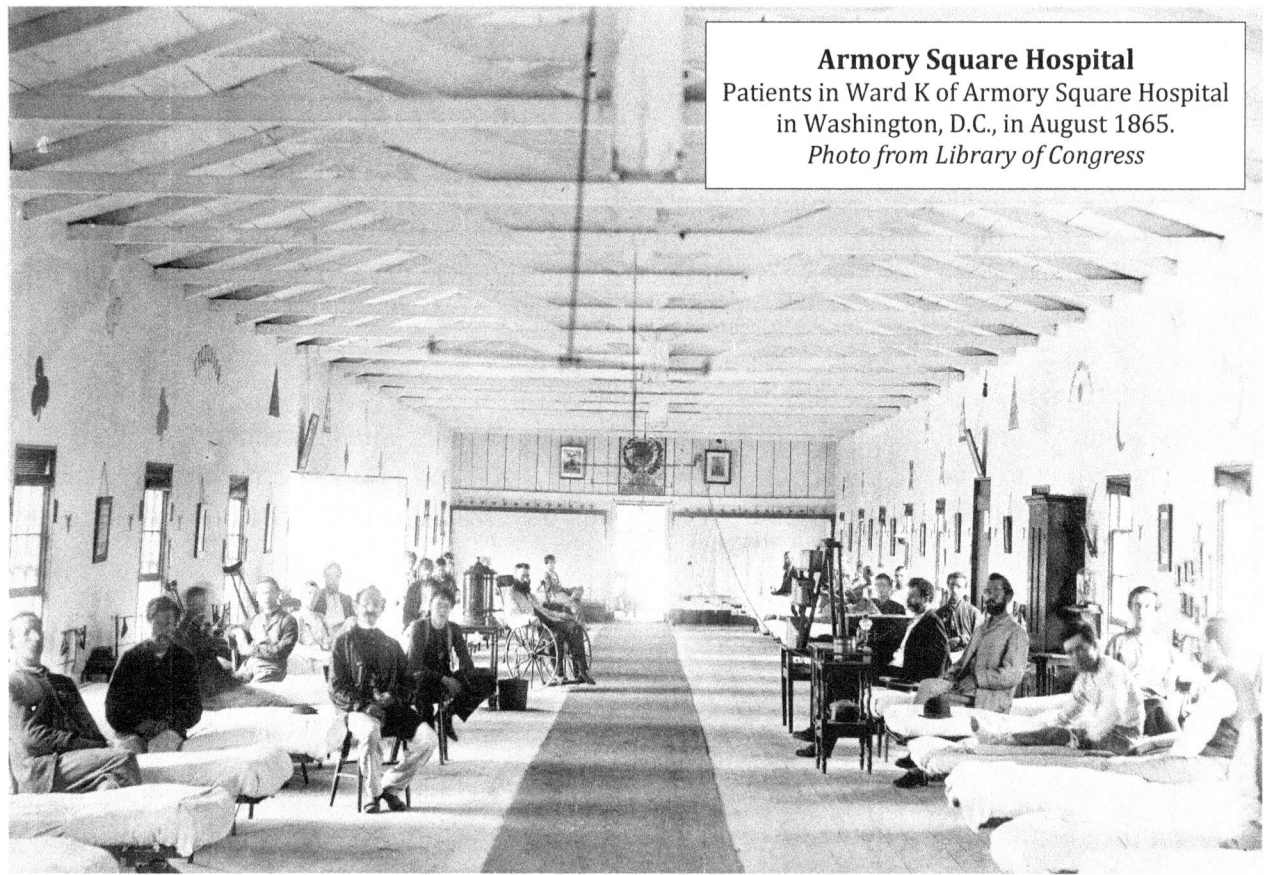

Armory Square Hospital
Patients in Ward K of Armory Square Hospital in Washington, D.C., in August 1865.
Photo from Library of Congress

revulsion they experienced in Berlin. "Here the misery and suffering beggars all description, the heart sickens at the sight," Fogg wrote as if she still walked amidst the horror.

"Taking a stroll through the town," she and Eaton "searched every old school house, log cabin &c [etc.] for the poor men who had been left behind, as our army moved on.

"In an old hut destitute of doors or windows and minus a part of the roof, we found 7 men, who had slept in the woods the night before, had crept in there, for the miserable shelter the place afforded," the aghast Fogg remembered.

She and Eaton sought "Maine men, and although these were not from our State, they claimed our sympathy." One soldier claimed he had the measles; Eaton believed he had smallpox, "which of course required immediate attention," Fogg realized.

"Finding the surgeon of the district" took some time. The doctor confirmed the patient had smallpox, Fogg said.

Eaton and Fogg "visited the Hospital of the 10th Maine" and found its patients "more comfortable than many others, but yet very much can be added to their comfort." The women (and likely Hayes) met with Lt. Col. James S. Fillebrown, "who expressed earnest thanks for our attention" to his men.

Resuming their building-by-building search of Berlin, Eaton and Fogg explored "a dilapidated school house, without [a] fireplace." The angels from Maine "found a man sick and old," a 57-year-old patriot "who had enlisted in the 12th Maine" Infantry a year earlier, the incredulous Fogg wrote Hathaway.[23]

Commanded by Col. George F. Shepley, the 12th Maine had served in Louisiana earlier that year. Apparently shipped east by midsummer, the grizzled old soldier "had been left, injured in the spine, at Fortress Monroe" in Virginia, Fogg noted. He "then knocked about from one Hospital to another" until his transfer to a New York regiment that had brought him to Maryland.

Abandoned at Berlin as too old and too slow to keep up with his new unit, the discouraged

Regimental hospital, 1863—viewed from entrance
Illustrations by James Fuller Queen via Library of Congress

veteran "knew not what to do," Fogg said. Hayes immediately started the appropriate paperwork to obtain an honorable discharge for the old soldier.[24]

That evening Fogg prepared gruel for the patients at the 10th Maine Infantry hospital. Walking to the 10th Maine camp, Eaton called at the tent belonging to Chaplain George Knox. "He went out and found Charles Tibbetts and Lieut. [John Mead] Gould," and the quartet had "quite a Portland chit chat."

Eaton, Fogg, and Hayes could have wrapped up their investigation at Berlin. Instead, after learning that Maine soldiers might be sick at Hagerstown, Fogg and Hayes headed there with a driver and an ambulance on Friday, November 7.

Staying at Berlin to care for the Maine boys found there, Eaton found "it is a luxury to be alone." She, the polished minister's widow, and Fogg, the blue-collar seamstress, had occasionally grated on each other's nerves during their epic up-country journey.[25]

Meanwhile, Fogg hoped for the best at Smoketown, "but how sadly we were disappointed.

"How I wish I could introduce you, and the Washington Com.[mission] to Smoketown Hos.[pital] in the midst of this driving snow storm!" she wrote John Hathaway. "You could have seen the poor fellows huddled together, with their pallets of straw on the ground, their tents connected by [tent] flyes, [sic] the same as erected in the heat of summer, many without walls and no stoves.

"Those who were able to creep out of their tents were crouched over fires, built in the woods, their heads covered with snow," and almost all the soldiers had only "thin muslin shirts on," Fogg wrote.

"The exposure has been such that diphtheria has broken out among them, and in nearly every case proves fatal," she noted. The patients lacked winter clothing, especially socks.

Did Fogg cry as she told Hathaway about "one of our poor Maine boys," a Smoketown patient who had diligently looked "up for us those belonging to Maine"? During Fogg's first visit to the hospital, the man had caught diphtheria, "caused by exposure, and lived but two or three hours."

Fogg and Hayes later reached Bakersville and the schoolhouse hospital operated by William Noyes. Fogg vented to Hathaway "our indignation" after learning that the local Sanitary Commission representatives had cut "fully one half on every article" requisitioned for the 5th Maine lads only a week or so earlier.[26]

But the "industrious" Noyes made do. Fogg and Hayes found him "grating corn on a grater he had made from an old canteen,[27] to furnish meal … to make gruel for his sick men."

Fogg urged Hathaway to cite Noyes "in your reports for he is worthy."

Fogg and Hayes traveled north to Hagerstown, where "we found several Maine men, but in a more comfortable condition than we had expected," Fogg said.

She and Hayes also found there three wooden boxes "for Maine regiments." Opening each box, Fogg and Hayes found in one "mostly old pillow cases," in another "chiefly muslin shirts," and in the third "upwards of a hundred flannel shirts, with some other useful articles," Fogg joyfully reported.

Chapter 47: Angels of Mercy

Union soldiers burying the dead
Confederate dead lie nearby while Union soldiers bury their own on the Miller farm.
Photo by Alexander Gardner via Library of Congress

"Imagine now, with what pleasure we retraced our steps to Bakersville and Smoketown!" she told Hathaway. "Could you have seen the happy faces and heard the thankful expressions of gratitude" from the Maine boys receiving the flannel shirts, "you would have felt that too much could not be done for their comfort."

Pushing east over South Mountain, Fogg and Hayes supplied flannel shirts to Maine soldiers they discovered hospitalized at Burkittsville in Middletown Valley. Finally, "after the tedious labor and hard exposure of three days" spent traveling on their final circuit, Fogg and Hayes reached Berlin on Monday, November 10.

The weary Isabella Fogg sat down to write her detailed report to Hathaway. Unafraid to express her opinions, she reminded him of the striking contrast between medical care in the nation's capital and in the hinterlands.

"You no doubt think your ladies in Washington are doing a great work, but I can assure you, if they were here, they would find the stern reality of want, privation and extreme suffering," Fogg wrote.[28]

Concluding her November 5 letter to Irene Bosworth, Harriet Eaton thought about the nightmares she had encountered at the so-called "hospitals" upriver from Berlin. She had crisscrossed rugged terrain and fast-flowing rivers, come close to blundering into Confederate pickets, and had seen sick men die who could have been saved with adequate nutrition and medical care.

"It is one vast hospital," Eaton described the human aftermath of Antietam. "I cannot picture it; my heart is sick.

"The great army must be attended to; but the thousands and tens of thousands who have fallen by the wayside, how few care for such!" she exclaimed.[29]

~~~

1. Inadequate medical care plagued sick and wounded soldiers from all loyal states in summer and autumn 1862. Soldiers feared being sent to hospitals, from which too many patients emerged in coffins.
2. Franklin Henry Eaton, *Soldiers' File,* Maine State Archives
3. The standard enlistment term for men joining most existing regiments was for three years or the war's duration.
4. Lynda L. Sudlow, *A Vast Army of Women: Maine's Uncounted Forces in the American Civil War,* Thomas Publications, Gettysburg, Penn., 2000, p. 86
5. Jane E. Schultz, editor, *This Birth Place of Souls: The Civil War Nursing Diary of Harriet Eaton,* Oxford University Press, New York, 2011, pp. 55-57
6. John W. Hathaway, letter to Governor Israel Washburn Jr., October 15, 1862, Maine State Archives
7. Captured soldiers were often paroled rather than sent to prison camps—or accepted parole to escape from such camps. A paroled soldier could not return to military service until exchanged for an enemy prisoner of equal rank. Paroled soldiers were often kept at a specific site, such as "Camp Misery."
8. Hathaway to Washburn, October 15, 1862, MSA
9. Underlined in diarist's original.
10. Schultz, *Birth Place,* pp. 60-70
11. Isabella Fogg, letter to John W. Hathaway, November 10, 1862, Maine State Archives
12. Schultz, *Birth Place,* p. 71
13. Fogg to Hathaway, November 10, 1862, MSA
14. Schultz, *Birth Place,* p. 71
15. Fogg to Hathaway, November 10, 1862, MSA
16. Schultz, *Birth Place,* p. 204
17. Fogg to Hathaway, November 10, 1862, MSA
18. Schultz, *Birth Place,* pp. 73-74
19. Fogg to Hathaway, November 10, 1862, MSA
20. Schultz, *Birth Place,* p. 75. Italics in original.
21. Fogg to Hathaway, November 10, 1862, MSA
22. Schultz, *Birth Place,* p. 75
23. This unfortunate soldier remains unidentified. According to the regimental returns for the 12th Maine Infantry Regiment as published in the *Annual Report of the Adjutant General of the State of Maine, 1861*, the only man older than age 50 who enlisted in the regiment was A.G. Robbins, 51, of Portland. He was a wagoner with Co. B. Many men in their mid-40s also joined the 12th Maine Infantry.
24. Fogg to Hathaway, November 10, 1862, MSA
25. Schultz, *Birth Place,* pp. 76-77
26. Fogg to Hathaway, November 10, 1862, MSA
27. Noyes drove a nail or spike into the canteen, then removed (grated) kernels from corn cobs by scraping them against the nail.
28. Fogg to Hathaway, November 10, 1862, MSA
29. Schultz, *Birth Place,* p. 205

Chapter 48

MAINE'S MOST HATED

"The character of Lunt was vile beyond description"

As Maine soldiers converged on Fredericksburg, deserter Albert W. Lunt learned his fate while incarcerated at St. Augustine, Florida.

After Confederates returned the 22-year-old Lunt to Federal lines in late April 1862, the wheels of military justice ground slowly to determine his fate. Captured by enemy cavalry after fleeing the 9th Maine Infantry, Lunt had betrayed seven comrades stationed at a rural house near Fernandina; Confederate cavalry swept in on April 10 and killed one soldier and captured the other six.

With Col. Alfred Terry of the 7th Connecticut Infantry presiding, a Union court-martial convened at St. Augustine, Florida to hear the indictments and sift through the evidence. Lunt listened as the military judges—senior officers drawn from various commands—heard testimony about the charges, including "Desertion" and "Highway Robbery."

The latter charge involved allegations that Lunt "did forcibly take from MRS. ELLEN MANNING" $268 at Fernandina "on or about the 6th of April, 1862." He was also charged with stealing the watch of a Confederate cavalry major.

Convicting Lunt for desertion and for robbing Manning, the Army judges sentenced him "to be shot to death at such time and place as the commanding general may direct."

Under congressional fiat, the "evidence and findings of the court" must be reviewed by President Abraham Lincoln. Back to his jail cell went Lunt and off to Washington, D.C. went the paperwork, but fighting in Tennessee and Virginia occupied the president's attention that spring and summer.[1] Lincoln took a while to confirm Lunt's fate.

Federal authorities transferred Lunt in September to Hilton Head, South Carolina, where provost marshal Maj. George Van Brunt of the 47th New York Infantry Regiment imprisoned him.[2] Not a particularly troublesome prisoner, Lunt displayed an insouciant attitude "respecting his fate," noted *New York Times* special correspondent Henry J. Wisner.

Lincoln approved the court-martial's findings in mid-November; at Hilton Head, Brig. Gen. John M. Brannan scheduled Lunt's execution for 11 a.m., Monday, December 1.

"The announcement he received carelessly—almost with insolent derision—saying that he might as well die at one time as at another," said Wisner, referring to Lunt.

Union Gen. Alfred Howe Terry
Photo from Library of Congress

Union Brig. Gen. John Milton Brannan
Photo from Library of Congress

Van Brunt ordered Lunt transferred under heavy guard from his cell to a tent "pitched in an isolated part of the Provost-Marshal's encampment," Wisner noted. The hope was that, with the transition, the deserter's "mind might be turned into reflection."

With the Reverend Joshua Butts[3] ministering to him, Lunt "underwent, to all outward appearance, a marvelous change. Seriousness took the place of levity," Wisner said. On November 26, Lunt "professed to see clearly the way of salvation and expressed himself as at peace with his Maker and the world."[4]

"Realizing his condition, he prayed for the forgiveness of God, and died professing his faith in the mercy of the Almighty," a Port Royal newspaper stated.[5]

In midafternoon on November 29, Wisner "received a note from the Provost-Marshal, inviting me to visit" Lunt, who wanted "to see a representative of the Press." Wisner "overcame a natural reluctance to call upon a person in his condition, and had the interview."

If Wisner expected to encounter a monster, he did not. "I found him [Lunt] perfectly composed, and during more than an hour I passed with him, not once did he lose his remarkable self-possession," Wisner noted.

Lunt gave Wisner six and a half pages "of closely written foolscap" and "asked me to print the paper," which iterated "his protestations of innocence of the crime of desertion."

As to the desertion charge, Lunt claimed a 9th Maine officer had sent him to Manning's house, where "a party of our own troops" might find him, "which would have placed him in difficulty." To avoid any approaching Union patrol, Lunt "pressed on further" until Confederate cavalry caught him.

"As far as the theft of the [Confederate] Major's watch was concerned, he did not consider that wrong, as it was filched while that officer had him under guard and was searching his pockets," Wisner noted.

Chapter 48: Maine's Most Hated

"For the sake of my family I want it to be published that I am innocent," Lunt said. "Tell my fellow-soldiers that I have been a hard boy, and have done a great many wicked things, and they must take my death as a warning not to be led astray by bad company."

Lunt claimed that witnesses had lied about him at the court-martial, "but I have no ill-feeling toward them. I am resigned to my fate."

Joining Lunt on Sunday, November 30, Reverend Butts and Reverend Henry Hill, the chaplain of the 3rd New Hampshire Infantry, remained with the doomed soldier until 3 a.m. Monday, when he finally fell asleep. Slowly passed the night, "hours of which each minute must seem a year," Wisner said.

Clad in his uniform, "a blue army overcoat and … a black felt hat," Lunt left his tent at 10:30 a.m., Monday and walked to a horse-drawn ambulance while guarded by two soldiers armed with pistols. "Not a muscle of his features moved, not a limb trembled," a reporter noticed.[6]

The ambulance was parked inside a square "formed by the firing party of twenty-four men of the Provost Guard" drawn from the 47th New York, according to Wisner. The soldiers stood "at open order, with pieces [firearms] reversed."[7]

Walking through his executioners, Lunt climbed into the ambulance "sedately and unaided, seating himself upon the rough coffin which was destined for his remains," Wisner said. There Lunt sat with "his face reclining upon his right hand, and his elbow supported upon his knee."

Van Brunt took a position on the right side of the ambulance, and the funereal procession stepped off. For the next 30 minutes, "the mournful tap of muffled drums" resounded as the ambulance traveled slowly "to the place selected for the execution," Wisner said. The soldiers from the 47th New York Infantry marched in front of the ambulance, the two chaplains and several "medical officers" behind it.[8]

"As the procession slowly made its way … the guards and sentinels along the route, presented arms and crowds of soldiers, civilians and contrabands pressed forward eagerly to gratify a morbid curiosity and catch a glimpse" of Lunt, a reporter observed.[9]

Finally the ambulance rumbled past the Federal earthworks crossing Hilton Head and halted in "a spacious field" on the south end of the island. Army authorities had already marched out several regiments to form a three-sided "hollow square."[10] Summoned to witness the punishment meted out by his military court, Alfred Terry waited near the square's center with his staff and several high-ranking officers.[11]

The ambulance stopped on the open side of the square. The waiting soldiers—"veterans, undaunted in battle, but now timorous and stricken with dread," according to Wisner—silently watched as Lunt "alighted without assistance, and his coffin was placed beside him," Wisner said. Lunt displayed "no dampness upon his brow, no tears upon his cheek."[12]

The soldiers did not want to be there, but their presence was mandatory. "All the troops at Hilton Head were called out to witness a very painful scene … the execution of a hardened criminal," said Frederic Denison of the 3rd Rhode Island Heavy Artillery Regiment, assigned to the island garrison.

"The desperate character was William W. Lunt (true name Albert Lunt), of Company I, Ninth Maine Regiment," Denison noted. "He was duly convicted by court-martial, and sentenced to be shot for the double crime of desertion and highway robbery."[13]

Wisner watched the execution because he recognized the incredible story it entailed. Denison and his comrades watched because their superiors sought to instill the fear of the firing squad in soldiers who might be tempted to get into serious trouble.

The drama played out too long. Lunt listened as a lieutenant read the court-martial proceedings, and then Van Brunt asked the deserter if he wanted to speak. Addressing the assembled soldiers "in a loud, clear tone," Lunt proclaimed, "I want you to take warning of me and seek salvation from the Lord before it is too late.

"I am not guilty of the crime which I am condemned to death for," he stated.

Doffing his overcoat, Lunt knelt on his coffin. "In this position a bandage was fastened over his eyes, and at the same moment a squad of twelve men were silently motioned to post themselves in front of him at a distance of fifteen paces," Wisner scribbled in his notebook.

Actually comprising 24 men—a 12-man squad and a backup squad—the firing squad had been "selected by the Provost-Marshal with a view to nerve and good marksmanship," and the soldiers had practiced shooting at a stationary target set "at the designated distance," Wisner said. Capt. Edward Eddy Jr. commanded the firing squad.

As the chaplains quietly prayed with Lunt, the twelve soldiers cocked their rifled muskets. Eleven were fully loaded; the twelfth contained "a blank cartridge and a heavy wad" so that as each soldier received a musket, he could not tell if it contained the blank or not, Wisner later learned.

Shaking Lunt's hand, Van Brunt moved out of the line of fire. Eddy waved his sword, and the twelve soldiers raised their muskets to their shoulders and aimed at the silent Lunt. Wisner watched closely as Van Brunt dropped "his pocket handkerchief" to signal Eddy to shoot.

"Fire!" he shouted. Eleven muskets roared; the percussion "cap of one musket exploded without discharging the piece," Wisner noticed.

"Six or eight dark splotches" suddenly appeared "as if by magical power ... upon the body," and Lunt "lies lifeless upon the ground," Wisner said.[14] Denison remembered that Lunt fell forward on the top of his coffin.[15]

The second twelve-man firing squad was not needed; the medical officers who had accompanied Lunt from his prison tent declared him dead. They spent considerable time examining the body and determining how many bullets struck Lunt and where. Eight bullets "passed entirely through the body" and a ninth lodged in it, Wisner later wrote in his detailed description of the lead musket balls' passage through Lunt.

At many other military executions undertaken during the Civil War, the watching soldiers were marched past the corpse to remind them what fate awaited deserters. Terry waived this practice post-Lunt; once the casket was nailed shut, six soldiers escorted it without "the usual military honors" to a graveyard for burial, Wisner noted.

He expressed his pleasure that "the barbarous custom of allowing the corpse to lie where it fell until the entire command should march by" was proscribed by Terry, who also "wisely refused permission to civilians to see the execution."

By doing so, Terry effectively barred the human vultures, "those whom of a depraved

Execution of deserters from the 118th Pennsylvania at Beverly Ford
Alfred Lunt's fate was much the same as these deserters. Soldiers were marched out in formation, much as with Lunt, to witness the execution. The six deserters at middle right are kneeling on their coffins, to fall in when shot.
Illustration by Edwin Forbes via Library of Congress

taste would have been drawn to the scene," Wisner realized.[16]

Some eyewitnesses approved of the execution. "Desertion on the front is a crime that may not be measured," opined Denison. "The character of Lunt was vile beyond description."[17]

People agreed in Maine, where no politician wanted to admit Lunt's connection with the state. The *Annual Report of the Adjutant General of the State of Maine, 1861* had listed Orono as the town in which Lunt had lived before enlisting.[18] Patriotic Orono residents were now aghast that Albert W. Lunt was "on our list of men furnished for the war" in 1861, Samuel Libbey protested to Adjutant Gen. John L. Hodsdon on November 19, 1862.

"He is the infamous scoundrel who was recently sentenced to be shot, for desertion, etc and has no reason to hail from here," Libbey snorted. "His father Henry Lunt moved from here in [18]48 or 49. The young man hasn't ever worked here since; but lived in Old Town and lastly in Hampden.

"I wish our town might be spared the disgrace of such fellows hailing from it by putting them where they belong," Libbey wrote. "I merely state the facts ... as I understand them and you will of course dispose of this case as you think best."[19]

Like other Maine newspapers, the *Portland Daily Press* drew heavily on Wisner's account of the execution. To reinforce "the depravity to which the victim had sunken," the editors added a claim by "another correspondent" that Lunt had "on various parts of his body ... obscene pictures, in India ink, [tattoos] of the most revolting and disgusting character."[20]

Such lurid detail provided additional evidence to horrified Mainers that Albert W. Lunt was a man to be most hated.

The 9th Maine's returns published in the *Annual Report of the Adjutant General of the State of Maine, 1862* indicated that 22-year-old "William W. Lunt" of "Plattsburg, N.Y." had joined the regiment in September 1861. He had "deserted April 7; returned April 20 by Col.

Davis of the rebel army; now in arrest for desertion."

The six surviving men of Co. I whom Lunt had betrayed at Fernandina—Orderly Sgt. Richard Webster, Corp. James Bowman, and privates C. Wesley Adams, John Kent, Alonzo Merrill, and Isaac Whitney—still languished in a Tallahassee prison in late 1862.[21] And Pvt. Ansel Chase was eight months' dead.

The capture of six soldiers and the killing of Ansel Chase "was occasioned by a deserter of the company named Albert W. Lunt, giving information to the enemy of their whereabouts," Hodsdon stated.

"Lunt was afterwards caught, and for this and other crimes which he was proved guilty of, was shot," the angry Hodsdon reminded Mainers still stunned by Lunt's treachery.[22]

The deserter, thief, and traitor had received his just reward. No other Mainer would be so hated in his home state during the Civil War.

~~~

1. Henry J. Wisner, "Interesting from Port Royal," *New York Times,* Monday, December 1, 1862
2. "Execution Of A Soldier," *The New South,* Vol. 1, No. 16, Saturday, December 6, 1862. The New South article reveals that another person was present when Wisner interviewed Lunt.
3. Butts was the chaplain of the 47th New York Infantry Regiment, then stationed on Hilton Head.
4. Wisner, *NYT,* Monday, December 1, 1862
5. *The New South,* Saturday, Dec. 6, 1862
6. *The New South,* December 6, 1862
7. Reversed here means "muzzles pointed at the ground."
8. Wisner, *NYT,* Monday, December 1, 1862
9. *The New South,* December 6, 1862. This paper apparently drew heavily on Wisner's account, some of which it published verbatim without crediting the New York Times' correspondent.
10. Wisner, *NYT,* Monday, December 1, 1862
11. A brigadier general of volunteers since spring 1862, Terry remained in the Army after the Civil War. He led the Army column that discovered the Custer massacre site at the Little Big Horn in late June 1876.
12. Wisner, *NYT,* December 1, 1862
13. Rev. Frederic Denison, *Shot and Shell: The Third Rhode Island Heavy Artillery Regiment,* J.A. & R.A. Reid, Providence, R.I., 1879, p. 128
14. Wisner, *New York Times,* December 1, 1862
15. Denison, *Shot and Shell,* p. 128
16. Wisner, *NYT,* December 1, 1862
17. Denison, *Shot and Shell,* p. 128
18. *Annual Report of the Adjutant General of the State of Maine, 1861,* pp. 429-430
19. Samuel Libbey, letter to Adjutant Gen. John L. Hodsdon, November 19, 1862, Maine State Archives
20. "Execution of a Maine Soldier," *Portland Daily Press,* Wednesday, December 17, 1862
21. *Annual Report of the Adjutant General of the State of Maine, 1862,* pp. 254-255
22. Ibid., p. 66

Chapter 49

THE BLANKET BRIGADE PRESSES ONWARD

"All that time God was busy making heroes"

As a frustrated Charles Tilden watched his 16th Maine Infantry Regiment disintegrate in fall 1862, he likely wondered why War Department bureaucrats were killing or disabling Maine soldiers.

Was that not the job of the enemy?

Crossing the Antietam battlefield on Friday, September 19, the 16th Maine lads camped near Sharpsburg that night and, after bouncing around the landscape a bit, settled into a semi-permanent camp on the Potomac River, about three miles west of town. Duty for the 16th Maine Infantry should have been idyllic, yet the regiment immediately crumbled on its feet.

The officers had tents. Under official orders, the enlisted men had left their knapsacks, overcoats, and tents in Arlington, Virginia; every 16th Maine lad not wearing shoulder straps suffered for that error.

Sharpsburg lies in Washington County, the fertile 467-square-mile agricultural and wooded region bordered by South Mountain to the east, Pennsylvania to the north, and the Potomac River and West Virginia to the south and west. The town stands 420 feet above sea level, 30 feet higher in elevation than Houlton on the southern Aroostook plateau in Maine.

But Sharpsburg lies at 39.457 degrees latitude and Houlton at 46.122 degrees latitude, a difference of 6.6 degrees or about 460 miles, south to north, from central Maryland to northern Maine. Spring comes earlier and autumn lingers longer in Sharpsburg than in Houlton, to which mid-19th century winters usually brought deep snow, howling wind, and subzero cold.

Similar wintry weather prevailed elsewhere in Maine in mid-century. Intimately acquainted with winter, Maine lads knew how to live with bone-chilling cold, but not in the 16th Maine camp, where enlisted men lacked even a tent's canvas walls to ward off autumn's sinking temperatures.

"Our regiment was overlooked," and Adjutant Abner R. Small could not understand why.

"The property that we had left behind, as ordered, was not sent to us; neither were other supplies."

The 16th Maine belonged to the 3rd Brigade (Col. Richard Coulter) of the 2nd Division (Brig. Gen. James Ricketts), which belonged to I Corps, commanded by Maj. Gen. Joseph Hooker. Coulter had replaced Brig. Gen. George Lucas Hartsuff, wounded in the hip at Antietam. Assigned to the 3rd Brigade were four veteran infantry regiments from other states.

"We were bitterly chagrined ... to see others well supplied while we were neglected," Small said. "Some of our sister regiments [in the 3rd Brigade], fully clothed and blanketed and tented, were secure against the weather.

"Our men, with nothing but their blankets and the clothing they stood in, were suffering for lack of their tents, overcoats, and the knapsacks that held their extra wear [clothing]," he complained.[1]

Soldiers from veteran regiments camped nearby started referring to the 16th Maine Infantry as the "Blanket Brigade," an appellation that stung. Already struggling to stay dry, many Maine lads stood guard duty with thin blankets wrapped around their shoulders in lieu of missing overcoats. Healthy soldiers wore weather-rotted clothing. Hats and shoes fell apart, men lacked warm flannel blouses, and although they built roaring fires at night, soldiers accustomed to frigid Maine winters could not get warm in lower-latitude Maryland.

Charles W. Tilden
Photo courtesy of Maine State Archives

The verbal bullying by other Union veterans cut as deep psychologically as the Sharpsburg cold did physically. "How those men suffered!" Small said. "Hunger, daily felt,[2] was nothing compared with it.

"Men of education, refinement, and wealth, who willingly and cheerfully gave up home, with all its love and comfort, made to feel degraded for want of proper clothing!

"The men were made to feel mean and despicable, and felt as does a poor boy at school, when the well-dressed student resents the contact of blue jeans with broadcloth," Small said.

He laid the blame for the regiment's breakdown on "the inefficiency and neglect" of quartermasters scattered all the way from Washington, D.C. to the 3rd Brigade headquarters near Sharpsburg. Out in their rude hovels of "cornstalks and boughs," enlisted men "accused their immediate commanders" of neglecting them and cursed the officers "as the authors of their miserable condition."

Chapter 49: The Blanket Brigade Presses Onward

Wildes and Tilden came in for particular condemnation—and Small knew the accusations were untrue. As adjutant, he wrote the orders dictated by both officers as they doggedly tried to retrieve the tents and baggage.

On October 2, the ailing Asa Wildes ordered Capt. Stephen Whitehouse of Co. K and Newcastle to "proceed at once" to Washington, get the regiment's "company books and papers," and identify the sick 16th Maine lads scattered "in various hospitals" between Sharpsburg and the capital.

Wildes dutifully sent his order up the chain of command. After sitting on the order for four days—and without citing a reason—division commander James Ricketts denied the request.[3]

By then the 16th Maine was already fading away. In Co. A, James Witham of Township 3, Range 3 died on Tuesday, September 30.[4] In Co. D, Capt. Moses Rand of Waterford—remembered by Pvt. Henry Franklin Andrews of Lovell as "a splendid specimen of humanity, physically"[5]—fell so seriously ill that he was confined to Seminary Hospital in Georgetown near Washington, D.C.

Only three days after her arrival in the capital, nurse Harriet Eaton visited Seminary Hospital and "found there a very sick man, Capt. Rand of Waterford, Maine, belonging to 16th Maine Company D.

"[I] don't believe he is having suitable medical treatment, sat by him about two hours," Eaton said.[6]

Later sent home to Maine, Rand died in Portland on December 8.[7]

Sick for much of his tenure with the 16th Maine, Asa Wildes took a leave of absence on October 10.[8] Tilden replaced him immediately and on October 13 ordered Whitehouse to travel to Washington, D.C. to get the regiment's books, papers, and "knapsacks packed with clothing."

Forwarding that order to Brig. Gen. Nelson Taylor (the current 3rd Brigade commander), Tilden indicated that the "men in my command are suffering for a want of a change of clothing." By October 13, in fact, many 16th Maine boys no longer had "underclothes."

Taylor approved the request later that day. Writing via his own adjutant that "these articles can be telegraphed for from Sharpsburg," Ricketts denied Tilden's request before going to bed that night.[9]

Lacking extra clothing, the 16th Maine

Union Brig. Gen. James Brewerton Ricketts
Pictured here as a major general.
Photo by Mathew Brady via Library of Congress

429

boys seldom washed their existing clothing and themselves. Sweat-encrusted grime clung to men and, especially in conjunction with the filthy underwear that could not be changed, left a stench wafting through the camp.

"The rapid decline from fastidious neatness to filthiness of condition and habits changed some of them [16th Maine boys] beyond recognition," Small observed.[10]

Mental disorders afflicted many men. Dr. William Eaton, an assistant regimental surgeon, noticed that "uncleanliness, despondency, and gloom prevailed" among the patients he treated at Sharpsburg. Becoming "so fearful in its severer types," homesickness struck hard, he said. Men so afflicted sank into "unbearable" despair, and while "weaker constitutions succumbed at once, the stronger bore up for a while," only to bear "the full fruits of those days" later in life.

Small remembered "a college graduate, a royal good fellow" who gradually exhibited a personality change ("lost his self-respect"). The soldier "was only brought to himself and obedience by the free use of a corn broom and brook water."[11]

The nutritional deficiency continued well into October—and likely exacerbated the mental and physical breakdowns of many 16th Maine boys. One day "there was a flurry of hope when cases of hardtack were distributed in the camp," Small noticed.

Then the cheers faded, and men cursed. Every case bore the word "Yorktown," indicating that the contents had been issued to the Army of the Potomac early in the spring 1862 Peninsula Campaign.

Small took a bite; "I learned then ... why 'worm castles' was the popular name for hardtack," he said.

Although foraging was banned,[12] starving 16th Maine lads took their chances with the army provosts. "Many a choice fowl, an occasional lamb, and any amount of garden truck mysteriously satisfied the hunger of our troops," Small admitted.

Snatching empty sardine tins "in the rear of brigade headquarters"—where the staff ate well—Maine soldiers would "with a nail convert the tins into graters" and on them rub the corn stolen from local farms, Small recalled. With this method the enlisted men got enough corn to prepare "a genuine Maine hasty pudding."[13]

Charging two dollars for a bushel of potatoes, 40 cents per pound for butter, and 10 cents for a quart of milk,[14] Army sutlers made a killing at the 16th Maine's expense.[15]

Tilden tried again on October 18 to alleviate the regiment's suffering by ordering Capt. John Ayer of Co. H and Bangor to fulfill the same mission as that fruitlessly assigned twice to Capt. Whitehouse earlier that month. In a passionately detailed preface addressed to Nelson Taylor, Tilden explained why the regiment needed the missing clothing, knapsacks, and tents.

Taylor, Ricketts, and I Corps commander Brig. Gen. John Reynolds endorsed Tilden's request on Sunday, October 19. Stipulating that Ayer must "return in five days," George B. McClellan added his approval on Tuesday, October 21.[16]

Ayer immediately decamped for Washington, D.C., and the 16th Maine "received marching orders" that same day. Albeit too late, McClellan was going after Robert E. Lee; brigades and divisions were crossing the Potomac River, and only heavy rain kept the 16th Maine from

Thanksgiving surprise
While working as a combat artist during the Civil War, Winslow Homer drew this amusing sketch of Union soldiers celebrating Thanksgiving at the sutler's tent set up near their regiment's camp. When their long missing clothing and tents arrived at their camp on Thanksgiving Day 1862, the men of the 16th Maine Infantry Regiment rejoiced.
Illustration by Winslow Homer

departing Sharpsburg on October 22.[17]

After their officers struck their tents, the 16th Maine lads stepped out at 4 a.m., Sunday, October 26 "and marched through … Sharpsburg in a torrent of rain," Small said. Shuffling in ankle-deep mud through Rhorersville, the soldiers climbed South Mountain via Thornton's Gap and "by common consent and instinct" sought shelter in "the woods on the west side" of the mountain after enduring an hour-long halt around 8 p.m.

In those woods Small and his comrades "passed a dismal night" during "a furious storm of wind and rain."

And the regiment's disintegration continued. The 24-year-old captain of Co. A, Charles Williams of Skowhegan, was probably sick when he left Sharpsburg; his friends left him "at a citizen's house in Rhorersville," Small remembered.[18]

Bivouacking at Burkittsville, Maryland on October 27, the 16th Maine lads left there at 6 a.m. the next day and camped in "the village of Berlin [now Brunswick, Maryland], under a hill on the north bank of the Potomac River," he said. A quartermaster issued "shelter tents and shoes"—not enough to go around—to the men, and for the first time in almost eight weeks, some soldiers spent a night beneath canvas.[19]

During the regiment's brief stopover in Berlin, Co. C privates Albion Bean of Wilton and William Carpenter of Jay were discharged for disabilities.[20] The remaining 16th Maine boys broke step to cross a Potomac River pontoon bridge at 4 p.m., October 30; Small commented on the "the tall stone piers" of a Confederate-wrecked railroad bridge rising from the river just downstream from where the 16th Maine crossed.

Survivors would remember the ensuing march across Virginia as "cold, hard, wearisome going ... the roads were muddy, and our marches and bivouacs were miserable," Small groused. Spirits lifted briefly on Wednesday, November 5, after the 16th Maine boys "halted to let a wagon train pass," he said. Suddenly George Brinton McClellan and his glittery cavalcade rode past the Maine soldiers.

"A great wave of cheering swept with him into our hearing, and was loud with the shouts of our men, and swept away down the road," Small described the joyous scene. The Maine lads "went on after that with livelier spirit."

That night the 16th Maine camped near "the home of a rebel colonel." Small said. Searching the property before the provosts arrived, famished 16th Maine foragers discovered a treasure trove of corn and potatoes concealed in the outbuildings.

"Hunger knew no discipline," Small commented. "The buildings were ransacked."[21]

The next day, Pvt. Leonidas Wentworth of Hope succumbed to sickness. He was the first man from Co. D to die.[22] Friends buried him; amidst "a blinding snowstorm" and bitter cold that froze water in the men's metal canteens, the 16th Maine marched on to Warrenton on Friday, November 7.[23]

The next morning, every man from Co. H turned up sick. Tilden evidently delayed the regiment's departure until medical personnel evaluated the Co. H lads; then the 16th Maine stepped out at 4 p.m. and, "led by a stupid guide," marched six miles in the wrong direction until someone figured out the correct road to Rappahannock Station, Small remembered.

Suffering "in a blinding storm of snow and hail," the 16th Maine lads marched into Rappahannock Station at 1 a.m., Sunday, November 9, he recalled. They now camped on the river's north bank; their long march from Maryland was over.

Later that Sunday, fewer than 200 "ragged, dirty, half fed, [and] half clothed" soldiers reported for duty, Small noticed. But "they are cheerful and plucky."

Having dug deep into their psyches, the survivors realized the great transformation they had undergone since jauntily marching out of Fort Tillinghast eight weeks earlier.

"We learned obedience, we were taught patience through suffering, courage came to us by exposure to danger; and, somehow, we were better men for these weeks of vicarious atonement," Small said.[24]

"Out of all this suffering ... came a lasting patriotism and courage that no privation, no danger could abate," he believed. "The few short months developed a new set of men, and what kind of men let Fredericksburgh tell.

"All that time God was busy making heroes," Small concluded.[25]

Chapter 49: The Blanket Brigade Presses Onward

But the heroes kept fading away. On Monday, November 10, Charles Williams died in Rhorersville, Maryland, and Josiah Nutting, an 18-year-old private from Canaan, was discharged for disability from Co. A.[26] Sgt. Walter E. Stone of Co. D and Waterford had fallen ill in Maryland; he would die in a Virginia hospital in June 1863.[27]

The 16th Maine lads who reached Rappahannock Station would remember one particular detail. "Through all that long, sad, and weary tramp [from Sharpsburg], we were jeered at, insulted, and called the 'Blanket Brigade!'" Small exclaimed.[28]

Meanwhile John Ayer had successfully completed his mission in Washington; the Army forwarded the 16th Maine's baggage and tents from Arlington to Hagerstown. Unfortunately, the freight arrived a day after the regiment departed Sharpsburg.

And when Quartermaster Tucker hustled to Hagerstown to have the gear forwarded to the regiment, the post quartermaster refused to do so. Meanwhile, the 16th Maine went into camp near Stafford Court House, Virginia.

So on Tuesday, November 11, Charles Tilden again asked Nelson Taylor to resolve the supply problem. Letters flurried across the desks of John Reynolds and other generals; Tilden received approval to send 1st Lt. Oliver Lowell of Co. F and Gorham to Hagerstown, get the missing baggage and tents, bring the gear via Berlin, "and return, without delay, to his regiment."[29]

Then the 16th Maine shifted campsites, transferred to a brigade commanded by Col. Adrian Root, and lost track of Lowell—and vice versa. At yet another new camp site at Aquia Creek, Virginia, Charles Tilden even wrote John Hathaway of the Maine Soldiers' Relief Agency on November 24 and asked, "Has Lieut. Lowell left Washington with the clothing for this regiment?"

On Thursday, November 27, remembered by Small as "both the national and State 'Thanksgiving Day,'" Lowell suddenly "arrived from Washington with knapsacks and overcoats.

"Seldom have men greater cause for gladness," Small joyfully wrote. "The overcoats gave warmth and respectability, while the knapsacks supplied underclothing in place of that worn [for] eleven long weeks."

The men's moods changed. "Despondency gives place to a buoyancy hitherto unknown," according to Small. "Shelter, food, and clothing have done their perfect work, and a feeling of satisfaction and contentment envelops the command."[30]

The Blanket Brigade was now clothed—and bound for Fredericksburg.

~~~

1. Major Abner R. Small, *The Road to Richmond,* editor Harold Adams Small, reprinted by Fordham University Press, New York, 2000, pp. 48-49
2. To add insult to injury, the War Department often failed to supply adequate rations to the 16th Maine during its Sharpsburg sojourn. The lack of adequate nutrition plagued Union troops well into the war.
3. Major A.R. Small, *The Sixteenth Maine Regiment in the War of the Rebellion 1861-1865,* editors Peter and

Cyndi Dalton, B. Thurston & Company, Portland, Maine 1886, pp. 36-40

4. *Maine Adjutant General's 1862,* Appendix D, p. 543
5. H.F. Andrews, *Company D 16 Maine Vols.,* Exira Printing Co., Exira, Iowa 1906, p. 3
6. Jane E. Schultz, editor, *This Birth Place of Souls: The Civil War Nursing Diary of Harriet Eaton,* Oxford University Press, New York, 2011, p. 58
7. Andrews, *Company D,* p. 3
8. *Annual Report of the Adjutant General of the State of Maine, 1862,* Appendix D, p. 541
9. Small, *Sixteenth Maine Regiment,* pp. 40-41
10. Small, *Road to Richmond,* p. 49
11. Small, *Sixteenth Maine,* pp. 37-38
12. This was to avoid irritating civilians who might take up arms and become guerrillas. This was not an issue in Maryland, but in northern Virginia ("Mosby's Confederacy") and elsewhere in the occupied South, it was indeed.
13. Small, *Road to Richmond,* p. 51
14. Small, *Sixteenth Maine,* p. 50
15. Civilian merchants authorized to sell food and supplies, ostensibly at affordable prices, to Union soldiers. Only too anxious to buy "fresh" food, desperate men willingly paid outrageous prices, a practice that drained many soldiers of their pay. In autumn 1862, a Union private was paid $13 per month.
16. Small, *Sixteenth Maine,* pp. 41-43
17. Small, *Road to Richmond,* p. 52
18. Small, *Sixteenth Maine,* pp. 50-51
19. Small, *Road to Richmond,* p. 53
20. *Annual Report of the Adjutant General of the State of Maine, 1862,* Appendix D, pp. 547
21. Small, *The Road to Richmond,* p. 53
22. Andrews, *Company D,* p. 15
23. Small, *Road to Richmond,* pp. 53-54
24. Small, *Sixteenth Maine,* pp. 51-52
25. Ibid, p. 39
26. *Annual Report of the Adjutant General of the State of Maine, 1862,* Appendix D, pp. 542-543
27. Andrews, *Company D,* p. 6
28. Small, *Sixteenth Maine,* p. 38
29. Ibid., pp. 45-47
30. Ibid., pp. 55-56

Chapter 50

THEY WANTED TO FIGHT

"They are smart and intelligent, they are <u>Maine men</u>"

About a week before Charles Tilden's 16th Maine Infantry lads celebrated the delivery of tents and overcoats and clean underwear to their Virginia camp, overstuffed mail bags thumped onto the floors at the State House offices occupied by the aides of Governor Israel Washburn Jr.

Delivered to Augusta by stage, train, and an occasional rider, mail arrived daily at the State House. Most went to Washburn or Maine's adjutant general, the administratively brilliant John L. Hodsdon. Letters, reports, muster rolls, regimental returns: military-related correspondence usually crossed his desk. But on this particular mid-November morning, a Washburn aide slit open a particular envelope to discover that a senior officer had written the governor directly from a "Camp near Rappahannock Station Va." on November 16, 1862.

"Our Regiment is in a very bad condition," proclaimed the lead sentence in the third paragraph. *Uh-oh—a complaint from a soldier,* the aide probably thought. The letter went into the "must-see" pile.

Every weekday, Washburn's aides sorted the diverse correspondence addressed to Maine's chief executive. As the war spread its bloody tentacles across the state, taciturn Mainers who would never have thought about bothering the governor certainly did so now.

"Our Husbands are in the army," six patriotic women from Cutler on the Washington County coast had succinctly informed Washburn in their collective October 14 letter. "We are entirely dependent up on them for the support of ourselves and families. While they were at home we were well cared for; at the present time we are really in want."

That last sentence hinted at hungry children, empty larders, and little hard cash as the women held home and hearth together with winter lurking just below the Down East horizon. Impoverished, they now sought help after asking Washburn to "pardon us for troubleing [*sic*] you with wants, wishes and complaints."

Abigail C. Ramsdell, Lydia Maker, O.P. Perkins, E.A. Ramsdell, and Pheby Suffell had sent their men—husbands, sons, and, in the case of elderly widow Emmy B. Maker, a grandson—to serve the United States. The women reminded Washburn "that the state has made some provision for us [and other military families] so that we might not become paupers."

Unaware as to the program's exact details, but anxious to read the fine print, "some of us called on the Fathers of the town [the Cutler selectmen]." Apparently "the Fathers" cared not a whit about their destitute constituents; "all the satisfaction we could get, was, 'go to the overseers of the poor,'" the women said, likely quoting a town official.

Proud of their roles as homemakers, the women refused to declare themselves as paupers unable to feed or clothe their families. "We think it rong [sic] for us to be compeled [sic] to do so as well as very trying," they wrote Washburn.

Could he help? "Will you be so very kind to inform us what course we are to take in order that we may obtain the amount we should receive from the state," the women asked the governor for whom they could not vote.

"Any favor that you may be able to render us will be greatfully [sic] appreciated by us," the Cutler women told Washburn.[1]

The November 16 letter from Virginia brought a different complaint to Washburn, yet contained a heartening message. With the 1st Maine Cavalry Regiment "in a very bad condition," Lt. Col. Calvin Douty beseeched the governor to lobby for the unit's inclusion in "an expedition being fitted out for Texas ... under the command of Major General [Nathaniel] Banks.

"Every officer present with the Regiment" had signed the petition circulated by Douty to load the entire 1st Maine Cavalry onto the next transports sailing for the Gulf of Mexico.

Why did the regiment's officers want to exit Virginia for Texas?

Because they wanted to fight as cavalrymen, not serve as glorified guards and messenger boys.

Charles Watson
Co. K, 11th Maine Infantry
(Bangor Public Library)

Pvt. John H. Annis
Co. F, 6th Maine Infantry
(Bangor Public Library)

Sgt. Joshua P. Graffam
1st D.C. & 1st Maine Cavalry
(Library of Congress)

Chapter 50: They Wanted to Fight

Douty detailed for Washburn how "we ... are broken up into squads of from four to twelve men each and scattered throughout our Army of the Potomac as 'orderlies' and cattle drivers ..."

In its collective wisdom, the War Department had scattered the 1st Maine Cavalry to the wind; Co. G pulled provost duty and Co. L orderly duty with I Corps, Fitz John Porter used companies "H and M" as he saw fit at V Corps, "and Co. I" performed similar duty for Gen. Ambrose Burnside, the new Army of the Potomac commander.

Five companies remained with Douty at the regimental headquarters, but with so many men away on detached duties, "our companies are ... reduced to about twenty men each for duty," Douty told Washburn.

A particular "'misfortune'" was "the cause of our disorganization," Douty explained. "Our men make good 'Orderlies'—they are smart and intelligent, they are Maine Men—they can read and write, and they can act equal to any men in the service."

For these reasons "our regiment is broken up," so if "Your Excellency" could arrange that the 1st Maine Cavalry "be brought together so that it may be effective as a regiment," the mounted warriors of Maine could fight effectively and honorably for their state and their nation, Douty said.[2]

Anxious to rejoin the 1st Maine Cavalry Regiment in the field, the badly wounded Maj. Jonathan Prince Cilley had "arrived home" in Thomaston in summer 1862. "Now fast improving in general health," he was "unable as yet to make any use of his wounded arm, from which

Capt. Winslow P. Spofford
11th Maine
(Betsy Coe)

2nd Lt. Horace G. Jacobs
Co. G, 6th Maine Infantry
(Bangor Public Library)

Sgt. Sewell Hubbard
Unit unknown
(Bangor Public Library)

eighteen pieces of bone have been taken," a Maine newspaper reported.[3]

Deciding he had rested sufficiently at home, Cilley returned to Washington, D.C. More bone and "metal fragments" had exited his arm via multiple surgeries by mid-November, yet despite the pain—and perhaps to focus his attention past it—Cilley took the offered position of War Department paper shuffler.[4]

The Confederacy had not seen the last of Jonathan Prince Cilley, Charles Tilden, Elijah Walker, Sarah Sampson, Harris Plaisted, Isabella Fogg, John Mead Gould, Oliver Otis Howard, Harriet Eaton, Ira Gardner, Thomas Hyde, and the tens of thousands of other Mainers stepping forward to defend the United States, in the field or at home.

~~~

1. Abigail C. Ramsdell et al. to Governor Israel Washburn Jr., October 14, 1862, Maine State Archives
2. Lt. Col. Calvin Douty to Governor Israel Washburn Jr., November 16, 1862, MSA. Underlines in earlier passages were in the original.
3. *Maine Farmer,* Thursday, Sept. 4, 1862
4. Eve Anderson, *A Breach of Privilege: The Cilley Family Letters,* Seven Coin Press, Spruce Head, Maine, 2002, pp. 444-445

Sgt. Noah W. Jordan
Co. A, 12th Maine Infantry
(Bangor Public Library)

Jeptha Murch
1st Maine Heavy Artillery,
originally 18th Maine Infantry
(Bangor Public Library)

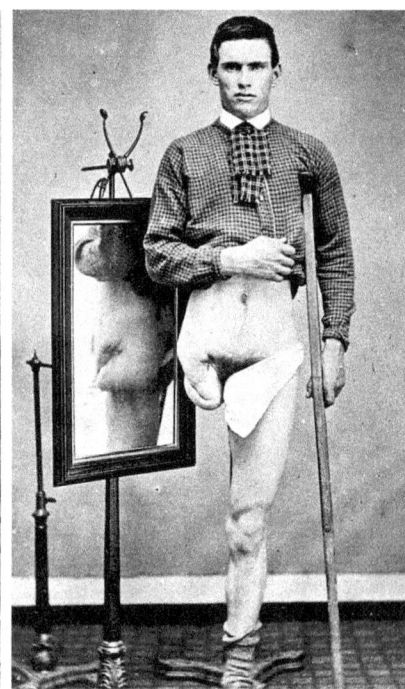

Pvt. Eben Smith
Co. A, 11th Maine Infantry
(Library of Congress)

Bibliography

Alexander, Col. Barton, *The Peninsula Campaign*, Atlantic Monthly, Vol. 13, No. 77, March 1864

Ames, Judson, *History of the Fourth Maine Battery Light Artillery in the Civil War 1861-1865*, Burleigh & Flynt, Augusta, Maine, 1905

Anderson, Eve, *A Breach of Privilege: The Cilley Family Letters*, Seven Coin Press, Spruce Head, Maine, 2002

Andrews, H.F., *Company D 16 Maine Vols.*, Exira Printing Co., Exira, Iowa, 1906

Annual Report of the Adjutant General of the State of Maine, 1861, Stevens & Sayward, Augusta, 1862

Annual Report of the Adjutant General of the State of Maine, 1862, Stevens & Sayward, Augusta, 1863

Annual Report of the Adjutant General of the State of Maine, 1864-1865, Stevens & Sayward, Augusta, 1866

Bailey, Ronald H. and the Editors of Time-Life Books, *The Civil War—The Bloodiest Day: The Battle of Antietam*, Time-Life Books, Alexandria, Va., 1984

Banks, Robert F., *Maine Becomes a State: the movement to separate Maine from Massachusetts, 1785-1820*, Maine Historical Society, Wesleyan University Press, 1970

Bath Independent, The
    —August 18, 1906: *Famous Nurse*

Bearss, Edwin C., *The Battle of Baton Rouge*, The Journal of the Louisiana Historical Association, Vol. 3, No. 2, Spring 1962

Belfast Historical Society, Belfast, Maine
    —Joseph B. Wilson, application for Original Invalid Pension

Bicknell, Rev. George W., *History of the Fifth Maine Regiment*, Hall. L. Davis, Portland, Maine, 1871

Bowdoin College, O.O. Howard Papers, George J. Mitchell Department of Special Collections & Archives
    —April 4, 1862: Sarah Sampson to Guy Howard
    —May 7, 1862: Oliver Otis Howard to Elizabeth Anne Howard
    —October 22, 1861: Sarah Sampson to Oliver Otis Howard

Brady, Robert Jr. and Maxfield, Albert, *The Story of One Regiment: The Eleventh Maine Infantry Volunteers in the War of the Rebellion*, J.J. Little & Co., New York, NY, 1896

Brockett, Dr. L.P. and Vaughan, Mary C., *Women's Work in the Civil War: A Record of Heroism, Patriotism and Patience*, Ziegler, McCurdy & Co., Philadelphia, and R.H. Curran, Boston, 1867

Butler, Benjamin F., *Autobiography and Personal Reminiscences of Major-General, Benj. F. Butler*, A.M. Thayer & Co., Boston, 1892

Cilley, Brevet Brig. Gen. Jonathan P., *The Dawn of the Morning at Appomattox*, Military Order of the Loyal Legion of the United States, Bowdoin College, Maine, 1886

Clark, Charles A., *Campaigning With the Sixth Maine*, The Kenyon Press, Des Moines, 1897

Congressional Globe, House of Representatives, 25th Congress, 2nd Session, Library of Congress, 1838

Courier-Gazette
- —May 26, 1891: William E. Crockett

Daily Whig & Courier
- —July 24, 1861
- —July 27, 1861
- —August 2, 1861: Stephen to editors
- —August 3, 1861
- —April 24, 1862
- —April 26, 1862: *Letter from the Eighth Maine*
- —April 30, 1862
- —May 3, 1862
- —May 18, 1862: George A. Bartlett letter
- —May 19, 1862: Capt. James G. Swett to William H. Wheeler
- —May 29, 1862
- —May 30, 1862
- —May 31, 1862
- —June 2, 1862: Capt. George M. Brown letter to wife
- —June 2, 1862: Capt. Sidney W. Thaxter to father
- —June 3, 1862
- —June 5, 1862: Clifford N. Mayo letter
- —June 7, 1862
- —June 9, 1862
- —June 13, 1862
- —July 8, 1862: Col. Charles W. Roberts to Amos M. Roberts
- —July 18, 1862
- —July 19, 1862
- —July 22, 1862
- —July 24, 1862
- —July 24, 1862: *Letter from the Sixth Maine Regiment*
- —August 7, 1862: Dr. William H. White to Israel Washburn Jr.
- —August 12, 1862
- —August 12, 1862: *The Eighteenth*
- —August 15, 1862
- —August 18, 1862: *Presentation*

Dalton, Peter P., *With Our Faces to the Foes: A History of the 4th Maine Infantry in the War of the Rebellion*, Union Publishing Co., Union, Maine, 1998

DeKay, James Tertius, *Monitor*, Walker and Company, New York, N.Y., 1997, p. 173

Denison, Rev. Frederic, *Shot and Shell: The Third Rhode Island Heavy Artillery Regiment*, J.A. & R.A. Reid, Providence, R.I., 1879

DiMeglio, John, *Civil War Bangor*, University of Maine graduate thesis, 1967

Eastern Argus

—July 18, 1861

Eastport Sentinel

    —July 24, 1861

Ellsworth American

    —June 30, 1862: *From the 11th Me. Regiment*

    —July 4, 1862: *From the 11th Maine Regiment*

    —August 1, 1862

    —August 9, 1862: *From the 10th Maine*

    —August 22, 1862: *From the 10th Maine Regiment*

    —August 29, 1862: *From the 10th Maine Regiment*

Gardner, Ira B., *Recollections of A Boy Member of Co. I, Fourteenth Maine Volunteers*, Lewiston Journal Company, Lewiston, Maine, 1902

Gottfried, Bradley M., *The Maps of First Bull Run*, Savas Beattie, New York and California, 2009

Gould, Maj. John M., *History of the First-Tenth-Twenty-Ninth Maine Regiment*, Stephen Berry, Portland, Maine, 1871

Gould, John Mead, *Gen. Mansfield at Antietam*, S. Berry, Portland, Maine, 1895

Haley, John, *The Rebel Yell & the Yankee Hurrah*, edited by Ruth L. Silliker, Down East Books, Camden, Maine, 1985

Howard, Oliver Otis, *Autobiography of Oliver Otis Howard, Major General United States Army*, Baker & Taylor Company, New York, 1907

Hyde, Thomas Worcester, *Following the Greek Cross: Or, Memories of the Sixth Army Corps*, Houghton, Mifflin, United States, 1894

Jaeger, Michael, Lauritzen, Carol, and Lowe, T.S.C., *Memoirs of Thaddeus S.C. Lowe, Chief of the Aeronautics Corps of the Army of the United States During the Civil War: My Balloons in Peace and War*, Edwin Mellen Press, Lewiston, N.Y., 2004

Johnston, Gen. Joseph E., *Manassas to Seven Pines, North to Antietam: Battles and Leaders of the Civil War, Vol. II*, Thomas Yoseloff, New York and London, reprinted 1956

Jordan, William B., *The Civil War Journals of John Mead Gould 1861-1866*, Butternut & Blue, Baltimore, 1997

Kilby, William Henry, *Eastport and Passamaquoddy: A Collection of Historical and Biographical Sketches, 1888*, reprinted by Border Historical Society, Eastport, Maine, 2003

Knight, Larry

    —August 12, 1862: Pvt. Adelbert Knight to Julia Ann Fletcher Knight

Lattimore, Ralston B., *Fort Pulaski National Monument*, U.S. Department of the Interior, Washington, D.C., 1954

Lewiston Daily Evening Journal

    —August 12, 1861: Frank E. Lemont to father

Lewiston Falls Journal

    —Lt. Col. James S. Fillebrown to Anna Fillebrown

Machias Republican

    —April 8, 1862

Maine Farmer

    —April 24, 1862

MAINE AT WAR - Volume I: Bladensburg to Sharpsburg

—May 8, 1862: *Ship Island*

—June 5, 1862

—June 12, 1862

—June 19, 1862: *Official Report of Col. Plaisted*

—June 26, 1862 *From the 8th Maine*

—June 26, 1862: *An Important Order*

—June 26, 1862: *To Returned Maine Soldiers*

—July 3, 1862

—July 10, 1862: *Aid for Maine Soldiers*

—July 17, 1862: *The Fifth Maine in Battle*

—July 31, 1862: Maj. Edwin Burt report to Gen. D.B. Birney

—July 31, 1862: Rev. Henry C. Leonard, *Third Maine*

—August 28, 1862: *The Evacuation of Harrison's Landing by McClellan's Army*

—November 13, 1862: *Fate Of A Deserter*

—January 15, 1863

Maine State Archives

—December 19, 1860: Davis Tillson to Lot Morrill

—March 20, 1861: William L. Tobey to John L. Hodsdon

—April 18, 1861: Augustus C. Hamlin to John L. Hodsdon

—April 19, 1861: John F. Mines to Israel Washburn Jr.

—April 21, 1861: H.W. Cunningham to John L. Hodsdon

—May 6, 1861: George W. Dyer to Israel Washburn Jr.

—May 11, 1861: Edwin M. Smith to John L. Hodsdon

—May 16, 1861: A.D. Manson and Arad Thompson to John L. Hodsdon

—June 14, 1861: Sarah Sampson to Dr. Alonzo Garcelon

—October 7, 1861: Benjamin Freeman to Israel Washburn Jr.

—November 18, 1861: John I. Perry to Israel Washburn Jr.

—November 21, 1861: R.K. Goodenow to Israel Washburn Jr.

—January 16, 1862: Thomas Hollis transcript

—May 24, 1862: Col. Hiram Burnham to Israel Washburn Jr.

—June 4, 1862: Archibald G. Spalding to Israel Washburn Jr.

—June 5, 1862: Col. John Goddard to Israel Washburn Jr.

—June 15, 1862: Joseph B. Wilson to parents

—June 20, 1862: Adjutant General John L. Hodsdon, General Order No. 15

—July 7, 1862: Governor Israel Washburn Jr., executive order

—July 10, 1862: Sarah Sampson to John L. Hodsdon

—July 14, 1862: Joshua L. Chamberlain to Israel Washburn Jr.

—July 18, 1862: Maj. Robert F. Campbell to Israel Washburn Jr.

—July 21, 1862: Josiah H. Drummond to Israel Washburn Jr.

—August 1, 1862: Augustus Stevens to John L. Hodsdon

—August 7, 1862: John Gilman to John L. Hodsdon

Bibliography

    —August 8, 1862: Dr. Nathan F. Blunt to Dr. A Garselin

    —August 9, 1862: Col. Frank Nickerson to Israel Washburn Jr.

    —August 16, 1862: Lt. Col. William H. Shaw to John L. Hodsdon

    —August 16, 1862: George Washington Bartlett to Israel Washburn Jr.

    —September 20, 1862: Jeremiah Bartlett to John L. Hodsdon

    —October 15, 1862: John W. Hathaway to Israel Washburn Jr.

    —November 10, 1862: Isabella Fogg to John W. Hathaway

    —November 19, 1862: Samuel Libbey to John L. Hodsdon

    —June 20, 1863: Jonathan P. Cilley to Abner Coburn

Marks, Rev. James Junius, D.D., *The Peninsula Campaign in Virginia*, J.B. Lippincott & Co., Philadelphia, 1864

Maxfield, Albert and Brady, Robert Jr., *Company D of the Eleventh Regiment Maine Infantry Volunteers in the War of the Rebellion,* Press of Thos. Humphrey, New York, NY, 1890

Moore, Frank, *Women of the War: Their Heroism and Self-Sacrifice*, S.S. Scranton & Co., Hartford, Conn., 1866,

Mundy, James H., *No Rich Men's Sons: The Sixth Maine Volunteer Infantry*, Harp Publications, Cape Elizabeth, Maine, 1994

Mundy, James H., *Second To None*, Harp Publications, Scarborough, Maine, 1992

New South, The

    —December 6, 1862: *Execution Of A Soldier*

New York Times

    —June 22, 1862: Gen. Casey's Division at the Battle of Fair Oaks

    —August 11, 1862: Brig. Gen. Henry M. Naglee to Lt. B.B. Foster, *The Battle of Seven Pines.; Report of Brig-Gen. Naglee*

    —December 1, 1862: Henry J. Wisner, *Interesting from Port Royal*

Picerno, Nicholas

    —Harrison Hume letter to parents, June 2, 1862

    —Harrison Hume letter to brother, June 7, 1862

    —Harrison Hume letter to father, June 19, 1862

Phelan, Helene, editor, *Tramping Out The Vintage, 1861-1864: The Civil War Diaries and Letters of Eugene Kingman*, Almond, N.Y., 1983

Portland Daily Express

    —June 30, 1862: Col. Harris Plaisted letter to Israel Washburn Jr.

Portland Daily Press

    —June 28, 1862

    —July 11, 1862

    —July 12, 1862

    —July 14, 1862

    —July 16, 1862: *Letter from the Maine 7th*

    —December 17, 1862: *Execution of a Maine Soldier*

Porter, Lt. Horace, April 12, 1862 report to Brig. Gen. Quincy Gillmore, *Papers on Practical Engineering, No. 8, Appendix D*, D. Van Norstrand, New York, N.Y., 1862

Sawyer, Candace, *The Civil War Letters of Capt. John Franklin Godfrey*, Candace Sawyer and Laura Orcutt, Portland, Maine, 1993

Schultz, Jane E., editor, *This Birth Place of Souls: The Civil War Nursing Diary of Harriet Eaton*, Oxford University Press, New York, 2011

Sears, Stephen W., *To the Gates of Richmond: The Peninsula Campaign*, Ticknor & Fields, New York, N.Y., 1992

Small, A.R., *Sixteenth Maine Regiment in the War of the Rebellion 1861-1865, Volume I*, edited by Peter and Cyndi Dalton, B. Thurston & Company, Portland, 1886, reprinted by Union Publishing Co.

Small, Henry Adams, *The Road to Richmond: The Civil War Letters of Major Abner R. Small of the 16th Maine Volunteers*, Fordham University Press, New York, 2000

Stanley, R.H. and Hall, George O., *Eastern Maine and the Rebellion*, Heritage Books, Maryland, reprinted 2008

Staples, Horatio G., *Reminiscences of Bull Run*, Maine M.O.L.L.U.S., War Papers, Vol. III, Portland, Maine, 1898

Sudlow, Lynda L., *A Vast Army of Women: Maine's Uncounted Forces in the Civil War*, Thomas Publications, Gettysburg, Penn., 2000

Tobie, Edward Parsons, *History of the First Maine Cavalry*, 1861-1865, Emery & Hughes, Boston, 1887

Townsend, George Alfred, *Campaigns of a Non-Combatant and His Romaunt Abroad During the War*, Blelock & Company, New York, NY, 1866

Tripp, H.A., *Cedar Mountain*, National Tribune, Thursday, May 6, 1886

Walker, Elijah, *The Old Soldier: History of the Fourth Maine Infantry*, Tribune, Rockland, Maine, 1895

War of the Rebellion, The: a Compilation of the Official Records of the Union and Confederate Armies, Government Printing Office, Washington, D.C., 1880-1901

Whitman, E.S. and True, Charles H., *Maine in the War for the Union: A History of the Part Borne by Maine Troops in the Suppression of the American Rebellion*, Nelson Dingley Jr. & Co., Lewiston, Maine, 1854

Young, George F.W., *The British Capture & Occupation of Downeast Maine 1814-1815/1818*, Penobscot Bay Press, Blue Hill, Maine, 2014

Military Units Index

This index features all military units mentioned in this volume in three sections. Refer to the General Index following for all other references.

Maine Military Units

All military units from Maine are listed here in numerical order.

1st Maine Battery: 92, 348

1st Maine Cavalry Regiment: vi, 1, 11, 83, 85-91, 116, 143, 145, 146, 148, 153-155, 159, 161-166, 242, 243, 348, 352, 375, 412, 436, 437

1st Maine Infantry Regiment: 24, 27, 36, 51, 52, 70, 75-79

2nd Maine Battery: 87

2nd Maine Infantry Regiment: 20, 25, 27, 35-41, 49, 52, 54, 59, 63, 67, 70, 86, 117, 118, 163, 195, 251, 257, 262, 275, 283, 285-287, 291

3rd Maine Battery: 87, 347-349

3rd Maine Infantry Regiment: 29, 31-33, 45-47, 60-65, 80, 117, 124, 135, 136, 139, 141, 195, 196, 226, 227, 229, 230, 233, 248, 262, 268-271, 284, 305, 307, 308, 316-318, 331, 335, 339

4th Maine Battery: 86-88, 90, 92, 347-349, 353-355, 357, 359, 360, 370, 371

4th Maine Infantry Regiment: 21, 25-27, 29, 30, 43-47, 49, 59, 75, 81, 116, 117, 123, 124, 141, 195-197, 207-212, 214, 216-220, 226, 227, 233, 268-271, 283, 284, 302, 305, 308, 314, 317, 332, 333, 335

5th Maine Battery: 87, 92, 347

5th Maine Infantry Regiment: 29, 43-47, 49, 52, 53, 75, 76, 117, 136-138, 142, 258, 281, 287-293, 297, 300, 329, 332, 414, 418

6th Maine Battery: 87, 347, 348, 359, 370, 371

6th Maine Infantry Regiment: 65, 67, 69-72, 76, 81, 101, 123, 125-128, 131-133, 142, 201, 264, 265, 280, 282, 287, 296, 309, 329, 330, 409, 410

7th Maine Infantry Regiment: 101, 123-132, 140, 280, 300, 302, 309, 311, 330, 387-392, 394, 396-399, 401, 403, 404; Illus.: 388

8th Maine Infantry Regiment: 77, 101-105, 107-110, 112, 119

9th Maine Infantry Regiment: 101-103, 119, 120, 421-423, 425

10th Maine Infantry Regiment: 78-79, 144, 161, 162, 164, 165, 347, 350-355, 358, 359, 362, 363, 365-371, 374-376, 379-385, 390, 401-403, 415, 416, 418

11th Maine Infantry Regiment: vi, 167-171, 173, 177-179, 181-187, 189, 190, 237, 238, 266, 267, 276, 281, 295-297, 299, 300, 308-313, 330, 333-335; Photo: 180; Illus.: 312

12th Maine Infantry Regiment: 95-97, 99, 416, 417

13th Maine Infantry Regiment: 87, 90, 95, 98, 99, 116

14th Maine Infantry Regiment: vii, 80, 97, 90-92, 95, 98, 99, 100, 275, 322, 324-327

15th Maine Infantry Regiment: 87, 90, 95, 99, 345

16th Maine Infantry Regiment: 247-51, 254, 255, 257, 258, 273, 344, 404-407, 430-433, 435

17th Maine Infantry Regiment: 250, 256, 258, 276

18th Maine Infantry Regiment: 250, 256-259

19th Maine Infantry Regiment: 250, 259, 345, 412, 415

20th Maine Infantry Regiment: vii, 252, 257, 259, 414

25th Maine Infantry Regiment: 410

Limerock Regiment (4th Maine Infantry Regiment): 195

Other Union Military Units

Military units from Union states are listed here numerically by state.
Federal forces are included under United States (Federal).

Connecticut

1st Connecticut Infantry Regiment: 35, 38
2nd Connecticut Infantry Regiment: 35, 38
3rd Connecticut Infantry Regiment: 35, 39
5th Connecticut Infantry Regiment: 350, 361
6th Connecticut Infantry Regiment: 104
7th Connecticut Infantry Regiment: 107, 421
21st Connecticut Infantry Regiment: 321

District of Columbia

1st District of Columbia Volunteers: 380

Indiana

21st Indiana Infantry Regiment: 322-325

Maryland

1st Maryland Light Artillery, Battery A: 391-393
3rd Maryland Infantry Regiment: 357

Massachusetts

2nd Massachusetts Infantry Regiment: 367
6th Massachusetts (Carruth's) Light Artillery: 322, 324
6th Massachusetts Infantry Regiment: 22, 23
12th Massachusetts Infantry Regiment: 405
13th Massachusetts Infantry Regiment: 405
20th Massachusetts Infantry Regiment: 210
35th Massachusetts Infantry Regiment: 375

Michigan

2nd Michigan Infantry Regiment: 195
3rd Michigan Infantry Regiment: 195
5th Michigan Infantry Regiment: 195
6th Michigan Infantry Regiment: 327

New Hampshire

1st New Hampshire Infantry Regiment: 79
3rd New Hampshire Infantry Regiment: 423
5th New Hampshire Infantry Regiment: 193, 199, 218, 219
9th New Hampshire Infantry Regiment: 405

New York

1st New York Artillery, Battery K: 359
1st New York Battery: 127
1st New York Engineers: 112
1st New York Light Artillery, Battery E: 127
1st New York Light Artillery, Battery H: 181, 183, 184
5th New York Cavalry Regiment: 149
13th New York Infantry Regiment: 209, 286
16th New York Infantry Regiment: 287, 288, 293
20th New York Infantry Regiment: 388, 390, 391, 397
27th New York Infantry Regiment: 287, 290, 291, 293
28th New York Infantry Regiment: 350, 361
33rd New York Infantry Regiment: 127, 128, 130, 132, 388, 390
37th New York Infantry Regiment: 195
38th New York Infantry Regiment: 124, 195, 217, 226
40th New York Infantry Regiment: 124, 195, 226, 270
43rd New York Infantry Regiment: 72, 125
46th New York Infantry Regiment: 107, 110
47th New York Infantry Regiment: 421, 423
48th New York Infantry Regiment: 104
49th New York Infantry Regiment: 388
56th New York Infantry Regiment: 171, 182, 186
61st New York Infantry Regiment: 193, 221, 223, 225
63rd New York Infantry Regiment: 205, 309
64th New York Infantry Regiment: 193, 221, 223, 225
71st New York Infantry Regiment: Photo: 117
77th New York Infantry Regiment: 388-390

Indices

87th New York Infantry Regiment: 195
100th New York Infantry Regiment: 171, 182, 183
101st New York Infantry Regiment: 270
102nd New York Infantry Regiment: 357
105th New York Infantry Regiment: 383
107th New York Infantry Regiment: 384
Irish Brigade: 218, 391

Pennsylvania

1st Pennsylvania Artillery: Photo: 363
1st Pennsylvania Artillery, Battery F: Photo: 362
1st Pennsylvania Cavalry Regiment: 369
1st Pennsylvania Light Artillery: 232
1st Pennsylvania Light Artillery, Battery H: 296
11th Pennsylvania Infantry Regiment: 405
13th Pennsylvania Infantry Regiment: 196
23rd Pennsylvania Infantry Regiment: 136
45th Pennsylvania Infantry Regiment: 376
46th Pennsylvania Infantry Regiment: 350, 361, 368
49th Pennsylvania Infantry Regiment: 125, 127
52nd Pennsylvania Infantry Regiment: 171
53rd Pennsylvania Infantry Regiment: 219, 223, 227
54th Pennsylvania Infantry Regiment: 144
57th Pennsylvania Infantry Regiment: 195
63rd Pennsylvania Infantry Regiment: 195, 314
81st Pennsylvania Infantry Regiment: 193, 219-221, 226
85th Pennsylvania Infantry Regiment: 209
96th Pennsylvania Infantry Regiment: 287, 288, 293
104th Pennsylvania Infantry Regiment: 169, 171, 173, 181, 183, 185
105th Pennsylvania Infantry Regiment: 195, 231
109th Pennsylvania Infantry Regiment: 357
111th Pennsylvania Infantry Regiment: 357
118th Pennsylvania Infantry Regiment: Illus.: 425

Rhode Island

1st Rhode Island Light Artillery, Battery E: 316
3rd Rhode Island Artillery: 104, 107, 112
3rd Rhode Island Heavy Artillery Regiment: 423

Vermont

1st Vermont Calvary Regiment: 147-149, 154, 155
2nd Vermont Infantry Regiment: 29, 33, 44
7th Vermont Infantry Regiment: 326
Vermont Brigade: 280, 391-393, 397

United States (Federal)

1st United States Artillery Battery I: 201
2nd U.S. Artillery, Battery G: 314
4th U.S. Artillery, Battery F: 358, 361
5th U.S. Artillery: 252
5th U.S. Cavalry Regiment: 127
11th U.S. Infantry Regiment: 332
17th U.S. Infantry Regiment: 342

Wisconsin

3rd Wisconsin Infantry Regiment: 361, 367
5th Wisconsin Infantry Regiment: 125, 127, 128, 131

Confederate Units

Military units from Confederate states are listed here numerically by state.

Alabama
3rd Alabama: 225
5th Alabama Infantry Regiment: 251, 287
31st Alabama Infantry Regiment: 326

Florida
1st Florida Cavalry Regiment: 121

Georgia
7th Georgia Infantry Regiment: 393
18th Georgia Infantry Regiment: 138
20th Georgia Infantry Regiment: 382

Kentucky
4th Kentucky Infantry Regiment: 326

Mississippi
2nd Mississippi Battalion: 393
2nd Mississippi Infantry Regiment: 218
31st Mississippi Infantry Regiment: 326

North Carolina
5th North Carolina Infantry Regiment: 132

South Carolina
2nd South Carolina Infantry Regiment: 45
6th South Carolina Infantry Regiment: 196
8th South Carolina Infantry Regiment: 45

Texas
1st Texas Infantry Regiment: 138, 393
2nd Texas Infantry Regiment: 218
4th Texas Infantry Regiment: 138
5th Texas Infantry Regiment: 138, 218

Virginia
5th Virginia Infantry Regiment: 40
12th Virginia Infantry Regiment: 225
24th Virginia Infantry Regiment: 132
41st Virginia Infantry Regiment: 225
42nd Virginia Infantry Regiment: 366
48th Virginia Infantry Regiment: 366

General Index

Refer to the Military Units Index preceding for indexed military units.

A

Abbot, Maine: 90
Abbott, Willis J. (illustrator): Illus. by: 203
Adams, C. Wesley: 120, 426
Adams, Frances Caroline: 252
Aldie, Virginia: 1; Illus.: 3
Alexander, Barton: 201
Alexander, Dr. Charles: 406, 407
Alexander's Bridge (Chickahominy River crossing): 291, 292, 295
Alexandria, Virginia: 65, 124, 135, 139, 169, 347, 373, 411
Alleghany Mountains (Virginia): 159
Allen, James: 209-212
Allen, Samuel H.: 353, 354
Allen, Susan: 196
Allen, William H.: 53
ambulance: 43, 205, 233, 241, 282, 298, 309, 333, 334, 376, 384, 411, 412, 414, 415, 418, 423; Photo: 233
Amelia Island, Florida: 119, 121
Amelia River (Florida): 119, 120
Ames, Adelbert: 252, 255; Photo: 249
Ames, Judson: 87, 88, 92, 347, 348, 350, 354, 355, 357, 359-361, 370
Anderson, Eve: vii
Anderson, Robert: 19
Andrew, John Albion: 22
Andrews, Henry Franklin: 429

Androscoggin County (Maine): 17, 30, 85, 136, 255, 342
Androscoggin Valley (Maine region): 101
Annapolis Junction, Maryland: 101
Annapolis, Maryland: vi, 66, 87, 101, 185, 233, 264, 265, 273, 274
Annis, John H.: Photo: 436
Annis, Jotham S.: 175
Anson, Maine: 254
Antietam Creek (Maryland): 379, 387, 390, 403
Antietam, Battle of: 387, 401, 405, 412, 414, 419, 427, 428; Photos: 403-406, 414, 419; Illus.: 388, 396
Antietam, Maryland: vi
Appalachian Mountains: 247
Appleton, Maine: 144
Aqueduct Bridge (Potomac River): 404
Aquia Creek (Virginia): 170, 334, 433; Photo:174
Ariel (steamer): 101
Arlington Heights (Virginia): 35, 53
Arlington, Virginia: 404, 406, 410, 427, 433
Armory Square Hospital (Washington, D.C.): 410; Photo: 416
Army of Northeastern Virginia (U.S. Army Command): 29
Army of Northern Virginia: 271,
373, 379
Army of the Potomac: 123, 140, 145, 170, 171, 174, 193, 210, 213, 247, 262, 263, 266, 279, 292, 295, 299, 305, 306, 334, 335, 373, 374, 379, 388. 407, 414, 430, 437
Army of Virginia (U.S. Army command): 349, 351, 373, 374
Army, United States: v, 6, 29, 92, 99, 102, 120, 135, 153, 169, 207, 231, 242, 263, 264, 278, 331-333, 347, 380, 410, 421, 433; Photo courtesy of: 282
Aroostook County (Maine): 15, 19, 84, 387, 427
Aroostook County Historical & Art Museum of Houlton: vii; Photo courtesy of: 84
Aroostook, Territory of: 13, 14
artillery (military): see Military Units Index, q.v.
Ashby, Turner: 148, 150, 154; Illus.: 147, 157
Atlantic Ocean: 99, 103
Atlantic wharf (Rockland, Maine): 27
Auburn Artillery (militia): 24
Auburn, Maine: 17, 340
Augur, Christopher C.: 350, 353, 357, 358, 362; Photo: 349
Augusta House (Augusta, Maine): 32
Augusta, Maine: 13, 21, 24, 31-33, 60, 68, 80, 85-93, 115-117,

143, 167-170, 175, 249-252, 254, 255, 258, 273-276, 322, 422, 344, 345, 347, 387, 435
Avery, Columbus: 91
Ayer, John: 430, 433

B

Bacon, Harriet Agnes Hope (see also Harriet Eaton): 409
Bacon, James and William: 36
Baker, Scollay D.: 119-121
Bakersville, Maryland: 414, 418, 419
Balaklava, Crimea: 387, 392, 398
Bald Hill Cove (Maine): 5
Balloon Corps, Union Army: 193, 207
balloons: 210; Photo: 210
Ball's Bluff (Virginia): 130
Baltimore & Ohio Railroad: 61, 143, 144, 374
Baltimore Riot of 1861: Illus.: 23
Baltimore, Maryland: 22, 33, 76, 140, 162, 261-263, 265, 339, 340, 373, 410; Illus.: 79
Bangor Band (Bangor, Maine): 25
Bangor Daily News: iii, v
Bangor House (Bangor, Maine): 343
Bangor Light Infantry (militia): 16, 36
Bangor Public Library: iii, v, vii; Photos courtesy of: 14, 78, 255, 436-438
Bangor, Maine: vii, 2, 5, 6, 13, 15, 20, 21, 25, 26, 35, 36, 40, 41, 53, 54, 56, 57, 59, 67-70, 75, 80, 92, 107, 117, 118, 120, 150, 153, 162, 163, 174, 250-252, 257, 258, 291, 343, 344, 430
Bangor, Port of: 257
Bangs, Algernon S.: 347, 360
Banks, Nathaniel P.: 145-148, 150, 161, 164, 247, 349, 350, 358, 363, 436; Photo: 144
Banks, Ronald F.: 6
Barker, Charles: 76
Barker, David (poet): 344; Illus.: 345
Barker, Lewis: 344
Barlow, Francis C.: 221-223, 225; Photo: 226
Barnard, George N. (photographer): Photos by: 41, 48, 52, 222, 228
Bartlett, George A.: 145
Bartlett, George Washington: 322, 324-327; Photo: 323
Bartlett, Jeremiah: 276-278
Bartlett, Joseph J.: 287-293, 300; Photo: 283
Bassett, Abner F.: 238
Bath Grays (militia): 21
Bath, Maine: 21, 60, 65, 124, 135, 250, 261, 336, 344, 387, 321-324, 327
Baton Rouge, Battle of: Illus.: 326
Baton Rouge, Louisiana: Illus.: 326, 327
battery (military): see Military Units Index, q.v.
Battery Burnside (Tybee Island, Georgia): 107, 109
Battery Halleck (Tybee Island, Georgia): 108
Battery Hamilton (Bird Island, Georgia artillery post): 105
Battery Lincoln (Tybee Island, Georgia): 107
Battery Lyon (Tybee Island, Georgia): 107, 108
Battery McClellan (Tybee Island, Georgia): 108
Battery Scott (Tybee Island, Georgia): 108
Battery Sigel (Tybee Island, Georgia): 108, 110
Battle of Aldie: 1; Illus.: 3
Battle of Friday on the Chickahominy (illustration): Illus.: 290
Baxter, Dr. Joseph: 406
Bay of Fundy (Canada): 84
Bay State (Massachusetts): 409
Bay State (steamer): 77
Bayard, George D.: 352; Photo: 353
Bayou Sara Road (Baton Rouge, Louisiana): 321
Beal, George Lafayette: 164, 165, 347, 352-354, 358, 362, 363, 365, 368, 370, 371, 379, 381, 382, 390; Photos: 165, 348
Beal, George Lafayette: Illus.: 79
Bean, Albion: 432
bean-hole beans: 89
Beauregard, Pierre Gustave Toutant: 1, 29; Photo: 4; Illus.: 44
Beaver Dam Creek (Virginia): 279, 280, 283, 297
Beaver Dam Station (Virginia): 271
Begg, Johnny: 392, 397
Belfast Historical Society: vii
Belfast, Maine: 16, 21, 59, 75, 91, 208, 295, 296
Belmont, Maine: 22
Belvidere (vessel): 102
Benham, Henry W.: 110-112
Benson, Nathan and Stephen: 36
Benton, Maine: 254
Bentonville, North Carolina: vi
Berkeley Plantation (Virginia): 331; Photo: 332

Indices

Berlin, Maryland: 415, 417-419, 431-433
Berry, Hiram: 19, 27, 29, 124, 195, 214, 233, 279, 284, 308, 314; Photo: 280
Bethel, Maine: 86
Bethel, Virginia: 347
Betsy Coe: Photo by: 437
Beverly Ford (Virginia): Illus.: 425
Bible: 30
Bicknell, George W.: ii, 136, 137, 139, 142, 281, 288-292, 297, 300, 303, 329, 332; Photo: 136
Bill 376-174 (Maine Legislature): 60
Billings, Ezra: 75
Bird Island, Georgia: 104, 105, 112
Birney, David: 141, 195, 197, 217, 219, 220, 270, 284, 307, 308, 313, 317; Photo: 195
Bisbee, Horatio: 119, 121, 122; Photo: 121
Black Creek (Virginia): 267
Blackwell, Charles: 99
Bladensburg Dueling Grounds: Photo: 9
Bladensburg, Maryland: 1, 8, 11
Blaine, James G.: 31, 32; Photo: 31
Blaisdell, George I.: 136
Blake, Rev. Charles E.: 116
Blanket Brigade: 427, 428, 433
Bloodless Aroostook War: 1, 13, 17, 18, 69
Bloody Lane: Photo: 408
Blue Hill Bay (Maine): 275
Blue Hill, Maine: 275
Blue Ridge Mountains (Virginia): 146, 159, 247, 349, 350, 374
Blunt, Dr. Nathan F.: 276
Boatswain's Creek (Virginia): 283, 285, 287, 288, 291; Photo: 289

Boonsboro, Maryland: 378, 379
Boston & Maine Railroad: 32
Boston Common (Massachusetts): 387
Boston Harbor: 92
Boston Journal (newspaper): 123
Boston, Massachusetts: 3, 5, 6, 21-23, 27, 32, 77, 79, 92, 96, 98, 99, 387
Bosworth, Irene Francis: 413, 414, 419
Bottoms Bridge (Virginia): 172, 267, 300, 306, 311
Bowden, Sewall: 41
Bowdoin College (Brunswick, Maine): 6, 54, 251, 252, 322, 387
Bowman, James W.: 120, 426
Bradbury, Alden W.: 348
Bradbury, C.: 230
Bradford, Warren W.: 118
Bradley, Elwin: 54
Brady, James: 296
Brady, Mathew (photographer): 297; Photos by: 124, 194, 195, 210, 239, 253, 283, 343, 351, 377, 391, 429
Brady, Robert: 167, 168, 179, 186, 187, 237, 238
Brady, Robert Jr.: 167-175, 177-179, 181, 182, 186-189, 237, 238, 296, 330
Brannan, John M.: 421; Photo: 422
Bratton, John: 196
Bray, A.C.: 230
Breckinridge, John C.: 322-324, 326; Photo: 323
Brent Point, Virginia: 170
Brewer Light Artillery (militia): 39
Brewer, Maine: v, 6, 54
Brickett, Dr. George E.: 292

Bridgton, Maine: 118
Broad Street (Bangor, Maine): Photo: 56
Broadway (Bangor, Maine): 27, 56, 57
Brooke, John R.: 219, 223, 227
Brooks, Thomas Harbraugh: Photo: 393
Brooks, William T.H.: 393
Brooksville, Maine: 41
Brown Theatre (Portland, Maine): 25
Brown, George M.: 40, 150, 153, 154, 156, 161-163
Brown, Harlan: 397
Brown, John: 348
Brown, Rev. T.J.: 345
Brownville, Maine: 67, 69
Brunswick, Maine: 6, 85, 251, 406
Brunswick, Maryland: 415, 431
Bryant, John E.: 106
Buck, Harriet: 387
Buckfield, Maine: 106
Bucksport, Maine: 25, 67, 68, 70, 257, 296, 387
Budge, Gibson S.: 168
Bull Run (Virginia): 29, 38, 39, 41, 43, 44, 51, 79, 117, 130, 251, 276, 335; Illus.: 46
Bull Run, Battle of: 143, 276
Bullfinch, Charles: 115
Burd, Charles: 75
Burgess, T.Y.: 54
Burke, John: 309
Burkitt's Run (Maryland): 388
Burkittsville, Maryland: 374, 388, 419, 431
Burley, Elizabeth Ann: 11
Burnham Tavern (Machias, Maine): 69
Burnham, Henry A.: 383, 384

Burnham, Hiram: 69, 70, 72, 123, 125-129, 131-133, 142, 282, 296, 329; Photo: 69
Burnham, Job: 69
Burnham, Maine: 163
Burnside, Ambrose Everett: 103, 375, 391, 403, 407; Photo: 391; Illus.: 46, 341
Burnside's Bridge: Photo: 398
Burr, William P.: 359
Burrill, William I.: 157, 159
Burt, Edwin: 270, 306-308, 316, 317; Photo: 306
Burton, Albert G.: 70
Burying the Dead (illustration): Illus.: 236
Butler, Benjamin F.: 95-98, 100, 116, 275, 321; Photo: 96; Illus.: 341
Butler, Joseph G.: 392
Butterfield, Daniel A.: 283, 291; Photos: 282, 287
Butts, Rev. Joshua: 422, 423

C

Cabinet of the Confederate States of America: Illus.: 297
Calais, Maine: 65, 68, 264, 409, 410
Caldwell, John C.: 168-171; Photos: 170, 173
California Flag: 35, 37, 39, 40, 54; Photos: 38, 39
Camden Station (Baltimore, Maryland): 22, 23
Camden, Maine: 104
Cameron, Simon (Secretary of War): 83, 102; Photo: 86
Camp Allen (Virginia): 144
Camp Chase (Lowell, Massachusetts): 96

Camp Chase (Portland, Maine): 95
Camp Howard, District of Columbia: 136, 139
Camp John J. Andrew: Illus. by: 89
Camp King (Cape Elizabeth, Maine): 256
Camp Knox (Rockland, Maine): 27
Camp Knox (Washington, D.C.): 169
Camp Langford (Florida): 121
Camp Moore (Virginia): 322
Camp No. 19 (Virginia): 123
Camp Penobscot (Augusta, Maine): 85-87
Camp Preble (Cape Elizabeth, Maine): 70-72
Camp Roberts (Bangor, Maine): 257
Camp Seward (Washington, D.C.): 35
Camp Washburn (Baltimore, Maryland): Illus.: 79
Camp Washburn (Bangor, Maine): 25, 27, 67
Campbell Photo Service: Photo from: 125
Campbell, Harry: 394, 395, 397, 399
Campbell, John W.: 136
Campbell, Lucy: 136
Campbell, Robert F.: 181, 185, 238, 267, 333
Campbell, Thomas: 112
Campobello Island, New Brunswick: 68
Canaan, Maine: 255, 433
Canada: 3, 5, 7, 13, 254, 350
Cape Charles, Virginia: 139
Cape Elizabeth, Maine: 70, 85, 252, 256, 258
Cape Horn: 322

Capitol (Maine): 85
Capitol (United States): 33, 341; Illus.: 8
Capitol Park (Augusta, Maine): 32, 80, 115, 116
Capitol Street (Augusta, Maine): 115
Capture of Secession Varmints (illustration): Illus.: 277
Caran (Ireland): 167
Carey, Theodore: 68
Caribou, Maine: 14
Carpenter, William: 432
Carruth, William: 324, 325
Carter, John J.: 275
Carver Barracks (Washington, D.C.): 169; Illus.: 168, 169
Carver, Edwin: 305
Carver, Leonard: 40
Casco Bay (Maine): 77, 78, 96
Casco, Maine: 76
Casey, Silas: 169, 172-175, 177, 179, 181-183, 186, 187, 194, 195, 223, 239, 267, 333; Photos: 171, 238
Castine Light Infantry (military): 15, 25, 36
Castine, Maine: 4-6, 15, 25, 36, 41, 54, 251
Catoctin Mountain (Maryland): 374, 375
cavalry (military): see Military Units Index, q.v.
Cedar Keys, Florida: 119
Cedar Mountain (Virginia): vi, 335, 352-355, 357, 358, 360, 361, 369; Photo: 360; Illus.: 358
Cedar Mountain Battlefield (Virginia): Photos: 355, 359
Cedar Mountain, Battle of: Illus.: 368, 369

Indices

Cedar Run (Virginia): 353, 355, 357, 370
Cedarville, Virginia: 147, 148
Central Road (Virginia): 214
Central Street (Bangor, Maine): 57, 59, 343
Centreville, Virginia: 29, 33, 35, 40, 48, 49, 75
Chamberlain, Grace: 252
Chamberlain, Harold: 252
Chamberlain, Joshua Lawrence: i, v, 252; Photo: 253
Chancellorsville, Virginia: vi
Channing, John: 397
Chapel Road (Virginia): 147
Chaplin, Daniel: 257; Photo: 255
Chapman, George D.: 350
Chapman, Milton: 163
Chapman, Stephen: 24, 45
Charles City Road (Virginia): 214, 306-308, 313
Charles Town, Virginia: 348
Charleston, South Carolina: vi, 1
Charlottesville, Virginia: 159
Chase, Ansel: 120-122, 426
Cheever, David: vii
Cherryfield Light Infantry (militia): 68
Cherryfield, Maine: 68, 69, 267, 333
Chesapeake Bay: 101
Chesapeake Hospital (Union hospital, Virginia): 140
Chester Gap (Virginia): 350
Chicago University: 387
Chicago, Illinois: 387
Chickahominy fever: 330
Chickahominy River (Virginia): 141, 167, 171-174, 177, 179, 180, 183, 193, 195, 199-201, 205, 207, 211, 213-215, 218, 247, 267, 271, 279-281, 283-285, 288, 290, 292, 295, 296, 299, 300, 302, 303, 305-311, 335; Illus.: 202
China, Maine: 397
Chinn Ridge (Manassas, Virginia): 45, 47, 49, 52, 75, 195
Christ Church (Augusta, Maine): 322
Christianity: 375
Cilley, Bowdoin Longfellow: 7
Cilley, Deborah Prince: 7, 8, 11; Illus.: 2
Cilley, Elizabeth Ann: 6
Cilley, Greenleaf: 6, 11
Cilley, Jane Nealley: 7
Cilley, Jonathan: 6-9, 11; Illus.: 2
Cilley, Jonathan Prince: vi, 1, 3, 6, 7, 11, 21, 22, 81, 83, 85, 86, 88, 91, 93, 143-145, 147-151, 153, 159, 164, 241-243, 245, 437, 438; Photos: 10, 242; Illus.: 82
Cilley, Julia Draper: 7, 11, 21, 22, 81, 83, 85, 88, 91, 93, 241-243, 245; Photo: 242
Citizens Band (Augusta, Maine): 342
Clark, Charles (Confederate general): 324, 325; Photo: 325
Clark, Charles A.: 69, 70, 72, 126, 128, 132, 133, 141, 142, 287
Clark, Daniel: 68
Clark, David R.: 126
Clark, J.G.: 56
Clark, Thomas: 327
Clark, William: 75
Clay, Sen. Henry (Kentucky): 8
Cloudman, Andrew: 365
Coatzacoalcos (vessel): 102
Cobb, Amasa: 127, 131
Cobb, Charles: 126
Coburn, Gov. Abner: 1, 2, 11; Photo: 4
Coburn, Hiram: 317
Cochrane, Granville: 397
Cockspur Island, Georgia: 103, 104, 107, 108
Colburn, Albert V.: Photo: 335
Cole, Dennis W.: 276-278
Cole, J.E.: 230
Coleman, William: 86
Collins, William: 148, 150, 153
Columbia Street (Bangor, Maine): 21
Columbia, Maine: 257
Colvin's Tavern (Virginia): 353, 370
Comanche (Native American tribe): 153
Comite River (Louisiana): 323
Concord Township, Maine: 255
Confederacy: 321, 438
Confederate prisons: Illus.: 158
Confederate States of America: Illus.: 297
Congress, United States: 6, 7, 15
Connor, Selden: 387, 403; Photo: 402
Consitution (Maine): 54
Constitution (balloon): 209, 211, 212
Constitution (steamer): 95-97, 169, 170
Convalescent Hospital (Arlington, Virginia): 410
Cook, John: 397
Cook, Melville B.: 85
Cook, William: vii
Coombs, Asa: 349
Coombs, Charles: 349
Copeland, Edward and Edwin: 36
corduroy road: 199, 201, 202, 205,

453

284; Photo: 204
Corinth, Maine: 67, 185
Cornwallis, Charles: 137
Corps (Roman numeral): see I, II, III, IV, V, VI, IX, and XII Corps
Corydon, Indiana: Photo: 187
Couch, Darius N.: 181
Coulter, Richard: 428
Courier and Enquirer (newspaper): 7, 8
Covell, James E.: 384
Cowan, Andrew: 127, 130
Crampton's Gap (Maryland): 374, 388, 389, 391, 412
Cranberry Isles, Maine: 185
Crawford, Samuel W.: 350, 352, 353, 358, 361, 362, 370, 371, 374, 380, 383; Photo: 351
Crescent City (New Orleans, Louisiana): 100
Crimea: 387, 392, 398
Crimean War: 60, 65
Croasdale Knoll (Sharpsburg, Maryland): 383
Crocket, Albert: 90
Crockett, William E.: 43, 45-48
Crosby, Charles: 56
Cross, Edward Ephraim: 218, 219; Photo: 218
Crossing the Chickahominy (illustration): Illus.: 202
Crossman, Christopher V.: 257
Crounse, Lorenzo: 359
CSS Arkansas: 323; Illus.: 327
CSS Virginia: 125, 170
Cub Creek (Virginia): 127, 129, 130-132
Cub Run (Virginia): 29
Culpeper Court House (Culpeper, Virginia): 351, 352, 354
Culpeper Road (Virginia): 352, 354, 355, 357-359, 361, 362, 369
Culpeper, Virginia: 347, 350, 352-355
Cumberland County (Maine): 76, 77, 256
Cumberland Landing (Virginia): 261
Cunningham, H.W.: 21, 26
Cunningham, Owen: 254
Currier & Ives: Illus. by: 128, 184, 326, 327, 368, 369
Custer, George Armstrong: 127; Photo: 178; Illus.: 341
Custis, Martha: 138, 141
Cutler, Frank: 86, 145, 151, 153, 241, 243, 245
Cutler, Maine: 435, 436

D

Daggett, Aaron: 45
Daily Union, The (newspaper): 54
Daily Whig & Courier (newspaper): 53, 54, 59, 107, 109, 110, 112, 163, 252; Illus. by: 345
Dakin, Freeman R.: 238
Dalton, Peter and Cyndi: vii
Daniel Webster (steamer): 27, 336
Darbytown Road (Virginia): 306, 307, 313
Daufuskie Island (South Carolina): 104, 112
Davis, Abel: 360
Davis, Jefferson: 56
Davis, Lewis: 347, 348
Davis, Matthew L.: 7, 8
Davis, R.P.: 275
Davis, William G.M.: 121, 122
Day, Charles: 68

Dead River Plantation, Maine: 90
Dealing, John: 41
Deane, James: 36
Deane, Sarah Dustin: 54
Deane, William J.: 36, 37, 39, 40, 54
Death of Ashby, The: Illus.: 157
Deer Island, New Brunswick: 68
Deer Isle, Maine: 68, 296
Deering Oaks (Portland, Maine): 383
Delmarva Peninsula: 139
Democrat, The (newspaper): 51, 54, 56, 57; Photo: 55
Denison, Frederic: 423-425
Dennis, John: 317
Dennysville, Maine: 68
Department of the South (U.S. Army command): 110, 113
Department of Virginia (U.S. Army command): 101
Deray, Thomas: 239
deserter, desertion: 49, 68, 81, 102, 117, 118, 121, 122, 127, 274-276, 278, 349, 352, 380, 421, 422, 424, 425; Illus.: 425
Desjardin, Tom: vii
Destruction of the Rebel Ram 'Arkansas,' The (illustration): Illus.: 327
Detroit, Maine: 254
Devereaux, Seth: 16, 25
Devereaux, Warren: 41
Dexter, Maine: 36, 95
Dice Head (Castine, Maine): 4
Dickinson College: Photo courtesy of: 232
Dirigo Engine Company (Rockland, Maine): 19
Dispatch Station (Virginia): 300
District of Columbia: 8, 101
District of Maine: 3, 4, 6

Dix, Dorothea: 62, 63, 65; Photo: 62
Dix, Joseph: 62
Dogan House (Manassas, Virginia): 44
Donnelly, Dudley: 350
Douglas Hospital (Washington, D.C.): 410
Douty, Calvin: 2, 145, 147-150, 153, 154, 161, 162, 164-166, 436, 437; Photo: 146; Illus.: 3
Dover, Maine: 1, 67, 145
Down East (Maine region): 67, 68, 409, 435
Drew, Alonzo: 163
Drummond, Josiah H. (Maine attorney general): 252; Illus.: 251
Du Pont, Samuel Francis: 102, 103
Duane's Bridge (Chickahominy River crossing): 287, 288
Dunbar, Benjamin F.: 295, 296, 300, 308
Dunker Church (Antietam battlefield): 390, 391, 396, 397, 402, 405; Photos: 394, 405
Durham, Maine: 384
Dyer, George W.: 25, 26

E

Early, Jubal A.: 129
East Machias, Maine: 173
East Side (Bangor, Maine): 37
East Woods (Sharpsburg, Maryland): 381-384
Eastern Argus (newspaper): 70, 72
Eastern City (steamer): 70
Eastern Express Office (Portland, Maine): 71
Eastern Sentinel (newspaper): 72
Eastport Harbor (Maine): 5

Eastport Light Infanty (militia): 17
Eastport, Maine: 5, 6, 17, 68-70, 257, 274
Eaton, Agnes: 409
Eaton, Dr. William: 406, 430
Eaton, Franklin: 409
Eaton, Frederick: 410
Eaton, Hamlin F.: 359, 361
Eaton, Harriet (daughter): 409
Eaton, Harriet (mother): 409-416, 418, 419, 429, 438
Eaton, Jeremiah Sewall: 409
Eddy, Edward Jr.: 424
Edwards, Clark S.: 291
Edwards, Gary: vii
Elba Island, Georgia: 104
Ellsworth American (newspaper): 359
Ellsworth, Maine: 67, 181, 184, 185, 257, 359
Elm City (steamer): 262, 264, 265
Elm Grove Cemetery (Thomaston): 11
Eltham Plantation, Virginia: 137, 138
Eltham's Landing (Virginia): 137, 261
Ely, S.B.: 111, 112
Emerson, Charles S.: 79, 366
Emery, Augustus F.: 391
Emery, Ellen Vesta (Hannibal Hamlin's second wife): 344
Emery, Marcellus: 54, 56, 57
Emery, Sarah Jane (Hannibal Hamlin's first wife): 344
Empty Sleeve, The (poem): 344; Illus.: 345
Enfield, Maine: 167
Epping, New Hampshire: 81, 83, 241
Erwin, John: 110

Essex Street (Bangor, Maine): 25
Estes, Llewellyn G.: 153, 163
Europe: 387
Evelynton Heights (Virginia): 329
Ewell, Richard S.: 147-149, 300; Photo: 146
Excelsior (balloon): 210
execution: 274, 421, 423-425; Illus.: 425
Executive Council (Maine): 116
Exeter, Maine: 344

F

Fair Oaks Station (Virginia): 172, 186, 202, 212-214, 218, 219, 222, 228, 231, 233, 237, 265, 310, 339, 340; Photos: 175, 188, 190; Illus.: 174, 206
Fairfield, James: 99
Fairfield, Maine: 254, 387, 391, 397
Fall River, Massachusetts: 77
Falls Church, Virginia: 35
Falls, Richard J.: 369, 370
Falmouth, Maine: 5
Farmington, Maine: 76, 91, 116, 170, 343, 406
Farnham, Augustus B.: 251
Farragut, David: 99
Farrow, George: 239
Fauquier County (Virginia): 350
Fennell, John: vii
Ferguson, C.B.: 135, 139
Fernandina, Florida: 119, 121, 421, 426; Illus.: 120
Ferry Point (Virginia): 261
Fessenden, Menzies: 24, 25, 77
Fessenden, Rep. Samuel Clement: 164; Illus.: 164
field hospital: 53, 227-229, 231-

233, 263, 266, 268, 298, 409; Photos: 188, 235, 299
Fillebrown, James S.: 382, 384, 390, 416; Photo: 383
First Baptist Church (Augusta, Maine): 342
First Baptist Church (Hartford, Connecticut): 409
First Manassas (battle): 257, 275
First Parish Church (Bangor, Maine): 27, 56
Fisher's Ford (White Oak Creek, Virginia): 305, 308
Fitzpatrick, David M.: iii, iv, vi, vii; Digital art: front cover, back cover
Flagg, John: 239
Florence, Italy: 387
Florida Railroad: 119, 121
Fogg, Hugh Morrison: 65, 68, 264, 282, 410
Fogg, Isabella: vi, 65, 66, 263-265, 268, 282, 297, 299, 303, 309, 333, 335, 409-419, 438; Photos: 65, 410
Fogg, William: 65
Fogler Library, University of Maine: Photo courtesy of: 275
Folsom, James C.: 366
Footman, William M.: 121
Forbes, Edwin (illustration credits): Illus. by: 244, 358, 425
Ford, Moses: 196
Fore River (Maine): 256
Forest City (Portland, Maine): 70, 71
Forest City (steamer): 96
Fort Buffalo (Virginia): 347
Fort Corcoran (Virginia): 118
Fort Fisher (North Carolina): vi
Fort George (Castine, Maine): 4, 5

Fort Gregg (Morris Island, South Carolina): Photo: 106
Fort Kent, Maine: 78
Fort Knox (Maine): 103
Fort Madison (Maine): 5
Fort Magruder (Virginia): 129
Fort Monroe (Virginia): 96, 97, 101, 123-125, 139-142, 170, 230, 247, 261, 262, 331-333, 336, 339, 417
Fort Pickens (Florida): 97
Fort Pulaski (Georgia): vi, 103, 104, 106-112; Photos: 108, 109, 111
Fort Ramsey (Virginia): 347
Fort Richardson (Virginia): Photo: 228
Fort Sullivan (Eastport, Maine): 5, 68, 70
Fort Sumter (South Carolina): 1, 13, 19, 20, 26
Fort Tillinghast (Virginia): 404, 432
Fort Ward (Virginia): 373
Fourteenth Street (Washington, D.C.): 169
Foxcroft Academy: 69
Foxcroft, Maine: 87, 347
Fox's Gap (Maryland): 374-377
Franconia, Virginia: 208
Frankfort, Maine: 36, 54
Franklin, William B.: 138, 280, 388, 389, 398, 399; Photo: 284
Frederick, Maryland: 164, 373-375, 411, 412
Fredericksburg, Virginia: vi, 73, 349, 421, 433
Fredericton, New Brunswick: 14, 26
Free Bridge (Augusta, Maine): 170
Free Street Baptist Church

(Portland, Maine): 409, 410
Freeman, Albert W.: 366
Freeman, Benjamin: 86, 87
Freeman, D.: 230
Fremont, John: 247
French and Indian War: 3
French, Evander L.: 163
French, William: 200, 218-222; Photos: 219, 220
Frick, Jacob G.: 288, 293, 300
Front Royal Pike (Virginia): 147, 148
Front Royal, Virginia: 146, 148, 165, 243, 351
Fry, J.B.: 44, 45
Furbish, Nehemiah Thompson: 385
Furlong, Reuel W.: 68

G

Gagnon, Joseph E.: 118
Gaines Hill (Virginia): 201
Gaines Mill (Virginia): 251, 279, 283, 291, 292, 295-297
Gaines, Dr. William Fleming: 207, 210, 214
Garcelon, Alonzo (Maine surgeon general): 60-63, 65, 276; Photo: 61; Illus.: 276
Gardiner, J.H.: 230
Gardiner, John: 248, 258, 273
Gardiner, Maine: 31, 318, 406
Gardner, Alexander (photographer): 402, 403; Photos by: 403-408, 414, 419
Gardner, Almy Evelyn: 19
Gardner, Eva Elberta: 19
Gardner, Ida Rosalee: 19
Gardner, Ira: vii, 19, 20, 77, 80, 92, 98, 99, 321-328, 438; Photos:

20, 78, 322
Gardner, John: 20
Gardner, John and Mary: 19, 77
Garlick's Landing (Virginia): 266
Garnett's Hill, Battle of: 302
Geary, John W.: 354, 362; Photo: 354
General Court, Massachusetts: 3, 4
General Order No. 106 (Maine): 83
General Order No. 11 (Maine): 247
General Order No. 12 (Maine): 247
General Order No. 13 (Maine): 250
General Order No. 15 (Maine): 273
General Order No. 16 (Maine): 250
General Order No. 46 (Maine): 83
General Order No. 47 (Maine): 83
General Order No. 48 (Maine): 83
General Order No. 5 (Maine): 351
General Order No. 50 (Maine): 78
General Order No. 54 (Maine): 168
General Order No. 61 (United States): 273
Gentleman Jim: 39
George III, King: 6
George Washington Parke Custis (coal barge): 209
Georgetown, Maryland: 404, 429
Gettysburg (film): v
Gettysburg, Pennsylvania: i, vi; Photos: 362, 363
Gholson, Rep. Samuel Jameson (Mississippi): 7
Gibson, Elizabeth: 297
Gibson, James F. (photographer): 297; Photos by: 173, 178, 188, 190, 235, 265, 299
Gillmore, Quincy A.: 103-109, 111, 112
Glendale, Virginia: 314, 315
Goddard, John (colonel): 85, 89, 159, 163-165, 242; Photo: 162

Goddard, John H. (lieutenant): 156, 161
Godfrey, John Franklin: 92
Goff, Lindsey O.: 106
Golding's Farm, Battle of: 296
Golding's Farm, Virginia: 296, 301
Goodenow, R.K.: 87
Goodwin, Charles: 397
Gordon, G.H.: 229, 230
Gordon, George H.: 358, 380; Photo: 381
Gordon, John: 367
Gorham, Maine: 406, 433
Gould, John Mead: ii, iv, 20, 22-27, 51-53, 75, 76, 78, 79, 347, 350-352, 354, 361-363, 365-367, 370, 373-384, 401, 403, 418, 438; Photos: 22, 78, 380
Gould, Samuel: 112
Gov. Goodwin (locomotive): 72
Graffam, George W.: 291
Graffam, Joshua P.: Photo: 436
Graffam, Leander L.: 118
Grand Patriotic Rally (Portland, Maine): 342
Granite State (New Hampshire): 81
Grant, Dr. Gabriel: 227, 229
Grant, Ulysses S.: Photo: 256
Grapevine Bridge (Chickahominy River, Virginia): 183, 199, 200-202; Photo: 200
Grattan Guards (militia): 16
Graves, Rep. William Jordan (Kentucky): 8, 9, 11, 242; Illus.: 5
Gray, Daniel: 238, 239
Gray, David: Photo: 301
Gray, Maine: 106
Great Britain: 3, 5, 6, 13-15, 65
Great Cacapon River (Virginia): 143-145

Great Famine (Ireland): 167
Greene, George S.: 380, 384
Greene, Maine: 45
Greenhalgh, J.B.: 47
Greenwell Spring Road (Baton Rouge, Louisiana): 321, 323
Greenwood, Maine: 276, 277
Griffin, Charles: 291
Griffin, Warren: 41
Grimes, Elizabeth T.: 243
Grover, Cuvier: 270
Gulf Coast: 95, 99, 116, 119
Gulf of Maine: 261
Gulf of Mexico: 92, 99, 436
Gunn, Thomas Butler: Illus. by: 277

H

Hackett, Alden: 254
Hager, Sewall B.: 75
Hagerstown Pike (Sharpsburg, Maryland): 393, 394, 402
Hagerstown, Maryland: 164, 374, 418, 433
Haley, George (assistant surgeon): 153, 159, 243, 245
Haley, John W.: 255-259
Halifax, Nova Scotia: 68
Hall, B.H.: 229, 230
Hall, Cyrus: 255
Halleck, Henry: 334; Photo: 334
Hallowell, Maine: 15, 115
Halpine, Charles G.: 111, 112
Hamilton Hospital (Union hospital, Virginia): 140
Hamlin, Charles: 257
Hamlin, Dr. Augustus Choate: 21, 24, 25, 53
Hamlin, Hannibal: 2, 21, 344, 411; Photo: 343
Hampden Academy: 6

Hampden, Maine: 5, 6, 62, 75, 120, 150, 257, 344, 425
Hampton Roads (Virginia region): 101, 102, 125, 140, 170
Hampton, Virginia: 124, 209
Hampton's Legion: 138
Hancock Barracks (Houlton, Maine): 14
Hancock County (Maine): 66, 67
Hancock, Maine: 182, 185
Hancock, Winfield Scott: 125-132, 282; Photo: 125; Illus.: 341
Handy, Levin Corbin: Photo by: 343
Hanover County (Virginia): 265
Hanover Court House (Virginia): 163, 251, 266, 283
Hanson, Aaron: 68
Hardee hat: 365; Photo: 366
Harper, Kenton: 40
Harpers Ferry (Virginia): vi, 143, 144, 163, 348, 374, 388, 389, 402, 403, 411, 415
Harper's Weekly: Illus. by: 46, 98, 158, 330
Harris, Alburn P.: 138
Harris, Benjamin: 68
Harris, Ellen Orbison: 262, 268, 269, 271, 272, 302, 331
Harris, Isaac B.: 144, 153, 159, 243, 245
Harrisburg, Pennsylvania: 373
Harrison's Landing (Virginia): 254, 272, 276, 317, 318, 329-336, 409; Photo: 335; Illus.: 330
Hartford, Connecticut: 409
Hartsuff, George Lucas: 402, 405, 428
Harvard College Divinity School: 322
Harvey, George W.: 268

Harvey, Leonard S.: 168, 177, 237
Haskell, Almon: 91
Haskell, William L.: 392, 393, 397
Hatch, John Porter: 146, 147, 149, 150, 153, 154, 165; Photo: 147
Hathaway, John W.: 410-412, 415, 417-419, 433
Hawes, Dr. John Q.A.: 415
Hawthorne, Nathaniel: 6
Haxall's Landing (Virginia): 315
Haycock, George: 35, 36
Haycock, Joel A.: 68
Hayes, Charles C.: 410, 412, 415, 416, 418, 419; Photo: 411
Haynes, Lucius M.S.: 360, 361
Hazzard, George W.: 202, 205, 219
Heald, Mrs.: 62, 63
Heath, Mr.: 119
Heath, William S.: 47, 288, 290-292
Heintzelman, Samuel P.: 29, 48, 141, 173, 195, 231, 263, 268-270, 284, 309, 329; Photo: 47
Helm, Hardin: 323
Hempstead, Long Island, New York: 101
Henry House Hill (Virginia): 29, 39, 44, 47, 75; Photo: 49
Henry House ruins: Photo: 52
Hero (tugboat): 170
Herring Creek (Virginia): 329
Hildreth, Dr. Thaddeus: 318
Hill, Ambrose Powell Jr.: 313; Photo: 314
Hill, Daniel Harvey: 181; Photo: 182
Hill, Dwight Harvey: 129
Hill, Henry F.: 396
Hill, James B.: 80, 99, 323
Hill, Jonathan: 281, 295
Hill, Joseph C.: 159
Hill, Lorenzo B.: 163

Hill, Rev. Henry: 423
Hilton Head, South Carolina: 103, 104, 107, 119, 421, 423
History Channel: Photo from 218
HMS Margaretta: 69
Hobbs, Harrison: 307, 317
Hodsdon, Isaac: 15
Hodsdon, John L.: vi, 13, 15, 17, 18, 20, 23-27, 61, 65, 66, 69, 78, 83-85, 101, 116-118, 122, 164, 168, 169, 247, 250, 252, 254, 256, 257, 273-278, 336, 337, 425, 426, 435; Photos: 14, 78
Hollis, Thomas: 90
Holmes, Ezekiel: 117, 230, 241, 242, 255, 273, 342, 344; Illus.: 274
Holmes, Theophilus: 313, 315; Photo: 315
Holt, Samuel: 106
Homer, Winslow (illustration credits): Illus. by: 64, 431
Hood, John Bell: 138; Photo: 138
Hooker, Joseph: 269, 270, 333, 380-382, 405, 428; Photo: 269; Illus.: 341
Hope, James: Illus. by: 388
Hope, Maine: 432
Hopkins, Dr. William: vii
hospital: Illus.: 417
Houlton, Maine: 14, 84, 117, 153, 159, 163, 167, 427
House, Mathew P.: 238
Howard, Charles: 61, 135, 202, 222, 223, 227, 233, 262, 339, 340
Howard, Elizabeth Anne: 31, 135, 136, 339-343; Photo: 340
Howard, Grace Ellen: 136, 339
Howard, Guy: 135, 136, 339
Howard, James Waite: 136, 339

Howard, Oliver Otis: vi, 29-34, 43-49, 61, 63, 65, 75, 135, 136, 139, 193, 194, 199, 200, 202, 205, 214, 216, 218-223, 225-229, 231, 233, 234, 262, 339-346, 438; Photos: 30, 340
Howard, Rev. Rowland: 343
Howland, Maine: 67
Hubbard, Sewall: Photo: 437
Hudson House (Virginia): 357-359, 370, 371; Photo: 360
Hudson River (New York): 32, 77, 340
Hudson, Maine: 296
Huger, Benjamin: 307, 313, 315, 317; Photo: 306
Hume, Harrison: 173, 178, 179, 181, 183, 184, 239
Humphreys, Andrew A.: 213, 214; Photo: 213
Hunter, David: 107
Hutchins, Charles: 249
Hyde, Jonathan: 387
Hyde, Mary Eleanor: 387
Hyde, Thomas W.: ii, 124-126, 128, 129, 131, 132, 279, 280, 285, 287, 301, 302, 309, 310, 312, 313, 387, 389, 390-399, 402, 403, 438; Photos: 124, 389
Hyde, Zina Jr.: 387
Hygeia Hospital (Union hospital, Virginia): 140

I

I Corps: 247, 380, 405, 428, 430, 437
Idaho (ship): 92
II Corps: 173, 183, 193, 199, 218, 263, 309, 349, 358, 374
III Corps: 124, 141, 173, 174, 179, 193, 195, 200, 212, 217, 231, 233, 263, 265, 269, 279, 284, 302, 329, 352, 370
Ijamsville, Maryland: 374
Indian Town Island, Virginia: 261
Indians (Native Americans): 3, 84
Industry, Maine: 91
infantry (military): see Military Units Index, q.v.
Intrepid (balloon): 210, 212, 213, 215; Photos: 210, 211
Ireland: 167
Ireland, Lawson G.: 179
Irwin, William H.: 388, 390, 392, 393, 397-399
Island Park (Cape Elizabeth, Maine): 252
Isle au Haut, Maine: 5
Italy: 387
IV Corps: 169, 172-174, 177, 179, 193, 195, 196, 199, 200, 212, 214, 223, 229, 239
IX Corps: 375, 391

J

Jackson, Andrew: 7
Jackson, Nathaniel James: 51, 281, 287-290, 292; Photos: 53, 282
Jackson, Thomas "Stonewall": 40, 145-149, 153, 156, 165, 245, 247, 254, 288, 291, 307, 311, 313, 315, 349, 353, 357; Photo: 145
Jacksonville, Florida: 121
Jacobs, Horace G.: Photo: 437
Jamaica Plains (Boston, Massachusetts): 387
James River (Virginia): 125, 141, 172, 215, 247, 254, 272, 276, 284, 292, 295, 302, 306, 311, 315, 317, 329-331, 334
Jameson, Charles D.: 20, 27, 35, 36, 40, 41, 53, 63, 86, 195, 214, 233, 262; Photo: 36
Jay, Maine: 432
Jennings, Reuben: 90
Jersey City, New Jersey: 76
Jesperson, Hal: Photo by: 366
Jewell, Linda and John: vii
John Brooks (steamer): 137
John Bull: 15
Johnson, Charles F.: 221
Johnson, Francis M.: 178, 182, 190, 237, 238
Johnston, Joseph: 171, 174, 177, 179, 181
Jones Island, Georgia: 104, 105, 112
Jones, David R.: 296, 301
Jones, Edward: 22
Jones, George W.: 8, 9
Jones, James Parnell: 397
Jordan, Noah W.: Photo: 438
Jordan, William P.: 383, 384
Jordan's Ford (White Oak Creek, Virginia): 285, 302, 305, 307
Jose, Jim: 258
Jose, Martin: 75
Judge O'Neal place: 119, 121

K

Katon, Alexander: 183-185
Kealiher, John: 254
Kearny, Philip: 195, 196, 217, 233, 268, 270, 279, 284, 285, 302, 305, 307 313, 314; Illus.: 232, 341
Keedysville, Maryland: 380, 412
Keene, Elden A.: 118
Keene, Josiah: 182

Keith, John: 324
Kennebec Arsenal (Augusta, Maine): 87, 115; Photo: 90
Kennebec County (Maine): 254, 274
Kennebec Journal (newspaper): 255
Kennebec River (Maine): 60, 87, 170, 254, 261, 387
Kennebec Valley (Maine): 31, 33
Kennebunk, Maine: 159
Kent (steamer): 170
Kent, John E.: 120, 426
Kentucky: 242, 254
Kentwood, Virginia: 322
Kernstown, Virginia: 254
Ketch, Elias: 296
Keyes, Erasmus Darwin: 35, 37-41, 125, 169, 173, 263; Photo: 172
Kilby, William Henry: 17
Kimmage's Creek (Virginia): 329, 330
King George III: 6
King, Jabez: 41
Kingman, Eugene Kincaide: 95-98
Kingman, Rev. Lebbeus: 95
Kingman, Ruth: 95
Kirby, Edmund: 201, 202, 205; Illus.: 206
Kittery Point, Maine: 17
Kittery, Maine: 17
Knap, Joseph: 358, 369
Knapp, Frederick: 265
Knap's Pennsylvania Independent Battery E: 352, 354, 358, 369; Illus.: 358
Knight, Adelbert: 332, 334, 335
Knight, Storer S.: 384
Knipe, Joseph: 350
Knowles, Abiather: 40
Knowles, Abner: 69, 72

Knowlton, Wayland: 208, 209
Knowlton, William: 366
Knox County (Maine): 81
Knox Flying Artillery (proposed company): 21
Knox, Chaplain George: 418
Kuprovich, Robert: vii
Kurz & Allison: Illus. by: 44, 130, 396

L

Ladd, Luther: 23
Ladies' Aid Society of Philadelphia: 262
Ladies Committee (Free Street Baptist Church): 410
Ladies' Volunteer Aid Society, The (Belfast, Maine): 59
Lafayette Square (New Orleans, Louisiana): 100, 321
Lagrange, Maine: 40
Lake Borgne (Louisiana): 97
Lake Wassookeag: 96
Lakeman, Moses: 195
Lang, James: 239
Latham, Henry Grey: 39
Lawrence, Massachusetts: 22
Lawrence, William H.S.: 35, 40
Lawson Hill (Virginia): 208
Leavitt, James: 255
Lee, Henry "Light Horse Harry": 84
Lee, Maine: 167
Lee, Mary: 141
Lee, Robert E.: 84, 103, 138, 141, 213, 254, 271, 272, 279, 280, 283, 295, 300, 306, 307, 313-316, 373, 374, 379, 380, 399, 430; Photo: 280
Lee, Robert M. Jr.: 221, 226
Lee, William "Rooney": 138, 142

Leeds, Maine: 30
Leesboro, Maryland: 405
Leesburg, Virginia: 373
Leighton, Stephen: 75
Lemont, Frank L.: 43-47
Leonard, Rev. Henry: 317-319
Letter for Home (illustration): Illus.: 64
Letterman, Dr. Jonathan K.: 333
Leuzarder, Julius M.: 163
Levant, Maine: 157
Lewiston Journal (newspaper): 339
Lewiston Light Infantry (militia): 17, 24
Lewiston Zouaves (militia): 17, 24
Lewiston, Maine: 17, 43, 51, 68, 83, 117, 143, 255, 340, 341, 365, 366, 382, 397
Lexington Township, Maine: 91
Libbey, Samuel: 425
Libby Prison (Richmond, Virginia): 75
Libby, Arthur: 124, 207-209, 212
Limington, Maine: 109
Lincoln County (Maine): 6, 75
Lincoln Patriot (newspaper): 11
Lincoln, Abraham: 17, 22, 29, 62, 75, 76, 78, 96, 139, 145, 247, 250, 254, 321, 334, 344, 345, 373, 379, 407, 421; Photos: 406, 407
Lincoln, John: 68
Lincoln, Maine: 163, 255, 257, 297
Lincoln, Mary Todd: 323
Lincoln, Theodore Jr.: 68
Lincolnville, Maine: 332
Line, George: 380, 385
Lisbon, Maine: 156
Litchfield, J.B.: 24
Litchfield, Maine: 322

Little Tybee Island, Georgia: 103
Little Washington, Virginia: 350
Little, Eleanor Maria: 387
Littlefield, Jeremiah and Dorothy: 15
Littlefield, John: 15
Livermore, Maine: 13, 101, 136, 342
Lockes Mills (Greenwood, Maine): 276
Logan, John A.: Illus.: 341
London, England: 14, 15, 26
Lonely Grave, A (photograph): Photo: 404
Long Branch (steamer): 125
Long Bridge (Washington, D.C.): 169
Long Bridge Road (Virginia): 306, 307, 313, 314
Long Island (Blue Hill Bay, Maine): 275
Long Island, Georgia: 105
Long, William H.: 399
Longfellow, Henry Wadsworth: 6
Longstreet, James: 313
Longstreet, James: Photo: 314
Loudon Valley (Virginia): 415
Louisiana (steamer, hospital transport): 262, 331
Lovell, Maine: 429
Lowe, Charles: 317
Lowe, Prof. Thaddeus Sobieski Constantine: 124, 193, 207-215, 218; Photos: 125, 209, 210, 215; Illus.: 197
Lowell, Massachusetts: 23, 96
Lowell, Oliver: 433
Lower Canada (Canada): 14
Lubec Rifles (militia): 17
Lubec, Maine: 17, 68
Luce, William H.: 163

Lumley, Arthur: Illus. by: 197, 229
Lunt, Albert W.: 119-122, 421-426; Illus.: 425
Lunt, Henry: 425
Lunt, William W.: See Lunt, Albert W.
Luray Valley (Virginia): 146, 350
Lynchburg Artillery (Confederate unit): 39

M

Mace, Andrew C.: 170, 171
Machias Rifles (militia): 68, 69
Machias, Maine: 4, 5, 68, 69, 125
Macky, Thomas: 68
Maddocks, Willis: 184, 185, 239, 240
Madison, James (U.S. president): 5
Madison, Maine: 254
Magnus, Charles (illustration credit): Illus. by: 168, 169
Magruder, John B.: 126, 279, 295, 309
Mahan, Dennis Hart: 124
Main Street (Bangor, Maine): 343
Maine at War (column): iii, v
Maine Central Railroad: 343, 344
Maine Coast Guards: 344
Maine Farmer (newspaper): 117, 123, 132, 163, 230, 241, 255, 273, 342
Maine Farmer (newspaper): Photo: 275
Maine Historical Society: Photo courtesy of: 413
Maine Hotel (Auburn, Maine): 341
Maine House of Representatives: 7, 31
Maine Legislature: 15, 23, 59, 60, 115, 410; Photo: 92

Maine Soldiers' Relief Agency: 66, 410, 433; Photo: 413
Maine State Agency Sanitary Commission: Photo: 413
Maine State Archives: iii, v, vii; Photos courtesy of: 15, 20, 21, 36, 37, 60, 61, 69, 78, 87, 90-92, 116, 124, 131, 136, 146, 162, 172, 183, 186, 248, 281, 282, 322, 323, 348, 389, 411, 428; Illus. by: 352
Maine State Capitol: Photo: 116
Maine State Library: Photos courtesy of: 104, 105
Maine State Museum: Photos courtesy of: 38, 39, 180
Maine State Prison: 120
Major (dog): 79, 162
Maker, Emmy B.: 435
Maker, Lydia: 435
Malvern Hill (Virginia): 118, 306, 307, 313, 316, 317, 329, 330, 333; Photo: 319
Malvern Hill House: Photo: 310
Manassas Gap (Virginia): 349
Manassas Junction (Virginia): 29
Manassas, Virginia: 41, 43, 51, 53, 54, 56, 65, 75, 76, 81, 118, 124, 137, 195, 207, 208, 222, 248, 252, 373; Photo: 50
Manassas-Sudley Road (modern Virginia Route 234): 45
Manners-Sutton, John: 26
Manning, Ellen: 120, 121, 421, 422
Mansfield, Joseph King Fenno: 378-384; Photo: 377
March to Seven Pines (illustration): Illus.: 203
Marcy, Randolph B.: 214, 215; Photo: 213
Maritimes (provinces): 14

Marks, Rev. James Junius: 297, 299, 300, 302, 303, 309-311
Marsh Island (Maine): 67
Marshall, Thomas: 208
Marston, Charles: 365
Martindale, E.: 399
Martindale, John H.: 283, 285, 286, 291; Photo: 286
Martinsburg, Virginia: 161, 164
Maryland Heights (Maryland): 389, 403
Mason, Edwin C.: 131, 387, 403; Photo: 131
Massachusetts General Court: 3, 4
Massanutten Mountain (Virginia): 146
Mattaponi River (Virginia): 137, 261
Mattawamkeag, Maine: 14, 163
Matthews Hill (Manassas, Virginia): 43
Maurer, Louis: Illus. by: 316
Maxfield, Albert: ii, 334
Mayhew, Rev. Andrew: 66
Mayhew, Ruth: 66, 264
Mayo, Clifford N.: 150, 151, 154-157, 159
McArthur, William: 109, 110, 112; Photo: 105
McCall, George: 297, 314, 315, 334; Photo: 315
McCarty, Jerry: 239
McClellan, George B.: 123, 126, 133, 135, 137, 138, 141, 171-173, 179, 193, 207, 209, 210, 212, 214, 239, 247, 250, 254, 263, 266, 267, 269, 272, 279, 283-285, 292, 295, 300, 302, 306-309, 312, 315, 329, 330, 333, 334, 342, 373, 374, 379, 388, 399, 402-405, 407, 430, 432; Photos: 124, 239, 406, 407; Illus.: 316, 341
McCrillis, William: 56, 57, 59
McDavitt, William Jr.: 307, 317
McDonald, George F.: 163
McDowell, Irvin: 29, 30, 34, 35, 44, 53, 54, 75, 247, 352, 370; Photos: 76, 353; Illus.: 44
McFarland, John D.: 196
McGehee Farm (Richmond, Virginia): 290, 291, 292
McGilvery, Freeman: 347, 348, 359, 370, 371; Illus.: 352
McIntyre, Charles A.: 147, 148
McIntyre, William: 225
McKeen, John: 254
McKnight, Armor A.: 231
McLellan, William: 76
Meade, George G.: 315
Meader, W.F.: 230
Meagher, Thomas F.: 200, 202, 205, 218; Photo: 201
Mechanic Blues (militia): 17
Mechanicsville, Virginia: 210, 211, 213, 215, 275, 283
Meduxnekeag River (Aroostook County, Maine): 14, 84
Meigs, Montgomery C.: 102
Memnon Sanford (steamer): 25
Mercer, Maine: 366
Merchants' and Traders' Bank (Portland, Maine): 20
Meridian Hill (Washington, D.C.): 33, 35, 51, 61, 63, 169
Merrill, Alonzo B.: 120, 426
Merrill, Joseph: 384
Merrill, Simeon H.: 179, 189, 190
Mexican-American War: 226
Mexico, Maine: 91
Midcoast (Maine region): 1, 83, 97, 98, 98, 345

Middletown Disaster: 163, 242
Middletown Road (Maryland): 388
Middletown Valley (Maryland): 374, 375, 388, 419
Middletown, Maryland: 374, 412
Middletown, Virginia: vi, 1, 147-150, 153-156, 159, 161, 163-166, 241, 243, 245, 348; Photo: 155
Miles, Dixon S.: 143, 145; Photo: 144
Miles, Nelson A.: 205, 221, 226
Military Road (Maine): 14, 15, 84
Miller farm (Antietam): Photo: 419
Miller, David: 381
Miller, James: 219-221
Miller, Theodore: 232
Millett, Joseph: 91
Milo Artillery (militia): 17
Milo, Maine: 17, 54, 275
Mines, Rev. John F.: 21
Mississippi (steamer): 98
Mississippi Delta: 97
Mississippi River: 97, 100, 321, 322; Illus.: 327
Missouri Compromise: 6
Mitchell Station Road (Virginia): 357
Mitchell, Charles: 296
Mitchell, O.P.: 24, 30
Molly Camel Run (Virginia): Photo: 149
Monmouth, Maine: 397
Monocacy River (Maryland): 374
Monroe, Maine: 75
Monroe, R.A.: 275
Moore, Americus: 40
Moore, James: 69
Moore, John F.: 239
Moose River Plantation, Maine: 254

Morgan County, Virginia: 144
Morgan, John Hunt: 254
Morrell, George W.: 283
Morrill, Lot: 15, 138, 139
Morrill, Maine: 254
Morris, Charles: 5, 41
Morris, James A.: 185
Morrison, Isabella (see Fogg, Isabella): 65
Morse, Llewellyn J.: 54
Mount Jackson (Virginia): 159, 163, 245
Mount Vernon, Maine: 249
Mount Vernon, Virginia: 138
Mowat, Henry: 5
Mud River (South Carolina): 104
mud season (Maine): 193
Mudgett, Lewis P.: 291
Muhlenberg, Edward D.: 358, 361, 362
Mundee, Charles: 392
Mundy, James: vii, 69, 70
Murch, Jeptha: Photo: 438
Museum of Fine Arts (Boston): Photo courtesy of: 103

N

Naglee, Henry M.: 169, 172, 173, 179, 180, 182, 183, 187, 239, 267; Photos: 171, 238
Napoleon cannon: 201, 202, 314, 325, 361; Photo: 319
Narraguagus River (Maine): 68, 69
Narraguagus, Maine: 68, 69
National Air & Space Museum: Photo courtesy of: 215
National Archives: Photos courtesy of: 106, 146, 267, 280, 314
National Park Service: Illus. by: 388

National Pike (Maryland): 374, 376, 378
Navy, United States: v, 5, 69, 97, 110, 119, 122, 137, 284, 313, 323, 334
Needham, Sumner: 22, 23
Nelly Baker (steamer): 234, 262, 336, 337, 339, 340; Photo: 234
Nelson, William: 255
New Bridge Road (Virginia): 213
New Brunswick (Canada): 13, 14, 65, 68, 254, 257, 352
New England: 3, 4, 8, 59, 96, 122, 322
New France: 3
New Ireland (Maine colony): 4, 5
New Kent County (Virginia): 138
New Kent, Virginia: 266
New Market, Virginia: 145
New Orleans, Louisiana: 96, 97, 99, 100, 113, 321
New River (South Carolina): 104
New York City: 7, 32, 33, 77, 84, 255, 340, 410
New York Times (newspaper): 119, 421
Newburgh, Maine: 238
Newcastle, Maine: 429
Newcomb, Lemuel E.: 311, 312
Newport News, Virginia: 170
Newport, Maine: 254
New-York Tribune (newspaper): 231, 286, 334
Nicholson, Asa: 54
Nickerson, Albert: 397
Nickerson, Franklin S.: 80, 92, 275, 321, 324-328; Photo: 322
Nightingale, Florence: 60, 65
Nine Mile Road (Virginia): 172, 181, 183, 186, 187, 269
North America (sailing vessel): 92, 98, 99

North Island, Georgia: 104
North Yarmouth Academy: 16, 54
Norumbega Hall (Bangor, Maine): 56, 343; Photo: 342
Norvell, J.M.: 340
Norway Light Infantry (militia): 24
Norway, Maine: 22, 274, 379
Nottingham, New Hampshire: 6, 81
Nova Scotia (Canada): 26
Noyes, H.K.: 230
Noyes, William: 414, 418
Nutter, Robert: 159, 245
Nutting, Josiah: 254, 433

O

Oak Grove (Virginia): 279, 297, 307
Oak Grove, Battle of: 269
O'Brien, Jeremiah: 69
Old Church, Virginia: 265, 266
Old Dominion State: 355
Old Point Comfort, Virginia: 96, 125, 140
Old Sharpsburg Road (Maryland): 374, 376
Old Tavern, Virginia: 270
Old Town, Maine: 14, 20, 27, 40, 67, 70, 153, 195, 425
Olmstead, Charles H.: 107, 108, 111, 112
Olmstead, Frederick Law: 263; Photo: 267
Orchard Station (Virginia): 196, 197, 207, 217, 263
Orland, Maine: 257
Orono, Maine: 36, 53, 120, 163, 257, 425
O'Rorke, Patrick H.: 105
Orrington, Maine: 6, 36, 41

Osborn, Juliette: 16
O'Sullivan, Timothy: Photo by: 355
Otto Boetticher: Illus. by: 158
Outer Banks (North Carolina): 81
Owen, Jere: 360
Owens, John Algernon: Illus.: 3
Oxford County (Maine): 22, 87, 256, 276, 343, 344

P

Pacific Mail Steamship Company: 169
Page, Gilman J.: 274
Page, Silas: 296
Paine, R.E.: 257
Palmer, Dr. Alden D.: 286
Palmer, Dr. Gideon S.: 62-65
Palmyra, Maine: 91
Pamunkey River (Virginia): 136-138, 141, 233, 261, 266, 280, 284, 303
Paris, Maine: 87, 344
Parker, Thomas J.: 221, 223, 225
Parker, William: 185
Parrot gun/rifle: 105, 110, 183, 369; Photos: 106, 362, 363
Parsons, John B.: 397
Passamaquoddy (Maine region): 17
Passamaquoddy Bay (Maine): 4, 5, 68
Patten, Maine: 19, 20, 77, 80, 99, 255
Peck, John J.: 267, 330, 333; Photo: 331
Peerless (vessel): 102
Peirce, Frank: 68, 69
Pelouse, Louis H.: 103, 363
Pembroke Rifles (militia): 68
Pembroke, Maine: 17, 68

Peninsula (Virginia): vi, 123, 135-137, 139-141, 145, 170, 208-210, 230, 263, 264, 334, 335
Peninsula Campaign: 124, 208, 209, 252, 257, 276, 333, 342, 414, 430
Pennsylvania Avenue (Washington, D.C.): 61, 63
Pennsylvania Reserves: 314
Penobscot Bay (Maine): 3, 4, 15
Penobscot County (Maine): 14, 19, 56, 67, 77, 85, 95, 254
Penobscot Expedition: 4
Penobscot Narrows (Maine): 67
Penobscot River (Maine): 3, 4, 5, 25, 67, 70, 120, 167
Penobscot Valley (Maine region): 14, 84, 167, 296
Penobscot, Maine: 41
Perkins, Eben: 41
Perkins, Elisha: 36
Perkins, John: 36, 41
Perkins, O.P.: 435
Perry, Joe: 256
Perry, John I.: 87
Perryville, Battle of: Photo: 318
Perryville, Kentucky: Photos: 318, 371, 385
Pert, William G.: 275, 276
Pettit, Rufus D.: 219
Philadelphia, Pennsylvania: 33, 76, 238, 262, 278, 335, 373, 410
Philbrook, D.W.: 230
Phillips, Byron: 360
Picerno, Nicholas P.: I, ii, vii; Photos courtesy of: 22, 78, 165, 348, 367, 380, 381, 383
Pierce, Frank: 70
Pierce, Franklin: 6
Pillsbury, John: 91
Pine Tree State: v, 31, 67, 80, 101, 117
Pinnette, Megan: vii
Piper, Henry: 392-394, 397-399
Piscataqua River (Maine/New Hampshire): 3
Piscataquis County (Maine): 2, 17, 67, 72, 75, 87, 90, 95, 274, 275
Piscataquis River (Maine): 67
Pitcher, Horatio: 257
Pitcher, William: 196, 197, 217, 219-221, 226
Pittston, Maine: 183
Plaisted, Harris M.: 171, 179, 181-186, 189, 237-240, 276, 300, 308, 311, 312, 334, 438; Photos: 172, 238
Plattsburg, New York: 425
Pleasant River (Maine): 67
Pleasant Valley (Maryland): 389
Poems by David Barker (book): Illus. by: 345
Poffenberger, John: 381
Poffenberger, Samuel: 381, 384
Poor, Austin: 255
Poor, Russell: 118
Pope, John: 349, 351, 373; Photo: 350
Poquosin Flats (York River, Virginia): 137
Port of Bangor: 257
Port Royal, South Carolina: 103, 119, 422
Porter, David: 35
Porter, Fitz John: 207, 215, 279-281, 283-285, 288, 291, 437; Photos: 208, 209
Porter, Horace: 107
Portland Armory (Portland, Maine): 24
Portland City Hall (Portland, Maine): 25, 342

Portland Daily Press (newspaper): 251, 425
Portland Harbor (Portland, Maine): 96
Portland Light Guards (militia): 17, 24, 25, 78
Portland Light Infantry (militia): 17
Portland Rifle Corps (militia): 17
Portland Rifle Guards (militia): 17, 24
Portland Transcript (newspaper): 123
Portland, Maine: 5, 6 14, 17, 20, 24-26, 36, 40, 47, 66-68, 70-72, 77-79, 92, 95, 96, 115, 117, 137, 250, 252, 256-258, 277, 291, 342, 347, 365, 383-385, 387, 392, 409, 410, 413, 415, 418, 429
Portsmouth, New Hampshire: 79
Potomac River: 36, 93, 138, 139, 159, 162, 165, 170, 334, 373, 374, 379, 389, 402-404, 406, 410, 411, 415, 427, 430-432
Pottle, Simon II: 68
Powers, Hannibal: 360
Powhite (Virginia farm): 207
Powhite Creek (Virginia): 210-212
Pratt, George W.: 118
Pratt, Reuben: 366, 367
Prentiss, Henry E.: 56
Prentiss, Maine: 167
Prescott, Henry G.: 185
President Street Station (Baltimore, Maryland): 22
Presque Isle, Maine: 392
Prince Edward Island, Canada: 68
Prince, Deborah: 6
Prince, Henry: 349, 354, 355, 357, 371

Prince, Hezekiah: 6
Prince, Isabella: 6
Province of Lower Canada: 14
Pry's Ford (Antietam Creek, Maryland): 390
Pulaski, Casimir: 103
Putnam, Aziel: 84
Putnam, Black Hawk: 84, 86, 153, 155, 159, 163; Photo: 84
Putnam, John: 85
Putnam, John and Elizabeth: 84
Putnam, Osceola: 84
Putnam, Sarah: 84
Pysell, William: 68

Q

Quaker Road (Virginia): 306
Queen (steamer): 68
Queen City (Bangor, Maine): 59, 257
Queen, James Fuller: Illus. by: 417
Queen's Creek (Virginia): 127, 132
Quint, Luther: 91

R

Ramsdell, Abigail C.: 435
Ramsdell, E.A.: 435
Ramsdell, Seth B.: 118
Rand, Moses: 429
Randolph, George E.: 316
Rankin, Abel: 365
Rapidan River (Virginia): 352, 355
Rappahannock River (Virginia): 349
Rappahannock Station (Virginia): 432, 433, 435
Rawlins Mill Pond (Virginia): 329
Raymond H. Fogler Library (University of Maine): vii

Readfield, Maine: 249, 384
reenactors: Photos: front cover, 187, 318, 362, 363, 371, 385, 395, back cover
regiment (military): see Military Units Index, q.v.
Regimental Order No. 1: 124
Reno, Jesse Lee: 375; Photo: 375
Revolutionary War: 4, 14, 69, 84, 103, 137, 406
Reynolds, Charles: 99
Reynolds, John: 430, 433
Rhorersville, Maryland: 431, 433
Rice, William H.H.: 181, 184, 185
Rich, Rishworth: 101, 119
Richardson, Israel B.: 193, 199, 200, 218, 219, 221, 339, 340; Photo: 194
Richardson's Civil War Round Table: vii
Richmond & York River Railroad: 137, 138, 141, 172, 196, 199, 205, 215, 217, 218, 233, 238, 261, 263, 265, 266, 280, 281, 284, 295, 308, 309, 409; Illus.: 312
Richmond, Kentucky: 254
Richmond, Maine: 143
Richmond, Virginia: 75, 135, 138, 140, 142, 145, 159, 171, 172, 210-213, 215, 237, 247, 254, 263, 264, 266, 267, 269, 270, 279-282, 295, 306, 307, 315, 333, 340, 410; Photo: 204; Illus.: 158
Ricker, Edward: 275
Ricketts, James: 428-430; Photo: 429
Ridgeville, Maryland: 405
Riley, George: 126
Ring, Warren: 397

Ripley, Maine: 118
River Road (Virginia): 306, 307, 313, 329
Roanoke Island, North Carolina: 103
Robbinston, Maine: 68, 178
Roberts, Charles: 53, 54, 283, 285, 291; Photo: 281
Roberts, Jim Sr.: vii
Roberts, Winslow: 80
Robie, Charles: 347, 348
Robinson House (Manassas, Virginia): Photo: 41
Robinson, James: 75
Robinson, James ("Gentleman Jim"): 39
Robinson, John C.: 307, 313, 314; Photo: 308
Robinson, O'Neil W. Jr.: 86, 87, 347, 349, 353-355, 357, 359, 361, 370, 371; Photos: 87, 348
Roche, Thomas: 68
Rockland City Guards (militia): 19
Rockland Harbor (Rockland, Maine): 27
Rockland, Maine: 15, 19, 24, 25, 27, 45, 66, 68, 117, 195, 252, 264, 279, 412
Rockville Turnpike (Maryland): 374
Rockville, Maryland: 373, 374
Rodgers, John: 315
Rogers, Fred H.: 196
Rogers, James and Joseph: 36
Rogers, John (sculptor): Sculpture by: 256
Root, Adrian: 433
Rosecrans, W.S.: Illus.: 341
Roulette, William: 390
Rowe, Dr. Ephraim: 54
Royal Army: 26

Royal Navy: 5
Ruggles, Sen. John (Maine): 7
Russell, Andrew J.: Photo by: 360
Rust, John: 104, 107, 109, 110, 112; Photo: 104

S

S.R. Spaulding (steamer): 335
Sabine, Francis W.: 174, 178, 179, 186, 189, 190; Photo: 186
Sacket, Delos B.: Photo: 335
Saco Water Power Shop: 256
Saco, Maine: 78, 255, 259, 414
Sagadahoc County (Maine): 143
Saint John, New Brunswick: 26, 84
Sally, Charles H.: 360
Sampson, Charles A.L.: 60, 135, 139, 141, 270, 284, 306, 307, 317, 335, 336
Sampson, Sarah: vi, 60-66, 135, 136, 139-142, 251-263, 265-272, 302, 303, 331-333, 335-337, 438; Photo: 60
San Francisco, California: 35, 37
Sandpits, Battle of the: 169
Sanger, Dr. Eugene F.: 72
Sangerville, Maine: 69, 72, 257
Sanitary Commission (Maine): Photo: 413
Sanitary Commission (U.S.): 263, 264, 411, 412, 414, 415, 418
Santa Rosa Island, Florida: 97
Sargent, Herbert: 365
Sauk (Native American tribe): 84
Savage Station, Battle of: Illus.: 271
Savage Station, Virginia: 263, 265, 266, 268-272, 282, 296, 297, 306, 309-312, 318, 331, 409; Photo: 265, 297, 299
Savannah River (Georgia): 104, 107
Savannah, Georgia: 103, 104
Sawyer, George: vii
Sawyer, N.K.: 359
Saxton, Rufus: 102
Scamman, Edward S.: 291
Schaumberg, James W.: 9
Scholten, John A.: Photo by: 334
Scott, Winfield: Illus.: 341
Scoullar, James A.: 239
Searsport, Maine: 80, 321, 347
Sebasticook River (Maine): 254
Sebec, Maine: 75, 274
secesh, secess: 245, 251, 273, 278, 348
secession: 401
secessionist: 273, 278, 373; Illus.: 277
Second Bank of the United States: 8
Second Manassas (battle): 207, 254
Sedgwick, John: 173, 183, 189, 199, 201, 202, 205, 218, 228; Photo: 183, 335
Sedgwick, Maine: 350, 358
Seminary Hospital (Georgetown, Maryland): 429
Seminole Wars: 31
Senate, United States: 13
Serrell, Edward W.: 112
Seven Days Battles: 233, 409
Seven Pines, Battle of: 231, 318; Illus.: 184, 229
Seven Pines, Virginia: 141, 172, 173, 175, 177, 180, 183, 186, 187, 189, 193, 195, 199-201, 205, 207, 211, 212, 214, 215, 218, 223, 225, 229, 232-234, 237, 238, 262, 267, 269, 279, 295, 305, 318, 333, 341, 343,

344; Photo: 222; Illus.: 203
Severn River (Maryland): 101
Sewall, F.D.: 234
Sewall, Frederick: 259, 339, 341
Seward, Frances "Fanny" Adeline: 35
Seward, William (U.S. Secretary of State): 35
Sharpsburg, Maryland: 377-380, 388, 389, 391, 401-407, 414, 427-431, 433; Photo: 395
Shattuck, Luke: 317
Shaw, Elijah: 52, 76
Shaw, Richard R.: vii; Photos courtesy of: 56, 342
Shaw, William H.: 276
Sheldon, J.A. (photographer): Photo by: 138
Shenandoah River (Virginia): 415
Shenandoah Valley (Virginia): vi, 145, 146, 157, 159, 161, 163-165, 241, 245, 247, 254, 348-350
Shepherd, Russell B.: 257
Shepley, George Foster: 95, 96, 417; Photo: 97
Sheridan, James: 384
Sherman, Moses E.: 238
Sherman, Thomas W.: 81, 83, 101-103, 107
Sherman, William (Maine private): 238
Sherman, William Tecumseh: 38; Photo: 37
Shields, James: 245
Ship Island (Mississippi): 92, 95, 97, 98, 100; Illus.: 98
Sibley tent: Photo: 117; Illus.: 89
Skowhegan, Maine: 249, 254, 344, 431
skulkers: 286, 295, 367

Slaughter, Rev. Philip: 352
Slocum, Henry W.: 138, 287, 288, 291, 300, 303, 388, 389, 391, 415; Photos: 137, 283
Small, Abner R.: ii, 248-251, 258, 404-407, 427-433; Photo: 248
Smart, Benjamin: 40
Smith, Charles: 2, 80; Photo: 5
Smith, Charles (14th Maine Infantry): 99
Smith, Eben: Photo: 438
Smith, Edmund Kirby: 254
Smith, Edwin: 27
Smith, John Rubens: Illus. by: 8
Smith, Lewis B.: 51
Smith, Perley: 317
Smith, Samuel: 57
Smith, William F. ("Baldy"): 125, 280, 296, 300, 309, 310, 312, 388, 393, 397-399; Photo: 281
Smoketown Hospital (Smoketown, Maryland): 412, 414, 418
Smoketown Road (Maryland): 380-383, 390
Smoketown, Maryland: 407, 418, 419
Sneden, Robert Knox: 329
Snow, Edward A.: 412
Soldiers at Harrison's Landing (illustrations): Illus.: 336, 337
Somerset County (Maine): 90, 254, 344
South Anna Bridge (Virginia): 266
South Mountain (Maryland): vi, 374, 375, 379, 388, 389, 403, 412, 419, 427, 431
South Mountain, Battle of: Illus.: 376
Spalding, Archibald G.: 147, 151, 163-165, 242
Special Order No. 262: 405

Special Order No. 271: 404
Spofford, Winslow P.: Photo: 437
Spring, Park: 207, 212, 213
Springfield, Maine: 167, 178
Sproul, Hiram: 68
St. Augustine, Florida: 421
St. Croix River (Maine/New Brunswick): 14, 65, 68, 254
St. Francis River: 254
St. John River (Maine/New Brunswick): 14, 84
St. John Valley (Maine): 14
St. Lawrence River (Canada): 14
St. Mary's River (Florida): 119
St. Stephen, New Brunswick: 68
Stafford Court House (Virginia): 433
Stanton, Edwin M. (secretary of war): 96, 145, 250, 252, 254, 411; Photos: 249, 256
Stanwood, John D.: 168, 178
Staples, Henry G.: 226, 227, 230
Staples, Horatio: 35, 37, 38, 40
State Arsenal (Bangor, Maine): 25
State House (Augusta, Maine): 32, 80, 85, 87, 91, 115-117, 248, 250, 251, 387, 435
State of Maine (steamer): 169, 331
State Street (Augusta, Maine): 32, 87, 115
State Street (Bangor, Maine): 56, 257
State Street Avenue (Bangor, Maine): 37
Steamer Eastern City, The (illustration): Illus.: 71
Stetson, Charles W.: 163
Stetson, Isaiah: 56, 57
Stevens, Augustus: 275, 276
Stevens, Elizabeth: vii
Stewart Horse Artillery: 265

Stinson, Alonzo: 47, 48
Stinson, Harry: 48
Stockton Springs, Maine: 41, 291
Stone Bridge (Bull Run): 38
Stone, Walter E.: 433
Strasburg, Virginia: 145, 146, 245
Strickland, Lee: 101, 104, 119
Strickland, Robert: 238
Stuart, James Ewell Brown: 265-267, 279, 280, 300, 331; Photo: 267
Sudley Church (at Sudley Ford): 43
Sudley Ford (Bull Run): 29, 34, 43, 48; Photo: 48
Suffell, Pheby: 435
Summat, George J.: 153, 154
Summer Street (Bangor, Maine): 57
Sumner, Edwin V.: 193, 199, 201, 202, 214, 215, 218, 219, 309; Photo: 194
Sunken Road: Photo: 408
Swartz, Brian F.: v, vii; Photos by: front cover, 49, 50, 55, 109, 149, 155, 187, 289, 318, 319, 332, 359, 362, 363, 371, 385, 394, 395, 398, back cover
Swartz, Christopher: vii
Swartz, Susan: vii
Swett, James G.: 349
Swinburne, Dr. John: 265
Sykes, George: 288; Photo: 285

T

Tabor, John: 57
Talbot, Thomas Hammond: 257
Tallahassee, Florida: 121, 426
Taylor, Charles: 23
Taylor, Ephraim H.: 156, 161
Taylor, Nelson: 429, 430, 433

Tenleytown, Maryland: 373
Tennallytown, Maryland: 373
Tennessee (ship): 99
Terrapin Point (Virginia): 261
Territory of Aroostook: 13, 14
Terry, Alfred: 421, 423, 424; Photo: 422
Thanksgiving Surprise (illustration): Illus.: 431
Thaxter, Sidney W.: 162, 163
Third District (Maine congressional): 7
Tholey, Augustus: Illus. by: 341
Thomas, George H.: Illus.: 341
Thomas, Lorenzo (U.S. adjutant general): 247, 250; Photo: 248
Thomaston (Elm Grove Cemetery): 11
Thomaston Historical Society: vii; Photos courtesy of: 9, 10, 422; Illus. by: 2, 82
Thomaston, Maine: 1, 6, 7, 21, 81, 84, 85, 120, 243, 245, 437
Thompson, Albert V.: 349
Thompson, Arad: 27
Thompson, James: 314
Thompson, Rev. Zenas: 70
Thornton's Gap (Maryland): 431
Tibbetts, Charles: 418
Tides Institute & Museum (illustration credit): Illus. by: 71
Tiger Island, Georgia: 119
Tilden, Charles W.: vi, 16, 25, 27, 36, 41, 251, 255, 405, 407, 427, 429, 430, 432, 433, 435, 438; Photos: 36, 428
Tilden, Mary: 16
Tilley, Samuel Leonard: 26
Tillson, Davis: 17; Photo: 15
Titcomb, William H.: 18, 24

Tobey, William L.: 17
Tobie, Edward Parsons: 83, 85, 87-91, 93, 143-145, 148, 150, 151, 153-155, 159, 161, 245; Photo: 91
Todd, Alexander H.: 323
Todd, Emilie: 323
Tolman, Eliazer: 275
Tomlinson, William P.: Illus. by: 164
Tompkins, Charles H.: 201
Tom's Brook (Virginia): 146
Toombs, Robert Augustus: 296, 301; Photo: 296
Topsfield, Maine: 167
Townsend, Eliza: 208
Townsend, George Alfred: 302; Photo: 301
townships: 91, 254, 429
Treasury Department, United States: 149
Treaty of Ghent: 6, 7, 13
Tripler, Dr. Charles S.: 263
Tripp, Alonzo: 254
Tripp, Harrison A.: 350-352, 358, 362, 366-370; Photo: 367
Tucker, Isaac: 31-33, 406, 433
Tukey's Bridge (Portland, Maine): 258
Tunstall's Station (Virginia): 266, 267, 280
Turner, Gilman: 117
Turner, Hiram A.: 317
Turner, J.S.: 342
Turner, John Wesley: 110
Turner, Maine: 106
Turner's Gap (Maryland): 374, 375, 378, 379
Turtle Island, Georgia: 104
Twain, Mark: Photo: 301
Tybee Island, Georgia: 103, 106,

107, 112
Tyler, Daniel: 35, 37, 38

U

Uncle Sam: 59
Union (steamer): 102
Union Army Balloon Corps: 193, 201, 207, 210; Photo: 210
Union cavalryman: Illus.: 244
Union Street (Bangor, Maine): 343
Union, Maine: 145
unit (military): see Military Units Index, q.v.
United States: v, 435, 438
United States Capitol: Illus.: 8
United States Sanitary Commission: 263, 264, 411, 412, 414, 415, 418
University of Maine: vii; Illus. by: 274
Upton, Emory: 391
Urbana, Maryland: 374
USS Adams: 5
USS Chocura: 141
USS Cumberland: 140, 170
USS Essex: Illus.: 327
USS Galena: 315, 336
USS Galena: Illus.: 316
USS Katahdin: 326
USS Kineo: 326
USS Maratanza: 141
USS Marblehead: 141
USS Monitor: 125, 170
USS Sebago: 141
USS Wabash: 110

V

V Corps: 145, 161, 279, 280, 292, 295, 300, 305, 437

Valley Campaign: 247
Valley Pike (Virginia): 147-150, 153, 154, 156, 159, 161
Van Brunt, George: 421-424
Van Vliet, Stewart: 263, 268, 302; Photo: 266
Vanderbilt (vessel): 102
Vannerson, Julian: Photo by: 280
Varney, George: 40, 291
Venus Point (Jones Island, Georgia): 105
VI Corps: 280, 281, 388, 389, 397-399
Vicksburg, Mississippi: 323
Viele, Egbert Ludovicus: 101, 104, 105; Photo: 102
Vienna, Maine: 249
Vienna, Virginia: 35
Vinton, Francis L.: 72
Virgin, Wirt: 18
Vittum, Ambrose: 360
Von Vegesack, Ernst Mathias Peter: 390; Photo: 390

W

Wade, William: 385
Waite, Henry H.: 68
Waldo County (Maine): 22, 75, 80
Waldoboro, Maine: 339, 345, 346
Walker, Annie: 19
Walker, Charles: 383, 385
Walker, Elenor: 19
Walker, Elijah: vi, 19, 20, 22, 24, 25, 27, 29, 30, 33, 34, 45, 124, 195-197, 207, 208, 214, 216-218, 221, 226, 227, 284, 285, 302, 305, 307, 308, 314, 317, 330, 331, 333-335, 438; 21
Walker, F.F.: Illus. by: 23
Walker, Frank: 19

Walker, Ireson: 19
Walker, Narcissa: 19
Walker, Susan: 19
Walker, William: 19, 27
Walker, Winfield: 19
Wallace, Lew: Illus.: 341
War Council, The: Photo: 256
War Democrats: 87
War Department: 1, 17, 21, 23, 25, 33, 35, 53, 54, 66, 76, 81, 83, 87-89, 104, 107, 117, 143, 145, 171, 207, 247, 250, 255, 273, 334, 344, 346, 349, 403, 406, 427, 437, 438
War of 1812: 1, 5, 6, 13, 387
Ward, John Henry Hobart: 217, 221, 226, 227; Photo: 227
Wardwell, Duane: vii
Warren, Alanson M.: 159
Warren, George W.: 239
Warren, Maine: 147
Warrenton Turnpike (Virginia): 29, 37, 38, 44, 53
Warrenton, Virginia: 349-351, 432
Warwick Court House (Virginia): 209
Warwick River (Virginia): 125, 126
Washburn, Israel Jr.: vi, 13, 17, 18, 21, 25, 26, 31-33, 65, 76, 81, 83, 86, 87, 91, 96, 97, 112, 116-118, 122, 123, 127, 129, 132, 133, 139, 147, 151, 159, 163-166, 168, 242, 248-250, 252, 254, 273, 274, 322, 325, 327, 333, 342, 344, 345, 347, 403, 404, 411, 435-437; Photo: 16
Washburn, Sarah: 9
Washington (balloon): 211, 212; Illus.: 214
Washington County (Maine): 17, 67-69, 178, 254, 435

Washington County (Maryland): 427

Washington, D.C.: 1, 2, 7, 8, 14, 22, 23, 25, 27, 33, 35, 41, 51, 54, 59, 61-64, 66, 75, 76, 78, 81, 84, 101, 118, 123, 135, 137, 139, 145, 164, 169, 171, 243, 245, 247, 297, 335, 344, 347, 373, 404, 405, 410, 411, 419, 421, 428, 429, 433, 438

Washington, George: 84, 137, 138, 141, 142

Washington, James Barrall: 177; Photo: 178

Wassaw Island (Georgia): 103

Wassaw Sound (Georgia): 103

Water Street (Augusta, Maine): 115

Waterford, Maine: 429, 433

Waterville, Maine: 47, 182, 248, 254, 288

Watson, Charles: Photo: 436

Watson, Leonard: 66, 412, 415

Watt House (Sarah Watt): 285

Watt, Sarah: 283

Waud, Alfred R.: Illus. by: 126, 174, 202, 236, 290, 312, 336, 337

Waynesboro, Virginia: 159

Webb, Glenn: vii

Webb, James Watson: 7-9; Photo: 7

Webber, Eli: 397

Webster, Daniel: 208

Webster, Richard: 120-122, 426

Webster-Ashburton Treaty: 15, 254

Wentworth, Leonidas: 432

Wentworth, Polly: 15

West Market Square (Bangor, Maine): 56, 57

West Point (military academy): 29-33, 103, 252

West Point, Virginia: 136-138, 261

West Woods (Sharpsburg, Maryland): 398

West, J. William: 173, 184, 239, 240

West, Robert M.: 232

West, William H.: 125

Westbrook, Maine: 385

Weston, Maine: 237

Westover Landing (Virginia): 331

Wheat, Chatham Roberdeau: 154; Illus.: 154

Wheat's Tigers (Confederate unit): 149, 154

Wheeler, Charles C.: 127, 130

Wheeler, Henry: 40

Wheeler, William H.: 54, 163, 252, 254

Wheelwright & Clark Block (Bangor, Maine): 56, 57

Wheelwright, Clark & Company (Bangor, Maine): 26

Whipple, A.W.: 30, 34

Whitcomb, John Jr.: 238

White House (Washington, D.C.): 33

White House Landing, Virginia: 138, 141, 185, 233, 234, 238, 261-268, 271, 272, 284, 297, 299, 300, 302, 309, 331; Photos: 140, 141, 263, 264

White House Plantation, Virginia: 141

White House, Virginia: 138, 142, 302, 303

White Oak Bridge (White Oak Creek): 312, 313

White Oak Creek (Virginia): 284, 285, 302, 305-308, 313

White Oak Swamp (Virginia): 172, 181, 284, 302, 305-307, 312

White, Dr. William H.: 286

Whitehall (Royal Army): 26

Whitehouse, Stephen: 429, 430

Whitney, Addison: 22, 23

Whitney, Isaac: 120, 426

Wicklow Mountains (Ireland): 167

Wikipedia: Photo courtesy of: 314, 402

Wilderness, The (Virginia): vi

Wildes, Asa W.: 249, 251, 404, 405, 407, 429

Wilkeson, Samuel: 231-234; Photo: 232

Willard Hotel (Washington, D.C.): 61

Williams, Alpheus Starkey: 350, 353, 361, 371, 374, 380, 405; Photo: 349

Williams, Charles: 254, 431, 433

Williams, George: 392, 397

Williams, Thomas: 321; Photo: 324

Williamsburg Stage Road (Virginia): 172, 181-183, 187, 214, 270, 306

Williamsburg, Battle of: 123, 133; Illus.: 126, 128, 130

Williamsburg, Virginia: 123, 126, 127, 129, 132, 137, 140, 145, 171, 180, 261, 264

Williamsport, Maryland: 162, 163, 165, 242, 245

Willis Church Road (Virginia): 306, 307, 313, 316

Wilmington Island (Georgia): 103

Wilmington River (Georgia): 103
Wilson, Aaron: 275
Wilson, Jesse: 208
Wilson, John (grandfather): 208
Wilson, John (grandson): 208
Wilson, Jones: 208
Wilson, Joseph B.: 207-213, 215
Wilson, Joseph H.: 107
Wilson, Julius: 208
Wilson, Justus: 208
Wilton, Maine: 66, 432
Winchester, Virginia: 145-147, 149, 150, 156, 157, 159, 161-163, 242, 347, 355
Windham, Maine: 22
Wingate, Ada: 257
Wingate, William P.: 257
Winslow & Co. (Portland, Maine): 71
Wiscasset, Maine: 27, 75
Wise, Rep. Henry (Virginia): 7, 8, 9
Wisner, Henry J.: 119, 120, 122, 421-425
Wiswell, Francis W.: 179
Witham, James: 254, 429
Wolcott, John: 391, 392
Woodbury, David B. (photographer): Photos by: 200, 204, 335
Woodbury, Maurice: 106
Woodbury's Bridge (Chickahominy River crossing): 288, 295
Woodman, Ephraim W.: 104
Woodstock, New Brunswick: 84
Woodstock, Virginia: 145
Wool, John E.: 101, 102
Worcester County (Maryland): 415
World's Work: Photo courtesy of: 267
Wright River (South Carolina): 104
Wright, Anna: 243, 245
Wright, John W.: 153, 159, 243
www.civilwararchives.com (photo credit): Photo courtesy of: 325
www.generalsandbrevets.com (photo credits): Photo courtesy of: 182, 201, 324, 353, 393

X

XII Corps: 374, 378-380, 383, 384, 405, 415

Y

York County (Maine): 255, 256
York River (Virginia): 127, 136, 137, 247, 261, 303, 340
York, Rosalvo: 91
Yorktown, Virginia: 137-139, 145, 194, 207, 209, 261, 331, 334, 335, 430
Young, Ralph: 68
Young's Branch (Bull Run): 39, 44

Z

Zouaves: 17, 24; Photo: 233

The story of Maine's involvement
in the American Civil War
will continue in

MAINE AT WAR
Volume II

and conclude in

MAINE AT WAR
Volume III

 Brian F. Swartz was a reporter and an editor with the Bangor Daily News for 27 years. He is the author of *An American Homecoming; Celebrating 50 Years: Bangor International Airport;* and *Where Good Means the Best: 70 Years at Frank's Bake Shop.* In collaboration with Richard R. Shaw, he is the co-author of *Legendary Locals of Bangor.* A Civil War historian, Brian writes weekly posts about Maine's involvement in the war at maineatwar.bangordailynews.com. Brian lives in central Maine with his wife and their butternut-colored cat, Miss Gettysburg.

www.ingramcontent.com/pod-product-compliance
Lightning Source LLC
Chambersburg PA
CBHW080538230426
43663CB00015B/2629